Like no other text, *American Education* prepares your students to step into their first classroom—ready and confident.

Activity 3.1

Intelligence is genetic, behavioral, and tested. It is also a highly personal issue. Most people hold strong feelings about their intelligence as an essential part of who they are. After reading the section on intelligence, how does your new understanding of intelligence affect the way you view yourself and others?

Answer the following questions:

A. When did you first think about intelligence as something related to you? Were you at home? In school? How did the subject arise? What did you think about your own intelligence?

B. What evidence did you gather to determine how intelligent you were—or were not? Did you use objective measures such as formal IQ tests? Did you compare your schoolwork with that of your brothers or sisters? With that of your classmates? Was there another way you judged your own intelligence?

C. Which definitions of intelligence presented in this chapter do you find most meaningful and true for you? Which definitions do you like the least?

D. Describe in which ways and situations you find yourself intelligent and in which you feel yourself to be less intelligent.

E. How can you become more intelligent?

◀ **Fresh, active-learning approach**

The authors connect educational foundations material to contemporary school issues to create immediacy and relevance. Activities ask students to reflect on their own professional values and future practices—and hone the critical thinking skills they will need as teachers.

▼ **The latest research and topical coverage**

As part of presenting current knowledge in such fundamental areas as finance, school structure, legal issues, and ethics, the book's *A Closer Look* presents or summarizes primary sources, encouraging analysis of key issues related to education, teaching, and learning.

▼ **Unique chapter on misconceptions about teaching**

Chapter 3 identifies and dispels some common, yet entrenched misconceptions about education.

A CLOSER LOOK

Cultural conservatives criticize public schools because they believe educa benefits should rest upon individual merit, family, free enterprise, patrio Christianity. They believe that public schools undermine traditional valu on religious morality and individual merit.

Liberal critics believe public schools must level the playing field betw ent and disadvantaged students through policies and programs that give taged students a better chance to make the most of their educational opp They see education as balancing the individual and social needs in ways with democracy and meritocracy.

Critical theorists would change both schools and the society that ma keep people unequal. They believe that the traditional curriculum aims t students conforming and docile. Instead, they suggest, schools should be just, and inclusive of those who most need access to the educational proc Schools can be a vehicle for social change when they implement curricul teaching that are multicultural, antiracist, antisexist, and antitraditional, the diversity of today's students in the United States.

Considering the information in this text, answer the following questi

1. On which issues do you agree with each of the three different perspe

2. On which issues do you disagree with each of them?

3. Where do you see each perspective's influence in today's public scho

4. In what ways do you think public schools would change if schools a each approach's ideas regarding curriculum, library resources, need f academic support for minority and disadvantaged students, school r prayer in schools, achievement testing, and availability of school sup personnel (counselors, nurses)?

Misconception 3: Teachers Teach; Students Learn

What Many People Believe

Education occurs when teachers present information to students, and students receive the information. Receiving the information is the same as learning it. Students are, in effect, containers into which teachers convey knowledge.[21]

What Is True

Learning is an active and highly personal process. Cognitive research has provided much new information about how it actually occurs. Teachers must do more than just understand their material; they must also understand their students as learners so that they can organize and present the content in ways that students can actually learn it.

How Students Learn

"The cognitive sciences are discovering all sorts of things that good teachers have always intuitively known," giving our profession "strong scientific support."[22] Many research findings have emerged from studies of the human brain that were not available to previous generations of teachers. Although a discussion of brain anatomy and its neurological functioning is too complex and tangential for our purposes, we will give a simple, clear explanation here of how people learn from a cognitive perspective. Recognizing the basics of how students learn will give future teachers insight into how to organize and deliver instruction to maximize student learning, and how to increase their own learning.

The Brain and the Mind

The **brain** is biology—it is a physical organ that controls all body functions in humans as well as their ability to think and to reason. The brain consists of massive networks of neurons that work in conjunction with other cells and structures such as blood vessels. The **mind**, by contrast, is psychology—it is our consciousness, the thinking you that experiences your thoughts and feelings. The mind includes the psychological processes that structure our awareness of the world, our reasoning and

---

[21] This belief underpins policy decisions to let individuals who have a college degree in a subject and work experiences in the related profession enter the classrooms without "teacher education" courses.
[22] Sylwester, R. (1995). *A celebration of neurons: An educator's guide to the human brain*. Alexandria, VA: Association for Supervision and Curriculum Development, p. viii.

Strong focus on diversity and equality

Two chapters (11 and 12) on equality of educational opportunity are complemented by diversity topics integrated throughout the text. In addition, distinctive coverage of the history of American schools pays special attention to how public schools have educated women, African Americans, and persons with disabilities—topics often overlooked in Foundations texts.

Figure 5.6	Children Involved with the Brown v. Board of Education Case Which Challenged the Legality of Public School Segregation.

would help to equalize their educational resources and improve their academic outcomes.

Ruby Bridges and school desegregation. Although school desegregation was a societal issue, it was also a personal one affecting actual children. In Figure 5.7, first-grader Ruby Bridges walks from her elementary school, escorted by federal marshals who were ordered to protect her by President Dwight D. Eisenhower. Court-ordered integration in New Orleans schools began in November 1960. Ruby was the first African American child enrolled in the William Franz Elementary School, and she needed an armed escort to keep her safe. The New Orleans and Louisiana police refused to help. The large angry white crowds who gathered every day outside the school grounds to yell and intimidate Ruby had the potential for physical violence. Consequently, the marshals carried guns and often threatened arrests to keep the protesting crowds back.

Later that year, two white boys joined with Ruby at the school. As expected, the mob became very upset upon first seeing them. Other children soon followed. The following school year, the onlookers gave up their struggle to scare Ruby or to defeat the judge's order. Ruby finished Franz Elementary School and went on to graduate from high school.[64]

While this particular experience was Ruby's, African American students entering formerly all-white schools faced similar difficulties. The undoing of cultural norms about keeping the races separate raised tremendous anger and moved very slowly. **Massive resistance**—closing public schools to keep African American students

[64] Bridges Hall, R. (2000, March). The education of Ruby Nell. Ruby Bridges Foundation. Retrieved May 12, 2008, from http://www.rubybridges.org/story.htm.

ure 12.6	Respect and Family Loyalty Contribute to Latinos' Identity and Well-Being.

eachers can help Latino students succeed in school if they look for and work the students' cultural and personal strengths rather than their shortcomings. xample, when teachers recognize that Latino culture values the extended fam- d social network for self-definition, teachers can construct classroom practices work *with* instead of *against* that orientation.[101] Peer helping and sharing are d.[102] The family notion of working together for mutual benefit of all is easily ed to groupwork in schools. Saying, "Good work—your family will be proud u," and encouraging the child to bring the work home to show the parents play tino students' cultural strengths.

ecause authentic relationships matter to Latinos, teachers are more effective in uraging Latino students to "care" about their schoolwork when these students ience genuine "caring" relationships and compassion from their teachers.[103] ers show real caring when they offer regular after-school consulting and tu- g, encourage students to ask questions and seek assistance.[104] Other effective ices include setting high expectations for achievement, attendance, and disci- ; helping students envision a positive future; providing access to a rigorous cur- m; providing tutors and mentors for students; valuing students' linguistic and ral heritage; and increasing parent involvement.[105]

eachers need to understand that Latino parents' reluctance to attend teacher rences may result from language difficulties, complicated by many low-income o parents' belief that they have no right to question the teacher or school deci- . This reluctance to meet should not be interpreted as a lack of caring or par- volvement in the child's education. Instead, scheduling conferences at flexible , making child care and interpreters available if the teacher is not bilingual,

G. (2006). Connections between classroom management and culturally responsive teaching. In Evertson & C. S. Weinstein (Eds.), *Handbook of classroom management: Research, practice, and con- ry issues* (pp. 343–370). Mahwah, NJ: Lawrence Erlbaum Associates.
pit, L. (1995). *Other people's children: Cultural conflict in the classroom.* New York: New Press, p. 170; ein-Fisch & Trumbull, 2008, p. 22.
nzuela, A. (1999). *Subtractive schooling: U.S.–Mexican youth and the politics of caring.* Albany, NY: Iniversity of New York Press.
aff, K. P. (2008, June). Supportive schooling: Practices that support culturally and linguistically students' preparation for college. *NASSP Bulletin*, 92(2), 95–100.
kwood, A. T., & Secada, W. G. (1999). *Transforming education for Hispanic youth: Exemplary practices, ns, and schools* (NCBE Resource Collection Series No. 12). Washington, DC: NCBE; Gandara, P., & . (2001). *Paving the way to postsecondary education; K–12 intervention programs for underrepresented NCES 2001205).* Washington, DC: National Center for Education Statistics.

Emphasis on multiple perspectives

Kaplan and Owings believe that presenting multiple perspectives helps your students develop an open-minded and perceptive consciousness necessary to adapt to the 21st-century classroom. For instance, here are the section titles of Chapter 12, "Equality of Educational Opportunity—Diverse Students' Perspectives."

Diverse Students' Achievement
Developing Cultural and Racial Identities
Minority Students' Perceptions and Academic Performance
Low Income Students' Perspective
African American Students' Perspectives
Latino Students' Perspectives
Special Needs Students' Perspectives
Discarding the Deficit Model
Fostering Diverse Students' Resilience
Strategies for Helping Diverse Students Succeed in School

Support from media resources

Premium Website—In addition to password-protected teaching resources, the **Premium Website** offers students access to ABC® News Videos and chapter-specific study resources. You and your students also gain access to **InfoTrac® College Edition**, an online library featuring over 20 million articles from nearly 6,000 publications. *Make sure your students have access to the site by packaging a printed access code card with each new text—use this ISBN when placing your textbook order:* ISBN: 978-0-538-46323-2.

PowerLecture™ PowerLecture™ with ExamView® and JoinIn™—This one-stop digital library and presentation tool includes PowerPoint® lecture slides, an image library with graphics from the text, ABC News Videos, the **Instructor's Manual and Test Bank**, ExamView® computerized testing software, and JoinIn™ **Student Response System** content (for use with most "clicker" systems). ISBN: 978-0-495-80864-0.

American Education
Building a Common Foundation

American Education
Building a Common Foundation

Leslie S. Kaplan

Administrator, Newport News Public Schools (Retired)

William A. Owings

Old Dominion University

WADSWORTH
CENGAGE Learning

Australia • Brazil • Japan • Korea • Mexico • Singapore • Spain • United Kingdom • United States

American Education: Building a Common Foundation
Leslie S. Kaplan and William A. Owings

Education Editor: Linda Schreiber-Ganster

Developmental Editor: Lisa Kalner Williams

Assistant Editor: Caitlin Cox

Editorial Assistant: Linda Stewart

Media Editor: Ashley Cronin

Marketing Manager: Kara Kindstrom Parsons

Marketing Assistant: Dimitri Hagnere

Marketing Communications Manager:
   Martha Pfeiffer

Content Project Manager: Tanya Nigh

Creative Director: Rob Hugel

Art Director: Maria Epes

Print Buyer: Linda Hsu

Rights Acquisitions Account Manager, Text:
   Roberta Broyer

Rights Acquisitions Account Manager,
   Image: Leitha Etheridge-Sims

Production Service: Pre-Press PMG

Text Designer: Tani Hasagawa

Photo Researcher: Pre-Press PMG

Cover Designer: Lee Friedman

Cover Image: Getty Images

Compositor: Pre-Press PMG

For product information and technology assistance, contact us at
Cengage Learning Customer & Sales Support, 1-800-354-9706.

For permission to use material from this text or product, submit all requests online at **www.cengage.com/permissions**
Further permissions questions can be e-mailed to
permissionrequest@cengage.com

Library of Congress Control Number: 2009934267
ISBN-13: 978-0-495-59939-5
ISBN-10: 0-495-59939-5

Wadsworth
20 Davis Drive
Belmont, CA 94002-3098
USA

Cengage Learning is a leading provider of customized learning solutions with office locations around the globe, including Singapore, the United Kingdom, Australia, Mexico, Brazil, and Japan. Locate your local office at **www.cengage.com/global**.

Cengage Learning products are represented in Canada by Nelson Education, Ltd.

To learn more about Wadsworth, visit **www.cengage.com/wadsworth**
Purchase any of our products at your local college store or at our preferred online store **www.ichapters.com**.

Printed in the United States of America
1 2 3 4 5 6 7 13 12 11 10 09

Brief Contents

Contents

PART 4 Social Foundations

PART 5   Curricular and Instructional Foundations

American Education: Building a Common Foundation *was written to make educational foundations' topics relevant and personally meaningful to young adult learners while offering the comprehensive scope, scholarly depth, and insightful analysis that demanding professors require.*

College students taking their first education course do not often see how foundations topics connect to their future careers. While preparing to write American Education, *the authors saw why. Many of the available textbooks for the foundations course read like encyclopedias. They seemed to have been written for fellow professors or for doctoral students. Less encyclopedic textbooks had attention-grabbing photos but little in-depth discussion of vital concepts pertinent to college-age students or future educators.*

With these concerns in mind, the authors decided to create an educational foundations textbook which met both students' needs for relevance and *meaning* and *professors' needs for respected foundations' content.*

The text's authors and instructors teaching an introductory course in education share many common goals for their students:

- Use a textbook that college students will find readable, interesting, and scholarly.

- Address what future educators need to know and understand that will help them smoothly transition into the education profession.

- Respect the traditional educational foundations' content.

- Give immediacy, relevance, and meaning for today's college students by continually linking foundation' issues to "hot-button" contemporary educational concerns.

- Provide scholarly support for important concepts with current research findings.

- *Educate,* not *inculcate* [1] by introducing students to varied perspectives on American public education and the larger social and political context by which to assess and draw their own conclusions.

- Infuse teaching's and learning's "best practices" to continuously engage students and professors in applying the content and reflecting on its personal meaning.

- Develop culturally responsive teachers who respect and understand diverse students and recognize the cultural assets they bring to school.

- Cultivate reflective practitioners by providing frequent, on-going occasions for students to create the personal meaning that will increase their retention of important concepts and help them develop a philosophy of education.

- Include varied learning styles in the instructional activities, including visual, auditory, graphic, and interpersonal learning and technology.

---

[1] Liston, Dan, Whitcomb, Jennie, and Borko, Hilda. (2009). The end of education in teacher education. Thoughts on reclaiming the role of social foundations in teacher education. *Journal of Teacher Education,* *60* (2), 107–111.

Features of American Education

This text offers special features to help educational foundations students learn the content of each chapter.

- _A Closer Look._ Seen in nearly every chapter, this feature's primary source material gives students and instructors opportunities to think in-depth about a key aspect under discussion, develop a fuller understanding of the issue, and reflect and share its personal meaning and relevance to them as students and as future educators.

- _Activities_. Located immediately following major concepts in each chapter, these practical activities help students find relevance and construct personal meaning from the ideas just discussed. Most associated questions have several correct answers that readers can develop by relating text information to personal ideas and experiences. Professors can adapt and revise activities as they desire to accomplish their instructional goals.

Organization

The text is organized into five parts.

Part 1 – Understanding the Teaching Profession

Chapter 1, So You Want to Be a Teacher? describes how teaching is an inspiring, satisfying, and important profession. It discusses the qualities of effective teachers as persons and introduces education's moral purposes. It considers varied perspectives on globalization's recent technological and economic changes and their implications for teaching and learning. The Interstate Core Standards for New Teachers (INTASC) that prepares teachers to work effectively in today's challenging classrooms are also presented.

Chapter 2, Teaching as a Profession, considers who becomes a teacher, the nature of teaching, and the profession's cultural shifts. The chapter describes how teachers are best prepared for classroom success, discusses state and national board certification and licensure, and presents the research findings on teacher preparation, retention in the profession, and student achievement. The chapter also considers the teaching field's increasing professionalization and the organizations and agencies which promote this.

Chapter 3, Misconceptions About Education and Teaching, explores and rebuts the following three commonly held misconceptions about public education: (1) The intelligence you're born with is the intelligence you keep; (2) Race is a biological fact that determines many traits including intelligence and achievement; and (3) Teachers teach; students learn. Credibly challenging these ideas will help prospective teachers better understand their diverse students as well as the teaching and learning process.

Part 2 - Historical and Philosophical Foundations

In **Chapter 4 & Chapter 5, The History of American Public Education, Parts 1 and 2**, we look at public education from the earliest days through the current high stakes No Child Left Behind Act era. **Chapter 4** examines the emerging public school in early American colonial and national periods through Horace Mann and the movement towards universal public schooling. Education of women, African Americans, Native Americans, and special needs students receives clear attention.

Chapter 5 considers educational changes in the 20th and 21st centuries. Topics include the societal and political influences on public school curriculum and the swings between subject-centered and student-centered pedagogy. Also discussed are: the educational impacts of World War I and II, the Great Depression, vocational education, and technology; how underserved student populations have gained access to public schools through African American leaders and 1954 *Brown vs. Board of Education* decision; the Coleman Report; *A Nation at Risk*; the Individuals with Disabilities Education Act (IDEA); and No Child Left Behind Act.

Chapter 6, Philosophy of Education, looks at four major educational philosophies that influence American public education – traditional, progressive, existential, and critical theory. Varying beliefs about the purposes of school, the criteria for excellence, the practice of democratic citizenship, the knowledge most essential for students to learn, and other value-laden questions play essential roles in how teachers translate their knowledge and skills into classroom practice. Readers will consider each philosophy's contributions and begin developing a personal philosophy of education.

Chapter 7, The Purposes and Promises of Public Education, discusses public education's intellectual, social, political, economic, and personal purposes. Public schools are an agency to transmit the American culture, prepare students to live as responsible citizens, and advance social justice to improve society. We also introduce the concept of education as an investment in human capital.

Part 3 – Political, Legal, and Economic Foundations

Chapter 8, Teaching, Ethics, and the Law, covers the essentials of what every new teacher needs to know about professional ethics and school law. The chapter addresses professional concerns about using social networking sites. The chapter also speaks of teacher employment contracts, tenure, negligence, freedom of expression, students' rights, and other professional and classroom issues.

In **Chapter 9, Governance and Structure of Schools**, we look at the federal role in education, state boards of education, local school boards, the consolidation of schools and school districts, and the roles of superintendents, school board personnel, and principals. Also discussed are additional educational professionals who work with teachers to help students and how they contribute to student learning and achievement.

Chapter 10, School Funding, reviews federal, state, and local responsibilities for funding education and describes how education dollars are spent. Equality and equity issues in school funding, educational adequacy, and "taxpayer revolts" are considered. Data about education as an investment in human capital supports the idea that education improves a community's quality of life.

Part 4 – Social Foundations

Chapter 11, Equality of Educational Opportunity: Societal and School Practices, describes how society and school present obstacles which limit minority and low-income students' educational opportunities. The chapter reviews the ethnic and racial makeup of today's and tomorrow's students, social class and the achievement gap, teachers' expectations and student achievement, and school practices that reduce students' opportunities to learn. The chapter also discusses institutional perspectives that foster inequity, and explains multicultural education's academic and social benefits.

Chapter 12, Equality of Opportunity: Diverse Students' Perspectives, reviews current student achievement data for traditionally underserved student groups. It explores how persons develop their racial and cultural identities and how these impacts their school achievement. The chapter considers stereotype threat; cultural opposition theory; coping strategies; how the cultural assets of African Americans, Latinos, low-income, and students with disabilities can contribute to their school success; and offers teachers culturally responsive strategies for increasing diverse students' achievement.

Part 5 – Curricular and Instructional Foundations

Chapter 13, Curriculum, explains how curriculum reflects a society's values and political beliefs about schools' major goals and looks at various curricula types. The chapter looks at the core curriculum of reading, math, science, and social studies and considers the relationship between the arts and student achievement.

Chapter 14, Instruction, considers the research on teaching effectiveness and student achievement, the research on teacher preparation and student achievement, and describes behaviorist, cognitive, and constructivist instructional models. The chapter also relates research-affirmed best teaching practices to help teachers become more effective educators.

Chapter 15, Achievement and Accountability, discusses how assessment can be an integral part of teaching and learning and used to increase student achievement. This chapter considers the role of standards in driving accountability, and the variable nature of "proficiency." The chapter argues the cases for and against standardized testing for making important educational decisions, articulates equity and ethical issues in testing and accountability, and presents the case for developing a holistic accountability system.

In **Chapter 16, Effective Schools**, considers how today's schools can make a difference in student achievement – in spite of students' family backgrounds. The chapter reviews the Effective Schools Movement's emergence and its research-affirmed correlates for increasing student achievement: safe & orderly climate; clear focused mission; instructional leadership; climate of high expectation for success; opportunity to learn & student time-on-task; frequent monitoring of student progress; and home-school relations. Finally, the chapter shows what these factors look like in today's schools.

Supplements to the Textbook

Teaching Tools for Instructors

Premium Website with Infotrac®

The instructor area of the premium website offers access to such password-protected resources as an electronic version of the instructor's manual and PowerPoint® slides. Go to www.cengage.com/login to access these resources.

PowerLecture™ with ExamView® and JoinIn™

This one-stop digital library and presentation tool includes PowerPoint® lecture slides, an image library with graphics from the text, and ABC® News Videos. In addition to a full Instructor's Manual and Test Bank, this resource also includes ExamView testing software. ExamView enables you to create customized print or online tests. PowerLecture also includes JoinIn Student Response System content (for use with most "clicker" systems).

WebTutor for WebCT™ or Blackboard®

Jumpstart your course with customizable, text-specific content within your Course Management System. Whether you want to Web-enable your class or put an entire course online, WebTutor offers a wide array of resources including media, quizzes, web links, exercises, and more.

Instructor's Manual with Test Bank

The Instructor's Manual with Test Bank contains resources designed to streamline and maximize the effectiveness of your course preparations. The contents include chapter objectives, focusing questions, summaries, bonus activities and discussion topics, important lecture points, and the test bank.

Learning Resources for Students

Premium Website with Infotrac®

The premium website offers access to video segments from ABC® News on relevant topics, including guiding questions to help you relate the videos to chapter content. Other study tools and resources on the premium website include links to related sites for each chapter of the text, tutorial quizzes, interactive glossary/flashcards, and information about education standards in the US and Canada. Your access comes with **InfoTrac® College Edition**, an online research and learning center featuring 24/7 access to over 20 million full-text articles from nearly 6,000 journals. Log in at www.cengage.com/login using the access code packaged with your new text, or purchase access at www.iChapters.com.

Acknowledgements

Writing this book has been a genuinely interesting, enjoyable, and collaborative experience. Our sincere thanks and appreciation to:

Dan Alpert, our former Wadsworth editor for American Public School Finance (Cengage, 2006), who gave us invaluable suggestions about creating a winning content and format for this endeavor. Dan has become a dear friend.

Lisa Kalner Williams, our highly talented and always conscientious Cengage editor and partner. Lisa knowledgeably guided us through the review and revision process with always-excellent suggestions, consistent encouragement, sunny good humor, a capable eye for excising text, and clear deadlines. Lisa has become a good friend.

Diahanne Dowridge, Marie Desrosiers, Caitlin Cox, and Ashley Cronin were invaluable resources during the production phase. Their ideas, persistence, and organizational skills secured beautiful and insightful artwork to illustrate the text plus constructing additional materials for professors and students. Diahanne, Marie, Caitlin, and Ashley were always open to our suggestions.

Additional thanks go to other members of the Cengage team who put forth great contributions to this first edition, namely Kara Kindstrom Parsons, Tanya Nigh, and Linda Stewart.

Our peer reviewers provided extremely valuable and useful feedback. They told us when we were on the right track, when we needed to rethink and revise, and which key topics their students really wanted to understand. These reviewers became welcome and virtual collaborators as we developed and refined this text.

Reviewers

Jim Barrett, *Fort Hays State University*

Marilyn Bartlett, *University of South Florida*

Jerome Cammarata, *West Chester University of Pennsylvania*

Theresa Canada, *Western Connecticut State University*

Wei Cao, *University of Michigan-Flint*

Teri Castelow, *University of Memphis*

Donald R. Clerico, *Charleston Southern University*

Roger Cleveland, *Eastern Kentucky University*

Jim Codling, *Mississippi State University*

Howard Coleman, *University of North Carolina Wilmington*

Debra Cunningham, *Pima Community College*

Charlotte Danielson, *Educational Consultant*

Barry S. Davidson, *Troy University*

John Dublanica, *East Stroudsburg University*

Jay Feng, *Mercer University*

Julie J. Flynn, *Plymouth State University*

Olive Gahungu, *Northern Arizona University*

Michael Tlanusta Garrett

Ron Germaine, *National University*

Barbara Graham, *Ball State University*

Saul B. Grossmann, *Temple University*

Marsha L. Heck, *Indiana University South Bend*

Jennifer Herring, *University of Illinois*

Peter Hessling, *North Carolina State University*

Carole Hillman, *Elmhurst College*

Warren A. Hodge, *University of North Florida*

Judith Z. Hotz, *Xavier University*

Michael Jacobs, *University Northern Colorado*

Hal E. Jenkins, II, *Mississippi University for Women*

Kristi Johnson, *Marymount University*

Natalie Johnson-Leslie, *Arkansas State University*

Susan Kalsow, *Buena Vista University*

Jeffrey Kaplan, *University of Central Florida*

Bob Lake, *Georgia Southern University*

Brian Leavell, *Texas Woman's University*

William G. Leewer, Jr.

Huey-li Li, *University of Akron*

Jonathan Lightfoot, *Hofstra University*

Delores Liston, *Georgia Southern University*

Mary Nell McNeese, *University of Southern Mississippi*

Robert Moody, *Fort Hays State University*

Diane B. Napier, *University of Georgia*

K. A. Okrah, *Indiana University South Bend*

Darlene Peters, *University of West Florida*

Kristen Ramirez, *California State University Bakersfield*

Sara Salbego, *University of Missouri, St Louis*

Jeff Sapp, *California State University Dominguez Hills*

Chrystal Soltero, *Pima Community College*

Terry Stahler, *Kutztown University*

Rosita Tormala-Nita, *University of Wisconsin*

Curt Visca, *Saddleback College*

Joan Rudel Weinreich, *Manhattanville College*

H. Jeanette Willert, *Canisius College*

Locord D. Wilson, *Jackson State University*

Finally, Leslie and Bill want to thank each other for that special "teamwork" which is personally and professionally rewarding, even without words.

So You Want to Be a Teacher?

Most U.S. students attend public schools. Public schools educate nine out of every ten K–12 students in this country. Forty-nine million students attend 54,000 elementary schools and 18,000 secondary schools in the United States. Another 6.1 million students attend private/independent schools, and approximately 1 million are home-schooled.[1] It is not through the "school" that real learning occurs, however, but rather through the caring, one-to-one teacher–student relationship.

Being a teacher is important and challenging work. "It takes a great deal of dedication to walk into school every day with enthusiasm, energy, and love, often in spite of conditions that make doing so a constant struggle. Yet some teachers do it all the time, and many remain in the classroom for years with a commitment that is nothing short of inspirational."[2]

Noted education professor Sonia Nieto observes that teachers' values, beliefs, and dispositions energize them to stay in the profession. Their love for children, desire to engage with intellectual work, hope of changing students' lives, strong belief in public education's democratic potential, and anger at public education's shortcomings all lie at the heart of what makes for excellent and caring teachers.[3] Having a sense of mission, solidarity and empathy for students, the desire to be lifelong learners, the courage to challenge conventional thinking, improvisation ability, and a passion for social justice motivate and keep teachers in the profession.[4] Comfort with uncertainty, endless patience, and a sense of humor also help.

And students know the difference when they have teachers who care about them and want to help them learn. When asked how they make this determination, they answer: The teacher *teaches well* (makes the class interesting, stays on task, stops to explain sometimes) and the teacher *treats them well* (is respectful, kind, and fair).[5] In these ways, a "caring teacher" models how children can become both smart and good.

The need for excellent public school teachers has never been greater. More students and increasingly diverse students are sitting in today's classrooms. Becoming educated and employable in the twenty-first century requires knowledge and skills beyond those needed even one generation ago. Our communities and our country's well-being depend on educating all students for full participation in our economy and democracy. Teaching is a critically important career where the challenges—and the satisfactions—are many.

This chapter discusses the crucial importance of education for today's world and describes the social context in which we work. We will look at how teaching inspires its best practitioners; effective teachers' personal qualities; education's moral purposes; education's role in an interconnected, global environment; and core standards for new teachers.

---

[1] Hodgkinson, H. (2006). *The whole child in a fractured world*. Alexandria, VA: Association for Supervision and Curriculum Development, p. 2.
[2] Nieto, S. (2009). From surviving to thriving. *Educational Leadership, 66*(5), 8–13.
[3] Nieto, S. (2003). *What keeps teachers going?* New York: Teachers College Press.
[4] Nieto, S. (Ed.). (2005). *Why we teach*. New York: Teachers College Press.
[5] Davidson, M., Lickona, T., & Khmelkov, V. (2007, November 14). Smart schools and good schools: A paradigm shift for character education. *Education Week, 27*(12), 31, 40.

- Why is teaching an inspiring, satisfying, and important profession?
- What are qualities of effective teachers as persons?
- What are education's moral purposes?
- How does the trend toward globalization affect what it means to be educated for the twenty-first century?
- What are core standards for new teachers?

As you begin your induction into our profession, these perspectives will help you better understand your role and determine how you can create the conditions for high levels of student learning and your own professional satisfaction.

Inspiring New Teachers

Since 1952, the National Teacher of the Year Program has focused public attention on excellence in teaching. As part of its 50th Anniversary Celebration, each National Teacher of the Year winner from past years was invited to submit a letter "for the future." One of the teachers' options was to write to an elementary or secondary student whom they knew would make a wonderful teacher or a newly trained teacher getting ready to begin their classroom career. Their letter would offer insights to what motivates successful teachers.[6]

The 1997 National Teacher of the Year, Sharon M. Draper, chose this option. In her "Letter to a Prospective Teacher," she writes:

Dear Friend:

. . . I was probably born to be a teacher. As a child, I taught my dolls, my dogs, and the kids next door. I never wavered in my desires and determination to become not just a teacher, but a really good teacher who made memories in the minds of children. From my early days of student teaching when I learned that acting out history made it memorable for me as well as my students, to my first teaching assignment where I broke down and cried in front of the class because forty-two disruptive students in a makeshift, renovated classroom did not fit my glossy vision of educational excellence, to today where my seniors wear T-shirts, proudly proclaiming, "I Survived the Draper Paper," I continued to try to make a difference—one child at a time. For our greatest accomplishments in education are not the plaques and awards, but the smiles and hugs and memories of children touched today and somehow influenced tomorrow.

They ask me about the lack of respect for the profession. I respond with, "Raise your hand if you don't respect me!" They grin and see my point. They want to know about the lack of financial rewards. I tell them honestly, "I'll never make what a basketball player makes, but then neither will most of you. It's not fair that our society pays its entertainers more than its educators, but I make a good living, can support a family, and send my children to college. And I get extra benefits—smiles, hugs, and the knowledge that what I do really matters.

[6] National Teacher of the Year Program. *Voices for the future*. Washington, DC: Council of Chief State School Officers. Retrieved January 28, 2009, from http://www.ccsso.org/projects/National_Teacher_of_the_Year/Voices_for_the_Future/.

I once asked a class of fourth graders to give me their definition of a good teacher. These are their responses:

- A good teacher is soft enough to hug, but too hard to punch....
- A good teacher is not scared of thunder and lightning and knows what to do when the lights go out.
- A good teacher never makes fun of you when you do dumb stuff like throw up or forget the answer...
- A good teacher makes you have so much fun you don't know you're learning, and then when you've learned it, you realize it wasn't hard at all.
- A good teacher never has bad breath.
- A good teacher loves you and you know it.

If we could all live up to this simple list, we'd be successful teachers. The children are waiting."[7]

| Figure 1.1 | "I was probably born to be a teacher." |

Kendra Dew/Photolibrary

Similarly, John A. Ensworth, 1973 National Teacher of the Year, recalls:

Dear New Teacher:

. . . It all started with the death of a banty hen on my forty-acre ranch. I brought the dead hen to the fifth-grade classroom where we removed the skin and feathers and cooked the chicken until the meat fell off the bones. Several students who were interested reconstructed the skeleton. One of the students was Karen Gunson. She was just named Oregon's first female State Medical Examiner. In the state-wide article "Bend Doctor Owes Much to Grade School Teacher" (Monday, September 27, 1999, *Bend Bulletin*), [the reporter wrote of Gunson]: "But a small portion of the credit for her success goes to the teachers she studied with along the way, in particular Mr. Ensworth, whose talent made her fifth grade year so pivotal in her life. . . ."

---

[7] Draper, S. M. (2000). *Teaching from the heart: Reflections, encouragement and inspiration.* New York: Heineman. Excerpted in National Teacher of the Year Program. *Voices for the future.* Washington, DC: Council of Chief State School Officers. Retrieved January 28, 2009, from http://www.ccsso.org/projects/ National_Teacher_of_the_Year/Voices_for_the_Future/.

Glen Burleigh, a former student, and I were fishing one day. He started talking about the time he spent in my classroom. Glen said, "Mr. Ensworth, the one thing I remember about our class was that you were having as much fun as we were. . . ."

Our class motto was as follows: "Do your best even if it falls short of what the experts think is excellent. The forest would be far too quiet if only the most beautiful birds sang."[8]

Looking at teaching from a different framework, Myrra Lee, 1977 National Teacher of the Year, reminds the future teacher that professional excellence and satisfaction take time to grow:

Dear Brave and Idealistic Soul:

The road to excellence in teaching can be difficult and it can't be traveled overnight. The first few years have to be ones of experimentation and self-examination. Once you realize what your strengths are, you must continue to improve upon them . . . We all have our individual styles and if you are genuine, your students will sense this and respond with respect and will desire to work for your approval and their success. If something works well one year, do try to incorporate it in succeeding years—but experiment and make it better. . . . Don't ever be embarrassed because you are excited by what you are doing—even after twenty or more years in the classroom. Enthusiasm for what you are doing is an important key to success.

One of the reasons teachers leave the profession is because they fail to see where they have made a difference. One never knows, entirely, how one has affected another person. However, students come back to teachers many years later to tell them how their lives have been affected and even changed. It isn't subject matter which changes people's lives. Skills change people's lives. Competence and self-esteem enable students to gain confidence. Knowing a teacher who can be trusted changes student's lives.

You need to face this fact—you may be the one steady influence in your student's lives. This may be true whether you are teaching elementary or secondary school. The home situation, of too many of today's young people, is unstable and dangerous. If you can provide a measure of stability, your students will find it easier to learn and will then test well. The best way to accomplish this is to be "real." Acknowledge from the beginning of the year that you and your students are on this life journey together. Too many teachers view their students as adversaries, not partners. If you can convey this partnership relationship to them, you will find that the validation of knowing that you have made a difference. It will make up for all the frustrations you will encounter. The high that comes about when understanding lights up a student's face cannot be duplicated. Validation is the key for both the student and the teacher. May you and your students experience this high repeatedly.

My best wishes to you as you start upon this journey![9]

For a final look at how teaching inspires its best practitioners, Jennifer Wellborn, a middle school science teacher, writes about why she teaches:[10]

I may be naive, but I believe that what I do day in and day out *does* make a difference. Teachers *do* change lives forever. And I teach in public school because I still believe in public school. I believe the purpose of public school, whether it delivers or not, is to give quality education to all kids who come through the doors. I want to be part of that lofty mission. The future of our country depends on the ability of public schools to do that.[11]

---

[8] E., Jack (2002). In National Teacher of the Year Program. *Voices for the future*. Washington, DC: Council of Chief State School Officers. Retrieved January 28, 2009, from http://www.ccsso.org/projects/National_Teacher_of_the_Year/Voices_for_the_Future/.

[9] Lee, M.. (2002). In National Teacher of the Year Program. *Voices for the future*. Washington, DC: Council of Chief State School Officers. Retrieved January 28, 2009, from http://www.ccsso.org/projects/National_Teacher_of_the_Year/Voices_for_the_Future/.

[10] Wellborn, J. (2005). The accidental teacher. In S. Nieto (Ed.), *Why we teach* (pp. 15–22). New York: Teachers College Press.

[11] Wellborn, 2005, p. 17.

Activity 1.1

Discuss in pairs and then as a class:

A. What satisfactions and cautions do these four excellent teachers offer prospective educators?

B. What motivates you to consider a teaching career?

C. Describe an experience you had as an elementary or secondary student with an exceptional teacher that had a meaningful impact on who you are as a person, or describe who influenced you to become a teacher.

These teachers, and countless thousand others, give clear voice to the belief that teaching is an inspiring, satisfying, highly demanding, and vitally important profession.

Qualities of Effective Teachers as People

In their letters to the future, the most vivid memories that these Teachers of the Year described were about their students. The reverse is true for students, too. Although we may not always remember specific facts learned in a particular class, most of us can easily recall volumes about the teacher's personality.

Before any individual becomes a professional, he or she is first a unique person of distinct appearance, personality, interests, abilities, talents, and ways of interacting with others. A teacher's personality is one of the first characteristics that students, parents, and administrators notice. Who the teacher is as a person has a tremendous influence on the classroom climate and students' learning experiences. Even more impressive, teachers' psychological influence on students has been linked to student achievement in various studies of educational effectiveness.[12] While many aspects of effective teaching can be taught and developed, changing an individual's personality is difficult.

Here are some of the research-based findings about effective teachers' personal qualities.[13] See if you can identify some of your own favorite teachers here:

- *Effective teachers care about their students.* They show their caring in ways that students understand, see, and feel. These teachers bring out the best in students by affirming and encouraging them with patience, trust, honesty, courage, listening, understanding, and knowing their students as persons and as learners.

- *Effective teachers show all students (and colleagues) fairness and respect.* They establish rapport and credibility by emphasizing, modeling, and practicing fairness and showing esteem. For instance, they respond to student misbehavior on an individual level—rather than by punishing the entire class. They tell students what they need to do right—and get all the facts before speaking with students about what they did wrong. And they treat students equitably and do not show favoritism.

- *Effective teachers show interest in their students both inside and outside the classroom.* When students are having difficulties, these teachers work with them—rather than scold or ignore them. Attending football games, plays,

---

[12] We will discuss teachers' psychological influence on student achievement in Chapter 11, Equality of Educational Opportunity: Societal and School Practices.

[13] Stronge, J. H. (2002). *Qualities of effective teachers.* Alexandria, VA: Association for Supervision and Curriculum Development.

Figure 1.2	Teachers Show Interest in Students Both Inside and Outside the Classroom

ColorBlind Images/Iconica/Getty Images

and choral concerts in which their students participate also shows students that their teachers genuinely care about them, and it increases students' feelings of belonging in their classrooms. At the same time, teachers maintain the appropriate professional role with students. The ability to relate in these positive ways creates a learning environment that promotes student achievement.

- *Effective teachers promote enthusiasm and motivation for learning.* Teacher enthusiasm has been shown to increase both positive relations with students and student achievement. Effective teachers know how to motivate all students—by understanding their individual interests and making connections whenever possible to familiar and valued prior knowledge. These teachers also give students choices about what and how they will study, thereby creating intrinsic motivation for students to learn. Students want to work hard and learn for teachers they think like them and who believe in their ability to learn.

- *Effective teachers have a positive attitude toward their own learning and to the teaching profession.* They have a dual commitment to student learning and to personal learning. They believe that all students can learn—and this is not just a slogan to them. Furthermore, effective teachers see themselves as responsible, capable, and willing to deliver for their students' success. They also work collaboratively with other teachers and staff, sharing ideas and assisting to resolve difficulties.

- *Effective teachers are reflective practitioners.* They continuously and thoughtfully review their teaching practice daily, class by class. Research consistently affirms the value of reflection in developing effective teaching.[14] Self-evaluation and

---

[14] Korthagen, F. A. J., & Wubbels, T. (2001). Evaluative research on the realistic approach and on the promotion of reflection. In F. A. J. Korthagen (Ed.), *Linking practice and theory: The pedagogy of realistic teacher education* (pp. 88–107). Mahwah, NJ: Lawrence Erlbaum Associates.

self-critiquing are essential learning tools. Effective teachers seek greater understanding of teaching through experience, scholarly study, professional reading, and observing master teachers. Likewise, they desire feedback to improve their performance. As they become better, their sense of **efficacy**—their belief in their own ability to make a difference—increases. They gain confidence both in their skills and in their results. Their students and colleagues see this transformation in action.

Teaching is more than what you know and can do in the classroom. Who you are as a person greatly affects how effective you are as a teacher.

Activity 1.2

A. Describe your favorite teacher—the one who was most influential in motivating you to become a teacher. Use the information in the list to describe this teacher's characteristics. Using the chart below, respond in a word, picture, or cartoon to the following questions about your favorite teacher: How did that teacher become so influential to you? Which behaviors and attitudes did the teacher regularly use in class?

B. Describe the worst teacher you had in school, and fill in a second column in the chart by answering the same questions for that teacher.

My Most Influential Teachers		
Teacher Characteristics	Favorite Teacher	"Worst" Teacher
What influenced me the most		
How the teacher made me feel in class		
Teacher's excitement about the subject taught		
Made learning personally meaningful		
Presented challenging work I wanted to learn		
Delivered work of an appropriate difficulty for my experience and age		
Gave me some control and choice over my learning		
Used my prior knowledge		
Provided opportunities for interaction		
Gave helpful feedback		
Taught me new ways to learn better		
Created a positive emotional climate		
Created a positive class environment		

Activity 1.3

Getting to know a teacher's personality is one of students', parents', and administrators' first priorities. Working individually for 3 minutes, complete the "Positive Teacher Qualities" chart by filling in qualities *that you see in yourself.* Then, working in pairs, discuss the five characteristics you see as your strengths now and the five characteristics that you want to develop more fully.

Report both sets of characteristics to the large group, and have a person tally them for the class as a whole. Discuss where and how in your teacher preparation program you can find resources, people, or environments where you can more fully develop those qualities that still need strengthening or refinement.

	Personal Assessment: The Degree to Which I Have the Quality		
Positive Teacher Qualities	Less Developed	Moderate	High
1. I have personal experiences working with students as a tutor, teacher, counselor, or mentor.			
2. I assume responsibility for my students' success.			
3. I understand students' feelings.			
4. I am a good listener.			
5. I communicate clearly.			
6. I admit my mistakes and quickly correct them.			
7. I think about and reflect on my behavior so I can improve.			
8. I have a sense of humor.			
9. I dress appropriately for the teaching position.			
10. I am structured but also flexible and spontaneous.			
11. I expect to enjoy teaching and expect students to enjoy learning.			
12. I look for a win-win resolution in conflict situations.			
13. I listen carefully to students' questions and comments.			
14. I respond to students with respect, even in difficult situations.			
15. I consistently express high expectations and high confidence.			
16. I treat students equally and fairly.			
17. I have positive dialog with students outside the classroom.			
18. I maintain a professional manner at all times.			

The Moral Purpose of Education

Teaching deliberately affects both the local community and the larger society. Michael Fullan, Professor Emeritus at the University of Toronto and an international leader in teacher education, explains that schools have a moral purpose. Schools are charged with improving their students' lives, regardless of those individuals' background, and developing citizens who can live and work productively in increasingly dynamic complex societies.[15] The individual teacher is the building block of this educational endeavor, linking caring and competence through professional practice. In this view, teachers' personal purpose has a social dimension: They are the agents of educational change and societal improvement.

Likewise, John Goodlad, an influential author and researcher on teacher education, believes that schools have four moral imperatives: preparing students for responsible citizenship, providing essential knowledge and skills, building effective relationships, and practicing sound stewardship.[16]

Preparing Students for Responsible Citizenship

First, a public school is the only national institution specifically assigned to prepare students to live responsibly in a democratic republic. Our federal government, state, and local communities have charged public schools as the agents of societal well-being. Children need to develop the information, skills, and habits of mind that make them informed citizens who can effectively participate in our representative government and can constructively fulfill their obligations as voters, law-abiders, and taxpayers. Through school, students acquire the knowledge and reasoning skills that allow them to become self-supporting and productive contributors to our society.

Living in the U.S. democracy requires getting along with other people who hold different viewpoints. Students tend to live in neighborhoods with others like themselves. Schools, by contrast, gather several neighborhoods together into a larger and more diverse educational community. In schools, students develop the interpersonal skills they need to understand and appreciate the common ties they share with classmates from different families, genders, races, and economic backgrounds. Schools help both native-born individuals and immigrants, as well as people from different regions of the same state and the country, to identify and celebrate their unifying American traditions and beliefs and to build a common civic purpose. Students also get to know unfamiliar peers with different backgrounds as pleasant individuals much like themselves and learn how to show respect and appreciation for their individual traditions.

Providing Essential Knowledge and Skills

U.S. schools also offer students access to knowledge. Schools help students learn about the earth as a series of physical and biological systems and develop communication skills through verbal and numerical fluency. They help students learn the historical, political, social, economic, and cultural realities in which they live. In addition, schools provide students with instruction on how to gather, assess, and judge information and to express informed opinions. They also ensure that no belief, attitude, or practice keeps students from getting the necessary knowledge.

Building Effective Relationships

Goodlad also notes that American schools build effective teacher–student connections. Although teaching is a professional activity, it is also an acutely personal

[15] Fullan, M. (1993). Change forces: Probing the depths of educational reform. London: Falmer Press.
[16] Goodlad, J. (1990). Studying the education of educators: From conception to findings. *Phi Delta Kappan 71*(9): 698–701.

Figure 1.3   Classrooms Create Diverse Communities with Common Ties

one. Teaching entails much more than just the mechanics of delivering content: It involves caring about and interacting with individual students in a group setting. The teacher–student relationship can either help or hurt learning. Effective teachers create and sustain a safe, caring, and intellectually challenging environment. If students feel frightened, humiliated, or discounted by their teacher, they won't learn. Students know when teachers respect and like them. They know when teachers hold high expectations for students' achievement—and when they don't. And students respond accordingly—by engaging the material or by withdrawing from it. While important interpersonal and professional boundaries exist, good teachers combine teaching's generalizable principles and subject-specific instruction with a genuine sensitivity to their students' uniqueness and humanness as learners.

Practicing Good Stewardship

Goodlad affirms that schools and teachers must practice good **stewardship**.[17] A steward is a caretaker who looks out for and manages an estate's or organization's affairs. Similarly, teaching involves more than working with students behind the classroom door. By virtue of their faculty membership and school district employment, teachers have ethical duties and obligations that go beyond the classroom. As good stewards, they attend to the school's mission and protect the school's reputation in the community it serves. Similarly, teachers have an ethical obligation to protect the reputation of the teaching profession as a whole.

As stewards, teachers ensure that their school is committed to students' advancement and to society's well-being. To do so, they assure the highest-quality teaching

---

[17] For a fuller discussion of Goodlad's view of stewardship, see Fenstermacher, G. D, (n.d.). Teaching on both sides of the classroom door. Retrieved September 18, 2006, from http://www-personal.umich.edu/~gfenster/jigms.pdf.

and learning for all students in the school (not just those inside their own class-rooms). Meeting this goal means that teachers must be constructive and helpful colleagues who share the mutual goal of making the school an increasingly effective and satisfying place for everyone to learn and work. Stewardship also means keeping the community informed about the school's accomplishments and activities and enlisting local support to make school even better. It means practicing responsible citizenship, thinking critically, and acting deliberately in a pluralistic world—and educating students to do the same.

Finally, fulfilling the demands of teacher stewardship means becoming a transformational learner. Changing the world begins with changing oneself. Teachers must be enthusiastically engaged with their own learning, continue to learn, and show students how to learn. Teachers ought to learn their material three times—the first time to understand it, a second time to master it, and a third time to organize it for teaching. Students are more likely to find learning a specific subject fascinating and motivating when they see that their teacher finds it fascinating as well. Put simply, teachers encourage student learning by being enthusiastic learners themselves.

Enacting these four moral imperatives—acculturating students, providing essential knowledge and skills, developing effective relationships with students, and providing stewardship—are more than a matter of teachers' personal preferences. Fullan and Goodlad believe teachers are morally obligated to take on these roles. Teaching is clearly more than a job or career. Teachers touch our entire community and nation through the students we educate.

Activity 1.4

John Goodlad talks about four moral imperatives for schools and teachers:

1. To prepare students to live in a democracy
2. To provide students with essential knowledge and skills
3. To develop effective relations with students
4. To practice good stewardship

A. In groups of four, discuss these four imperatives. Which have you experienced as a student in elementary school, secondary school, and college? From your own school experiences, which imperative had the greatest impact on you as a person? Which had the least impact? Report your group's findings to the class and discuss how they compare with the other groups' findings.

B. With the other members of your four-person group, describe teacher behaviors that you have seen inside or outside your classrooms during your lives as students that illustrate each of the imperatives. Also describe teacher behaviors that you have seen that might have acted against the moral imperatives. Report these examples back to the class. Which behaviors are most common? Which are least common? Which do you think are the most difficult behaviors for teachers to enact, and why?

C. Working in the same groups of four, select one of the moral imperatives to illustrate on paper with images, colors, words, and other decorations to communicate its message through examples of teachers successfully enacting—or not enacting—the moral imperative. Report back to the class, and display and explain your group's illustration.

Enacting Schools' Moral Purpose Through Caring

Nel Noddings, a Stanford University Education Professor, has focused on the relationship aspect of teachers' moral purpose, reflecting the belief that teaching has a human outcome. Contemporary teachers enact schools' moral purpose through *caring*.[18] Our schools should produce competent, caring, loving, and lovable people.[19] In addition to developing academic adequacy, all children must learn to care for other human beings as well as for animals, plants, the physical and global environments, objects, instruments, and ideas. By furthering students' development in this way, schools produce people who can care competently for their own families and contribute effectively to their communities, both local and international.

In Noddings' view, American schools have traditionally promoted the belief that students develop character through academic skills and intellectual pursuits.[20] Historically, educators assumed that knowledge of "the basics" (whether classical studies or fundamental reading and math) along with self-sacrifice, success, determination, ambition, and competition would enable students to build the attitudes and skills appropriate to life in a capitalist society. The school was not expected to cure social ills; instead, it was expected to vigorously teach the values that society deemed important. In this way, teaching academic skills reinforced the society's desired moral ends.[21] To Noddings, schools should address human values and concerns, not merely cognitive ones.

Ethical caring and relationships. Caring relationships involve moral and ethical behaviors. Ethics and morals are analogous to theory and practice, respectively. That is, **ethics** denotes the theory of right and wrong actions, while **morals** indicate those actions' practice within guidelines. Relationships connect individuals with an emotion. For example, they may involve love or hate, anger or sorrow, admiration or envy. In some situations, the feelings may be mixed, with each party feeling different emotions. According to Noddings, a person who behaves ethically seeks to preserve or transform the relationship into a caring one. This ethical caring is more highly abstract than mother–child caring, also known as natural caring. **Ethical caring** is neither as intense nor as intimate as natural caring. With an ethic of caring, one acts out of affection or inclination rather than simply from duty and principle. For teachers and students, these caring relationships occur within the school and classroom settings during the teaching and learning process.

Ethically caring teachers enjoy working with students. To them, teaching encompasses more than just doing their job and earning a paycheck. With caring, the relationship itself is important—how the other person feels and responds. The caring teacher responds to his or her students' needs, wants, and requests. The student, ideally, recognizes and responds to the teacher's caring by thoughtfully completing the assigned work. The ethic of caring, therefore, is often characterized as responsibility and response. Students learn and develop this caring outlook and behaviors through their relationships with their teachers.

Caring teachers extend their goals for students beyond simply learning the content and performing well on the test. They want to help their students grow into likeable and ethical persons: "persons who will support worthy institutions, live compassionately, work productively but not obsessively, care for older and younger generations, be admired, trusted and respected."[22] For this type of development to happen, however, teachers need to know both their subjects and their students very well.

---

[18] Noddings, N. (1988, February). An ethic of caring and its implications for instructional arrangements. *American Journal of Education, 96*(2), 215–230.
[19] Noddings, N. (1995, January). A morally defensible mission for schools in the 21st century. *Phi Delta Kappan, 76*(5), 365–368.
[20] For a fuller discussion of the traditional view of "mental discipline" and the classical curriculum developing students' character, see Chapter 5, History of American Education, Part 2.
[21] Noddings, 1988.
[22] Noddings, 1988, p. 221.

Figure 1.4 | **Ethically Caring Teachers Enjoy Working with Students**

Jupiterimages/Photos.com/Jupiter Images

Caring relationships place cognitive and emotional demands on both teacher and student. Both parties allow themselves to be known as persons within their different roles and responsibilities. Every interaction then brings with it the possibility of deeper caring. In turn, each party must decide how to respond to the other while maintaining the appropriate role boundaries. Teachers do not strive to be students' pals, however, but rather to be their caring adult educators.

How teachers model caring. Teachers model caring for students in many ways. First and foremost, they consistently treat students with respect and consideration, and expect them to treat other students in the same way. Of course, one sees teachers model caring in other ways, too. Teachers show students how intellectual activity is useful, fun, and important. They limit lectures to the presentation of essential information and then use class time for students to interact and explore how the information addresses issues that are real and relevant to them. Teachers work with students to develop learning objectives that meet both the school's and the students' needs; when they use discussion to elicit and respond thoughtfully to students' ideas; and when they give students timely, specific written feedback on their work. They try to understand and meet the needs that underlie students' sometimes annoying behaviors rather than responding quickly and punitively to the behavior itself.

Fostering caring relationships requires open dialog. In this type of exchange, neither the teacher nor the student draws conclusions before opening the discussion. This does not mean that all viewpoints and choices are equally acceptable or that one party in the relationship must give in to the other's views or wishes. It does mean, however, that teachers and students must trust and respect each other well enough to express differing viewpoints or decisions and will thoughtfully consider the reasons given that oppose their original stand.

In addition, the caring teacher wants students to practice caring. Such teachers encourage students to support one another. They offer opportunities for students to interact as peers working collaboratively on projects of shared interest. The quality of their interactions reflects the respect and appreciation required to build their classroom community. Teachers encourage students to care for animals, plants, and the environment in ways consistent with caring for humans. Likewise, teachers help students feel at home in and appreciate the technical, natural, and cultural worlds.

Further, teachers help students understand that caring in every domain implies competence. When we care, we accept the responsibility to work continuously on our competence so that the recipient of our care—whether a person, animal, object, or idea—is enhanced. Caring is the strong, resilient backbone of human life.

Finally, caring teachers support students by responding to their actions in ways that reinforce the type of individual we want them to be. Caring teachers assume that students are well intentioned and act from worthy motives. When teachers respond to students with respect for the quality person that student either is now or can become, the student feels confirmed, validated as worthy and competent. What teachers reveal to students about themselves as ethical and intellectual beings has the power to either nurture that ideal or destroy it. Through their interactions, the teacher and the student become partners in fostering the student's growth.

For the relationship between teachers and students to develop, they need to spend more time together. Creating opportunities to greet and interact with students every day through welcoming them into the classroom and providing engaging lessons are positive starting points for forging such a connection. Similarly, creating smaller schools, limiting class sizes, and keeping students and teachers working together over multiple years can provide the extra time needed to develop a strong teacher–student relationship. In addition, schools can organize their curriculum around themes of care rather than traditional disciplines.[23] Working to create more caring schools would help both teachers and students develop more ethical selves.

Activity 1.5

Nel Noddings believes that schools should produce more competent, caring, loving, and likeable people. Teachers enact their moral purpose by developing caring relationships with their students.

A. Explain the different behaviors that characterize "ethical caring" and "natural caring." How can teachers recognize the "line" between the two? How can crossing this boundary confuse both teacher and student?

B. As a class, identify the behaviors that one might observe in classrooms that are characterized by caring and respectful teachers and students.

C. Discuss how a teacher knowing individual students well can improve the quality of student learning and the relationships in the classroom.

Moral Purpose and Economic Well-Being

Many people that believe schools' moral purpose is to prepare children to contribute to their own economic well-being when they reach adulthood and to ensure a thriving national economy. They assert that "prosperity must have a moral purpose" to make its economic gains available to as many citizens as possible.[24] Certainly, government has a responsibility to provide young people with skills and opportunities

---

[23] Noddings, 1995.
[24] Goldsmith, S. (2000). What compassionate conservatism is—and is not. *Hoover Digest. Research and Opinion on Public Policy.* Retrieved October 9, 2009, from http://www.hoover.org/publications/digest/3492491.html.

to create their own wealth by providing them with the education, information, and resources they need to make informed decisions and advance their economic destinies. Apart from this purpose, government and government agencies such as the public schools should have a limited role in people's lives. Marketplace competition is the most effective means of producing social and economic progress.

In this vein, public schools' "moral purpose" is to be accountable for all their students' performance through rigorous standardized testing, with scores from that testing being posted for all parents and the community to see. If schools don't show measurable increases in performance, then the parents should have control over those public dollars and be allowed to make the decisions about their children's education. If public schools do not educate their children to state standards, then the state should send parents vouchers or other financial means that enable them to send their children to private schools that can raise their achievement.[25] If we give individuals the education and other tools they need for success, allow them to control their own dollars, and help them enter the mainstream of American life, then we will produce a more prosperous and forward-looking country.

The debate about public schools' moral purpose can be addressed from varied perspectives. A pluralistic society expects and welcomes differing viewpoints. In all of these views, however, schools and the quality of our students' education remain essential keys to our children's and our nation's future.

Education for an Interconnected, Global Environment

Throughout most of human history, people lived and organized their lives around boundaries structured by local geography and topography, family and kinship, community social organizations, religions, and local worldviews. This is no longer true, however. Today's world is changing, and so is our understanding of what it means to be "educated." Today, youth grow up linked to economic realities, social processes, technology and media practices, and cultural movements that spill over local and national borders.

Just to get a sense of how the world has changed, consider this example: In 1969, an international telephone call from Hong Kong to Chicago cost nearly $10 per minute. In 2009, the same call cost between 1 and 15 cents per minute, depending on the phone company.[26] In the 1960s and 1970s, immigrants working in London relied on the postal system and personal letter carriers to communicate with family back home in India, Malaysia, or China. They waited two months to receive a reply to each letter. Calling by phone was not even possible. By the late 1990s, however, their grandchildren used mobile phones that linked them instantly with their cousins in Calcutta, Singapore, or Shanghai.[27]

Today, helping young people become fully educated is especially critical. Unlike when your parents were in K–12 schools, today you will teach in an interconnected, globalized world. "Education's challenge will be to shape the cognitive skills, interpersonal sensibilities, and cultural sophistication of children and youth whose lives will be both engaged in local contexts and response to larger transnational processes."[28]

---

[25] Goldsmith, 2000.

[26] Retrieved October 9, 2009, from http://www.vonage.com/lp/US/searchinternational995/ir.php

[27] Watson, J. L. (2004). Globalization in Asia: Anthropological perspectives. In M. M. Suarez-Orozco & D. B. Qin-Hilliard (Eds.), *Globalization: Culture and education in the new millennium*. Los Angeles: University of California Press, p. 147.

[28] Suarez-Orozco, M. M., & Qin-Hilliard, D. B.. (2004). *Globalization: Culture and education in the new millennium*. Los Angeles: University of California Press, p. 3.

Technology and the Workplace

According to Thomas Friedman, the three-time Pulitzer Prize–winning *New York Times* columnist and best-selling author, the "world is flat."[29] The flat world occurred when the Internet, broadband connectivity, inexpensive and widely dispersed computers, email, and software that could chop up any piece of work and send one part to Boston, Massachusetts, and the other to Bangalore, India, came together around the year 2000. This convergence created a platform for intellectual work that could be delivered from anywhere to anywhere. The flattening world means we are connecting together all the planet's knowledge centers into a single global network.

Friedman's use of the phrase "flat world" set many back on their heels. After all, don't American children learn that Christopher Columbus sailed from Spain in 1492 to prove that the world was *not* flat? The clash between our traditional views and this novel image certainly makes the concept of a "flat world" catchy—and highly controversial.

Technology is clearly changing the workplace, by virtue of its ability to connect people together in a virtual environment. Thanks to computer networks, people no longer have to be physically next to one another to work together. Standardized protocols can now connect everyone's machines. Software applications encourage the development of standardized business processes for how certain kinds of commerce or work will be conducted, allowing people to work seamlessly together. Companies have access to talent sitting in different parts of the world, and these widely dispersed workers can complete needed tasks in real time.

Naturally, **globalization**—that is, the trend of de-territorializing skills and competencies so that people working anywhere in the world can collaborate with those working elsewhere—affects what students worldwide need to know.[30] Globalization has major implications for American education and students' eventual careers. Anything that can be digitized[31] can be outsourced to either the smartest producer or the cheapest producer—or the producer that fits both descriptions. Many manufacturing jobs that traditionally provided middle-class salaries for relatively low-skilled workers have already been automated (using fewer workers) or moved offshore. Increasingly, jobs that require a college education are going to well-educated, highly trained, English-fluent workers with a strong service orientation around the world who are willing and able to work for much less money than their U.S. counterparts, yet who still manage to have a relatively high standard of living in their own country. The wages and rents in Bangalore, India, for example, are less than one-fifth what they are in Western capital cities. An investment analyst in Bangalore earns about $15,000 in total compensation, as compared with $80,000 for a person filling the same position in New York or London. Even for jobs remaining in the United States, salaries for highly skilled workers are much higher than those for low-skilled workers.[32] Learning that enables students to develop high levels of knowledge and skills is a necessary condition for obtaining well-paying employment—but it is not a guarantee that such opportunities will open up when students are ready to join the work force.

How Does Globalization Affect American Students?

What type of education do students need to survive and succeed in this globalized environment? For one thing, cognitive flexibility will be extremely important. Multitasking, learning how to learn, learning from failures, lifelong learning, and the

---

[29] For a full and insightful look at this concept, its practice, and its many implications for business, politics, and education, read Friedman's book: Friedman, T. L. (2006). *The world is flat: A brief history of the twenty first century, updated and expanded.* New York: Farrer, Straus and Giroux.
[30] Suarez-Orozco & Qin-Hilliard, 2004, p. 6.
[31] Digitization is the process by which words, music, data, films, files, and pictures can be manipulated on a computer screen, stored on a microprocessor, or transmitted over satellites and fiber-optic lines. This process allows you to browse online for books or download your favorite songs onto an MP3 player.
[32] Greenspan, A. (2007). *The age of turbulence.* New York: Penguin Press.

ability to make connections between different ideas and processes will be essential skills. In addition, education for globalization will require learning the higher-order thinking and interpersonal skills needed for problem finding, problem solving, and articulating arguments with verifiable support.

Should America's teachers and best students worry? Maybe. This new reality poses a challenge to all industrialized nations. Although Americans and Western Europeans produced many twentieth-century innovations, we have no guarantee that they will remain permanently in the lead in terms of technological development. After World War II, the United States had no serious economic or intellectual competition. In recognition of its dominance, the twentieth century was often called the American Century. Some believe that this economic, military, and cultural preeminence "bred a sense of entitlement and cultural complacency" in the United States.[33] Achieving a preeminent place in the world of tomorrow will not be as easy for Americans as it has been the last 50 years.

Certainly, education encompasses much more than securing a well-paying job. Nevertheless, "learning more to earning more" is still a realistic goal. Americans who want to compete successfully for decent-paying jobs will need the right attitudes, knowledge, and skills to vie for the information-rich careers in new specialties that will likely become available in this country. Individuals with low-knowledge skills, whose jobs can be moved elsewhere, however, have reason to worry. For example, the accounting profession is currently in transformation. The "grunt work" (i.e., bookkeeping, preparing payrolls) has been moving overseas. Meanwhile the job of designing and creating complex tax sheltering strategies with quality-time discussions with clients remains anchored in the United States.

"The ovarian lottery has changed—as has the whole relationship between geography and talent,"[34] argues Bill Gates, Microsoft's originator and former chairman. As the world has become globalized, people can "plug and play" from anywhere, and natural talent has started to become more important than geography. "Now, Gates says, "I would rather be a genius born in China than an average guy born in Poughkeepsie (New York)."[35]

Likewise, Thomas Friedman writes that when he was young, his parents used to tell him to finish his dinner because people in China and India would love to have his food. Now his advice to his daughters is, "Finish your homework. People in China and India would love to have your jobs."[36]

Activity 1.6

A globalized, interconnected "flat world" brings new challenges to today's teachers and learners.

A. In a group of four, explain how a "flat world" becomes both larger and smaller? How does it affect today's learners and tomorrow's workers?

B. As a group of four, draw, decorate, and color a picture to represent your answer.

C. Present the final product, along with a verbal explanation, to the rest of the class.

D. Discuss the group's views on living, working, teaching, and learning in this interconnected world.

---

[33] Friedman. 2005, p. 325.
[34] Bill Gates, cited in Friedman, 2005, p. 226.
[35] Bill Gates, cited in Friedman, 2005, p. 226.
[36] Friedman, 2005, p. 277.

"Everyone has to focus on what exactly is their value-add."[37] In the future, that special talent will distinguish a more employable from a less employable college graduate. Given our interconnected world economies, technology's reach and power, and good jobs spread across the globe, today's and tomorrow's teachers face the critical challenge of preparing all our students for personal satisfaction and economic survival in this high-information, highly competitive world.

Challenges to Globalization's Assumptions, Analysis, and Conclusions

The view of a globalized world that requires high intelligence, flexible skills, and more education to secure worthwhile employment is a controversial one. While many agree that globalization is changing the world's economy, work patterns, and education, people interpret the meaning of this transformation according to their various belief systems. They remind us to think more deeply and in more complex ways about why we have schools and what we want our teachers to accomplish.

| Figure 1.5 | In a Globalized World, the Ability to Get Along and Work with People Different from Oneself is an Important and Marketable Skill |

Comstock Images/Jupiter Images

---

[37] Jaithirth "Jerry" Rao, cited in Friedman (2005). p. 15.

First, globalization critics correctly observe that higher skills and more education do not guarantee higher wages. Data indicate that earning a college degree does not guarantee getting a college-level job. Since the early 1970s, a growing proportion of college graduates have taken jobs that usually do not require at least a bachelor's degree. Bureau of Labor Statistics, news reports, and private organizations indicate that there are more jobseekers with college degrees than there are openings in jobs requiring them.[38] While individuals who have earned college degrees still fill college-level jobs, increasingly they accept employment that does not require that level of formal education. Usually, however, they are well paid for their knowledge and skills, at whatever level they find employment. The trend in which the number of college graduates outstrips the number of college-level jobs available is expected to continue into the twenty-first century.

A 2007 Educational Testing Service study clarifies this situation. It observes that although the changing economy has seen an increased financial return on schooling and skills, even among adults with college degrees, college graduates with weaker literacy and numeracy skills are more likely to be employed in jobs that do not require a college degree than their college-educated peers who possess stronger skills. College graduates with weaker skills tend to find employment in lower-paying, low-end jobs.[39] The gap between high skills and low income is likely to grow. Higher skills are necessary to earn (but do not guarantee) higher wages.

Next, critics challenge the very assumption that schools' purpose is to prepare students for employment. Critical theorists Henry Giroux and Stanley Aronowitz reject the premise that U.S. schools should be preparing students to meet America's "corporate needs." Knowledge, they assert, is more than "economic capital" or preparation for employment.[40] Giroux argues that corporate power is encroaching on our culture, penetrating deeper into the education system, displacing the goals of democratic citizenship with the preparation of human capital for industry, and replacing concern for community with narrow self-interest.[41]

To **critical theorists**—a group of like-minded educators who believe that schools and teachers should serve the interests of social justice—knowledge has ethical value that includes self-definition, social responsibility, and individuals' capacities to expand the range of freedom, justice, and democratic practices.[42] Critical theorists see education as a political force that helps teachers and students push against the oppressive boundaries of gender, class, race, and age domination. Instead of training students for specific labor tasks, they suggest, schools should educate students to think differently about the meaning of work, preparing them with the skills and attitudes they will need to hold multiple jobs over the course of their careers.[43]

In 2007, the *Washington Post* wrote that the myth that the U.S. students will not be well prepared for the modern work force has been bandied around since at least the turn of the nineteenth century by business leaders who blame schools for inadequately preparing workers. The U.S. economy has grown "faster than any other

[38] Dolton, P., & Vignoles, A. (2000, April). The incidence and effects of overeducation in the U.K. graduate labour market. *Economics of Education Review, 19*(2), 179–198. For instance, studies have found that from 11 percent to 40 percent of U.S. white males were overeducated for their jobs; see Hecker, D. E. (1992). Reconciling conflicting data on jobs for college graduates. *Monthly Labor Review, 115,* 3–11. Retrieved October 9, 2009, from http://www.bls.gov/opub/mlr/1992/07/art1full.pdf.

[39] Olson, L. (2007, February 7). ETS study warns of growing inequality in income, skills. *Education Week, 26*(22), 7.

[40] Giroux, H. (n.d.) Doing cultural studies: Youth and the challenge of pedagogy. Retrieved October 9, 2009, from http://www.gseis.ucla.edu/courses/ed253a/Giroux/Giroux1.html; Aronowitz, S., & Giroux, H. (1985). *Education under siege: The conservative, liberal, and radical debate over schooling.* South Hadley, MA: Bergin & Garvey.

[41] Giroux, H. (2006). America on the edge: Henry Giroux on politics, culture, and education. New York: Palgrave Macmillan.

[42] Giroux, n.d.; Aronowitz & Giroux, 1985.

[43] Giroux, H. (1994, Fall). Slack off: Border youth and postmodern education. Retrieved October 9, 2009, from http://www.gseis.ucla.edu/courses/ed253a/Giroux/Giroux5.html.

advanced economy" over the past two decades and generated a third of the world's economic growth. A dynamic economy, the *Post* adds, is much more than the sum of its test scores. It's part of a culture that rewards innovation, risk taking, and unconventional problem solving. "Much of this is nurtured in our schools, even if it can't be quantified on a test."[44]

Where All Agree

Whatever the viewpoint or ideology, the high-tech, high-information, interconnected world has major implications for schools and teaching:

- Different viewpoints about education's purposes lead to different conclusions about how globalization will affect our students.
- Earning a college degree does not guarantee that the individual will find employment in a job requiring a college degree.
- Globalization impacts the way employees will work and learn. This has implications for education.
- Globalization is changing the nature of life from labor to knowledge.
- A globalized economy will increase international competition for well-educated and highly skilled workers who can provide the best, user-tailored products for the most reasonable costs, accessing work across a virtual world without moving physically.
- The ability to understand, communicate, work with, and get along with people different from oneself is an important and marketable skill.
- High-level knowledge and skills and the ability to keep learning are necessary conditions to secure a well-paying career.
- High-level skills and knowledge and the ability to keep learning do not guarantee that anyone possessing them will secure or keep a well-paying career.
- Education necessary for satisfaction and success in this changing world is broader than education for employment. It is lifelong, and focuses on living an aware, productive, personally and socially responsible, and satisfying life.

Activity 1.7

On one national 2000 teacher survey, only 32 percent of teachers responded that they felt prepared to address the needs of students from diverse cultural backgrounds.[45] Is this also true for the members of your current class?

A. Describe your personal experiences knowing or working with individuals from races, ethnic backgrounds, or religions different from your own. Did you know these persons from school? From your neighborhood? From a sports team? From your church? From your parents' work? From the media? From somewhere else?

B. How do these experiences—or lack of them—influence your present comfort level with individuals from these groups?

---

[44] *Washington Post.* (2007, January 24). Retrieved July 30, 2009 from: http://www.sptimes.com/2007/01/24/Opinion/Never_mind_the_doomsa.shtml.
[45] Teacher quality: A report on the preparation and qualifications of public school teachers. (2000). Washington, DC: National Center for Education Statistics. Retrieved July 30, 2009 from: http://nces.ed.gov/surveys/frss/publications/1999080/6.asp.

C. How do you plan to become more comfortable working with members of such diverse cultural groups? How can this class and your teacher education program increase both your comfort and professional skills levels with diverse student learners?

INTASC Model Core Standards for New Teachers

New teachers enter the profession inspired and excited about their new role. They want to be prepared and confident to meet the classroom demands they will face. Recognizing and responding to new teachers' challenges, the profession has built frameworks to support this effort.

In 1992, the Interstate New Teacher Assessment and Support Consortium (INTASC), a program of the Council of Chief State School Officers, developed model standards for licensing new teachers. These represent the common core of teaching knowledge and skills that will help their future students learn the twenty-first-century skills appropriate for a knowledge-based economy. These INTASC standards were designed to be compatible with those set by the **National Board for Professional Teaching Standards (NBPTS)**, a national professional organization that certifies teachers who can document meeting advanced standards of practice that improve teaching and learning through intensive study, expert evaluation, self-assessment, and peer review. NBPTS certification is the highest level of professional teaching practice now available.

INTASC standards address the knowledge, dispositions, and performances common to all teachers, regardless of academic discipline or specialty area, who are able to ensure that all their students learn to high levels. These include knowledge of student learning and development, curriculum and teaching, and contexts and purposes that create a set of professional understandings, abilities, and ethical commitments that all teachers share.

The INTASC standards are performance based.[46] They describe what teachers should know and be able to do. These behaviors are assessable. The INTASC standards also permit states and schools to incorporate more innovation and diversity in their teacher education programs by looking at teacher outcomes rather than lists of courses taken or other inputs. These standards are based on five propositions:

1. Teachers are committed to students and their learning.
2. Teachers know the subjects they teach and know how to teach those subjects to diverse learners.
3. Teachers are responsible for managing and monitoring student learning.
4. Teachers think systematically about their practice and learn from experience.
5. Teachers are members of learning communities.

Within this context, INTASC has identified ten principles that guide teacher education and teacher licensing. Teacher education programs following these principles work toward helping their students gain the knowledge, skills, dispositions, and behaviors that lead to greater teaching effectiveness in today's diverse classrooms. Future educators and their professors would do well to consider how effectively candidates are learning these principles in their college and teacher preparation courses.

- **Standard 1: Content Pedagogy.** The teacher understands the central concepts, tools of inquiry, and structure of the discipline(s) he or she teaches and can create learning experiences that make these aspects of subject matter meaningful to students. The teacher also recognizes that the subject matter is always

---

[46] Miller, J. M., & Darling-Hammond, L. (1992). Interstate New Teacher Assessment and Support Consortium: Draft. Retrieved October 9, 2009, from http://www.ccsso.org/content/pdfs/corestrd.pdf.

evolving, conveys multiple perspectives, understands that students bring misconceptions that may interfere with learning, and connects the content to students' daily lives.

- **Standard 2: Student Development.** The teacher understands how students learn and develop, and can provide learning opportunities that support their intellectual, social, and personal development. The teacher understands how students construct knowledge; recognizes how students' physical, social, cognitive, moral, and emotional development affect learning; and knows how to address these factors when making instructional decisions.

- **Standard 3: Diverse Learners.** The teacher understands how students differ in their approaches to learning and creates instructional opportunities that are adapted to diverse learners. The teacher understands and can identify different approaches to learning, such as learning styles and learning exceptionalities; recognizes how prior learning, experiences, language, values, family, and culture affect learning; and uses teaching approaches that are appropriate to these experiences.

- **Standard 4: Critical Thinking Skills.** The teacher understands and uses a variety of instructional strategies to encourage students' development of critical thinking, problem-solving, and performance skills. The teacher carefully evaluates how to achieve learning goals and chooses alternative teaching strategies and materials to achieve these goals and meet students' needs.

- **Standard 5: Motivation and Management.** The teacher uses an understanding of individual and group motivation and behavior to create a learning environment that encourages positive social interaction, active engagement in learning, and self-motivation. The teacher creates a smoothly functioning learning community in which students assume responsibility for both themselves and other students, work collaboratively and independently, make decisions, and engage in purposeful learning activities.

- **Standard 6: Communication and Technology.** The teacher uses knowledge of effective verbal, nonverbal, and media communication techniques to foster active inquiry, collaboration, and supportive interaction in the classroom. The teacher models effective communication and supports and expands the learners' expression in speaking, writing, and other media.

- **Standard 7: Planning.** The teacher plans instruction based on knowledge of the subject matter, students, the community, and curriculum goals. The teacher plans for learning opportunities that recognize and address variations in students' learning styles and performance modes.

- **Standard 8: Assessment.** The teacher understands and uses formal and informal assessment strategies to evaluate and ensure the learner's continuous intellectual, social, and physical development. Use of techniques including observation, portfolios of student work, teacher-made tests, performance tasks, student self-assessment, peer assessment, and standardized tests enables the teacher to enhance his or her knowledge of the learners, evaluate student progress and performance, and modify teaching and learning strategies as necessary.

- **Standard 9: Professional Development.** The teacher is a reflective practitioner who continually evaluates the effects of his or her choices and actions on others (students, parents, and other professionals in the learning community) and who actively seeks out opportunities to grow professionally. The teacher uses classroom data, collegial feedback, and the professional literature to support his or her own development as a learner and as a professional.

- **Standard 10: School–Community Involvement.** The teacher fosters relationships with school colleagues, parents, and agencies in the larger community to support students' learning and well-being. The teacher acts as an advocate for students.

If these ten standards reflect what a newly licensed teacher must know and be able to do, what does a mature and effective teacher need to know and be able to do? INTASC debated this question, asking what distinguished the beginning practice of a competent, newly licensed teacher from the advanced levels of teaching performance expected of a Nationally Board Certified teacher. The members of this organization concluded that the differences between beginning and advanced practice resided more in the degree of sophistication teachers used in applying their knowledge than in the kind of knowledge they needed. All teachers must be able to meet these ten standards, but they will differ in the expertise with which they do so.

For example, advanced practitioners have developed the ability to deal simultaneously with more of the complex facets of teaching. They can more effectively integrate and adapt their understandings and performances to meet students' individual needs. To eventually become an expert practitioner, beginning teachers must have at least an awareness of the kinds of knowledge and understandings needed—as well as the resources available—to develop these skills, knowledge, dispositions, and behaviors that increase all students' learning. Having a core content of common knowledge gives teachers a professional base from which to learn, grow, and perform.[47]

The INTASC competencies accurately reflect the complex and high-stakes world of today's diverse classrooms. What is more, many content areas have their own additional standards that teachers must meet. Learning to become an effective newly licensed teacher takes time, learning experiences, quality feedback, and increasingly extended doses of reflection and practice.[48] Becoming a teacher blends the individual's personality with the professional attitudes, knowledge, and skills shared by the profession as a whole. Becoming an educator takes a moral and ethical commitment for a lifelong journey.

Activity 1.8

The INTASC standards provide clear principles for teacher education and prospective teachers to build the essential knowledge, skills, dispositions, and performances necessary to be effective educators in today's diverse classrooms.

A. Individually reread the ten principles and identify for yourself which ones you believe you already know something about and which ones you will have to learn "from scratch." Discuss with other members of the class where they gained knowledge, skills, dispositions, and performances already in each of the areas—at least at a basic level—from their previous student, family, or worker experiences.

B. As a class or individually, discuss with your professor or college advisor the ten principles and identify which courses or experiences in your teacher preparation program you can expect to find opportunities to learn and build knowledge, skills, dispositions, and performances in each area.

C. With your professor or advisor, identify which principles—if any—are not addressed in the course content or pre-professional experiences your teacher education provides. Where can you find learning experiences to help you meet the standards where you currently fall short?

---

[47] For a description of how effective teachers can produce powerful learning in their classrooms, see the Supplement to Chapter 1, So You Want to be a Teacher, item C, on the Web site.
[48] For a fuller discussion on becoming a reflective teacher and reflection's value to continued professional growth, see Chapter 14, Instruction.

A CLOSER LOOK 👁

Is teaching an art or a science? Read the following passages and answer the questions below.

I began to wonder, was teaching a science or an art? Unfortunately as my medical educator colleagues used to comment, there is no protocol for good teaching that ensures success as there is for strep throat. There is science: knowledge about how learning occurs and research literature on good teaching practices. There is art: previous experiences to draw on, "gut" instinct or what . . . (is called) . . . reflective practice, and maybe a pinch of luck. We often think of artistic endeavors as being subjective—I don't like Picasso's cubist period, but my friend does. But are they really? In reality there are basic tenets of good practice and fundamentals that must be mastered for any art, whether it's painting, film, architecture, or teaching. One must explore the science of the field before one can practice the art.

Source: Qualters, D. (2002). The art and science of teaching with a little help from my friends. Retrieved July 30, 2009 from: **http://www.stthomasu.ca/publications/teaching/spring2002/qualters.htm**.

Some say that teaching is a science. These people stress the scientific aspects of teaching and focus on ways to systematize the communication between teacher and student. They believe that it is possible, through careful selection and pacing of materials, to regulate interactions among the student, the teacher, and materials to be learned, thus reducing the possibility that learning occurs by chance. . . . Others say that teaching is an art. These people believe that "scientific" teaching ends up in formalized, cookbook approaches that force students to perform and bureaucratizes learning. Besides, they argue, actual teaching involves great amounts of intuition, improvisation, and expressiveness, and effective teaching depends on high levels of creativity, sound judgment, and insight. Elliot Eisner, a professor of education at Stanford, has likened the artistic aspects of teaching to the activity of a symphony conductor. The teacher, like the conductor, draws upon a repertoire of skills and orchestrates a highly complex process.

Source: Davis, J, R. (1997). *Better teaching, more learning*. Phoenix: American Council on Education, Series on Higher Education. Retrieved July 30, 2009 from: **http://www.ntlf.com/html/lib/btml_xrpt.htm**.

Questions

1. Do you think that teaching is an art or a science? Which aspects of the profession require art and which aspects require science?

2. In what ways is effective teaching both an art and a science?

3. As a future teacher, which aspect—art or science—do you think you have more of naturally, and which aspect will you have to learn in formal and informal ways?

Activity 1.9

Below are the qualities that principals and human resources personnel want to observe in their teachers. During this semester, each student should visit and observe teachers at two different levels—elementary, middle, or high school. Use this checklist to document the teacher behaviors you see. Also note how the students appear to be responding (behaving and learning) to teachers in these classrooms. What do you see as the connections between teacher and student behaviors?

Check below if the teacher's behavior is present:

_____ **Exhibit enthusiasm.** Show your enthusiasm for teaching. Make learning fun.

_____ **Know your content.** Keep up with your field of expertise.

_____ **Be organized.** Established routines keep the class on track. Give students responsibility for maintaining their classroom.

_____ **Teach actively.** Be visibly and energetically involved with students and staff.

_____ **Show a good attitude.** Let your tone of voice and body language say you are in a good mood, showing care, concern, and respect.

_____ **Establish successful classroom management.** Establish and enforce your classroom management system. Be consistent and fair.

_____ **Pace instruction.** Considering the content and the learners, teach rapidly enough to keep students interested but not so fast that learners become confused and can't keep up.

_____ **Maintain good people skills.** Work collaboratively and respectfully with others.

_____ **Communicate clearly.** Convey information clearly. Be concise. Demonstrate.

_____ **Question effectively.** Ask questions directed to the whole class as well as to individuals. Ask the question first before calling student names. Wait 3–5 seconds for an answer.

_____ **Differentiate instruction.** Mix auditory, visual, and hands-on techniques. For specific lessons, subgroup students with similar weaknesses or skill gaps.

_____ **Build success into your class.** Continue to increase task difficulty with success at each step until students reach and exceed the standard.

_____ **Hold high expectations.** Communicate high expectations for good performance.

_____ **Create a pleasant atmosphere.** Cheerful, happy, and attractive classrooms will stimulate learning.

_____ **Be flexible.** Be sensitive enough to student needs to vary from your routines and rules when necessary to help a child.

Summary

As a future teacher, you are preparing to enter a respected and challenging profession that can significantly affect the quality of life for your students, their communities, and yourself.

Schools and teaching have moral purposes. Teachers are the agents of societal well-being—helping students develop the cognitive and interpersonal skills they need to thrive as persons, workers, and citizens. To be effective, teachers themselves must become lifelong learners. With this perspective, teaching evolves into more than a career; it becomes a means to enact social justice. Schools prepare students to successfully live in a democratic republic and help them learn the cognitive skills and attitudes that will allow them to lead personally satisfying and socially productive lives outside school.

The ongoing trend of globalization is already affecting the way employees work and learn, and changing the nature of life from a focus on brute labor to an emphasis on knowledge. High-level knowledge and skills and the ability to keep learning are necessary conditions for—but not a guarantee of—securing a well-paying career. This transformation has enormous implications for education worldwide.

The Interstate New Teachers Assessment and Support Consortium has developed ten principles to guide teacher education. They clearly articulate the knowledge, skills, dispositions, and performances that newly licensed teachers need to support high rates of learning in classrooms filled with diverse students. These principles can serve as powerful guidelines to help prospective teachers plan their professional preparation programs and offer benchmarks to note progress in the teacher's professional growth. The INTASC principles differ only in intensity (but not in type) from those that characterize an advanced professional teacher.

The teacher as a person and as a classroom manager has an enormous impact on the classroom climate and students' learning experiences. Teachers' psychological influence on students has been linked to student achievement in numerous effectiveness studies. Recognizing the qualities of effective teachers in themselves—and creating occasions to further develop and refine these aspects—can assist teachers in finding more personal and professional satisfaction in their work.

Conclusions

- Teaching is an inspiring as well as intellectually and emotionally challenging profession.
- Teachers are the means by which schools transmit our cultural heritage and instill in students the attitudes, knowledge, and skills they need to become informed citizens and economic contributors to our society.
- Teachers serve as both moral and ethical progenitors who contribute to the development of students and the advancement of the larger community.
- Effective teachers have much to learn personally and professionally to prepare themselves to accept this responsibility.

Teaching as a Profession

The teaching profession has become the focus of national attention. As one journalist recently wrote, "Teacher quality is not just an important issue in addressing the many challenges facing the nation's schools: It is *the* issue."[1]

Teacher and teaching quality are related policy challenges from the statehouse to the schoolhouse. Significant research evidence suggests that teacher and teaching quality are the most powerful predictors of student success.[2] Research also describes superlative teachers' characteristics and explains which classroom behaviors result in high student learning.[3] Better teaching is the key to higher student achievement. And better teaching depends, in part, on viewing teaching as a profession.

The perception of teaching as a profession depends, largely, on practitioners receiving adequate and appropriate preparation. New teachers agree. As one beginning teacher who entered the classroom through an alternative-route teacher preparation program reflected:

> I knew if I wanted to go on teaching there was no way I could do it without training. I found myself blaming my kids because the class was crazy and out of control, blaming the parents as though they didn't care about their kids. Even after only three-fourths of a semester [in a teacher preparation program] I have learned so much that would have helped me then.[4]

Another once-new teacher wrote of her early teaching experience in Philadelphia:

> My impeccably planned morning went smoothly for a grand total of eight minutes . . . then chaos ensued. We entered into negotiations. Would they work for a prize? How about a ten-minute break afterward? . . . I stood in a classroom wearing ugly, rubber-soled shoes, shouting at eleven-year-olds. I felt I had aged twenty years in two months. . . . Who ever thought this could be done by anyone, and without any training?"[5]

Teaching as a profession has never been stronger. The profession knows how to prepare effective teachers and how to support them once they enter their own classrooms. It knows how to keep teachers developing their expertise and leadership throughout their careers. This chapter will consider the factors that make it so.

Focus Questions

- How has teaching as a profession changed over the past decades?
- How is the teaching career changing?
- How do we prepare teachers for the profession?

---

[1] Minner, S. (2001, May 30). Our own worst enemy: Why are we so silent on the issue that matters most? *Education Week, 20*(38), 33.

[2] For a more complete literature review on teacher quality, see Kaplan, L. S., & Owings, W. A. (2002). *Teacher quality, teaching quality, and school improvement.* Bloomington, IN: Phi Delta Kappa Educational Foundation; and Kaplan, L., & Owings, W. (2003). The politics of teacher quality. *Phi Delta Kappan, 84*(9), 687–692.

[3] See Marzano, R. J. (2003). *What works in schools: Translating research into action.* Alexandria, VA: Association for Supervision and Curriculum Development.

[4] Darling-Hammond, L. (2006). *Powerful teacher education: lessons from exemplary programs.* San Francisco, CA: John Wiley and Sons, p. 14.

[5] Asquithy, C. (2005). *The emergency teacher.* Washington, DC: West Paley Press, pp. 47, 68–70.

- What does research say about how teacher preparation affects student achievement?
- Which factors contribute to new teachers leaving their classrooms?
- How do states license or certify teachers?
- What are teachers' standards of professional excellence?
- Which professional organizations support teachers?
- What does the research say about professionally endorsed teachers' impact on student achievement?
- How can schools' induction programs and professional development strengthen and keep the teachers they hire?

Teaching as a Profession

Teachers are professionals with expert knowledge about instruction and curriculum in their particular disciplines. They understand child development and the ways in which learners learn. As a group, teachers are well organized and participate in decision making about educational practices and their work conditions.

Defining a Profession

Sociology professor Andrew Abbott defines a **profession** as an exclusive occupational group that applies abstract knowledge to particular cases and has expertise and influence to practice in a given domain or field.[6] Establishing a profession means that individuals in a certain field of work claim an authority—power, confidence, and right—to practice that work. Because they can demonstrate expertise, these individuals receive the opportunity to do the profession's work.

Professionalism can be broadly defined as accepting responsibility for one's own professional development and growth. For teachers, professionalism means incorporating specialized knowledge, self-regulation, special attention to students' unique needs, autonomous performance, and responsibility for students' welfare into their practice.[7] In addition, teacher professionalism implies a sense of stewardship, of caring and doing everything possible to improve teaching and learning. Accomplishing all this requires values such as honesty, fairness, and integrity in the practitioner.[8]

A profession can keep its authority if the public accepts its claims of expertise and if the profession's internal structure of well-defined and agreed-upon knowledge and skills support it. For instance, people believe that physicians are professionals because they know anatomy, physiology, biochemistry, and pathology, and have specialized information and abilities gained through their study in an accredited medical school. The medical profession includes organizing groups that provide written and performance tests that enable doctors to become board certified and earn advanced credentials.

"Few would require cardiologists to deliver babies, real-estate lawyers to defend criminal cases, chemical engineers to design bridges, or sociology professors to teach

[6] Abbott, A. (1988). The system of professions: An essay on the division of expert labor. Chicago: University of Chicago Press.

[7] Darling-Hammond, L., & Goodwin, A. L. (1993). Progress toward professionalism in teaching. In G. Cawelti (Ed.), *Challenges and achievements of American education* (pp. 19–52). Alexandria, VA: Association for Supervision and Curriculum Development.

[8] Sergiovanni, T. J. (1992). *Moral leadership: Getting to the heart of school improvement.* San Francisco: Jossey-Bass.

English. The commonly held assumption is that such traditional professions require a great deal of skill and training; hence, specialization is assumed to be necessary."[9]

Characteristics of a profession include the following elements:[10]

- Autonomy in making decisions about selected aspects of work
- A clearly defined, highly developed, specialized, and theoretical knowledge base beyond that understood by laypersons
- Agreed-upon standards of professional practice shaped by practitioners
- A code of ethics to help clarify ambiguous issues related to services rendered
- A lengthy period of specialized training
- Control of licensing and certification standards and entry requirements
- Control over training new entrants
- Self-governing and self-policing authority by members of the profession, especially about professional ethics (acceptance of responsibility for judgments made and acts performed related to service rendered)
- A commitment to public service
- Professional associations and elite groups that provide recognition for individual achievements
- High prestige and economic standing

Let's see how the teaching profession compares with other fields such as law and medicine in four key areas: (1) a defined body of knowledge and skills beyond that which laypersons recognize as unique and special; (2) control over licensing standards and/or entry requirements; (3) autonomy in making decisions about certain work areas; and (4) high prestige and economic standing.[11]

A defined body of knowledge. All professions have a certain knowledge specialty that separates their members from the general public. When members make this clearly defined expertise widely known, they protect the public from untrained amateurs by denying them professional membership.

Until relatively recently, however, "teaching" had no agreed-upon specialized body of knowledge.[12] Traditionally, teaching has not been guided by extensive procedural rules and established methods such as those found in the physical sciences and health care. As a result, many people talk about education as if they—the laypersons—were also experts. To them, teaching holds no mystery because they have all had personal experiences as students. Because they cannot see teachers' complex planning decisions or thinking choices made in a dynamic classroom, laypeople assume that teaching does not require any extraordinary knowledge or skills apart from knowing their subject. In fact, Daniel C. Lortie, professor emeritus of education at the University of Chicago, has coined the phrase **"apprenticeship of observation"** to describe the phenomenon where laypersons who have spent

---

[9] Ingersoll, R. M. (2008, January). A researcher encounters the policy realm: A personal tale. *Phi Delta Kappan, 89*(5), 371.

[10] The definition of *profession* is compiled from the following resources: Abdal-Haqq, I. (1991) Professionalizing teaching: Is there a role for professional development schools? Retrieved October 9, 2009 from http://library.educationworld.net/a12/a12-170.html; Corwin, R. G. (1965). *Sociology of education.* New York: Appleton-Century-Crofts; Darling-Hammond, L. (1987). Schools for tomorrow's teachers. *Teachers College Record, 88*, 356–358; Howsam, R. B., Corrigan, D. C., & Denemark, D. W. (1976). *Educating a profession.* Washington, DC: American Association of Colleges for Teacher Education; Levine, M. (1988). Introduction. In M. Levine (Ed.), *Professional practice schools: Building a model* (pp. 1–25). Washington, DC: American Federation of Teachers; and Rosenholtz, S. J. (1989). *Teachers' workplace: The social organization of schools.* New York: Longman.

[11] Yinger, R. J., & Nolen, A. L. (2003, January). Surviving the legitimacy challenge. *Phi Delta Kappan 84*(5), 386–390.

[12] Yinger & Nolen, 2003; Johnson, S. M. (2001, January). Can professional certification of teachers reshape teaching as a career? *Phi Delta Kappan, 82*(5), 393–399.

thousands of hours as schoolchildren watching and judging teachers in practice develop many false preconceptions about teaching and mistakenly consider themselves to be "experts."[13]

Furthermore, teaching's less well-defined body of knowledge has allowed teacher education course requirements to vary from state to state, and even among teacher training institutions within a given state. While teacher education usually includes three major components—general education, specialized subject education, and professional education—heated discussions frequently arise over which is more important and by how much. For instance, how many credit hours should a prospective teacher have in professional practice (pedagogy) compared to course hours in a specialized subject field? How much clinical experience in actual school settings should be required? Should students learn the subject discipline in a liberal arts college or within specialized teacher education schools? One might logically ask, if leaders in teacher education cannot clearly agree on the profession's body of knowledge, how can the general public expect to see teachers as true professionals?[14]

Notably, this situation is improving as states increasingly are adopting a common set of high-quality, national professional benchmarks. The **National Council for Accreditation of Teacher Education (NCATE)**, a national teacher education accrediting organization, has set high, clear standards that specify the courses to be taken and the faculty qualifications for teaching them. By 2006, 25 states had adopted or adapted the NCATE standards and processes to evaluate institutions that do not seek national accreditation.[15] Having a recognized, respected, and clearly defined body of knowledge strengthens teaching as a profession.

Controlling requirements for entrance and licensing.

Unlike other professions, teaching has historically lacked uniform requirements for professional entry and licensing. Certification requirements vary from state to state, and the trend toward testing teachers remains controversial. Recent reforms, however, have required prospective teachers in most states to pass minimum competency tests. States control the "cut scores" that mark the difference between passing and failing, so a teacher who receives a certain score may "pass" in one state but "fail" in another.

In short, the teaching field does not consistently control professional entry and licensing. For the most part, states make these decisions based on political influences and other local considerations.

Autonomy in deciding work responsibilities.

Every profession considers all group members qualified to make expert judgments about their work; outsiders, by contrast, are deemed unqualified to make such decisions. Teachers, in comparison, traditionally have had little input about what they teach or the resources they use. School officials often hire outside "experts" with little teaching experience to help teachers select textbooks, write grant proposals, or resolve local community issues. Likewise, school reform ideas often come from government officials, business leaders, and civic groups—not from teachers.

As teachers increase their knowledge about effective teaching and learning practices and actively participate in school improvement teams and site-based management, they are likely to increase their autonomy in deciding their own work responsibilities.[16]

Prestige and economic standing.

Prestige is the level of social respect or standing, the good reputation and high esteem accorded to an individual or a group because of

---

[13] Lortie, D. (1975). *Schoolteacher: A sociological study*. London: University of Chicago Press.
[14] Yinger & Nolen, 2003; Johnson, 2001.
[15] Honawar, V. (2006, October 11). Teacher-prep field of two minds over replacing NCATE. *Education Week, 26*(7), 1, 18.
[16] Darling-Hammond, L. (1994). Who will speak for the children: How "Teach for America" hurts urban schools and students. *Phi Delta Kappan, 76*(1), 21–33; Luke, A., Luke, C., & Mayer, D. (2000, April). Redesigning teacher education. *Teaching Education, 11*(1), 5–11.

| Figure 2.1 | Today's Teachers Enter the Profession from a Variety of Backgrounds, Including Prior Careers |

Yellow Dog Productions/Riser/Getty images

their position's status. Occupations have high prestige if the public believes the people who fill them make especially valuable contributions to society. Similarly, the most prestigious occupations require a high level of education or skill and little physical or manual labor.

Today's elementary and secondary teachers rank relatively high in prestige.[17] In 2004, one poll found that Americans view doctors, scientists, fire fighters, teachers, and military officers as the professions and occupations with the most prestige. Since 1977, the percentage of the public that sees teachers as having "very great" prestige has increased 19 points, from 29 percent to 48 percent. What is more, teachers are the only occupation whose prestige rating has improved since 1977.[18] Clearly, occupational prestige is strongly associated with respect, public service, and good work—all qualities associated with teachers.

Teachers clearly appreciate their prestigious standing. A 2008 MetLife Survey of the American Teacher found that the proportion of teachers saying they are "very satisfied" with their careers increased from 40 percent in 1984 to 62 percent in 2008, while more teachers today (66 percent) feel respected by society than did their peers back then.[19]

Several factors account for this trend. First, teachers' average education level has increased significantly over the past century. Now, all teachers have bachelor's degrees; many have master's degrees and even doctorates. Second, teaching has

---

[17] Harris Interactive Poll. Doctors, scientists, firemen, teachers, and military officers top list as "Most Prestigious Occupations." These are some of the results of the annual Harris Poll measuring public perceptions of 22 professions and occupations, conducted by telephone between August 10 and 15, 2004, by Harris Interactive® with a sample of 1,012 U.S. adults. Retrieved October 9, 2009, from http://www.harrisinteractive.com/harris_poll/index.asp?PID=494.
[18] Harris Interactive Poll, 2004.
[19] Rebora, A. (2009, March 4). Survey shows teacher satisfaction climbing over quarter century. *Education Week, 28*(23), 12.

become increasingly complex. Teachers use high-level thinking in planning, delivering, and assessing lessons. They have high levels of language skills in reading, writing, and speaking. Teachers also work effectively with a variety of people—students, colleagues, parents, and administrators.

Nevertheless, several factors limit teachers' status and prestige in the public's eyes. First, their clientele's size and nature play a role in determining a group's occupational prestige. For instance, people accord more prestige to occupations in which the individuals deal with one person at a time and that person comes voluntarily. For example, a doctor treats a patient with an illness, and a lawyer litigates on the client's behalf. Teachers, by comparison, tend to work with groups of young persons who are required to attend school, a captive audience. As a result, the public grants teachers relatively lower prestige. Further, because most adults have seen teachers in action, teaching holds no "mystique" while less familiar professions do.[20]

Teacher salaries. Salary plays a role in determining an occupation's prestige. Teachers are not as highly paid as physicians, lawyers, engineers, and college professors because the public believes that these other professionals deal with more abstract and complex material. In addition, these fields require more demanding academic preparation and licensure than does public school teaching.[21]

In addition, the teaching profession is large, and schools run on taxpayers' dollars. These factors also limit what teachers can earn. Teacher salaries typically lag behind inflation. Over the past 10 years, the average salary for public schoolteachers increased only 1.3 percent after adjusting for inflation.[22] An analysis of U.S. Census data shows that over the past 60 years, the annual salary teachers receive has fallen sharply relative to the annual pay of other workers with college degrees.[23] In 2006, public school teachers earned, on average, 15 percent less than workers in other professions that require similar education and skills, including accountants, reporters, nurses, and computer programmers.[24] Economic downturns like those that occurred in 2007, 2008, and 2009—also mean less public money is available for school budgets, teachers' salaries, and benefits increases.[25]

Nevertheless, the percentage of teachers agreeing that they can earn a "decent salary" has nearly doubled since 1984, to 66 percent, and far more teachers today (75 percent, compared with 45 percent in 1984) say they would recommend a career in teaching to a young person.[26]

Table 2.1 shows the starting salaries for teachers and some other college-educated professions. Beginning teachers earn $6,000 less than the next closest profession, registered nurse, and almost $16,000 per year less than a public accountant—even though entry into each of these fields requires a four-year college degree. Studies have also found that teacher salaries are important in attracting individuals to teaching from the college-educated pool and in influencing early career behavior.[27]

An individual with similar credentials in anther profession could earn roughly $175 more in one week than a teacher.[28] An original analysis by the EPE Research Center found that public school teachers across the United States make 88 cents for

---

[20] Hoyle, E. (2001, April). Teaching: Prestige, status and esteem. *Educational Management and Administration, 29*(2), 139–152.

[21] Hoyle, 2001.

[22] Alvarez, B. (2007, December 10). Teacher salary lags behind inflation. National Education Association. Retrieved May 19, 2008, from http://www.nea.org/newsreleases/2007/nr071210.html.

[23] Hurley, E. (n.d.). Teacher pay 1940 to 2000 losing ground, losing status. National Education Association, Education Statistics. Retrieved December 14, 2006, from http://www.nea.org/edstats/losingground.html.

[24] Honawar, V. (2008, March 12). Teachers found to face "penalty" in salaries. *Education Week, 27*(27), 5.

[25] DeVise, D. (208, May 9). A school budget era may be over. WashingtonPost.com. Retrieved October 9, 2009, from http://www.washingtonpost.com/wp-dyn/content/article/2008/05/08/AR2008050803006_pf.html.

[26] Rebora, 2009.

[27] Darling-Hammond, L., & Sykes, G. (2003). Wanted: A national teacher supply policy for education: The right way to meet the "highly qualified teacher" challenge. *Educational Policy Analysis and Archives. 11*(33). Retrieved October 9, 2009, from http://epaa.asu.edu/epaa/v11n33.

[28] Mihans, R. (2008, June). Can teachers lead teachers? *Phi Delta Kappan, 89*(10), 762–765.

Table 2.1	Trends in Starting Salaries Across Professions, 2008
Profession	National Average Starting Salary
College graduate	$51,000
Teachers	$43,000
Researcher (nontechnical)	$62,000
Registered nurse	$49,000
Public accountant	$59,000
Engineer	$66,000
Systems analyst and designer	$63,000

Sources: U.S. Census Bureau. Average salaries. Simplyhired. Retrieved May 27, 2009, from http://www.simplyhired.com/a/salary/search/q-teacher; http://www.simplyhired.com/a/salary/search/q-Registered+nurse; http://www.simplyhired.com/a/salary/search/q-Engineer; http://www.simplyhired.com/a/salary/search/q-Public+Accountant; http://www.simplyhired.com/a/salary/search/q-Researcher; http://www.simplyhired.com/a/salary/search/q-college+degree.

every dollar earned in 16 comparable occupations. Ten states reach or surpass the pay-parity line, meaning teachers earn at least as much as comparable workers.[29] Although analysts have repeatedly attempted to examine the competitiveness of teacher pay, a variety of factors complicate this research.[30]

For example, teacher salaries vary by location. In New York, the median kindergarten teacher salary is more than $71,000 per year, and New Jersey middle school vocational teachers make more than $60,000 per year. In Montana and Arkansas, by contrast, teacher salaries rarely exceed $40,000 per year, even after individuals have been teaching for many years. The cost of living in different areas can also have a significant effect on teacher salaries.[31]

Making sense of teachers' salaries requires an appropriate frame of reference. The Bureau of Labor Statistics (BLS) estimates that full-time public teachers work an average of 36.5 hours per week during the school year, which usually lasts fewer than 200 days.[32] From a different perspective, Stanford University professor Linda Darling-Hammond asserts that teachers work 10-12 hours per day.[33] That totals an extra 12.5 weeks of work each year not accounted for in the BLS figures. In addition, these numbers don't account for the benefits that most school districts offer their educators: comprehensive health and life insurance; solid retirement and pension plans; opportunities to earn stipends as club sponsors, department heads, coaches, and summer school instructors; and additional money for earning advanced degrees. Many school districts offer opportunities for continuing education as well.[34] According to a recent Manhattan Institute for Policy Research study of teacher salaries, public school teachers are paid 11 percent more than the average professional worker.[35] While teachers

[29] Swanson, C. B. (2008, January 10). Teacher salaries: Looking at comparable jobs. Quality counts 2008: Tapping Into teaching. *Education Week.* Retrieved October 9, 2009, from http://www.edweek.org/ew/articles/2008/01/10/18salaries.h27.html.
[30] Complicating factors include whether teachers are 9-month or 12-month workers, whether fringe benefits should be considered in addition to salary, and whether to analyze hourly, weekly, or annual pay.
[31] Halsted. K. (2008). Learn the truth about teacher salaries. All Star Directories. All Education Schools. Retrieved October 9, 2009, from http://www.alleducationschools.com/faqs/teacher-salary.php.
[32] National compensation survey: Occupational wages in the United States, June 2005: Supplementary tables, 2006. (2006). Retrieved February 15, 2009, from www.bls.gov/ncs/ocs/sp/ncbl0831.pdf.
[33] Interview with Linda Darling-Hammond (n.d.). PBS "Only a teacher" series. Retrieved September 14, 2009 from: http://www.pbs.org/onlyateacher/today2.html
[34] Halsted, 2008.

can make a good living depending on their subject specialty, their state and school district, and their initiative, recruiting and keeping capable, qualified, and committed teachers is critical. Given our market-driven economy, however, the law of supply and demand does not stop at the schoolhouse door.[36]

Increasingly, teaching is strengthening many factors that enhance its professional status. Understanding the teaching career's historical changes—its maturation—helps explain just how much how far the profession has progressed along these four dimensions.

The Changing Nature of Teaching

As an occupation, teaching is highly demanding, exciting, and important. Teachers bear society's burden of newer, higher expectations for schools.[37] Nevertheless, teaching and schooling have changed more dramatically in the past few decades than they did in the two centuries before. Today's teachers are working by a whole new set of rules.

Teaching's Career Structure

Although the first American teachers were male "schoolmasters," by 1870 women outnumbered men as teachers across the nation—an imbalance that has not been reversed since it began.[38] As a result, teaching has been a profession largely shaped by a "gendered bureaucracy" in which men, viewed as professionals, supervised and trained women, who actually taught.[39] For the most part, young women teachers did not remain in their classrooms for long. Many married and left to have families. Female teacher turnover was an expected part of the school culture. Because they were seen as a source of cheaper and less aggressive labor than men throughout the nineteenth century and into the twentieth century, women teachers were paid less than their male counterparts.[40]

The U.S. educational system of the early twentieth century organized teaching and learning in simple and mechanistic ways. Administrators—usually men—maintained their schools' continuity. They hired departing teachers' replacements and tried to get newcomers up to speed as efficiently as possible. To achieve this feat, schools typically took an unsophisticated view of teaching. The hiring protocol addressed basic questions:

- Did teachers know their subjects (at least better than their students)?
- Did teachers keep their classrooms orderly, quiet, and purposeful?
- Did teachers move all students out of the halls by the time the next class's bell rang?
- How well did their students score on tests (so administrators could infer what they learned)?

Thus, while teachers considered themselves to be professionals, the organizations in which they worked—schools—often did not treat them accordingly.

---

[35] *How much are public school teachers paid?* (2007, January). Washington, DC: Manhattan Institute for Policy Research, U.S. Bureau of Labor Statistics.
[36] Mishel, L., Allegretto, S., & Corcoran, S. (2008, April 30). The teaching penalty: We can't recruit and retain excellent educators on the cheap. *Education Week, 27*(35), 30.
[37] Hargreaves, A. (2003). Teaching in the knowledge society: Education in the age of insecurity. New York: Teachers College Press.
[38] Donahue, D. M. (2002, Spring). Rhode Island's last holdout: Tenure and married women teachers on the brink of the women's movement. *History of Education Quarterly, 42*(1), 50–74.
[39] Blackwell, P. J., Futrell, M. H., & Imig, D. G. (2003 January). Burnt water paradoxes of schools of education. *Phi Delta Kappan, 85*(5), 357.
[40] Donahue, 2002.

In the two decades following World War II, teaching changed from an occupation requiring little specialized training to a profession that demanded increasing levels of preparation and competence. Yet partially in response to the earlier political and life-choice realities, teaching remained an "unstaged" career, lacking a progression of steps through which one could advance.[41] Unlike most other professions, teaching does not have career ladders that employees climb as they mature, become more productive, and show leadership. Teachers' responsibilities seldom change over the years, from their first to their last workdays.

Analysts offer differing explanations for teaching's traditional lack of career stages.[42] Some say teaching, because its was widely regarded as "woman's work," did not require the same kinds of promotions that signaled advancement in male-dominant careers.

Next, because child rearing has traditionally shaped women's employment patterns, teaching has been a high-turnover field, not easily plotted out into stages. A national survey of first-year teachers in 1956 found that while 80 percent of the male respondents expected to remain continuously employed as teachers or administrators, only 25 percent of the female respondents had similar expectations. The vast majority of women who planned to leave education listed raising a family as their reason, even though many of those same women returned to teaching after their children were in school.[43] With women living in a society that expected mothers to stay home with their children, personal and family changes dictated career changes.

Other analysts point to schools' customary "egg crate" structure, in which teachers work alone rather than as members of an integrated and tiered organization, for the lack of career stages. In this view, hiring teachers to fill vacant classrooms could supposedly occur with relatively little disruption to the rest of the organization. Others note the influence of teaching's conservative milieu, which discourages efforts to distinguish individuals by competence. Finally, some analysts conclude that the unstaged nature of teaching careers results from teachers' tendency to define their success based on their work inside the classroom rather than their ability to move up to higher-status positions outside it. Such has traditionally been teaching's professional culture: rationalizing and minimizing the absence of teaching career stages, promotions, and tangible rewards.[44]

Changing Career Expectations

Not only has the teaching profession changed, but future teachers have changed, too. Those entering teaching today have different expectations for their careers than did the teachers who entered the profession a generation ago.

Until the mid-1960s, teaching was the primary career option for large numbers of well-educated women and people of color to whom other professions were formally or informally closed. This is no longer true. Today, persons considering teaching have many more career options than did the retiring veterans of the current school system. Many of these alternative careers offer higher salaries, greater status, and better working conditions than does teaching. As a result, today's prospective teachers are drawn from a different population than the one that filled the teaching ranks decades earlier.

---

[41] Lortie, 1975, p. 85.

[42] Johnson, S. M. (2001, January). Can professional certification for teachers reshape teaching as a career? *Phi Delta Kappan, 82*(5), 393–399; Donohue, 2002.

[43] Simpson, R. L., & Simpson, I. H. (1969). Women and bureaucracy in the semi-professions. In A. Etzioni (Ed.), *The semi-professions and their organization* (p. 209). New York: Free Press.

[44] Johnson, 2001.

In addition, today's new and prospective teachers differ from retiring teachers in other important ways: They enter teaching at different career stages, they take multiple routes to the classroom, and they plan to spend fewer years in the classroom.[45]

First, more new teachers already have worked several years in other career fields and are entering teaching at a midcareer point in their lives. In one sample of 50 first- and second-year teachers, 52 percent entered teaching as a first career, on average at age 24, while 48 percent entered it at midcareer, on average at age 36.[46] Midcareer new teachers came to teaching believing that it offered more meaningful work than their previous employment.

Second, new teachers are reaching the classroom by taking a variety of paths. Most new teachers enter the profession using the traditional pathways of undergraduate or graduate teacher preparation programs. These programs include at least one academic year of specific coursework, opportunities to practice their skills under an experienced teacher's supervision during 6 to 10 weeks of student teaching, and state certification. By contrast, approximately 36 percent of teachers in one study entered teaching through an alternative route.[47] These teaching newcomers relied more on their innate teaching ability and other work experiences than on professional teacher education to prepare them for successful teaching.

Third, in contrast to veteran teachers who expect to remain in their classrooms until retirement, many new teachers approach teaching tentatively, conditionally, or as one of several careers they expect to have over their working lives. Few see themselves remaining in the classroom for the long term. Even first-career teachers do not expect to be full-time teachers until they retire. Although they expect to be excellent teachers, they do not plan to make a teaching their life's work.[48]

In summary, new teachers have more career choices available to them and do not expect to make classroom teaching their life's work. Many have solid work experiences in other career fields and arrive at teaching with a maturity born of greater chronological age and life-earned wisdom. Given these factors, it is the school's professional culture that often makes the difference between teachers who leave and teachers who stay.

How We Prepare Teachers: Traditional Teacher Education

Quality teacher preparation programs are essential if we are to educate teachers to successfully handle the varied challenges they will face in modern-day schools. In this section, we look at how teacher preparation programs developed and examine the data supporting their effectiveness.

Early Teacher Training and Normal Schools

In the early 1800s, American society did not require a highly educated work force. Instead, it needed large numbers of people with basic skills to drive its economy. The schools met this need.

Beginning in the early 1800s, states saw the need to train teachers to be more effective. Recognizing that educated citizens were essential to protect and preserve our democratic institutions, New York Governor DeWitt Clinton advocated that "the

---

[45] Peske, H. G., Liu, E., Johnson, S. M., Kauffman, D., & Kardos, S. M. (2001, December). The next generation of teachers: Changing conceptions of a career in teaching. *Phi Delta Kappan, 83*(4), 304–311.

[46] Johnson, S. M. (2006, Summer). *American Educator*. Retrieved October 9, 2009, from www.aft.org/pubs-reports? american_educator/issues/summer06/Teacher.pdf.

[47] Johnson, 2001.

[48] Johnson, 2001.

mind and morals of the rising and perhaps the destinies of all future generations, be not entrusted to the guardianship of incompetence."[49]

By 1810, the Lancastrian higher schools in New York and elsewhere had developed classes for training monitors as teachers. While they offered an extremely narrow concept of what teaching should be, these schools represented the only teacher-training institutions available at the time. In 1827, Governor Clinton recommended the creation of a "central school in each county for the education of teachers," and the New York legislature appropriated the state funds necessary to fulfill this goal.[50] Similarly, in 1834, the New York legislature enacted the country's first law providing for elementary school teachers' professional education in a teacher training institute called a normal school.[51]

Normal schools and academies. **Normal schools** were one- or two-year training institutions for prospective teachers. The term "normal school" comes from the French model, *ecole normale*. Literally, as normal school graduates, teachers were expected to uphold and teach society's norms and rules.[52]

The first normal schools were actually secondary schools that prepared teachers for elementary schools; they were not college-level institutions. Most of their students had only an elementary education. Because a high proportion of normal school students needed remediation, the curriculum included an eclectic mix of basic subject matter and pedagogy. Normal schools operated locally and enrolled neighborhood students who would teach for community schools.[53]

Prospective teachers could also receive training in academies. The academy teacher training program was entirely academic, because no professional body of teaching knowledge existed at the time. In these institutions, lecturers taught principles of teaching and school management primarily by using personal anecdotes drawn almost entirely from their own school experiences. Future teachers reviewed elementary school subjects and advanced academic studies.[54]

Because education was a state responsibility, each state decided how to prepare teachers for its public schools. By 1860, nine states had established state normal schools. By 1865, the United States had 22 state normal schools. After that time, however, public and private teacher training schools grew rapidly.

Teachers' colleges. In the late nineteenth century, colleges and universities claimed the right to prepare new teachers. To compete with colleges, normal schools transformed themselves by adopting the newly developed accrediting and professional standards. They also raised their admissions standards, requiring all applicants to have a high school diploma, and extended their teacher-training programs to two years for elementary school teachers and four years for high school teachers. They added research, liberal arts departments, and professors to their organizations. In short, they become teachers' colleges.[55]

Teacher Education in the Twentieth Century

In the late nineteenth and early twentieth centuries, American universities began to study education and develop more sophisticated teacher preparation programs. Given that only 4 percent of the college-aged population attended college in 1900,

---

[49] Cubberley, E. P. (1947). *Public education in the United States.* Cambridge, MA: Houghton Mifflin, p. 375.
[50] Cubberley, 1947, p. 376.
[51] Cubberley, 1947, p. 377.
[52] The term "normal school" is now largely obsolete. By the end of the nineteenth century, most normal schools had become four-year teacher education colleges.
[53] Levine, A. (2006). Educating school teachers. The Education Schools Project. Retrieved October 9, 2009, from http://www.edschools.org/pdf/Educating_Teachers_Report.pdf.
[54] Cubberley, 1947, p. 378.
[55] Public normal schools first became state normal colleges, then state teachers' colleges, then state colleges and universities. Private normal schools closed. See Levine, 2006, p. 25.

college and universities saw teacher preparation as a possible source of students and income and competed to enroll them.[56]

Until 1900, education studies were largely devoted to history and philosophy of education, teaching methods, and school management. After 1900, because high school teaching depended on mastering a subject or discipline, teacher education began to include more advanced content, including testing and measurement, educational philosophy, school surveys, and educational research. By 1915, a majority of colleges provided teacher education coursework.[57]

In 2006, Arthur Levine, former president of Columbia University Teachers College, surveyed principals and found that 60 percent thought education schools were doing a good job in preparing future teachers in mastery of subjects, understanding of how students learn, ability to use different pedagogies, and capacity to implement state standards.[58] Levine also found that strong teacher preparation programs integrate and balance academic and clinical instruction.

A telling anecdote highlights the importance of connecting theory and practice. As one teacher preparation alumnus reported, "I could talk about (influential psychiatrist) Carl Jung, scaffolding, cooperative learning groups, [and] the advantages of constructivism," but had no idea what to do "when Johnny goes nuts in the back of the class, or when Lisa comes in abused, or when Sue hasn't eaten in three days."[59]

Today's schools of education are in the business of preparing teachers for a new world in which all students are expected to learn to high levels. Joining teaching theory with real-world application and practice as well as expert supervision and feedback gives future teachers the basic knowledge and skills necessary to ensure their effectiveness in the modern-day classroom.

Research Studies: The Importance of Teacher Preparation

In *Doing What Matters Most: Investing in Quality Teaching*, Linda Darling-Hammond concludes that reviews of more than 200 studies contradict the myth than "anyone can teach" and that "teachers are born and not made":

> Teachers who are fully prepared and certified in both their discipline and in education are more highly rated and are more successful with the students than are teachers without preparation, and those with greater training . . . are more effective than those with less.[60]

Teacher Quality, Teacher Preparation, and Student Achievement

Darling-Hammond's research connects effective teacher preparation and teaching behaviors to student achievement. In a national survey, Darling-Hammond found that factors such as student poverty, minority status, and language background appear less important in predicting individual achievement levels than "teacher quality" variables. Fully certified teachers who had a college major in the subject they were teaching had

---

[56] Levine, 2006, p. 25.
[57] Clifford, G. J., & Guthrie, J. W. (1988). *Ed school: A brief for professional education*, Chicago: University of Chicago Press, p. 63.
[58] Levine, 2006.
[59] Levine, 2006, p. 39.
[60] Darling-Hammond, L. (1997). *Doing what matters most: Investing in quality teaching.* New York: National Commission on Teaching and America's Future, p. 10. A copy of the complete report, *What Matters Most: Teaching and America's Future*, can be found at http://www.nctaf.org/documents/WhatMattersMost.pdf.

a greater positive impact on student achievement than could be predicted from students' poverty, minority status, or language. Similarly, teacher preparation had a stronger connection with student achievement than class size, overall spending, or teacher salaries, even after taking students' backgrounds into account.[61]

In addition, Darling-Hammond and University of Washington professor John Bransford studied the research on the ways in which students learn and teacher education. They found that the following teacher quality and teacher preparation factors related to increased student achievement:[62]

- The teacher's verbal ability
- The teacher's knowledge of the content and understanding of how to teach it to a diverse range of students
- Education coursework on teaching methods in the teacher's discipline, the ways in which students learn and develop, and assessment
- The teacher's scores on state licensing exams that measure both basic skills and teaching knowledge
- Teaching behaviors including purposefully, diagnostically, and skillfully using a broad repertoire of approaches that respond to student and curricular needs, and giving student opportunities to learn criterion material
- The teacher's ongoing voluntary professional learning
- The teacher's enthusiasm for learning
- The teacher's flexibility, creativity, and adaptability
- Amount of teaching experience (teachers with fewer than three years of classroom practice are less effective, though there is little difference after this point)
- The teacher asking students higher-order thinking questions and probing their responses
- The teacher's class sizes, planning time, opportunities to work with colleagues, and curricular resources
- The interaction among these variables

Darling-Hammond believes that effective teacher education requires students to integrate and relate knowledge of the learners' characteristics with knowledge of the subject taught, and then to connect both of these factors to the relevant teaching practices. Only when these three dimensions overlap and interact in professional practice can effective teaching and learning occur.

Learning How to Teach Well

In 2003, the Education Commission of the States reviewed the entire body of teacher preparation research to see its findings and determine policy implications. The members of the Commission found that teachers' subject matter knowledge, preparation in how to teach a particular subject, and core teaching skills such as how to manage a classroom, assess student learning, and develop curriculum are all supported by research as making key contributions to effective teaching.[63]

---

[61] Darling-Hammond, L. (2000, January 1). Teacher quality and student achievement: A review of state policy evidence. *Education Policy Analysis Archives, 8,* 1. Retrieved July 30, 2009 from: http://www.epaa.asu.edu/epaa/v8n1.

[62] Darling-Hammond, L. (1996). *What matters most: Teaching and America's future.* National Commission on Teaching and America's Future. Columbia University: Teachers College, p. 28; Darling-Hammond, L., & Bransford, J. (Eds.). (2005). *Preparing teachers for a changing world: What teachers should know and be able to do.* National Academy of Education. San Francisco: CA: Jossey-Bass.

[63] Allen, M. (2003). *Eight questions on teacher preparation: What does the research say? A summary of the findings.* Denver, CO: Education Commission of the States. Retrieved May 19, 2008, from http://www.ecs.org/html/educationIssues/teachingquality/tpreport/home/summary.pdf. The full report can be retrieved from www.ecs.org/treport.

Likewise, in a study on mathematics teaching, Dan Goldhaber and Dominic Brewer concluded that the effects of teacher licensure on student achievement are greater than the effects of having a content major in the field; this finding suggests that what licensed teachers learn about teaching methods, in education coursework and in practice, adds to their actual abilities in the classroom.[64] In another study that gathered data for more than 2,800 students, David Monk determined that courses in methods of teaching math and science shared the same positive relationship to student achievement as actual content preparation in those fields. In mathematics, additional teaching methods courses had "more powerful effects" than additional preparation in the content area.[65]

The results in several other research reports reinforce these findings. For example, the National Research Council's Division of Behavioral and Social Sciences and Education found that effective teaching requires teachers with a deep knowledge of the subject, an understanding of how people learn, and an ability to use principles of learning and teaching to stimulate student learning and achievement.[66]

In another study, an American Educational Research Association Panel of nationally recognized scholars analyzed the empirical evidence related to practices and policies in preservice U.S. teacher education. They found that education programs that produce successful teachers include collaborative arrangements between university programs and local school districts—known as **professional development schools** (PDSs)—that have a positive impact on K–12 students in measurable ways, such as increases in standardized test scores.[67] They also found positive correlations between licensure and student achievement, especially in mathematics education. These results led the Panel to conclude that licensure in the field, gained by university-based teacher preparation, is a predictor of effective teaching and student achievement.[68]

Similarly, the Center for the Study of Teaching and Policy analyzed 57 studies published in peer-reviewed journals. Researchers found that a teacher's pedagogical preparation—that is, training in how to teach—had a positive impact on both teaching practice and student achievement. The report concludes, "The solution [to becoming an effective teacher] is more complicated than simply requiring a major or more subject matter courses."[69]

Preparedness and Teaching Longevity

Teachers' ages and years in their career are major influences on their decisions whether to leave the profession.[70] Beginning teachers leave their classrooms at higher rates. In his 2003 study, Richard Ingersoll, a University of Pennsylvania professor, observed that 14 percent of beginning teachers left after one year, and an-

[64] Goldhaber, D. D., & Brewer, D. J. (2000). Does teacher certification matter? High school certification status and student achievement. *Educational Evaluation and Policy Analysis, 22,* 129–145.

[65] Monk, D. (1994). Subject area preparation of secondary mathematics and science teachers and student achievement. *Economics of Education Review, 13*(2), 125–145.

[66] Schneps, M., & Sadler, P. (2000). *A private universe: Minds of our own.* In J. D. Bransford, A. L. Brown, & R. R. Cocking (Eds.). *How people learn: Brain, mind, experience, and school* (pp. 15–16). Washington , DC: National Academies Press.

[67] Cochran-Smith, M., & Zeichner, K. M. (2005). *Studying teacher education: The report of the AERA Panel on Research and Teacher Education.* American Educational Research Association. Mahwah, NJ: Lawrence Erlbaum Associates, p. 329.

[68] Cochran-Smith & Zeichner, 2005.

[69] Wilson, S. M., Floden, R. E., & Ferrini-Mundy, J. (2001). *Executive summary: Teacher preparation research: Current knowledge, gaps, and recommendations.* Center for the Study of Teaching and Policy, University of Washington, in collaboration with Michigan State University. The report is available at http://depts. washington.edu/ctpmail or look up the Center for the Study of Teaching and Policy.

[70] Murnane, R., Singer, J., Willett, J., Kemple, J., & Olsen, R. (Eds.). (1991). *Who will teach? Policies that matter.* Cambridge, MA: Harvard University Press.

Figure 2.2	Cumulative Percentage of Beginning Teachers Leaving the Profession

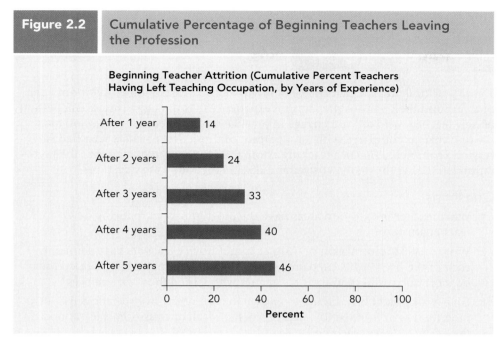

Source: Ingersoll, R. (2003). Is there really a teacher shortage? Retrieved December 12, 2006, from http://www.ncctq.org/issueforums/atrisk/presentations/keynoteIngersoll.ppt#291,6,Beginning Teacher Attrition (Cumulative Percent Teachers Having Left Teaching Occupation, by Years of Experience).

other 10 percent left after the second year; thus a cumulative total of 24 percent of all new teachers had abandoned teaching after only two years in the classroom. After five years, fully 46 percent of the original teaching pool had exited the profession (see Figure 2.2).[71]

Importantly for prospective teachers, research finds that well-prepared graduates are more likely to remain in teaching and contribute to developing a strong professional learning community in their schools. In 2003, Jianping Shen, a professor at Western Michigan University, examined new-teacher attrition rates five years after college graduation and found that teachers with no pedagogical training were three times more likely to leave teaching during any given year. By comparison, those who completed student teaching, acquired certification, and participated in a new teacher induction program were four times more likely to stay in teaching than those who had no training.[72]

Similarly, Richard Ingersoll found that when first-year teachers' preparation includes five key elements—training in selection and use of instructional materials, training in child psychology and learning theory, observation of other classes, feedback on teaching, and practice teaching—the attrition rate for those teachers is cut in half (see **A Closer Look**).[73]

[71] Ingersoll, R. (2003). Is there really a teacher shortage? Retrieved October 9, 2009, from http://www.ncctq.org/issueforums/atrisk/presentations/keynoteIngersoll.ppt#291,6,Beginning Teacher Attrition (Cumulative Percent Teachers Having Left Teaching Occupation, by Years of Experience).
[72] Shen, J. (2003, April). New teachers' certification status and attrition pattern: A survival analysis using the Baccalaureate and Beyond Longitudinal Study 1993–97. Paper presented at the AERA annual meeting, Chicago.
[73] Ingersoll., R. (2003, January). Original analysis for NCTAF of the 2000–2001 Teacher Follow-up Survey. In National Commission on Teaching and America's Future. *No dream denied*. (p. 84). www.nctaf.org.

A CLOSER LOOK

Figure 2.3 compares the percentage of novice teachers leaving the classroom after one year and their various preparation experiences. As the figure shows, 25 percent of new teachers who did not engage in practice teaching left the profession after the first year, as compared with 11.6 percent of those new teachers who had successfully completed practice teaching. More than twice as many without the preparation left. Using the figure, answer and discuss the following questions.

Questions

1. What teacher preparation areas have the most impact in reducing new teacher attrition?

2. What specific information or insights might novice teachers have gained in each of the five teacher preparation experiences that might have helped them be more successful than their colleagues who lacked those experiences?

3. Give examples of how failure to engage in each of the five specific activities might have contributed to a novice teacher's lack of classroom success and the desire to leave teaching.

4. In which teacher preparation courses will you be receiving these five professional education and related experiences?

Figure 2.3	Teacher Preparation Reduces Attrition of First-Year Teachers

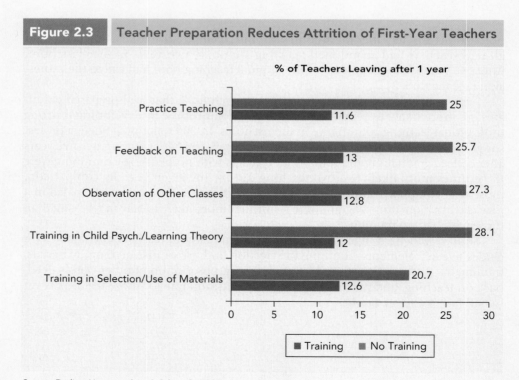

Source: Darling-Hammond, L., & Sykes, G. (2003). Wanted: A national teacher supply policy for education: The right way to meet the "highly qualified teacher" challenge. *Educational Policy Analysis and Archives, 11*(33). Retrieved October 9, 2009, from http://epaa.asu.edu/epaa/v11n33.

What the research shows. The research on teacher preparation and teaching effectiveness is clear and consistent. High-quality preservice teacher preparation provides beginning teachers with the knowledge and skills needed for effective teaching in today's diverse classrooms. Effective teachers know their subjects very well, and they are able to teach them so that students learn and increase their measured achievement. Teachers understand and apply knowledge of child and adolescent development to motivate and engage students. They are able to diagnose individual learning needs. They know how to make their classroom a safe and stimulating learning environment. In addition, when prospective teachers have sufficient opportunities to practice their learning in real classroom settings with effective supervision from experienced teachers and mentors, both they and their students are more likely to be successful.

While content knowledge is important and necessary, by itself it cannot ensure that the teacher is able to teach or that their students will learn.

How States License or Certify Teachers

If students are to be held to high standards, their teachers must also be held to high standards. **Licensure** and **certification** indicate the state's formal approval of teaching candidates for professional practice. These two terms are often used interchangeably.

States have a compelling interest in setting meaningful teacher standards. Students and communities cannot afford to work with unqualified teachers. We expect our schools—when successful—to provide benefits to society that go beyond the sum of those conferred upon individual students.

Similarly, states license individual teachers and accredit their teacher preparation programs. Without strong, meaningful, and well-enforced licensure and accreditation requirements, not only will districts lack important information about

Figure 2.4	Research Findings Show Teaching Requires Knowledge of Subject, Pedagogy, and Learner

Hill Street Studios/Harmik Nazarian/Jupiter Images

Activity 2.1

The research on teacher education clearly supports the need for future teachers to learn both content knowledge and pedagogical skills.

A. Divide the class into two groups. One group will consider those characteristics of the teacher as an individual that research finds contribute to teaching effectiveness. The other group will consider those teaching behaviors and practices that research finds increase student achievement. Each group will take 10 minutes to discuss, list, and describe the characteristics and behaviors in their area of study. It will then report its findings to the entire class.

B. Working as a group, discuss which characteristics or behaviors a person must develop through personal and professional experiences, feedback, and reflection, and which can be taught in a classroom. Which characteristics and behaviors need both personal and classroom learning?

---

the teacher candidates, but parents will also lack important information about the individuals to whom they entrust their children. Likewise, states will lack the policy tools needed to encourage improvements in teacher training and make quality teachers available to all schools.

Brief History of Teacher Licensure

Nineteenth-century teachers usually achieved licensure or certification by taking an examination administered by the local employing school system or county board of education. The number of education courses the candidate had taken did not matter. In 1898, only four states had state-centralized licensing.[74]

In the late nineteenth and early twentieth centuries, as the United States evolved from a rural to an industrialized nation, responsibility for teachers' professional qualifications moved from the localities to the states. By 1933, 42 states had centralized their teaching licensing at the state level. At that time, completion of most teacher education and other courses became the key criterion for awarding certification.[75]

States often use licensure tests for several purposes: for admission to teacher education programs, as a condition of graduation, and for initial teacher licensure.[76] Educational Testing Service's (ETS) Praxis II and National Evaluation Systems (NES) develop most of these licensing tests, which measure basic skills, content knowledge, and knowledge of teaching strategies. Thus licensing tests serve a critical purpose: They provide the public with assurance that the person meets the minimal qualifications to be a teacher.

State Variations in Licensing Teachers

Wide state-by-state variations exist in teacher licensure requirements.[77] Similarly, states differ on how much content and pedagogical knowledge they expect their beginning teachers to have. New York requires new teachers to pass exams in general

---

[74] Elsbree, W. S. (1939). *The American teacher: Evolution of a profession in a democracy.* New York: American Book. Cited in Spring, J. (2001). *American education* (10th ed.). Boston: McGraw Hill, p. 26.

[75] Elsbree, 1939.

[76] *Testing teacher candidates: The role of licensure tests in improving teacher quality.* (2001). National Academies Press. Retrieved August 6, 2008, from http://books.nap.edu/openbook.php?record_id=10090&page=57.

[77] Castle, J., & Jacobs, S. (2007). *State teacher policy quality yearbook 2007: Progress on teacher quality.* Washington, DC: National Council on Teacher Quality, pp. 7, 79. Retrieved August 6, 2008, from http://www.nctq.org/p/publications/docs/stpy_national_20071129024206.pdf.

Activity 2.2

In 2006, Arthur Levine showed principals, education school faculty, deans, and alumni a list of the skills and knowledge believed essential for prospective teachers. Then Levine asked them to evaluate how well schools of education prepared their graduates in each area, with the levels ranging from "very well" to "not well at all."

A. Working in groups of four, read the items in the following list and write at least three descriptive behaviors for what these skills and knowledge would *look like* if they were happening in a class. Which teacher and student behaviors would you *see and hear*?

B. Working individually, identify whether you could presently meet this expectation *if you were a teacher right now*. When and where (through which courses, experiences, and other means) do you plan to develop of refine your skills and knowledge prior to graduation from college so that you will be prepared to the "very well" level?

C. Discuss your findings as a class to determine additional relevant classroom behaviors and college/community resources you will need to engage to help yourself and your classmates develop these skills.

Teaching Knowledge and Skills

Essential Knowledge/Skill	Three Examples of What the Knowledge/Skill Would Look and Sound Like in the Classroom	My Present Knowledge and Skill Level in This Area (Low, Medium, High)	Where/When Can I Develop and Refine This Skill
Subject matter mastery	1. 2. 3.		
Ability to integrate technology into your teaching	1. 2. 3.		
Ability to apply different pedagogical approaches	1. 2. 3.		
Ability to employ assessment techniques	1. 2. 3.		
Ability to implement a standards-based curriculum	1. 2. 3.		
Understanding of how students learn	1. 2. 3.		
Capacity to work with diverse groups including parents	1. 2. 3.		
Capacity to work with diverse groups including children with disabilities	1. 2. 3.		
Capacity to work with diverse groups including children with limited English proficiency	1. 2. 3.		

liberal arts knowledge, teaching pedagogy, and pedagogical content knowledge and general subject knowledge. Meanwhile, neighboring New Jersey assesses only subject-matter knowledge.[78]

How Does a New Teacher Become Licensed?

"Are you licensed?" is one of the first questions candidates applying for teaching positions will be asked by most school district employers. Becoming licensed or certified usually means the individual has completed the appropriate academic training and satisfied the requirements specified by internal state procedures and regulations. Each state has its own specific rules and regulations for teacher certification, but most require a combination of some or all of the following:[79]

- Formal academic training. General elementary teachers need a major or minor in education and must have taken college-level courses in math, science, English, and social studies. To become a secondary teacher, one usually is required to major in the subject area to be taught.

- Completion of an accredited teacher preparation program. Traditional college and university teacher education programs are designed so students can work toward the major or minor coursework while also taking teacher preparation courses. These programs include practicum (a required number of hours) and a student-teaching internship, usually a semester in length. Many education programs lead to teacher certification upon graduation. One-year teacher preparation programs after a person has obtained a bachelor's degree are also available.

- Statewide assessments and testing. Each state requires teachers to pass a series of tests that evaluate their basic liberal arts knowledge as well as their teaching skills. Many states use ETS's Praxis series. Some states allow candidates to take the test within a year or two of being granted a provisional license.

- Additional checks. Many states now require applicants to complete a background check and undergo fingerprinting to assure that only persons without a criminal record are working with children.

Because each state has different licensure or certification requirements, it is best to contact the education department or licensing office in the state where one plans to teach for more information about its teacher-related requirements.

"Highly Qualified" Teachers

In the past, many states required a bachelor's degree in a content area for teacher certification,[80] but these standards were not always enforced. In 2002, however, the federal government's No Child Left Behind Act (NCLB) specified new definitions of "highly qualified" teachers.

According to NCLB, teachers are "highly qualified" when they meet three conditions.[81] A "highly qualified" teacher has

- A college degree.
- Full state certification or licensure, which specifically does not include any certification or licensure that has been "waived on an emergency, temporary, or provisional basis."

---

[78] Castle & Jacobs, 2007, pp. 46, 48.
[79] Sasson, D. (2007, April 27). How to become a certified teacher. Suite101.com. Retrieved May 22, 2009, from http://preservice-teacher-training.suite101.com/article.cfm/how_to_become_a_certified_teacher.
[80] Efforts to improve teacher quality. (2006, January 5). *Education Week: Quality Counts 2006*, 86–90.
[81] Education Commission of the States. (2002). *No state left behind: The challenge and opportunities of ESEA 2001*. Denver, CO: Author, p. 30.

- Demonstrable content knowledge in the subject the teacher will be teaching or, for elementary teachers, in at least reading, writing, and mathematical ability and teaching skills. Middle and secondary school teachers do not have to demonstrate teaching skills.

Teachers may demonstrate their content knowledge in several ways:

- New elementary teachers must pass a state test of literacy and numeracy.
- New secondary teachers must either pass a rigorous test in the subject area or have a college major in that subject.
- Veteran teachers may either pass the state test, or have a college major, or demonstrate content knowledge through some other uniformly applied process designed by the state.

Not everyone believes that NCLB's "highly qualified" definition actually assures teacher quality.[82] For example, only elementary school teachers must demonstrate their ability to teach. Some have called this requirement "an exercise in meeting the lowest common denominator of quality."[83] While the federal program does improve the odds that low-income and minority students will have a teacher who has studied the subject he or she is teaching, the law does not guarantee that the 3 million teachers in classrooms nationwide will know *how* to teach. "Highly qualified" teacher does not mean "highly qualified" teaching.

Research on Teacher Certification and Student Achievement

Although states try to increase teacher quality by setting licensure and certification requirements, the literature on the relationship between teacher certification and student achievement has produced mixed and controversial results. On the one hand, Darling-Hammond and colleagues have found that teacher preparation and certification are the strongest correlates of students' math and reading achievement.[84] On the other hand, little research on teacher testing or licensing has met the standard for scientific evaluation.[85] The research that does meet this standard has yielded tentative and inconclusive results.[86] Overall, the teacher certification evidence suggests that existing credentialing systems do not distinguish very well between effective and ineffective teachers.

---

[82] Although NCLB does not permit temporary, emergency, or provisional teacher certifications, it does not require a teacher to attain the highest level of certification to be considered "highly qualified." NCLB regulations state that under most circumstances, teachers who participate in alternative certification programs and who have a college degree in the subject they are teaching are also considered "highly qualified." That means a college graduate who is *enrolled* in an alternative certification program—but has not yet completed the first course, demonstrated the ability to teach, or met the state's standards for a professional license—can be considered "highly qualified" and assigned to a classroom. Such teachers may "assume the functions of a teacher" for up to three years without having received full certification and still be considered "highly qualified." See Darling-Hammond & Sykes, 2003.

[83] Barnes, R. E., & Aguerrebere, J. A. Jr. (2006, November 15). Sidetracking the debate on teacher quality. Education Week, 26(12), 34, 44.

[84] Darling-Hammond, L. (2002, September 6). Research and rhetoric on teacher certification: A response to "Teacher certification reconsidered." *Education Policy Analysis Archives. 10*(36). Retrieved January 17, 2003, from http://epaa.asu.edu/v10n36.html; Darling-Hammond, L. (2000). Teacher quality and student achievement: A review of state policy evidence. *Education Policy Analysis Archives, 8*(1). Retrieved October 9, 2009 from http://epaa.asu.edu/epaa/v8n1; Darling-Hammond, L. Berry, B., & Thoreson, A. (2001). Does teacher certification matter? Evaluating the evidence. *Educational Evaluation and Policy Analysis, 23*(1), 57–77.

[85] Much research in this area lacks the scientific rigor associated with randomized experimental study design or non-experimental longitudinal data on participants. Essentially, comparing apples to oranges makes conclusions difficult to draw.

[86] Podgursky, M. (2003). *Improving academic performance in U.S. public schools: Why teacher licensing is (almost) irrelevant.* Paper presented at the Teacher Preparation and Quality: New Directions in Policy and Research Conference, Washington, DC, October 18–20, 2003.

Professional Teaching Organizations

Over the years, the rules governing teachers' behavior and working conditions have evolved. For example, a 1922 Wisconsin teacher's contract forbade a female teacher from dating, marrying, staying out past 8 P.M., smoking, drinking, loitering in ice cream parlors, dyeing her hair, and using lipstick or mascara.[87] More significantly, until the mid-twentieth century, married women teachers were not allowed to earn tenure.[88] Professional organizations for teachers, such as the National Education Association and the American Federation of Teachers, have long worked to improve teachers' quality of work life and advance teaching as a profession. National accrediting associations and the National Board for Professional Teaching Standards (NBPTS) have also increased teacher professionalization.

Teachers' Organizations

Requirements for teachers in colonial America and in the United States' early days of nationhood were the ability to read, write, and stay out of trouble. The mid-1800s saw widespread education reforms, an emerging public school system, and the need to professionally train teachers. In 1857, while state education associations existed in 15 of the 31 states, no national organization spoke for America's teachers.[89]

National education association. Started in 1857, the National Education Association (NEA) today has 3.2 million members who work at every level of education.[90] Primarily suburban and rural in membership, the NEA represents the fifth-largest lobbying force in the United States.[91] In 1966, the NEA merged with the American Teachers Association (ATA), whose membership was predominantly African American, so that it could better promote the human and civil rights of educators and students of all ethnicities.

By 1900, teachers were still struggling with workplace and professional issues. Most salaries remained less than $50 per month, and women received less pay than men for doing the same jobs. Within their classrooms, teachers often had to educate more than 60 students with little support. In 1903, the NEA created a national committee and allocated funds to work on improving teacher salaries, tenures, and pensions.[92]

In 1926, the NEA and ATA persuaded the Southern Association of Colleges and Schools (SACS) to evaluate and accredit African American schools, allowing many African American students to gain college admissions and improving educational quality in many minority-dominated areas. In 1954, the NEA and ATA supported the Supreme Court's ruling in *Brown v. Board of Education* (1954), which led to school desegregation in the United States.

Today, NEA has more than 14,000 affiliates and an annual budget of approximately $150 million.[93] The organization raises funds for scholarship programs, conducts professional workshops, and negotiates contracts for school district employees. At the state and national levels, NEA and its affiliates regularly lobby legislators for

---

[87] *Chicago Tribune.* (1975, September 28). Section 1, p. 3. Cited in Ornstein, A. C., & Levine, D. U. (2006). *Foundations of education.* New York: Houghton Mifflin, p. 46.
[88] Donahue, 2002.
[89] Holcolm, S. (2006, January). NEA today: The history of the NEA. Part I. Retrieved May 22, 2008, from http://www.nea.org/neatoday/0601/neahistory.html.
[90] For more information on the National Education Association's history, see http://www.nea.org/neatoday/0601/neahistory.html.
[91] See www.nea.org/publications (2003).
[92] Donahue, D. M. (2002, Spring). Rhode Island's last holdout: Tenure and married women teachers at the brink of the women's movement. *History of Education Quarterly, 42*(1), 50–74.
[93] National Education Association. (2007). *Columbia encyclopedia* (6th ed.). Retrieved October 9, 2009, from http://www.encyclopedia.com/doc/1E1-NatlEduc.html.

school resources, campaign for higher professional teaching standards, file legal actions to protect school employees' academic freedom and rights, support and coordinate innovative projects, and publish literature about professional issues.

Nonetheless, critics complain that NEA is primarily interested in protecting and advancing teachers' interests—and only secondarily interested in improving public schools. Some argue that NEA is trying to create a national system of education, thereby removing schools from local control, and promotes an "ultra-liberal social agenda."[94] In addition, NEA's assertion that its membership is "voluntary" belies the reality that in some situations, school boards require teachers to pay NEA dues as a condition of employment.[95]

American federation of teachers. Founded in 1916, the American Federation of Teachers (AFT) represents the economic, social, and professional interests of classroom teachers. Affiliated with the AFL-CIO[96] (a labor union), AFT was the first national teachers union. Although it was originally open only to classroom teachers, in 1976 AFT welcomed nurses, cafeteria, custodial, maintenance, and transportation workers into its membership. By 2004, this organization had more than 3,000 local affiliates nationwide, 43 state affiliates, and more than 1.3 million members.[97]

AFT advocates public education policies including high academic and conduct standards for students and greater professionalism for teachers and school staffs. It has argued for teacher tenure laws to give teachers legal protections that could prevent them from being arbitrarily fired. Like the NEA, AFT strongly supported the *Brown* decision when it was handed down in 1954.

Activism has dramatically expanded AFT membership. Growing from fewer than 60,000 members in 1960 to more than 200,000 members by 1970, AFT affiliates spearheaded the drive toward increased power and public visibility for teachers, as evidenced by an increase in teacher strikes and other headline-grabbing actions. As a result of its success in negotiating grassroots workplace contacts, visible female leadership, and observable teacher advocacy, AFT became the dominant teacher organization in many large cities.

During the 1980s, AFT worked to advance educational reform, placing contract-related "bread-and-butter" issues side-by- side with professional concerns. Similarly, throughout the 1990s, this organization continued its push for clear standards, higher academic achievement and excellence.

Although the two groups had early and substantial differences over the years, NEA and AFT have successfully collaborated at both local and national levels to win higher teacher salaries, increase benefits for teachers, improve working conditions, and promote effective educational practices to increase student achievement. In fact, nearly one-third of NEA's 3.2 million members are dues-paying members of the AFL-CIO as a result of many state-level mergers of NEA and AFT affiliates.[98]

Should Teachers Strike?

Teachers face ethical dilemmas when they are expected to behave in ways about which they have mixed feelings. Participating in a teachers' strike is one example. Acting professionally in problematic situations involves thoughtfully addressing issues of personal, moral, and ethical significance.

---

[94] Moo, G. G. (1999). Power grab: How the National Education Association is betraying our children. Washington, DC: Regnery Press, p. i.

[95] Moo, 1999, p. xviii. In fact, Peter Brimelow and Leslie Spencer entitled their June 7, 1993, *Forbes* (vol. 151, no. 12) article, "The National Extortion Association."

[96] AFL-CIO stands for American Federation of Labor–Congress of Industrial Organizations.

[97] To learn more about the American Federation of Teachers, see "Who We Are: About the AFT," found at http://www.aft.org/about/index.htm.

[98] Honawar, V. (2008, September 3). NEA locals slowly start to join giant labor federation. *Education Week, 28*(2), 10.

Causes of teacher strikes. Between 1918 and 1960, more than 120 teacher **strikes**—that is, employee work stoppages in support of demands made on their employer, such as higher pay or improved conditions—occurred. Usually, teachers were responding to economic hardships, such as lagging or unpaid salaries.[99]

Teachers also strike to express their strong objections to educational policy and practices over which they feel powerless to influence. They want more input into their schools' decision making about educational programs and improved educational services for students. They want higher salaries, better benefits, and improved work conditions. Research finds that teachers who reported feeling powerless were more likely to become involved with their teachers' unions than were teachers who did not feel this way.[100]

The legality of strikes varies from state to state. Teachers who decide to strike in states where this practice is illegal can be fired from their jobs. Likewise, the public often reacts negatively to striking teachers. They accuse teachers of striking illegally, victimizing children, violating their contracts, disregarding their districts' poor financial circumstances, and following small groups of "malcontents."[101]

What strikes can accomplish. Teachers strike because it produces results. Having the legal right to strike affords teachers greater power to increase the dollar value of their work. Even where strikes are illegal, teachers who strike win better salaries and working conditions. A national 43-state analysis conducted in 1996 found evidence that when teachers go on strike, whether legally or illegally, or have a neutral party arbitrate their dispute, they win salary increases of 3.6 to 11.5 percent and reduce class hours between 37 and 70 minutes per day. In contrast, fact-finding missions and voluntary arbitration have no significant influences on outcomes.[102]

The dilemma for teachers. Considering whether to participate in a strike requires teachers to ponder several ethical and moral dilemmas involving their personal and professional code of ethics, their employment, their colleagues, their students, and their administrators.[103] For professionals, the first ethical principle is "Do no harm." Teachers must consider all of the following as they make their decisions:

- Personal/professional ethics. As individuals and as professionals, teachers develop a set of ethical guidelines that influence their thoughts and actions about what is "right and appropriate." Professionalism and individual values define what they consider to be the correct behavior in this situation.

- Employment. If participating in a strike is not legal, teachers who strike may be fired from their jobs. An individual teacher must consider whether participating in an illegal walkout is worth the possibility of losing one's job (and perhaps future jobs if the teacher cannot get a letter of recommendation from the previous employer).

- Colleagues. Some teachers interpret "collegiality" as having unquestioned loyalty, group solidarity, and the belief that teachers as professionals should not interfere in other teachers' business, criticize them or their practices, even at the expense of students' well-being. Individual teachers may feel helpless in the face of this "peer pressure" and forced to not "break ranks" with colleagues, even if such loyalty compromises students' needs and welfare.[104]

---

[99] Oakes, R. C. (1960, March). Should teachers strike? An unanswered question. *Journal of Educational Sociology, 33*(7), 339–344.
[100] Jessup, 1978.
[101] Oakes, 1960, p. 343.
[102] Zigarelli, M. A. (1996, Winter). Dispute resolution mechanisms and teacher bargaining outcomes. *Journal of Labor Research, 17*(1), 135–148.
[103] Campbell, E. (2005, September). Challenges in fostering ethical knowledge as professionalism within schools as teaching communities. *Journal of Educational Change, 6*(3), 207–226, p. 208.
[104] Louis, K. S., Kruse, S. D., & Bryk, A. S. (1995). Professionalism and community. In K. S. Louis, S. D. Kruse, et al. (Eds.), *Professionalism and community: Perspectives on reforming urban schools* (pp. 3–42). Thousand Oaks, CA: Corwin Press, p. 16.

- Students. Teachers' practice strongly influences the moral lessons students learn both directly and indirectly in the classroom. Teachers transmit societal values by providing formal instruction and by becoming moral role models (when children watch their actions). When deciding whether to join a strike, teachers may feel torn between advocating for improved personal and professional benefits and meeting their responsibilities toward their students. Teachers are aware that their respect (or lack of it) toward school rules and commitment to their students' well-being sends powerful messages to students about integrity and appropriate behavior.[105]

- Administrators. Walking out in a strike may place teachers in an adversarial relationship with their administrators and school boards. Teachers must consider whether participating in a strike is worth jeopardizing the collaborative and trusting relationship they have built with their principal and the school board (the teacher's actual employer).

Applying abstract ethical standards to actual situations is very difficult. When teachers are not sure how to act, they need to be able to rely on their own sense of what is right and appropriate as well as on the expressed and shared professional norms about what constitutes ethical behavior. Prospective educators—in fact, all educators—can develop a more mature sense of ethical judgment when they seriously reflect on their own values, expectations, and professional norms and consider together how to act ethically and professionally in given situations.[106]

National Accreditation Organizations

Receiving a public or private accrediting body's endorsement is one way that teacher education programs show their worth. Like most other academic fields, teacher education programs use accreditation as a means for engaging in self-policing. **Accreditation** is a form of quality control. Two principal independent accrediting bodies serve teacher education: the National Council for Accreditation of Teacher Education and the Teacher Education Accreditation Council. The two associations have different philosophies, structures, and practices.

National council for accreditation of teacher education. The National Council for Accreditation of Teacher Education (NCATE), founded in 1954, is an independent organization has accredited more than half (650) of the United States' 1,200 college and university teacher education programs; 100 more programs are also seeking accreditation.[107] More than two-thirds of the nation's new-teacher graduates come from NCATE-accredited institutions.[108] The Washington, D.C.–based group is a coalition of 33 member organizations, making NCATE the teaching profession's largest collective educational organization.

NCATE's mission is to judge the degree to which colleges of education and the individual programs that prepare P–12 school personnel meet professional and public expectations. In contrast to the states' tradition of setting their own teacher licensing requirements—often based on "seat time" in teacher preparation courses, the number of books in the college library, or local political realities—NCATE judges teacher education programs based on national professional standards. Its standards are tied to state standards, the ETS's Praxis II exam, and the Interstate Teacher Assessment and Support Consortium (INTASC) standards.

---

[105] Campbell, E. (1997, September–October). Connecting the ethics of teaching and moral education. *Journal of Teacher Education, 48,* 255–264.
[106] Campbell, E. (2001, October). Let right be done: Trying to put ethical standards into practice. *Journal of Education Policy, 16*(5), 395–411.
[107] Honawar, V. (2008, June 18). Unified teacher-college accrediting system urged. *Education Week, 27* (42), 9.
[108] Wise, A. E. (2005). Establishing teaching as a profession: The essential role of professional accreditation. *Journal of Teacher Education, 56*(4), 318–331.

Since the late 1980s, 48 states, the District of Columbia, and Puerto Rico have partnered with NCATE to increase their teacher preparation programs' rigor.[109] Twenty states now require all of their teacher programs to be NCATE accredited. Additionally, 39 states have adopted or adapted NCATE's standards and process to evaluate institutions that do not choose to seek national accreditation.[110] As a result, NCATE standards are becoming *the* standard for professional teacher preparation practices, defining a body of knowledge that unites and further professionalizes teaching. [111]

NCATE and new teachers. NCATE standards focus on assuring that prospective teachers are learning the knowledge and skills that promote classroom learning.[112] NCATE-accredited programs are able to produce evidence showing that their future teachers know their subject matter, demonstrate effective teaching practices, reflect on their practice, adapt their instruction, teach students from different backgrounds, have been supervised by master teachers, and can integrate technology into instruction.[113] Likewise, NCATE-accredited programs gather and use all performance data to refine and improve their teacher preparation programs.[114]

This rigorous accreditation process comes with certain costs, however. Some colleges have complained that the process of NCATE accreditation is tedious, expensive, and time-consuming.[115] In response, NCATE plans to redesign and streamline its accreditation process so as to make it more cost-effective.[116]

Research on NCATE-accredited programs. Data are mixed but mostly positive about whether NCATE-trained teachers are superior to those from non-NCATE-endorsed teacher education programs. For example, studies find that individuals from NCATE-accredited institutions passed the Praxis II licensing exams at a higher rate (91 percent) than those from unaccredited institutions (84 percent) or those with no teacher preparation (74 percent).[117] A study of student achievement conducted in 2004–2005 found slight gains in K–12 reading and math test scores for students whose teachers graduated from these NCATE-approved programs.[118] A 2000 study showed that teachers from NCATE-accredited programs can help all children from different cultural, ethnic, and socioeconomic backgrounds learn to high levels,[119] and NCATE's standards have been connected to increases in measured student achievement.[120]

On other measures, two U.S. Department of Education surveys observe that little difference exists between NCATE and non-NCATE teacher groups in their desire to remain in a teaching career.[121] Nevertheless, because small liberal arts colleges and more

---

[109] In 1989, NCATE established a state partnership program. Since then, 48 states plus the District of Colombia and Puerto Rico have integrated NCATE's professional review of teacher education colleges with their own.

[110] NCATE at 50. Retrieved October 9, 2009, from http://www.ncate.org/documents/15YearsofGrowth.pdf.

[111] Further raising the bar, in 2004 NCATE and the National Board for Professional Teaching Standards (NBPTS) aligned their standards, including an emphasis on clinical practice.

[112] Wise, A. E. (2006, October 11). Letters: NCATE already is doing what Levine suggests. *Education Week, 26*(7), 36.

[113] NCATE standards include teacher preparation in assessment systems that analyze and use data on a variety of areas.

[114] Honawar. V. (2006, October 11). Teacher-prep field of two minds over replacing NCATE. *Education Week, 26*(7), 18.

[115] Honawar, 2008, "Unified teacher-college accrediting system urged."

[116] Honawar, V (2008, December 3). NCATE commits to streamlining accreditation process. *Education Week, 28*(14), 6.

[117] Wise, A. E. (2001, June). Standards or no standards? Teacher quality in the 21st century. *NCATE Newsbriefs, 27*, 3. Cited in L. S. Kaplan & W. A. Owings. (2002). *Teacher quality, teaching quality, and school improvement.* Bloomington, IN: Phi Delta Kappa Educational Foundation, p. 16.

[118] Honawar, 2006; Levine, 2006, pp. 67–68.

[119] Weglinsky, H. (2000). *Teaching the teachers: Different settings, different results.* Princeton, NJ: Educational Testing Service. Retrieved October 9, 2009, from http://www.ets.org/Media/Research/pdf/PICTT.pdf.

[120] Weglinsky, H. (2000). *How teaching matters: Bringing the classroom back into the discussion of teacher quality.* Princeton, NJ: Educational Testing Service and the Milkin Family Foundation. Retrieved October 9, 2009, from http://www.mff.org/pubs/ets_mff_study2000.pdf.

[121] Ballou, D., & Podgursky, M. (1997). Reforming teacher training and recruitment: A critical appraisal of the recommendations of the National Commission on Teaching and America's Future. *Government Union Review, 17*(4), 22.

selective universities are less likely than larger colleges to seek NCATE accreditation, the study shows differences in teacher race and ethnicity between NCATE and non-NCATE teachers. While NCATE schools supply only 41 percent of all teachers, NCATE schools supply 52 percent of minority teachers and 65 percent of Latino teachers.[122] Their graduates tend to work in inner cities and to teach in schools with large numbers of minority and limited-English speaking students in their classrooms.

Teacher education accreditation council. Established in 1997 as an NCATE competitor, the Teacher Education Accreditation Council (TEAC) offers an alternative teacher education accreditation process. Formed by a group of college presidents who wanted a less intensive certification approach,[123] TEAC accredits teacher education programs; in contrast, NCATE accredits whole institutions with teacher education programs. To date, TEAC has approved 80 teacher education programs, with 100 more in the pipeline.[124]

TEAC's approach to accreditation differs significantly from that employed by NCATE. Instead of providing the professional standards that teacher education programs must meet, as does NCATE, TEAC believes that the teacher preparation knowledge base is not complete. Therefore, the colleges can decide for themselves what their standards are. In short, TEAC standards are institutionally driven rather than professionally driven. To obtain TEAC accreditation, teacher education programs define what they are seeking to achieve and are expected to present rigorous evidence of their accomplishments. TEAC then evaluates their programs' adequacy. Because faculty must provide multiple measures of their students' competence, corroborating information can either clarify—or contradict—the evidence provided by the program's administrators.[125]

Critics charge that TEAC lacks both a rigorous set of national standards[126] and a rigorous program evaluation process.[127] As a result, some doubt TEAC's effectiveness.[128] While certain schools appreciate TEAC's flexible approach to standards setting and meeting, others believe that this same looseness undermines the concept of professionalism. They argue, instead, that this approach gives ammunition to teacher education opponents who claim that teaching does not have a well-defined, agreed-upon body of knowledge.[129]

Research on TEAC programs. The effectiveness of TEAC accreditation is not yet confirmed in the professional literature. Its relative newness on the scene as well as the few programs that have sought and received its accreditation do not permit enough data to be gathered for a representative sample. Nonetheless, TEAC notes that it would not claim superiority for those programs that have received TEAC accreditation to the unaccredited program or to the NCATE-accredited program, but only to those programs that have been denied TEAC accreditation.[130]

Both NCATE and TEAC seek to advance the professionalization process as teacher education schools review and evaluate their own programs in light of relevant standards. In 2008, a panel of teacher education stakeholders asked these two national teacher-college accreditors to work together on creating a unified system of accreditation. This work has begun.[131]

---

[122] Ballou & Pdogursky, 1997.

[123] Wise, 2005.

[124] Honawar, 2008, "NCATE commits to streamlining accrediting process." For a thoughtful comparison of NCATE versus TEAC accreditation, see Wise, 2005.

[125] For a thorough discussion of TEAC, see Murray, F. B. (2005). On building a unified system of accreditation. *Journal of Teacher Education, 56*(4), 307–317.

[126] Honawar, 2008, "Unified teacher-college accrediting system urged."

[127] TEAC responds to critics that it lacks standards by noting that both the Council on Higher Education and the U.S. Department of Education require that accreditors have standards. Both organizations have examined TEAC principles, and agreed that these meet their requirements. With circular reasoning, TEAC continues that because both groups recognize TEAC as an accreditation organization, TEAC has standards. See Murray, 2005.

[128] Honawar, 2006.

[129] Wise, 2005.

[130] Murray, 2005.

[131] Honawar, 2008, "NCATE commits to streamlining accreditation process."

Interstate New Teacher Assessment and Support Consortium

The Interstate New Teacher Assessment and Support Consortium (INTASC) is a group of state education agencies and national educational organizations dedicated to reforming teachers' preparation, licensing, and on-going professional development. Created in 1987, INTASC's primary clientele consists of state education agencies responsible for teacher licensing, program approval, and professional development. One basic premise guides its work: An effective teacher must be able to integrate content knowledge with students' specific strengths and needs to assure that *all* students learn and perform at high levels.[132]

INTASC has translated core academic content standards into model licensing standards in mathematics, English language arts, science, special education, foreign languages, and arts. It is developing standards for elementary education and social studies/civics as well. Thus, by adhering to these standards, all aspects of a state's education system become aligned with and organized to achieve the state's policy as embodied in its P–12 student standards.

INTASC has also developed principles for quality teacher preparation programs that explain how to incorporate its performance-based standards into teacher education. Finally, INTASC provides ongoing technical assistance to states as they implement standards-based licensing systems.

National Board for Professional Teaching Standards

The National Board for Professional Teaching Standards (NBPTS), established in 1987, operates a voluntary national system to assess and certify high-quality teaching. NBPTS sets high standards for what highly effective teachers know and do. Its goal is to improve the teaching profession and positively influence student learning. As of June 2008, nearly 64,000 teachers had earned their National Board Certification (NBC) in 24 fields.[133] Forty-one percent of these Board-Certified teachers teach in high-needs schools.[134] In effect, NBPTS spells out and recognizes the professional teaching expectations for highly effective teachers.

The voluntary certification process. The 10-month long certification process connects teaching and student learning by having applicants demonstrate knowledge of their subject matter and pedagogy; manage and monitor student learning; systematically think about classroom practice and learn from experience; and participate in learning communities. In addition, Board-Certified teachers must pass two assessments: a portfolio and a standardized test. The portfolio assessment requires candidates to videotape and analyze their lessons to diagnose student learning difficulties. Candidates then evaluate student data and reflect on how to improve both the lesson and the learning. The rigorous day-long, timed standardized test measures teachers' knowledge of content and how to teach it. The cut-off for passing is very high. Fewer than half of those candidates who sit for NBPTS certification for the first time ultimately achieve it.[135]

With widespread national professional support from major education associations, governors, state legislators, and school boards,[136] virtually every state and

---

[132] For more information on INTASC, see http://www.ccsso.org/projects/Interstate_New_Teacher_Assessment_and_Support_Consortium/.

[133] Viadero, D., & Honawar, V. (2008, June 18). Credential of NBPTS has impact. *Education Week, 27*(42), 1, 16. This number of NBPTS credential holders represents fewer than 3 percent of the nation's 3.7 million teachers.

[134] Honawar, V. (2008, August 13). NBPTS expands credentialing in high-needs districts. *Education Week, 27*(45), 8.

[135] Berry, B. (2005, December). Recruiting and retaining Board-Certified teaches for hard-to-staff schools. *Phi Delta Kappan, 87*(4), 290–297.

[136] National Board Certification has received recognition, support, and momentum from AFT, NEA, the Carnegie Foundation for the Advancement of Teaching, Columbia University's Teachers College, and NCATE. Some universities have incorporated the National Board standards into their teacher preparation and professional accreditation programs. Governors, state legislatures, and school boards help school districts provide a range of incentives encouraging teachers to earn NBPTS certification.

more than 25 percent of all U.S. school districts offer financial rewards or incentives for teachers seeking National Board Certification.[137] The Progressive Policy Institute estimated that states and districts are spending more than $100 million per year on assessment fees ($2,500 per teacher) and salary supplements for teachers who earn the certificate.[138]

Additionally, more minority teachers are earning national certification. Between 2005 and 2006, the number of African American teachers earning this credential rose by 24 percent, the number of Latino teachers increased by 13 percent, and the number of Native American teachers increased by 50 percent. Because African American, Latino, and Native American teachers are more likely to work in schools with minority populations and low-income families, this means more highly qualified NBC teachers are working in traditionally low-income, low-performing schools.[139] This development is important because only 19 percent of Board-Certified teachers work in their states' neediest schools (defined as schools where students score in the bottom third of achievement for their state).[140]

Research on NBPTS teachers. Understandably, the NBPTS has been under increasing pressure to demonstrate that the millions of state and district dollars spent on bonuses for nationally certified teachers buy the likelihood of greater student learning.[141] NBPTS notes that 150 research studies have examined its effectiveness, and more than 75 percent have found positive effects on teacher performance and student learning, engagement, and achievement.[142]

Results from studies focusing on the influence of National Board Certification on student achievement are mixed, but generally positive. Sample sizes tend to be small, limiting the ability to generalize conclusions. Research is consistently positive about National Board Certification's effect on teachers' instructional practices, professional development, and student achievement.[143] However, two major studies using large

[137] National Board for Professional Teaching Standards. (n.d.). Milestones: Raising the standard. Retrieved October 9, 2009, from http://www.nbpts.org/about_us/background/milestones.

[138] Harman, A. E. (2001). National Board for Professional Teaching Standards. National Teacher Certification. *ERIC Digest.* Retrieved July 30, 2009, from: http://www.eric.ed.gov/ERICDocs/data/ericdocs2sql/content_storage_01/0000019b/80/19/9d/f1.pdf; Viadero & Honawar, 2008.

[139] Keller, B. (2007, January 31). More minority teachers earn national certification. *Education Week, 26*(21), 5.

[140] Humphrey, D., Koppich, J., & Hough, H. (2005 March 3). Sharing the wealth: National Board Certified teachers and the students who need them most. *Education Policy Analysis Archives, 13*(18). Retrieved October 9, 2009, from http://epaa.asu.edu/epaa/v13n18.

[141] Keller, B. (2006, May 24). Under pressure, NBPTS to release full study. *Education Week, 25*(38), 5.

[142] National Board of Professional Teaching Standards. (2006, Fall). Making a difference in quality teaching and student achievement. Retrieved October 9, 2009, from http://www.nbpts.org; Viadero & Honawar, 2008.

[143] Bond, L., Smith, T., Baker, W. K., & Hattie, J. A. (2000, September). *Validation study: A distinction that matters.* University of North Carolina at Greensboro: Center for Educational Research and Evaluation. Retrieved October 9, 2009, from http://www.nbpts.org/UserFiles/File/validity_1_-_UNC_Greebsboro_D_-_Bond.pdf; Lustick, D., & Sykes, G. (2006, February 23). National Board Certification as professional development: What are teachers learning? *Education Policy Analysis Archives, 14*(5). Retrieved October 9, 2009, from http://epaa.asu.edu/epaa/v14n5; Sykes, G., et al. (2006, May). *National Board Certified teachers as organizational resource.* Grant # 61–5230. Final report to the National Board for Professional Teaching Standards; Cohen, C. E., & Rice, J. K. (2005, August). *National Board Certification as professional development: Design and cost.* Washington, DC: U.S. Department of Education and National Science Foundation. Retrieved October 9, 2009, from http://www.nbpts.org/UserFiles/File/Complete_Study_Cohen.pdf; Viadero & Honawar, 2008. Goldhaber, D., & Anthony, E. (2004, March 8). Can teacher quality be effectively assessed? Urban Institute. Retrieved October 9, 2009, from http://www.urban.org/publications/410958.html; Vandevoort, L. G., Amrein-Beardsley, A., & Berliner, D. C. (2004, September 8). National Board Certified teachers and their students' achievement. *Education Analysis and Policy Archives, 12*(46). Retrieved October 9, 2009, from http://www.nbpts.org/UserFiles/File/National_Board_Certified_Teachers_and_Their_Students_Achievement_-_Vandevoort.pdf; Smith, T. W., Gordon, B., Colby, S. A., & Wang, J. J. (2005, April). *An examination of the relationship between depth of student learning and National Board Certification status.* Boone, NC: Appalachian State University, Office for Research on Teaching; Cavalluzzo, L. (2004, November). *Is National Board Certification an effective signal of teacher quality?* Alexandria, VA: CNA Corporation. Retrieved October 9, 2009, from http://www.nbpts.org/UserFiles/File/Final_Study_11204_D_-_Cavalluzzo_-_CNA_Corp..pdf.

student samples found that students of Board-Certified teachers did not show statistically significant academic gains from working with these teachers.[144]

Gains from NBPTS certification. Apart from empirical measures of teachers' effect on student achievement, NBPTS certification provides a valid, reliable, and highly respected assessment and credentialing system to recognize "accomplished" teachers. It provides the teaching profession with a way to create stages to an otherwise "unstaged" profession, while keeping excellent teachers teaching.

Similarly, schools and school districts frequently use Board-Certified teachers for instructional leadership. They can model excellent classroom practice that increases students' learning, mentor novice teachers, provide professional development to their colleagues, serve as peer assessors, and work as curriculum coordinators. When used (and appropriately compensated) in these ways, Board-Certified teachers can help transform schools into high-achieving and professionally rewarding learning communities.

Schools' Professional Culture and Teacher Retention

Teaching is the only profession without a built-in apprenticeship period. Schools expect new teachers to do the same job as 15-year veterans—a tall order. New-teacher initiation is often a trial by fire.[145]

As discussed earlier, teaching has an unusually high attrition rate, with as many as 50 percent of new teachers leaving the field within their first five years on the job.[146] If school districts want to keep and develop the teachers they hire, schools need ways to support new teachers as they begin working.

Induction, Mentoring, and Professional Development

The terms "induction" and "mentoring" are often used interchangeably. In reality, the two terms mean slightly different things.

Induction is a comprehensive, coherent, and sustained professional development process that the school district organizes to train, support, and retain new teachers. Good induction seamlessly moves new teachers into a lifelong learning program. Beginning before the first day of school and continuing through the first two or three years of teaching, induction includes new teacher orientation, support, and guidance programs.

Mentoring is a specific type of induction program. It consists of a collegial, supportive relationship developed between a veteran and a new teacher to ease the transition into the realities of daily classroom teaching. Typically, mentoring includes giving moral support and practical suggestions.

In both induction and mentoring, teachers "who know the ropes" help novices understand and successfully handle events happening in their classrooms and schools. These programs acculturate the new teachers, who learn to prevent and solve problems on their own. With a variety of caring and knowledgeable colleagues to help the novice make transition to teaching make sense, learn new skills, and gain insights, a new teacher can quickly build competence and a feeling of "I can do this!" No wonder that more than half of the deans, faculty, alumni, and principals

[144] Sanders, W. L., Ashton, J. J., & Wright, S. P. (2005, March 7). Comparison of the effects of NBPTS certified teachers with other teachers on the rate of student academic progress. SAS Institute. Retrieved October 9, 2009, from http://www.nbpts.org/UserFiles/File/SAS_final_NBPTS_report_D_-_Sanders.pdf; McColsky, W., Stronge, J. H., et al. (2005, June). *A comparison of National Board Certified teachers and non-National Board Certified teachers: Is there a difference between teacher effectiveness and student achievement?* Greensboro, NC: University of North Carolina at Greensboro/SERVE. Retrieved October 9, 2009, from http://www.nbpts.org/UserFiles/File/Teacher_Effectiveness_Student_Achievement_and_National_Board_Certified_Teachers_D_-_McColskey.pdf.
[145] Ingersoll, R. M., & Smith, T. M. (2004, March). Do teacher induction and mentoring matter? *National Association of Secondary School Principals Bulletin, 88*(638), 28.
[146] Ingersoll, R., & Smith, T. (2003). The wrong solution to the teacher shortage. *Educational Leadership, 60*(8), 30–33.

| Figure 2.5 | Induction Programs Provide Caring, Knowledgeable Colleagues Who Help Ease the Transition into Teaching |

Lon C. Diehl/PhotoEdit

believe that inadequate induction and mentoring are among the key reasons why so many new teachers leave the profession so rapidly.[147]

Induction. Effective induction programs recognize that the art and craft of teaching develops over time. Typically, induction programs focus on easing the novice's transition into teaching and improving the novice's teaching effectiveness. They also help the beginning teacher learn the district's culture—its philosophy, mission, policies, procedures, and goals.

No two induction programs are exactly alike. Effective induction programs may include any or all of the following components:[148]

- Offer seminars or classes for beginning teachers
- Provide study groups in which new teachers can network and build support, commitment, and leadership in a learning community
- Integrate a mentor who is a successful teacher in the same subject area as the new teacher and who is willing to put in the time and patience to help the novice
- Supply common planning time with other teachers in their subject area
- Provide common planning time with a mentor
- Participate with a network of teachers, such as one organized by the school, an outside agency, within the larger school division, or over the Internet

[147] Levine, 2006, p. 42.
[148] Wong, 2004; Ingersoll & Smith, 2004.

- Offer regular supportive communication with the principal, other administrators, or department chair
- Present a structure for modeling effective teaching during professional development activities

Strong induction programs understand that new teachers want to become good at what they are doing and experience success. They also want to connect with colleagues and contribute to a group. Therefore, the best induction programs structure new teachers' ties within learning communities that allow new and veteran teachers to interact respectfully and to value one another's contributions. Teachers remain in teaching when they belong to professional learning communities based in high-quality interpersonal relationships founded on trust and respect.[149]

Mentoring. Although mentoring has become the most popular teacher induction practice during the past 20 years, the format of these programs varies widely. They may be a more or less structured coaching relationship. Mentoring may consist of only one hasty meeting during the first week of school, or it may involve regularly scheduled, weekly hour-long meetings during time provided apart from teachers' regular teaching schedules. Some mentoring programs include any teachers new to the schools; others focus solely on teachers new to the profession. Some programs train the mentors to increase their effectiveness—certain school districts devote from 40 to 100 hours of training for each mentor.[150]

While offered as a stand-alone activity, mentoring does not automatically help novice teachers adjust successfully or persuade them to stay in teaching. In many school districts, mentors are not part of a comprehensive induction program. Instead, they are simply veteran teachers whom principals assign to work with newcomers—like a blind date. Without strong administrative support, mentoring does not work.[151]

Research on induction and mentoring. The quality and effectiveness of local schools' induction and mentoring programs vary. Their success with new teachers depends on the funding availability, the quality and number of mentors, and principals' and superintendents' commitment to make the programs work.[152]

Increasingly, research is showing that well-conceived and -implemented teacher induction and mentoring programs successfully increase new teachers' job satisfaction, efficacy, and retention rates.[153] Comprehensive induction programs move beyond the new teachers' initial classroom management concerns to helping teachers better focus on student learning. A 2003 study reveals that the more helpful induction or mentoring supports that new teachers received, the lower the likelihood of their leaving teaching or moving to other schools after their first year.[154] New teachers participating in an induction program reduce their attrition rate within the first three years to 15 percent, compared with 26 percent for teachers who do not receive any induction support.[155] School districts including Cincinnati, Columbus, and Toledo, Ohio, and Rochester, New York have reduced beginning teacher attrition rates

---

[149] Wong, H. K. (2004, March). Induction programs that keep new teachers teaching and improving. *National Association of Secondary School Principals Bulletin, 88*(638), 41–58.

[150] Wong, 2004.

[151] North Carolina Teaching Fellows Commission. (1995). *Keeping talented teachers.* Raleigh, NC: Public School Forum on North Carolina. Cited in Wong, 2004, p. 44; Schlager, M., Fusco, J., Koch, M., Crawford, V., & Phillips, M. (2003, July). *Designing equity and diversity into online strategies to support new teachers.* Paper presented at the National Educational Computing Conference (NECC), Seattle, WA.

[152] *Education Week* quality counts 2003. (2003, January 9). *Education Week, 22*(17), 70.

[153] Alliance for Excellent Education, 2008; Strong, M. (2004). *Induction, mentoring, and teacher retention: A summary of the research.* Santa Cruz, CA: Association of Teacher Educator's Commission on Mentoring and Teacher Induction and the New Teacher Center, University of California, Santa Cruz; Wong, 2004.

[154] Ingersoll & Smith, 2004.

[155] National Center for Education Statistics. (2000). Progress through the teacher pipeline: 1992–93 college graduates and elementary/secondary school teaching as of 1997. Washington, DC: U.S. Department of Education.

from more than 30 percent to less than 5 percent by providing an induction program with expert mentors and release time to coach first-year teachers.[156] A 2008 study found that urban teacher residency programs in Boston and Chicago that focus heavily on classroom-based training and on-the-job support for new teachers had increased new-teacher retention in their districts to 90 percent and 95 percent, respectively, after just three years.[157]

The New Teacher Center, a national resource center on teacher induction, has found that the productivity of new teachers in comprehensive induction programs rivals that of their third- and fourth-year peers.[158] Thus an inducted first-year teacher is likely to produce the same levels of student achievement as a non-inducted fourth-year teacher. Comprehensive induction programs help young teachers stay in the profession at higher rates and become competent more quickly than those who learn by trial and error.

Likewise, research shows that teachers learn more in teacher networks and study groups than with mentoring. They learn more in professional development programs that are longer, more sustained, and more intensive than they do in shorter ones. They learn more when there is collective participation, and when they see teacher learning and development as part of a coherent professional growth program. Demonstrating that quality teaching is a group responsibility—not just an individual concern—is another hallmark of successful induction programs.[159]

What do these data mean? First, effective teacher induction programs can help teachers successfully adjust to their new careers. The most effective induction programs include a package of supports, especially mentors from the same field, the chance to participate in group or collective planning, and collaborative learning activities. Novice teachers need stronger teacher–teacher relationships that promote trust, motivation, commitment, and collective sense of their own capacities to do their job well.[160] Beginning teachers are more likely to stay in schools where they feel they can succeed.

Professional Development

For new and veteran teachers alike, lifelong professional learning is an essential part of becoming a skilled professional. Learning the teaching "basics" is critical before reaching the job setting. Developing the know-how to do the job well once in the field builds new teachers' competence and confidence. Whether called "professional development," "staff development," or "in-service programs," these adult learning activities convey to new teachers the professional culture of shared responsibility for mutual growth and increased student achievement.

High-quality professional development that enhances teaching practices and increases student achievement is not one-shot "sit-and-get" or "workshop" activity in which teachers listen to an outside expert explain how to do things. **National professional development standards** define effective teacher learning as a comprehensive system of consistent and sustained job-related activities directly related to teachers' actual classroom responsibilities. This high-quality professional

---

[156] Darling-Hammond, L. (2001, June). The challenge of staffing our schools. *Educational Leadership, 58*(8), 12–17; National Commission on Teaching & America's Future. (2003). *No dream denied: A pledge to America's children.* New York: Author.

[157] Honawar, V. (2008, September 17). Boston, Chicago teacher "residencies" gaining notice. *Education Week, 28*(4), 13. The studies were conducted by the Washington-based Aspen Institute and the Center for Teaching Quality in Hillsborough, North Carolina.

[158] Villar, A., & Strong, M. (2007). Is mentoring worth the money? A benefit–cost analysis and five-year rate of return of a comprehensive mentoring program for beginning teachers. Santa Cruz, CA: New Teacher Center.

[159] Garet, M., Porter, A. Desmoine, L., Birman, B., & Kwang, S. K. (2001). What makes professional development effective? *American Educational Research Journal, 38*(4), 915–946; Palumbo, M. (2003). A network that puts the Net to work. *Journal of Staff Development, 24*(1), 24–28; Rothman, R. (2002/2003). Transforming high schools into small learning communities. *Challenge Journal, 6*(2), 1–8.

[160] Bryk, T., & Schneider, B. (2002). *Trust in schools: A core resource for improvement.* New York: Russell Sage Foundation.

development is driven by data concerning what teachers' own students need to know and be able to do. It involves teachers working and learning together in collegial conversations about their actual students' work and then designing and practicing strategies to improve their own classroom practices and student learning. Instead of calendar days set aside for staff development events, professional development involves "just-in-time" learning that occurs during the regular workday. Teacher learning in this manner benefits both educators and all their students.[161]

To be successful, professional development programs must include four components: theory, demonstration, practice, and feedback.[162]

- *Theory.* Teachers need to understand how this new information fits with their professional knowledge and connects to their beliefs about teaching and learning.

- *Demonstration.* Teachers need to watch an expert enact the instructional practice in question. They need to see what it looks and sounds like so they will have a visual and auditory model upon which to draw as they practice the technique themselves.

- *Practice.* Teachers need opportunities to try out the new approach using role play, or visualization in their own classrooms.

- *Feedback.* Teachers need clear and accurate feedback on how well they accomplished their goal. Did they do everything they planned to do? How did the students respond during the activity? What does assessment of student learning show they gained? Collecting feedback from caring and informed colleagues, thinking about how to use it, and making adjustments before the next attempt can bring the new practice slowly into the classroom.

Research on professional development. A growing body of research shows that improving teacher knowledge and teaching skills are essential to raising student performance.[163] For example, Eric Hanushek, Senior Fellow with the Hoover Institution at Stanford University, estimates that "the difference between a good teacher and a bad teacher can be a full level of [student] achievement in a single year."[164] The National School Boards Foundation calls investment in teacher learning "the primary policy lever that school boards have to raise student achievement."[165]

In one study, sustained participation in professional development activities tied to a state's elementary school mathematics curriculum successfully improved teachers' knowledge of mathematics and their ability to transfer this knowledge to students.[166] Similarly, 65 percent of teachers who participated in professional development activities focused on standards were much more likely to teach using three or four "mathematics reform" activities that raised students' achievement, as compared with 35 percent of teachers *without* professional training.[167] Teachers report that professional development improves their teaching practices and encour-

[161] Roy, P. (2004, September). Move beyond workshops with NSDC standards: Results. National Staff Development Council. Retrieved May 20, 2008, from http://www.nsdc.org/library/publications/results/res9-04roy.cfm.

[162] Showers, B., Joyce, B. R., & Bennett, B. (1987 February). Synthesis of research on staff development: A framework for future study and a state of the art analysis. *Educational Leadership, 45*(3), 77–87.

[163] For a more complete discussion of studies showing that increased teacher knowledge and skills leads to increased student achievement, see Chapter 14, Instruction. See also Kaplan & Owings, 2002.

[164] Haycock, K. (1998, Summer). Good teaching matters . . . a lot. *Thinking K–16, 4.* Washington, DC: The Education Trust.

[165] National School Boards Foundation. (1999). *Leadership matters: Transforming urban school boards.* Alexandria, VA: Author.

[166] Cohen, D. K., & Hill, H. C. (1998). *Instructional policy and classroom performance: The mathematics reform in California.* Philadelphia: Consortium for Policy Research in Education.

[167] Alexander, D., Heaviside, S., & Farris, E. (1998). *Status of education reform in public elementary and secondary schools: Teachers' perspectives.* NCES 1999-045. U.S. Department of Education, National Center for Education Statistics, Fast Response Survey System. Washington, DC: U.S. Government Printing Office.

ages more learning, causing them to change their teaching practices, seek more information or training, and alter their views on teaching.[168]

Professional development and school culture. A school in which teachers value a professional learning culture enhances both teachers and students. New teachers can get better, marginal teachers can improve, and successful teachers can keep strengthening their expertise through well-designed programs. In addition, the professional culture that supports all teachers' learning provides the moral and technical support that new teachers desperately need to survive their first classroom days and become competent and confident. This school climate helps reduce teacher turnover and attrition and allows more students to work with effective, maturing teachers.

According to Linda Darling-Hammond, "An occupation becomes a profession when it assumes responsibility for developing a shared knowledge base for all of its members and for transmitting that knowledge through professional education, licensing, and ongoing peer reviews."[169] Today, teachers have clear articulated standards for what they should know and be able to do that are empirically tied to student learning. The alignment of NCATE, INTASC, and NBPTS standards has established a powerful professional model. These principles can guide preservice and practicing teachers along a continuum of professional growth from novice to master teacher. Together, they provide the profession with a defined body of knowledge, influence teacher entry and licensing requirements, affect teachers' autonomy in deciding work responsibilities, and provide higher prestige and increased economic benefits for teachers. As a result, teaching, as a profession, has never been better positioned to make a difference to teachers, students, and their communities.

---

[168] Choy, S. P., & Xianglei, C. (1998). *Toward better teaching: Professional development in 1993–94.* NCES 98-230. U.S. Department of Education. National Center for Education Statistics. Washington, DC: U.S. Government Printing Office.
[169] Darling-Hammond, 1997, p. 30.

Summary

Within the past few decades, teaching has enhanced its professional status. It has developed a clearly defined, specialized knowledge base, established practitioner-shaped and agreed-upon standards of professional practice, enlarged its influence on licensing/certification standards and entry requirements, and improved autonomy in deciding work responsibilities. Although the prestige attached to a teaching career has grown, teachers' occupational status and financial compensation remain below those of other college graduates.

In the past, teachers were prepared in normal schools, which eventually evolved into teachers' colleges. Today, teacher education programs are found in many colleges and universities. Ample research finds that strong teacher preparation programs produce effective teachers who can raise student achievement.

Licensure and certification are the states' formal processes for admitting teaching candidates into professional practice. Teacher shortages or other political factors play roles in setting state licensure requirements. Overall, the teacher certification evidence suggests that existing credentialing systems do not distinguish very well between effective and ineffective teachers.

The National Education Association (NEA) and the American Federation of Teachers (AFT), two organizations for professional teachers, have successfully worked to gain higher salaries, increased benefits, and improved working conditions for teachers. Both are committed to improving public schools and supporting democracy and social justice through political and professional activities.

National accrediting associations, such as National Council for Accreditation of Teacher Education (NCATE) and the Teacher Education Accrediting Council (TEAC), as well as the Interstate Teacher Assessment and Support Consortium (INTASC), have developed integrated standards that are improving teacher education programs and practice. The National Board for Professional Teaching Standards (NBPTS) sets and assesses high standards for what very effective teachers know and do. Experienced teachers voluntarily seek this advanced certification. Research on National Board Certification has found that it has a positive impact on teacher performance and student learning, engagement, and achievement.

Induction programs in the employing public schools help new teachers manage their transition into the profession. Induction programs are comprehensive, coherent, and sustained professional development services that aim to train, support, and retain new teachers. Mentoring is one type of induction program. Increasingly, research shows that well-designed and -implemented teacher induction and mentoring programs are proving successful in increasing new teachers' job satisfaction, efficacy, and retention rates.

Both teachers and students gain when all staff members participate in sustained, intellectually rigorous professional development about what they teach and how they teach it. Effective professional development is collaborative, tied to standards that students must meet, and results driven. A school climate in which everyone learns helps reduce teacher turnover and attrition and allows more students to work with effective, maturing teachers.

Conclusions

- Teaching as a profession has never been in a stronger position.
- Today's teachers have both increasing expertise and influence.
- The profession has a defined body of knowledge, influences the requirements for its professional entry and licensure, has growing autonomy regarding work responsibilities, and is increasing its prestige and economic standing.
- A variety of professional organizations and teachers' commitment to enhanced practice are making these gains for educators and students possible.

Misconceptions about Education and Teaching

Chapter 3

Conventional wisdom is what most people think about a certain topic. People hold many different beliefs about education—about intelligence, about race, and about the way in which students learn. Unfortunately, conventional wisdom is occasionally wrong—though it is seldom in doubt.

Three widely held misconceptions exist about education and teaching:

- A person is born with a certain amount of intelligence, and that amount does not change throughout life.
- Race is a biological fact that determines many traits, including intelligence and achievement.
- Teachers teach, and students learn. Students are vessels into which teachers convey knowledge. When they are filled, they have learned.

Of course, these myths are not the public's only misconceptions about education. These three points can, however, seriously affect how teachers view their students and how the public views its teachers. Challenging one's own beliefs about intelligence, race, and learning—and developing an accurate understanding of these dimensions—will help prospective teachers become better educators and more informed professionals. It will also help them become better citizens.

Focus Questions

- What is incorrect about the following statement: The intelligence you are born with is the intelligence you keep throughout life.
- What is incorrect about the following statement: Race is a biological fact that determines many traits, including intelligence and achievement.
- What is incorrect about the following statement: Teachers teach; students learn.

Misconception 1: The Intelligence You Are Born with Is the Intelligence You Keep Throughout Life

What Many People Believe

Intelligence means how smart you are. A person's genetic makeup—his or her DNA—determines that individual's intelligence. As a consequence, a person's capacity to learn is fixed and cannot be changed. No matter how motivated or how hard a student works, he or she cannot learn more than he or she is genetically able to learn. Having high expectations for some students' achievement is, therefore, a waste of time, money, and energy.

What Is True

Intelligence has many meanings. It can grow or be limited, depending on the environment in which a person is born, raised, and educated. Effective schools and excellent teaching can increase a student's intelligence.

Intelligence

Looking more closely at intelligence can help future teachers develop more accurate, realistic, and higher expectations for all students' learning and achievement.

What Is Intelligence?

Intelligence is a complex issue. The American public has strong cultural views—that is, it has developed conventional wisdom—about students' intelligence and the way in which they learn. These beliefs may or may not fit with the way learning really happens. Anne Lewis, a national education policy writer, challenges American teachers to confront their own attitudes toward learning.[1] She uses math as a case in point.

Compared with students in high-achieving countries, Lewis writes, American students (and many of their teachers) believe more strongly that mathematical talent is innate. In other words, they think that certain individuals are born with the ability to do math, whereas the rest of us are not. Many people believe that effort does not make much difference when the innate ability is not there. Instead, they believe, students either "get math" or they don't. This "get-ability" is set by their genes. All the effort, attention, and motivation in the world, they conclude, won't enhance a student's capacity to learn how to correctly solve math problems because their math ability was immutably set before birth. This belief is incorrect.

Similarly, most U.S. students believe that there is only one right way to solve any math problem and that math is best learned alone. Both notions are also incorrect. Many ways exist to solve a math problem. When students learn to solve math problems simply by "plugging numbers into a formula," however, their confusion is understandable. Likewise, teachers who understand the developmental process that students go through in coming to understand math concepts—which is best accomplished through group discussion—will be more successful in teaching math.

Meanings of Intelligence

Psychologists and educators sometimes disagree about what *intelligence* really is. For our purposes, we will consider the definitions upon which most agree.

Intelligence has three meanings: genetic, behavioral, and tested.[2] All refer to the individual's ability to learn. Individuals have all three types at the same time, and they interact.

Genetic intelligence is an individual's innate capacity, his or her DNA-determined equipment. The genetic component influences the speed and precision with which an individual learns. Also, the unique ways in which an individual's brain grows affect how it works. The brain's distinctive genetically determined mental and

---

[1] Lewis, A. (2005, February). Washington commentary: Endless ping-pong over math education. *Phi Delta Kappan, 86*(6), 420–421.

[2] Sattler, J. M. (1974). *Assessment of children's intelligence.* Philadelphia: W. B. Saunders Company, pp. 8–15. For a more in-depth discussion of intelligence, see Sattler, J. M. (2001). *Assessment of children: Cognitive applications* (4th ed.). San Diego, CA: Author.

biological structures, in combination with the physiological processes involved in the brain's development and functioning, may create the capacity for different individual talents. Genetic intelligence can never be directly measured.

Behavioral intelligence refers to what the individual does—that is, the person's observed actions. This is intelligence made visible. Behavioral intelligence results from the interaction of the individual and his or her genetic makeup with the environment, both inside the mother's womb before birth and with the family and larger world as the child grows and matures. Psychologically, this intelligence comprises the cumulative mental maps the individual builds up through interactions with the environment, to the extent that the person's constitutional equipment permits. The ability to construct mental maps can be hampered by physical or biological disabilities, such as brain damage. It can also be negatively influenced by detrimental environmental factors. For example, not having enough to eat, not having primary caretakers frequently touch and talk to you from birth onward, not having teachers encourage and stimulate learning, not being able to speak fluently with those around you, and believing on the basis of varied experiences that you are stupid and cannot learn may all affect an individual's mental maps and later behaviors.

Tested intelligence refers to a person's score on an intelligence test. A tested intelligence score is usually represented by one or two numbers, and it represents a very narrow sample of intelligent behavior. Tested intelligence encompasses behavior on a standardized instrument that is designed to elicit a person's responses to a variety of stimuli at that time. All intelligence, ability, and achievement tests measure what the individual has learned.[3] The score received on an intelligence test does not directly tap any innate potential that is genetically determined.

Issues in Measuring Intelligence

Obtaining accurate measures of intelligence is difficult. Several outside factors, especially true for disadvantaged children, can lower a person's performance on a standardized intelligence test. These include being unfamiliar with the test situation, lack of motivation, lack of familiarity with the test items or test format, mistrust of the examiner, and difficulties in understanding the instructions or communicating the answers.

In addition, many believe that different population subgroups have different cultures. Everyday experiences that are familiar to affluent or suburban students, for example, may not be familiar to poor, rural, or urban students. A farmer's child may know what a silo is; a city bus driver's child may not. This reality makes a standardized test "culturally biased" toward students who share the same experiences as those students who made up the original test **norm group**, the unique collection of individuals on whom the test was originally used to determine test items and derive scores.[4] Students who are not the same as members of the norm group—whether in terms of age, gender, socioeconomic status, geography, ethnicity, or other factors—may score lower on the test. As a result, intelligence scores are not necessarily accurate or valid for every person and should not be used without other information for making important decisions.

When people talk about intelligence, they often mention "IQ." **IQ**—more formally, the intelligence quotient—is one example of an intelligence test score. Alfred Binet, an early twentieth-century French psychologist (Figure 3.1), wanted to find a way to measure the ability to think and reason in any particular field, apart from

---

[3] Sattler, 2001, p. 135.
[4] The norm group is those individuals on whom the test was developed. Their responses formed the basis for assigning scores to categories indicating the level of performance. The closer the test taker is (e.g., in age, gender, or socioeconomic background) to the members of the norm group, the more valid and reliable the test scores will be.

| Figure 3.1 | Alfred Binet, Developer of the Intelligence Quotient (IQ) Test |

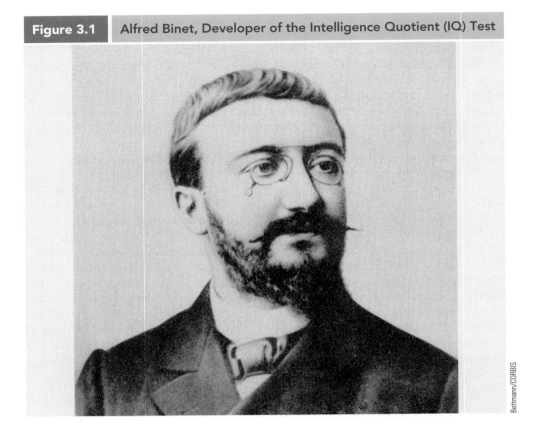

Bettmann/CORBIS

education. In 1905, he developed a test that asked children do tasks such as follow commands, copy patterns, name objects, and put things in order or arrange them properly; all of these activities shared the underlying fact that they did not depend on rote memory. Binet gave the test to Parisian schoolchildren and created a standard based on his data, which he suggested could be used to measure a particular child's performance against the trend of other children.

For example, if 70 percent of 8-year-olds could pass a particular test, then success on the test represented the 8-year-old level of intelligence. The IQ is the ratio of "mental age" to chronological age, with 100 being average. An 8-year-old who passed the 10 year-old's test would have an IQ of $10/8 \times 100$, or 125. For Binet, IQ was a measure of convenience that captured the character of a person's intelligence in a limited way. Today, we generalize the concept and consider persons with a high intelligence as having a high IQ, regardless of—whether the person ever took the intelligence test. Figure 3.2 illustrates how to calculate Binet IQ scores.

Intelligence in Daily Life

Our own experiences with intelligence also tell us what it is. We see more or less intelligent behavior every day. Different people show consistently more or less intelligent behaviors across a range of ordinary situations. Many are quick to call their own responses to new events "dumb" or "smart." People can learn to behave more intelligently when they eat well, sleep well, get enough exercise, and maintain good health. We know that the better we learn the rules and the more we practice what interests us (such as playing chess, learning complex rap lyrics, playing baseball, writing term

Figure 3.2	Calculating IQ Scores

Calculating IQ Scores

$$\frac{\text{Mental Age (MA)}}{\text{Chronological Age (CA)}} \times 100 = \text{IQ}$$

Examples:

A very bright
10-year old $\quad \frac{15}{10} \times 100 = 150$

A bright
12-year old $\quad \frac{15}{12} \times 100 = 125$

A slow learning
15-year old $\quad \frac{12}{15} \times 100 = 80$

papers, or listening to our friends' complaints), the faster, more knowledgeable, and more insightful we become at doing those things. We may not be able to attach a number to it, but we know more or less intelligence when we see it. These are examples of the second meaning for intelligence.

Many variations on the definition of intelligence exist. Some definitions differ only slightly, but in important ways, from each other. Most commonly, intelligence has alternately been defined as follows:

- The ability to carry on abstract thinking (Terman, 1921)[5]

- A collection of faculties—judgment, practical sense, initiative, and the ability to adapt oneself to circumstances (Binet & Simon, 1905)[6]

- The aggregate or global capacity of the individual to act purposefully, to think rationally, and to deal effectively with his or her environment (Wechsler, 1958)[7]

- The extension of biological adaptation, consisting of the processes of assimilation (responding to internal cues) and accommodation (responding to environmental cues) (Piaget, 1929)[8]

- A mental activity directed toward a purposive adaptation to, selection of, and shaping of real-world environments relative to one's life (Sternberg, 1985)[9]

- Your skill in achieving whatever it is you want to attain in your life within your sociocultural context by capitalizing on your strengths and compensating for, or correcting, your weaknesses (Sternberg, 2004)[10]

- Eight different intellectual competencies used to resolve genuine problems and create an effective product (Gardner, 1983)[11]

---

[5] Terman, L. M. (1921). A symposium: Intelligence and its measurement. *Journal of Educational Psychology. 12,* 127–133.

[6] Binet, A., & Simon, T. (1905). Methodes nourvelles pour le diagnostic du nuveau intellectual des anormaux. *L'Annee Psychologique. 11,* 191–244.

[7] Wechsler, D. (1958). *The measurement and appraisal of adult intelligence* (4th ed.). Baltimore: Williams & Wilkins.

[8] Piaget, J. (1929). The *child's conception of the world.* New York: Harcourt, Brace Jovanovich.

[9] Sternberg, R. J. (1985). *Beyond IQ: A triarchic theory of human intelligence.* New York: Cambridge University Press.

[10] Interview with Dr. R. J. Sternberg, Retrieved October 10, 2009, from http://www.indiana.edu/~intell/sternberg.shtml.

[11] For a complete understanding of Howard Gardner's theory of multiple intelligences, see Gardner, H. (1983). *Frames of mind: The theory of multiple intelligences* (10th ed.). New York: Basic Books; Gardner, H. (n.d.). Multiple intelligences. Retrieved October 10, 2009, from http://www.thomasarmstrong.com/multiple_intelligences.htm.

Likewise, when 1,020 experts in psychology, education, sociology, and genetics rated 13 behavioral descriptions of intelligence dimensions, their ratings showed a high degree of consensus[12]:

1. Abstract thinking or reasoning (99.3 percent agreement)
2. Problem-solving ability (97.7 percent)
3. Capacity to acquire knowledge (96.0 percent)
4. Memory (80.5 percent)
5. Adaptation to one's environment (77.2 percent)
6. Mental speed (71.7 percent)
7. Linguistic competence (71.0 percent)
8. Mathematical competence (67.9 percent)
9. General knowledge (62.4 percent)
10. Creativity (59.6 percent)
11. Sensory acuity[13] (24.4 percent)
12. Goal-directedness (24.0 percent)
13. Achievement motivation (18.9 percent)

Different intelligences emerge from different combinations of genetic and environmental influences. Environmental experiences (such as schooling) vary among individuals in terms of their intensity, length, and quality. The different degrees and forms of intelligences that result reflect the variety of neurological, experiential, developmental, genetic, and life influences, as well as their interactions. The different patterns of our achievement echo some of these differences. In all cases, environment interacting with genetic capacity plays an important role in bringing intelligence to its maturity and influencing its actions on the world.

Intelligence Depends on Nature and Nurture

As you see, intelligence is much more than a test score, and it is also more than biology. The consensus reached by developers of intelligence theories stresses the importance of both innate and developmental influences in determining how intelligent or competent a person is. Research suggests that intelligence is not fixed at birth, but rather can be learned. Intelligence is a central, flexible, genetically determined basic ability that is modified by experience. Individuals' unique learning history, however, determines how they use their intelligence. A person's environment and experiences may have either a positive impact or a negative impact on how the person expresses his or her genetic capacity in the real world. For example, an enriched environment enables more of the person's genetic capacity to grow and become realized. In contrast, a depressed, resource-poor environment limits this potential for growth. If a person's intelligence can be increased by the right experiences, then school can make students smarter.

Along these lines, David Perkins, a Harvard researcher on thinking, learning, and education, affirms that intelligence is not genetically fixed. In fact, intelligence can be taught.[14] Synthesizing the existing studies on intelligence, Perkins' research suggests that 50 to 60 percent of the variation in measured intelligence is genetically determined. Therefore, 40 to 50 percent of measured intelligence comes from environmental nurturing.[15] Parenting, the process of learning one's cultural norms, and formal education can make big differences in a person's IQ. Not only can IQ

---

[12] Sattler, 2001, p. 137. The percentage in parentheses indicates the percent agreement among experts.
[13] Sensory acuity means using the five senses of seeing, hearing, feeling, smelling, and tasting—that is, having conscious awareness of what is going on inside and around you.
[14] Perkins, D. (1995). Outsmarting IQ: The emerging science of learnable intelligence. New York: Free Press.
[15] Perkins, 1995, p. 55.

(as measured on an intelligence test) change, but—more importantly—behaviors identified as intelligent can also change. Improving a test scores is not the point; increasing intelligent behaviors is.

Teachers Can Increase Students' Intelligence

In sum, intelligence is both genetic and experiential, influenced by the twin forces of nature and nurture. The right environment can markedly increase intelligent behaviors, whereas a poor environment limits its growth and expression. But what does this mean for teachers?

First, teachers can make students more intelligent. Given the right environments, students' learning potentials are greater than the limits imposed by their family backgrounds and DNA inheritance. Remember, 40 to 50 percent of a student's capacity to learn can be significantly influenced by the environment—namely, the environment in your classroom. Students may not necessarily gain IQ points through their formal education, but they can learn the content you are teaching. They can grasp how to use what they learn and use this learning to behave intelligently in both simulated and real-world situations. When high expectations are set for all students and effective teaching practices are employed, all students can master the subject matter. Then, they can use the subject to think logically, reason clearly, solve problems accurately and effectively, and use the correct vocabulary. In short, students can learn how to behave intelligently with the content.

In this way, teachers serve as critical agents in increasing student learning. Their high expectations for all students' achievement and effective teaching practices are vital elements in making students intelligent. Nevertheless, these two factors are not present in every classroom. Perkins makes a compelling analogy: "Conventional instruction in the subject matter comes close to providing a heap of facts and skills, not so different from a heap of bricks, with the main hope that the learner will magically transform the heap into a building."[16] (See Figure 3.3.) Some students will make this leap—mostly the better ones, fueled by their genetic intelligence and rich array of experiences brought from home. Many other students will not—often because teachers do not spark the meaningful and exciting experiences, create the enriching environments, or provide the clear rules with ongoing feedback and opportunities to practice that those students need to successfully structure their learning.

Figure 3.3	Facts are Just a Heap of Bricks Until a Teacher Helps Students Transform Them into a Building

istockphoto.com

---

[16] Perkins, 1995, p. 117.

Unfortunately, not all teachers take advantage of the 40 to 50 percent of students' intelligence that they can influence. These teachers misunderstand intelligence. They mistakenly think their students either "get it" or they don't. They assume that all students come to the classroom with the same experiences and can learn the curriculum in the same way and in the same amount of time. Because they believe that some students have intellectual limitations, teachers don't use the range of powerful instructional practices that would help slower-learning students find meaning in the lesson and work at learning it. This faulty belief that students either have intelligence or they don't then becomes a self-fulfilling prophesy that leaves many students lagging behind their peers.

Clearly, we humans are not as intelligent as we need to be. No other species gets itself into trouble as an entire species! Intelligence consists of whatever factors contribute to intelligent behavior. Better understanding of intelligence can help teachers make their students more so.

Activity 3.1

Intelligence is genetic, behavioral, and tested. It is also a highly personal issue. Most people hold strong feelings about their intelligence as an essential part of who they are. After reading the section on intelligence, how does your new understanding of intelligence affect the way you view yourself and others?
Answer the following questions:

A. When did you first think about intelligence as something related to you? Were you at home? In school? How did the subject arise? What did you think about your own intelligence?

B. What evidence did you gather to determine how intelligent you were—or were not? Did you use objective measures such as formal IQ tests? Did you compare your schoolwork with that of your brothers or sisters? With that of your classmates? Was there another way you judged your own intelligence?

C. Which definitions of intelligence presented in this chapter do you find most meaningful and true for you? Which definitions do you like the least?

D. Describe in which ways and situations you find yourself intelligent and in which you feel yourself to be less intelligent.

E. How can you become more intelligent?

Activity 3.2

Intelligence is an important, but often misunderstood dimension in schools.

A. Discuss the following questions as a class:

- What is intelligence?
- How does the definition of intelligence as adaptive and purposeful behavior influenced by genes and experiences compare with what you thought defined intelligence?
- How does this definition of intelligence affect the way teachers may interact with students who come from different backgrounds than themselves?

- After reflecting on this chapter, describe to your group how your intelligence has grown as a result of a positive experience with a teacher.
- After reflecting on this chapter, describe to your group how your intelligence has been limited as a result of certain teacher practices.
- In what ways will this understanding of intelligence influence the ways you work with students?

B. Have each student select his or her favorite definition of "intelligence." Ask the student to explain why this way of viewing intelligence is his or her favorite. Also ask students to select their least favorite definition of intelligence and explain why it is their least favorite.

Misconception 2: Race Is a Biological Fact That Determines Many Traits, Including Intelligence and Achievement

What Many People Believe

Racial differences are important biological variations that determine many human traits, including intelligence. Different races, therefore, have different degrees of intelligence. As a result, students of certain races have biological limits on what they can learn. Regardless of students' motivation or work ethic, certain students will never be able to meet high standards because of their inherent racial limitations.

What Is True

Race is a cultural invention with no influence on intelligence and what students—or adults—can learn. Ability when joined with motivation, effort, and opportunities to learn, make the difference in students' achievement.

Race: More Social Than Biological

Many people in our society misunderstand the nature of race, and prospective teachers are not exempt from this problem. The U.S. Census divides us into groups based on race, and observable physical differences among people certainly do exist. People have different skin color, nose and eye shapes, body types, hair color and texture, and so on. The No Child Left Behind Act focuses on **disaggregating**, or separating out, achievement test scores for students from varied racial groups, so students' race is an important factor when talking about teaching and learning.

Race Is a Human-Constructed Concept

Race comprises two concepts—biological and social. **Anthropologists** say that, from a biological standpoint, races do not exist. They reject the concept of race as a scientifically valid biological category. Instead, they argue that race is a human-made, socially constructed concept.[17] People, not nature, they say, invented the idea of race to help make sense of their experiences in a world filled with people who lived elsewhere, looked different, and behaved in ways unlike the way they did. Anthropologists study and compare humans' biological and evolutionary history as

---

[17] Mukhopadhyay, C., & Henze, R. C. (2003, May). How real is race? Using anthropology to make sense of human diversity. *Phi Delta Kappan, 84*(9), 669–678.

Figure 3.4   **The Idea of Race Emerged in the Seventeenth and Eighteenth Centuries in Conjunction with the Growth of the Slave Trade**

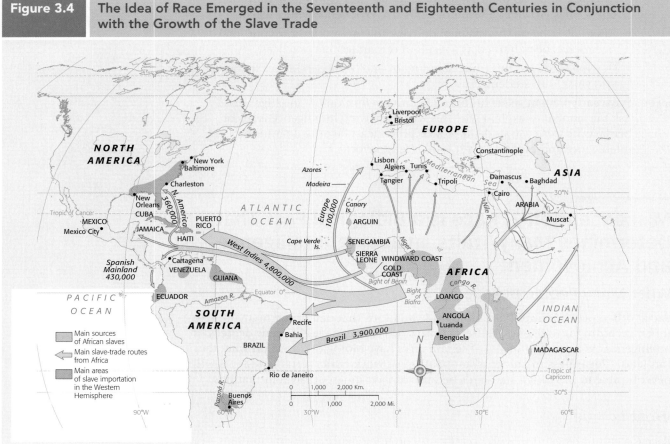

Homo sapiens to today's societal and cultural features, which decisively distinguish humans from other animal species. Through this work, they find a deeply embedded ideology that Europeans and Americans hold about race.

Historically, the idea of race emerged in the seventeenth and eighteenth centuries with the growth of colonialism and the slave trade. Figure 3.5 shows a map of the slave trade from Africa to South America, Europe, and the United States over the period 1711–1810. Europeans tried to classify humans into geographically distinct "races." Nineteenth-century evolutionary scientists began to claim multiple origins of humankind, with distinct races evolving in different places and times. By the beginning of the twentieth century, European and American scientists viewed races as a natural, long-standing division of the human species, evolving at different biological and cultural rates, given that biology drives changes in culture. "By such logic was racial inequality naturalized and legitimized."[18]

When today's scientists and anthropologists say that races are not scientifically valid, they reject the idea that humans were originally divided by nature or God into small sets of biologically distinct, fixed species or subspecies (or races). In fact, DNA evidence shows that contemporary humans are one variable species whose roots lie in Africa. Some human groups moved out of Africa into a wide range of environments around the world, producing hundreds—perhaps thousands—of culturally and genetically distinct populations. Through natural selection and genetic mutation in varied environments, local populations acquired some distinctive genetic traits. Some developed slanted eyes; others developed uniquely pigmented skin. In short, there are no basic or ancient biologically determined races. There are

---

[18] Mukhopadhyay & Henze, 2003, p. 670.

Figure 3.5   The Concept of Race and Racial Criteria are Subjective, Arbitrary, and Inconsistently Applied

Patrick Robert/Sygma/CORBIS

Malcolm Hanes/Etsa/CORBIS

Gideon Mendel/CORBIS

no stable, natural, permanent, or even long-standing groups called races. All human populations are historically specific mixtures of the human gene pool.

Like their ancestral forbearers, contemporary humans are not divisible into biological races. No naturally occurring clusters of racial traits exist. For races to be real as biological categories, classifications must be based on objective, consistent, and reliable biological criteria. These classifications must have predictive value that will make them useful for research. This does not hold true for race. Scientists have shown that the concept of race and racial criteria are subjective, arbitrary, and inconsistently applied. For example, the U.S. Census racial categories rely on only few visible, superficial, genetic traits, such as skin color and hair texture, and ignore the remaining enormity of human variation.

Extending this argument, equally visible racial classifications could have been constructed using such criteria as height, weight, ear shape, and hairiness! Less visible genetic traits, such as the presence or absence of the Rh factor in blood, susceptibility to diabetes, or the ability to digest milk (lactose), also could have been used to develop classifications. The potential biologically based racial groupings number in the millions, because each trait could produce a different racial classification. For instance, if height were a criterion for a racial category, the northern Afghan population would be placed in the same racial category as Swedes and the Rwanda Tutsi (See Figure 3.5). At first glance, a tall dark-skinned, dark-haired Caucasian; a tall light-skinned, blonde-haired Caucasian; and a tall dark-skinned, dark-haired African would not seem to have much in common apart from their height.

Racial classifications are also unscientific because they are unreliable and unstable over time. In one study, a medical anthropologist found that 37 percent of babies described as Native American on their birth certificate ended up in a different racial category on their death certificates.[19] Likewise, the racial categories used by the U.S. Census have changed over time. For example, "mixed race" is now an available category, whereas "Asian/Pacific Islander" is not. If racial classifications were truly biologically based, how could they change every decade?

Finally, and perhaps most importantly, no substantial evidence supports the notion that race as a biological category (including "racial" characteristics, such as skin color, hair texture, and eye shape) is causally linked to behavior, to capacities, to individual and group accomplishments, to cultural institutions, or to propensities to engage in any specific activities. One classic study that controlled for socioeconomic and other environmental variables eliminated the alleged "racial" differences in IQ scores and academic achievement between African Americans, Mexican Americans, and European American students.[20] In addition, the practice of people from different groups marrying into dissimilar groups means that two individuals from unlike "races" are just as likely to be more similar to one another genetically than two individuals from the same "race." Race, from the standpoint of biology, has no predictive value.

Race and Education

How does race influence education? The concept of race is a culturally and historically specific way of thinking about and relating to other human beings. It reflects a society's social divisions, identities, privilege, and power. Consequently, race is a major system of social identity, affecting one's own perceptions about oneself and others. It also affects how one is perceived and treated by others.

Race as a social construct does have a biological component in geographically localized populations. This results from adaptation, migration, and chance. Because ethnic groups from northwest Europe first settled the United States, they became the dominant culture. They used convenient (if unreliable) visible biological markers—especially skin color—to indicate themselves as distinct from immigrant (voluntary and involuntary) populations that immigrated later from southern and eastern Europe, Africa, Asia, India, and Latin America.

For the most part, classifications are neither bad nor good. People have always grouped others in ways that mattered to the society. However, the myth of race as biology is dangerous because it confuses superficial characteristics, such as skin color, with unrelated qualities, such as intelligence. Historically, U.S. society equated race with intelligence. It used this mistaken belief to justify slavery and to practice

---

[19] Robert Hahn, cited in Mukhopadhyay & Henze, 2003, p. 672.
[20] Mercer, J. (1998). Ethnic differences in IQ scores: What do they mean? (A response to Lloyd Dunn). *Hispanic Journal of Behavioral Sciences, 10.* 199–218.

educational and employment discrimination. Until 1954, U.S. schools were separate but unequal. This "racially different" rationale also supported Adolph Hitler's genocide of Jews, Africans, gypsies, and members of other supposedly "inferior races."

Educators need to understand that race is a historical, cultural, and social creation and remains a powerful social, political, economic, psychological reality. Race and racism profoundly affect how we see ourselves, how others see us, how we are treated, and how accessible our resources are. Sometimes, race and racism determine whether we get to use our civil rights. Despite the pervasiveness of these beliefs, we have the ability to change—or end—this racially charged system through our own behaviors. Teachers as transmitters of the official culture are well positioned to be active change agents to end racism.

Teachers must avoid thinking about students primarily as members of racial categories because doing so oversimplifies and masks complex human differences. Saying that someone is Asian tells us almost nothing concrete about that person. It may, however, elicit stereotypes such as "model minority" and "good at math." Yet "Asian" can mean Korean, Japanese, and Vietnamese, all of these groups have their own distinct histories, languages, and cultures. The same is true for the racial labels "white," "African American," and "Latino": The differences within members of each group are actually greater than the similarities among them.

Whether racial labels are good or bad depends on what we do with them. During the 1960s civil rights movement, ethnic pride and slogans such as "Black Power" were forces that raised consciousness and united people in efforts to improve our society. Today, racial classifications assist educators in monitoring how equitably our schools are serving the public. Disaggregating data based on achievement, attendance, discipline, course placement, and college attendance rates can help determine whether certain groups of students are disproportionately represented in any outcome areas. For example, is something happening at a school that has too few Latino students enrolled in AP classes? Is something happening between teachers and students that is leading to too many African American students being suspended from school for "disrespectful behaviors"? With these data in hand, the school can plan how to change this outcome. In this way, racial classifications as a social construct can be used to make a positive difference.

Dismissing the myth of race as biology also allows teachers to look at the underlying causes of social inequality in the United States. It allows us to look at the social, economic, political, and historical conditions that have encouraged and sustained social inequality in this country. As part of their roles as change agents, teachers can help students identify and understand others as individuals, rather than as stereotypes. The more teachers and students show genuine respect for other individuals' talents, abilities, backgrounds, and contributions to the classroom, the more likely we are to end racial discrimination on a personal level, on a school level, and in the community. It is within our power to help create a more socially just world.

Understanding race as a social—not biological—construct can help teachers respect each student's potential and create the learning environment that allows each student to grow, learn, and meet high standards.

Activity 3.3

Race is primarily a cultural—not a biological—construct. The following activities will help you clarify your ideas about how race plays an important role in American society, and particularly in American schools.

A. Explain how "race" is a historical, cultural, and social construct, rather than a biological outcome. Discuss how the race concept developed and how its continued use today in American society is helpful or hurtful.

B. Divide the class into two working groups. One group will argue why racial classifications should remain part of today's American culture, and specifically part of the school culture. The other group will argue the opposite position. What do you find is the class consensus on this question?

C. Discuss as a class the following question: What are the political and practical realities that would confront educators if they were to remove gender and racial classifications from student records, student achievement data, special education documents, and other school documents?

D. Working in groups of four persons, illustrate the actual concept of race with images, colors, shapes, words, and other media. Present this depiction to the class and explain.

Misconception 3: Teachers Teach; Students Learn

What Many People Believe

Education occurs when teachers present information to students, and students receive the information. Receiving the information is the same as learning it. Students are, in effect, containers into which teachers convey knowledge.[21]

What Is True

Learning is an active and highly personal process. Cognitive research has provided much new information about how it actually occurs. Teachers must do more than just understand their material; they must also understand their students as learners so that they can organize and present the content in ways that students can actually learn it.

How Students Learn

"The cognitive sciences are discovering all sorts of things that good teachers have always intuitively known," giving our profession "strong scientific support."[22] Many research findings have emerged from studies of the human brain that were not available to previous generations of teachers. Although a discussion of brain anatomy and its neurological functioning is too complex and tangential for our purposes, we will give a simple, clear explanation here of how people learn from a cognitive perspective. Recognizing the basics of how students learn will give future teachers insight into how to organize and deliver instruction to maximize student learning, and how to increase their own learning.

The Brain and the Mind

The **brain** is biology—it is a physical organ that controls all body functions in humans as well as their ability to think and to reason. The brain consists of massive networks of neurons that work in conjunction with other cells and structures such as blood vessels. The **mind**, by contrast, is psychology—it is our consciousness, the thinking you that experiences your thoughts and feelings. The mind includes the psychological processes that structure our awareness of the world, our reasoning and

---

[21] This belief underpins policy decisions to let individuals who have a college degree in a subject and work experiences in the related profession enter the classrooms without "teacher education" courses.
[22] Sylwester, R. (1995). *A celebration of neurons: An educator's guide to the human brain*. Alexandria, VA: Association for Supervision and Curriculum Development, p. viii.

beliefs. Certainly, brain and mind are related. Different parts of the physical brain control different aspects of being alive; certain brain parts control what happens in the mind. In other words, "The brain is what we have; the mind is what it does."[23]

"Each of us is born with a highly complex, inborn circuitry—creating innumerable branching pathways of options and obstacles."[24] Some of us have brains that are wired to handle a lot of information at once. Others can absorb and process only a little information at a time (albeit often with greater accuracy). Some of us have brains that can store and retrieve information from memory with speed and precision. Others have brains that access facts more slowly or with less precision. Some brains like to dream up their own ideas, while others prefer to use others' ideas. No two brains are alike, and no two work exactly the same.

"The adult human brain is a wet, fragile mass that weighs a little over three pounds. It is about the size of a small grapefruit. . . . Although it represents only about 2 percent of our body weight, it consumes nearly 20 percent of our calories!"[25] The brain uses one-fifth of the body's oxygen, and high levels of mental functioning require high-quality air (more oxygen, less carbon dioxide).[26] Figure 3.6 shows a cross section of the human brain.

The brain's natural function is to learn. Each healthy human brain, regardless of a person's age, gender, nationality, or cultural background, has the mental capacity to perform the following tasks:

- Detect patterns and relationships and make approximations
- Self-correct and learn from experience by analyzing outside data and reflecting on them
- Create[27]

Figure 3.6	Cross Section of the Human Brain

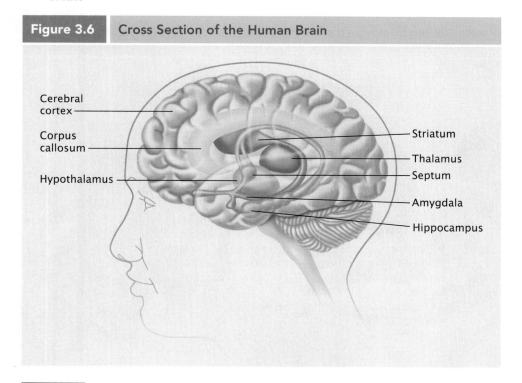

---

[23] Jensen, E. (1998). *Teaching with the brain in mind*. Alexandria, VA: Association for Supervision and Curriculum Development, p. 15.
[24] Levine, M. (2002). *A mind at a time*. New York: Simon & Schuster.
[25] Sousa, D. A. (1995). *How the brain learns*. Reston, VA: National Association of Secondary School Principals.
[26] Jensen, 1998, p. 10.
[27] Caine, R. N., & Caine, G. (1994) *Making connections: Teaching and the human brain*. New York: Addison-Wesley, p. 3.

Learning Changes the Brain

The brain can rewire itself when it encounters a new stimulation, experience, and behavior. To our brain, either we are already doing something we know how to do or we are doing something new. If we are reviewing an earlier learning, there is a good chance the **brain cells** (**neurons**, the compact cell bodies that process information by converting chemical and electrical signals back and forth) have already created well-connected, efficient pathways in our brain along which the information can travel. Thus, with familiar information, the message moves more swiftly over a well-traveled connection. In contrast, learning **new information**, by taking in novel or unfamiliar data, goes more slowly because the neural pathways have yet to be built.

When we say that cells "connect" with other cells, we really mean that they are in such proximity that their ends (**synapses**) are easily and almost effortlessly used over and over. New learning creates new synapses.

The key to getting smarter is growing more synaptic connections between brain cells and not losing existing connections. The brain connections that we have formed by making sense of our experiences allow us to solve problems and figure things out. It is estimated that we use less than 1 percent of 1 percent of our brain's projected processing capacity.[28]

We Screen Out What Is Not Important to Us

When we learn, we take in information through one or more of our **senses**, usually sight, hearing, and touch. During our lives, these three senses contribute to approximately 95 percent of all new learning.[29] Our eyes hold 70 percent of our body's

Figure 3.7   Seeing, Hearing, and Touching Contribute to 95 Percent of A New Learning

JLP/Jose L. Pelaez/Ivy/CORBIS

---

[28] Jensen, 1998, p. 15.
[29] Sousa, 1995, p. 10.

sensory receptors, which begin the cognitive process of transforming reflected light from images in our environment into a mental image of the objects that reflected that light. Meanwhile, our senses are constantly collecting bits of information, even while we sleep—approximately 40,000 bits of information each second averaged over the course of one day.[30]

The human brain cannot realistically attend to all that information at once: We would be overloaded! To help us, our brains have evolved a structure that screens all of these data to determine their importance to us. This structure is called a **perceptual** or **sensory register**. It uses our own experiences to decide whether the new data matter to us and, if that information does matter, how much. This sorting out of information lets us focus on what is significant to us.

Figure 3.8 gives a model of how external information tries to get through our perceptual register. Any information that doesn't make it through this register is gone for good, so it has no chance of being remembered after this encounter. By contrast, data that do make it through the perceptual register move to the next level.

If the new data get past the perceptual register, they next enter short-term memory. **Short-term memory** is a mental process that operates unconsciously and can hold information for approximately 30 seconds. This time span is long enough to look up the phone number for your favorite pizza place, dial the number, and forget it before you even reach for your car keys. Whether the information gets passed along to the next level—the working memory—depends on how important the person thinks it is. If the individual is facing a survival crisis, such as a fire or a medical emergency,[31] the brain will give its full attention. Any incoming information that is not related to that immediate need will be lost, however.

Emotions and Learning

Emotional data have a high priority in humans' information-processing system. An **emotion** is a mental state or affective feelings of psychological arousal in response to an event or thought. When a person responds emotionally to a situation, the complex thinking processes tend to shut down, making learning much more difficult to happen. When the student feels strong emotions—the teacher is yelling in her face, he does not want to look foolish in front of his friends, she has negative feelings about the subject because of repeated failures, or he has just broken up with

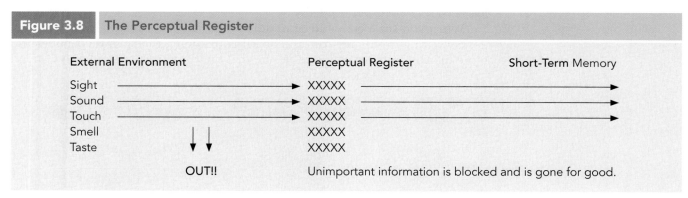

| Figure 3.8 | The Perceptual Register |

External Environment	Perceptual Register	Short-Term Memory
Sight	XXXXX	
Sound	XXXXX	
Touch	XXXXX	
Smell	XXXXX	
Taste	XXXXX	

OUT!!   Unimportant information is blocked and is gone for good.

Source: Adapted from Sousa, D. A. (1995). *How the brain learns.* Reston, VA: National Association of Secondary School Principals, p. 11.

---

[30] Sylwester, 1995, p. 61.
[31] Or whatever the individual thinks or feels is an emergency or crisis—this is a subjective experience that involves strong emotions.

his girlfriend—the person will tend to ignore the incoming data. The new information is lost forever. Information may be sent, but it is not received.

Emotions can sometimes override rational thoughts, leaving one "frozen" or "dumbfounded." A highly emotionally charged incident can reduce student learning to the level of a "deer caught in the headlights." That is, the student freezes. In such a case, survival data and emotional data are processed ahead of data for new learning. That information that does make it through the short-term memory during this period moves to the working memory.

Emotions and learning are like a two-way street. Emotional problems may interfere with a student's ability to take in new information. Conversely, the inability to grasp the new information can cause more stress and more emotional turmoil. This increasing downward spiral of emotions blocking learning can take a huge toll in the classroom. It is a situation teachers must recognize and avoid.

Working Memory and Learning

Working memory is where deliberate, conscious information processing happens. The working memory is temporary. It is limited both in how much information it can deal with at one time and in how long it can remain focused on that information. In general, both of these limits tend to increase, up to a point, with age. Table 3.1 shows how long we tend to keep information in our working memory as a function of our age. The younger the learner, the shorter the time available in working memory. On average, a preschooler can keep only two items at a time in working memory, whereas a high school student can keep seven items in this part of memory.

We can keep these data in our working memory for 18 to 36 hours on average, although we have to vary the way in which we are processing the information every 20 minutes or so. Otherwise, we will get bored and lose it. Attention span plays a major role in keeping the focus on the new data. Preadolescents tend to have a 5- to 10-minute time span to think about new information before they get bored. Adolescents normally can process an item in working memory intently for 10 to 20 minutes before their minds start to drift. For focus to continue, the individual must change the way he or she is dealing with the material.

For example, the person may switch from thinking about the subject, to physically manipulating it (writing, drawing, and handling), to talking about it, to relating it to different ideas or events already known. If, however, nothing else is done with the item after the 10 or 20 minutes (whether the person is a preadolescent or a teenager), the item is likely to drop from working memory. Once again, the message has been sent but is not learned.

When you see a class full of middle school students silently sitting at their desks, writing problems from the board and solving them on their papers for more than 10 minutes, you can be sure that their minds have started to wander!

Table 3.1	Changes in the Capacity of Working Memory with Age		
Approximate Age Range in Years	Capacity of Working Memory in Number of Items		
	Minimum	Maximum	Average
Younger than 5	1	3	2
Between 5 and 14	3	7	5
14 and older	5	9	7

Source: Sousa, D, A. (1995). *How the brain learns.* Reston, VA: National Association of Secondary School Principals, p. 15.

Most are probably no longer fully engaged. They may appear busy, but little learning is occurring.[32]

Sense and Meaning in Learning

After being processed, practiced, and manipulated, some of the information moves on to the next level: **long-term memory**. Before information can be learned, however, it must be stored. Teachers hope that students will understand and retain the information in long-term memory—that is, learn it—so they can recall the information for future use.

Which factors determine whether the information will reach long-term memory and be stored? Our total set of experiences and beliefs influence our working memory. These beliefs unconsciously filter information in working memory to determine if an item will be saved or dropped based on the answers to the following two questions:

1. Does this make sense?
2. Does this have meaning?

"Does this make **sense**?" asks whether the learner can understand the item based on experience. Is it comprehensible? Does the student understand what the teacher is saying? Does it "fit" into what the learner knows about how the world works? Just because the information makes sense to the teacher does not guarantee that it makes sense to the learner. Also, just because the student says, "That makes sense," when the teacher says it or answers "Yes" when the teacher asks, "Do you understand?" does not mean the student will be able to recall the information while attempting to complete homework at the kitchen counter after school or will remember it for tomorrow's quiz.

"Does it have **meaning**?" refers to whether the student finds the item relevant to his or her life, past learning, or experiences. Why should the learner remember the information? Meaning is very personal, and our experiences determine what is meaningful to us. Students find new information meaningful when it is clearly relevant to their previous experiences, whether in life or in school. In such a case, the new information fits in with what we already know and what matters to us. Conversely, if a student asks, "Why do I have to know this?" the student has not yet found this learning personally important. For instance, if you tell a student that you will accept word-processed term papers, that instruction makes sense to the student. It will only have meaning, however, if the student has access to a word processor.

Look into this classroom: When students hear the teacher take 10 minutes to explain several ways to solve a certain type of problem, and that information makes sense and has meaning to them, then—and not until then—students can begin to work. To learn how to make a bar graph in a seventh-grade classroom, the teacher might survey the class to see which music groups the students like best, tally the responses on the board as each student votes for his or her favorite group, and work with students to use these data to construct a bar graph for "Favorite Musical Group." Students could then copy the graph onto their own papers. Next, students could survey the class for their favorite actor, write the data on the board, and work with partners to create bar graphs for the new topic. The teacher would walk around the room monitoring students' understanding and progress, giving needed feedback to encourage, praise, and make corrections. The variety of activities all focused on the same learning—what is a bar graph and how do you make one correctly to communicate important information—sustains students' attention longer. Learning will be more likely occur with this teaching practice.

---

[32] For an in-depth discussion of "chunking," the process of teaching and learning discrete related groups of information, see Jensen, E., & Nickelson, L. (2008). *Deeper learning: 7 powerful strategies for in-depth and longer-lasting learning.* Thousand Oaks, CA: Corwin, p. 85.

Working memory goes into overdrive during exam time as students cram as much information as possible into their clogged brains at the last minute. Because this information is placed only in the working memory, rather than in long-term memory, within 48 hours most of it will be gone.

Caine and Caine offer the schema depicted in Figure 3.9 as an example of teaching for superficial meaning. Try to memorize the figures and relationships in Figure 3.9. Unless you can invent some significance, the information given is surface knowledge, and the exercise is rather pointless. It neither makes sense to the reader nor has meaning, unless you can design one. Yet many students' learning experiences in the classroom resemble this example. To see how having sense and meaning can help learning Figure 3.9, see Figure 3.11 on page 85.

Sense and meaning are independent of each other. One can remember an item that makes sense but has no meaning. Sometimes the bits of information that we have in long-term memory surprise us, such as when we come up with correct answers to

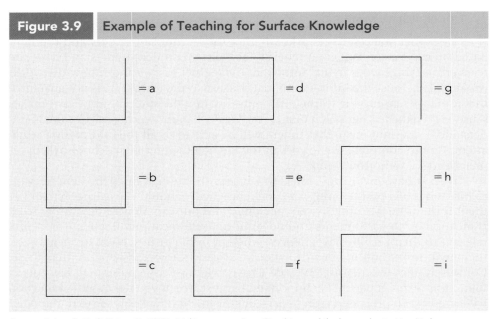

| Figure 3.9 | Example of Teaching for Surface Knowledge |

Source: Caine, R. N., & Caine, G. (1991). *Making connections: Teaching and the human brain.* New York: Addison-Wesley, p. 102.

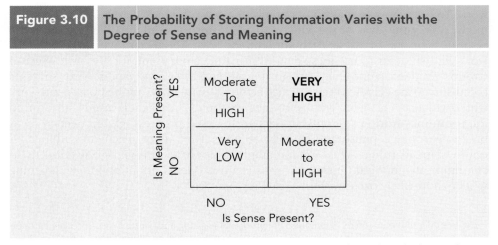

| Figure 3.10 | The Probability of Storing Information Varies with the Degree of Sense and Meaning |

Source: Sousa, D. A. (1995). *How the brain learns.* Reston, VA: National Association of Secondary School Principals, p. 18.

Trivial Pursuit. It is also possible to remember things that have meaning but that make no sense. Memorizing a nonsense poem such as Lewis Carroll's "Jabberwocky"—"Twas brillig, and the slithy toves did gyre and gimble in the wabe"—is one example. Carroll follows the English language rules by using nonsense sounds that resemble real words (meaning), allowing us to better remember them.

Of the two criteria, meaning has the greater amount of influence on whether we store the information. Most of us can remember ourselves as learners and see how this is true. Relevance matters. Our teacher might explain new information clearly and it might make sense to us when he or she says it. We can take notes on the information. We can follow the directions for solving the problems and even get the right answers. But when asked to solve the same type of problem several days later, or when asked to apply this learning to solve related problems, we cannot. We have forgotten. Because the process made sense but had no meaning for us, we never moved it into long-term memory. For some of us, when the next year's teacher asks whether we have learned the material in the previous grade, many of us can honestly say, "No!" Last year's teacher may have taught it, but we didn't learn it. When the current teacher explains it again, the information seems brand new. Figure 3.10 illustrates this relationship: The higher the meaning and sense, the greater the probability of storing the information in memory.

How do teachers get students to remember what they are teaching? They make students actively find personal meaning in the lesson. Shifting more of the classroom emphasis from listening to teacher explanations of content to students finding their own (accurate but personal) meaning for the learning will likely increase retention of learning.

Once the brain has assigned sense and/or meaning to the information, it moves into the long-term memory. Once the information is in, it is there to stay; it is available for later recall and use.[33] Ironically, the end of the process is also the beginning, because what we remember is often based on what we already know.

How and where we store information in our brains is another story, but it is worth noting that the process of storing information in our brains is not a single linear progression. A single memory might be broken up into many pieces, with each piece residing in a different part of the memory. Where information goes to be stored often depends on how and where we learned it. The more senses used in learning, the more places we will store the learning in our brains. When we listen to information, write it down, use it in a song, draw a picture of it, and trace its outline in the air, for example, we will store the learning in spots reserved for sound, movement, and sight. Storing information in many different mental locations increases the likelihood of it being remembered.

How do we know if information reaches long-term memory for storage? Research on retention shows that the greatest loss of newly acquired information or skills happens within 18 to 24 hours after the new learning occurs. Twenty-four hours is a reasonable guideline. If the learner can recall new learning the next day in class, a high probability exists that it was stored and can be recalled.

Furthermore, a difference exists between long-term memory and long-term storage. Long-term memory is the process of storing and retrieving information, whereas long-term storage consists of the brain sites that keep memories. The long-term storage sites are like the library, while the long-term memory is like the librarian.[34]

The Personal Process of Learning

As you see, the learning process includes both physiological and psychological components. Learning is a highly personal process. The psychological part—our **cognitive belief system**—is the total construct of how we see the world.

---

[33] Information will remain accessible unless the person experiences traumatic brain injury, stroke, or another brain-injuring syndrome.
[34] Sousa, 1995, p. 19.

The entirety of the information found in our brains' long-term storage areas forms the basis for our unique view of the world around us. Our cognitive belief system contains all our experiences, ideas, and feelings about these factors. Taken collectively, they form our point of view. Our cognitive belief system helps us make sense of new events, understand natural laws, and recognize cause and effect. It enables us to make decisions about what we think is good, important, or beautiful.

No two people have exactly the same data in our long-term memory. Not even identical twins raised in the same home have identical memories. No two people see the world in exactly the same way. These differences reflect the ways individuals use their experiences to interpret the world around them.

Self-concept is part of our cognitive belief system. It describes the way we see ourselves in the world. We might see ourselves as loyal friends, popular, so-so baseball players, strong social studies students, and procrastinators. Self-concept can be positive, neutral, or negative, depending on the situation and the feelings we have about ourselves in similar situations. Our experiences shape our self-concepts. Successful and rewarding experiences can raise our self-concept, whereas failure and humiliation can lower our self-concept. Not surprisingly, our self-concept affects how well we learn.

When we are in a new learning situation, our cognitive belief system and self-concept act as **perceptual filters** in our perceptual registers and short-term memories. They serve as screens to determine the incoming information's importance to us. If our previous dealings with similar information were positive and successful, the information is very likely to pass along to the working memory. We consciously recognize that we were successful in handling this information. We feel comfortable with it, and we focus on it for further processing. But if our past experiences with this information produced failure, the self-concept signals to the perceptual register (see Figure 3.8) to block the incoming data, because the information feels dangerous and unsettling. In this situation, we close our perceptual register just as we would close a Venetian blind to keep out light. The learner resists being part of the unwanted learning experience and mentally avoids the situation. When a concept comes in conflict with an emotion, the emotion almost always wins.

Finally, teaching that considers how students actually learn, as described earlier in this chapter, can create learning experiences that students perceive as joyful, interesting, and fun. This can be true even though the content is rigorous and intellectually challenging. Teaching in ways that allow students to learn lets students experience a high degree of self-motivation. Such teaching acknowledges the brain's ability to integrate large amounts of information, given the right learning conditions.

Effective teaching considers the whole learning environment and the whole student. It simultaneously involves the intellect, creativity, emotions, and body. It recognizes that learning takes place within many different contexts—classroom, school, community, home, country, and planet. Effective teaching connects what is learned to the big picture and allows learners to investigate the parts within the whole. When new information makes sense and has meaning to the student, students will remember it (Figure 3.11). And isn't this what we—and our students—need?

The message from brain research to prospective teachers about learning is clear. The choices you make about planning and delivering meaningful instruction and creating a positive class climate deeply affect student learning. The more interesting and relevant the learning activities are to students, the more energy they will invest in practicing, applying, and mastering them. When you can maintain a positive and safe class environment, students' emotions (no threats, no undue stress, no fear, no embarrassment) are less likely to interfere with their learning (their perceptual filters will stay open). Likewise, when you provide students with opportunities for success, you encourage your students to open their perceptual registers and participate in

Figure 3.11	An Example of How Providing Sense and Meaning Increases Learning

Note: This graphic provides reader with a familiar image—a tic-tac-toe diagram—that has meaning and makes sense based on many past personal experiences. Now, remembering the relationship between the letters and the figure becomes easy because the relationship has meaning.

Source: Caine, R. N., & Caine, G. (1991). *Making connections: Teaching and the human brain.* New York: Addison-Wesley, p. 104.

the learning. This can be true even if the student failed with similar content in another teacher's class.

Providing a safe and encouraging learning environment, and structuring instruction to have sense and meaning for each student increases learning. Including activities that enable students to become familiar with the material and that keep students' attention also increases student achievement. Teachers cannot merely "transmit" content to their students. Rather, they must recognize the conditions under which learning most optimally occurs and orchestrate those conditions in the classroom. We must know the "what" of teaching and the "how" of teaching.

When the "what" and "how" come together, disadvantaged students, minority students, English language learners, special education students, and traditional "college bound" middle-class students will all benefit from high teacher expectations and teacher behaviors that actually support their learning to high levels. Not only will the joy for teaching and learning increase, but achievement will grow as well.

Activity 3.4

The learning process is complex and involves more than just a teacher delivering a curriculum to passive student recipients.

A. Divide the class into three teams. Each team will design and enact the learning process, using the descriptions of learning from this chapter as students role-play the following characters: new information, senses, perceptual filter, short-term memory, emotions, working memory, long-term memory, sense, meaning, cognitive belief system. Be sure the audience can understand the process as you enact it.

B. Discuss what the learning process means for teaching and learning.

C. Discuss how this class can be adjusted to make better use of the way individuals actually learn. What would the students and the professor have to do differently to create more opportunities for learning?

Summary

The following statements are correct:

- Intelligence is not fixed: It can be increased with enriching life and school experiences.
- Race is a social—not biological—condition that places no limits on students' ability to learn.
- Teaching requires helping students find sense, meaning, and safety in their classrooms to facilitate learning.

First, *intelligence* is a central, flexible genetically determined basic ability that is modified by experience. People's intelligence can grow when they learn in supportive and stimulating environments. Intelligence changes with life situations and conditions, meaning that a person's environment and experiences have a positive or negative impact on how the person expresses his or her genetic capacity in the real world.

Individuals' unique learning histories determine the ways they use their intelligence. Intelligence is not fixed at birth; it can be learned. Research suggests that 50 to 60 percent of the variation of measured intelligence is genetically determined and 40 to 50 percent of measured intelligence comes from environmental nurturing. Not only can IQ (as measured on an intelligence test) change, but—more importantly—behaviors identified as intelligent can also change given the right environments and beliefs.

Second, race is a social construct. Race is not a scientifically valid biological category. Scientists have shown that the concept of race and racial criteria are subjective, arbitrary, and inconsistently applied. Contemporary humans are all members of one variable species.

The myth of race as biology is dangerous because it confuses superficial characteristics, such as skin color, with unrelated qualities, such as intelligence. Thinking in racial categories oversimplifies and masks complex human differences. Understanding race as a social—not biological—construct can help teachers respect each student's potential and create the optimal learning environment that allows each student to grow, learn, and meet high standards.

Third, teachers can either facilitate or hinder student learning. The learning process is physiological, psychological, and highly personal. Learning changes the brain, which rewires itself with each new stimulation, experience, and behavior encountered. Information must both make sense and have meaning to the person before it can be learned. Teachers' choices about how to teach their content and how to build a positive class climate must, therefore, consider how these factors affect students' brains, if they are to enhance student learning.

Conclusions

- These three misconceptions of education prevent people from seeing complex individual differences.
- Clarifying and removing these misconceptions help professional educators use their skills to help students learn beyond limitations placed on them by their backgrounds, skin colors, or ethnicities.

The History of American Public Education, Part 1

We can better understand where U.S. education is today by seeing where we have been. To a large extent, today's education reflects its roots.

This chapter looks at American education from the colonies' earliest days through the movement toward universal public schooling. We will consider how the earliest settlers brought European educational ideas and institutions to their new homeland, and how our American environment transformed these Old World beliefs and practices. We will see how the early interaction of three key factors—the economy, religion, and the view of governmental control—led to the types of schools that each community developed. In addition, we will discuss how our forbearers' attitude about the type of democracy and the government they wanted affected the educational system. The extension of the right to vote, the rise of manufacturing, and the increasingly diversity of the American population all encouraged public schools' expansion to higher grades and spread across the nation. Many of the educational challenges we face and are overcoming today had their roots in these earlier schools.

Focus Questions

- How did the local economy, religion, and views about who should control education influence the type of public schools that emerged in early America?
- What were the characteristics of education in the early New England Colonies?
- What were the characteristics of education in the middle colonies?
- What were the characteristics of education in Virginia and the other Southern colonies?
- What did teaching and learning look like in the early colonial schools?
- How did the early colonies and early national period address the process of educating girls, African Americans, and Native Americans?
- How did public schooling change during the early national period?
- How did student discipline change from the colonial time to the late nineteenth century?
- Which factors influenced the U.S. movement toward universal public schooling?

The Emerging Public School in Early America

The North American continent was not empty when the European settlers arrived. Native Americans had been here for centuries, developing their own civilizations. Culture contact was the initial reality of American education, but also proved to be its ongoing challenge.

Settling North America

When the Pilgrims came to America in December 1620, they were a community seeking to preserve its religious and cultural integrity. Although the Pilgrims were only a minority of the Plymouth, Massachusetts, population, their views dominated the colony's character. As in the earlier (but failed) Jamestown settlement in Virginia, family and church initially were responsible for the education of the colony's children, rather than any school or college. A key reason: The settlers included few men with formal learning.[1]

Like the Pilgrims before them, the Puritans who settled Massachusetts in later years arrived as a community tied by family, friendship, and common loyalty. They were attempting to preserve their religious and cultural heritage by creating a Christian commonwealth. Within such a society, education would transmit their intellectual traditions and prepare young people to pursue the Puritans' cultural ideal. Family, church, school, university, and community all provided education dedicated to molding men.[2]

American settlers also came from other countries. The Spanish founded the first permanent European settlement north of the Gulf of Mexico at St. Augustine, Florida, as early as 1565. The French had permanent colonies in Nova Scotia and Quebec in 1605 and 1608. By 1664, New Amsterdam (later renamed New York) was a prosperous Dutch market town of about 1,500 inhabitants. Englishmen, Swedes, French, Portuguese, and Africans lived in its extensive colonial province. The Swedes founded New Sweden along the Delaware River in 1638. There were scattered settlements of French Huguenots, Spanish and Portuguese Jews, Scottish Presbyterians, and German sectarians. These early immigrants came as individuals, as independent families, and in groups of families looking to share a common life in a new land under unfamiliar but tolerant civil authorities.[3]

From its inception, diversity and its necessary cultural competition, accommodation, and blending were fundamental facts of American life.[4]

English influence. By 1689, English settlements stretched from Maine to the Carolinas and east to the West Indian Islands. Of the 200,000 Europeans on the North American continent, the English represented the largest group. Owing to their greater numbers than the French, Dutch, and Spanish settlers and their technological superiority to the Native Americans and the Africans, the English were uniquely positioned to influence colonial development.

England's decisive cultural influence in North America was spread through the educational system developed by English colonists. By the 1620s, England saw its colonies as permanent, self-sustaining communities. These communities came to embrace families, churches, missions, print shops, and schools, which would systematically advance English ideas, customs, language, law, and literature. While settlers from other countries had families in North America during the seventeenth century, and some had churches, missions, and schools, none of these groups managed to develop an educational system as extensive as the English version. As a result, England achieved intellectual as well as political influence that, although challenged, would not be overthrown.[5]

---

[1] Cremin, L. A. (1970). *American education: The colonial experience 1607–1783*. New York: Harper & Row.
[2] Cremin, 1970, pp. 15–16.
[3] Many contemporary historical scholars acknowledge the need for a more comprehensive approach to American history than the narrow focus on British New England settlements and seek to include Spanish, Dutch, French, West African, and other influences. See MacDonald, V-M. (2001, Autumn). Hispanic, Latino, Chicano or "other"?: Deconstructing the relationship between historians and Hispanic-American educational history. *History of Education Quarterly, 41*(3), 365–413.
[4] Cremin, 1970, pp. 21–22.
[5] Cremin, L. A. (1977). *Traditions of American education*. New York: Basic Books, pp. 1–10.

Renaissance Influences on Early Colonists' Intellectual Traditions

The Renaissance and its contradictions influenced those who came to America. Colonists were both overly believing and skeptical, idealistic yet pragmatic. Colonists accepted witchcraft and the new sciences. They believed in improving themselves while preserving valued customs. Their books included Christian classics and ancient texts. Renaissance scholarship looked backward toward the past exemplars and focused on contemporary religious works, as well as manuals of law, medicine, politics, surveying, agriculture, and conduct. Poetry, drama, history, and fiction offered colonists opportunities to experience refined living once basic survival was assured. Colonists wanted to ensure their civilization's continuity in the New World. As the colonies evolved into full-fledged communities, these books played a fundamental role in expressing their shared aspirations and the forms of education they would support.[6]

The early settlers' intellectual tradition included humanistic ideas about education developed by Desiderius Erasmus, Sir Thomas Elyot, and John Locke. Erasmus's *The Education of a Christian Prince* (1516) identified education as the critical agency to prepare the future king and a just state. To fulfill this essential educational responsibility, a tutor of fine character, high morals, pure life, and affable manner was widely sought and highly valued. The curriculum taught by such a tutor would include the Bible, Greek and Roman literature, and classical historians.[7]

Influenced by Erasmus, Sir Thomas Elyot's *The Boke Named the Governour* (1531)[8] extended a good education's value from hereditary monarchy to those who would govern. The key idea was that common-born administrators and professionals needed a proper education if they were to join with traditional aristocracy in government service.

British philosopher John Locke believed in the principle that the people, not their kings, had civil and political rights.[9] As a result of his contractual theory of government, some would consider Locke to be the grandfather of the American Declaration of Independence.[10] Locke believed education had useful purposes—for the business of living (not simply for the university) and for the possibility of advancing progress. In *Some Thoughts Concerning Education* (1693), Locke advised parents on how to raise their children into moral, social persons with the virtue (have a good life based on Christian principles) and the wisdom (able management of one's business affairs) necessary for living in the world. In his view, education helped shape the child's psychological and motivational structure, enabling the child to take rational control over his or her own life.[11]

The Renaissance's religious conflicts also contributed to America's educational influences. The sixteenth century's Protestant Revolution challenged the Catholic Church's authority, and this revolt did not stop at the Atlantic Coast. Individual responsibility for salvation became more dominant than the church's collective influence. Individual responsibility required all people to be educated. Education became viewed as a vital necessity, requiring a new type of school—elementary, for the masses, and in the native tongue. The American colonies would faithfully reflect this belief.[12]

An important humanistic shift eventually occurred in sixteenth-century English educational thought. The same education that Erasmus, Elyot, and Locke

---

[6] Cremin, 1970, p. 29.

[7] Erasmus, D. (1936). *The education of a Christian prince*, translated by L. K. Born. New York: Columbia University Press, pp. 140–141.

[8] T. Elyot, (1883). *The Boke named the governor*, edited by H. H. S. Croft. London: Kegan Paul, Trench, & Co. Cited in Cremin, 1970, pp. 61–63.

[9] Barzun, J. (2000). *From dawn to decadence: 1500 to the present*. New York: HarperCollins.

[10] Darnton, R. (2003). George Washington's false teeth: An unconventional guide to the eighteenth century. New York: Norton, p. 97.

[11] Cremin, 1970, pp. 276–278.

[12] Cubberley, E. P. (1947). *Public education in the United States*. Cambridge, MA: Riverside Press, pp. 6–10.

realized would prepare the aristocracy to rule could also prepare common persons to rule and live productive lives. Convinced of education's value, "it is but a short step from an education that confirms status to an education that confers status."[13] Education, it was realized, could lift men up to a higher station in life. It did not just humanize those who ruled; rather, education could *qualify* men to rule, whatever the circumstances of their birth and the conditions of their early life.

Activity 4.1

A. Discuss the difference between "an education that confirms status to an education that confers status."

B. How does this idea fit with the American belief in the values of meritocracy and social mobility?

C. If you were living in colonial America in a family of modest means, what would belief in "education that confers status" mean for your own schooling and life opportunities?

Schooling in the Early Colonies: Three Key Factors

Available schooling in the early colonies depended on three key factors that influenced people's thoughts and actions about educating their children: the local economy, local religious practices, and the locality's views on government involvement in their schools. Table 4.1 clarifies these relationships and identifies the type

Table 4.1   Types of Early Colonies and Types of Schools

Factors Influencing the Type of School Desired	Geographic Regions		
	New England*	Middle Colonies (Pennsylvania, New Jersey, New York, Delaware, Maryland)	Virginia and Southern Colonies
Economy	Small farms, trades, lived in small villages, towns, cities.	Small farms, trades, lived in small villages, towns, cities.	Large plantations, highly stratified society of great wealth, servants, slaves.
Religion	Mostly Puritan. Calvinist; wanted a church-based society.	Varied. Did not want religion dominating the others.	Varied. Did not want religion dominating the others.
Community's desired level of government involvement in its schools	State and local control favored to require, pay for, and maintain public schools.	No governmental involvement with schools wanted.	No government involvement with schools wanted.
Type of school	Church-run, later becoming public schools for all.	Parochial or charity schools for the few.	Parochial and charity schools for the few.

* New England is generally considered to include Maine, Vermont, New Hampshire, Massachusetts, Connecticut, and Rhode Island.

---

[13] Cremin, 1970, p. 67.

Figure 4.1	Immigrant Groups in the U.S. Colonies, 1775

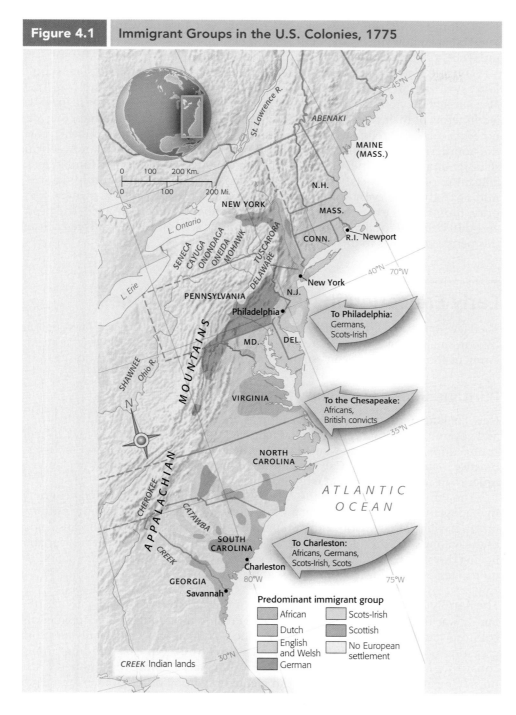

of schooling each region developed.[14] Of course, diverse viewpoints existed in every region, but general trends can be described.

Early American public education arose from collaboration between churches and colonial governments. Most of the first colonists arrived from Western Europe and had a range of ideas about what education in the New World should be. Figure 4.1 shows their settlements along the Atlantic Coast.

---

[14] Cubberley first defined the four basic types of schooling practices that we cite here: Cubberley, E. P. (1947). *Public education in the United States: A study and interpretation of American educational history.* Cambridge, MA: Houghton Mifflin, pp. 97–105.

Colonists' differing views of what schools were for and whose purpose they served shaped how American public schools developed. Each view reflected the local influences of religion, the economy, and perspectives on governmental control.

Outside New England, settlers rejected the idea that church and state should join as partners in running the colonies, including their educational systems. They also rejected the notion of using public monies for public schools. Because they varied in terms of their religious backgrounds, social classes, and economies, they did not want one sect's religious leaders controlling all students' learning. Furthermore, the Southern caste system in which wealthy whites ruled over African American slave labor and white indentured servants made the idea of publicly funded mass education of varied social and economic classes and races totally unthinkable.[15] Adding to the mix, every colony had private venture schools whose owners, for a price, promised to teach their students whatever they wanted to learn.[16] The push-and-pull between local and state control of public schooling that emerged during this period continues to this day.

Early Education in New England Colonies

The New England colonies shared a small farm and trades economy. Most people lived in small villages. Many shared a common religious faith and believed that government should have a role in establishing and maintaining public schools.

Puritans Shape Early New England Education

New England's Puritans valued education as the essential backbone of their society and government. While still living in England, Puritans opposed close church–state connections. Instead, they wanted their churches and congregations to be free to practice their own style of Calvinist Protestantism. Many Puritans fled England for America to save their lives and religious liberty.

The Puritans settled along the Atlantic Coast in a small farm-based economy, living together in villages, sharing a similar religious background and the philosophy that education, religion, and the state all served a common good. Because most of the colony's early residents were English Calvinist Puritans, they felt comfortable having the state or locality collect fees or taxes to pay for, build, maintain, and require attendance in local church-run schools.

The family as an educational agency. In the early New England colonies, the family was the principal means of educating children. Through home instruction, colonists taught their children to read the Bible and participate in family and congregational worship. Families often used a **hornbook** (an early reading primer consisting of a single page protected by a transparent sheet of flattened cattle horn), the alphabet, and a primer (an elementary book of religious material) or catechism (a series of questions and answers giving the fundamentals of religious belief) to teach reading.[17] In this way, children learned to read using passages with which they were probably familiar. The early colonial family also undertook training children for labor or employment, with fathers teaching their sons the multiple arts required to manage the household, farm, and shop, while mothers instructed their daughters in domestic skills.

---

[15] Cubberley, E. P. (1920). *History of education.* New York: Houghton Mifflin, p. 457.
[16] Herbst, J. (2002, Autumn). Nineteenth century schools between community and state: The cases of Prussia and the United States. *History of Education Quarterly, 42*(3), 317–341; Leslie, B. (2001, Summer). Where have all the academies gone? *History of Education Quarterly, 41*(2), 262–270.
[17] Cremin, 1970, p. 129.

When they wished to follow a vocation not pursued in their own homes, children would apprentice in another household, where a parent-surrogate systematically taught the new trade. Young men who wanted to enter a more learned profession might substitute a period of formal schooling for the apprenticeship. The masters of the school stood in *loco parentis (in place of the parents)*, and the curriculum of reading, writing, and principles of religion either incorporated or supplemented the trades portion of the education. Apprentices learned by direct example with immediate participation and appraisal by the parent or master.

This educational arrangement did not hold for all New England families, however. The English settlers sharply disrupted the Native Americans' family life and education, and many indigenous people eventually withdrew from the tribal environment and attempted to live as Europeans did. An even sharper rupture of family life and education occurred among the Africans who were brought forcibly to America as servants or slaves and placed within colonial households. We know practically nothing about the education provided in such families. Often the instruments of white households and white missionaries, these involuntary immigrants likely transmitted African stories to their children, and adapted their tribal lore to their New World circumstances.[18]

New England laws regarding town schools. In New England, the Plymouth Colony originally left education to households and churches. Different towns experimented with providing grammar (elementary) schools, however. By the end of the settlement's first decade, 7 of the 22 Massachusetts towns had taken some public action on behalf of schooling, although not all of these attempts survived.[19]

Because most colonial townships had not provided formal schooling for their residents, the state government felt compelled to act. In 1642, Massachusetts passed ground-breaking legislation that empowered the selectmen of each town to periodically visit local homes where they expected parents or masters to explain how they were providing for their children's education. Children were to learn how to read well enough to understand religion and secular laws.

With this law, education became compulsory for all youths in the Massachusetts Bay Colony—boys and girls alike.[20] To the Puritans, both genders' eternal souls were at stake. Most notably, the responsibility for encouraging and overseeing family education now moved from the clergy to secular officials.

Intended more for parental guidance, these laws were not usually enforced. From time to time, Massachusetts towns would crack down on parents and masters whose dependents remained ignorant and illiterate. After five years, the general court realized that the school law was not working as intended.

The first school finance laws. Acting more firmly, the court established the law of 1647—the famous "Ye Olde Deluder Satan" law. Because Puritans saw children as depraved—prone to idleness and foolishness—the law assumed that those who could read and understand the Bible could not be lured to follow Satan's temptations (and possibly offend God and neighbors).

The 1647 law required towns that had at least 50 households to appoint and pay for a teacher to instruct all children to read and write. Any town with 100 or

[18] Vaughan, A. T. (1965). *New England frontier: Puritans and Indians, 1620–1675*. Boston, MA: Little, Brown; Degler, C. N. (1959–1960). Slavery and the genesis of American race prejudice. *Comparative Studies in Society and History, II*, 49–66.
[19] Cremin, 1970, p. 180.
[20] The law of 1642 made no distinction between educating boys or girls because both genders needed to be able to read the Bible to practice their religion appropriately. In practice, however, its application may have been more arbitrary.

more households was required to set up a grammar school and hire a teacher to prepare youth for university. Towns generated school funds by direct taxation of the entire town, by taxing all those with boys of school age (typically 6- to 12-year-olds), by charging tuition, by selling some town land, or by some combination of such measures.[21]

Selectmen were authorized to impose fines on those parents who were not educating their children. Violators might endure public humiliation in the stockades.[22] Despite the legal penalties, most towns responded with a variety of strategies, ranging from outright noncompliance to meeting the letter of the law but compromising on its spirit.[23]

Most importantly, civil authorities—not religious ones—retained functional control over schools. Town funds—not church funds—financed schools. Elected local officials now had the duties that had formerly belonged to ministers—inspecting schools, supervising curriculum, and encouraging student attendance.

The Puritans had few objections to moving the school into civil government's hands. After all, they saw religious and civic government as one in the same. To the community, the local government and the local church shared a common purpose in educating children to prepare them for a righteous religious and civic life. Not until 1789, after the American Revolution, did Massachusetts require community (secular) sponsored schools.

Initially, Massachusetts's approach to state-controlled education had limited impact outside what are now the neighboring states. In Connecticut, the law of 1650 ordered that children and apprentices be taught to read. Like its neighboring colony to the north, Connecticut established Latin grammar schools to prepare male students for the state college, Yale College,[24] where they would study for the ministry.

To the New England Puritans, education's primary goal was not to advance a child's personal interests, but rather to protect and enhance the community and the state. Public schools were not supposed to replace parents' role in teaching and socializing their children. An educated populace was as much a moral issue as a civic necessity. The state, however, was in a better position than parents to enforce this expectation for learning. State oversight and control of schools began.

Four Types of Schools

Most New England colonials saw the family unit as the source for all education—practical, moralistic, and religious. The family controlled its children's future social and economic mobility. Wealthy (and many middle-class) families could afford for their children to get an education rather than to work as laborers or apprentices. They could pay for private tutors, send their children to private tuition-based schools, or send them to Europe to receive a cosmopolitan education. If they wanted their sons to become lawyers, physicians, or ministers, they could send them to college.

Not all families believed that women needed an education to meet their household and social responsibilities.[25] Families with means who wanted to educate their daughters could send them to an entrepreneurial school, if one were available.[26] As for children from poor families, unless they lived in a town that required school attendance for a few years, they received no formal instruction at all. Their future economic survival depended on gaining an apprenticeship or undertaking hard, backbreaking manual or household labor.

---

[21] Perlman, J., Siddali, S. R., & Whitescarver, K. (1997, Summer). Literacy, schooling, and teaching among New England women, 1730–1820. History of Education Quarterly, 37(2), 117–139.

[22] Cubberley, 1920, p. 365.

[23] Perlman, Siddali, & Whitescarver, 1997.

[24] Yale was the only college in Connecticut at that time.

[25] Sklar, K. K. (1993, Winter). The schooling of girls and changing community values in Massachusetts towns, 1750–1820. History of Education Quarterly, 33(4), 511–542.

[26] Preston, J. A. (2003, September). "He lives as a *Master*": Seventeenth century masculinity, gendered teaching, and careers of New England schoolmasters. History of Education Quarterly, 43(3), 360–371.

New England colonists re-created the dual-track system they had seen in England. The dual track included a minimum education for most children (at the English elementary, town, or common school) and preparation for college for affluent young men (at the Latin grammar school). A third type of school, the dame school, became available to prepare young children with the skills to enter elementary (common) school. A fourth type, the academy, was a newer and less well-defined institution for older students not attending college.

English (Elementary) Town Schools

The New England town (elementary) school was controlled locally and welcomed both boys and girls, ages 6 through 13 or 14. Attendance was irregular, depending on the weather and the need for children to work on their families' farms. The schools' curriculum included reading, writing, arithmetic, catechism, and religious hymns. Children learned the alphabet, syllables, words, and sentences by memorizing the hornbook. Older children read the *New England Primer,* which included the Ten Commandments, the Lord's Prayer, and the Apostles' Creed. Math went as far as counting, adding, and subtracting.

Town school teachers. Initially, all teachers in New England town schools were men. Some were earning a living as a teacher while preparing to become ministers or enter another profession. Some became teachers to repay debts owed for their trips from Europe to North America. In the late seventeenth century when a few towns did hire women ("school dames") for teaching, they employed them only as adjuncts to the town schoolmaster who remained the "revered and accepted instructor of children."[27]

Eventually, the schoolmasters' jobs went to itinerant teachers and college students in the winters and to women teachers in the summers. Girls were usually admitted to the summer school with the female instructors but not to the winter schools.[28] Girls, therefore, learned a small amount of reading, writing, religion, and ciphering.[29] Only toward the end of the colonial period—and then only for girls "from the best families"—did girls receive education beyond domestic training for the home.[30]

Teaching salaries remained modest. Reading and writing masters in smaller rural communities could earn 10 pounds per year, while distinguished grammar school masters could earn a more generous 25 to 50 or 60 pounds per year. Given colonial New England's labor shortages, salaries for competent teachers could sometimes approach 75 to 100 pounds per year.[31] Unfortunately, because parents did not always pay their school fees, teachers were often not paid on time. On the plus side, teachers occasionally received special grants and benefits such as gifts of land, houses, and firewood; a share of tuition fees; and exemptions from taxes and military service.[32]

Teacher turnover was high during this era. In fact, most schoolmasters changed jobs yearly.[33] Only about 3 percent of the graduates remained in teaching permanently, because ongoing labor shortages opened attractive alternatives to talented schoolmasters. The result was a chronic scarcity of schoolmasters and the presence of many transient, part-time teachers. The best teachers soon left the classroom for higher-paying careers in medicine, business, public service, and the ministry. Many teachers "doubled up," simultaneously serving as ministerial assistants, practicing

---

[27] Preston, 2003, p. 371.
[28] Sklar, 1993.
[29] Ciphering = adding and subtracting.
[30] Cubberley, 1947, p. 52.
[31] Cremin, 1970, p. 558.
[32] Cremin, 1970, pp. 187–188.
[33] Preston, 2003.

law and medicine, acting as justices of the peace and captains of the militia, and working as brewers, tailors, innkeepers, and gravediggers.[34]

As a result, pupils were taught by anyone and everyone, including parents, tutors, clergymen, lay readers, physicians, lawyers, artisans, and shopkeepers. In large towns such as Boston, New York, and Philadelphia, "virtually anyone who could command a clientele could conduct classes."[35] The content and sequence of learning remained fairly well defined, and each student progressed from textbook to textbook at his or her own pace.[36]

School buildings. Formal schools started wherever space could be found: a meeting room, a barn, or a spare room in a large home. Without models for schools to copy, townsfolk built utilitarian and practical shelters—one room, with benches and a stove. Multiple grades of students attended the same school, where they were taught by a single teacher.[37]

More often than not, these schools were built cheaply and quickly, and deteriorated almost as quickly. In 1681, one Roxbury, Massachusetts, citizen complained that the local schoolhouse was "not fitting for to reside in; the glass broken and thereupon very raw and cold; the floor very much broken and torn up to kindle fires; the hearth spoiled; the seats, some burnt and others out of kilter, so that one had as well nigh as good keep school in a hog-sty as in it."[38]

In most cases, school furnishings were threadbare, consisting of a rough floor and planks on barrels or stakes for desks, and benches running around the walls for seats. Paper greased with lard often substituted for windows.[39] In the winters, many schools went unheated. Those that were heated often relied on poorly vented fireplaces or stoves, sometimes making breathing difficult. Heating the school building used much wood, which sometimes led to a wood tax levy on families with children attending school.[40]

If the town did not build schoolhouses, summer school might be held in barns, watch houses, or meeting houses. In winter, however, classes needed warmth as well as space, so schoolmasters rented a room with a fireplace—sometimes a kitchen.[41]

Teaching resources. Teachers had an almost complete lack of teaching supplies, books, and effective teaching methods. Desks would not appear for many years, and blackboards did not appear until 1820s. Pencils and steel pens were not available until later still. Paper was expensive and of poor quality, so pupils used it as little as possible. Sometimes students wrote their letters and numbers on birch bark or traced letters in sand. One of the schoolmaster's job requirements was the ability to make and repair goose quill pens. Meanwhile, the ink was homemade and often poor quality.[42]

Instructional methods. Instructional methods in the colonial era were relatively unsophisticated. The vast majority of schools were ungraded, and most instruction was individual, with pupils approaching the master's desk or lectern and reciting orally or displaying their work for praise or correction.[43] Other students practiced their drills and waited their turns. Memorizing was the norm. The teaching and

[34] Cremin, 1970, pp. 188–189; Preston, 2003.
[35] Cremin, 1970, p. 558.
[36] Cremin, 1970, p. 558.
[37] One room schoolhouses. (2003). *John's History of Education.* Retrieved May 24, 2007, from: http://historyeducationinfo.com/edu6.htm.
[38] Small, W.H. (1969). *Early New England schools.* New York: Arno Press & *New York Times,* p. 258.1969, p. 258.
[39] Cubberley, 1947, p. 56.
[40] Small, 1969.
[41] Small, 1969.
[42] Cubberley, 1947, p. 56.
[43] Cremin, 1970, p. 505.

learning process was so inefficient and ineffective that students could attend school for years and gain only the most minimal reading and writing skills.[44]

Teachers' time was spent on listening to individual students' recitations, assigning students new tasks to learn, preparing copies, making quill pens, dictating math addition problems, and keeping order.[45]

Classroom management. Townsfolk considered teachers to be failures if they could not keep their students under tight control. As a consequence, school discipline was severe. Even college men occasionally received whippings. Whipping, standing in the corner, wearing a dunce cap, and other humiliating behaviors were commonplace.[46] Some schoolrooms even had their own whipping posts in the classroom—or the post stood in the school yard or street.[47]

Because the New England Puritans believed that children were born sinful, Puritan teachers believed that students were better off whipped than eternally damned. Oftentimes, the punishments were administered in a highly arbitrary fashion. One story tells of a boy who made mistakes on his recitation, so his teacher flogged another boy "for not exercising a better influence over the delinquent."[48] One schoolmaster gathered several offending students. He had one student get on all fours, another mount the first student's back, and the third whip the other two around the room. They then changed positions until each boy had his turn at whipping once and being whipped, twice.[49]

Milder punishments included forcing students to sit on air or "standing in the corner, face to the wall; stooping down to hold a nail or peg in the floor, the culprit often getting a stinging slap on his rear to keep him from bending his knees. Another punishment included being forced to sit among the girls, which in time came to be called *capital* punishment."[50] In colonial schools, students frequently received blistered hands, swollen ears, and throbbing limbs along with their ABCs.

Dame (Primary) Schools

Town schools made no provisions for beginning learners. Students were supposed to learn how to read at home before they entered the town school at age 8.[51]

Providing something between day care and primary reading instruction, dame schools began to prepare certain students for the town school. These schools were fee-based lower elementary or primary schools typically held in a widowed or otherwise unmarried townswoman's home. If young children could "stand up and keep their places," they could attend.[52] For a few pennies a week from parents or the town treasury, the dame took neighbors' children into her home and helped them learn the beginnings of reading and spelling, basic writing, and counting. More often, dames taught what they knew best—and students learned rudimentary sewing and knitting. In time, schoolmasters' daughters were trained to keep a dame school to prepare boys for the town's grammar school.[53]

Unlike today's kindergartens and early primary grades, the dame schools were not pleasant, colorful, child-friendly places. The alphabet and the Bible formed the heart of the curriculum, and the atmosphere was stern and dogmatic.[54]

---

[44] Cubberley, 1947, p. 57.
[45] Cubberley, 1947, pp. 57–58.
[46] Small, 1969, p. 386.
[47] Cubberley, 1947, p. 57.
[48] Small, 1969.
[49] Small, 1969, pp. 389–390.
[50] Small, 1969, p. 391.
[51] Cubberley, 1920, p. 664.
[52] Cubberley, 1947, p. 29.
[53] Cubberley, 1947, p. 27.
[54] Rippa, S. A. (1984). Education in a free society: An American history. New York: McKay.

Figure 4.2 | Color Engraving of a New England Dame School, 1713

Learning the ABCs and basic reading and writing soon became a prerequisite for admission to the town grammar school. Eventually compulsory attendance legislation provided regular public funding for the dame school, and it evolved into the town primary school.

By 1750, most New England towns had elementary or common schools available to children, with primary schools available after 1820 to bring education down to beginning learners. For most children, however, formal education ended at age 7. Girls left school to attend to their household duties. They were generally excluded from Latin grammar schools and higher education. Similarly, after attendance at a dame school, most boys went on to apprenticeships or farm work. For both girls and boys, the household and workplace continued to be the strongest sources of education.

Latin Grammar Schools

While the more fortunate poor and middle-class students completed their education in the town schools, upper-class sons ages 7 or 8 went to Latin grammar schools, which prepared them to begin college at age 15. America's seventeenth- and eighteenth-century Latin grammar schools were often modest, one-room structures. The "Latin School" at Boston was established in 1635 (and still exists today as the nation's oldest school), with others soon following in Massachusetts towns.

Latin grammar school teachers. The towns' best teachers worked in Latin grammar schools, and their pupils called them "Master." These instructors were frequently well-educated men who held college degrees and enjoyed a higher social position than did the elementary teachers. They were strictly religious and capable instructors.[55] Because they served wealthy men's children, their salaries were

---

[55] Cubberley, 1947, p. 51.

relatively higher and more consistently paid than the salaries of their town school colleagues.[56]

Curriculum. Because Latin was considered the sacred language of religion and advanced learning, students studied works by Ancient Roman writers Cicero, Caesar, Virgil, and Horace. More advanced students studied works by Greek authors such as Socrates and Homer. Any given grammar school could include an additional offering that ranged from introductory reading and writing in English to arithmetic, geometry, trigonometry, navigation, surveying, bookkeeping, geography, rhetoric, logic, algebra, and astronomy.[57] Vocational subjects and instruction in fine arts were not available.

After Latin grammar school, upper-class boys often applied for admission to Harvard or Yale College to prepare for the ministry. Middle-class boys and girls did not expect to attend college. Students had to demonstrate competency in Latin and Greek to be admitted to Harvard, where they received an education in grammar, logic, rhetoric, arithmetic, geometry, astronomy, ethics, metaphysics, and natural science, in addition to Hebrew, Greek, and ancient history (useful for Bible study).

The middle and Southern colonies did not share New England's fondness for classical studies, but a few Latin grammar schools were founded in several large towns in those regions. These schools leaned toward more commercial and practical courses and introduced merchants' accounts, navigation, surveying, and higher math as subjects of study. In time, these schools evolved to become English grammar schools.[58] By the mid-eighteenth century, classical Latin grammar schools had declined in popularity, even in Massachusetts.[59]

The Academy

The **academy**, an institution providing "higher schooling," was the most flexible, fluid, and loosely defined of provincial schools. Academies were a good educational "fit" with commercial and early industrial economies, which demanded a modest number of people to fill those professions, later called "white-collar" positions, that required higher schooling. The academy was incorporated to ensure financial support beyond that available through tuition alone.[60] The families of small businessmen, merchants, professionals, and large landowners—that is, the "middling classes"—generated enough youths to provide the base population for an academy. In addition, by accommodating part-time and older students, academies fit the varied life cycles pursued by people of the time and maximized their attendance.[61]

Most academies catered to common school students. At their highest level, academies overlapped with colleges.[62] For the most part, early academies offered as their curriculum what the master was prepared to teach, what the students were prepared to learn, what the academy's sponsors were prepared to pay for, or some combination of the three.[63]

Governance. While open to the public, academies were not free; they were reasonably affordable, however.[64] Many academies were church-sponsored institutions. Other academies were supported by gifts or estates left by wealthy civic-minded

---

[56] Cubberley, 1947, p. 52.
[57] Cremin, 1970, p. 503.
[58] Cubberley, 1947, p. 31.
[59] Reese, W. J. (1995). *The origins of the American high school.* New Haven, CT: Yale University Press.
[60] Tolley, K. (2001, Summer). The rise of the academies: Continuity or change? *History of Education Quarterly, 41*(2), 225–239.
[61] Leslie, 2001; Beadie, Nancy. (2001, Summer). Academy students in the mid-nineteenth century: Social geography, demography, and the culture of academy attendance. *History of Education Quarterly, 41*(2), 251–262.
[62] Leslie, 2001.
[63] Cremin, 1970, p. 505.
[64] Leslie, 2001.

individuals in their wills for the purpose of educating children. Many others were organized by private subscriptions or as private stock companies. They usually retained private management.

In time, towns, counties, or states began to charter and help maintain the academies, and they evolved into semi-public institutions. Many mingled private and public funds to support their activities.[65] Almost all charged students a tuition or fee, and most had dormitories and boarding halls. A few even provided some form of manual labor—an early work–study program to defer school expenses.[66] Additionally, with the creation of boards of trustees to oversee the development of curriculum and assessment, academies became more accountable to the community for the quality of their students' learning.[67]

Curriculum and instruction. Academies maintained a degree of curricular choice and flexibility distinct from both the earlier Latin grammar schools and the later public high schools.[68] Unlike the Latin grammar schools, academies were not devoted solely to college preparation; they also sought to prepare students for business life and the rising professions. Teachers taught classes in English. While students might still have learned Latin and Greek, the curriculum now included English grammar, English literature, oratory, arithmetic, algebra, geometry, geography, botany, chemistry, general history, American history, surveying, rhetoric, and natural and moral philosophy.[69] Courses in navigation, needlework, vocal music, or dance might have been available as well. The curriculum was both traditional and, for its day, contemporary.

Rote memorization and student recitation remained the common practice in schools at all levels through much of the nineteenth century. The system of emulation—a form of competition in which prizes were generally awarded in public—was another popular instructional method. Teachers encouraged students to imitate and surpass their best peers.[70]

Women's education. Whereas the Latin grammar schools had been created exclusively for boys, the academies rather freely admitted girls.[71] Supply and demand played a role in bringing young women into this "advanced education." In 1800, the United States had only 25 colleges but hundreds of academies. The increased number of academies meant there was more competition for students, which in turn required academies to appeal to a broader constituency.[72] Thus academy education was the only form of higher schooling available to women in the early republic.

The academies soon became teacher-training schools, the chief supply source for the best-educated elementary teachers. Although they rarely offered instruction in how to teach, their advanced instruction in subjects related to the common schools' curriculum made their future common school teachers more knowledgeable about the subjects they would be teaching.[73] Normal schools would eventually replace academies as sources of teacher preparation. Likewise, the public high school became the main provider of what became known as "secondary" education. Eventually, academies were converted into high schools, became "prep" schools, or ceased to exist.[74]

---

[65] Leslie, 2001.
[66] Cubberley, 1947, p. 112.
[67] Tolley, 2001.
[68] Tolley, 2001.
[69] Cubberley, 1947, p. 113.
[70] Nash, M. A. (2001, Summer). Cultivating the powers of human beings: Gendered perspectives on curriculum and pedagogy in academies of the new republic. *History of Education Quarterly, 41*(2), 239–250.
[71] Because the grammar schools intended to prepare young men for the ministry, a wholly male occupation at that time, girls could not attend.
[72] Nash, 2001.
[73] Cubberley, 1947, p. 113.
[74] Leslie, 2001.

Facilities. Academies' special contribution to the U.S. educational system included its the facilities and resources for educating students. A larger school building replaced the resource-poor, one-room schoolhouse that had long served as the town school and Latin grammar school. Academies included a public hall for meetings and rhetorical exercises, and they provided maps, charts, globes, and libraries for students' use. The extra funds available to this kind of semi-public institution brought teachers and students a wider range of educational assets to improve their quality of learning.

Academies took students who had completed the common schools' English education and gave them an advanced education in modern languages, the sciences, mathematics, history, and the more useful subjects of the time. In this way, they built upon the common school courses but marked a transition from the aristocratic and largely exclusive college-preparatory colonial Latin grammar schools to the more democratic public high schools we have today.

Activity 4.2

A. Separate the class into three groups of early colonial New England children: those from poor families, those from middle-class families, and those from well-to-do families. Each group of "children" will prepare and give three-minute reports on the following topics:

Their educational experiences (which schools or training they received)

What they were taught and what they learned.

Their teachers and school facilities.

Their present life and/or career options

Their parents' reasoning for making these educational decisions for them

B. After the presentations, as a class discuss how children's social strata dramatically affected their educational, work, and life options in the early colonies.

C. As individuals, explain how this system would have personally affected you had you been living at that time.

Early Education in the Middle Colonies

In the heterogeneous middle colony communities, people believed that education, as a responsibility, belonged to the family, church, charitable organizations, or private efforts. Reflecting the many different religious sects represented by these immigrants, this region's early colonists did not want the state controlling education. They feared having one religion force its views on all students through a state-sponsored curriculum or teachers dedicated to a particular faith. Instead, the state's only responsibility was to maintain pauper schools for the students living in or near poverty. Colonies adhering to this view included Pennsylvania, New Jersey, New York, Delaware, and Maryland.

In the middle colonies, settlers supported church (parochial) schools. Each family paid tuition to send its children to the school run by its own religious denomination. Students often received lessons in the dominant community group's native language. Church schools also emphasized the sponsoring church's religious beliefs along with reading, writing, and math.[75]

Other students attended private or charity schools. A few of the larger towns opened private, tuition-based schools to educate children from more affluent families. Poor children, if their families allowed, could attend church or philanthropic charity-run schools (if available), where they received a minimal education. Many of the charity-run schools were geared toward sons and daughters of "middling income" who could not afford tuition but whose families were not in need of financial support.[76] These charity schools' curriculum were similar to dame schools, and they focused on teaching the ABCs, basic reading, and counting. Orphans and children in very poor families, however, typically received their education through apprenticeships.[77]

Teachers in the middle colonies' parochial schools were usually clergymen until a regular schoolmaster could be found and hired. The local churches employed schoolmasters if they were solid believers in their denomination's faith, had a respectable education of their own, and were willing to work hard. For a small extra fee, many parochial school teachers were part-time choir masters, church chorus members, bellringers, sextons, and janitors.[78]

Different middle colonies developed some unique educational features. In New York City, which served as a commercial port, several private, for-profit schools charged students fees to study navigation, surveying, bookkeeping, Spanish, French, and geography. In the seventeenth century, these private entrepreneurial schools came to shoulder an increasing share of New York City's formal education burden. During the eighteenth century, they expanded to educate more pupils.[79] These private schools were popular because teachers taught in English rather than in Latin or Hebrew as practiced in the church-run schools of the time, and because artisans, tradesmen, and shopkeepers taught the practical curriculum.[80]

Pennsylvania's Quaker settlers took a special interest in their local schools. Quaker schools, active since 1683, displayed a strong social justice bent, educated girls and boys, whites, African Americans, and Native Americans, emphasizing reading, writing, arithmetic, and religion as subjects of study. Quakers also sponsored a network of charity-run schools throughout the colonies to educate African American and Native American children. Reflecting the Quakers' practical-minded view, their curriculum included vocational training, crafts, and agriculture. Pacifists and conscientious objectors by religious principle, Quaker teachers did not use corporal punishment to control their students.

Centrally located between different colonies, New Jersey developed an educational system that reflected the many influences coming into the colony from varied directions. Each settler group brought its own education traditions. After the English colonized New York in 1664, however, English methods and practices came to control most of New Jersey. As a consequence, education in New Jersey became limited to families with money or was provided haphazardly through charitable schools for poor children.

Thus the middle colonies depended on a mixture of church-run and private schools for their educational opportunities. Without state involvement, education was very rudimentary, of limited availability, and often nonexistent. Each parochial (church) school did what it wished. Poor and orphaned children, if lucky, attended

---

[75] Hayes, W. (2006). *Horace Mann's vision of the public schools: Is it still relevant?* Rowman and Littlefield Education, Chapter 1. Retrieved March 17, 2006, from www.publiceducation.ord/newsblast/pdf/Chapter_One.pdf.
[76] Sundue, S. B. (2007, April). Confining the poor to ignorance? Eighteenth century experiments with charity education. *History of Education Quarterly, 47*(2), 123–148.
[77] Cubberley, 1947, p. 21.
[78] Cubberley, 1947, p. 53. This extra fee was often difficult to collect.
[79] Cremin, 1970, p. 537.
[80] Cremin, 1970, p. 537.

charity schools or entered apprenticeships. Meanwhile, children from wealthy families still had private tutors or attended private, tuition schools.

Early Education in Virginia and Southern Colonies

Colonized by wealthy, successful European immigrants, Virginia and other Southern colony settlers came to America with—or seeking—their fortunes. While religion was important to them, it was not the central guiding force in their lives.

Climate, crops, and social class influenced Virginians to develop large plantation-style settlements rather than the compact towns found in New England. The introduction of indentured servants and African slaves—along with well-to-do planters, landholders, and independently wealthy gentlemen—led to a highly stratified class-based society instead of New England's popular democracy. Given these social realities, early Virginians had no motivation, from a public policy standpoint, to provide free and common public schools. What is more, these settlers believed that education was the family's—not the state's—business.[81]

Virginians held traditionally English views about education. High-quality schooling was reserved for the elite. Wealthy students received private tutoring at home, attended small private or church-sponsored select schools, or received their education abroad. Young men learned basic academic skills, social graces and good manners, and management skills related to plantations and slaves. Daughters of wealthy families learned how to be successful hostesses. Children of self-taught, literate poor white farmers often learned from their parents. Students from meager backgrounds learned through apprenticeships, in charity-provided pauper schools, or in church-run schools. At best, impoverished children received a minimal education, lasting only a few years.[82]

With parents under no legal requirement to educate them, most children of penniless Southerners ended up as field laborers without any training in reading, writing, or arithmetic. In 1642, the Virginia legislature passed a law providing compulsory apprenticeship education to children of indentured servants, orphans, and poor children, usually little more than simple vocational training.

Meanwhile, girls' education in Virginia and the South was generally more restricted than it was in the North. Virginians' expectations for women's education were modest. Girls were expected to learn the domestic skills such as cooking and sewing. As far as schooling, girls could learn the basics of reading, writing, and arithmetic. If their parents permitted, girls were able to attend charity schools, private schools, and—for the wealthiest—tutoring, boarding, or finishing schools. Most young women received informal instruction at home to do those things that would make them better wives, mothers, and housekeepers.[83]

Early Education in Other States

Given their economies, religions, and views about government control, settlers in Rhode Island, North Carolina, Tennessee, Kentucky, Alabama, and Mississippi resisted the idea of the local or state government having a role in educating children. Among the New England states, only Rhode Island did not adopt the Massachusetts education laws. Desiring religious freedom, Rhode Island residents did not

---

[81] Cubberley, 1947, p. 22.
[82] Parts of New York, New Jersey, Delaware, Maryland, North Carolina, South Carolina, and Georgia also followed Virginia's example. In these colonies, however, some settlements offered a "free" school supported by assessments—fees paid by families who sent their children to the school.
[83] Cohen, S. S. (1974). *A history of colonial education, 1607–1776.* New York: Wiley.

want one religious group dominating thought in schools. Instead, their first public schools did not emerge until the early nineteenth century.[84]

Initially, these states were indifferent to providing a common education for their populace. As in other states, parents with money bought their children an education. If parents did not have the means, if parents did not want their children formally educated, or if no schools were available locally, however, children went without.

Farther west, Indiana and Illinois settlers held conflicting views about education, depending on their backgrounds before emigrating. Those coming from New England wanted a strong state hand in establishing and regulating schools. Those coming from the South believed the state had no legitimate role in educating children—and even if it did, mixing students from various social classes was unthinkable. In the end, settlers reached a stalemate, substantially limiting education's development in each state.

Although not all of the early states have been mentioned in these discussions, the economy, religion, and local views about government involvement in education contributed to the settlers' varying beliefs and practices regarding public schools.

Early Education of African Americans and Native Americans

Both schooling for democratic citizenship and schooling for second-class citizenship have been basic traditions in American education. . . . Both were fundamental American conceptions of society and progress, occupied the same time and space, were fostered by the same governments, and usually were embraced by the same leaders.[85]

Attempts to provide formal schooling for Native Americans or African immigrants and their descendants throughout the early 1700s were limited in scope and local in influence. Some missionary societies continually taught small numbers of free and unfree African Americans and Native Americans, eventually baptizing many of them. The pupils' day-to-day realities, however, often undermined their formal education.

Educating African American Slaves

The successful campaign to contain and repress literacy among enslaved Americans grew just as efforts to provide popular education for free people began to flourish. Between 1800 and 1835, most of the Southern states enacted laws making it a crime to teach enslaved children to read or write.[86] Wanting to create and maintain a submissive and obedient labor force, slave owners understood that education could undo their economic system by liberating African American slaves' thoughts. Learning to read, write, add, and subtract would give slaves "dangerous" notions about their own abilities and destinies. In addition, many Southern slaveholders believed that Africans were racially inferior to whites and did not have the intellect to learn. Some free Southern African Americans might attend Quaker schools and missionary schools set up by abolitionists. In spite of the dangers and difficulties, thousands of slaves somehow managed to learn to read and write. By 1860, approximately 5 percent of slaves were literate.[87]

Some education occurred as slave owners and their families taught African American children the lessons related to their status and work. Some lessons taught

[84] Cubberley, 1947, pp. 102–105.
[85] Anderson, J. D. (1988). *The education of blacks in the South, 1860–1935.* Chapel Hill, NC: University of North Carolina Press, p. 1.
[86] Anderson, 1988, p. 2.
[87] Anderson, 1988, p. 16.

the skills and manners required to properly complete their tasks, whether as field hands or as skilled and semi-skilled craftsmen, house servants, coachmen, midwives, preachers, healers, and parent-surrogates. All lessons were expected to nurture slaves' submissive and obedient attitudes toward the master in particular and toward white people in general.[88] For the most part, "it was the whip and the Bible that served as the two most important pedagogical instruments in instructing . . . [African Americans] in the White version of their place in the world."[89]

Although missionaries hoped that immigrant Africans and Native Americans would welcome conversion to Christianity, masters of African slaves objected. Owners feared that conversion would imply setting slaves free or at least impose certain obligations on owners such as charity, humanity, and potential future sale. Missionary societies did their best to convince slaveholders that baptism did not imply earthly freedom.[90] On some plantations, slaves were allowed to attend church services to learn their duties and obligations in Christianity that supported white oppression. At the same time, African Americans learned covert lessons necessary to their survival as a people and as human beings rather than as property through teachings by their slave community, their families, and their clandestine religious congregations.[91]

The pedagogy of the African American family helped their children learn gardening, hunting, fishing, quilting, sewing, cooking, and loyalty to kin that endured in spite of physical separation. Parents also taught their children lessons about personal dignity and pride, family and community solidarity, resistance to white oppression, and aspirations to freedom and salvation. Music and stories transmitted the African American culture from one generation to the next, perpetuating itself, expressing and inspiring an essential educational message. The pedagogy of their secret congregations located in the woods or swamps adjacent to their living areas provided adult slaves with emotional release, a sense of camaraderie and community support, and expression of the belief that they would transcend their daily miseries. The family and the church were also the chief institutions that free

| Figure 4.3 | In Spite of the Dangers and Difficulties, Thousands of African Americans Learned How to Read and Write |

Budding Scholar, Roseland, Henry Herman (1866–1950) / Private Collection / Photo © Christie's Images / The Bridgeman Art Library

[88] Cremin, 1980, pp. 221–222.
[89] Cremin, 1980, pp. 221–222.
[90] Cremin, 1970, pp. 348–349.
[91] Cremin, 1980, pp. 222–224.

African Americans relied on for their own education, with churches often establishing and maintaining schools for these individuals.[92]

Educating Native Americans

In New England, the Puritans remained ambivalent about the Native Americans' capacity to be educated or converted to Christianity. In the early years, the colony vigorously promoted Native American schooling. Evidence exists that as early as 1650, Native American children attended Massachusetts common schools alongside white classmates. Harvard's charter even mentions educating "English and Indian youth of this country."[93] Nevertheless, efforts to provide Native American youth with formal schooling had few permanent results because pupils' tribal folkways overwhelmed any white teachings.[94] The immense gap between what missionaries said about the brotherhood of man and how whites actually treated Native Americans and African immigrants made any religious teachings questionable to skeptical students. No other region did as well as New England in trying to educate the original inhabitants of America, although missionaries tried to provide schooling for Native Americans in all the colonies.

The Native American educational experience was no more successful in the South, although native children had an early history of education there. In 1622, Virginia settlers established a school, called Henrico, to educate native children in reading and knowledge of Christian principles.[95] The purpose was wholly evangelistic: to save these innocents' souls. This endeavor had limited success. Hostile relations frequently arose between the Native American population and the English settlers who wanted the young students to reject their tribal traditions in favor of the Western belief system. In addition, Native American children were highly susceptible to European diseases; as a consequence, many who attended the settlers' schools got sick and died.[96]

The large variety of Native American tribes and forms of social organization make generalizing about their education difficult, but for the most part, the family carried important teaching responsibilities in these groups. A clear division of labor occurred between the sexes. Women assumed responsibility for planting, cultivating, harvesting, preparing foods, and making clothes. Men engaged in hunting or fishing and making war. Training the young occurred continuously through showing, explaining, and imitating, with young men undergoing instruction in age cohorts. Most tribes relied on praise, reward, and prophesy rather than physical punishment to stimulate knowledge and skill mastery. Competition was an additional incentive. Likewise, tribes imposed meaning on the world through songs, stories, dances, and ceremonies. This family and community pedagogy was very powerful. Compared to it, any curriculum taught to Native American children by white "outsiders" in "school" appeared weak, disruptive, or meaningless.[97]

While many Native Americans and African Americans became Christian, only some of them became literate. A few were permitted to pursue decent careers as free tradesmen. A handful even influenced the thinking of their time, such as the Native American clergyman Samson Occom and the African American scientist Benjamin Banneker. Nevertheless, tribal values continued to dominate Native American thought and action, whereas most African Americans were constrained by the slave system and the attitudes toward race that supported it.[98]

---

[92] Cremin, 1980, pp. 224–229.
[93] Cremin, 1970, p. 194.
[94] Cremin, 1970, p. 350.
[95] Hlebewitsh, P. S. (2001). *Foundations of American education: Purpose and promise.* Belmond, CA: Wadsworth/Thomson Learning, pp.189–190.
[96] Hlebewitsh, 2001.
[97] Cremin, 1980, pp. 239–241.
[98] Cremin, 1970, pp. 353–354.

The early colonies took different approaches toward educating their young people. Much depended on how similar the settlers were—in terms of religion, ethnicity, and economic focus—to their town neighbors.

Given the realities of early colonial schooling, suppose you were growing up as a person of your same racial or ethnic background, socioeconomic class, and gender. Answer the following questions:

1. In which colony would you *most* preferred to have grown up? Which type of schooling opportunities would have been available to you? How would your educational opportunities made a difference in your adult lifestyle?

2. In which colony would you *least* preferred to have grown up? Which type of schooling opportunities would have been available to you? How would your educational opportunities made a difference in your adult lifestyle?

Public Schooling During the Early National Period

Schooling had been firmly transplanted to America during the initial decades of this country's settlement, especially in New England, by a population that highly valued education. As the colonies grew economically, the demand for schooling kept pace. People widely perceived and used schooling as a vehicle for personal advancement, such as moving artisans' children into the professions.[99] Schools also increased in number as competing Protestant sects used schools for missionary purposes. Finally, a growing interest in public affairs during the last half of the eighteenth century increased the incentive for schooling. One needed to know how to read to keep up with the almanacs, newspapers, pamphlets, and books dealing with current events, especially after the Stamp Act crisis of the 1760s.[100]

By the middle of the eighteenth century, secular schooling gained popularity. In New England, secular schools replaced earlier religious schools. In the middle colonies, many of the parochial schools had closed. In the Southern colonies, the highly stratified class-based society, the large distances between communities, and the ongoing presence of African American slavery still made common schools socially and politically unrealistic.

The Secular Mandate

Colonial leaders, proud of what they had accomplished in their new homeland, worked to gain their political and economic independence from England. The American Revolution, which took place from 1776 to 1781, ultimately ended British rule in the 13 colonies.

The new republic's leaders agreed that a self-governing people needed universal education that would motivate all men to choose public over private interest.[101] Although the U.S. Constitution does not mention education, the nation's leaders agreed that public education was essential to maintaining a republican form

---

[99] Cremin, 1970, p. 545.
[100] Cremin, 1970, pp. 545–546.
[101] *Education* meant the full array of institutions that helped shape human character, including families, churches, schools, colleges, newspapers, voluntary associations, and laws.

of government. This meant consciously fashioning schooling based on American art, history, and law, independent thinking, and commitment to the promise of an American culture.[102] Education's task was to erect and maintain the new American nation.[103]

The first U.S. President, George Washington, believed in widespread public education. A free people would inevitably have opinions about their government, and Washington preferred that these views be enlightened.[104] John Adams, the second U.S. President, observed that to act as a free person and participate in self-government, "I must judge for myself, but how can I judge, how can any man judge, unless his mind has been opened and enlarged by reading."[105] Continental Congress leaders and future presidents Thomas Jefferson and James Madison; Continental Congress President and future first U.S. Chief Justice John Jay; and revolutionary pamphleteer Thomas Paine all advocated for education as a necessary source of general knowledge for citizens in a democracy. By the 1820s, the need of a self-governing people for universal education had become a familiar part of American politics.[106]

Although united in purpose, the proponents of universal education disagreed about how to accomplish these ends. Washington was vague about what form the education to enlighten public opinion should take, but there is some evidence that he desired a national university located in the capital city. Jefferson was more specific, and in 1779 proposed a plan for public education in Virginia that mandated free public schooling for all free white children, at public expense, for three years. At that point, the best and brightest would be chosen for secondary education and later for attendance at the College of William and Mary, again at state expense. The Virginia legislature disagreed and did not ratify this plan.[107] Adams disagreed with Jefferson and Madison about the role of the church in universal education.

Consensus about the solution to this dilemma would not arrive until the early nineteenth century. Education for self-government would have three central parts: popular schooling for literacy along with a certain common core of knowledge, morality, and patriotism; a free press to express multiple views on important public issues to inform public opinion; and a variety of voluntary associations to serve the public good. Schooled for literacy and armed with newspapers containing up-to-date information, a free American citizenry would learn how to become self-governing by doing and experiencing it.[108]

Separating church and state. Separating church and state was on the framers' minds when they developed the U.S. Constitution. The new United States was a land of increasing religious and cultural diversity. The Constitution's authors supported the free exercise of religious faith for all by banning any state-sponsored religion. In this new nation, church and state could no longer be partners in public education. In turn, the public school began its transformation from an institution dominated by religious purpose and content into one charged with enlightening a diverse citizenry for civic participation. Its rationale became wholly civic, not religious. This essential idea laid the foundation for our system of free, common, public, tax-supported, nonsectarian schools that persists to this day.

---

[102] Cremin, L. A. (1980). *American education: The national experience, 1783–1876*. New York: Harper & Row, pp. 2–3.
[103] Cremin, 1980, p. 5.
[104] Cubberley, 1947, p. 89.
[105] McCullough. D. (2001).*John Adams*. New York, NY: Simon and Schuster, p. 223.
[106] Cremin, 1980, p. 103.
[107] Callahan, R. E. (1963). *An introduction to education in American society*. New York: Rinehart & Winston.
[108] Cremin, 1980, pp. 104–106.

Social, Political, and Economic Changes

After the Revolutionary War ended and the U.S. national government was formed, significant social, political, and economic movements continued to alter the fledgling nation's character and direction. Three of the most important influences were the rise of cities and manufacturing, extension of voting rights, and the growth of a new social class's demands for schools. All of these forces would change the U.S. system of public education.

Growth of city populations and manufacturing. When the U.S. national government was originally formed, almost every American lived on a farm or in a small village. As late as 1820, the country had only 13 cities of 8,000 people or more in 23 states, containing only 4.9 percent of the total national population.[109]

After 1825, an increasing number of little villages evolved into the cities of the future. Some developed near waterfalls where cheap power made large-scale manufacturing possible. For instance, Lowell, Massachusetts, did not exist in 1820. Yet by 1840, more than 20,000 people lived there, largely to work in the mills powered by the Merrimack River. Cincinnati and Detroit grew because their locations made them good trade and commerce centers. Driven by the improving economy after the 1812 War with Great Britain, U.S. cities increased rapidly in both size and number.[110]

The emergence of new cities and the rapid growth of older ones appreciably altered education by producing an entirely new set of economic, social, and educational conditions. Cities along the Atlantic Coast—especially in Pennsylvania, New York, and New England—rapidly developed a manufacturing economy. Factory work meant the beginning of the end of the home-and-village industries. Eventually the informal apprenticeship system foundered. Rural populations moved toward the cities and employment in large factories. More people lived and worked in close proximity with others different from themselves.[111]

The factory system altered village and home life as well as education. Living in large, crowded cities of diverse people brought to the fore many social and moral problems that were not evident when people lived in a small, familiar community. The villages' church, private, and charity school systems broke down under the strain of trying to educate many more children than they had the resources to do successfully. As a result, people started demanding that state funds or grants partially support both church and philanthropic society schools. Likewise, several charity organizations arose in various cities to help address poverty, juvenile delinquency, and other urban problems.[112]

These economic and societal changes did not affect everyone. The South's economy and society—which continued to be based on plantation life, African American slavery, indentured servants, and lack of manufacturing—remained largely unaffected by the changing economic and social conditions until well after the Civil War. Similarly, its educational practices changed very little over this period.[113]

Likewise, Native Americans were considered alien members of their respective tribes, with which the United States negotiated treaties. Nonetheless, they received few of the traditional benefits given aliens.[114]

Extending voting rights. Women, men who were not citizens or were not wealthy enough to own property, and non-whites could not vote in the nation's early days. Change in voting rights came slowly. Western states, which were formed by people who lacked "old money" or large estates, judged persons more on their earned merits than on their inherited family backgrounds, and they championed the voting rights movement. By 1828, all white men could vote, giving rich and poor,

---

[109] Cubberley, E. P. (1922). *A brief history of education.* Boston: Houghton Mifflin, p. 363.
[110] Cubberley, 1922.
[111] Cubberley, 1947, p. 148.
[112] Cubberley, 1947, p. 149.
[113] Cremin, 1980, pp. 6–7.
[114] Cremin, 1980.

Westerners and members of the Eastern manufacturing classes, employers and laborers greater influence in their government and their own affairs.

During the nation's early years, women could only vote in states where the constitutions did not specifically deny them this right.[115]

Poor and working-class demands for schools. Gaining the right to vote made white men of all social classes recognize that general education for knowledge and civic virtue was a basic necessity for their own and society's well-being. Governors began to recommend that their legislatures establish tax-supported schools. The new labor unions formed after 1825 joined in the demands for schools and education, as their members saw the free education of their own children as their natural right.

The nineteenth century's second quarter witnessed the movement for tax-supported, publicly controlled and directed, non-sectarian common schools. Bitter arguments, legislative fights, religious jealousies, and private interests characterized the process of establishing free public schools. By 1850, however, tax-supported, non-sectarian, public schools had become a reality in almost every Northern state. In North Carolina, free taxpayer-supported schools were established, marking the first implementation of this trend in the South.

Two developments—the newly invented steam printing press and the first cheap modern newspapers—also appeared at this time. These widely read publications strongly influenced popular opinion to support free common public schools. In time, the desirability of common, free, tax-supported, non-sectarian, state-controlled schools—open to all students—became clear to most American citizens as a means to perpetuate a free democracy and to advance public well-being.[116]

Developing a national educational consciousness. The post–Revolutionary War period signaled a turning point in American education. The schools' tradition of promoting religious doctrine could no longer hold, although it took time for this practice to fade.[117] Now, people would have to share a common loyalty and political allegiance with others whom they did not know, who did not live in their towns or states, and who saw and acted upon the world in different ways than they did. Secular purposes would direct schools. A new generation of young people had to be socialized to adopt the attitudes and behaviors needed to responsibly participate in the young constitutional democracy.

Before 1820, outside New England and New York, people had not developed an educational consciousness for a variety of reasons.[118] First, no economic demand for education existed. The era's simple agricultural life—the colonies' largest occupation—did not require formal schooling. A person who could read, write, and cipher was considered educated, and those who could not lost no respect.[119]

Second, after the Revolutionary War, the United States was very poor. The country had few industries and weak foreign trade. Political leaders focused on immediate problems: strengthening the existing government and finding necessary resources to make essential infrastructure improvements. These critical responsibilities demanded their attention at the expense of providing universal education.

Until this time, travel and communication were difficult, and people did not often interact with others holding differing views and values. They did not need formal schools to acculturate them to their shared society. Similarly, the early colonies had few cities that would bring diverse people together and socialization. Instead,

---

[115] Cremin, 1980, pp. 8–9.
[116] Cubberley, 1947, p. 167.
[117] That is not to say it was eliminated. Many of your parents and grandparents can remember prayer and Bible reading in schools as well as references to religious holidays (rather than winter and spring breaks).
[118] Cubberley, 1947, pp. 110–111.
[119] Cubberley, 1947, p. 111.

the colonial villages' isolation and independence allowed them to remain indifferent to providing a common, free education to their children unless, like the Puritans and Quakers, religious and humanity concerns motivated the residents.

In addition, no widespread voting eligibility, behaviors, or institutions existed in which citizens could publicly express their views or agitate for widespread education. The day's politics did not envision popular voting to settle important local or national questions. Political decisions, including those of war, taxes, the military draft, or writing a national Constitution, still remained in the hands of wealthy white men—and these influential individuals could always afford to educate their own children.

By the War of 1812–1814, when Americans finally pushed the defeated British out of the United States, they had built a democratic national consciousness. Confident that the Union would survive as a stable political entity, the citizens of the United States finally had the energy, the self-assurance, the money, and the interest in creating a democratic system of public schools. As a consequence, plans for education and national development began to receive serious consideration.

As the national consciousness began to rise, with it came a democratic awareness. People wanted something more practical and less exclusive than the Latin grammar schools, which had always been a European transplant and was never especially well suited to American needs. They wanted a school better adapted to the frontier, able to provide social mobility, and supportive of democratic environments.

Activity 4.3

During the colonial and early national periods in American history, public schools had distinctive philosophical underpinnings. Controversy still rages, however, about whether our public schools were—or should be—religious or secular in purpose and practice.

A. Discuss the extent to which early American colonists practiced religion in public schools. Where did it occur and for what reasons? Where did it *not* occur and for what reasons?

B. What ended the teaching of religion in U.S. public schools? Which reasons and conditions prompted this secular focus?

C. Why is it important to keep American public schools secular in outlook and practice?

Schools in the Early National Era

The early national era saw the common school, the Latin Grammar School, and the academy continue while three new types of schools began: the infant school, the public high school, and "supplementary" schools.[120]

Infant (primary) schools. Infant schools were an educational innovation that prepared very young children to attend the common school. In nineteenth-century England, children as young as five often worked up to 14 hours a day in factories. One philanthropic factory owner, Robert Owen, offered an education to children between ages three and five, partly to let youngsters have some fun before they entered factory life and partly to provide them with moral and intellectual training.

---

[120] Cremin, 1980, pp. 389–390.

These schools were known as infant schools because their students were virtually babies!

In 1816, infant schools arrived in America as an English import to supplement the common school. Established initially in the eastern cities, they were designed for children between the ages of four and seven. Women were the teachers. Infant schools created a home-like learning environment for young children, resembling a large nursery with the purpose of engaging and amusing the pupils.[121] The innovation flourished for a while, but then fell out of favor. Later, in the 1850s, the infant school was revived as the kindergarten.[122]

Infant schools tried to advance a new teaching theory propelled by a psychological view of children. For the first time, American schools considered the learner's needs and interests and the teaching methods needed to help them best learn.[123]

Over time, New England's infant schools evolved into kindergartens. Primary schools took over the dame school and infant school instruction as a public function and added the primary grades to the existing common schools. To this day, we still use the term "primary grades" to describe kindergarten through grade 3 of elementary school.

Public high schools. Empowered with new money and new political rights, middle-class and business people clamored for the taxpayer-supported public high school as a cooperative effort to offer something beneficial for their children.[124]

The public high school originated in 1821 in Boston as an alternative to the Latin grammar school. Its practical aim was to prepare young men for a private and public active life in a profession (not requiring college) at no fee. English was the only language taught, along with reading, writing, grammar, science, math, history, and logic. This type of school quickly developed into a public institution offering the option of an English or a classical curriculum.[125]

Under public control, the high school largely reproduced the academy's upper academic levels, making available to day students at modest cost or for free the same education that had once been available only to boarding students at a substantial cost.[126] Where high school extended education beyond primary, grammar, or intermediate school, it created an additional step on the American educational ladder, which was clearly evolving into a unitary school system for all the community's children.

A couple of factors provided the momentum for establishing public high schools. First, colleges required that students receive advanced education between elementary school and college, but no fully free, tax-supported schools yet bridged that gap. As city dwellers became more affluent and could afford to allow their children to attend school (rather than going to work), more students completed the elementary courses and wanted advanced training.

Second, the new manufacturing and commercial activities of the time called for more—and different—knowledge and skills that students needed to be effective workers. Workers in these emerging jobs needed learning beyond elementary school but not as much as college.

Supplementary schools. Supplementary schools were educational units that filled in the learning gaps for individuals whose school attendance had ended prematurely. Such schools emerged during the early national era under private, quasi-public, and public auspices for groups of students having special educational needs

---

[121] Cubberley, 1947, p. 138.
[122] Cremin, 1980, p. 389.
[123] Cubberley, 1947, p. 139.
[124] Cubberley, 1947.
[125] Cremin, 1947, p. 389.
[126] Cremin, 1980, pp. 389–390.

that the community thought best met in separate facilities. These students included children with disabilities, youths alleged to be delinquent, and African American and Native American children judged to be unacceptable in regular classrooms.[127]

Localities in the early 1800s also established several private or semi-private voluntary alternatives to tax-supported schools. These included the Sunday School Movement, the Public School Society, philanthropic societies for education, and monitorial schools. These innovations, however, remained local institutions rather than serving as national models.

Teaching and Learning in the Early National Era

Schooling's popularization brought a change in the teaching profession's character and composition. Teaching became an increasingly female-dominated profession, especially in the primary and intermediate grades.

Increase in women teachers. During this period, women, as compared to men, were considered more temperamentally and morally suited to work with younger children. They were also willing to work for half the salary (or sometimes one-third the salary) of men, and schools' male supervisors found women more open to suggestions. At the same time, teaching became more professional, making it a sacred calling second only to the ministry in its importance to society.

Particularly among male high school and academy teachers and state and city education leaders, providing teacher training for higher skills and standards became a priority. Intended or not, professionalism served to create an almost exclusively male-elite control of an increasingly female occupation.[128]

The learning environment. The one-room district school with one teacher instructing between 40 and 60 boys and girls of varying ages remained the rule in most parts of the United States during this time. Teachers informally grouped students for different subjects taught at different levels, trying to keep youngsters focused and working. Sometimes, the entire student group would learn through a sing-song drill together, spelling a group of words, reciting a multiplication table, or listing state capitals. At other times, groups of three or four students would recite together. Occasionally, individual students would take turns going through a question-and-answer drill with the teacher. Students occasionally helped one another. It was, however, a relatively inefficient process, especially for inexperienced teachers.[129]

Discipline problems often arose in these large classes. It was often the new teacher's job to test his or her charisma and classroom management skills against the "big boys" before the class could begin its serious work.[130]

Changes in student discipline. Successful efforts to limit physical punishment to control wayward student behaviors began in the 1820s and 1830s. By the last quarter of the nineteenth century, some urban schools had banned corporal punishment altogether. Where it was not forbidden, it fell into disrepute.[131]

After the American Revolution, order and authority no longer rested with the king and nobility and their agents, but rather was delegated to families and schoolmasters. The Enlightenment, American republicanism, the market economy, industrialism, and other factors came together to fundamentally alter colonial schooling. Social relationships were changing, and schools needed to reflect these changes.

---

[127] Cremin, 1980, p. 390.
[128] Cremin, 1980, pp. 397–398.
[129] Cremin, 1980, pp. 395–396.
[130] Cremin, 1980.
[131] Butchart, R. E. (1998). Punishments, penalties, prizes, and procedures: A history of discipline. In R. E. Butchart & B. McEvan (Eds.), *Classroom discipline in American schools* (pp. 19–49). Albany, NY: State University of Albany Press, pp. 21–23.

At this time, two different school discipline innovations occurred that altered the face of the classroom: bureaucratic discipline and affectionate discipline. In bureaucratic discipline, an impersonal institutional authority enforced the rules rather than the teacher. For example, in Joseph Lancaster's early nineteenth-century monitorial schools, which catered to the new industrial poor, students worked in a group relationship with **monitors**, more advanced pupils who earned their rank through merit. Surveillance of students was continuous and multiple, with each monitor responsible for teaching, assessing, and overseeing a small group of learners' study. In turn, higher-level monitors watched over them and multiple groups.

Instead of motivating students to achieve and behave appropriately through fear, Lancaster offered an elaborate system of rewards, prizes, and promotions. For example, a well-mannered student who mastered the assigned lessons could aspire to become a monitor, signified publicly by wearing a badge and chain around the neck. Students and classes competed against one another for public status. This kind of bureaucratic discipline, reinforced by ever-present surveillance and exams, encouraged students to internalize authority and prepared them for the larger world's "modicum of mobility . . . available to the diligent and fortunate."[132] Failure in the race for position brought students unpleasant consequences: Public humiliation was more unpleasant than beatings. Although monitorial schools fell into disfavor because they did not provide a reliable way of controlling costs or imparting instruction,[133] bureaucratic discipline became a common nineteenth-century school practice.[134]

Affectionate discipline, like the bureaucratic approach, sought to instill in students an internalized authority but without external scrutiny.[135] Instead, affectionate discipline depended on forging a deeply personal, warm, individualized relationship between teacher and student. Ideally, these positive emotional ties would trigger students' conscience, self-surveillance, and automatic obedience. In this disciplinary model, the ideal school—like the ideal family—showed love, affection, and intense emotional dependence on the authority figure. Students were self-disciplined by their fear of the teacher's withdrawal of affection and expressions of disappointment. The increasing presence of female teachers facilitated this disciplinary approach.[136]

Both types of discipline were introduced to manage classroom behaviors and motivate learning by creating incentives for students to manage themselves. Other aspects of nineteenth-century school life also advanced these approaches. For instance, where sufficient enrollment permitted, schools moved toward self-contained, graded classrooms, closely regulated school rituals and practices, and systems of promotion, retentions, and demotions. In these more intimate settings, teachers could better supervise students and interact with them more frequently. Forerunners of the modern report card and merit–demerit systems appeared as well. More whole-class teaching and learning-by-doing replaced the practice of memorization and recitation. Throughout the century, both bureaucratic and affectionate discipline approaches coexisted in the same classrooms.[137]

Varied Opportunities for Varied Students

Schooling was far less available for African Americans and Native Americans than for white children. Many Southern states made it illegal to teach slaves to read and write. Schooling was both less available and less used by first-generation immigrants than by their children and native-born whites. Finally, comparatively few women

---

[132] Butchart, 1998, pp. 23–25.
[133] Osgood, 1997.
[134] Butchart, 1998, p. 25.
[135] Sometimes called "New England pedagogy" or "soft pedagogy."
[136] Butchart, 1998, pp. 25–27.
[137] Butchart, 1998, pp. 27–28.

attended academies and colleges before the Civil War, and their choices among these institutions were limited.

Freed African Americans expressed their liberty through their struggle for education. After the Civil War, former slaves campaigned for universal schooling. The wealthy planters did not believe in state-enforced public education, however, and other classes of native white Southerners with whom they shared economic, psychological, and social interests did not disagree. Nevertheless, with help from Republican politicians, ex-slaves gained influence in state governments and laid the foundation for public schooling.

Without free schools, now-free African Americans taught themselves to read and write. By 1866, they had created at least 500 "native schools" in which the newly educated would teach other pupils. Ex-slaves also initiated free, church-sponsored "Sabbath" schools that operated mainly in the evening and on the weekend, providing basic literacy instruction. While newly liberated African Americans accepted help from Northern missionary societies, the Freedmen's Bureau, and certain Southern whites, their own actions were the primary force that brought schools to their children.[138]

The dilemma at the heart of both African American and Native American education was that nineteenth-century whites assumed that neither group could be assimilated into the larger society. The key issue, put simply, was race. To educate African Americans would raise their hopes for a lifestyle and privileges that they could never attain because of their former-slave status. Conversely, Native Americans who accepted the invitation to become educated to Western knowledge and skills in an effort to become part of the larger society found that no amount of "civilizing" would make their white neighbors accept them as equals. The prevailing assumption was clear. People could be educated to transcend ethnic and religious barriers to become full-fledged members of the American community, but they could not be educated to overcome the barriers of race.[139]

Increasing Access to Colleges

The earliest colleges—Harvard, William and Mary, Yale—were initially created with religious and state support to prepare men for ministry professions. Nationhood, however, brought a demand for more higher education opportunities for more citizens beyond those preparing for a religious vocation.

After nationhood, the nine original colonial colleges[140] reorganized to bring themselves more in line with the new government's ideas. Columbia and Pennsylvania changed for a time into state universities. At Harvard and Yale, divinity declined in importance while history and modern languages became more popular.[141]

The Western migration also influenced college availability. Immediately after the Revolutionary War, settlers began to move to the new western territories along the Ohio River. When "The Ohio Company" (a New England–based company) bought 1.5 million acres in south-central Ohio, the U.S. Congress granted it land for schools and a university. In 1788, upon the sale of 1 million acres near Cincinnati, Congress granted the township land for educational purposes. The former university became Ohio University at Athens, while the latter became Miami University at Oxford. The practice of granting townships land for schools and for state universities continued with the admission of each new Western and Southern state.

---

[138] Anderson, 1988, pp. 4–12.
[139] Cremin, 1980, pp. 242–245.
[140] The nine original colonial colleges were: Harvard (founded in 1636), William and Mary (1693), Yale (1702), Princeton (1746), University of Pennsylvania (1753–1755), Kings (later Columbia University; 1754), Brown (1764), Rutgers (1766), and Dartmouth (1769).
[141] Cubberley, 1947, p. 114.

After 1820, with the growing national consciousness favoring free public education, interest in founding new colleges increased. The already widespread dissatisfaction with colleges' exclusivity and curricular narrowness grew. Until about 1870, providing higher education was largely a private effort. Most colleges required students to pay tuition. Because most colleges were founded by different religious denominations, people viewed them as representing and advancing their own parochial interests rather than the state's—or general public's—interests.[142]

When some states discovered that they could not legally take over existing denominational colleges, they began to create their own universities. The University of Virginia, the University of North Carolina, and the University of Tennessee were just some of the resulting schools. The period of great state university expansion came after 1850. By 1860, the public educational stepladder spanning from first grade through college had become a reality.[143]

Over time, colleges opened their doors to women. In 1800, no college admitted women. By 1860, 61 colleges admitted women. After the Civil War, during which time many women filled work positions formerly held by men—especially in teaching—regular colleges began welcoming women as students. Every state west of the Mississippi River made its state university coeducational from its first days of admitting students. Many eastern universities followed suit in the nineteenth century.[144]

The new land-grant colleges. Before 1825, eight states had started building future state universities. The national government further encouraged the development of state-sponsored higher educational institutions by granting to each new state, beginning with Ohio in 1802, two entire townships of land to help endow a "seminary of learning" in each. This practice eventually led to the founding of a state university in every new state.

In 1862, the federal government granted funds under the Morrill Act to establish colleges of agriculture and the mechanical arts, thereby encouraging the founding of new institutions and the expansion of older ones. The Morrill Act granted 30,000 acres for each U.S. Senator and U.S. Representative that the state had. The result: more than 11 million acres of public land was given to states to endow institutions for teaching these new college subjects, an area half as large as the state of Indiana. The educational return on the land-grant colleges has been very large. Today, all states still receive federal money to carry on this work.

Movement Toward Universal Public Schooling

As public schools expanded in number and variety to meet increased workplace and literacy demands, immigrants from around the world began arriving in the United States. By the 1850s, more than 500,000 immigrants entered the United States each year, representing an increasingly wider range of backgrounds and cultures. Between 1840 and 1870, the country's population doubled; it then doubled again between 1870 and 1900. By 1900, one out of every seven Americans was foreign born.[145] It became clear that some socializing institution was needed to build political communities and help the newcomers adjust to their new homeland. The public school filled that gap, serving as a means to promote a common national experience.

The nineteenth century's second and third quarters saw the rise of local school districts. By the decade 1840–1850, however, serious organizational and practice

---

[142] Cubberley, 1947, pp. 270–271.
[143] Cubberley, 1947, p. 273.
[144] Cubberley, 1947, p. 275. Every state except for Missouri.
[145] Butts, R. F. (1955). A cultural history of Western education: Its social and intellectual foundations. New York: McGraw Hill.

defects had become obvious. State control of school systems would appear as a solution to better and more equitable education.

Creating School Systems

The formal legal movement toward the creation of public school systems was uneven. State constitutions would adopt principles, which their legislatures would then interpret or ignore.[146] For instance, Indiana's 1816 constitution made it the general assembly's duty to make a law for a general education system from township to state university "as soon as circumstances will permit." Circumstances did not "permit" for more than 30 years.[147]

Finding popular support for a state-governed education system was difficult. In the mid-1800s, political control remained firmly lodged at the district, town, or county level. The technology and concept of state control had not yet been fully developed. Local citizens squared off over highly divisive financial and symbol-laden issues, including levying taxes and allocating public monies, selecting curriculum, maintaining discipline, and drawing school districts.[148]

These growing state systems drew in an increasing number of amateurs, semi-professionals, and professionals advocating for public schooling. Before the Civil War, these "friends of education" appeared in every state, spearheading the public school movement, articulating and publicizing its goals. Horace Mann and Henry Barnard helped to make the public school movement one of the most enduringly successful of all pre–Civil War reforms.[149]

Horace Mann

In 1837, Massachusetts created the first State Board of Education. The state's first appointed Secretary of Education was Horace Mann. In the nineteenth-century, no one did more to convince the American people that education should be universal, nonsectarian, and free, and its aim should be social efficiency, civic virtue, and character. Under Mann's leadership, an unorganized and differing series of community school systems became a unified state school system, both in his state and throughout the Northern states. In recognition of his accomplishments, Mann is sometimes called "The Father of American Education."

Born in a small Massachusetts town in 1796, young Horace Mann was educated in the local one-room schoolhouse. Reading extensively at the town library, he learned enough to be admitted to Brown University. As a lawyer elected to the Massachusetts State Senate, and then as the Senate President, he had helped pass the bill creating the State Board of Education. In 1837, Mann shocked family and friends by taking the job of as the Board's first Secretary.

Neither the Massachusetts State Board of Education nor its Secretary had any powers to enforce their ideas. Their job was to investigate conditions, report facts, expose defects, and make recommendations regarding actions to the legislature. Any influence that they had would entirely depend on the Secretary's intellect, energy, and charisma.

As an educational leader, Mann's central purpose was to put Adams' and Jefferson's democratic educational vision into widespread practice. Aware of America's diversity in origins and traditions, he called for a publicly supported, publicly controlled "common school" that would be open to all students regardless of race, class, or sex, with

---

[146] Cremin, 1980, p. 171.
[147] Cremin, 1980.
[148] Cremin, 1980, pp. 174–175.
[149] Cremin, 1980, pp. 175–177.

| Figure 4.4 | Horace Mann, the "Father of American Education" |

The Art Archive/Culver Pictures

the goal of fostering a sense of community by sharing a "public philosophy."[150] This was not a school for the common people, but rather a school common to all the people, rich and poor alike.[151] According to Mann's vision, public schools would become "the great equalizer," helping end poverty and class distinctions.[152] By bringing children from such diverse backgrounds together, schools would develop friendships and mutual respect that would create social harmony and reduce adult life conflicts. Mann concluded, "As the child is father to the man, so may the training of the schoolroom expand into the institutions and fortunes of the state."[153]

To Mann, education and freedom were inextricably linked. Education was necessary for all citizens to learn the self-discipline required to live responsibly in a democratic republic. If the common people were wise, the problem of leadership would take care of itself.[154] He observed, "A republican form of government,

---

[150] Barzun, 2000, p. 489.
[151] Cremin, 1980, p. 138.
[152] Mann, H. (1848). *Report No. 12 of the Massachusetts Board of Education.* Boston, MA: Dutton and Wentworth.
[153] Mann, H. (1845). Ninth Annual Report of the Board of Education, Together with the Ninth Annual Report of the Secretary of the Board, p. 69. Cited in Cremin, 1980, p. 139.
[154] Cremin, 1980, p. 141.

without intelligence in the people, must be, on a vast scale, what a mad-house, without superintendent or keepers, would be on a small one."[155]

Mann did not like the self-regulating district system, which was not accountable to local or state concerns. Nor did he believe that such a system was an effective way to identify and spread successful teaching practices. Instead, Mann suggested, local schools needed a shared mission under an overseeing agency devoted to maintaining certain standards in all children's education. He advanced the idea of an education system, a functional organization of individual schools and colleges that put them into regular relationship with one another and with the state.

To this end, Mann articulated general principles on which intelligent educational choice could depend. His goal was to ensure educational equity and rationality (not uniformity) to all students in all locations.[156] In his *Fourth Annual Report*, in 1840, he asked small districts to consolidate into larger ones—and sought to bring them under state authority. The societal costs for not educating all students in effective schools, he reasoned, were greater than the cost of doing so.[157]

As an educational leader, Mann recognized individual student differences as an important factor in teaching and learning. He observed that children differed in temperament, ability, and interest, which meant that teachers needed to adapt their lessons to accommodate these differences.[158] Because his concern lay with the greatest general proficiency for average students rather than the remarkable progress of the few, teaching for all students' learning was of critical importance to Mann.[159]

The fundamental issues underlying the American Revolution spoke to human rights. As an outgrowth of this movement, some advocated that women were the natural equals of men in terms of rights, liberties, and abilities, and pointed out that a proper education (and employment) would make them equals in actuality. Mann asserted that mothers needed an education even more than leaders because of their critical influence on the next generation of citizens. Many disagreed with this view, however, and flatly opposed female education on the grounds that it was harmful and wasteful.[160]

Mann successfully met this challenge, making a difference through his intelligence, presentation of relevant data, personal charisma, excellent writing and speaking skills, and persistence. He held forums at teachers' institutes and public meetings in every county, raising public consciousness about the issues at hand. Besides public speaking, Mann's other instrument of persuasion and influence was his *Annual Report* (of which he wrote 12) that set out his vision of what education should be in a free society.

Mann's critics. In all his writings and commentary, Mann did not raise difficult questions that might have undermined the fragile coalitions he had cobbled together to support public schools. For example, he was unable to reconcile his desire to train students for responsible citizenship and his need to avoid controversial classroom topics.[161] Although Mann served in Congress after 1848 as an uncompromising abolitionist, he did not address providing education for African American children. Nor did he argue for public education exclusively.[162] He did not call for free higher education because his concern was with the greatest general proficiency of average students rather than the exceptional progress of a few.[163] While he exhorted against parental indifference

[155] Horace Mann (1796–1859): Only a teacher. Schoolhouse Pioneers. *PBS Online.* Retrieved October 12, 2009, from http://www.pbs.org/onlyateacher/horace.html.
[156] Cremin, 1980, pp. 153–157.
[157] Cubberley, 1947, pp. 225–226.
[158] Cremin, 1980, p. 140.
[159] Cremin, 1980, pp. 141–142.
[160] Cremin, 1980, pp. 143–144.
[161] Rothstein, R., Jacobsen, R., & Wilder, T. (2008). *Grading education: Getting accountability right.* New York: Economic Policy Institute and Teachers College Press.
[162] Barzun, 2000, p. 489.
[163] Cremin, 1980, pp. 141–142.

to schooling, he did not recommend compulsory attendance. Rather, he advocated regulations that would require children to attend either regularly or not at all. It was organized labor and reform groups that eventually pressed for compulsory school attendance to end youthful idleness and prevent youthful exploitation.[164]

Mann's contemporary critics viewed his call for school systems, educational consistency, and equity as partisan and political, rather than as common sense. Edward A. Newton and Matthew Hal Smith suggested that no idealistic equity could ever justify a rigid educational uniformity.[165] Likewise, Orestes A. Brownson, a Unitarian minister who later joined the Catholic Church, vigorously criticized Mann's advocacy children's attendance of state-sponsored secular schools, seeing them as promoting a "civil religion" that was a plot to end Christianity.[166]

Henry Barnard

At the end of the colonial period, Connecticut schools had greatly deteriorated. An 1838 investigation showed that only one-half of 1 percent of the state's children attended school. The available public schools were poor, private tuition-charging schools were increasing, the citizens objected to taxation, and teachers lacked training or professional interest.[167] Henry Barnard's work restored this state's educational effectiveness and its pride in its public schools.

Henry Barnard accomplished important educational improvements in both Connecticut and Rhode Island. A Yale-educated lawyer, he became deeply interested in teaching. For Barnard, public education was the means of ensuring that the American people remained capable of self-government. He subsequently spent much of his personal fortune to publish journals advocating educational reform. From 1835 to 1837, Barnard investigated schools in Europe, especially Johann Pestalozzi's work that respected children as learners. When Barnard returned to Connecticut, he helped pass the state law setting up the State Board of Education with a Secretary, like the Massachusetts plan. Barnard was then elected the first Secretary—at the grand salary of $3 per day plus expenses.[168]

As Connecticut's Secretary of the Board of Commissioners of the Common Schools, Barnard began to issue a series of reports identifying and detailing the problems he hoped to solve.[169] At that time, elementary education was the local school districts' responsibility. Their primary concern was cutting costs, as taxpayers generally did not want to spend money on either teachers' salaries or educational materials. Barnard invoked the state government's authority to force each district to meet certain standards for buildings, teachers, attendance, and textbooks. He delivered the unambiguous message that the state required each locality to fund its schools to the state's satisfaction.

As State Board Secretary, Barnard visited many schools and made numerous speeches championing public education. In 1839, he organized the first teachers' institute in America, which met for more than a few days—long enough for teachers to learn new instructional techniques. Barnard professionalized teaching by awakening teachers to learn and use appropriate pedagogical behaviors. Likewise, he worked to improve the physical conditions of schools by writing extensively about schoolhouse construction. He studied school data and used the statistical returns about school activities and accomplishments to engage public interest in education.[170]

---

[164] Cremin, 1980, pp. 156–157.
[165] Cremin, 1980, p. 155.
[166] Brownson, O. A. (1966). *The works of Orestes A. Brownson, vol. XIX*, collected and arranged by H. F. Brownson. New York: AMS Press, pp. 442–443.
[167] Cubberley, 1947, p. 227.
[168] Cubberley, 1947, p. 226.
[169] The Board of Commissioners of Common Schools was Connecticut's name for its State Board of Education.
[170] Cubberley, 1947, p. 227.

Figure 4.5	Henry Barnard, American Educational Scholar

Engraved by H W Smith

Henry Barnard

Hulton Archive/Stringer/Hulton Archive/Getty Images

Barnard's educational innovations met with active resistance. As backroom politics bended to the special interests on whose toes Barnard was stepping, he lost his job for a time when the legislature abolished both the Board and his position in 1842.[171]

Not willing to slow his mission to improve schools, in 1843 Barnard went to Rhode Island to examine and report on the conditions in that state's schools. He served as Rhode Island's Commissioner of Public Schools from 1845 to 1849. Like Mann, Barnard was a strong campaigner and fearless organizer, holding public meetings across the state to arouse interest in the state's educational system. He organized a series of town libraries throughout the state. In addition, he developed a traveling model school for his teachers' institutes, demonstrating lessons that showed current and prospective teachers how to teach.

In 1851, Barnard returned to Connecticut as head of the state normal school (teachers' college) and ex-officio Secretary of the State Board of Education. In this role, he rewrote school laws, increased taxation for schools, checked the power of local school districts, and laid the foundation for Connecticut's state schools system. In 1855, Barnard also began editing his *American Journal of Education*, a large encyclopedia of educational information. The *American Journal* reported on

---

[171] Cubberley, 1947, pp. 227–228.

every aspect of educational history from the earliest days of America's settlement by Europeans to 1870. This publication provided American educators with a necessary understanding of their educational inheritance and identified recent developments and practices in teaching. By some opinions, Barnard became American's first great education scholar.

Mann and Barnard were two highly visible, extremely influential leaders during the formative period of American education. Mann's and Barnard's work to build and strengthen state departments of education and create state-wide school systems inspired educators throughout the Northern states and encouraged friends of education elsewhere.

Activity 4.4

While the early days of our nation's history provided the foundation for our public schools, many important issues remained either partially addressed or ignored. These include, but are not limited to, religion in public schools, racial and gender discrimination in access to school enrollment and high-status curriculum, taxpayer ambivalence about paying for public schools, local control of school policy and curriculum, the relationship between schools and students' social mobility, the "achievement gap," teacher quality, and the tensions between creating a homogeneous or a diverse learning environment.

A. Form groups to address the different issues identified above that we are still trying to successfully address today. Each group should identify how its issue developed during the early colonial and national periods, and determine which aspects of the issue remain unresolved or partially resolved today.

B. Discuss the groups' findings as a class regarding which issues we are still working to address today. Which issues have been more successfully resolved and which have been less successfully resolved?

C. What is the value of a "school common to all the people" rather than a "school for common people"? How do the differences affect citizenship in a democratic republic?

The Status of Public Schooling in the Late Nineteenth Century

By the last half of the nineteenth century, regional differences existed in public schools. The Northern and Mid-Atlantic states saw substantial growth in their public school systems. Public schools in the Midwest expanded, while public schools in the South grew only modestly.

Within the various regions, schools differed in the school term's length and education's availability beyond the primary level. Significant racial, ethnic, gender, and religious differences continued to affect access to schooling. In addition, the differences in teacher qualifications made a year of schooling in one institution or locality significantly different from a year of schooling in another institution or locality.[172]

---

[172] Cremin, 1980, p. 180.

During this era, school was intended to prepare youngsters for productive work outside the household, where literacy and punctuality, the ability to follow rules and procedures, and cooperation with others would be expected. After receiving an education, American citizens could read and appreciate newspapers. They knew social norms beyond the family. Whatever their limitations, by the late nineteenth century public schools were preparing increasingly more students for adult life in a democracy. As Alexis de Tocqueville, the French political thinker and historian who toured the early nineteenth-century United States and wrote *Democracy in America* (1835), observed, if the United States had few individuals who could be described as learned, it also had fewer illiterates than anywhere else in the world.[173]

At the same time, the white community's cultural assumptions affirmed that people could be educated to transcend ethnic and religious barriers to become fully functioning American citizens, but they could not be educated to transcend the barriers of race.[174] African Americans, Native Americans, and other peoples of color largely remained outside this American cultural community and its public education system.

---

[173] De Toqueville, A. (1945). *Democracy in America,* edited by P. Bradley. New York: Alfred A. Knopf, vol. II, Chapter xvii.
[174] Cremin, 1980, p. 245.

Summary

In the colonial and early national period, three key factors—economy, religion, and local views about governmental involvement in societal matters—interacted to determine the type of education a colony provided its children. As a result, schools in New England, the middle colonies, and the Southern colonies differed greatly.

In the early colonial days, only the New England colonies provided free public schools for all residents' children. Early Massachusetts settlers saw publicly funded basic education for all students as a way to weave their cherished religion into the web of the community and civic life. Settlers elsewhere came from a wider range of religious and cultural backgrounds, prompting them to want to keep the state out of their church-sponsored education. Wealthy parents, meanwhile, could afford to provide their children with a quality private school or tutor.

In 1634 and 1638, Massachusetts passed laws establishing the principle of common taxation of all property for the town's and colony's benefit. This principle became the basis for all present-day taxation to support schools. Later, laws in 1642 and 1647 laid the basis for compulsory education of all children and established compulsory town maintenance of schools.

By 1750, most New England towns had primary and elementary schools available to all local children. Dame schools educated the youngest learners, teaching them how to read. Poor and middle-class students attended the town (elementary) schools, while wealthy sons attended the Latin grammar schools or received private tutoring to prepare them for college. Very poor and orphaned children went into apprenticeships. The academy, a quasi-private school, offered education beyond the town school for those wanting an advanced but more practical education.

In the middle colonies, families relied on church-run or charity-sponsored schools, where available, for their children's formal education. In Virginia and other Southern colonies with large plantations and highly stratified social hierarchies, residents did not advocate for any state role in education. Instead, wealthy students received private schooling. Students from poorer backgrounds learned through apprenticeships or in charity-provided pauper schools, if available.

Colonial teachers were poorly trained. Much of the teaching was accomplished by memorizing, and discipline was very harsh. School buildings and resources were often inadequate.

Not all children were welcomed in colonial schools. Education efforts aimed at African American and Native American were limited, sporadic, or banned. In New England, most free African Americans were educated in separate sectarian elementary schools. The few available Quaker schools welcomed African American and Native American students into their classrooms. In the Southern colonies between 1830 and the end of the Civil War, education of African American slaves was forbidden.

The mid-eighteenth century brought major social changes to America. Youth needed a secular, economic, and civic education. The public school began its transformation from an institution dominated by religious purpose and content into one charged with enlightening a diverse citizenry for civic participation and employment. Education became a state as well as a family responsibility.

In addition, the rise of cities and manufacturing businesses, extension of voting rights, and demands for new schools influenced education in the late 1700s and early 1800s. Cities that had expanded as a result of the Industrial Revolution demanded that state funds be allocated to support schools, and governors began to recommend establishing tax-supported schools. Infant schools, public high schools, and supplementary schools began. By 1850, tax-supported, non-sectarian, public schools had become a reality in almost every Northern state. Student discipline practices moved from physical punishment to more self-management through bureaucratic and affectionate discipline.

The founding of free public high schools and state universities created greater access to education, helped to unify the increasingly diverse American population, provided common ideals and a sense of community, created opportunities for learning and occupational and social advancement, and prepared people for civic leadership and service.

Horace Mann and Henry Barnard worked to broaden educational opportunities for all students, educate public opinion and thereby win public support for schools' value to the community, and provide professional training for teachers. Under their leadership, unorganized and differing community school systems evolved into unified state school systems, and teachers began to receive professional training.

Conclusions

- American education evolved from education for the few to education for many.
- However imperfect they remained, by the end of the nineteenth century, American public schools came to provide a free, non-sectarian, tax-supported education from primary years through high school to students from varied cultural, racial, ethnic, and economic backgrounds and on a scale not seen elsewhere in the world.
- More work to include all children remained to be done.

The History of American Public Education, Part 2

As a society, we have adopted Horace Mann's vision that public schools are our society's great equalizers. Our early national leaders believed universal education was necessary to ensure the United States' political and social well-being. They foresaw a country with a unified history, traditions, and common language—all rooted strongly on their own English traditions, religion, language, democratic principles, and school practices.

These ideals about education for all children, however, outran the early national leaders' abilities to put these values into action. Societal ignorance and prejudice prevented African Americans, economically disadvantaged students, and students with disabilities from attending—let alone benefiting from—America's public schools. To a large extent, the second part of American public schools' history demonstrates our nation's attempt to extend and address these unmet needs.

In this chapter, we discuss the changing concepts of schooling emerging from the late 1800s through the twenty-first century. Along the way, we look at educational figures who tried to remove obstacles to all students' learning. We consider the legal, legislative, and financial interventions used to increase access and success of all students, especially the underserved. Finally, we examine the ways American public schools have tried to meet these goals.

Focus Questions

- How did the view of education as human development challenge the traditional, subject-centered views and practices?
- How did *Cardinal Principles* report of 1918 and Frederick Taylor's scientific management theory influence the organization and curriculum of public high schools?
- Which legal, legislative, and fiscal actions in the twentieth and twenty-first centuries addressed the education of traditionally underserved students?
- How did World War I and the Great Depression contribute to American education?
- How did the concept of vocational education and the emergence of new technology contribute to American education?
- How did Booker T. Washington and W. E. B. DuBois influence public opinion about educating African American students?
- By what reasoning and events did the United States legally deny equal educational opportunity to African American and other minority students until 1954?
- How did the U.S. Supreme Court's *Brown v. Board of Education* ruling against "separate but equal" schools affect educational opportunities for African American students?
- How did the 1966 Coleman Report about educating the disadvantaged affect U.S. views about schools' capacity to make a difference with all students?

- How did PL 94-142 and IDEA make free and appropriate education available to students with disabilities?
- How did *A Nation at Risk* impact public schools?
- To what extent are the No Child Left Behind Act's expectations contributing to raising U.S. students' achievement?
- Where does the United States stand today regarding the quest to successfully educate all of its students?

Changing Concepts of Schooling in Late Nineteenth and Early Twentieth Centuries

Colonial and early national educators believed that certain book knowledge would give students the training necessary for life and citizenship. They assumed that all children learned in the same ways. Memorization and recitation—getting the facts into students' heads through practice and then repeating them back to the teacher—were the most frequently used teaching and learning techniques.

At the twentieth century's start, the idea of **pedagogy**—that is, teaching as a profession with certain methods, techniques, and materials to promote student learning—took new scientific and philosophical directions. Fresh ideas challenged traditionalist thinking about both curriculum and instruction. Heated debates would soon follow between those favoring a child-centered approach that considered how children learned and those who focused on a subject-centered approach for transmitting important cultural knowledge.

"Mental Discipline" and The Subject-Centered Education Approach

Between 1860 and 1890, **faculty psychology** became popular. This viewpoint believed that intellect, will, and emotions all had their own "place" or compartments in the mind. Thus, proponents of this view suggested, the mind could be trained by a uniform procedure of mental discipline and drill. According to **mental discipline** theory, building the "powers of the mind"—attention, will, memory, imagination, feelings, judgment, reasoning, ability in observation, and sense discrimination—through memorization, practice, and recitation developed children's moral character while they learned important information.

If "mental discipline" was the pedagogy, then traditional Western European subjects formed the curriculum. Latin, Greek, French, German, mathematics, rhetoric, grammar, history, physics, chemistry, government, biology, and the Great Books were seen as the anchors of a strong education. The rationale was simple and circular: The more difficult the curriculum, the more the students had to exercise their minds. The more exercise, the more value attributed to the subject. Any academic subjects that could not find a mental discipline rationale remained outside the curriculum.

The mental discipline approach required a very detailed set of courses that precisely spelled out the work that all pupils in each grade in all town or city schools would master. Regardless of students' age, past experiences, future prospects, or physical or mental condition, one course of study was perceived as fitting all. Proponents viewed this system as egalitarian because everyone received the "elite" curriculum. Teachers taught. Intensive drill, practice, and memorization were keys to learning. Students either learned or left school. Many aspects of this traditional approach remain to this day.

The Child-Centered Education Approach

In the late 1800s, a new academic discipline, psychology, made many educators rethink the processes of teaching and learning. **Psychology** entailed the scientific study of human behavior in general and the mind in particular. Reversing the traditional subject-centered model, psychologists now placed students—not subjects— at teaching's center. The educational focus moved to the learner and the ways the learners learned.[1] In turn, the view that a school's function was to assist children to develop their inborn capacities began to gain favor.

Many of the early impulses toward placing students rather than subjects at the center of education efforts came from Europe. Advocates of a "new education" insisted that young children should be educated in kindly and natural ways, and that they learned best not through books but through sensory experience and contact with real objects.[2] These concepts would profoundly influence American thinkers about the most effective ways of educating children.

G. Stanley Hall. In the 1880s and early 1890s, members of the **child study movement** investigated how children's minds and personalities developed. Their purpose was to help educators make practical judgments about how to best educate young people. G. Stanley Hall (1844–1924) and his students at Massachusetts' Clark University formed the leading center of this popular movement.

An American psychologist, Hall pioneered the experimental study of child development. In 1878, he earned Harvard's first doctorate in psychology.[3] Soon thereafter, he began to study children's minds at the age when they entered school. Using questionnaires, Hall and his colleagues systematically observed, questioned, and measured children, tabulating a variety of traits, opinions, and types of information along the way. Hall's scientific approach to observing children brought credibility to the child study movement. As a result, by 1900, the child study movement had become a key part of educational psychology.

Hall believed that a child's psychological life and behaviors develop through a series of stages that correspond more or less to the stages through which the human race has traveled from savagery to civilization. Children's normal mental growth requires living through each of the stages, and each stage provides the building blocks for the next. According to this view, the task of family and school is to adjust to and foster that development rather than to try to shape or control it.[4] "To a nation about to celebrate 'the century of the child,' his doctrines had enormous appeal."[5]

In 1882, Hall established his laboratory at Johns Hopkins University, concentrating on studying child development. When Hall became President of Clark University in 1889, that institution quickly evolved into a leading research and writing center for child study. Hall and his colleagues concluded that teachers using child study findings could be more effective by adapting their instructional practices to meet students' learning needs. For teachers, this meant extending kindergarten's informality upward into the elementary grades and adjusting the curriculum to fit children's natural rhythms of interest and need. Hall introduced art, music, gardening,

[1] Cremin., L. A. (1988). *American education: The metropolitan experience 1876–1980.* New York: Harper and Row, p. 226.
[2] Reese, W. J. (2001, Spring). The origins of Progressive education. *History of Education Quarterly, 41*(1), 1–24.
[3] Cremin, L. (1961). *The transformation of the school: Progressivism in education 1876–1957.* New York: Vintage, p. 101.
[4] Cremin, 1988, p. 279.
[5] Cremin, 1961, p. 102.

| Figure 5.1 | G. Stanley Hall, Child-Study Movement Pioneer |

Bettmann/CORBIS

manual training, domestic science, and physical education into the school program and encouraged development of parks and playgrounds.[6]

Hall's work helped shift teaching's focus from the subject to the student, through his assertion that no education could be worthy, much less efficient, if it ignored students' actual nature, needs, and development. His work placed a new emphasis on the scientific study of students' feelings, dispositions, and attitudes as part of the learning process. Most importantly, Hall's approach "subtly shifted the burden of proof in the educational situation, and in so doing, the meaning of equal opportunity as well."[7] This view would later lead to substantial changes in both curriculum and instruction.

Criticism of child-centered methods. Hall's child-centered approach risked moving school too close to the student, creating schools dedicated to allowing students to set all the terms and conditions on the learning content and process. Reacting to education's traditional overemphasis on control, order, and disregard for the learners' interests and welfare, the child-centered movement pulled too far in the other direction. Neither approach was fully in the students' best interests. The middle ground between the subject-centered and child-centered extremes would be a more reasonable place.

John Dewey. John Dewey brought education reform back to the middle. Dewey advanced a pedagogy that included both content and students within their social

---

[6] Cremin, 1988, pp. 280–306.
[7] Cremin, 1961, p. 104.

Figure 5.2	John Dewey, Educator and Philosopher, Focused on Subjects, Students in Their Social Context, and Effective Teaching

Hulton Archive/Getty Images

context. In turn, the struggle over school curriculum would become a broader struggle over how the schools would contribute to social progress. With Dewey, educational concerns affecting African Americans, women, the poor, and immigrants became public policy issues connected to social improvements.

John Dewey did not coin the term **progressive** (that credit goes to an educational movement that began in the late nineteenth century, in which children were seen to learn best from real-life experiences with other people), but it ultimately became associated with him.[8] Educated as a psychologist, Dewey completed his doctoral studies at Johns Hopkins University. He eventually set up a laboratory school at the University of Chicago to test his ideas about teaching children. In 1905, he left Chicago for Columbia University, where he worked until his death in 1952.

Dewey's era was characterized by many calls for educational improvement. Businesses and labor unions wanted schools to provide students with apprenticeships to prepare them for work. Settlement workers and municipal reformers wanted schools to provide poor residents and immigrants with instruction in hygiene, domestic science, manual arts, and child care. Patriots wanted schools to teach children how to become better Americans. Agrarians wanted schools to train students to appreciate country life and stop them from moving to the cities.

---

[8] For a full discussion of the progressive education movement and its origins, see Reese, W. J. (2001, Spring). The origins of progressive education. *History of Education Quarterly, 41*(1), 1–24.

All of these demands reflected a common message: The family, neighborhood, and workshop were no longing fulfilling their time-honored educational functions. Schools had inherited the educational role from other social institutions that could no longer do what they had always done because the modern world was too complex and too large.[9]

In *School and Society*,[10] Dewey blamed industrialism for education's then-current dilemma. He believed that society educates individuals by providing children with shared, meaningful work. According to Dewey, this close and intimate first-hand experience—doing important tasks with actual tools—built students' knowledge, character, and discipline. Now, schools would have to assume all the educative aspects of what the agrarian society had always provided. Achieving this goal meant both expanding the school curriculum and connecting school to the real world.

In Dewey's view, schools had the mission to advance democratic principles and form common democratic communities. Rather than strictly focusing on child-centered self-expression and self-development, or on the traditional curriculum that left students unconnected from their real world, Dewey believed that the larger society was vitally important. "Democracy has to be born anew every generation, and education is its midwife," Dewey observed.[11] He emphasized the importance of students developing social insights and a sense of community consciousness. Schools, he thought, could become a miniature democracy where students learned about their differences and commonalities, where vocational studies coexisted with academic ones, and where tolerance and diversity partnered with critical mindedness. To this end, Dewey pressed insistently for the type of common schooling that would bring the children of all classes, creeds, and ethnic backgrounds into little "embryonic communities."[12]

At the same time, Dewey viewed the traditional curriculum as undemocratic: "A democracy cannot flourish where there is a narrowly utilitarian education for one class and broadly liberal education for another. It demands a universal education in the problems of living together, one broadly human in outlook."[13] He recognized that the classical subject-centered curriculum served as a means to preserve social and class status through exclusivity and inequity. Unless students were planning to become statesmen, professionals, or intellectuals, they did not need to learn Latin and Greek languages. Instead, students needed to learn English and other practical knowledge and skills. Dewey believed in a common culture based on individual growth and development linked with social integration.

Effective teaching interested Dewey. Based on his laboratory work, he determined that good teaching must address three factors. First, teachers need to understand the learners' interests, problems, and developmental level. Second, teachers must present knowledge in ways that are relevant and make sense to the learners. Third, classrooms should reflect society's highest democratic values: tolerance, cooperation, critical mindedness, and political awareness.[14]

To connect formal learning and the real world, Dewey's lab school built its curriculum around social occupations such as cooking, carpentry, and sewing. From these occupations, students learned arithmetic, reading, writing, and sciences. Students learned subject matter as it developed from their experiences with their lives outside school. In this context, motivating student learning no longer depended on threats or punishments. Students were genuinely interested in the learning activities that they saw as worthwhile, relevant, and understandable. Likewise, Dewey believed that school should teach students how to be problem solvers by

---

[9] Cremin, 1961, p. 117.
[10] Dewey, J. (1899). *The school and society*. Chicago: University of Chicago Press.
[11] Dewey, 1899.
[12] Cremin, L. A. (1965). *The genius of American education*. New York: Vintage, p. 61.
[13] Cremin, 1961, p. 125.
[14] Cremin, 1961, p. 118.

helping them learn how to think rather than simply having them memorize large amounts of information.

Armed with this innovative perspective, Dewey merged ideas about science with those of democracy. He advocated using the scientific method in teaching and learning, believing that intelligent inquiry could transform problems into progress. Students in a healthy democracy needed to know how to think by themselves and act with social responsibility. Good learning, he concluded, originates in genuine life experiences, framed intellectually as problems to be investigated, hypotheses generated and tested to bring new insights on the original problem.

For Dewey, education did not consist solely of transmitting information to passive learners. Instead, education was an act of reconstruction: adding to experiences' meaning in ways that made sense to students and increased their ability to direct later experiences and control their surroundings. Active learning, Dewey insisted, was essential to education. Intelligence was the purposive reorganization of experience.

Dewey's educational ideas tried to reconcile the seemingly unworkable dualism between the wholly subject-centered and child-centered views. Over time, his work would change teaching and learning in American public schools.

Public School Life in the Early Twentieth Century

In the late 1800s and early 1900s, as waves of varied and impoverished newcomers arrived to make their homes and futures in America, well-to-do citizens realized that their country's best interests lay in educating the "lower" classes. To tackle this problem, communities widely adopted publicly supported education. In fact, between 1842 and 1918, all states passed compulsory education attendance laws.

At the same time, structural differentiation among schools increased. In the North, African American children were attending separate, segregated schools resulting from neighborhood segregation or gerrymandered school districts. Southern law and custom segregated that region's schools. Vocational high schools were becoming common in the larger cities, sorting students along class and gender lines, as did the vocational tracks within comprehensive high schools.[15] Curricular differentiation was imminent.

Liberal Arts and the High School Curriculum

In the 1890s, less than 5 percent of the U.S. student-age population attended high school.[16] Almost all of those individuals went on to graduate and then enroll in college. Because each college had its own requirements, a common high-status high school curriculum was just what they thought was needed to make sure that all prospective college students had a similar academic background.

Committee of Ten. In 1893, the National Education Association (NEA) appointed a Committee of Ten[17] to establish a standard high school curriculum for students planning to attend college. The Committee's final report advanced a highly traditional set of liberal arts studies: Latin, English literature, modern languages (such as German or French), algebra, geometry, physics, chemistry, natural history,

---

[15] Cremin, 1988, pp. 231–232.
[16] Mirel, J. (2006, Winter). The traditional high school: Historical debates over its nature and function. *Education Next, 6*(1). Stanford University, Hoover Institution. Retrieved October 10, 2009, from http://www.hoover.org/publications/ednext/3212486.html.
[17] Only one committee member actually worked in a public school. See Rippa, S. A. (1984). *Education in a free society: An American history.* New York: McKay.

history, and geography. All students were to take these courses, regardless of their background, educational plans, or career directions.[18]

Committee of Fifteen. Next, the NEA turned its attention to pre-high school education. It formed the Committee of Fifteen to address elementary education. In 1895, the Committee of Fifteen endorsed the traditional subject-centered courses: grammar, literature, arithmetic, geography, and history. Unlike the high school report, however, the elementary curriculum report urged that academic topics be "correlated" with—not taught in isolation from—the arts (vocal music, drawing, physical exercise, and hygiene). For seventh- and eighth-grade boys, it recommended manual training, such as woodwork; for girls, it recommended sewing and cooking.[19]

The Committee of Ten never imagined that secondary school would become universal or that students preparing for the work force would need such an academically-oriented curriculum. Nevertheless, the subject-centered emphasis of its report and its active disregard for students' needs would find a strong reaction among future educators.

The Cardinal Principles Report of 1918. During the early 1900s, high schools grew in number and popularity as they prepared increasing cohorts of middle-class students for work and college.[20] From 1890 to 1930, public high school enrollments virtually doubled every decade, bringing in more students who were not preparing for college.[21] High schools began to include alternatives to traditional liberal arts, permitting different students to study different subjects within the same school.[22]

Recognizing the trend toward a more diverse student body, the NEA sponsored a new report on high schools. The resulting *Cardinal Principles* report of 1918 became one of the twentieth century's most influential education documents. It called for expanded and differentiated high school programs that would better serve the new, highly diverse secondary school student population.[23]

The 1918 report recommended that high school adopt a more comprehensive approach, placing equal value on traditional liberal arts, vocational development, citizenship education, physical activity, and such personal needs as instruction in personal hygiene, the "worthy use of leisure," and wholesome boy–girl relationships.[24] *Cardinal Principles'* proponents believed that requiring all students to follow the same traditional academic course of study increased educational inequality. Their solution: allow students to follow programs and take courses suited to their interests, abilities, and needs.[25]

Cardinal Principles advocated a common core of knowledge and courses that would be far less academically substantial than the traditional college preparatory curriculum. Reflecting what was actually occurring in public high schools, *Cardinal*

---

[18] The Committee of Ten report indirectly highlighted a fundamental issue in schools' evolution. Should a school provide one unvarying curriculum for all students, treating everyone in the same way? Or should high schools broaden their course offerings to make learning more meaningful to a variety of students? What did educated students need to know? The report's writers writers came down in favor of the first position—uniformity of curriculum for all students.

[19] Committee of Fifteen. (1895). *Report of the Committee of Fifteen on elementary education.* National Education Association of the United States. New York: American Book Company.

[20] Crosby, E. A. (1993, April). The at-risk decade. *Phi Delta Kappan, 74*(8), 598–604.

[21] Cremin, 1988, p. 546.

[22] Cremin, 1988, p. 546.

[23] Mirel, 2006.

[24] Commission on the Reorganization of Secondary Education. (1918). *Cardinal principles of secondary education.* Department of the Interior, Bureau of Education, Bulletin No. 35. Washington, DC: U.S. Government Printing Office.

[25] Mirel, 2006.

Principles established a blueprint for the modern comprehensive high school.[26] Intending to develop the whole student for life and work, high school dropped its preoccupation with academic and intellectual disciplines and replaced it with a broadened curricular scope and a sorting function related to students' vocations and lifestyles.

This new vision of schooling affected high schools in several ways. Schools' differentiated curriculum allowed students to follow their own academic or vocational interests and plans. All students took courses in general education, designed as unifying learning experiences to promote the common knowledge and shared values needed for responsible democratic citizenship. To help students make curricular and career selections, guidance and counseling programs along with intelligence and achievement tests and other educational measurement instruments became integral parts of education.[27]

Criticism of the comprehensive high school. If the Committee of Ten's recommendations were weighted too heavily toward a classical academic curriculum, then the *Cardinal Principles* recommendations went too far in the opposite direction, diluting high schools' academic focus.[28] Designed to meet individual differences, the comprehensive high school developed a tracked curriculum and did not do enough to raise all students to high academic standards. The availability of advanced, average, and below-average courses assured that all students moved through the program at varying levels of intellectual rigor. The common learning intended to provide a shared experience in American ideas and values became a required core curriculum that "tracked" students did not share. Advanced, average, and below-average students might enter the same school building in the morning and never meet in the classrooms. Nevertheless, this commitment to educating all high school students under the same roof with a range of curricular choices has remained a mainstay of the U.S. educational system.

Scientific Management in Schools

Early twentieth-century business and industry leaders saw education as an important way to promote efficiency and profitability. Highly influenced by industrialization's mechanisms, factory productivity, and good organization, educators and business proposed applying **scientific management**, a process for increasing institutional competence, to assure quality, standardized school outcomes. This organizational approach fit well with the *Cardinal Principles* report in arranging high schools for maximum cost-effectiveness.

Frederick Taylor. Frederick Taylor (1865–1915), an engineer and the world's first efficiency expert, developed the concept of scientific management to provide businesses and factories with increased production and lower costs. To implement his ideas, Taylor contracted with companies to rearrange their production processes, simplifying each employee's tasks. According to Taylor, the "best practices" were those that gained the highest productivity with the least effort. Instead of doing many different things, workers in "Taylorized" factories executed the same simple tasks over and over. This increased production, reduced an employer's need for skilled labor, and lowered managements' costs.

Educators adapted Taylor's views on organizational efficiency to American schooling. For schools, however, scientific management was not a natural fit. Laboring on an assembly line was not the same as educating dissimilar children.

---

[26] Cremin, 1988, pp. 232–233.
[27] Cremin, 1988, p. 233.
[28] Rothstein, R., Jacobsen, R., & Wilder, T. (2008). *Grading education: Getting accountability right.* New York: Economic Policy Institute and Teachers College Press.

In making a factory model work in schools, teachers had to identify actual learning outcomes and take measurements to determine whether students had achieved those outcomes. The adaptation of Taylor's approach to the classroom, therefore, begat the science of school measurement: finding supposedly objective and numerical ways to demonstrate student achievement. Other efficiency reforms required teachers to document their teaching activities to prove that they were minimizing "waste." Because many of Taylor's education disciples were not educators themselves, however, they seldom tried to tell teachers what or how to teach.

How scientific management worked in schools. Scientific management in schools had curricular, instructional, and social implications. Schools developed tracking practices, placing students into unique programs of study, such as college-preparatory or vocational education, based on their demonstrated or assumed intelligence. In this way, high schools sorted and selected society's future leaders and workers.

Educators liked this system because it appeared to reward student merit. Students who learned well received rewards; students who did not learn as readily did not. Likewise, students saw themselves either as intelligent, superior, and worthy of a promising future or as not intelligent and unworthy. As a consequence, a self-fulfilling prophesy was set in motion.

Between 1900 and 1930, school administrators began to see themselves as managers, rather than as educators. They used scientific management ideas to help their schools accommodate the large numbers of immigrant children at low cost. Children entered school and moved through the grades with their age-peers, changing classes at predetermined intervals to ringing bells. Today we know that children grow and develop at different and variable rates, so automatically moving students in tandem with those of their chronological age rewarded students who showed quicker development. Those who developed more slowly fell behind and dropped out.[29]

The **factory model** idea reached its peak in 1908 in Gary, Indiana, where **platoon schools** became popular. Organized like factories, these schools used a bell schedule to organize learning time, provided a varied curriculum, organized academic departments to guide instruction in separate disciplines, and outfitted certain rooms for special uses. Hundreds of cities' schools adopted this plan, thinking that it made better use of schools' facilities. Many of these practices persist in schools today.

Criticism of scientific management. In the long run, the factory model proved ill suited to both business and schools. While mass production and its industrial ethos were brilliant innovations in their time, by the late twentieth century they had become liabilities for companies having to survive in competitive, rapidly evolving world markets. Daily work routines have a powerful impact in shaping an organization's culture. Instead of dividing work into smaller and less meaningful tasks in which quality was someone else's responsibility, organizations in the late twentieth and twenty-first century had to change their ways so as to educate, empower, and engage all of their employees in a process of continuously improving their product's quality.

Scientific management had a similar effect in schools, which became bureaucratic, impersonal, departmentalized, and increasingly isolated from the larger society. School codes and procedures spelled out exactly how to address every detail of school life. Students moved through the fragmented curriculum, and standardized tests purported to measure the quality of their learning. As learning became less meaningful to students, misbehavior increased, absences and dropouts increased, and academic quality and student achievement declined.[30]

---

[29] Gray, K. (1993, January). Why we will lose Taylorism in America's high schools. *Phi Delta Kappan, 74* (5), 370–374.
[30] Wilms, W. W. (2003, April). Altering the structure and culture of American public schools. *Phi Delta Kappan, 84*(8), 606–615.

A CLOSER LOOK

William Spady writes that the late nineteenth and early twentieth century produced a "paradigm that has defined, shaped, and sustained our public education system for over a century."

The paradigm took form in the late 19th century, during the optimistic adolescence of America's Industrial Age, and it embodies the leading ideas of that bygone era: a subject-structured curriculum, an age-based grade-level grouping and promotion structure, a time-based and time-defined form of organization, and a decidedly uniform pace of instruction, from September into June. All of these elements combined to mimic the much-admired factory assembly lines of the day, and within a few decades this industrial-age model of education became so institutionalized, legalized, internalized, and reinforced that it has been virtually impossible to change.

We simply know it as "school," and most Americans have spent at least 12 of their most formative years in it. Most of their schools looked like huge boxes containing a host of structural and operating elements that placed literal boundaries around the thinking and actions of educators, parents, policymakers, and the students themselves. These tightly bounded and self-constraining "boxes" of school included the content-subjects box, the grade-level box, the time box, the requirements box, the role box, the grading box, the credentialing box, the opportunity box, the classroom box, and (now ascendant) the test-score box—all intertwined in a web of mutually reinforcing boundaries and limits, something we know today as a closed system. Hence, the boxes have become the way we think, talk, and act whenever we deal with "schools."

www.PatriciaRainelIllustration.com

Source: Spady, W. (2007, January 10). The paradigm trap: Getting beyond No Child Left Behind will mean changing our 19th century closed-system mind-set. *Education Week, 26*(8), 27, 29. Illustration by Patti Raine. Available online from **http://www.edweek.org/ew/articles/2007/01/10/18spady.h26.html**.

Answer the following questions:

1. How does Spady's view explain the illustration? Do you agree or disagree with his position?

2. How did the liberal arts and mental discipline proponents influence the creation of this "box"?

3. How would American educators, including Hall and Dewey, address the "box"?

4. How did scientific management influence this paradigm?

5. In what ways do you see American education as still putting students into a "box"? In what ways do you see American education as removing the "box"?

Activity 5.1

The mid- to late nineteenth and early twentieth century saw many innovations in thought and practice that would define modern American public schools, at all levels (K–12).

A. Complete the following table, using the text and a partner as a resource.

Rationale/Philosophy	Description of Key Ideas and Practices		Major Proponent/s	Where This Aspect Seen in Public Schools Today
	Curriculum	Instructional Practices		
Mental discipline/ subject-centered education				
Child-centered education				
Scientific management and *Cardinal Principles*, 1918				

B. Discuss your findings as a class.

Which rationales and practices make sense to you?

Which criticisms and weaknesses does each approach contain?

As a student, under which educational system would you like to learn, and why?

The Myth of the Common School

John Dewey, like Horace Mann before him, believed in the common school's power to integrate students of varied ethnic and cultural backgrounds and help them become educated persons who were capable of living in and supporting a democratic republic. How well did this vision become a reality?

The common school was essentially a Northern and Western phenomenon, thriving best where a reasonable homogeneity of race, class, and religion already existed. Common schools were decidedly less common in the South and in America's large cities. Three trends undermined this ideal in those areas.

First, newly freed African Americans in the South were systematically barred from access to common schools. Public elementary schools became available to the majority of southern African American children only during the first third of the twentieth century, long after common schools became available for other American children.[31]

Second, on religious grounds, some parents would not forgo their own sacred doctrine for that of another group or for schools' secular needs. Roman Catholics created Catholic schools for all their children. Several ethnic groups—Pennsylvania Amish, for instance—resisted common schooling on the belief that it would prevent their children from properly appreciating their Old World language and customs.

---

[31] Anderson, J. D. (1988). *The education of blacks in the South, 1860–1935.* Chapel Hill, NC: University of North Carolina Press, pp. 148–149.

Third, members of the Eastern upper classes either sent their children to private schools while residential segregation separated students by social class on a geographic basis. Children of different classes went to different neighborhood schools. One celebrated common school, however, was the single-social-class slum schools that brought together immigrant children of different ethnic and religious backgrounds.[32]

Certain parents did not want their children to mix with students from other social classes. Others expressed genuine concern about the common schools' poor academic quality, preferring to educate their children in private schools rather than upgrade the public educational programs.[33] These arguments remain with us, influencing some of the most difficult educational and political problems of our time.[34]

The Struggle for African American Education

African Americans emerged from slavery with a strong belief in the desirability of learning how to read and write, and they demanded universal schooling. Mostly impoverished, they had to find a new way of life—one that included education to make the other promises possible.[35]

Seeking Educational Gains

From 1865 to 1872, the Bureau of Refugees, Freedmen, and Abandoned Lands (more simply called the Freedmen Bureau) helped resettle African Americans. It constructed and operated schools for African American children, collecting money from various private aid agencies and philanthropic societies to purchase buildings, providing curriculum materials, and hiring teachers. It had no Congressional appropriations during its first few years.

Without publicly supported Southern schools, many ex-slaves established their own educational collectives and associations and staffed schools entirely with African American teachers. At least 500 of these "native schools" were found throughout the South.[36] By the 1870s, African American Southerners had constructed and maintained a semblance of a common school system using their own scant resources.[37]

In the late nineteenth century, many Southern whites opposed universal schooling. They feared political instability if educated African Americans competed for jobs with white laborers. In addition, they recognized that teaching African Americans to read and write would enable them to read and sign their name to voting ballots. In many Southern states, African Americans accounted for 40 to 60 percent of the total population. The principle of "one man, one vote" had ominous implications in Southern states. Therefore, during the Southern education movement of 1901–1915, the region resisted educational reforms on African Americans' behalf, opposing public school appropriations, and excluding these students from compulsory school laws.[38]

Despite the Fourteenth Amendment's due process protections, African Americans were neither safe nor equal under the law. The South witnessed 49 lynchings in 1882 and 155 of these murders 10 years later.[39] In the South, "separate but equal" became the dominant social doctrine, officially approval in the *Plessy v. Ferguson* Supreme

---

[32] Cremin, 1965.

[33] Cremin, 1965.

[34] We will more fully discuss African American, Latino, Native American, and students with disabilities' experiences with U.S. education in Chapter 12, Equality of Opportunity: Diverse Students' Perspectives.

[35] Anderson, 1988.

[36] Anderson, 1988, pp. 4–7.

[37] Anderson, 1988, pp. 148–150.

[38] Anderson, 1988, pp. 98–101.

[39] Curti, M. (1968). *The social ideas of American educators*. Totowa, NJ: Littlefield, Adams, p. 294.

Court ruling in 1896. (This case is discussed in more detail later in this chapter.) Hate groups like the Ku Klux Klan became popular. It would take compelling African American leaders, later rulings by the U.S. Supreme Court, and federal legislation to make high-quality public education a possibility for African American students.

Booker T. Washington

Born in Virginia, son of an African American mother and a white father, Booker Taliaferro Washington (1856–1915) grew up as a slave. In 1865, when freedom came, his family moved to a West Virginia mining town, where his stepfather found work. As a young boy, Washington took a job in a salt mine that began at 4 A.M. so he could attend school later in the day. He learned to read and write at the local African American Baptist church. At age 10, he took a servant's job at a wealthy general's home. Washington had permission to use the family library, allowing him to further his self-education. These experiences formed Washington's intelligence and attitudes, likely giving him an early orientation in accommodation and compromise.

At 16, Washington's parents allowed him to quit work to go to school. He walked 200 miles to attend the Hampton Institute (now University) in Virginia, arriving with 50 cents in his pocket.[40] He paid his tuition and board by working as the janitor. The head teacher was suspicious of Washington's country ways and ragged clothes, and she admitted him only after he had cleaned a room to her satisfaction.[41]

At Hampton Institute, Washington aspired to become a lawyer but received a vocational education.[42] Hampton's mission was to provide an industrial education as a dignified pursuit and a reasonable first step in assisting African Americans to move out of poverty. Students learned vocational practices as well as attitudinal and moral ones: thrift, abstinence, order, and cleanliness. At Hampton, it was understood that once people of color had job skills, they could assimilate and become part of the larger culture.[43] Washington adopted this practical philosophy for himself.

Strongly believing that education would raise his people to equality in this country, Washington became a teacher. In 1881, he founded the Tuskegee Normal and Industrial Institute in Tuskegee, Alabama, with the goal of training teachers, farmers, and tradesmen.[44] He encouraged graduates to return as educated individuals to their communities to raise African American education levels in their hometowns. As the head of Tuskegee Institute, he traveled the country to raise funds from African Americans and whites alike, and through his journeys became a well-known speaker.

Washington's vision was pragmatic and sometimes controversial. A believer in self-reliance, he asserted that African Americans could secure their constitutional rights through their own economic and moral advancement rather than through legal and political changes. For instance, to prevent racial strife, Washington discouraged African Americans from voting, running for political office, and pursuing civil equality.[45]

A practical realist, Washington saw African Americans' social and economic improvement as a long struggle to be won one step at a time. Education for people of

[40] Curti, 1968, p. 288.
[41] Up from slavery: Booker T. Washington. (n.d.). Retrieved November 21, 2009, from http://www.nps.gov/archive/bowa/btwbio.html.
[42] Anderson, 1988, p. 102.
[43] Hampton Institute's founder, General Samuel Armstrong, had commanded African American troops in the Civil War, and was committed to providing an industrial education for African Americans and Native Americans. For a fuller discussion, see Hlebowitch, P.S. (2001). *Foundations of American education.* (2nd Edition). Belmont, CA: Wadsworth/Thomson Learning, p. 302.
[44] Washington's devotion to building his school saw Tuskegee grow from 30 students in 1881 to more than 1,000 in 1916.
[45] Anderson, 1988, pp. 102–103.

| Figure 5. 4 | Booker T. Washington, Educator, Developed Educational and Economic Opportunities for African Americans |

Library of Congress

color meant developing practical wage-earning skills and diligent work habits that set the foundation for self-sustaining, segregated communities. Only later could African American communities demand and expect increased political, educational, and economic opportunities.[46] Washington encouraged a peaceful apartheid between African Americans and whites and worked to develop educational and economic opportunities for his people.

In Washington's perspective, racial segregation had its advantages—specifically, it provided a business opportunity. African Americans' education, earnings, savings, and spending would be their political activity. By showing the white community their hard work, good business practices, and quality products, African Americans would be able to demand that whites grant them more civil rights.[47] In Washington's view, by working within the system, African Americans would transcend it.

To accomplish his ends, Washington advanced African American interests without offending whites who were in positions to stop African American progress. He wrote, "In all things that are truly social, we [African Americans and whites] are as separate as the fingers, yet one as the hand in all things essential to mutual progress."[48] This clear image suggesting racial separation made whites feel comfortable with African American progress. Washington's vision for African American advancement did not include competing with whites for higher education, professional

[46] Anderson, J. D. (1990, Summer). Black rural communities and the struggle for education during the age of Booker T. Washington, 1877–1915. *Peabody Journal of Education, 67*(4), 46–62.
[47] Harlan, L. R. (1988). *Booker T. Washington in perspective.* Jackson, MS: University of Mississippi Press.
[48] Washington, B. T. (1895/1969). The Atlanta compromise. In D. Calhoun, *Educating for Americans: A documentary history.* New York: Houghton Mifflin, p. 350.

jobs, or social status—so his message did not threaten them. His message was peaceful adjustment.

Although Washington's conciliatory stance angered some African American intellectuals who feared it would encourage the equal rights foes, his major achievement was to win over diverse elements among Southern whites, without whose support the programs he envisioned and brought into being would have been impossible. Other African American leaders like W. E. B. DuBois, however, wanted to move faster and farther.

W. E. B. DuBois

William Edward Burghardt DuBois was a scholar dedicated to attacking injustice and defending freedom. Endorsing a policy of "educate and agitate," he demanded full and immediate political and civil gains—including voting rights, access to liberal (not vocational) education, and equal economic opportunities—for African Americans.

DuBois (1868–1963) was born in Great Barrington, Massachusetts. DuBois's great-grandfather had fought in the American Revolution, and the Burghardts had been an accepted part of the community for generations. Yet from his earliest years, DuBois was aware of differences that set him apart from his Yankee neighbors. In addition to the hymns sung in his village Congregational Church, he learned his grandmother's songs passed through the generations from Africa. As a youngster, DuBois believed himself part of an earlier tradition that stood in sharp contrast to the detailed chronicle of Western civilization learned at school.[49]

At age 15, DuBois became the *New York Globe's* local correspondent. Intellectually gifted, he received a scholarship to attend Fisk College (now University) in Nashville, Tennessee. In DuBois's first trip south, he saw the discrimination, poverty, inferior land, ignorance, and prejudice directed toward African Americans. He also witnessed African Americans' desire for knowledge. In his roles as writer, editor, and dynamic orator, DuBois grew determined to speed up his people's emancipation. He completed his bachelor's and Ph.D. degrees at Harvard—DuBois was the first African American to earn a Harvard doctorate.

While on a University of Pennsylvania fellowship, DuBois conducted intensive social research on African Americans as a social system. His research marked the first time anyone had undertaken such a scientific approach to studying social phenomena.[50] While working as a sociology professor at Atlanta University, DuBois studied African American morality, urbanization, African Americans in business, college-bred African Americans, the African American church, and African American crime. He repudiated the widely held view of Africa as a vast cultural unknown by presenting a historical version of Africa's complex, civilizing development.

As a result of these rich and varied experiences, DuBois developed a broader and more radical perspective on American social reform than did Booker T. Washington. Essentially, they represented two sides of an ideological divide. DuBois rejected Washington's accommodation policy, calling instead for "ceaseless agitation and insistent demand for equality" and the "use of force of every sort: moral suasion, propaganda, and where possible even physical resistance."[51] DuBois asserted that Washington's emphasis on industrial education, conciliation, and silence about African American civil and political rights led to bad policy, which limited African Americans' advancement.

---

[49] Buckley, K. W. (n.d.). W. E. B. DuBois: A concise biography. University of Massachusetts, Amherst. Retrieved November 26, 2009, from http://www.library.umass.edu/spcoll/collections/dubois/biography.htm.
[50] As a consequence, DuBois is acknowledged as the "Father of Social Science."
[51] Biography: W. E. B. DuBois: African American perspectives: The progress of a people. (n.d.). Retrieved November 26, 2009, from http://memory.loc.gov/ammem/aap/dubois.html.

Figure 5.5 W. E. B. Dubois, Scholar and Writer, Agitated for African American Educational, Economic, and Civil Equality

Bettmann/CORBIS

DuBois stressed that African Americans needed a traditional liberal education so that they could advance intellectually, politically, and economically. At a minimum, he believed, 10 percent of the African American population—the "Talented Tenth"—should receive a classical education at the leading American universities, much like his own. In his view, this Talented Tenth would use their liberal education and knowledge of modern culture to guide the African Americans to a higher civilization.

DuBois kept pushing for African Americans' full civil and political rights. In January 1906, he and like-minded African American intellectuals formed the "Niagara Movement" to advocate civil justice and abolish caste discrimination. In 1910, the Niagara Movement joined with several white liberals and intellectual activists—including John Dewey—to form the National Association for the Advancement of Colored People (NAACP). DuBois became the Director of Publications and Research for the NAACP.[52]

World War I dramatically affected the lives of African Americans. Initially refusing to accept them as inductees, the Armed Forces finally accepted them into the military, albeit in subservient positions. At the same time, African Americans were moving from south to north in the United States, to areas where industry was desperately looking for workers. Ignorant, frightened whites feared that African Americans would take all available jobs, and lynchings were rampant.

---

[52] DuBois thought that African Americans should lead the NAACP and that if whites were to be included at all, they should serve in supportive roles.

After the war, DuBois's angry editorials about the injustices done to African American veterans in the NAACP magazine, *Crisis*, influenced Congress to act on their behalf. New legislation opened officer training schools for African Americans, law enforcement brought legal action against lynchers, and Congress established a federal work plan for returning veterans.

Over the years, DuBois concluded that only agitation and protest could bring social change in the racist culture of the United States. Although he supported integration and equal rights for everyone regardless of race, his thinking often exhibited black separatist–nationalist tendencies.[53]

Both Washington and DuBois saw school and educational opportunities as the foundation for improving African Americans' lives. Both advocated for improved African American schooling. It would take many years to accomplish even part of their goal, and decisions in groundbreaking court cases—rather than public opinion—would lead the way.

Gaining Access to Universal Education

In 1900, only 36 percent of African American children ages 5 to 14 attended school. Only 22 percent of those ages 5 to 9 years and slightly more than half of children ages 10 to 14 years attended school. Those fortunate enough to go received less than six months of instruction per year.[54]

From 1880 to the 1930s, almost all Southern rural communities with significantly large African American populations and more than half of the major Southern cities failed to provide any public high schools for African American youths.[55] By the early 1930s, state-sponsored and state-funded building campaigns had made public secondary schools available to all classes of white children, but generally excluded African Americans from the same benefits.[56] For African American youths in the South, the struggle to attain public high school enrollment would continue until after World War II. This lack of educational opportunity fundamentally hindered their social and economic adjustment.[57]

Meanwhile, courts were challenging discriminatory practices that affected African American students' access for free public schooling. The *Roberts* case, *Plessy v. Ferguson*, and *Cummings v. Board of Education* would pave the way for the 1954 U.S. Supreme Court's *Brown* ruling that desegregated America's public schools.

Roberts v. City of Boston.

The educational concept of "separate but equal" stems from the *Roberts* case, which was decided in 1849 in Massachusetts. Five-year-old Sarah Roberts had to walk past five Boston elementary schools for white children to reach Smith Grammar School, which had been established in 1820 for African Americans. Not only was Smith school far, but it was also in disrepair. Each time Sarah's father tried to enroll her in a nearby white school, his efforts were denied. Finally, Mr. Roberts contacted lawyer Charles Sumner to represent his child and challenge the unequal treatment.

Sumner eloquently argued that compelling African American children to attend separate schools was to virtually "brand a whole race with the stigma of

---

[53] In 1961, completely disillusioned with the United States, DuBois moved to Ghana and joined the Communist Party. A year later, he renounced his American citizenship. He died in 1963 at the age of 95.
[54] Anderson, 1988, pp. 148–152.
[55] For a thorough discussion with photos of African American education in the South between 1890 and 1940, and the unrealistic expectations placed on African American teachers, see Fultz, M. (1995, March). African American teachers in the South, 1890–1940: Powerlessness and the ironies of expectations and protests. *History of Education Quarterly, 35*(4), 401–422.
[56] Anderson, 1988, pp. 186–187, 235.
[57] Anderson, 1988, pp. 236–237.

inferiority and degradation."[58] Massachusetts Chief Justice Lemuel Shaw disagreed. He conceded that all citizens should have "equality before the law," but this did not mean that there could not be separate schools for African American children. With this decision, "separate but equal" entered our legal and educational culture, where it would remain entrenched for more than 100 years.

Plessy v. Ferguson. In 1868, Congress ratified the Fourteenth Amendment guaranteeing civil rights by affirming that no state shall deny equal protection under the laws to any person living within its jurisdiction. Unfortunately, the Amendment had little immediate impact, because it did not apply to discrimination in private enterprises such as hotels, restaurants, transportation, and entertainment.

The move legally approving state-sponsored discrimination came with a case having no connection to education. In *Plessy v. Ferguson* (1896), the U.S. Supreme Court decided that a Louisiana law requiring "separate but equal" accommodations for African Americans and whites on intrastate railroads was constitutional. This judgment established the earlier *Roberts* decision—"separate but equal"—as a national standard, providing a legal justification to socially and physically divide African Americans and whites in schools and society.

On June 7, 1892, a 30-year-old "colored" shoemaker, Homer Plessy, was jailed for sitting in the "White" car of the East Louisiana Railroad. Plessy had agreed to work with a small group of African American New Orleans professionals to challenge this law's arbitrariness. Plessy was one-eighth African American and seven-eighths white, but under Louisiana law, he was considered African American and was required to sit in the "Colored" car. When he identified himself as African American, he was promptly arrested.[59]

Plessy went to court and argued, in *Homer Adolph Plessy v. The State of Louisiana* that the Separate Car Act violated the U.S. Constitution's Thirteenth and Fourteenth Amendments. The court's majority opinion concluded that African Americans and whites were politically equal (they had the same political rights) but socially unequal (African Americans were not as socially advanced as whites).

Plessy then appealed to the Supreme Court of Louisiana, where Judge John Howard Ferguson upheld the *Plessy* decision. In 1896, the U.S. Supreme Court also affirmed the lower court's decision, allowing local custom and tradition rather than an objective and neutral law to win the day.

The *Plessy* decision set the precedent that "separate" facilities for African Americans and whites were constitutional as long as they were "equal." Public officials quickly extended the "separate but equal" doctrine to cover many areas of community life, such as public schools, restaurants, theaters, and restrooms. Nevertheless, the doctrine was a fiction: Facilities for African Americans were usually inferior to those for whites. Meanwhile, the *Plessy v. Ferguson* decision served as the organizing legal justification for more than 50 years of racial segregation.

Cummings v. Board of Education, Richmond County. With the U.S. Supreme Court now officially supporting racial discrimination in rationale and practice, Southern states began transforming the private custom of prejudice into state law. **Jim Crow laws**—a series of state and local laws mandating segregation—were soon practiced throughout the South and in border states. The precedent of racial separation quickly affected education as well.

In *Cummings v. Board of Education of Richmond County, Georgia* (1899), the Richmond County school board closed the African American high school and

---

[58] *Roberts v. City of Boston*, 59 Mass. (5 Cush.) 198. (1949). Cited in K. Alexander & M. D. Alexander. (2005). *American public school law* (6th ed). Belmont, CA: Wadsworth/Thomson Learning. p. 890.
[59] Zimmerman, T. (n.d.). *Plessy v Ferguson*. Retrieved November 27, 2009, from http://www.bgsu.edu/departments/acs/1890s/plessy/plessy.html.

turned the building into an African American elementary school rather than improve the original elementary school's facilities. The board recommended the displaced African American students try to enroll in church-affiliated schools.[60] When this decision was legally challenged, the U.S. Supreme Court replied that education was a state concern. Public school boards did not have to offer secondary education for African American youths. According to this ruling, a state could constitutionally maintain separate education systems for African Americans and white students in public and private institutions.[61]

The *Cummings* ruling confirmed that both the Fourteenth Amendment's equal protection clause and *Plessy*'s "separate but equal" rule were virtually meaningless.[62] Similar cases with similar outcomes followed in many states, in both the North and the South.

Until the U.S. Supreme Court decision in *Brown v. Board of Education* (discussed next), localities legally denied African American elementary and secondary school children equal educational opportunity. Owing to the *Cummings* precedent, African American children continued to attend schools in substandard facilities and receive poor instruction, frequently with school in session only a few months of the year. Additionally, funding for African American and white schools, although separate, was far from equal. In 1931, Southern states spent an average of $45.63 for each white child's education and only $14.95 for each African American student. Of the total school expenditures in the South, only 10.7 percent went to support African American students.[63]

Brown v. Board of Education, 1954

In *Brown v. Board of Education*, African American children of elementary school age living in Topeka, Kansas (see Figure 5.6), filed suit to be allowed to enroll in the public schools serving white children. They said that segregated public schools were not equal and could not be made equal, thereby depriving the children of the equal protection of the laws.

In a unanimous 1954 ruling, the U.S. Supreme Court wrote that "separate but equal" was "inherently unequal." According to this decision, the practice of segregating public school children solely on the basis of race deprived minority children of equivalent educational opportunities, even though the physical facilities and other "tangible" (material) factors might be identical. "Separate but equal" practices denied African American students equal protection under the laws, according to the Court. The ruling in the *Brown* case became a watershed moment for American education, and for larger society as well.

The Supreme Court decision saw education as the most important of state and local governments' functions to assure a democratic society, good citizenship, awaken children to cultural values, and prepare them for later professional training. Schools help children adjust to their environment. Without the proper education, students would have difficulty succeeding in life.

The Court concluded that segregated educational facilities provided unequal educational opportunities. To separate children from others of similar age and qualifications solely because of their race generated feelings of inferiority about their status in the community in ways that could not be repaired. These feelings, in turn, affected children's motivation to learn. Segregated schools, the Court determined, had the tendency to limit African American students' educational and mental development. Giving African American children access to racially mixed classrooms

---

[60] Alexander & Alexander, 2005, p. 891.
[61] For an example of the state mandating segregation in a private school, see *Berea College v. Kentucky,* 1908.
[62] Anderson, 1988, p. 192.
[63] Curti, 1968, pp. 306–307.

Figure 5.6	Children Involved with *Brown v. Board of Education* Which Challenged the Legality of Public School Segregation

Carl Iwasaki/Time Life Pictures/Getty Images

would help to equalize their educational resources and improve their academic outcomes.

Ruby Bridges and school desegregation. Although school desegregation was a societal issue, it was also a personal one affecting actual children. In Figure 5.7, first-grader Ruby Bridges walks from her elementary school, escorted by federal marshals who were ordered to protect her by President Dwight D. Eisenhower. Court-ordered integration in New Orleans schools began in November 1960. Ruby was the first African American child enrolled in the William Franz Elementary School, and she needed an armed escort to keep her safe. The New Orleans and Louisiana police refused to help. The large angry white crowds who gathered every day outside the school grounds to yell and intimidate Ruby had the potential for physical violence. Consequently, the marshals carried guns and often threatened arrests to keep the protesting crowds back.

Later that year, two white boys joined with Ruby at the school. As expected, the mob became very upset upon first seeing them. Other children soon followed. The following school year, the onlookers gave up their struggle to scare Ruby or to defeat the judge's order. Ruby finished Franz Elementary School and went on to graduate from high school.[64]

While this particular experience was Ruby's, African American students entering formerly all-white schools faced similar difficulties. The undoing of cultural norms about keeping the races separate raised tremendous anger and moved very slowly. **Massive resistance**—closing public schools to keep African American students

[64] Bridges Hall, R. (2000, March). The education of Ruby Nell. Ruby Bridges Foundation. Retrieved May 12, 2009, from http://www.rubybridges.org/story.htm.

| Figure 5.7 | U.S. Marshals Escort Six-Year-Old Ruby Bridges from Her Elementary School, November, 1960 |

AP Photo

from enrolling with white students—characterized several Southern states' efforts to block racially desegregated education.

Education after *Brown*. In spite of popular defiance toward the *Brown* decision, by 1970 Southern schools were less segregated than schools in any other region of the country.[65] Desegregation in the North, West, and Midwest faced different challenges. After World War II, many middle-class whites had moved out of cities and into the surrounding suburbs. As a consequence, meaningful school desegregation could not happen without crossing city–suburb lines. Because this kind of racial separation resulted from a "natural" outgrowth of individuals choosing where to live, courts considered it legally permissible. By 2001, many school districts, in both North and South, were at least as segregated as they were in 1954.[66] In fact, school districts in Boston, Chicago, and New York were more segregated.[67]

In a reversal of *Brown*'s intent, courts in the 1990s began releasing districts from desegregation orders issued in the 1970s. These later rulings allowed the return to neighborhood schools even if that meant that some schools re-segregated. As a result, the percentage of African American children attending mostly minority schools increased from 66 percent in 1991 to 73 percent in 2003.[68]

---

[65] Ferguson, R. F., with Mehta, J. (2004, May). An unfinished journey: The legacy of *Brown* and the narrowing of the achievement gap. *Phi Delta Kappan, 85*(9), 656–669.

[66] Clinchy, Evans (2001, March). Needed: A new educational civil rights movement. *Phi Delta Kappan, 82*(7): 494.

[67] Orfield, G., & Yun, J. T. (1999, June). *Resegregation in American schools.* Cambridge, MA: Harvard Civil Rights Project. See this report for data on increased racial, ethnic, and economic segregation.

[68] Marcus, R. (2006, November 29). A slide toward segregation. *The Washington Post*, p. A23. Retrieved November 26, 2009, from http://www.washingtonpost.com/wp-dyn/content/article/2006/11/28/AR2006112801275_pf.html.

Both federal and state courts are now declaring that formerly segregated districts have made "good faith"—if unsuccessful—efforts to desegregate. Called "unified," these school districts are relieved of any more duty to integrate their schools. These same courts are declaring "race-based admissions policies" unconstitutional, so that districts may now return to their policies of maintaining racially identifiable neighborhood schools.

In writing for the majority in one such 2007 case,[69] U.S. Supreme Court Chief Justice John Roberts affirmed, "The way to stop discrimination on the basis of race is to stop discrimination on the basis of race."[70] Even racial classifications that officials describe as benign or beneficial should be struck down, the Court's majority argues, because the act of classification itself is offensive.[71]

The *Brown* Legacy. In spite of the limited legal retreat since the 1954 ruling, *Brown*'s move to desegregate schools was appropriate, from both a moral and an educational standpoint. Current research shows that African American children achieve higher—and reduce the achievement gap between their test scores and those of white and Asian students—in racially integrated schools.

Since 1954, people have disagreed about whether *Brown*'s central meaning was to achieve a colorblind society or an integrated one. In the 2007 case, the Supreme Court firmly came down in favor of colorblindness.[72] Today, neither the government nor schools can use "a binary concept of race" to discriminate among individual students. Schools cannot put a collective social goal (racial balance) ahead of an individual's rights. Such racially based measures would now be considered "extreme."

Activity 5.2

"Separate but equal" was a social doctrine used to keep African Americans and whites physically apart in public (and private) spheres.

A Have the class reach a consensus on what they consider to be *Brown*'s top three compelling issues. Why are these issues the most forceful arguments?

B. Discuss the extent to which you think each issue *Brown* sought to improve is present in your home community and in the larger society. What evidence can you cite to support your view?

C. What do you think students—African American and white—felt and thought during the first few days and weeks after their schools became integrated? How do you think integration affected teachers' roles as instructors and classroom managers?

D. What do you think was *Brown*'s impact on other non-Caucasian students?

E. Discuss whether class members think that the U.S. schools should be *colorblind* or *integrated*. Why do you feel that way?

---

[69] Two cases were joined together as one case: *Parents Involved in Community Schools v. Seattle School District* (Case No. 05-908) and *Meredith v. Jefferson County Board of Education* (No. 05-915).
[70] Race and the Roberts Court: Opinion. (2007, June, 29). *The Wall Street Journal. 249*(151), A14.
[71] Bravin, J., & Golden, D. (2007, June 29). Court limits how districts integrate schools. *The Wall Street Journal, 249*(151), A1, A10.
[72] Rosen, J. (2007, July 1). Can a law change a society? Week in review. *The New York Times*, Section 4, pp. 1, 5.

World War I, the Great Depression, Vocational Education, and Public Education

World War I, the Great Depression, increased high school enrollments, and vocational education would all affect American public schools during the 1900s. These twentieth-century forces initiated important changes whose effects are still apparent today.

World War I and Standardized Tests

Modern standardized tests were a by-product of World War I. They emerged when military services needed to rapidly classify of millions of recruits based on their general intellectual level. In 1917, Army psychologists developed group tests to meet this urgent practical need.

In spite of their limitations, these early twentieth-century intelligence exams have remained the basis for standardized achievement tests ever since. Able to be efficiently administered to large groups and after many revisions, the Army Alpha and Army Beta intelligence tests became the models for most group intelligence tests. Soon, group intelligence tests were being devised for all ages and types of persons, from preschool children to graduate students. Designed for testing large numbers of individuals at the same time, through the use of simplified instructions and administrative procedures, the tests were both efficient and cost-effective.[73]

The Great Depression and Education

During the Great Depression in the 1930s, President Franklin D. Roosevelt and his advisors initially saw employment—rather than education—as the answer to the "youth problem." For this reason, they devoted their greatest attention to providing federal relief and creating jobs. Nonetheless, these jobs sometimes provided educational benefits to those most in need.[74]

For example, the Works Progress Administration (WPA) gave money to schools to hire more teachers and buy supplies. It also enabled public schools to provide free hot lunches for students. The WPA and Public Works Administration (PWA) built larger schools to replace the one-room schools that had prevailed in some parts of the country. Primarily to keep youths off the labor market, the National Youth Administration (NYA) provided work–study programs at the high school and collegiate levels. The Civilian Conservation Corps (CCC) put unemployed young men to work on conservation projects, while its voluntary education programs taught 35,000 illiterate youths how to read and write, and granted more than 1,000 high school diplomas and 39 college degrees. Thousands more studied everything from industrial trades to philosophy, economics, and social problems under these programs.[75]

Increasing High School Enrollments

After World War I ended, states began to enforce child labor and compulsory attendance laws. Secondary school enrollments in the United States rose from approximately 1.1 million in 1910, to 2.5 million in 1920, to 4.8 million in 1930.[76] Later, the Great Depression's economic collapse prompted an increase in high school enrollments, as large number of jobless adolescents returned to school. By 1940,

---

[73] For a fuller discussion of the early intelligence tests, standardized tests, and assessment in today's education, see Chapter 15, Achievement and Accountability.
[74] Kantor, H., & Lowe, R. (1995, April). Class, race, and the emergence of federal education policy: From the New Deal to the Great Society. *Educational Researcher, 24*(3), 4–11, 21.
[75] Cremin, 1988, pp. 312–313.
[76] Cremin, 1988, p. 311.

7.1 million students between the ages of 14 and 17 were enrolled in high school, representing more than 73 percent of that age group in this country. Amid this unprecedented enrollment surge, education leaders argued that the new high school entrants' intellectual abilities were weaker than those of previous student groups; they needed access to less-demanding courses.[77]

The economic crisis and resulting high school enrollment boom combined to produce a profound shift in high schools' nature and function. Increasingly, the schools' task became custodial in nature—to keep students out of the labor market instead of immediately preparing them for it. As a result, educators channeled increasing numbers of pupils into undemanding, nonacademic courses, while lowering standards in the academic courses required for graduation.

Proponents of these actions argued that these curriculum changes increased equal educational opportunities. In reality, they had a generally unequal impact on the low-income white and African American students who entered high schools in the 1930s and 1940s. These students were disproportionately assigned to nonacademic tracks and less demanding academic courses.[78] While high schools met their short-term goals of removing these students from the adult labor market, they failed to meet these students' long-term needs for appropriately rigorous and marketable knowledge and skills.

The Growth of Vocational Education

After the Civil War, rapid industrialization prompted many Americans to leave farming for factories.[79] The mechanization associated with this trend made on-the-job training realistic and low-skilled workers employable. By 1900, vocational school advocates argued that apprenticeship had become irreversibly inefficient, exploitive, and ineffective.[80] Public schools struggled to meet the demands for a labor force that was prepared to make the move from an agrarian society to an industrial economy.[81] To deal with this paradigm shift, the idea of vocational education took hold.

In 1906, the National Society for the Promotion of Industrial Education advocated vocational schools as the ideal way to prepare young people for work. Business and industry liked the idea of offering vocational courses in public schools because the availability of already-trained graduates helped minimize their own training costs and increase their profits. Politicians and economists encouraged these programs to increase their local and national competitive advantages. In addition, vocational education appeared to effectively train and integrate low-income and new immigrants' children who were seeking careers in the skilled trades or manual labor into the public school system.[82]

Since the passage of the Smith-Hughes Act of 1917, federal legislation has continued to provide funds to support vocational education in public schools.[83] Over the years, the Smith-Hughes Act and its successors have expanded these separate vocational education programs with the aim of keeping more students in secondary education and providing trained workers for a growing number of semiskilled occupations.

Since 1950, however, vocational education enrollment has declined. The current educational philosophy calls for all students to delay their occupational decisions

---

[77] Mirel, 2006.

[78] Mirel, 2006.

[79] See *Historical statistics of the United States, 1,* 138; and Nelson, D. (1975). *Managers and workers: Origins of the new factory system in the Untied States, 1880–1920.* Madison, WI: University of Wisconsin Press, pp. 6–9; cited in Cremin, 1988, pp. 480–481.

[80] Cremin, 1988, pp. 481–492.

[81] Gordon, Howard R. D. (1999). *History and growth of vocational education in the United States.* Needham Heights, MA: Allyn and Bacon.

[82] Benavot, A. (1983, April). The rise and decline of vocational education. *Sociology of Education, 56*(2), 63–76.

[83] The Smith-Hughes Act called for specific entry-level skill training for youths in separate vocational schools, teacher training, and separate state boards for vocational education.

and to "keep the doors open" to advanced education. The de-tracking movement and press for educational equality and equity for diverse students have significantly contributed to this view.[84]

As a result, today's vocational education in comprehensive high schools largely focuses on work-bound youth who will need education beyond a high school diploma (but not necessarily a college degree). To meet this demand, many public schools have organized their curricula so that students may develop both vocational and academic skills to prepare for both college and careers. For example, High Schools That Work (HSTW) is a national high school program that blends traditional college-preparatory studies with quality vocational and technical studies to improve learning and achievement for all career-bound students. Its research shows that vocational students in schools that participated in HSTW for at least two years exceeded the national average scores of vocational students in reading, math, and science achievement.[85]

Similarly, high school **career academies** are designed to equip each student for both college and career. These "schools within schools" combine core academic subjects with a career-technical class related to an occupational theme such as health and bioscience, business and finance, arts and communications, education and child development, or engineering and information technology. Longitudinal studies of matched comparison groups have found that academy students have better attendance, earn more course credits, receive higher grades, and are less likely to leave high school. In addition, four years after leaving high school, career academy graduates tend to be working and earning substantially more than their nonacademy counterparts.[86]

The Coleman Report: Family, School, and Educating the Disadvantaged

In the years after the *Brown* decision, many people wanted to know if school desegregation had actually improved learning opportunities for all American students. In 1964, the U.S. Office of Education commissioned James S. Coleman, a Johns Hopkins University sociology professor, to assess whether children of different races, income groups, and national origins had equal educational opportunities.[87] Published in 1966, the Coleman Report concluded that school might not be society's great equalizer.[88] Instead, it deduced that family background—not schools—was the most important determiner of children's academic success.[89]

---

[84] Benavot, 1983.

[85] Bottoms, G., & Presson, A. (2000). *Finishing the job: Improving the achievement of vocational students.* Atlanta, GA: Southern Regional Education Board, High Schools That Work, pp. 3, 6–7; Hoachlander, G., Alt, M., & Beltranena, R. (2001, March). *Leading school improvement: What research says: A review of the literature.* Atlanta, GA: Southern Region Education Board, High Schools That Work; Kaufman, P., Bradby, D., & Teitlebaum, P. (2000, February). *High Schools That Work and whole school reform: Raising academic achievement of vocational completers through reform of school practices.* ERIC # ED 438 418. Retrieved November 26, 2009, from http://eric.ed.gov/ERICDocs/data/ericdocs2sql/content_storage_01/0000019b/80/16/10/3d.pdf.

[86] Hoye, J. D., & Stern, D. (2008, September 10). The career academy story: A case study of how research can move policy and practice. *Education Week, 28*(3), 24–26.

[87] Coleman, J. S. (1966). *Equality of educational opportunity.* Washington, DC: U.S. Department of Health, Education, and Welfare, Office of Education/National Center for Education Statistics.

[88] Viadero, D. (2006b, June 21). Race report's influence felt 40 years later: Legacy of Coleman study was new view of equity. *Education Week, 25*(41), 1, 21–22.

[89] The Coleman study was the first time testing data were used to measure educational disparities by looking at what students actually learned. The data collected through Coleman's questionnaire addressed characteristics of schools, teachers and students, educational resources, physical facilities, socioeconomic backgrounds, racial composition, as well as attitudes toward race, integration, busing, and achievement.

Coleman Report Findings

Documenting an African American–white achievement gap, the Coleman Report found that African American children started out academically behind their white peers and stayed behind, regardless of whether equal resources were available in their schools. The achievement disparities were large. In sixth grade, the average African American student was 1.9 years behind his or her white peers. By twelfth grade, the average achievement gap had widened to nearly 4 years.[90] Desegregating schools did not appear to increase African American school achievement.

Additionally, the Coleman Report showed that African American children typically attended more poorly equipped schools—they had less access to physics, chemistry, and language; fewer laboratories available; and fewer books per pupil. But the differences were smaller than expected for African American and white schools in the same geographic regions. Few school inputs seemed to make a difference, except for teachers' verbal abilities. In addition, the report found that ten years after *Brown*, most students still attended segregated schools, and school segregation in the North was just as pervasive as it was in the South.[91]

Not all of the Coleman findings were discouraging. Its second most important finding was that after family characteristics, a student's sense of control of his or her own destiny was the most important determinant of academic achievement. The students with whom youngsters attended school were almost as important as family background in predicting academic success. African American students did better in schools that were predominantly middle class than they did in schools dominated by low-income students, even though the improvements were not large enough to make up for achievement differences due to family background. Desegregation advocates viewed this finding as a point in favor of their movement.[92]

The Coleman Report: A Second Look

Several attempts have been made to reanalyze the Coleman data to ensure that the original interpretations were correct. It is true that while the Coleman methodology would not meet today's standards for scientific research, it was considered to be in the "vanguard" in 1966.[93]

One study found that teacher bias might have possibly contributed to lower scores for African American students on Coleman's questionnaire.[94] Achievement gaps in the same school between African American and white students were higher where most of the teachers had expressed preference for teaching college-oriented children of white-collar professionals. Thus teacher expectations may have played an important role in influencing their students' outcomes.[95]

At the end of the day, what most people took away from the Coleman Report was that "schools don't matter"; smart families—not schools—make students smart. Considerable evidence suggests, however, that Coleman's conclusions greatly

---

[90] Viadero, 2006.

[91] Viadero, 2006.

[92] Viadero, 2006.

[93] Viadero, 2006.

[94] When Geoffrey Borman, of the University of Wisconsin–Madison, and his colleague N. Maritza Dowling reanalyzed the original Coleman data with more sophisticated statistical models than were available in 1966, they found they could attribute as much as 40 percent of the variation in achievement differences between students to in-school factors rather than to family background. For more details, see Viadero, 2006; and Borman, G. D., & Maritza Dowling, N. (2006, April). *Schools and inequality: A multilevel analysis of Coleman's equality of educational opportunity data.* Paper presented at the Annual Meeting of the American Educational Research Association, San Francisco, CA.

[95] Viadero, D. (2006, June 21). Fresh look at Coleman data yields different conclusions. *Education Week*, *25*(41), 21.

oversimplify and distort the findings. Even so, it is true that family systems do have critical and statistically significant associations with children's school success.[96]

Importantly, the Coleman Report's conclusions shifted the policy and research focus toward student achievement—as opposed to school facilities—as a measure of the public schools' quality. Stimulated by Coleman's findings, the "effective schools" research since the 1970s has shown how schools can make a difference—and even overcome—many students' background characteristics.[97]

Special Education: Providing Free and Appropriate Education to Students with Disabilities

Public prejudice and ignorance kept most students with disabilities from having access to a full and appropriate education until the late twentieth century. Until the mid-nineteenth century, only the least seriously handicapped students received public schooling.

Advances in Special Education in the Mid-twentieth Century

Inspired by the precedent set by the *Brown* ruling, parents of students with disabilities began to form organizations, such as the National Association for Retarded Citizens (The Arc), to advocate for publicly educating their children. Responding to their persistence, Congress authorized the 1958 Education of the Mentally Retarded Children Act (Public Law 85-926) to support the training and preparation of special education teachers. Special education leaders began arguing for the rights of students with disabilities to be educated alongside their nondisabled peers in more normal school settings.

Public Law 94-142; IDEA

The 1970s saw courts and Congress deciding in favor of special-needs students attending public schools based on equality of opportunity. Congress noted that of the more than 8 million children with disabilities in the United States in 1975, more than half did not receive appropriate educational services that would allow them to have full equality of opportunity. One million disabled children were excluded entirely from the public school system.[98]

---

[96] Epstein, J. L. (1991). Effects on student achievement of teachers' practices of parent involvement. In S. Silvern (Ed.), *Advances in reading/language research, vol. 5: Literacy through family, community and school interaction* (pp. 261–276). Greenwich, CT: JAI Press; Epstein, J. L. (1989). Family structures and student motivation: A developmental perspective. In C. Ames & R. Ames (Eds.), *Research on motivation in education: vol. 3: Goals and cognitions* (pp. 259–295). New York: Academic Press; Hoover-Dempsey, K. V., & Sandler, H. M. (1997). Why do parents become involved in their children's education? *Review of Educational Research, 67,* 3–42; Ketsetzis, M., Ryan, B. A., & Adams, G. R. (1998). Family processes, parent–child interactions, and child characteristics influencing school-based social adjustment. *Journal of Marriage and the Family, 60,* 374–387; Ryan, B. A., & Adams, G. R. (1995). The family–school relationships model. In B. A. Ryan, G. R. Adams, T. P. Gullotta, R. P. Weissberg, & R. L. Hampton (Eds.), *The family–school connection: Theory, research, and practice* (pp. 3–28). Newbury Park, CA: Sage.
[97] Brookover, W. B., Beady, C., Flook, P., Schweitzer, J., & Wisenbaker, J. (1979). *School social systems and student achievement: Schools can make a difference.* New York: Praeger; Clark, D. L., Lotto, L. S., & McCarthy, M. M. (1980). Factors associated with success in urban elementary schools. *Phi Delta Kappan, 61,* 469–470; Edmonds, R. (1979). Effective schools for the urban poor. *Educational Leadership, 37*(1), 15–24; Purkey, S. C., & Smith, M. S. (1983). Effective schools: A review. *Elementary School Journal, 83,* 427–454; Rutter, M., Maugham, B., Outson, J., & Smith, A. (1979). *Fifteen-thousand hours: Secondary schools and their effects on children.* Cambridge, MA: Harvard University Press. Chapter 16 provides a thorough look at the "effective schools" movement, including how it and contemporary versions of this movement seek to increase minority students' achievement.
[98] McCarthy, M. M. (1991). Severely disabled children: Who pays? *Phi Delta Kappan, 73*(1), 66–71.

Figure 5.8	A Special Needs Student Works on a Brailler with Her Teacher in a Regular Education Classroom

Robin Sachs/PhotoEdit

Early in this decade, court decisions in Pennsylvania (1971) and in the District of Columbia (1972) established the right of all children labeled as "mentally retarded" to a free and appropriate education. These rulings made it more difficult for public schools to exclude students with disabilities. Further, in 1973, the Rehabilitation Act, Section 504, and later amendments guaranteed the rights of disabled individuals in employment settings and in schools that receive federal monies. Finally, parental pressure, court decisions, and legislative actions persuaded Congress to pass the Education for All Handicapped Children Act (Public Law 94-142) in 1975. Amended several times, in 1990 it became the Individuals with Disabilities Education Act (IDEA).

PL 94-142 and beyond. PL 94-142 defined **children with disabilities** as those who are mentally retarded, hard of hearing, deaf, speech and language impaired, visually handicapped (including blindness), seriously emotionally disturbed, orthopedically impaired, or otherwise health impaired, as well as children with specific learning disabilities. To ensure their basic educational rights, this law specified that they must have the following requirements met and services made available to them:

- A free appropriate public education
- An individualized education program
- Special education services
- Related services
- Due process procedures
- The least restrictive learning environment (LRE) in which to learn

At last, all children with disabilities from ages 3 to 21, inclusive, were eligible to receive these educational services in public schools.

Over the years, additional amendments extended and clarified these rights. By 1976, all states had laws subsidizing public school programs for students with disabilities. IDEA amendments of 1997 (PL 105-171) addressed the need for high educational performance standards for all students and teachers, including those in special education. By the early 1980s, students considered to have mild or moderate disabilities were usually integrated into general education classrooms on at least a part-time basis. In addition, many students who were not served in the past—including those with severe disabilities—increasingly started receiving educational services in their local neighborhood schools, including participating in regular cafeteria, playground, library, halls, buses, and restroom activities.[99]

Court cases have subsequently tried to clarify the true intent of the IDEA statute. Cases have addressed issues such as free and appropriate education, procedural safeguards, individualized education program, LRE, separate school placement, related services, discipline, attorneys' fees, and tuition reimbursement. We will briefly clarify a few of the key findings here.

Free and appropriate education means an educational program of specialized instruction and related services purposely designed to meet the child with disabilities' unique needs. "Free and appropriate" does not mean the school has to maximize the child's potential by providing the best education that money can buy. Rather, this phrase specifies a "basic floor of opportunity" must be delivered.[100] The extent to which the education must "benefit" the child and what schools must do to make this happen, however, remain legally unclear and open to more challenges.

Procedural safeguards means using fair and proper steps in a highly regulated process to ensure that special-needs children receive appropriate educational services. The most important procedures include giving parents of special-needs children notice and an opportunity to participate in developing their child's individual educational plan. Parents must be told about the methods and procedures they can use to appeal and resolve any conflicts or grievances with the school officials if they disagree about how to best educate their child.

An **individualized educational program (IEP)** is a written educational plan that identifies the child's educational needs, the annual instructional goals and objectives, the specific educational programs and services to be provided, and the evaluation procedures that will measure the child's progress. Every year, parents work with a multidisciplinary team of their child's educators to develop this plan. Teachers are expected to implement the plan as written until the multidisciplinary team and parents change it.

The requirement that a child be taught in the **least restrictive environment (LRE)** means that special-needs children should be educated in the general education classroom with normally developing children whenever possible. This placement gives the child with disabilities more opportunities to socialize and interact with other typically developing children. It reduces the stigma of being "different," and offers students with disabilities the opportunity to learn the rigorous regular curriculum at the same pace as "normal" children.

Inclusion involves integrating students with disabilities into regular classrooms—the LRE—whenever possible, while providing them with the supports necessary for them to succeed.[101] The teacher's job is to arrange instruction that benefits all students, even though different students may gain different benefits from that teaching. Largely as a result of this mandate, from 1995 to 2005, the percentage

---

[99] For a more complete discussion of special education, see Chapter 12, Equality of Opportunity: Diverse Students' Perspectives.

[100] For more details on the interpretation of "free and appropriate education," see the U.S. Supreme Court decision, *Board of Education of Hendrick Hudson Central School District v. Rowley,* 1982, 458 U.S. 176, 102 S. Ct. 3034. Cited in Alexander & Alexander, 2005, pp. 499–502.

[101] Necessary supports to meet the inclusion mandate may include sending teachers, assistants, assistive technology, and adapted texts and curriculum into the general education classroom along with the student with disabilities.

of students with disabilities spending 80 percent or more of the school day in general classrooms increased from 45 to 52 percent.[102]

The 2004 IDEA legislation included provisions for a **response to intervention (RTI),** a pre-identification strategy to prevent unnecessary assignment to special education services for regular education students who have difficulties learning reading and math. RTI focuses on providing more effective instruction by encouraging earlier, structured, increasingly intense, and highly individualized interventions for students experiencing difficulty learning to read. Teachers monitor students' progress to see if the responses to this intervention bring adequate academic growth. If the student's progress does not seem adequate, an increasingly targeted and individualized approach is initiated and maintained until a multidisciplinary team determines that the student may be eligible for special education services. Critics of RTI focus on whether it will successfully identify—or over-identify—students needing special education services, note that it does not address students with neurologicallly-based disabilities, and wonder how it will fit with other subjects and older students.[103]

A Nation at Risk

In 1983, *A Nation at Risk*, a report of the National Commission on Excellence in Education, sharply criticized public schools.[104] It claimed that world competitors were challenging the United States' former preeminence in commerce, industry, science, and technological innovation. According to the report's authors, American students were scoring poorly on international tests, not taking enough science and math courses, and showing weak critical thinking skills, all of which placed the nation at risk. American schools, once a source of justifiable pride, were "presently being eroded by a rising tide of mediocrity that threatens our very future as a Nation and as a people."[105]

The report continued, "If an unfriendly foreign power had attempted to impose on America the mediocre educational performance that exists today, we might well have viewed it as an act of war."[106]

Complaining that U.S public schools had moved from standards centered to student centered, the authors of *A Nation at Risk* wanted the direction reversed. The report advocated high expectations for all students by having all complete a reasonably demanding academic curriculum. It also recommended the establishment of high standards that students must meet before they received a high school diploma, with textbooks and standardized tests being used to drive the improvement.

Responses to *A Nation at Risk*

As a report, *A Nation at Risk* was highly controversial. Some questioned the assumed cause-and-effect relationship between public schooling and market dominance or industrial productivity. Others raised broader issues, asking whether schools

---

[102] Indicator 31: Inclusion of students with disabilities in general classrooms. (2007). National Center for Education Statistics, Institute of Education Sciences, U.S. Department of Education. Retrieved April 1, 2009, from http://nces.ed.gov/programs/coe/2007/section4/indicator31.asp.
[103] Samuels, C. (2008, January 23). "Response to intervention" sparks interest, questions. *Education Week, 27*(20), 1, 13.
[104] National Commission on Excellence in Education. (1983, April). *A nation at risk*. Washington, DC: U.S. Department of Education.
[105] A nation at risk: The imperative for educational reform: An open letter to the American people. (1983, April). Retrieved February 6, 2009, from http://www.ed.gov/pubs/NatAtRisk/risk.html.
[106] "A nation at risk," 1983.

could either cause or cure America's social, economic, and political dilemmas.[107] Writers criticized the fallacy of comparing the highly dissimilar United States with European and Asian education systems.[108] Some observed that the report included a very narrow definition of "excellence".[109] Others noted that the report's recommendations placed an ever-growing group of educationally and economically disadvantaged students at even greater risk of failure.[110]

Many saw *A Nation at Risk* as propaganda meant to advance a political agenda[111] using a "golden treasury" of selective, distorted, and spun statistics.[112] It hyped bad news about schools, they said, while deliberately suppressing or ignoring the good news.[113] In addition, they pointed, the United States was not failing in the global marketplace.[114]

Despite these criticisms, *A Nation at Risk* delivered some key educational benefits. It spurred policy makers to increase public schools' accountability and educational rigor as evidence through standardized tests. By 1985, 35 states had implemented statewide minimum competency tests, and 11 required students to pass such tests to graduate from high school.

In the face of these new requirements for standardized tests, schools now perceived it to be in their best interests to provide extra help to low-scoring students, who were frequently low-income children and children of color. The emphasis on students mastering basic skills plus the new public accountability of published "school report cards" were important reasons why African American students' National Assessment of Educational Progress (NAEP, a common metric for all states) scores rose during the 1970s (for 9-year-olds) and during the 1980s (for 17-year-olds).[115]

A Nation at Risk put public education front and center on the national stage, by turning it into a highly visible topic for public discussion and allocation of resources. Although the report may have misrepresented what the public schools were accomplishing, it did focus national attention on ways to strengthen them.

No Child Left Behind 2002: Federal Support and Increased Accountability for Educating All Students

The No Child Left Behind Act of 2002 tied allocation of federal monies to rigorous and highly public school accountability for raising traditionally underserved students' academic achievement. It came about as a reauthorization of earlier legislation aimed at providing federal aid to public schools.

---

[107] Yeakey, C. C., & Johnston, G. S. (1985, February). High school reform: A critique and a broader construct of social reality. *Education and Urban Society, 17*(2), 157–170.
[108] Husen, T. (1983, March). School standards in America and other countries. *Phi Delta Kappan, 64,* 455–461.
[109] Yeakey & Johnson, 1985.
[110] Yeakey & Johnston, 1985.
[111] Writer Gerald Bracey concluded that *A Nation at Risk* was not intended to objectively examine the condition of American education, but rather to document the terrible things that Terrell Bell, President Ronald Reagan's Secretary of Education, had heard about schools.
[112] For specifics about how *A Nation at Risk* "spun" selective statistics, see the following article: Bracey, G. W. (2003, April). April foolishness: The 20th anniversary of *A Nation at Risk*. *Phi Delta Kappan, 84*(8), 616–21.
[113] For example, in 1990, politics delayed the Sandia Report's publication for several years because its positive findings about public schools might undercut the critical perspective taken by *A Nation at Risk*.
[114] Bracey, 2003.
[115] Ferguson & Mehta, 2004, p. 659.

1965 Elementary and Secondary Education Act

In 1965, President Lyndon Johnson led Congress to pass the Elementary and Secondary Education Act (ESEA), the parent of the No Child Left Behind Act of 2002. Part of Johnson's 1964 Civil Rights Act and the "War on Poverty" legislation, ESEA was possibly the most important congressional action to fund education programs until that time.

Head Start and Title I. ESEA introduced the federal **Head Start** programs, which were intended to give children from economically disadvantaged homes a "head start" on school success. The **Title I** legislation was intended to supplement academic resources for low-income children who needed extra reading and math help in the early grades. Although states received extra money to support low-income schools, the law did little to hold state governments responsible for academic outcomes at those schools.

While well intentioned, neither Title I nor Head Start has been as successful as hoped. The two large-scale Title I evaluations have concluded that it has not substantially narrowed achievement gaps between disadvantaged and middle-class students, as policy makers intended.[116] Reanalyses of the data and related studies have painted the findings somewhat more optimistically, concluding that Title I may have kept the achievement gap from widening.[117]

Head Start research findings are more positive. While the program improves school readiness as measured by achievement test scores, however, the initial advantages fade over the elementary years. The most likely explanation for the "achievement fade" is that Head Start graduates attend schools that do not effectively motivate learning or build on the academic skills that Head Start students bring upon their entry into school.[118]

National Education Goals

After *A Nation at Risk* warned of a "rising tide of mediocrity" in America's schools,[119] public attitudes about education began to change. In 1989, President George H. W. Bush and then–Arkansas Governor Bill Clinton (the National Governors Association's Chair) broke with tradition of local control and established national education goals. In 1994, President Clinton signed legislation that ordered states to set achievement standards, measure students' performance against them, and reform schools with students who did not make the grade. This law, however, did not require the states to move quickly to crack down on schools that didn't measure up.

No Child Left Behind Act

In 2002, President George W. Bush signed Congressional legislation reauthorizing the ESEA funds. Bush called the reauthorized funds program the **No Child Left Behind Act (NCLB)**, arguably "the most significant federal education policy

---

[116] See Puma, M. J., Karweit, N., Price, C., Ricciuti, A., Thompson, W., & Vaden-Kiernan, M. (1997, April). *Prospects: Final report on student outcomes.* Washington, DC: Planning and Evaluation Service, U.S. Department of Education; and Carter, L. F. (1983). *A study of compensatory and elementary education: The sustaining effects study.* Washington, DC: Office of Program Evaluation, U.S. Department of Education.
[117] Borman, G. D., et al. (2001). Coordinating categorical and regular programs: Effects on Title I students' educational opportunities and outcomes. In G. D. Borman, S. C. Stringfield, & R. E. Slavin (Eds.), *Title I: Compensatory education at the crossroads* (pp. 79–116). Mahwah, NJ: Lawrence Erlbaum Associates; and Borman, G. D., & D'Agostino, J. V. (2001). Title I and student achievement: A quantitative synthesis. In G. D. Borman, S. C. Stringfield, & R. E. Slavin (Eds.), *Title I: Compensatory education at the crossroads* (pp. 25–58). Mahwah, NJ: Lawrence Erlbaum Associates.
[118] Ferguson & Mehta, 2004, p. 658.
[119] National Commission on Excellence in Education. (1983, April). *A nation at risk.* Washington, DC: U.S. Department of Education. Retrieved November 30, 2009, from http://www.ed.gov/pubs/NatAtRisk/index.html.

initiative in a generation."[120] Seeking equity and excellence, NCLB represented the federal government's first serious attempt to hold states, districts, and schools accountable for remedying the unequal achievement among different student populations, especially low-income students, minority students, English language learners, and students with disabilities.

Basically, NCLB is a highly rigorous public accountability system. According to the legislation, all student subgroups must pass 100 percent of the state standards' assessments—and be performing at grade level—by the school year 2013–2014. The law requires schools to guarantee that only **highly qualified teachers**—individuals with documented subject-matter knowledge in the content they are teaching—be available in each core subject classroom.

Measuring student achievement. Operating under the slogan "what gets measured gets done," NCLB requires every state to develop a comprehensive system of standards and assessments in language arts, math, and science. Students are tested in grades 3–8 and once in high school in language arts, math, and science to measure their progress toward proficiency and to determine school accountability. States adopt criteria for improving test scores annually, a measure called **adequate yearly progress** (AYP). AYP gauges schools' and states' movement toward universal pupil proficiency and in closing achievement gaps. Each year, schools must show academic progress at all tested grades, in all tested subjects, by all tested student subgroups. If any one group fails to make the AYP goal (it can be a different subgroup from one year to another), the whole school receives a failing grade.[121]

Data disaggregation. NCLB's most dramatic innovation required schools to separate the results (**disaggregate the data**) for the following student subgroups:

- Students with disabilities (enrolled in special education)
- Minority students (usually African American, Latino, or Native American depending on the geographic region)
- Economically disadvantaged students (identified through participation in free and reduced-price lunch programs)
- English language learners (students speaking English as a second language)

The locality, state, and federal government monitor all students' achievement by school, grade, and subgroup within each school for each year. Students in each subgroup must make AYP each year. By requiring the achievement data to be separated in this way, policy makers sought to prevent schools from "hiding" or glossing over underserved students' low achievement by averaging their scores with the higher scores earned by more economically advantaged and better-achieving students.

Penalties for lack of achievement. In another innovation, NCLB makes schools that fail to move each student subgroup closer to proficiency in federally determined steps liable for a range of penalties. These include permitting in-district student transfers to more "successful schools" and requiring them to provide tutoring to failing students. Schools still "in need of improvement" after five consecutive years are forced to **restructure** by having the school district reassign the school administrators and teachers to other schools and restaff the school from the classroom up. Alternatively, the state can take over the school and make the necessary changes.

---

[120] *No Child Left Behind: The challenges and opportunities of ESEA 2001*. (2002 March). Denver, CO: Education Commission of the States, p. 1. For more NCLB details, see http://www.ed.gov/nclb/landing.jhtml and http://www.ed.gov/policy/elsec/leg/esea02/index.html.
[121] Schools must show that at least 95 percent of all students in each grade and in each subgroup participated in testing.

What the test data show. NCLB has produced some notable success stories. Despite poverty, high student mobility rates, and other challenges, urban school districts that focus attention, accountability, and support appropriately have been able to boost their students' achievement and narrow the achievement gap.[122] Test data support student achievement gains in these scenarios.

Nationally, elementary grades are showing consistent, overall achievement gains in reading and math and a reduced achievement gap between white and African American students and between white and Latino students. Most states have narrowed the achievement gap by raising achievement for all student groups. Less progress has occurred in middle and high schools, however.[123]

Similarly, **National Assessment of Educational Progress (NAEP),** a common metric for all states, shows achievement patterns consistent with the NCLB assessments.[124] Elementary-level reading and math scores show strong improvements between 1999 and 2004, with all student groups exhibiting strong performance. Results indicate the gaps separating African American and Latino students from white students during this period were the smallest in our nation's history.[125] Middle-level grades show higher achievement and narrowing gaps in math, but no gains in reading achievement. No real changes have appeared at the high school level. Because many state NCLB achievement scores are increasing while their NAEP scores are not, observers are left to wonder whether the learning gains are real.[126]

Limitations of NCLB 2002. While NCLB can claim some elementary school achievement gains, the accountability program is not always working as intended. NCLB appears to have "unforeseen problems, unintended consequences, and unworkable features" that limit its effectiveness.[127] Its practice of comparing one student group's performance against a different group's, the narrowing of the curriculum by placing an excessive focus on reading and math, statistical issues that interfere with drawing accurate conclusions, and a misleading definition of "teacher quality" all create difficulties in making school improvements that are meaningful for all students.[128]

Finally, "proficiency for all" may be neither logically nor practically possible. Every state defines "proficiency" its own way. What a student must know and be able to do in one state may or not match what a peer needs to accomplish in a neighboring state. Richard Rothstein, research associate for the Economic Policy Institute

---

[122] For examples of schools showing significant achievement gains from NCLB, see Haycock, K. (2006, November). No more invisible kids. *Educational Leadership, 64*(3), 38–42; and Zavadsky, H. (2006, November). How NCLB drives success in urban schools. *Educational Leadership, 64*(3), 69–73.

[123] Hall, D., & Kennedy, S. (2006, March). *Primary progress, secondary challenge: A state-by-state look at student achievement patterns.* Washington, DC: Education Trust. Retrieved December 1, 2006, from http://www2.edtrust.org/NR/rdonlyres/15B22876-20C8-47B8-9AF4-FAB148A225AC/0/PPSCreport.pdf; Haycock, 2006.

[124] *NAEP overview: NAEP: A common yardstick.* (2008, April). Washington, DC: National Center for Education Statistics. Retrieved May 14, 2008, from http://nces.ed.gov/nationsreportcard/about/.

[125] Perle, M., Moran, R., & Lutkus, A .D. (2005). *NAEP 2004, trends in academic progress: Three decades of student performance in reading and mathematics.* Washington, DC: National Center for Educational Statistics. Retrieved December 1, 2006, from http://nces.ed.gov/pubsearch/pubsinfo.asp?pubid=2005464.

[126] Lee, J. (2006). Tracking achievement gaps and assessing the impact of NCLB on gaps: An in-depth look into national and state reading and math outcome trends. Cambridge, MA: Harvard Civil Rights Project, Harvard Education Group, Retrieved December 14, 2007, from http://www.civilrightsproject.harvard.edu; Olson, L. (2007, April 18). Gaps in proficiency levels on state test and NAEP found to grow. Education Week, 26(33), 12; Matthews, J. (2007, April 16). Study shows more discrepancies between state, national assessments of student proficiency. Washington Post .com. Retrieved May 2, 2009, from: http://www.washingtonpost.com/wp-dyn/content/article/2007/04/15/AR2007041501099.html. For a more complete discussion of the NAEP/state achievement scores gap, see Chapter 15, Achievement and Accountability.

[127] Hess, F., & Finn, C. Jr. (2004, September). Inflating the life rafts of NCLB: Making public school choice and supplementary services for students in troubled schools. *Phi Delta Kappan, 86*(1), 34–58.

[128] We will more fully discuss the positives and negatives of standardized tests such as those used for NCLB accountability purposes in Chapter 15.

(a Washington think tank), believes that "'Proficiency for All' is an oxymoron because no goal can be both challenging to and achievable by all students."[129]

Recognizing the dilemma of determining ambitious but realistic goals, Rick Hess of the American Enterprise Institute believes that as the 2014 deadline for all students' full proficiency approaches, the commitment to complete proficiency may weaken, noting that it "was a nice aspirational goal, but it needs to be revisited."[130]

NCLB next steps. As we have seen, today's public schools organization and curriculum stem from early twentieth-century industrial beliefs and practices focused on efficiency. One of schools' key functions dating from that era was to sort and select children according to their perceived abilities. This process encouraged many students to drop out and go to work as laborers in a low-skill economy that had places for them. In short, public schools were designed specifically to leave many children behind.[131]

Although NCLB is not perfect, it commits us as a nation to ensure that all of our children receive a high-quality education. The legislation can certainly be improved. But in addition to measurable accountability, educators need to embrace a paradigm shift from an industrial schooling model to a postindustrial one that integrates personalization—academic and personal success for every child—with both common academic and individualized standards for all students.

Technology, Teaching, and Learning

Technology refers to computer-based tools, hardware, and software on which U.S. education spent approximately $12 billion in 2005 and was expected to spend $16.4 billion in 2010.[132] The Internet's emergence in the late 1980s and early 1990s linked computers and technology with educational reform, in a relationship that is transforming both teaching and learning.[133] More than 1 million students now take classes online, a 47 percent increase from the number doing so 2005–2006.[134] Some predict that by 2019, half of all high school classes will be taught over the Internet.[135] Most current research on the use of computer-based technology in K–12 education affirms that technology is a device for achieving instructional goals, not a goal in itself.[136] Using computers as a platform for learning offers teachers the chance to modularize and customize education to address differences in how individual students learn.[137]

Learning from and with Computers

Technology can help students learn in both basic and complex ways. Learning "from" computers is different than learning "with" computers, however.[138] When students are learning "from" computers, the technology serves as a tutor to increase students'

[129] Rothstein, R., Jacobsen, R., & Wilder, T. (2006, November 29). "Proficiency for all" is an oxymoron. *Education Week, 26*(13), 32, 44.

[130] Hoff, D. J. (2006, November 29). Researchers ask whether NCLB's goals for proficiency are realistic. *Education Week, 26*(13), 8.

[131] Marshak, D. (2003, November). No Child Left Behind: A foolish race into the past. *Phi Delta Kappan, 85*(3), 229–231.

[132] Hansen, S. (2006, October 24). Telecom trends and expenditures: US education. Figure 1. *InStat.* Retrieved May 15, 2008, from http://www.corp.att.com/edu/docs/Instat.pdf.

[133] U.S. Department of Education. (1993). *Using technology to support education reform.* Washington, DC: U.S. Government Printing Office. Available at http://www.ed.gov/pubs/EdReform Studies/TechReforms/title.html.

[134] Davis, M. R. (2009, January 28). Web-based classes booming in schools. *Education Week, 28*(19), 5.

[135] Trotter, A. (2008, May 7). Online education cast as "disruptive innovation." *Education Week, 27*(36), 1, 12–13.

[136] Ringstaff, C., & Kelley, L. (2002). *The learning return on our educational technology investment: A review of findings from research.* San Francisco, CA: WestEd RTEC. U.S. DOE Contract # R302A000021.

[137] Christensen, C. M., Horn, M. B., & Johnson, C. W. (2008, June 4). How "disruptive innovation" will change the way we learn. *Education Week, 27*(39), 25, 36.

[138] Reeves, T. C. (1998). The impact of media and technology in schools: A research report prepared for the Bertelsmann Foundation. Retrieved from http://www.athensacademy.org/instruct/media_tech/reeves0.html.

Figure 5.9 Computers Can Be a Powerful Tool for Learning Problem Solving, Concept Development, and Critical Thinking

Monkey Business Images, 2009/Used under license from Shutterstock.com

basic and advanced skills and knowledge. Online enrollments, which increased from 45,000 in 2000 to 1 million in 2008, now bring remedial and Advanced Placement courses to many small schools that are otherwise unable to offer them.[139] Working on-line, instruction is also available 24 hours a day[140] to homebound or home-schooled students, prekindergarten children, and students who need to make up course credits to graduate.[141] Students with disabilities, English language learners, and others with special needs can use computers to enlarge typographic fonts, translate to and from English, convert text to speech, correct mistakes, and help teachers individualize instruction.[142] The Web is also an indispensable ally for studying current events.[143]

In learning "with" computers, by contrast, students use the technology as a resource to help them develop higher-order thinking, creativity, and research skills in a variety of curricular areas.[144] Students learning "with" technology can efficiently and effectively create strategies for solving complex problems and develop a deep subject understanding. Digital tools such as "probes" help students collect, graph, and analyze science and math data. Today's interactive video combines the visual presentation's power with the computer's interactive and information-processing capabilities.[145] Students with Internet access can research topics of interest more deeply and widely than is possible in books; generate data for analysis, synthesis, and evaluation; and communicate through thoughtfully developed research papers, projects, and performances.

Research on Technology and Learning

Researchers have found that learning both "from" and "with" technology increases student achievement at all grade levels and in all subjects.[146] Many studies have

---

[139] Christensen, Horn, & Johnson, 2008, p. 25.
[140] Trotter, 2008, p. 12.
[141] Riley, R. W., Holleman, F. S., & Roberts, L. G. (2000). *The national educational technology plan: Putting a world-class education at the fingertips of all children*. Washington, DC: U.S. Department of Education.
[142] Zucker, A. A. (2008, April 2). Smart thinking about educational technology. *Education Week, 27*(31), 28–29.
[143] Zucker, 2008.
[144] Means, B., Blando, J., Olson, K., & Middleton, T. (1993). *Using technology to support education reform*. Washington, DC: Office of Educational Research and Improvement.
[145] Knapp, L. R., & Glenn, A. D. (1996). *Restructuring schools with technology*. Boston: Allyn and Bacon.
[146] Coley, R. (1997, September). Technology's impact. *Electronic School*. (pp. A30-A33). Alexandria, VA: American School Board Association.

revealed that learning "with" technology is most powerful when it is used as a tool for problem solving, conceptual development, and critical thinking.[147] Other studies have shown that technology has a positive effect on student attitudes toward learning, self-confidence, and self-esteem.[148] Other investigators report that technology can improve school attendance, decrease dropout rates, and positively influence students' independence and feelings of responsibility for their own learning.[149]

Learning "with" technology also has a constructive effect on the classroom environment. In numerous studies, teachers have reported that technology encourages them to be more student centered, more open to multiple perspectives on problems, and more willing to experiment in their teaching.[150] Students become more engaged and more active learners when their assignments place a greater emphasis on inquiry and focus less on drill and practice.[151] In addition, technology encourages student collaboration, project-based learning, and higher-order thinking.[152]

Successfully Educating All Students: Where We Stand Today

Today's achievement gaps between U.S. racial, income, and ethnic groups are smaller today than they were several decades ago, but little progress has been made in this area since 1990.[153] NAEP outcomes continue to show large differences between the scores earned by African American and Latino students and those earned by white and Asian students.[154] As of yet, only elementary schools have shown some success in narrowing these achievement gaps; middle and high schools, by contrast, show mixed or no progress.

Ultimately at stake is whether all children in our pluralist society will have access to high-quality schooling and achieve the knowledge and skills essential for twenty-first-century competence and a reasonably satisfying adult quality of life. As citizens, our students also need opportunities to share common educational experiences with peers who differ from themselves and learn the attitudes and skills needed to reduce tension and prevent conflict.

Today's achievement disparities will ultimately lead to socioeconomic differences among tomorrow's families. Such large discrepancies among families are both morally objectionably and politically dangerous for our society's future. This is part of the larger reality.

Educational change comes slowly. Because education is fundamentally and primarily about a society's values, educational consensus and adjustments are realized even more gradually in a diverse society. Nonetheless, change does occur.

Over the course of American history, this country's educational system has moved from a religious orientation to a largely secular one. In the twentieth and

---

[147] Culp, K., Hawkins, J., & Honey, M. (1999). *Review paper on educational technology research and development.* New York: Education Development Center, Center for Children and Technology; Means, B. (1994). *Technology and education reform: The reality behind the promise.* San Francisco: Jossey-Bass; Sandholtz, J. H., Ringstaff, C., & Dwyer, D. C. (1997). *Teaching with technology: Creating student-centered classrooms.* New York: Teachers College Press.

[148] Sivin-Kachala, J., & Bialo, E. R., *Report on the effectiveness of technology in schools, 2000.* Washington, DC: Software Information Industry Association.

[149] Coley, 1997.

[150] Knapp & Glenn, 1996.

[151] Sandholtz, Ringstaff, & Dwyer, 1997; Bozeman, W., & Baumbach, D. (1995). *Educational technology: Best practices from America's schools.* Princeton, NJ: Eye on Education.

[152] Penuel, B., Golan, S., Means, B., & Korbak, C. (2000). *Silicon Valley challenge 2000: Year 4 report.* Menlo Park, CA: SRI International.

[153] Ferguson & Mehta, 2004.

[154] NAEP is not identifying students according to disabled or nondisabled, so we cannot assess how well special needs students are achieving on this measure.

twenty-first centuries, court decisions, legislation, and case law have brought traditionally underserved students into our public schools. Today, we expect all students to master the high-status curriculum, and we are closer to making this goal a reality.

Summary

In the United States, ideals about educating all students for democracy have frequently extended beyond political leaders' or educators' abilities to put these values into practice. In addition, societal ignorance and prejudice prevented students of color and students with disabilities from attending or benefiting from public schools until the mid-twentieth century—failures that continue to have important implications for the current U.S. educational system.

During much of the late nineteenth and early twentieth centuries, U.S. educational reform focused on the nature of teaching and learning and defining the appropriate curriculum for all students. Between 1860 and 1890, teachers believed that the mind could be trained by mental discipline and drill using a traditional, liberal arts curriculum. In the 1890s, however, psychology's study of human behavior and the mind placed students—not subjects—at teaching's center. G. Stanley Hall proposed a child-centered curriculum tailored to children's nature, growth, and development, providing new approaches to teaching and learning.

John Dewey brought education reform back to the middle by placing subjects and students within their social context. He viewed the traditional curriculum as undemocratic, proposing one closer to real life along with effective teaching.

The modern high school has its roots in the 1918 *Cardinal Principles* report and in Frederick Taylor's views on organizational efficiency. *Cardinal Principles* recommended that high school place equal value on academic study, vocational development, citizenship education, and personal needs. Meanwhile, Taylor saw schools as factories. When his ideas were adapted to education, the results included organizational and curricular practices that actively worked against all students achieving to high levels.

Over the next 100 years, securing educational opportunities for African Americans, economically disadvantaged children, and students with disabilities required charismatic leaders, court decisions, and national legislation to overcome prejudice and ignorance. Although the former-slave community believed in learning and self-improvement as necessary for freedom and citizenship, Southern white opponents of universal schooling rejected public school funding and excluded freed African American students from compulsory attendance. Advancing different approaches, Booker T. Washington and W. E. B. DuBois saw education as the agency for African Americans' progress, providing opportunities for them to learn employable skills, become economically independent, and gain resources for their struggle for full equality.

Over the years following the Civil War, a series of court decisions closed schoolhouse doors, especially as a result of the *Roberts* and *Cummings* cases. In *Plessy v. Ferguson* (1896), the U.S. Supreme Court established "separate but equal" as a national standard. Finally, in *Brown v. Board of Education* (1954), the U.S. Supreme Court decided that "separate but equal" was "inherently unequal" and deprived minority group children of equal educational opportunities, even though the physical facilities and resources might be identical. Despite this ruling, negative public attitudes slowed progress toward full school desegregation for many years.

World War I, the Great Depression, vocational education, and technology had major impacts on schools. The Coleman Report of 1966 concluded that family background played the greatest role in student achievement. Although controversial, the report became widely popular.

In addition to desegregation and integration, African American students benefited from the establishment of educational accountability programs during the late twentieth century. Following their implementation, African American students' NAEP scores showed increased minority achievement and a decreased achievement gap.

In 1958, the Education of the Mentally Retarded Children Act authorized federal assistance for training teachers of handicapped students. In 1975, the Education for All Handicapped Children Act assured that all disabled children would be provided with a free appropriate public education, an individualized education program, special education and related services, due process procedures, and the least restrictive learning environment possible.

The publication of the report *A Nation at Risk* in 1983 challenged U.S. public schools to do better. Although most people consider it to be political in nature, its emphasis on high standards, testing, and a rigorous curriculum for all students dramatically influenced subsequent education reform and continues to shape today's educational climate.

Minority, economically disadvantaged, students with disabilities, and English language learners' achievement became central concerns with the No Child Left Behind Act in 2002. This legislation represented the first serious attempt to hold states, districts, and schools accountable for remedying disparities in the achievement levels of different student populations. While many students are benefiting from NCLB, especially in elementary school, other factors have limited its effectiveness.

Conclusions

- Many key concepts and practices that persist in our present-day K–12 public schools emerged during the nineteenth and twentieth centuries.

- Court decisions and legislation intended to better educate underserved students often moved faster than public consensus, but progress to ensure that all students meet high standards and receive a meaningful education continues to occur.

Philosophy of Education

No decision is more important than determining what to teach and toward what ends. The "right thing to do," regardless of context or profession, always relies on values as well as facts. Communities' system of values and beliefs about education—that is, their philosophy of education—influences what, how, and to what purposes schools teach. Different philosophies lead schools in different directions.

Competing views exist about schools' purposes and practices:

- Traditionalist educators believe that schools' purpose is to foster students' intellectual development by teaching the Western European classics and thought so as to prepare students for further education and work.

- Progressive educators believe that schooling is life, not preparation for life, and should be child centered, not subject centered. According to this view, schools should prepare students for an informed life in a democratic society.

- Existentialist educators believe that education's most important goals are to awaken human consciousness to the human condition and to the freedom to choose and create the personal self-awareness that helps make each person unique.

- Critical theorist educators believe that schools should create the conditions for teachers to act as public intellectuals to challenge the present power structure and create a more democratic society.

What our K–12 schools teach and why and how they teach it are normative questions. Decisions about what, why, and how to teach are an outgrowth of our beliefs, value systems, and worldviews. Teaching is a value-laden enterprise, influenced by plural beliefs available in a multicultural democracy.

Our philosophy shapes us and determines how we approach the world. Our philosophy of education influences our views about what schools are for and how we should educate our students.

Focus Questions

- What is an educational philosophy, and how does it differ from an opinion?
- What is the value of prospective educators having a philosophy of education?
- How does traditional education philosophy contribute to our understanding of school purposes and practices?
- How does progressive education philosophy contribute to our understanding of school's purposes and practices?
- How can educators successfully reconcile the traditional and progressive viewpoints?
- How does existential education philosophy contribute to our understanding of school's purposes and practices?
- How does critical theory education philosophy contribute to our understanding of school's purposes and practices?

Understanding the merits and limits of each approach will help prospective teachers develop and articulate their own views about education's purpose and process.

What Is an Educational Philosophy?

Philosophy comes from two Greek words: *philos*, meaning "love," and *sophy*, meaning "wisdom." Literally, philosophy means love of wisdom. In everyday usage, this term refers to the general beliefs, concepts, and attitudes that an individual or group possesses. Most people have a set of ideas, values, and attitudes about life and education.

What Is Philosophy?

Philosophy is difficult to define. **Philosophy** is "the investigation of causes and laws underlying reality" and "inquiry into the nature of things based on logical reasoning rather than empirical methods." It is also "a system of motivating concepts of principles" and "a basic theory or viewpoint" or "system of values by which one lives" as well as "the critique and analysis of fundamental beliefs as they come to be conceptualized and formulated."[1] In short, analytic questioning and reasoning about a reality's true nature creates a philosophy (a motivating viewpoint and value system), and that philosophy then directs one's beliefs and actions concerning that reality.

Having a philosophy involves more than simply having an opinion. An **opinion** requires only a point of view; it does not have to be supported by data or rational analysis. A philosophy, by contrast, requires intellectual and rational inquiry, a systematic critical thinking without reference to experiments or religious faith. A philosopher pursues knowledge for its own sake to more fully understand the world and its ideas. Having a philosophy or critically analyzed point of view gives people a frame of reference by which to make sense of their experiences and to chart a course for future ones.

What Is an Educational Philosophy?

Unlike philosophy as a discipline that stands on its own as a way of making abstract sense of the world, educational philosophy focuses on practice. **Educational philosophies** are viewpoints that help educators interpret, find meaning, and direct their work. Different educational philosophies exist because educators and policy makers hold different ideas and values about education's purposes and practices.

Educational philosophy asks many questions, such as these:

- What is education? What are its goals?
- What is school?
- What is an educated person?
- Which knowledge, attitudes, and skills should be taught?
- Who should decide what is taught?
- How should students be taught?
- What is the teacher's role?
- What is the student's role?

Educational philosophies reflect our society's pluralism. The philosophies considered in this chapter have well-established roots in educational thought and

[1] Philosophy. (1970). In *The American heritage dictionary of the English language* (p. 985). Boston: American Heritage Publishing & Houghton Mifflin.

practice. While science can provide guidance, it cannot yet verify that one educational philosophy is empirically and objectively superior to any other. Nor can science determine the world's "best" culture or the "truest" religious faith. All of these decisions are part of value-driven, affective belief systems. For most humans, our beliefs more powerfully determine our thoughts and actions than do any scientific conclusions—that is, unless scientific rationality as the basis for thought and actions is part of our belief system.

Influences on Educational Philosophies

As one might expect in a pluralistic society, Americans' sets of beliefs, concepts, and attitudes—the educational philosophies—about what should happen in schools vary greatly. Factors such as the historical era, the geographic location, the local and larger cultures, the ease of communication and travel between those cultures and others, and the specific persons involved all influence the prevailing educational philosophy. For example, an educational philosophy that grows and flourishes during an era of limited communication and transportation between and among different world cultures and limited education among its society's members may not be the same educational philosophy that develops in a more fluent, interconnected world which depends on a highly educated populace to survive economically and politically. Naturally, educational philosophies change over time as events and personalities emerge and affect thinking and living.

The Values Behind Education

Philosophy matters. Americans place great faith in education, in part because education prepares individuals to live as responsible and productive citizens in a democratic republic. At their best, public schools are the "great equalizer," bringing together students of diverse backgrounds and giving them a common American heritage. Indeed, schools have been the agency of Americanization for generations of immigrants. Likewise, a solid education can overcome limitations on students imposed by their background, creating opportunities for social and economic mobility. These beliefs and values underlie American schools.

Clearly, education is not a mechanical or neutral act. Rather, it is a value-laden process that influences the direction, knowledge, and nature of the students' learning experiences. Through a philosophy of education, or logical systematic point of view, a school, district, state, or nation selects which information and skills students will learn and how they will learn it. A philosophy of education provides answers about *why* one does things. Learning *why* to do something is an essential first step before teachers can learn *how* to do it. Educational philosophy offers the context or frame of reference that guides and makes sense of all other educational decisions. It provides a rationale and justification for making choices about curriculum, instruction, and student–teacher relationships.

Educational Foundations and Future Teachers

Educational foundations coursework has the potential to give prospective teachers the ability to make sense of pedagogy within the larger social context. It helps future teachers understand the ideologies and values that shape and inform their teaching choices. Effective foundations experiences encourage teacher education students to consider their personal values and determine how they want to relate to others and how the educational concepts they choose reflect these perspectives.[2]

---

[2] Tozer, S., Violas, P. C., & Senese, G. (1993). *School and society: Educational practice as social expression.* New York: McGraw-Hill.

As such, educational philosophy is an essential base for future teachers. A philosophy of education allows current and future practitioners to apply systematic approaches to making decisions in schools. It also highlights larger issues in the complex relationship between schools and society.

At the same time, understanding their own educational philosophy and being able to better articulate their beliefs and values can help future educators relate to those who view the world differently. Understanding and thoughtfully speaking about the teacher's educational philosophy can help defuse tensions among those who care about improving schools but who bring different perspectives and value sets to the discussion.

When looking at educational philosophies, it is tempting to oversimplify the arguments and define clear-cut "either–or" categories. The "traditional" educational philosophy versus the "progressive" educational philosophy, for instance, pits one set of views against a different set of views. To draw either–or comparisons between educational philosophies, however, would be imprecise and incorrect. In the real world, differences exist within each category as well as between the various categories. As so often happens with ideas in the real world, the process of drawing distinctions between philosophies is not always neat and orderly.

The following pages discuss four major perspectives on educational philosophy that have influenced—and continue to influence—the way people view and practice American education. The classical and contemporary educational philosophies affect the ways people today think about schools. Understanding these educational philosophies will make prospective teachers be both more knowledgeable educational consumers and more reflective practitioners.

Traditional Philosophy of Education

The conservative traditionalists adapt educational beliefs and practices extending back to ancient Greece and the Middle Ages.[3] The **liberal arts** vision of education believes that mastering the academic disciplines—mathematics, logic, philosophy, sciences, history, literature, and the arts—characterizes the educated person. Students pursue liberal studies to develop both their moral and intellectual excellence.

Traditional educational philosophies are incorporated into two educational approaches. **Perennialists** focus on teaching what they view as universal truths through the Western civilization's classics. **Essentialists** prefer to select those subjects from the Western tradition that would be most relevant to the current student generation. Table 6.1 compares the key ideas of these two traditional approaches that continue to influence contemporary U.S. education.

Essentialists

Both conservative in tradition, essentialists and perennialists view the Western classics and Western thought as the canon in which American children should be educated. The two approaches differ, however, in how they use the classics. As pointed out in Table 6.1, perennialists think students should learn the classics as timeless truths that are able to guide contemporary reasoning and life. Essentialists, in contrast, want to select from the Western classics those most suitable to adaptability and usefulness in contemporary life. Because essentialists adapt the classic

---

[3] This chapter uses the terms "conservative," "traditional", and "traditionalist" interchangeably when referring to this educational philosophy.

Table 6.1	Key Traditional Educational Ideas: Perennialist and Essentialist		
Key Ideas		Perennialist	Essentialist
Learning is subject centered. The teacher and the text are the classroom's central focus.		X	X
Western European civilization provides the core curriculum. It carries the accumulated universal and eternal truths and virtues that all students need to develop their minds and live good lives.		X	X
Schools' purpose is to transmit and preserve this common cultural knowledge. Teachers and curriculum socialize students into society's essential dimensions of truth, beauty, values, and wisdom.		X	X
Educators select the knowledge and skills most important to help students function successfully in a particular time and society.			X
Educators work with the community to identify essential knowledge and skills.			X
Schools' purpose is to prepare students for further education and work.			X

liberal arts curriculum to meet more focused, contemporary societal demands, they are sometimes called pragmatic traditionalists. The essentialist curriculum largely underlies today's U.S. public schools' curriculum.

The Essentialist Curriculum

Over time, society has found that certain skills—such as reading, writing, mathematics, and, most recently, computer skills—are essential for people to function effectively in their world. Both perennialists and essentialists share a basic commitment to train the intellect through subject-centered knowledge. Their differences revolve around what they consider to be most worth knowing.

Essentialist thinking has its roots in the **mental discipline** learning doctrine of early American schooling, which suggested that studying certain rigorous academic subjects strengthens the student's mind and character. According to the essentialist perspective, schools' focus should be very subject centered, academic, and mentalistic. Curriculum is a logically organized sequence of separate academic disciplines, such as one would see in a high school or college course handbook. Students experience highly structured study in language and grammar, mathematics, sciences, history, and foreign languages. The subject matter lays the intellectual foundation necessary for students to understand their society's shared common culture.

Essentialists believe that every student needs this general education to succeed in life in our democratic society. To deny this line of study to any student, essentialists argue, would be inequitable, regardless of that student's ability, interest, or career direction. The subject matter itself is the important variable, just as it would be for a perennialist.

At the height of essentialism's popularity, essentialist concerns were more nationalistic than democratic. During the Cold War (i.e., the latter half of the twentieth century), essentialists saw their discipline-centered academic education as a shield protecting the United States against Soviet imperialistic intentions. The

| Figure 6.1 | The Essentialist Curriculum Emphasizes Subject-Centered Learning to Build Reasoning Power, Character, and a Shared Culture |

Harrison/Hulton Archive/Getty Images

Soviets' 1957 launch of the Sputnik satellite humiliated the United States, which had fully expected to be first nation into space. Americans blamed the public education system for not producing enough sufficiently talented scientists and engineers to propel the United States into outer space ahead of its then-enemy.

Educators responded by developing a more intellectually demanding curriculum. The math, sciences, and reasoning skills fostered in the essentialist curriculum, proponents claimed, would produce the scientists, engineers, and technology workers who would defend and protect the United States from outside threats. Students' intellectual training became a critical weapon of national defense. To this day, most American high schools continue to rely on an essentialist curriculum.

Essentialist Instruction

The national security panic about schools' failings led in two directions. First, students would have to study math, science, and technology in greater depth and with more application to real situations. Instructionally, this meant an increase in inquiry teaching strategies to enhance thinking, reasoning, and problem solving by schools' high achievers.

Meanwhile, critics expressed concern that average and slower-learning American students were not mastering the basics in reading, writing, math, science, and other areas. The controversial report *A Nation at Risk* (1983), for example, suggested that U.S. children lagged behind other nations' achievement level when it came to basic subjects. Public schools needed to improve their teaching and improve students' skills in these areas, the report's authors said. Wide support for the "back to basics" curriculum followed.

Instructionally, essentialists support lecture, recitation, discussion, demonstration, question and answer, and competency-based assessments to determine student mastery of subjects. Drill and practice are also commonly employed learning strategies.

Essentialist teachers use a variety of learning materials to make sure that students learn the content. Typically, students learn from listening, talking, and watching rather than from engaging in first-hand exploration of the content. They demonstrate their learning of content and skills on achievement tests. Frequently, these are standardized tests used to make local, regional, statewide, and national comparisons.

Finally, essentialist schools are strictly academic learning centers. Teachers and administrators expect students to leave their emotional or behavioral concerns behind. Nonacademic activities interfere with schools' primary purpose, so schools' aim did not include remedying these types of problems in students' lives.

The Essentialist Teacher's Role

In the essentialist classroom, teachers transmit cultural and community-valued knowledge and expect students to learn it. To be successful, teachers must know their subjects very well. They organize the curriculum into a series of topics, taught in sequence, progressing from less complex to more complex ideas and skills through successive grade levels. The teacher's role is to engage students in high-level thinking, reasoning, questioning, evaluating, and problem solving. In addition, teachers show students that clear standards and criteria exist for judging art, music, poetry, and literature; and they show students how to evaluate and assess these works.

While the essentialist classroom might be intellectually satisfying for teachers of high-achieving students, helping more slowly achieving students can be more demanding. Slower-learning students typically spend more classroom time on lecture, drill, and practice, while their faster-learning peers devote more time to analysis, evaluation, and synthesis as they use their newly learned content in problem solving.

A Contemporary Essentialist

While the mid-1950s and 1960s focused on teaching students specific academic disciplines, by the late 1980s essentialists had returned to the idea of general education as necessary for students to participate responsibly in a democracy.

Spurred to action, essentialists identified two factors that had been neglected in youths' education in the previous decades. First, schools were not effectively training students' minds. Second, students were failing to gain the cultural background knowledge—that is, the shared information and vocabulary—they needed to develop a common national identity and participate fully in their culture. E. D. Hirsch proposed a remedy for this situation: bringing the academic disciplines back to the curriculum's center.

Eric Donald Hirsch, Jr. E.D. Hirsch (born 1928) is an American educator and literary critic. In his 1996 book *The Schools We Need and Why We Don't Have Them*, Hirsch suggests that the progressive and romanticized, anti-knowledge theories of education that prevailed in America for more than 60 years were the cause of America's lackluster educational performance as well as the widening inequalities in class and race that characterize the country. Hirsch believes that schools have placed more importance on self-esteem and freedom of expression than on hard work, learning the "basics," and academic achievement.

Further, Hirsch believes that American students have not been prepared to succeed in a highly competitive, information-based economy. This is especially true for disadvantaged children whose families cannot provide the "cultural capital" that more privileged children have available when they enter school. Hirsch views this

Figure 6.2   Eric Donald (E. D.) Hirsch, Jr., Advocate of Cultural Literacy

Polly Hirsch, 2009

basic knowledge as a "civil right." A definite correlation exists, he argues, between equality of opportunity and the learning of a core curriculum. To not teach all students the high-status curriculum hurts their chances of economic, social, and cultural advancement.

Hirsch proposes a common national core-knowledge curriculum that includes the basic principles of constitutional government; important events of world history; essential elements of math, and oral and written expression; masterpieces of art and music; and stories and poems passed down through the generations. He asserts that general factual knowledge is a vital part of learning, and suggests that schools should measure this learning with high-stakes standardized tests based on specific nationwide educational standards.

Criticism of Hirsch's ideas. Hirsch's educational ideas are extremely controversial. He has been attacked as a conservative advocate for a "lily-white" curriculum, a promoter of "drill and kill" pedagogy, and a reactionary force. By emphasizing content, critics claim, Hirsch underestimates the importance of pedagogy—that is, good teaching practices. Critics claim that Hirsch views schooling as simply **transmission of meaning:** Teachers hold meaning in their heads, and their job is to transmit it in the most efficient way into students' heads. Frequently, critics add, Hirsch's approach leads to whole-class instruction, telling, and rote memorization as the most effective means for accomplishing this transmission.[4]

Although Hirsch's critics agree that targeted ("rote") practice can be a useful learning tool, they observe that students must also actively manipulate the content if they are to understand and learn it. Likewise, critics have challenged Hirsch's theories for not addressing differences in learning styles and for omitting information about minorities.

---

[4] For a sample of Hirsch criticism, see: Kohn, A. (1999). *The schools our children deserve.* Boston, MA: Houghton Mifflin; Macedo, D. (1994). *Literacies of power.* Boulder, CO: Westview Press; Provenzo, E. (2006). *Cultural literacy: A critique of Hirsch and an alternative theory.* Boulder, CO: Paradigm Press.

ESSENTIALIST'S CONCEPTUAL FEATURES SUMMARY

Ideal of learner: a rational mind developed by studying the core academic disciplines of Western thought.

Ideal of subject matter: a strictly academic and discipline-centered curriculum that strengthens students' mental powers and is selected because of its relevance for today and its respect for yesterday.

Ideal of school: a rational, organized place that transmits important cultural knowledge and skills to students.

Ideal of society: a democracy depends on a common or shared core of academic knowledge.

A CLOSER LOOK

E. D. Hirsch believes that all school children should have rigorous, demanding academic learning in a core curriculum. He wrote:

> A child's mind is hungry for knowledge, stimulation and the excitement of learning. A child's school should provide these things. But most American schools do not. From Kindergarten through high school, our public educational system is among the worst in the developed world. For over 50 years, American schools have operated on the assumption that challenging children academically is unnatural for them, that teachers do not need to know the subjects they teach, that the learning "process" should be emphasized over the facts taught. All this is tragically wrong.
>
> American schools need to be transformed, and to accomplish that, many ideas need to be repudiated. The enemy is not the teachers; it is the controlling system of ideas that currently prevents needed changes from being made . . .
>
> Americans think kids shouldn't be asked to do difficult things with their brains while they are young. "Let them play; they'll study at the university." . . .

Source: Hirsch, E. D. Jr. (1996). *The schools we need and why we don't have them.* New York: Doubleday. Retrieved November 19, 2009, from **http://mwhodges.home.att.net/tracy/tracy-hirsch.htm.**

Answer the following questions:

1. What does Hirsch mean when he writes that American schools have operated on the assumption that challenging children academically is unnatural for them? Do you agree? What examples can you cite to support your opinion?

2. What does Hirsch mean when he says the enemy is not the teachers, but rather the controlling system of ideas that currently prevents needed changes? Do you agree? What examples can you cite to support your opinion?

3. How would you have responded as a student to a classroom that used Hirsch's educational approach and curriculum?

The Progressive Philosophy of Education

While the conservative traditionalists seek to preserve and transmit a core culture through schools, the progressive educational philosophy aims to change the society and culture. By definition, it is a relatively contemporary perspective. **Progressive** is defined as moving forward, ongoing, advancing; a person who favors or strives for reform in politics, education, or other fields.[5] Likewise, **progressive education** is "a set of reformist educational philosophies and methods that emphasize individual instruction, classroom informality, and the use of group discussions, children's experiences, and laboratories as instructional techniques."[6]

The term "progressive" arose from a period (roughly 1890–1920) during which many Americans took a careful look at the political and social effects of vast concentrations of corporate power and private wealth. From the inception of their movement, progressives argued that state systems of public schooling have primarily tried to achieve cultural uniformity, not diversity. The schools' goal, they proposed was to educate critical—not dutiful—citizens. Progressivism consistently rejected the traditional teacher-centered, curriculum-centered education in favor of a student-centered approach.

Briefly put, the **progressive philosophy** views students—rather than content—as education's focus. In this perspective, education's purpose is to prepare students to be lifelong learners in an ever-changing society.

As a movement, progressive education incorporated a variety of viewpoints and practices. Educational progressives were pluralistic and often self-contradictory, yet

| Figure 6.4 | Progressive Educators Focus on Both Students and Curriculum |

Tim Pannell/Corbis Premium RF/Alamy

---

[5] Progressive. (1969). In W. Morris (Ed.), *The American heritage dictionary of the English language* (p. 1045). New York: American Heritage Publishing & Houghton Mifflin.
[6] *Britannica concise encyclopedia.* (n.d.). Retrieved November 19, 2009, from http://www.answers.com/topic/educational-progressivism.

always closely tied to broader currents of social and political progressivism.[7] In this section, we first discuss the generic progressive philosophy. Next, we review John Dewey's approach. Later, we will investigate the critical theory, a radical contemporary offshoot of progressive philosophy.

Key Ideas of Progressivism

During most of the twentieth century, progressive educators shared the belief that democracy means active participation by all citizens in social, political and economic decisions that will affect their lives (see Table 6.2). This progressive approach contrasted with the U.S. educational model that prevailed in the early 1900s, which was based in **social efficiency**—that is an emphasis on classroom control, management, obedience to authority, and a structured curriculum that focused on memorization and rote skills.

The progressive curriculum. Progressives believe that because learning is a natural response to students' curiosity and their need to solve problems, students' interests and desire to seek solutions should guide the curriculum. Accordingly, the progressive curriculum focuses on adapting the program of study to students' needs—academic, social, and physical. The formal written curriculum is interdisciplinary, as knowledge appears in the real world. The teacher, the student, and the curriculum need to work together to find the best fit to promote the most learning.

In addition, progressives believe that although the past produced great ideas and thoughts, knowledge constantly changes.[8] Given this dynamic nature, reliance on a classical Western—or any—tradition of thought would quickly lead to an outdated curriculum. Students' job is to learn how to learn so they can cope successfully with new life challenges and discover relevant truths in the present. Learning how to learn and making learning personally meaningful to students are more important than transmitting a set body of once-valued knowledge to students.

Table 6.2	Progressive Educators' Key Ideas

- **Education should be child centered.** Each individual has unique creative potentialities. Pupils should be free to develop naturally. Students' interests should guide teaching. There is some debate on the extent to which a school should encourage children to freely develop these potentialities.
- **Schools are a means of social reform and improvement.** A child-centered school is the best guarantee that the larger society will be truly devoted to human worth and excellence.
- **Education's purpose is to create engaged citizens for a democratic republic.** Schools create small communities in which students and teachers show respect for one another and work together in mutually beneficial ways.
- **Educators should respect diversity.** They should recognize each individual for his or her own abilities, interests, ideas, needs, and cultural identity as well as encourage students to be independent thinkers and creative beings.
- **Students are whole people.** Developing the whole student—physically, mentally, socially, and morally—is essential for the student's intellectual growth.
- **Teachers should motivate learning.** In this role, they should serve as guides, not taskmasters.
- **Schools and homes should cooperate to meet students' needs.**

[7] Cremin, L. A. (1961). *The transformation of the school: Progressivism in American education 1876–1957.* New York: Random House, Vintage Books.
[8] For more information on the speed of knowledge growth, see Costa, A., & Liebman, R. (1995). Process is as important as content. *Educational Leadership, 52*(6), 23–24.

Progressive instruction. Progressives believe that education's aim is to prepare students for life. For this reason, they suggest, instruction should begin with real-world objects rather than abstractions. Teachers show young children how to observe, describe, classify, assess, and eventually generalize what they see and touch. Older children's education includes the traditional curriculum but taught in an interdisciplinary fashion. Teachers help students learn appropriate moral behavior by connecting students' acts with natural consequences. Because bodily health is essential to cognitive health, teachers also encourage students in physical play and activity. In these ways, teachers provide the range of knowledge that will enable people to adapt more readily to their circumstances.[9]

Progressive teachers engage students in inquiries or investigations that the students develop themselves. Students learn from one another in cooperative learning groups. This approach fosters both intellectual and social learning. In the progressive classroom, the teacher becomes a facilitator, a resource person, and a co-inquirer. Through students' own investigations, they continuously develop new and deeper understandings. Students learn in a hands-on, interactive classroom.

The progressive teacher's role. From the beginning, progressive approaches placed high demands on teachers' knowledge, time, and ability. Teachers must know their subjects inside and out to integrate them with related disciplines and, at the same time, connect them to students' social, physical, and cultural environments. Teachers must be lifelong learners so they can continually introduce students to new scientific, technological, literary, and artistic developments to illustrate that knowledge is constantly changing. Similarly, teachers need a repertoire of effective instructional skills and an extensive array of teaching materials to accommodate students' preferred learning styles.

In addition, teachers should get to know their students very deeply as individuals and as learners, looking for opportunities to connect students to content through these learner-centered factors. Because students' needs have academic, social, and physical aspects, teachers must design learning activities to have children interact with one another around the content in cognitive, social, hands-on, and minds-on ways.

Progressive Education Critics

In the hands of first-rate instructors, progressive innovations were highly successful. In the hands of average teachers, however, they led to chaos. Done poorly, progressive education could be worse for children's learning than the formalism it sought to replace.

Some progressive advocates greatly expanded this perspective's child-centered focus. In doing so, they unwittingly turned progressive education into a gross and anti-intellectual caricature, quickly and inaccurately popularized as the child controlling the classroom. As a result, in too many classrooms, "license began to pass for liberty, planlessness for spontaneity, and chaos for education."[10] Phrases such as "whole child" and "creative self-expression" became clichés, too vague to serve as useful guides to constructive educational practice.

Critics claimed that progressive educators were trying to reengineer society along collectivist lines by eliminating competition and independent thought from schools.[11] A few even attacked progressive educators as Communists. For example, pamphlets bearing slogans such as "Progressive education increases juvenile delinquency"

---

[9] Cremin, 1961, pp. 93–94.
[10] Cremin, 1961, p. 207.
[11] Golub, A. B. (2004, August). *Into the blackboard jungle: Educational debate and cultural change in 1950s America*. Unpublished dissertation. University of Texas, Austin, TX, p. 63. Retrieved November 19, 2009, from http://www.lib.utexas.edu/etd/d/2004/goluba86500/goluba86500.pdf.

and "The commies are after your kids" appeared.[12] By the mid-1950s, the progressive movement had lost its central influence on school practice, and it eventually disintegrated as an identifiable educational movement.

Enduring Progressive Contributions

By the end of World War II, much progressive philosophy had become conventional wisdom. Education policy discussions routinely included phrases such as "recognizing individual differences," personality development," "the whole child," "social and emotional growth," "the learners' needs," "intrinsic motivation," "bridging the gap between home and school," and "teaching children, not subjects." Many aspects of progressive education had become accepted as simply good education.[13]

In the late twentieth and early twenty-first centuries, various educational groups rediscovered and revised progressive beliefs and practices to address the changing needs of schools, children, and society. Open classrooms, schools without walls, cooperative learning, multiage approaches, whole language, the social curriculum, experiential education, and numerous forms of alternative schools all have important philosophical roots in progressive education. The progressive philosophy offers hopeful alternatives to the one-size-fits-all curriculum and assessments, the mechanized school organization that characterize today's schools.

A Notable Progressive Educator

John Dewey. In the 1920s and 1930s, John Dewey (1859–1952), a philosopher and educator, became one of the key figures in the progressive education movement. Considered an American pragmatist (pragmatism was a very influential philosophy during his time), Dewey inspired but did not lead the progressive education movement. In fact, over time he became one of the movement's most vocal critics. Through his writings and laboratory work at the University of Chicago, Dewey tested and refined his ideas about how to best help students learn.

PROGRESSIVISM'S CONCEPTUAL FEATURES SUMMARY

Ideal of the learner: the student is a whole person with cognitive, emotional, social, and physical needs central to learning to use his or her mind well and interact well with others.

Ideal of the subject matter: interdisciplinary, problem focused, inquiry based in a real-life context and using real-world resources so students learn to use their minds well.

Ideal of the school: a small community that teaches the cognitive and interpersonal skills necessary for all students to live American democratic life.

Ideal of the society: a democratic society made up of caring, responsible, interacting intelligent citizens working for the common good.

---

[12] 1919. The Progressive Education Association is founded. *History of education: Selected moments of the 20th century.* Retrieved January 18, 2007, from http://www.wier.ca/~%20daniel_schugurensky/assignment1/1919pea.html.
[13] Cremin, 1961, p. 328.

A CLOSER LOOK

A. S. Neill, founder of Summerhill School in the United Kingdom, uses a romantic version of the progressive philosophy, creating a free learning and living environment for his pupils.

I would rather Summerhill produced a happy street sweeper than a neurotic prime minister. In all countries, capitalist, socialist or communist, elaborate schools are built to educate the young. But all the wonderful labs and workshops do nothing to help Jane or Peter or Ivan surmount the emotional damage and the social evils bred by the pressure on him from his parents, his schoolteachers, and the pressure of the coercive quality of our civilisation. The function of the child is to live his own life—not the life that his anxious parents think he should live, nor a life according to the purpose of the educator who thinks he knows best. All this interference and guidance on the part of adults only produces a generation of robots.

We set out to make a school in which we should allow children freedom to be themselves. In order to do this we had to renounce all discipline, all direction, all suggestion, all moral training, all religious instruction. We have been called brave, but it did not require courage. All it required was what we had—a complete belief in the child as a good, not an evil, being. Since 1921 this belief in the goodness of the child has never wavered; it rather has become a final faith.

Source: A. S. Neill's Summerhill School. Retrieved November 19, 2009, from **http://www.summerhillschool.co.uk/ pages/school_policies.html.**

Answer the following questions and explain your views:

1. What do you think our society and world would be like if schools produced large numbers of "happy street sweepers" rather than "neurotic prime ministers"?
2. How do you think schools should respond to parental and societal pressures placed on young people?
3. With which of Neill's beliefs do you agree?
4. With which of Neill's beliefs do you disagree?
5. With which students do you think Neill's school would be successful?
6. What do you think would happen if U.S. public schools followed Neill's model?

Dewey's view of education. To Dewey, education's aim was ultimately to make human beings who would live life to the fullest, continually add to the meaning of their experiences, and increase their abilities to direct their lives. Educated students had both personal initiative and adaptability, and were able to control their surroundings, rather than simply adjust to them. Likewise, Dewey saw intelligence as the purposive reorganization, through action, of actual world-based experience.[14] Dewey believed:

- **Each student is unique,** both genetically and experientially.[15] Children have cognitive, emotional, social, and physical differences and growth rates. Even when teachers present a standard curriculum using established pedagogical methods, each student will respond uniquely to the experience. Thus teaching and curriculum must be designed in ways that allow for such individual differences if all students are to learn effectively.

---

[14] Cremin, 1961, p. 123.
[15] Dewey called his educational approach "experientialist" rather than "progressive."

- **Education must serve a broader social purpose.** Education must help people become more effective members of a democratic society. Democracy, for Dewey, is more than just a form of government; it incorporates all of the associated living and shared communicated experiences. Students practice successful democratic citizenship through their classroom behaviors. Schools that place students in the center of active, meaningful, shared learning become levers of social change.

- **Teaching practices must be democratic.** Dewey argued that authoritarian schools' one-way delivery style does not provide a good model for life in democratic society. Instead, students need educational experiences that will enable them to become valued, equal, and responsible citizens.

- **Students' experiences affect their learning.** There is no one, common reality of experience for all people. Instead, each person experiences his or her own reality, depending on his or her previous experiences; these experiences, in turn, influence the individual's perceptions and actions in the present situation.

- **Curriculum includes real-world experiences.** Each school is an embryonic community, active with the various types of occupations that reflect the larger society. Through interaction, students learn the spirit of service and the capacity for self-direction. Increasing the number of student viewpoints, their number of shared interests, their freer interactions, and mutual adjustments will eventually create a more democratic society.

- **Schooling is life, not preparation for life.** Learning's outcome is behavior. Schooling is a means to improve students' thinking, skills, capacities, democratic interactions, and eventually to improve society.

- **Curriculum integrates culture and vocation.** Curriculum should be both egalitarian and democratic, always stressing use of the mind and applying learning to real-world situations.

Defining a balance. Dewey rejected the idea that traditional liberal arts curriculum was the only education students needed. He also challenged the age-old separation between culture and vocation. For centuries, "culture" and higher social standing had meant possessing certain kinds of knowledge associated with wealth, leisure, and theory—as opposed to poverty, labor, and practice. In Dewey's view, while the traditional curriculum was thoroughly useful to statesmen, professionals, and intellectuals, it was largely irrelevant for other persons. Dewey, therefore, rejected it as both exclusive and inequitable.

Dewey did not simply discard the traditional subject matter but rather sought to balance it with teaching that accounted for the principles of children's growth and development, children's needs and interests, and learning styles at different ages. Schools became "child centered" to the extent that teachers tailored the curriculum and instruction to facilitate the individual student's development. This "child-centered" curriculum considered the child's physical, intellectual, and emotional growth as these forces interacted with the curriculum. In this context, the curriculum's role was seen as developing children's own capacities and intelligence and nurturing children's own thinking rather than simply transmitting knowledge and facts. Dewey's educational vision included was "both–and," not "either–or."

When following Dewey's approach, teachers designed learning experiences for students that would provide data for students' observations, reflections, meaning creation, and learning. The resulting curriculum was both hands-on and minds-on. The younger the students, the more concrete and hands-on the curriculum. As a result, the curriculum was largely interdisciplinary, problem focused, and inquiry based, and it connected students to the real world outside the classroom.

Dewey believed in three types of subject matter:

- The active pursuit of occupations, such as carpentry, sewing, or cooking
- Studies dealing with the background of social life, such as history and geography
- Studies that provided command of the forms and methods of intellectual communication and inquiry, such as reading, grammar, and arithmetic

Generally, this curriculum moved from the concrete, which was immediately knowable by physical experience, to the social, which focused on a more abstract knowing, to intellectual abstraction and reasoning.

The importance of teaching and learning. The child-centered approach contrasted in key ways with the traditional "teacher-centered" classroom. In teacher-centered classrooms, the teacher transmitted skills, facts, and values largely through lecturing and seatwork. Thus knowledge was transferred from teacher to students; it went in a one-way direction, with teachers determining the subjects, standards, and methods of teaching. Children's participation in deciding on learning processes and purposes was minimal.

By comparison, in a "child-centered" classroom, the teacher considered both the individual children's needs and the prescribed curriculum. Therefore, the teacher's role changed from transmitter of the official curriculum to facilitator of student learning. Teachers now designed and enacted ways to connect students to content through activities that made sense and had meaning to the learners. In addition, they encouraged student collaboration in real-world problem solving with learned content to build deeper understanding, analysis, synthesis, evaluation, and application of what they learned. At the same time, teachers helped students work collaboratively to increase their interpersonal skills. This knowledge and skill base, Dewey thought, would best prepare students to live responsibly in a democratic society.

Dewey believed that teachers needed thorough knowledge of two arenas: subjects and students. First, teachers needed a deep and wide knowledge of their academic disciplines. They needed to understand how to connect their subject content to the meaningful themes and related disciplines that students studied. Second, teachers needed a strong awareness of those common childhood experiences that they could use to lead children toward understandings that the knowledge represented. Making this connection successfully required teachers to know sufficient detailed information about children's physical, cognitive, psychological, and social growth and development.

Beyond the "Paradigm War." Progressive education accommodated a substantial variety of curricula and teaching approaches While many people identify John Dewey with progressive education, throughout the 1920s he became less the progressive education movement's interpreter and synthesizer and more its prime critic.

Dewey saw traditional educational philosophy and progressive education philosophy as representing two extremes in the education paradigm. The traditional philosophy encouraged a relatively structured, disciplined, ordered, didactic, teacher-directed education, whereas the progressive philosophy advanced a relatively unstructured, free, student-directed education. While each approach might have some merit, neither approach alone could be successful.

On the one hand, in Dewey's view, the traditional education brought a constructive structure and order to learning, though it lacked a holistic understanding of students. Further, the traditional approach led to design of a curriculum that was too focused on content and not enough on how teachers could help diverse students learn it. Dewey suggested that teachers must consider both the subject and the learners' needs it if they were to make a positive difference in their students' lives.

On the other hand, Dewey argued that progressive education misapplied freedom. He disapproved of completely "free, student-driven" education. He recognized that students often did not know how to structure their own learning experiences for maximum benefit. Many progressive teachers did not sufficiently direct or constrain students. All too often, they provided freedom without really knowing how or why freedom could be most useful to promote student learning. Freedom, without structure and focus, was no solution.

Dewey proposed that education move beyond this "paradigm war," and seek first to understand the nature of human experience. Learning needed structure and awareness of how children learned, both–and, not either–or. Learning should be based on a clear theory of experience, not simply teachers' or students' whims.

Discarding the traditional versus progressive paradigm, Dewey suggested that American education follow a middle ground. According to him, teachers need content knowledge along with strong attention to students' subjective experiences, present and past. With these factors in mind, educators can design an effective sequence of learning experiences that will allow their students to learn to their full potential. Education needs some systematic organization of activities and subject matter for students to become thinking and knowledgeable individuals. Individuality, Dewey argued, is continuously attained and is not something given all at once and ready made. Furthermore, education becomes scientific, Dewey observed, only as teachers attempt to be more intelligent about their goals and practices used to achieve these ends.

In Dewey's synthesis view, schooling's goal was an educated person, able to reason effectively, act creatively, behave responsibly within a democratic society, adapt when necessary, initiate and control when possible, and continue lifelong learning.

Reconciling Traditional and Progressive Viewpoints

The pendulum has continued to swing between traditional and progressive educational approaches for more than 100 years. One approach takes hold, influences school programs, and inevitably has some glaring failings in its outlook and implementation. Then, its opponents reject the approach and substitute its opposite. A while later, the cycle repeats itself, exasperating educators, policy makers, teachers, students, and parents.

Good intentions are one of the teaching profession's strengths. Both traditionalists and progressives continue to offer educational theories based on sincere positive aims. Both viewpoints have cadres of dedicated and enthusiastic supporters. Yet, no evidence exists that good intentions increase learning beyond a basic level.

Clearly frustrated by the tug of war over American educational philosophy, Stanley Pogrow, Education Professor at San Francisco State University, writes, "Pure traditionalists are brain dead. Pure progressives live in a fairy-tale land. And while good intentions are better than bad intentions, relying primarily on their power is not effective."[16] Likewise, as the late-writer Michael Crichton, author of *State of Fear* has observed, the combination of good intentions and bad information is "a prescription for disaster."[17]

In reality, both traditional and progressive approaches have strengths and weaknesses. Each philosophy supplies an important piece of the puzzle in our quest to create better schools. Although these two educational philosophies appear at loggerheads, they are, in fact, complementary. "They are intertwined taproots of our professional outlook, the warp and woof of the fabric of beliefs that guide us when

---

[16] Pogrow, S. (2006, October). The Bermuda Triangle of American education: Pure traditionalism, pure progressivism, and good intentions. *Phi Delta Kappan, 88*(2), 142.
[17] Crichton, M. (2004). *State of fear*. New York: Avon Books, p. 531.

we walk into a classroom."[18] In their extreme versions, however, neither approach works. In their reasonable versions, one approach will not work without the other.

The problem comes when influential groups seeking to establish their philosophical dominance take their ideas to illogical extremes. Educators and policy makers all too often use exaggerated rhetoric as a means to capture the most followers. As Dewey and others observed, extremist traditional and progressive positions are mistaken on how teaching and learning occur for most students. The vast majority of students do not function or learn best in a purely structured or purely unstructured approach. Meanwhile, the current research cannot smooth out the pendulums' oscillations.

Here are each view's enduring and valid insights:[19]

Traditionalists:

- **Teach students what is of deepest value.** Choose texts that will pass along to young people the best of the world's thoughts and words with the power to help students understand truth, beauty, goodness, meaning, and pleasure. Choose content that will lift students beyond themselves, thereby creating a sensibility and vision of a thoughtful and well-lived life.

- **Teach with rigor.** Tactfully insist that students and teachers express their thoughts clearly to better express ideas and open minds.

- **Uphold standards of excellence.** Hold students' work to high standards to promote real achievement.

- **Use instructional time in meaningful ways.** Lecture is not inherently "bad" and cooperative learning is not inherently "good." In the time available, identify and use the pedagogical pathways most likely to lead all students to the most learning.

- **Acknowledge that discipline-based knowledge is the firm foundation for any transdisciplinary learning.** It is a necessary but not a sufficient condition for learning. Subject disciplines provide important intrinsic knowledge about the nature of human beings and the world as well as powerful, indispensable perspectives and tools of inquiry.

Progressives:

- **Children are whole people.** Students have intellectual and psychological characteristics that are at least as important as wise content selections. These characteristics affect how well students learn.

- **One standard does not fit all.** While standards of excellence are absolute, individual students' performance standards may differ at a particular time. We teach individual students, not categories of them.

- **A child's mind is not a receptacle.** Students need to think about what they have heard or read to create sense and meaning from it, comprehend it, and learn it. They need to be minds-on.

- **Children bring their unique beliefs and attitudes into the classroom.** Teachers must consider these existing assets as part of students' learning experiences.

- **Students find holistic knowledge more meaningful.** Teachers need to help students connect disciplinary knowledge fragments into a versatile, coherent, relevant, and harmonious set of lenses for understanding the world.

An educational philosophy that takes the best of both approaches values an active mind during the learning process. It provides a strong disciplinary focus as well as knowledge integration. It understands the values and limitations of both content

---

[18] Ackerman, D. B. (2003, January). Taproots for a new century: Tapping the best traditional and progressive education. *Phi Delta Kappan, 84*(5), 346.
[19] Ackerman, 2003, pp. 344–349.

"depth" and "coverage" and balances the necessary tradeoffs. It uses student ability grouping—and ungrouping—when appropriate to the learning tasks at hand. It evaluates students on the progress they have made toward achieving personal excellence as they grow toward meeting standards of measurable excellence.

In this way, prospective teachers can find the positive aspects in varied educational philosophies. It is not necessary to take each approach as absolute and extreme. Rather, it is important to acknowledge that each can make a positive contribution in the classroom. Although existential and critical theory approaches do not routinely appear in American public schools, they offer perspectives that can give teachers more choices about ways to make learning more attainable and meaningful for our diverse students.

The Existential Philosophy of Education

As a philosophy, existentialism represents both the desperation and the hope inherent in modern living. An **existential educational philosophy** is a viewpoint in which curriculum and instruction encourage deep personal reflection on one's identity, commitments, and choices. Its approach is cognitive, affective, and highly individual.

Existential Philosophy Beliefs

Existentialism is a relatively modern philosophy that became prominent after World War II. Its roots, however, trace back to the Bible. As a philosophy relevant to today's education, one may date its modern influences to the nineteenth-century European philosopher Soren Kierkegaard (1813–1855). More recently, philosophers advocating this approach include Martin Buber (1878–1965), Karl Jaspers (1883–1969), Jean Paul Sartre (1905–1986), and the contemporary educator, Maxine Greene.

Existentialist philosophy reacts against two factors. First, it rejects the conservative education tradition that respects only the Western classics and shows little regard for the individual. Second, it recoils from the horrors of World War II and the Holocaust as vivid examples of a world gone mad. Instead of the world's chaos, **existentialism** focuses on the existence of the individual and individual responsibility. Existentialists believe that people must create themselves by creating their own meaning and choices. The key ideas associated with this perspective appear in Table 6.3.

Table 6.3	Key Ideas of Existentialism

The world is chaotic, producing anxiety and hurt. People free themselves from this disorder through awareness and choices.

People are responsible for defining themselves through their choices. They create their own self-definition by the personal choices they make. Choosing is an act of creating personal meaning and value. The individual chooses the knowledge he or she wishes to possess.

People's most significant realities are personal and nonscientific. Although people live in a world of physical realities and have developed scientific and useful knowledge about these realities, their subjective experiences are their most meaningful to them.

Education's most important goal is to awaken human consciousness to the human condition and to the freedom to choose and create the personal self-awareness that helps make each person authentic, genuine, and unique.

Education should focus on both cognitive and affective dimensions. Both aspects are necessary for a meaningful whole.

Existentialism rejects any source of allegedly objective, authoritative truth about the world. Instead, existentialists emphasize that people are responsible for defining themselves. The only "truth" is the "truth" that the individual determines is true. To exist is to choose. The choices people make will define who they are as individuals.

According to existentialists, people have two choices. They can either define themselves or have others define them. Humans always face the threat of people, institutions, and agencies imposing an artificial truth on them and restricting their individual freedom. Existentialists believe that individuals are in a constant state of becoming, creating chaos and order, creating good and evil. Each person has the potential for loving, creating, and being an inner-directed, authentic person. An authentic person recognizes this freedom and knows that every choice is an act of personal value creation.[20] The choice is up to the individual.

Education, say existentialists, should focus on individuals' cognitive and affective needs, stressing students' individuality. It should include topics about the rational and irrational world and the anxiety that conflict generates. Through education, individuals can liberate themselves from a chaotic, absurd world. By making choices, individuals have the power to create meaning in their lives.

Existential Versus Traditional Views

Existentialists and traditionalists view the world and education very differently. Existentialists reject the traditionalists' views about the primacy of Western classics as the source of universal virtue and wisdom. To existentialists, one curriculum does not fit all. Instead, existentialists see each student as a separate individual needing a highly personalized education. Whereas conservatives see the world as stable and able to benefit from unchanging truths, existentialists see the world as indifferent to human wishes and anarchic. Individuals, however, have the responsibility to impose a meaning and order on the world. Death is the only given.

The existential curriculum. Existentialists believe that the great thinkers of the past had their own ways of considering life and the natural world. In short, they developed their own conclusions. Likewise, today's students need to find their own ways of thinking about these issues and develop their own conclusions. To this end, the existential curriculum is heavily geared toward the humanities.

The humanities provide students with vicarious experiences that will help them find and use their own creativity and self-expression. For example, rather than emphasizing historical events, existentialists focus on historical figures' actions, which serve as possible models for students' own behaviors. In deference to the humanities, the existential curriculum may de-emphasize math and the natural sciences, presumably because their subject matter would be considered "cold," "dry," "objective," and, therefore, less useful to increasing students' self-awareness.

Existential educators regard vocational education as a method of teaching students about themselves and enabling them to recognize their own potential, rather than as a means for earning a livelihood. Similarly, as part of the emphasis on teaching art, existentialism encourages individual creativity and imagination more than copying and imitating established models.

Literature, especially biography, has important meaning in an existential classroom. Drama and films also provide ample material illuminating the human condition. Because these media recreate the author's experiences, thoughts, emotions, and images around meaningful life issues, they illustrate conditions in which individuals make choices. As such, media can evoke readers' responses that increase

---

[20] Greene, M. (1978). *Landscapes of learning*. New York: Teachers College Press.

Figure 6.5	In Existentialist Classrooms, Students Learn About Choice, Meaning, and Self-Expression Through the Arts

Comstock Images/Getty Images

their levels of awareness. What is more, art, drama, and music encourage personal interaction with the content. From an early age, teachers expose students to life's problems and possibilities, humanity's horrors and accomplishments. In such contexts, students can better learn about choice and meaning.

Likewise, students must create their own means of self-expression. They must be able to freely employ artistic media to illustrate and communicate their emotions, feelings, and insights. Educational technology and use of multimedia enhance students' range of self-expression. In such classrooms, students write plays, create graphic images, produce films, and craft poems to express their own voices.

In the existentialist classroom, subject matter takes second place to helping students understand and appreciate themselves as unique individuals who accept complete responsibility for their thoughts, feelings, and actions. The existential curriculum is a means to an end, not an end in itself, as conservative educators would have it. Teachers and schools offer the topics they consider appropriate for students at each grade level to study. From these subjects, students make meaningful choices and decide what they need to study. Because every student is different, no single set of learning outcomes is appropriate for all students. Likewise, because feeling is not divorced from reason in decision making, the existentialist expects the school to educate the whole person—mental, emotional, social, and physical.

Although many existentialist educators provide some curricular structure, existentialism—more than other educational philosophies—affords students great latitude in their choice of subject matter. Students have a wide variety of curricular options from which to choose. As a result, in the existential classroom, students do many different things and study many different topics at the same time. In one classroom, several students may watch a video of Martin Luther King, Jr.'s "I Have a Dream" speech, two or three may listen on headphones to Abraham Lincoln's Gettysburg Address, several students may dissect a frog, others may read books, and a few others may draw pictures of the human skeletal system. The teacher moves from group to group, working to help advance students' understandings, furthering their investigations, and asking questions to challenge their conclusions and prompt them to refine their products.

The existential teacher's role. Existentialists believe that both teachers and students should have opportunities to ask questions, suggest answers, and participate in dialog about humanity's important issues—namely, life, love, and death. An existential teacher encourages students to philosophize, question, and discuss life's meaning. The answers to these questions are personal and subjective, of course; they are not measurable by standardized tests. The teacher uses whatever curriculum engages students in that dialog.

As a resourceful guide and facilitator, the teacher's role is to help students define their own essence by exposing them to various paths they may take in life. To do so, teachers create an environment in which students may freely choose their own preferred way. Teachers work with each student to help him or her find appropriate materials and the best study methods to address the student's interests. In this kind of classroom, the teacher is a resource—along with other students, books, great works, contemporary works, the Internet, television, newspapers, magazines, and other people.

Obviously, existential educators reject the standards movement, opposing the imposition of one common curriculum and the use of standardized testing as a way to measure meaningful academic success. They see this movement as a trend away from individuality, personal choice, and freedom, and toward conformity and loss of freedom.

Additionally, teachers in an existential classroom face demands on their own affective and cognitive dimensions. When teaching under the existential umbrella, teachers need to understand their personal lives and the meanings they have constructed from their personal experiences. Without this personal experience and introspection, they cannot help their students make sense and reasonable choices in their own lives. Teachers need to be able to take intellectual and emotional risks to open their thinking and feeling to students, to let students know them as thinking and feeling individuals. Such intimate sharing helps students become awake to the possibilities within themselves in their own worlds. In this role, teaching is intensely personal and carries significant responsibility, as the line between the teachers' personal and professional behaviors is notably more fluid than in a traditional classroom.

Existential instruction. Existential classrooms are open learning environments. Instruction is largely self-directed and self-paced, and includes a great deal of individual contact with the teacher. Existentialist methods focus on the individual. Because each student has a different learning style and different learning topic, the teacher's primary job is to discover what works for each student and then provide the student with the necessary resources to let learning happen.

Instruction is frequently informal and highly interpersonal in this kind of environment. The teacher relates to each student openly and honestly. In an intense relationship with each student, the teacher helps each pupil understand the world by posing questions, generating activities, and working together. Martin Buber, an existential philosopher, wrote about an "I–thou" approach, in which student and teacher learn cooperatively from each other in a nontraditional, nonthreatening "friendship."[21]

Maxine Greene. One influential contemporary existential educator is Maxine Greene, a professor emeritus of philosophy and education at Teachers College, Columbia University. Greene believes in the intersection of the arts with social action. Her philosophy sees education as a process of awakening diverse persons, enabling

---

[21] Buber, M. (1923/2004). *I and thou.* New York: Paulist Press.

| Figure 6.6 | Maxine Greene, a Proponent of Existential Education |

AP Photo/Kathy Willens

them to develop their talents, and work with one another. Their common goal is to bring a better and more just social order and more meaningful way of being in the world into existence.

Greene sees education's goals as helping students to realize their deep responsibility for themselves and recognize their connections to other human beings who share this world. Learning's purpose, in her view, is to nurture students' intellectual talents so they can construct a more democratic, just, and caring society. Citizens must be well informed and have the educational abilities and sensitivities needed to critically examine our world.

Further, Greene sees education that stresses self-defining, choosing, and acting upon the world as crucial, especially in a global environment. In today's hyperconnected world, finding a calm, optimistic, personal space can be difficult. Technology makes everyone's pain and society's violence visible to anyone with a TV, Internet hookup, or iPod. As a result, the current world is a challenging place to live and to teach children to have a positive outlook.

Greene has put her beliefs into action. The Maxine Greene Foundation for Social Imagination, the Arts, and Education doles out awards of as much as $10,000 to everyday educators who are capable of inventiveness and who go "beyond the standardized and ordinary."[22] The Foundation also supports artists whose works embody new social visions, and individuals who radically challenge or alter the public's imagination around social policy issues.

Greene writes, "As a teacher and teacher educator, never certain about right and wrong, I am very concerned about how we teach the young at a time when we are surrounded by obvious lies and manipulations. How can children be encouraged to discover some authentic way of being in a world that is so decayed?"[23] She sees the existential classroom as being rich in humanities and the arts, and staffed by caring, aware teachers; in these refuges from the unsafe external world, teachers help students find constructive possibilities in spite of the discouraging realities outside.

---

[22] For more information on the Maxine Greene Foundation, see http://www.maxinegreene.org/fdn_mission.htm.
[23] Greene, M. (2005, November 23). Retrieved November 20, 2009, from http://maxinegreene.blogspot.com/.

EXISTENTIALISM'S CONCEPTUAL FEATURES SUMMARY

Ideal of learner: a unique individual, who discovers his or her identity, makes choices, creates his or her own meaning, and brings order to the world's chaos.

Ideal of subject matter: the humanities bring opportunities for students to explore life's heights and depths, and to develop personal insights for future choices.

Ideal of school: schools create an environment for individuals to learn how to define self and create meaning for their life choices in a disorderly world.

Ideal of society: the world is chaotic and absurd, and individuals must decide who they are and how they wish to respond to events in their lives.

Greene's curriculum and instruction. Greene's existential curriculum is strongly rooted in the humanities. Using literature, students and teachers challenge the "taken for granted," explore the text's meaning, share insights with others, and reevaluate their thinking in light of various ideas. Likewise, Greene believes that the arts and humanities bring human life to a deeper level of experience and knowing. They break through routine and conventionalized consciousness. Art brings proof that problems have solutions, and that individuals' choices can make the world a better place. Through the arts, music, and drama, students have myriad opportunities to clarify themselves as individuals, to make choices, and to express their thoughts and feelings. Freedom does not mean absence of responsibility, however.

What is more, Greene expects teachers to create communities in their classrooms. Acting as resources, guides, and facilitators, teachers help students share experiences and reflections, seek patterns of meaning, and conduct a dialog around the arts in an effort to connect themselves to others.. Students and teachers listen carefully to one another as they try to make sense of their unique experiences. In these ways, teachers help students respect their own as well as others' individual differences. With their teachers' guidance, students feed their responses to these experiences into their intellectual and emotional quests for decency and social justice.[24]

Criticism of existential philosophy in schools. Although existentialism is a highly individualistic philosophy, it does have educational implications. Although elements of existentialism occasionally appear in public schools, this philosophy has found wider acceptance in private schools and in some alternative public schools founded in the late 1960s and early 1970s. To be effective as an educational approach, existential philosophy requires a smaller, more homogeneous school environment where students have family backgrounds rich in learning experiences before they come to school so they do not need to spend much time mastering basic skills.

The Critical Theory Philosophy of Education

Critical theory is social theory oriented toward critiquing and changing society and increasing human freedom from domination through education.

The progressive education movement led to the development of a more radical offshoot in the 1930s, known as **social reconstruction.** These progressive

---

[24] Greene, M. (n.d.). The arts and the search for social justice. Retrieved January 24, 2007, from http://www.maxinegreene.org/pdfs/socialjustice.pdf.

educators looked to schools for leadership in creating a new and more equitable society than the one that had given birth to the Great Depression. As a consequence, social reconstructionists advocated for serious societal reform. Critical theory developed from this progressive offshoot.[25]

Critical Theory

Critical theory is well known within the education mainstream, as its development revitalized the debate about democratic schooling in this country.[26] The late 1970s saw a reaction to the conservative movement of the 1950s and 1960s, which sought to strengthen public schools' liberal arts and sciences curricula. Working independently, a group of American scholars began to critique public schooling. They saw public school as an arena for ideological struggle, with a hidden curriculum and socialization for capitalistic needs that neglects issues of class, race, and gender.

Key Ideas of Critical Theory

Critical theorists reject schools' transmission of traditional mainstream culture and values as indoctrination. They see schools' traditional purpose as way for the wealthy, powerful elites to convince most people that their privileged interests are also society's interests. As a result, these culturally influential and powerful persons shape our schools by making their curriculum our "official knowledge."[27]

Critical theorists believe that students from less privileged socioeconomic backgrounds begin school with unequal opportunities. These limitations, they argue, can be removed only by changing the society's political and economic systems (Table 6.4). Critical theorists would change both schools and the society that makes and keeps people unequal.[28]

Critical theory suggests that schools can sow the seeds of societal transformation. Peter McLaren, Michael W. Apple, and Henry Giroux, for example, see schools'

Table 6.4	Critical Theory's Key Ideas[37]

Education is values based. It takes place within a particular culture. True education, rather than pursuing child development or human achievement in a vacuum, revolves around the particular culture's values.

Education involves types of imposition and indoctrination. Because education has its roots in both culture and values, the real question is not whether imposition and indoctrination will take place, but rather from which source it will come.

Education represents a political activity. It involves degrees and types of imposition and indoctrination that follow the ruling groups' and classes' wishes.

Teachers engage in political activity. This action usually occurs without conscious awareness of their work's political nature. Teachers are not teaching "truth," but rather the social elites' values. Teachers need to respond to the genuine interests of people other than the upper-middle-class and upper-class interests who use schools to keep their power by reproducing the status quo.

Teachers should work for social justice. Teachers can help students critique the status quo and unequal power relations and work for social justice in their society. Schools can transform society.

---

[25] In the United States, progressivism begat *social reconstructivism*, which begat *critical theory*.

[26] Berube, M. R. (2004). *Radical reformers: The influence of the left in American education.* Greenwich, CT: Information Age Publishing.

[27] The term "official knowledge"—the formal curriculum that the society's dominant culture transmits in schools—was coined by Michael W. Apple: Apple, M. W. (1993). *Official knowledge: Democratic education in a conservative age.* New York: Routledge.

[28] Counts, G. S. (1932). *Dare the school build a new social order?* New York: John Day, pp. 11–26.

potential as serving as a positive power for social justice.[29] As presently organized, public schools simply replicate, and thereby reinforce, the status quo, including its inequities and undemocratic practices. Sounding the call for pedagogical empowerment, these critical theorists see teachers' role as helping students make sense of and engage the world around them. When necessary, they add, teachers should help students change the world for the better. In this way, schools can become the agents that raise children to question and challenge their society's limitations and failings. When students learn how to push against the status quo's "fit," they will be well prepared to improve their communities and the nation as a whole. Thus adoption of the critical theory perspective raises educators' consciousness beyond the classroom and school yard to consider broader social and cultural concerns.

Critical theory curriculum. A curriculum based on critical theory is designed around contemporary social life rather than academic disciplines. It includes whatever will help a culture to evolve, change, and solve real problems.

A critical theory curriculum incorporates several organizing ideas. First, it views culture as a product of power relations. Next, it helps students investigate issues of inequality in their own environments and encourages them to take action against those conditions. It conceptualizes culture and identity as complex and dynamic, and it considers all cultures to be integral parts of the curriculum.

In addition, a curriculum based on critical theory organizes studies that incorporate students' backgrounds, learning styles, and experiences. It purposely uses schools as laboratories to prepare students to participate actively in a democratic society and become change agents in their culture. Finally, such a curriculum creates an environment that celebrates diversity, and it teaches students to build coalitions and develop cooperative learning strategies.[30]

To accomplish these goal, the critical theory curriculum integrates all traditional subjects into single-theme, interdisciplinary units. By interacting with this highly relevant, contemporary, and interdisciplinary curriculum, teachers can help their students understand current social problems' validity and urgency. With teachers' guidance, students decide which problems to study and which educational objectives they want to reach.

For example, a mathematics lesson on "sweatshop accounting" could help students look closely at profit distribution for shoes and clothes in different areas of the world. The class might receive sets of data to extract and analyze what the price of a brand-name shoe represents and determine the relative salaries going to the shoe-making workers, retail store owners, and marketing spokespersons.[31] A social studies class could consider the world's distribution of wealth, where cookies represent wealth and students are assigned to different continents. Some continents would receive more cookies than others, and students can eat what they have been given. When one or two students receive many cookies apiece while many students have to share only a few, the obvious unfairness becomes apparent.[32] Similarly, issues such

[29] McLaren, P. (1994). *Life in schools*. New York: Longman; McLaren, P. (2000). White terror and oppositional agency: Toward a critical multiculturalism. Apple, M. W. (1990). *Ideology and curriculum*. London: Routledge; Apple, M. W. (2000) *Official knowledge: Democratic education in a conservative age* (2nd ed.). New York: Routledge; Giroux, H. (1988). *Teachers as transformative intellectuals: Towards a critical pedagogy of learning*. Westport, CT: Bergin & Garvey; Giroux, H. (1983). *Theory and resistance: Towards a pedagogy for the opposition*. South Hadley, MA: Bergin & Garvey; Giroux, H. (2002, October). The corporate war against higher education. Retrieved November 20, 2009, from http://louisville.edu/journal/workplace/issue5p1/giroux.html.
[30] Sleeter, C. E., & Grant, C. A. (1994). Making choices for multicultural education: Five approaches to race, class, and gender (2nd ed.). New York: MacMillan.
[31] Gutstein, E., & Peterson, B. (2005). *Rethinking mathematics: Teaching social justice by the numbers*. Milwaukee, WI: Rethinking Schools. Cited in Adair, J. K. (2008, November/December). Everywhere in life there are numbers: Questions for social justice educators in mathematics and everywhere else. *Journal of Teacher Education, 59*(5), 408–415.
[32] Gutstein & Peterson, 2005.

as terrorism, violence, hunger, poverty, inequality, racism, sexism, homophobia, and homelessness might all become relevant topics for class study.

Working together, the teacher and students explore the issues at hand, suggest alternative viewpoints for fuller understanding, analyze the topic, and form conclusions. Throughout this endeavor, the teacher models the democratic process, listening carefully and respecting diverse viewpoints.

Curriculum materials may come from a variety of sources inside and outside the school. Students can learn through internships, work–study programs, and other cooperative relationships with the community and outside resources.

Critical theory instruction. Critical theorists believe that students learn through a cultural context and participation in a democratic process. Key elements of this type of learning include use of a problem-based framework and cooperative investigation. As exemplified by the "sweatshop accounting" case, students learn that history is influenced by past and present cultural and societal environments, analyze the data, and use their findings to inform their decision making. Along the way, students acquire skills and knowledge as they continually interact between their school and their community.

Similar to what happens in an existential classroom, students in a critical theory–based classroom engage in many different activities to study the agreed-upon topic. Teachers guide and facilitate them to learn how the scientific method applies not just to physics, chemistry, or biology, but to the whole of life, including students' personal and social lives.

For example, one math lesson grew out of student-raised real-life concerns about how fast the middle school was growing. The school district's lack of space forced the school to occupy the top floor of an older building with a leaky roof. The student body doubled in size, from 100 to 200 students. After the terrorist attacks on September 11, 2001, the students worried about being trapped in a fire and stampeded in an emergency. Their teacher organized them into groups and challenged them to use math to make their case for more school space. After taking measurements, comparing their school with one in a more affluent neighborhood, and collecting and analyzing data, the sixth graders compiled their findings and presented their report to the school advisory council, which reported directly to the school board.[33]

Critical theory recommends use of a variety of instructional methods, including simulations, demonstrations, group research, reports, analysis of current issues, reading, guest speakers, small-group discussion, field trips, interviews, internships, and essay writing; it also advocates students reformulating ideas and providing strategies for implementation. In addition, students can conduct Internet research, read case histories, analyze multiple aspects of the topic, formulate predictions, propose and justify revisions and solutions, and act to implement these solutions.

The critical theory teacher's role. Critical theory sees teachers as change agents and the classroom as a site for political action. Critical theorists encourage teachers to empower themselves by conducting a challenging review of their school's purpose, its curriculum content and organization, and the teaching profession's role and mission. Critical theorists recommend that teachers take responsibility for shaping their own futures and for helping students shape their own lives and the world in which they will live.

To make this happen, critical theorists believe that teachers need greater self-awareness regarding their political role in maintaining the existing political and social power structure. Teachers must understand how a society constructs knowledge from

---

[33] Gutstein & Peterson, 2005.

various positions if they are to understand how to create equitable and culturally representative teaching strategies.

In this regard, many U.S. teachers may be at a significant disadvantage. Critical theorists claim that because most prospective teachers are heterosexual white women from European American, middle-class backgrounds, they may not immediately recognize the unique ways in which their racially privileged, class-dominant, gender (either an advantage or disadvantage), and heterosexually oriented positions influence and transform their teaching. How they teach influences how their students view and experience the world—specifically, it encourages students to adopt the teacher's own perspective.[34]

The task of teacher-training programs, critical theorists argue, is to awaken prospective teachers' awareness of the same oppression that they might potentially reinforce in their classrooms.[35] This process can be very difficult, and even threatening to undergraduates who are still forming their collegiate and young adult identities. In fact, *every individuals' identity has multiple aspects that must be considered:* a person can be a son or a daughter; male or female; brother or sister; Caucasian, African American, Latino, Asian, or mixed race; thin or stout; marathon runner or couch potato. Each individual has more than one persona; reality is complex. To emphasize only one of these aspects of self, instead of recognizing and accepting them all, critical theorists claim, leads to cognitive dissonance.

Henry Giroux's critical pedagogy. Henry A. Giroux, a professor at McMaster University in Ontario, Canada, offers a clear definition of the public schools as a battleground of political ideas. With a thorough understanding of public school education from life experiences as a teacher and intellectual experiences as a scholar, Giroux developed a **critical pedagogy,** an instructional perspective whose purpose is to transform teachers, schools, and society into agents for social justice.

Giroux clearly articulates his views about critical pedagogy.

- **Struggling for democracy is both a political and educational task.** For a vibrant democratic culture to arise, education must be treated as a public good. More than a place to benefit individual students, schools are a crucial site where students gain a public voice and come to understand their own power as individual and social agents. Giroux believes that incorporating different groups' experiences and voices into the curriculum and having students reflect on these perspectives helps build a democratic community.[36]

- **Teaching is a political activity.** Teaching is not objective and value neutral. Instead, teachers are cultural producers who are deeply implicated in public issues. Public schools' purpose is to indoctrinate students into preserving the society and political power structure as they are.[37] Therefore, teachers are transformative intellectuals, helping students identify where their society's power is located and how the power structure communicates its ideology and values. Educators should teach "students how to think in ways that cultivate the capacity for judgment essential for the exercise of power and responsibility by a democratic citizenry," expanding the possibilities of a radical democratic society and social transformation.[38]

---

[34] Martin, R. J., & Koppelman, K. (1991, Spring) The impact of a human relations/multicultural education course on the attitudes of prospective teachers. *Journal of Intergroup Relations, 43*(1), 16–27.
[35] Martin, R. J., & Van Gunten, D. M. (2002). Reflected identities: Applying positionality and multicultural and social reconstructionism in teacher education. *Journal of Teacher Education, 53*(1), 44–54.
[36] Giroux, 2002.
[37] Giroux sees the traditional "Americanization" of diverse students into a common American democratic culture, which has been the guiding purpose of American public schools since the eighteenth century, as indoctrination.
[38] Giroux, H. (n.d.). Doing cultural studies: Youth and the challenge of pedagogy. Retrieved November 20, 2009, from http://www.gseis.ucla.edu/courses/ed253a/Giroux/Giroux1.html.

- **Ethics is a central concern of critical pedagogy.** Education is more than just "economic capital" necessary to get a job. Education should be about self-definition, social responsibility, and individuals' capacities to expand the range of freedom, justice, and democratic practices. Knowledge has ethical value. Without an ethical perspective, students cannot see a society's ideology as being deeply implicated in individuals' struggles for identity, culture, power, and history. Nor can knowledge without ethics help teachers and students push against the oppressive boundaries of gender, class, race, and age domination. Education is a moral and political practice with serious implications for individual and social change.[39]

- **The curriculum should include diverse student voices.** The curriculum should expand beyond the Western European tradition. In 1940, 70 percent of new U.S. immigrants came from Europe. In 1992, by comparison, only 15 percent came from Europe, while 44 percent came from Latin America and 37 percent came from Asia.[40] The "melting pot" metaphor, in which schools "Americanize" all newcomers to accept traditional Western thought and values, no longer works for such a diverse population with multiple narratives, cultural myths, and beliefs. Schools need adopt a multicultural curriculum to accommodate their more diverse populations.

- **Critical pedagogy should be politically transformative.** Knowledge is not just to *learn*; it is to *use* to make the world better and more democratic. Students need to understand how the curriculum presents different viewpoints, voices, and identities; how these relate to historical and social forces; and how they can be used as the basis for change. In addition, teachers and students need to critically address issues related to life in a vastly more globalized, high-tech, and racially diverse world than has existed at any other time in history.[41]

- **An interdisciplinary curriculum permits students to consider important social issues.**[42] While the traditional curriculum does contain some content useful for the critical theory classroom, the curriculum best suited to developing critical reflection among students and the community is interdisciplinary in scope and recognizes that knowledge is partisan and culturally determined. It should examine the hidden examples of power in everyday life.[43] Although this sounds inconsistent with previous writings, Giroux believes that reading the liberal curriculum as popular culture rather than viewing it as an immutable canon or great narrative could be useful.

Finally, Giroux says public schools need to rethink their purpose. Educators should abandon the long-held assumption that school credentials provide the best route to economic security and class mobility. In his view, the U.S. economy has experienced long-term stagnation, with real incomes declining for low- and middle-income groups. Given this reality, schools should reexamine their mission. Instead of training students for specific labor tasks, they should facilitate students in thinking differently about the meaning for work and prepare them to demonstrate the skills and attitudes necessary to hold multiple jobs over the course of a career. Achieving this goal will require a curriculum characterized by new forms of literacy, vastly expanded understanding of how power works within a culture, and an appreciation for how the mass media play a decisive role in constructing multiple and diverse social identities.[44]

---

[39] Giroux, 2002.
[40] Giroux, H. A. (1994, Fall). Slacking off: Border youth and postmodern education. Retrieved November 20, 2009, from http://www.gseis.ucla.edu/courses/ed253a/Giroux/Giroux5.html.
[41] Giroux, "Doing cultural studies."
[42] Giroux, "Doing cultural studies."
[43] Aronowitz, S., & Giroux, H. (1985). *Education under siege. Critical studies in education and culture.* South Hadley, MA: Bergin and Garvey Publishers.
[44] Giroux, 1994.

CRITICAL THEORY'S CONCEPTUAL FEATURES SUMMARY

Ideal of learner: a liberated individual seeking genuine meaning and identity in a diverse and complex world

Ideal of subject matter: knowledge understood in relation to its connection to the society's dominant ideology and power structure.

Ideal of school: an agency of societal transformation to provide more economic and political equality in a democratic society.

Ideal of society: individuals and groups finding identity, understanding, and meaning in an unjust society.

Criticism of critical theory. Like other educational viewpoints, critical theory has its opponents. First, according to many of these critics, critical theory education writers use a language that is difficult to understand, which in turn makes it difficult to clearly comprehend what they are saying and use it as an agenda for changing public schools.

Second, critical theories usually avoid using empirical research methods to study schools. As a consequence, they have much to say, but little evidence to back it up. Finally, critical theories of education often fail to connect theory to practice in ways that practitioners can find meaningful or useful.

Reflections on Educational Philosophies

Educational philosophies become a lens through which a teacher filters ideas about teaching, learning, and education's purpose.

Not all educational philosophies have equal respect and standing in today's public schools. Any philosophy may have some merit. If taken to illogical extremes, however, no educational philosophy can support all students' learning. In addition, philosophies that seek to overturn the prevailing culture are not well received by those who stand to lose their influence and social or political power under the new schema. Where educational philosophy seeks to improve a classroom, it must offer insight into the learner, the society, and the subject matter.

Four traditions inform the educational philosophy that governs today's public schools: traditional, progressive, existential, and critical theory.

Traditional views are deeply subject centered, anchored in the psychology of mental discipline and the purpose of transmitting the Western European culture through knowledge of the time-honored academic subjects. They attempt to build a common set of understandings and loyalty among diverse students to a shared American society.

Progressives—in many varieties—focus less on the strict academic disciplines and mental exercises and rely more on the learners' needs. They seek to teach the skills, competencies, and attitudes needed to lead an intelligent life in a pluralistic democratic society. Part of this approach entails applying the scientific method to social thinking.

Existentialists stress the importance of individuals' choices in creating their identity, values, and personal meaning. The humanities and arts form the basic curriculum with this perspective. Because this approach is so highly individualized, it is not widely used in today's public schools.

Finally, critical theorists see public schooling as a political activity. By using a relevant and varied curriculum and engaging in intellectual inquiry, teachers have the power to challenge the inequitable power bases inherent in schools' structure and curriculum; give diverse students a voice; and use problem solving, intellectual growth, and social action to radically improve our society as a whole.

Activity 6.1

Educational philosophies are theoretical maps that guide opinions about schools' purpose and the nature of learning. They vary according to our beliefs, values, and circumstances. How would you define education's goals?

A. Divide the class into two groups. Each group should then be assigned one of the following questions, for which they will compose will write a 25- to 100-word statement describing their answer:

1. What are the goals for U.S. public education, K–12?

2. What is an educated person?

B. Have each group present its statement to the class. Write the statements on the board so all can see and refer to them during the following discussion.

C. In their answers, to what extent did each group consider the needs of the individual, the society, the economy, and the democracy?

D. As a class, develop a consensus statement to answer each question and write it on the board.

E. Identify which aspects of the answer statements you can attribute to each of the educational philosophies considered in this chapter. Some aspects may refer to several philosophies.

F. For each answer statement, describe what the teacher's role should be.

Activity 6.2

Each educational philosophy discussed in this chapter has both merits and limitations. Let's take a closer look at each.

A. Divide the class into four groups. Each group should adopt one of the following educational philosophies:

Traditional (includes perennialist and essentialist)

Progressive

Existential

Critical theory

B. Have each group identify and illustrate in words and graphics the three to five top strengths and three greatest weaknesses they see in each approach. A weakness or strength can come from theory or from its use or misuse in actual classroom practice.

C. Have groups present their findings to the whole class.

D. As a class, discuss the positives and negatives of each educational theory.

E. Identify the commonalities you find among the various educational philosophies.

F. On the board, create a graphic illustration of a continuum. Label the far left side of the continuum as "Student"; label the far right side as "Curriculum." Decide as a group where on the continuum to locate each of the educational philosophies discussed.

Activity 6.3

Many educational philosophies differ in their views about how school should influence or change society. As a class, discuss how each approach views the relationship between school and society.

A. Draw a continuum on the board. Label the left end as "Focus on individual"; label the right end as "Preserve and transmit society's values and culture." Decide where to place each educational philosophy along this continuum and mark them accordingly on the board.

B. Discuss the decisions made as a class.

Activity 6.4

Clarify your own "philosophy of education" by considering your own K–12 educational experiences.

A. Which aspects of your school experiences can you attribute to each of the educational philosophies discussed?

B. Give examples of curriculum, teacher behaviors, classroom activities, pupil and teacher interactions, and your feelings about school to illustrate your answer. Use the chart to help you reflect on your experiences.

C. Highlight the ideas that you strongly believe from each of the four traditions and that may become part of your own "philosophy of education."

Philosophy of Education	Key Ideas and Practices
Traditional	Subjects are the center of learning. Western European civilization is the core curriculum. Schools' purpose is to transmit and preserve the common cultural knowledge. Teacher-centered classrooms use lectures and interactive approaches.
Progressive	Interdisciplinary curriculum using real-world problem solving. Educate the whole child—physical, intellectual, and emotional aspects. Schools' purpose is to create engaged citizens in a democratic community that respects diversity. Schools are means of social reform and improvement. Students learn through hands-on and minds-on experiences where they use what they learn.
Existential	The world is chaotic. People create meaning and take responsibility for defining themselves through their choices. People's subjective experiences are what is most important to them. Education should focus on the cognitive and affective dimensions found in the humanities and the fine arts.
Critical theory	Education is based on culture and values (rejects Western European classics as the core curriculum because they typically ignore gender and racial/ethnic issues). Curriculum should be designed around contemporary social life rather than academic disciplines. Teachers are potential change agents and classrooms are sites for political action. Teachers should foster critical reflection, awaken students' intellectual capacities, promote reflective action, and make a more democratic and socially just society.

Activity 6.5

Design and articulate your own philosophy of education.

A. Many interviews with principals for teaching positions ask for your "philosophy of education." As a future teacher, which components of the educational philosophies discussed in this chapter would you include?

B. Which aspects would you definitely leave out? Why?

C. Role-play an interview with a principal in which you have to speak about your philosophy of education. You can prepare and use a single note card or piece of notebook paper to help you. After the interview, ask for feedback from your interviewer, classmates, and professor about which aspects of your answer are strong and believable and which aspects need more thought.

Summary

Teaching is a value-laden enterprise, and it is always influenced by the myriad beliefs available in a multicultural democracy. An educational philosophy is a theoretical map that guides opinions about schools' purpose and the nature of learning. It also guides teachers as they seek to implement these purposes in the classroom. Many different viewpoints about education's purposes and practices exist.

People live in a social context that is characterized by common norms, beliefs, and practices about how to think and how to act. Individuals may accept their culture's norms, accept some and reject others, or reject them all. Philosophy and ideology help people make sense of their surroundings, provide a moral and ethical compass, and strongly shape individuals' identities and behaviors.

Traditional educational philosophy has two perspectives: perennialists and essentialists. Perennialists believe that education should teach the enduring, universal truths evidenced in Western European civilization's "classics." With this perspective, learning is subject centered, and the teacher and the text are the classroom's central focus. Schools' purpose is to transmit and preserve the common cultural knowledge and socialize students into society's ideas of truth, beauty, values, and wisdom.

In contrast, essentialists want to select from the Western classics those most adaptable and useful in contemporary life. Like perennialists, essentialists believe that learning is subject centered, and they also place the teacher and the text at the center of the classroom's focus. Schools' purpose is to transmit and preserve this common cultural knowledge. Unlike perennialists, however, essentialist educators work with the community to select the knowledge and skills deemed necessary for students to function successfully in a particular time and society. Ultimately, schools function to prepare students for further education and work. E. D. Hirsch is a contemporary essentialist.

While conservative traditionalists seek to preserve and transmit a core culture through schools, advocates of the progressive philosophy aim to change the larger society and culture. Progressive educators reject the traditional teacher-centered, curriculum-centered education in favor of a student-centered approach. In this perspective, education's purpose is to prepare students to be lifelong learners in an ever-changing society.

Generally, progressive educators believe that education should be child centered. The development of students' physical, mental, social, and moral aspects is seen as contributing to their intellectual growth. Students' needs and interests should guide teaching. In addition, schools serve as a means of social reform and improvement. Education's purpose is to create engaged citizens for a democratic republic. Schools create small communities in which students and teachers respect one another and work together in mutually beneficial ways. In these classrooms, teachers motivate learning and serve as guides, not taskmasters. Finally, schools and homes cooperate to meet students' needs. John Dewey was an influential educator who argued in favor of this perspective.

Some progressive educators misapplied progressive philosophy, expanding its child-centered approach too far. In doing so, they turned what should have been deliberately designed flexibility into planlessness and chaos. To many onlookers, this caricature of progressive education became what they mistakenly considered as the sum total of the progressive approach.

An existential educational philosophy encourages deep personal reflection on one's identity, commitments, and choices. Education's most important goals are to awaken human consciousness to the human condition and to the freedom to choose. This means educating both cognitive and affective dimensions. It is the teacher's job to discover what works for each student and then to provide the student with the necessary resources to let learning happen. In this type of classroom, instruction is frequently informal and is typically highly interpersonal. Maxine Greene is an influential existential scholar.

Critical theorists believe that education is culture-based and value-based, and indoctrinates students to accept their culture's norms, beliefs, and power structure. They see public schools as arenas for ideological struggle, with a hidden curriculum that socializes students for capitalistic needs while neglecting issues of class, race, and gender. Accordingly, they view schools and teachers as being engaged in political activity. As public intellectuals, teachers need to respond to the genuine interests of the people other than the upper-middle-class and upper-class interests who use schools to keep their power by reproducing the status quo. Henry Giroux is a critical theorist who writes about how to teach with this philosophy.

Because educational philosophies create educational viewpoints, having one's own philosophy of education can inform one's decisions about teaching and learning.

Conclusions

- All of the educational philosophies discussed in this chapter have both strengths and weaknesses.
- When considered deeply, these philosophies can be seen as complementary, with each serving as an important piece of the puzzle for creating better schools and a more equitable culture.
- Taken to its illogical extremes, any approach becomes ineffective as a guide to increase student learning and create educated persons, responsible citizens, and a more democratic society.
- The educational philosophy teachers develop will guide their beliefs and classroom practices.

Chapter 7

The Purposes and Promises of Public Education

For more than 300 years, Americans have expected much from our schools. Starting with narrowly academic and religious goals in the seventeenth century, we added vocational and social goals in the eighteenth and nineteenth centuries. Personal or self-realization goals entered the picture in the twentieth century. "These goals now encompass such a wide range of knowledge, skills, and values along with a kaleidoscopic array of scientific, humanistic, and aesthetic sources of human enlightenment."[1] It seems as if public education is trying to do it all.

With so many purposes and goals, it is understandable that we would occasionally disagree about which are more important and how well our schools are accomplishing them. Some critics, however, are very impatient. "We can all agree," recently wrote a contributing editor for *The Weekly Standard*, "that American public schools are a joke."[2]

It is difficult not to feel defensive or outraged when reading such an overstatement. Certainly, schools are not accomplishing everything our society expects them to do. While most communities remain proud of their local schools, some people consider schools in general as failing to fulfill their mission. Relentless attacks on public schools since at least Sputnik's launch in 1957—along with disillusionment with public institutions and public life born of high-profile government scandals and bureaucratic inefficiency—have made people question all public institutions.

"In the midst of the culture wars that swirl around schools; the fractious, intractable school politics; the conservative assault on public institutions; and the testing, testing, testing—in the midst of all this, it is easy to lose sight of the broader purpose and grand vision of the common public school."[3] It is also easy to lose sight of the value of respectful dialog.

As citizens in a democratic republic, it is our responsibility to continually assess how well our public institutions are performing. We need to repeatedly review their purposes and gauge the extent to which they are fulfilling their promises. At times, we need to revise the purposes we as a society decide upon in response to our changing world. To do this is natural—and does not imply failure. Rhetorical overkill like the *Weekly Standard*'s unequivocal statement, however, is so broad and inflammatory that it makes thoughtful analysis and reflection more difficult. Only when we can listen thoughtfully and respectfully to those with whom we disagree can we avoid the false choices and find better, more meaningful solutions for our national community.

What are public education's purposes? Short answer: to equip all children with the intellectual, cultural, and interpersonal knowledge and skills that will enable them to become self-directed, employable, and contributing citizens.

What are public education's promises? Short answer: to enable all students to turn its purpose into personal realities.

---

[1] Goodlad, J. I. (1979, January). Can our schools get better? *Phi Delta Kappan. 60*(5), 342.

[2] Gelernter, D. (2006, January 2). Misinformation age: More computers, less learning. *The Weekly Standard, 11*(16). Retrieved October 16, 2006, from http://www.weeklystandard.com/Utilities/printer_preview.asp?idArticle=6532&R=EDEBCB4.

[3] Rose, M. (2006, October 11). Grand visions and possible lives: Finding the public good through the details of classroom life. *Education Week, 26*(7), 32–33. Retrieved October 1, 2009, from http://www.edweek.org/ew/articles/2006/10/11/07rose.h26.html.

Education is society's best investment in itself and its future. In a democratic republic, education ideally provides a meritocracy in which individuals have equal chances to develop their abilities and advance in the society through their own talents and efforts. Education has social, political, economic, and personal purposes. Having an education not only improves the individual's quality of life, but also enhances the community's quality of life.

Education can also become an agent for societal improvement. Advocates on both the political left and the political right criticize public education according to their own agendas. Critics on the left see education as falling short of the goal of making our society fair and just for all those persons who are now marginalized and disadvantaged. Critics on the right see education as too secular and fostering a society without morals, respect for authority, or tradition. Considering these and other perspectives about public school's purposes and promises will help us clarify what we want our schools to accomplish—so we can hold them accountable for meeting these aims.

Focus Questions

- What are the purposes of public education?
- What are the major goals of American education?
- What are the *America 2000* goals?
- What are the 12 major comprehensive goals for U.S. public schools?
- How can one define education's intellectual, political, personal, social, and economic goals?
- How is reconciling competing goals for education difficult?
- How do conservative, liberal, and critical theorists view education's goals? What valuable contribution does each perspective make?
- How is education is an investment in human capital?
- In what ways is education still the key to achieving the American Dream (i.e., the dream of upward social mobility and economic opportunity)?

The Purposes of Public Education

Education exists to serve society by socializing each generation in the knowledge and skills required for mature citizenship and economic participation in that society. In a diverse society, however, finding a common set of values and purposes for schools to address presents many challenges.

Defining a Set of Common Values

American public schools have many responsibilities. Their historical mandate requires that they offer learning experiences that contribute to students' intellectual, academic, personal, social, and vocational growth. Students clearly need the skills and habits that will make them productive employees. In fact, society has charged schools with remedying virtually every societal ill, while simultaneously providing students with the intellectual and creative capacities they need to lead and defend our nation.

The idea of education to serve the social order has been handed down through many generations. In Plato's time, the idea of a good society implied a set of educational policies and practices that would support the public's highest ideals. In those days, societies could only exist through the conscious, deliberate socialization process, established on a community-by-community basis.

In the early United States, the idea of common public school became popular. American intellectuals like Thomas Jefferson advanced the widespread availability of public schooling as essential to an enlightened citizenry. Democracy could not exist, he avowed, unless future generations had the knowledge, skills, and ethical beliefs needed to support this form of self-government. Thus mass public schooling was viewed as a way to continue our form of government and culture.

This notion extended into the nineteenth century when Horace Mann, as Massachusetts Superintendent of Schools, used his position to require public school attendance through the elementary grades. Mann envisioned public schools as teaching common political values, with the ultimate aim to maintain public order. Other thinkers agreed with him, framing education's purposes even more broadly.

Defining a shared set of political values has become more difficult in more recent times. Since the nineteenth century, community debates over what schools should teach have shaken the schoolhouse. During the late twentieth century, conservative political groups pressured public schools not to teach what they considered to be "left-wing ideas." On the other side, liberal organizations and labor unions pressed the schools to teach their type of political ideology. The range of educational alternatives now available—including private schools, home schooling, and parochial schools—means that a community's children do not all attend a common school. Economically, ethnically, and racially segregated neighborhoods also keep children from sharing universal educational experiences.

Nevertheless, in spite these societal realities and so that the United States can survive as a democratic republic, we all must live together in an economically viable, law-abiding, patriotic, fair, and civil society. Public schools' purpose, then, is to attempt to create a more democratic, integrated society in what is arguably a less than a perfect world.

Defining Schools' Purposes

Societies always make ongoing distinctions between what schooling's purposes are and what they ought to be. For example, many believe that schooling should educate citizens to fit into the existing society. Others believe that schools should educate citizens to improve—not reproduce—the society. Different educational visions mean different ideas of what makes a "good society," and varying social visions influence what makes a "good education."

Schools' **intellectual purposes** are to teach basic cognitive skills such as reading, writing, and mathematics. Schools are charged with transmitting the culture's knowledge and values through reading and discussing the society's literature, history, sciences, and other disciplines. Schools also address intellectual purposes when they teach students to use higher-order thinking and reasoning by using analysis, synthesis, and evaluation to manipulate and use information to solve problems.

Similarly, schools' **political purposes** are to instill allegiance to the existing political order. Schools are supposed to encourage patriotism and responsible public behaviors. They are tasked with preparing children to become citizens who will participate in our civil processes by obeying the laws, paying taxes, and voting for persons to represent them in the state and national government. In schools, our young citizens learn how to appropriately express their views about important issues of the day. Likewise, schools help assimilate different cultural groups into a shared political society with unifying traditions and values.

Figure 7.1	Schools' Political Purposes Encourage Patriotism and Responsible Public Behaviors

Fred Prouser/Reuters/Landov

Many believe that schools' **social purposes** include helping prevent or solve societal problems. Schools work as one of many institutions—which also include the family and religious organizations, among others—to socialize children into society's various roles, behaviors, and values. By bringing the community's children together in a common facility to pursue a common endeavor, schools teach students how to respect and work effectively with people from other backgrounds or traditions. This **socialization process**—developing in its members a shared culture, behaviors, values, and loyalty—is essential to any society's stability.

Finally, schools' **economic purposes** are to prepare students for their later occupational roles and to select, train, and distribute individuals into the division of labor. The extent to which schools directly prepare students for their work varies from society to society, but most schools have at least some indirect role in this process.

Ironically, these purposes sometimes produce contradictory impulses. If schools are to increase students' intellectual ability by teaching and encouraging critical thinking, reasoning, and evaluating, they can also create students who thoughtfully challenge—rather than accept—their society's norms and rules.

As Lawrence A. Cremin, an education historian, noted: [4]

Schooling, like education in general, never liberates without at the same time limiting. It never empowers without at the same time constraining. It never frees without at the same time socializing. The question is not whether one or the other is occurring in isolation but what the balance is, and to what end, and in light of what alternatives.

The natural tension between schooling's role in maintaining the status quo and its potential to bring about change lies at the heart of differing views of education and schooling. Those who support society tend to stress school's role in preserving it. Those who believe that society needs improvement stress schools' role in either

---

[4] Cremin, L. A. (1977). *Traditions of American education*. New York: Basic Books, p. 37.

improving or transforming it. In this chapter, you will read about how different political perspectives on education view its purpose and goals.

Major Goals of American Education

Today, American schools' basic governance is decentralized, with most power wielded at the state level. As a result, we actually have 50 school systems, one for each state. All regulate themselves in slightly different ways. Given this context and America's wide diversity, any effort to advance a single set of educational goals for American schools is likely to promote disagreement and debate.

National Goals in a Decentralized Education System

Communications and travel improvements over the years have allowed some nationalizing influences to affect schools in similar ways. In addition, federal legislation and designated funding have encouraged certain school reforms. The national popularity of certain exams and textbooks in the school curriculum has also contributed to a degree of consistency among schools. To an extent, national schooling exists—if we all believe that public education is an agency of democracy and our country's chief engine for societal improvement.

In our decentralized school governance system, the challenge is to provide a set of national educational goals for schools that gives guidance and direction, without giving requirements or prescriptions. The national goals have to be general enough to mean different things to different people. To gain widespread acceptance, these goals must leave room for interpretation and adaptation according to the state and local circumstances. At the same time, they must be clear enough to give a shared sense of national purpose and identity.

When we talk about **educational purposes,** we refer to goals and objectives. Both terms describe a direction—what we are seeking to accomplish. Many educators use the terms **goals** to refer to broad directions, whereas **objectives** are more specific. Many educators refer to these as the "ends" of education.

Goals for U.S. Education

All education endpoints reflect two major influences—current social forces and prevailing educational philosophies or theories. Social forces and philosophies interact to shape the goals which are adapted at the national or state levels. These goals, in turn, affect the more specific school and classroom goals and objectives. As time passes, changes in society, knowledge, and beliefs about the nature of learning may produce changes in educational theories and purposes.

U.S. Department of Education's *America 2000* Goals

The U.S. Department of Education continues to monitor the nation's progress on a set of national education goals adopted in 1990, which provide national-scale benchmarks for performance and progress. Originally published in a report, *America 2000: An American Educational Strategy,*[5] these goals are now well established. Even though we are now living in the twenty-first century, these ambitious educational targets are still used to judge our national, state, and local school performance because they have yet to be fully met.

---

[5] U.S. Department of Education, (1990). *America 2000*. Washington, DC: U.S. Government Printing Office. Retrieved October 1, 2009, from http://www.answers.com/topic/department-of-education. These goals refer to national goals that public schools were to have reached by the year 2000.

The *America 2000* goals are as follows:

1. All children will start school ready to learn, with their preparation being ensured by participating in preschool programs.

2. The national high school graduation rate will increase to at least 90 percent.

3. All students will leave grades 4, 8, and 12 having demonstrated competency in English, mathematics, science, foreign languages, civics and government, economics, art, history, and geography.

4. Teachers will have opportunities to acquire the knowledge and skills needed for preparing students for the twenty-first century.

5. U.S. students will be first in the world in mathematics and science achievement.

6. Every American adult will be literate and will possess the knowledge and skills necessary to compete in a global economy.

7. Every school will be free of drugs, violence, and the unauthorized presence of firearms and alcohol.

8. Every school will promote partnerships to increase parental involvement in the social, emotional, and academic growth of children.

To assess how well U.S. schools are meeting these goals, the National Center for Education Statistics (NCES) has developed a set of performance benchmarks. This organization collects data on an ongoing basis to allow states and policy makers to determine how well schools are meeting these goals.

Comprehensive Education Goals

Comprehensive goals of education still exist. While studying school goals in 1979, John Goodlad, a noted education professor, researcher, and writer, reviewed lists of desired outcomes published by local school boards across the country. From these, Goodlad identified a cluster of 12 major American schools' goals that reflect a complete, humanistic perspective about what communities wanted their schools to accomplish and gave each a rationale.[6] These American public schools' purposes remain valid today:

1. **Mastery of basic skills or fundamental processes.** In our technological civilization, an individual's ability to participate in society's activities depends on mastering these fundamental processes.

2. **Career or vocational education.** An individual's satisfaction in life will be significantly related to satisfaction with her or his job. Intelligent career decisions will require knowledge of personal aptitudes and interests in relation to career possibilities.

3. **Intellectual development.** As civilization has become more complex, people have had to rely more heavily on their cognitive abilities. Full intellectual development of each member of society is necessary.

4. **Enculturation.** Studies that illuminate our relationship with the past yield insights into our society and its values; moreover, these strengthen an individual's sense of belonging, identity, and direction for his or her own life.

5. **Interpersonal relations.** Schools should help every child understand, appreciate, and value persons belonging to social, cultural, and ethnic groups different from his or her own.

6. **Autonomy.** Schools must produce self-directed citizens, or else they have failed both society and the individual. As society becomes more complex, demands on individuals increase. Schools help prepare children for a rapidly changing

---

[6] Adapted from Goodlad, J. I. (1979). *What are schools for.* Bloomington, IN: Phi Delta Kappa Educational Foundation, pp. 44–52. Reissued in 2006 by Phi Delta Kappan International, Bloomington, IN.

world by helping them develop the capacity to adapt to new situations and assume responsibility for their own needs.

7. **Citizenship.** To counteract the present human ability to destroy humanity and the environment requires citizen involvement in this country's political and social life. A democracy can survive only through its members' participation.

8. **Creativity and aesthetic perception.** The abilities to create new and meaningful things and appreciate other people's creations are essential both for personal self-realization and for society's benefit.

9. **Self-concept.** An individual's self-concept serves as a reference point and feedback mechanism for personal goals and aspirations. The school environment can help facilitate development of a healthy self-concept.

10. **Emotional and physical well-being.** Emotional stability and physical fitness are perceived as necessary conditions for attaining other goals, and they are also worthy ends in themselves.

11. **Moral and ethical character.** Individuals need to develop the judgment that allows them to evaluate behavior as right or wrong. Schools can foster the growth of such judgment as well as a commitment to truth, moral integrity, and moral conduct.

12. **Self-realization.** Efforts to develop a better self contribute to the development of a better society.

Ideally, during the process of developing a school district's or individual school's goals, local citizens, parents, and students are invited to give meaningful input. Working as partners with professional educators who understand child development and the learning process, the community members can provide valuable perspectives on what the local schools should teach.

Whether school goals are formulated at the national, state, school district, or school level, the goals are written generally. That is, they are not directly connected

| Figure 7.2 | John Goodlad, Education Scholar, Defined Comprehensive American Education Goals |

Courtesy of John Goodlad

Activity 7.1

Schools' purpose is to contribute to students' growth in five areas—intellectual, social, political, personal, and economic growth.

A. Working in groups of four students, organize Goodlad's "12 major goals of American schools" into these five categories. Which of the five categories has the most of Goodlad's 12 goals under it? Which has the least?

B. Have each student in the group give specifics of how his or her personal K–12 educational experiences did or did not contribute to meeting each of these 12 goals. To what extent did your schools do what these goals intended them to do? What might you do now and while in college to increase your growth in domains that you identify as less well developed?

C. Compare your assignment of goals with those from the rest of the class. How are they different? How are they alike? Are there better or worse arrangements—or are there several logical ways to organize these goals? Based on which criteria can you make your decision? Discuss how school boards can use these goals to identify key purposes for their own schools.

to any particular content or subject matter; instead, they are intended to be long-lasting guides, providing direction for what the school is supposed to accomplish. Such goals are too vague for teachers and students to directly apply them in the classroom. For their part, teachers must translate these broad goals into more specific objectives—and consider the best way for students to learn them.

Personal Goals of Education

While Goodlad provides a comprehensive look at American public schools' goals, Elliot W. Eisner, Stanford University Professor of Education and Art, brings the goals down to the individual student level. Eisner sees schools' purpose as helping students to live personally satisfying and socially productive lives by fully developing their minds.

"Mind is a form of cultural achievement," says Eisner.[7] Humans are *born* with brains, but their minds are *made*. In other words, the cultures into which they are born shape their minds. For children, school is the primary culture for their mind's development. Therefore, school decisions about its priorities are fundamental decisions about the kinds of minds our children will have the opportunities to develop.

Eisner also believes that "schools are part of the furniture of our communities, historically rooted institutions that we take as much for granted as the streets upon which we walk."[8] Their aims, dominant practices, organizations, and reward systems have an extraordinary impact on how the young come to think about knowledge, how they view success, what they consider intelligent, and how they see their place in the world.

Likewise, schools are cultures for growing minds. The opportunities that schools and teaching provide influence the direction this growth takes. Both the curriculum schools teach and the time allotted for different subjects tell children what adults believe are important for them to learn. These factors also influence the kinds of mental skills children have the opportunity to acquire.[9]

---

[7] Eisner, E. W. (1992, April). The misunderstood role of the arts in human development. *Phi Delta Kappan, 73*(8), 592.
[8] Eisner, E. W. (2003, May). Questionable assumptions about schooling. *Phi Delta Kappan, 84*(9), 648–657.
[9] Eisner, 1992.

Eisner argues that an education which develops the students' minds helps them live well outside school. Education involves both cultural transmission and self-actualization.[10] Schooling's aim is not merely to enable our children to do well in school; it is also to enable our children to do well in life.[11] In this view, students' test scores are merely proxies (stand-ins) for learning; the scores themselves are not learning.

Developing the mind is related to the modes of thought that teachers enable and encourage students to use. A valuable education uses a curriculum that encompasses various ways of thinking and knowing the world, including exploration of both the arts and the sciences. The thought processes that occur in both realms can deepen and extend children's education and prepare them to live in a complex and changing world. These thought processes incorporate the rational and the affective, the planned and the serendipitous. In the last analysis, the most important curriculum is the one that will help students compete successfully in the lives they lead outside school, so students can ably and continually adapt to changing circumstances.

To allow such mental development to occur, insightful teachers understand that not all problems have a single answer, purposeful flexibility is an important learning tool, and students need opportunities for varied types of self-expression.

First, not all problems have a single answer. Solutions to problems take many forms. Whereas spelling, arithmetic, writing, and reading are taught with conventions and rules, the arts celebrate imagination, multiple perspectives, and the importance of personal interpretation. Both sets of knowing are important. Students need opportunities to see and explore the world in a variety of formats so they can think in unique ways.

Next, in a technologically-oriented world, people tend to believe that objective rationality is the shortest distance between two points. This view is illustrated by the scientific method: define, hypothesize, experiment, and evaluate. While this is a solid approach to solving certain problems, it is not the only way to understand experiences. Wise teachers realize that rationality is broader. In the arts (as in scientific research), for instance, goals need to be flexible and surprise can be valuable. Educated individuals are open to unanticipated opportunities that inevitably emerge and that increase insight. The work of art is an act of creation, an unfolding journey. Ending a learning experience too soon short-circuits the potential of greater and more personal understanding.

"While we say that the function of schooling is to prepare students for life, the problems of life tend not to have fixed, single correct answers" like the problems students find in school, Eisner remarks. The problems students find in life are much more like the problems they find in the arts[12]; they are often subtle and occasionally ambiguous. "Life outside school is hardly ever like a multiple-choice test."[13]

Effective teachers create learning experiences for students that increase their opportunities to experience the world fully and meaningfully. They make schools intellectual, rather than merely academic places. They understand that students' minds can be developed, knowledge is greater than what literal language might convey, and intelligence deepens and expresses itself in many forms. For students, education means learning how to use their minds well. This is the best preparation for life.

Human intellectual capacity is much wider than schools' traditionally narrow emphasis on reading and math achievement test scores would suggest. Reading and math are certainly essential skills, but they are not all an educated person needs to know. Schooling's purpose is to prepare students for lives in a complex and changing world. As educators and citizens, we must view education's purpose broadly and in human terms. "What's at stake is not only the quality of life our children might enjoy but also the quality of the culture that they will inhabit."[14]

---

[10] Eisner, E. W. (2001, January). What does it mean to say a school is doing well? *Phi Delta Kappan, 82*(3), 367–372.

[11] Eisner, E. W. (1999, May). The use and limits of performance assessment. *Phi Delta Kappan, 80*(9), 658–660.

[12] Eisner, 1992, p. 595.

[13] Eisner, 1992, p. 595.

[14] Eisner, 1999, p. 660.

Activity 7.2

Education leads students to more personally satisfying and socially productive lives. Elliot Eisner observes that education's goal should be for young people to do well outside school by developing and expanding their minds in a nourishing school culture.

A. As a class, describe the types of thinking, problem-solving skills, and a deep awareness and appreciation of life experiences that a successful young adult such as you will need to live a personally satisfying and socially productive life as that person deals with relationships, a career, a home, and the world at large.

B. Divide the class into three groups. One group will consider the traditional English, math, and science curriculum (those subjects traditionally covered by high-stakes achievement testing). The second group will consider the fine arts (poetry, music, visual arts, theater). The third group will consider examples that integrate traditional content subjects with fine arts. Reflecting on their experiences in high school and college, the members of each group should identify the types of thinking, problem solving, and life appreciation most developed by high school and college students studying the disciplines each group represents.

C. Have all groups report their findings back to the class.

D. Working as a class, discuss how the benefits of each approach to the curriculum can enhance college students' thinking, problem-solving skills, and deep appreciation for life experiences.

E. Discuss as a group how you as future teachers can use this awareness to increase your students' meaningful and mind-developing learning experiences in your classes.

Social Goals of Education

Schools have long had social goals. In 1900, Edward Alsworth Ross, an American sociologist, referred to education as "an economical system of police."[15] He divided social control into internal and external forms. Traditionally, he asserted, internal forms of social control centered on the family, the church or synagogue, and the community. The family and religious institution inculcated moral values and social responsibility into the child. This process ensured social stability and cohesion. In modern society, however, school has largely replaced the family and church as the community's most important institution for instilling internal values. In this sense, the school exerts external social control. "The ebb of religion is only half a fact," Ross observed. "The other half is the high tide of education. While the priest is leaving the civil service, the schoolmaster is coming in."[16]

Whether the family and religious institutions are collapsing is debatable. Yet our society often views education as assuming the responsibility for teaching moral values, thereby enacting a social role. Historically, public schools have delivered moral and social instruction in a variety of ways. Horace Mann, for example, believed schools were the key to reforming society; he assumed that properly trained youths would not want to commit criminal acts. As a consequence, required school attendance evolved as a means to reduce juvenile delinquency. Similarly, the need to keep young people off the streets was cited as a justification for starting summer

---

[15] Ross, E. A. (1900, January). Social control XIV: Education. *American Journal of Sociology, 5*(4), 483.
[16] Ross, 1900, p. 485.

schools in the late nineteenth and early twentieth centuries. More recently, schools have assumed the responsibility for reducing traffic accidents by drivers' training programs, improving family life through courses in home economics, and ending drug abuse, preventing sexually transmitted diseases, and reducing teen pregnancy through health education.[17]

Frequently, schools are asked to solve social problems by finding solutions that do not challenge economic and political interests. For instance, alcoholism might result from family stresses or other adverse conditions. For schools to solve the problem of alcoholism through health classes assumes that the problem is one of individual training, unrelated to other causes. It is easier for a community to provide and require students to take a health course than to change job conditions, improve urban environments, or send a family into counseling. Schools are less threatening than direct interventions that target businesses, unions, city government, or family privacy.

Schools are often the safest and least controversial way of planning for social improvement. Assigning these responsibilities to schools allows legislators, policy makers, and local government officials to give the appearance of doing the right thing without offending any important interests. Yet regardless of schools' good intentions, their social influence has only gone so far toward remedying society's ills.

For instance, our society has used schools to help end poverty. The relationships between schools and poverty are many and complex. Inadequate education is linked to low-income jobs, low-quality housing, poor diet, poor medical care, and high rates of school and work absenteeism. The community finds it difficult and expensive to intervene to break these interactions, even though programs such as Medicare and Medicaid, food stamps, and public housing subsidies try to make a difference. Meanwhile, schools offer Head Start and other compensatory education programs for low-income children who begin school at a disadvantage in comparison to children from middle- and high-income families. These programs' success, however, has been either limited or mixed.

In addition, not all societal groups agree on which social values schools should teach. Horace Mann argued that all religious groups could agree upon certain moral values, and these shared values would become the backbone of schools' moral teachings. Religious groups, however, disagreed with his supposition. The Catholic Church, which voiced the strongest opposition to this notion, established its own school system. More recently, the 1990s witnessed heated value conflicts about AIDS education, with those who believed in a strong moral code to control sexual behavior taking up opposition against those who believed in the right of free sexual activity between consenting adults.

Viewing American education as a cure-all for America's social ills raises questions about whose social and moral values and goals our schools should reflect. It also raises the question of whether using schools for social control is actually a way to avoid more direct and controversial approaches to solving societal problems. These questions remain unanswered. American educators, however, would prefer that schools be part of the solution.

Economic Goals of Education

Public schools also have economic goals. Economists note that schools can advance economic growth in two ways. First, they can socialize future workers for the workplace. Through their academic curriculum, attendance requirements, tardiness rules, practice in completing assigned tasks and following directions, and emphasis on obedience to authority, schools provide the preparation and training future workers need. Second, schools can increase national wealth by sorting, selecting, and training students for the labor force. Schools sort students by identifying their indi-

---

[17] Spring, J. (2002). *American education.* New York: McGraw-Hill, pp. 10–15.

vidual abilities and interests and determining the best type of education and future employment that is appropriate for each student.

Both of these goals have historical support. In the nineteenth century, schools emphasized marching, drills, and orderliness as preparation for factory work. In the twentieth and twenty-first centuries, public schools have served as a "**sorting and selecting** machine" that separates "human capital" (students) by their abilities and interests into certain curricular programs matched to appropriate future jobs. Standardized tests determine students' abilities, aptitudes, and interests, and counselors or other school officials then match these factors to the suitable school programs. When schools act as sorting machines in this way, proponents of this goal suggest, the economy will prosper and workers will be happy.

In the twenty-first century, while the "sort and select" process appears much the same as in the previous century, the economic environment into which U.S. students graduate is clearly changing. Chapter 1 discussed how American workers are now competing in a global labor market. Globalization exposes the average U.S. worker to much more competition and job insecurity. As the world becomes more interconnected, jobs become more mobile. U.S. companies seek cheaper labor in foreign countries, even for white-collar professional jobs, and American workers are forced to take reductions in benefits and wages to compete with foreign workers.

In response to this trend, policy makers and schools have called for world-class standards and raising the educational level of U.S. workers to the levels achieved in other industrialized countries (usually identified as Canada, Europe, or Japan). This move is intended to make U.S. workers more competitive in world labor markets. Having U.S. students take international achievement tests and comparing their scores with those of other industrialized nations is one way to monitor our students' performance against their international competition.

In addition, a learning society and lifelong learning are considered essential parts of global education systems. Both concepts assume a world of constant technological change that will require workers to continually update their skills. This assumption means that schools will be required to teach students how to learn, so that they can keep learning throughout their working lives.

Likewise, American society is much different today than it was 50 years ago, when a one-income household could support the American working- and middle-class family. To maintain our standard of living, members of the American working- and middle-class populace now work more than 600 hours in a year than their counterparts in the 13 industrialized nations. The United States is the only industrialized nation whose worker hours have increased since 1980.[18]

These new economic and global demands on education raise unsettling questions about treating students as human capital. Should schools emphasize a broad liberal education, or should they prepare students for a specific career? In a labor market based on educational attainment, will inequality of educational opportunity cause increased stratification between the educational haves and have-nots? Will producing many well-educated graduates lead to **educational inflation**, in which the supply of well-educated individuals increases yet employee wages and advanced degrees' value decline because so many qualified and available persons exist to fill the positions? Should economic opportunities be based on the outcomes on high-stakes tests? These are important questions on which a national consensus is lacking.

Certainly, students need to learn the intellectual tools and knowledge for making decisions about the quality of their lives. What is more, given the wide variations in school quality in the United States (in terms of cognitive readiness for school, teacher quality, class size, resources, counseling, and preparation for college admissions, for instance), if the ability to compete in the labor market depends on

---

[18] Ornstein, A. (2007). *Class counts: Education, inequality, and the shrinking middle class.* Lanham, MD: Rowman & Littlefield, p. 178.

Activity 7.3

Society has assigned schools many purposes and goals—perhaps too many for schools to do well.

A. Assign one major purpose to each group—intellectual, social, political, personal, or economic. In small groups, brainstorm all the school goals or objectives that fit into the category your group is assigned.

B. Identify and discuss the following issues:

Which goals had the most impact on you as a K–12 and college student, and how?

Which goals have had the greatest impact on who you are today?

Which goals you think are realistic and achievable? Which are beyond the school's means to achieve?

Which goals reinforce the "status quo"?

Which goals are likely to reduce the "achievement gap"?

Which goals have the potential to change the society?

Which goals have the most community support in your hometown? Which goals have the least support in your hometown?

the quality of education, then some school graduates will be more advantaged than others. Those persons with access to better schools will end up with access to better jobs. These important issues should influence our ongoing discussions about schools' economic purpose.

In the future, schools will continue to serve comprehensive, political, personal, social, and economic purposes. It remains critical for prospective and present educators, policy makers, and our society as a whole to consider these purposes, some of which are contradictory, when deciding how to move forward.

Educational Critics: Differing Views of Society

While public schools intend to transmit our best traditions and values, public schools are not static. Rather, schools reflect changes in their host society—from putting computers into every classroom to having security guards patrol the halls. What is more, the "official knowledge" included in the school curriculum is often contested—and changed. Struggles over curriculum, teaching, and policy are actually battles for power over children's thoughts and for the direction of society's future.

For all, knowledge is power. Whoever controls the knowledge—and the policies, textbooks, and lessons that contain it—holds the power. In fact, vigorous community debates over textbook adoptions illustrate cultural politics in action. They are skirmishes in the national conflict for cultural authority. The winners' views will prevail.

Debates about educational issues often focus on different ideas about what schools' goals—and what our society—should be. From our early days as a young republic through today, many different visions of U.S. education and school's role in society have been advanced. While the views are complex, it helps to simplify and frame them by using a political typology—specifically, conservative, liberal, and critical theory perspectives. The remainder of this section presents broad and general descriptions of how each viewpoint sees education.

The Conservative Perspective

The origins of the conservative perspective lie in the nineteenth-century Darwinist view that individuals and groups must compete in the social environment to survive. According to this view, human progress depends on individual initiative and effort. Conservatives also believe the capitalist free market as the economic system is most respectful of human needs. They see individuals as rational actors who can make decisions on a cost–benefit scale.[19] Finally, conservatives see social problems as stemming from individuals. They believe that people create problems by making uninformed choices; accordingly, individuals are responsible for their own well-being.

Conservatives believe that schools should provide the educational training necessary to ensure that the most talented and hard-working individuals receive the tools they need to become the most socially and economically productive. Under this approach, schools socialize children into the adult roles needed to maintain society as it is. Students learn the cultural traditions through the curriculum. Schools are essential to both economic growth and social stability. Nevertheless, individuals or groups of students rise or fall based on their own intelligence, hard work, and initiative. Achievement requires hard work and sacrifice. Schools give students the opportunity to succeed, but it is the individual's responsibility to do the work to make it happen.

Generally, conservative critics believe today's educational problems have occurred for the following reasons:

- Schools have watered down the curriculum and lowered academic standards in response to "liberal and critical theorist" demands in the 1960s and 1970s for greater equality.
- Multicultural education that responds to the needs of all groups has weakened the traditional curriculum, reducing the school's ability to pass on the American and Western civilization's heritage.
- Liberal demands for cultural relativism (the belief that every culture's values and beliefs are equally valid) are forcing schools to lose their traditional role of teaching absolute ("correct") values and moral standards.
- Schools' acceptance of individuality and freedom means the loss of traditional discipline and decline of authority.
- Schools are state-controlled public institutions, immune from laws of a competitive free market, and choked by bureaucracy and inefficiency.

Many of today's religious and social conservatives express strong views about public schools, bringing their views of faith and ethical behavior into the political arena. They criticize public schools for undermining what they see as traditional values. Further, they believe that society would be better if schools contained more religion (typically Protestantism)—or at least did not advance ideas, values, or practices that undermine it. They believe schools should return to more traditional religious values and practices as they attempt to bridge the doctrine of separation between church and state.[20]

Indeed, some conservatives no longer want to send their children to American public schools. They worry that our public schools have turned away from the country's educational foundation. It is true that today's public schools are no longer

---

[19] *Cost–benefit scale* is an economics term meaning that a person makes decisions by taking into account the relative advantages as compared to the expenses (financial, emotional, physical, social) of making a particular decision.
[20] The phrase "a wall of separation between church and state" does not appear in the U.S. Constitution. The phrase comes from a letter written by Thomas Jefferson on January 1, 1802, to the Danbury Baptist Association. For that reason we refer to that concept as a *doctrine*.

church-run small schools that teach right and wrong using the Judeo-Christian Bible as the basic text. The publication of a report called *A Nation at Risk*[21] nearly 25 years ago confirmed conservatives' deepest fears about public schools' harmful effects on their children. The report, compiled by a panel appointed by President Ronald Reagan, sharply criticized American education—and gave many conservatives a scapegoat on which to pin society's problems. Similarly, the report blamed the "rising tide of mediocrity" in schools for skyrocketing divorce rates, teenage pregnancy, and sexually transmitted diseases.

Finally, conservative educational reformers want to make the following changes to modern-day public schools:

- Return to the basics—reading, writing, math, and other traditional learning.
- Return to the traditional academic curriculum, which focuses heavily on Western civilization's history, thought, and literature.
- Make students and schools accountable for minimum performance standards at specific grade levels (i.e. fourth, eighth, and eleventh grades).
- Introduce free-market mechanisms into the education marketplace, including tuition tax credits and vouchers to support parents who wish to send their children to private schools and public school choice programs (allowing parents to send their children to the public school of their choice, regardless of where they live).

Questions of larger social and political movements cannot be divorced from educational philosophy, nor should educational philosophy and reflection on practice simply be reduced to acting according to the day's prevailing political winds. As thoughtful citizens, we need to examine these issues carefully and diligently. We must take seriously the various critics' motives and reasons, rather than replying defensively. As we have said, the problems of learning in contemporary U.S. schools actually stem from competing social visions. In a diverse society, this debate is both expected and beneficial.

The Liberal Perspective

In the twentieth century, liberal perspectives on education arose as an outgrowth of the works of U.S. philosopher and educator John Dewey and the New Deal politics of President Franklin Delano Roosevelt. While supporting the conservative view of a market capitalist economy, liberals believe that an unregulated free marked is open to abuses. It is particularly hurtful to economically and politically disadvantaged groups. Recognizing this potential for harm, society needs government involvement in economic, political, and social arenas to ensure fair treatment of all citizens and to guarantee a healthy economy. Liberals, therefore, balance economic productivity of capitalism on the one hand with individuals' social and economic needs on the other hand.

By placing a strong emphasis on equity and equality of opportunity, liberals try to minimize the differences in life outcomes between the country's richest and poorest citizens. Unlike conservatives, they believe that although individual effort is very important, it is not enough. When individual effort falls short, government must sometimes intervene on behalf of those in need. Liberals also believe that groups, rather than individuals, are affected by society. Accordingly, solutions to social problems must address group dynamics rather than individuals alone.

Liberals value schools for their ability to train and socialize students into the society, as do conservatives. Liberals, however, stress the school's role in creating equal

---

[21] National Commission on Excellence in Education. (1983). *A nation at risk.* Washington, DC: U.S. Government Printing Office.

opportunities for all students to succeed in society. They recognize America's pluralism and emphasize the schools' role in helping students thrive in a diverse society. They argue that individual students or groups of students begin school with different life advantages. Schools must be equitable to all of these children—leveling the playing field through policies and programs that give disadvantaged students a better chance to make the most of their educational opportunities. According to this perspective, education entails balancing individual and social needs in ways consistent with democracy and meritocracy. School is a means for all students to receive a fair and equal opportunity for upward mobility—economically, politically, and socially.

Liberals believe that today's educational problems exist for the following reasons:

- Schools need to even the playing field experienced by economically disadvantaged or culturally different students, as their backgrounds have limited these students' chances for a good life by allowing them to underachieve.

- Schools place too much emphasis on discipline and authority, not allowing students to develop fully as individuals.

- Academic quality and climate differences between schools serving affluent as opposed to low-socioeconomic-status students creates unequal achievement.

- The traditional curriculum leaves out the diverse cultures of groups that make up our pluralistic society. Students need to see and feel that they have value before they can learn.

The "achievement gap"—the unequal achievement shown by different student populations—greatly concerns liberals. At present, liberal critics strongly influence educational policy and practice. In particular, they have focused on the federal approaches to support disadvantaged students. For example, liberal critics voted for categorical funds, such as Title I aimed at improving education for schools with a high percentage of students living in poverty. Likewise, liberals helped write and pass the 2002 federal No Child Left Behind Act (NCLB).[22] NCLB is supposed to make sure that all students, including traditionally underperforming students

| Figure 7.3 | **Liberals Support Education Policies That Connect Equity and Excellence** |

Jani Bryson/istockphoto

---

[22] We discuss NCLB more fully in Chapters 5 and 15.

(minority, economically disadvantaged, special education, and English language learners), get the high-quality education they need.

Liberals and conservatives worked closely together to write and pass NCLB. During this process, conservatives focused on the high accountability requirements and sanctions for public schools not successfully meeting these requirements. For their part, liberals approved making the schools more accountable for assuring the high achievement of the traditionally underachieving student groups.

Liberal critics want education reforms that include the following measures:

- Policies that connect equity with excellence, making quality education a reality for all students. Treating different students the same is inherently unequal, they say.

- Policies that lead to improving failing schools, especially urban schools. Programs should include site-based management (decentralized school control), teacher empowerment (teachers have a say in the way schools run), effective schools programs (based on research about what works),[23] and public school choice programs that support public education.

- Policies that compensate high-quality teachers who work in high-challenge urban schools to create a stable culture of achievement.

- Programs that create more equal opportunity for disadvantaged students, such as Head Start,[24] Advancement via Individual Determination (AVID),[25] affirmative action, and compensatory higher education programs.[26]

- A curriculum that balances Western thought and values along with readings and history of other groups in a culturally diverse setting.

- Policies that strike a balance between setting acceptable performance standards and ensuring that all students can meet those standards (by providing needy students with additional academic supports rather than lowering standards).

Liberals are currently reaching some of their objectives with the practices that support diverse students learning to high levels. These purposes, however, are only in the process of being achieved; much remains to be done.

The Critical Theory Perspective

Critical theory is an educational philosophy that concerns itself with issues of struggle, power, culture, domination, and critical consciousness. Historically, schools transmitted a society's culture—the one usually belonging to society's dominant group. Education extends the dominant group's norms, values, and practices into the future. As a result, the culturally influential and powerful shape our schools and determine our "official knowledge."[27] Critical theorists reject this dominance by one group. They believe that students from lower socioeconomic backgrounds begin school with unequal opportunities. These limitations can be removed only by changing the society's political–economic system. Liberals would adapt school practices to increase disadvantaged students' achievement, but critical theorists would go even further: They would change both schools and the society that make and keep people unequal.

Critical theorists believe that our public schools practice a **cultural hegemony** (control by one dominant worldview) by imposing the colonial Western European settlers' traditions on today's ethnically and culturally diverse students. What is more,

---

[23] See Chapter 16, Effective Schools.
[24] Head Start is a preschool program for students from lower-socioeconomic-status backgrounds. It is intended to prepare students to be ready to learn in a formal school environment.
[25] AVID is an academic support program for middle and high school minority students that enrolls them in high-challenge academic classes while simultaneously teaching them note-taking skills and other academically essential work habits, providing tutoring, and offering positive peer pressure.
[26] Compensatory higher education programs for disadvantaged students, such Upward Bound, prepare middle school– and high school–aged minority students for college.
[27] The term "official knowledge"—the formal curriculum that the society's dominant culture transmits in schools—comes from Apple, M. W. (1993). *Official knowledge: Democratic education in a conservative age.* New York: Routledge.

according to critical theorists, the dominant class deliberately controls, shapes, and manipulates the subordinate groups' beliefs to ensure that the dominant group's views become familiar, common sense, accepted, and taken for granted. In these ways, critical theorists argue, schools perpetuate the socioeconomic conditions that keep poor people poor and ignorant.

Critical theorists believe that school and society have problems for the following reasons:

- The educational system has failed the poor, minorities, and women through continuation of classist, racist, and sexist policies and practices.

- Schools have stifled analysis, deep understanding, and criticism of American society's problems through implementation of a curriculum and teaching practices that promote conformity and docility.

- The traditional curriculum ignores cultures, genders, and races that are present in the classroom and that have contributed to society. It leaves out minority and culturally marginal voices, which disrespects diverse students.

- The educational system promotes inequality of both opportunity and results.

Critical theory developed in the United States as an offshoot of the progressive education movement.[28] Critical theorists recognize that humans are the architects of their own destinies. They urge individuals to develop a critical consciousness that can create new truths both for themselves and for society. As part of their perspective, they hold dual views of schools.

First, critical theorists believe that schools are a means to reproduce oppressive social patterns. Education favors the dominant culture's **cultural capital**— its language, values, and meanings. As such, schooling confirms, legitimizes, and reproduces the status quo. This domination does not happen through force or coercion, but rather occurs through a process of gaining the students' passive, legitimate consent. In short, through schooling's socialization, all social and economic classes learn to accept the dominant social group's beliefs, values, and practices as right and natural.

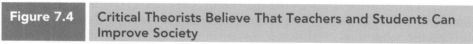

| **Figure 7.4** | **Critical Theorists Believe That Teachers and Students Can Improve Society** |

Jose Gil, 2009/Used under license from Shutterstock.com

---

[28] Critical theory is a specific type of political perspective that stands to the left of liberalism. We have used the term to stand for all similar views. This discussion of critical theory is adapted from: Abrahams, F. (2004, January). The application of critical theory to a sixth grade general music class. *Visions of Research in Music Education.* Volume 4. Retrieved October 1, 2009, from: http://www.rider.edu/~vrme/articles4/abrahams/index.htm

For example, critical theorists see school practices such as **tracking** (placing poor and minority students into a low-status, low-interest, low-ability dead-end curriculum) and assigning "special education" labels to students who cannot keep up with the traditional curriculum as grave injustices. In their view, schools are instruments of oppression, designed to keep certain groups down while lifting up others.

Similarly, critical theorists contend that a U.S. history course that reflects only the white Euro-American experience does not show respect for the contributions of other races and cultures in creating today's America. Such a course delivers an implicit message to students: This is a Caucasian society; if you are not white, you are marginal in tradition and importance. Similarly, critical theorists assert that the decision to teach literature primarily reflecting Western experience tells students that Western thought and culture are superior to any other traditions and cultures.

Differential access to knowledge and opportunities to learn, differential opportunities to think and use language, and differential access to high-quality curriculum are all part of this educational process, say critical theorists, deliberately designed to keep "less desirables" out of the cultural mainstream.

Second, and on a more positive note, critical theorists believe that schools contain the seeds of societal transformation. Henry Giroux and Peter McLaren, for example, see schools as able to exert positive power for social justice.[29] Sounding the call for pedagogical empowerment, they see teachers' role as helping students make sense of and engage the world around them and—when necessary—change the world for the better. Through this type of effort, schools can become the agents that raise children to question and challenge their society's limitations and failings. When students learn how to push against the status quo's "fit," they can improve both their community and the nation as a whole. In this way, critical theory raises our consciousness beyond the classroom and schoolyard to broader social and cultural concerns.

Critical theorists such as diverse as Jonathan Kozol and Paulo Friere agree that poverty, social class division, unequal distribution of labor, poor teacher working conditions, poor student learning conditions, and gender and race divisions are powerful but destructive realities in U.S. schools. They call on educators to resist the dominant class's cultural reproduction and instead, to develop a curriculum that provides the conditions in schools necessary to transform the institution of school as well as students' lives and the society in which they live. In other words, people are capable of creating and transforming their own culture because people are both the products and the creators of their social world.[30]

"Schools must be moral, just, and inclusive of those who most need access to the educational process that is imperative to sustaining a democratic community," says educator Louise Anderson Allen."[31] Schools can be a vehicle for social change.

---

[29] Giroux, H. (1994, Fall). Slack off: Border youth and postmodern education. Retrieved October 1, 2009, from http://www.gseis.ucla.edu/courses/ed253a/Giroux/Giroux5.html; Giroux, H. (n.d.). Doing cultural studies: Youth and the challenge of pedagogy. Retrieved October 1, 2009, from http://www.gseis.ucla.edu/courses/ed253a/Giroux/Giroux1.html; McLaren, P. (1994). *Life in schools.* New York: Longman; McLaren, P. (2000). White terror and oppositional agency: Toward a critical multiculturalism. In E. Duarte & S. Smith (Eds.). *Foundational perspectives in multicultural education.* Newbury Park, CA: Sage.

[30] Kozol, J. (1967). *Death at an early age: The destruction of the hearts and minds of Negro children in the Boston Public Schools.* New York: Bantam Books; Kozol, J. (1985). *Illiterate America.* Garden City, New York: Anchor Press; Kozol, J. (1991). *Savage inequalities: Children in American schools.* New York: Crown; Kozol, J. (1995). *Amazing grace: The lives of children and the conscience of a nation.* New York: Crown; Kozol, J. (2000). *Ordinary resurrections: Children in the years of hope.* New York: Crown; Freire, P. (1970). *Pedagogy of the oppressed.* New York: Continuum; Freire, P. (1973). *Education for critical consciousness.* New York: Herder and Herder; Freire, P. (1985). *The politics of education.* New York: Bergin & Garvey; Freire, P. (1998). *Pedagogy of freedom.* Boston: Rowman & Littlefield.

[31] Allen, L. A. (2006). *The moral life of schools* revisited: Preparing educational leaders to "build a new social order" for social justice and democratic community. *International Journal of Urban Education Leadership, 1,* 1–13.

Critical theorists believe that schools can improve by focusing on the following goals:

- **Changing society.** For the most part, critical theorists do not believe school reform alone can solve educational problems because many problems begin with the society at large. Many radicals seek significant social change.

- **Implementing programs that lead to more democratic schools**—with teachers, students, and parents having more input into decision making (teacher empowerment, school-based management, school-community cooperation).

- **Developing curriculum and teaching that involve "critical pedagogy"**—allowing teachers and students to understand the social and educational problems and see potential (radical) solutions to these ongoing issues.

- **Developing curriculum and teaching that are multicultural, antiracist, antisexist, and anticlassist**—offering a positive curricular treatment of the diverse groups the make up U.S. society.

Critical theory can provide current and future educators with a lens through which to view, test, and challenge their assumptions about diversity and find better answers to inform school practices that can help all students learn to high levels.[32] As critical theorists observe, although schools' curriculum conveys the dominant

A CLOSER LOOK

Cultural conservatives criticize public schools because they believe educational benefits should rest upon individual merit, family, free enterprise, patriotism, and Christianity. They believe that public schools undermine traditional values based on religious morality and individual merit.

Liberal critics believe public schools must level the playing field between affluent and disadvantaged students through policies and programs that give disadvantaged students a better chance to make the most of their educational opportunities. They see education as balancing the individual and social needs in ways consistent with democracy and meritocracy.

Critical theorists would change both schools and the society that made and keep people unequal. They believe that the traditional curriculum aims to make students conforming and docile. Instead, they suggest, schools should be moral, just, and inclusive of those who most need access to the educational process. Schools can be a vehicle for social change when they implement curriculum and teaching that are multicultural, antiracist, antisexist, and antitraditional, respecting the diversity of today's students in the United States.

Considering the information in this text, answer the following questions:

1. On which issues do you agree with each of the three different perspectives?
2. On which issues do you disagree with each of them?
3. Where do you see each perspective's influence in today's public schools?
4. In what ways do you think public schools would change if schools accepted each approach's ideas regarding curriculum, library resources, need for extra academic support for minority and disadvantaged students, school rules, prayer in schools, achievement testing, and availability of school support personnel (counselors, nurses)?

---

[32] Allen, 2006, p. 9.

Table 7.1	Comparing Education Critics' Perspectives		
	Conservative	**Liberal**	**Critical Theory**
Role of individual and government	Individuals must compete in social environments to survive. Individuals are responsible for their own choices.	Individual effort is not enough. Government and school must assure fair treatment of citizens in economic, political, and social arenas.	Need to change schools and society that make and keep students unequal.
Role of school	Provide opportunities for educational training to become economically and socially productive. Socialize children into adult roles. Provide opportunities to let individual initiative and effort lead to success (or not).	Provide educational training and socialization. Schools must create equal and equitable opportunities for all students to succeed in a diverse society by leveling the playing field for economically and culturally disadvantaged students.	Public schools wrongly practice a Western cultural hegemony of the dominant class that allows this class to perpetuate its power through injustices of race, class, gender, and culture. Schools and teachers need to instill in students a critical awareness that can help them understand, challenge, and transform their society.
Curriculum	Curriculum should meet high standards and follow the traditional Western European/American curriculum.	Curriculum should meet high standards, while including diverse voices along with traditional Western European and American history, thought, and values.	Move beyond white European/American experiences to include diverse cultures and voices. Give all students access to high-quality curriculum and learning experiences.
Accountability	Make schools and students accountable for meeting acceptable standards of minimum academic performance.	Government and schools have major roles in reducing "achievement gaps" by assisting traditionally underperforming students. Ensure that all students can and do meet high standards.	Teachers should help students develop a critical awareness of society's power and inequalities so they can challenge and transform their society for the better.

cultural values through its choice of subjects and topics for study, it also teaches the cognitive and intellectual means to challenge those assumptions.

Learning from the Critics

All critics—conservative, liberal, and critical theorists—offer perspectives on how to improve schools (see the summary in Table 7.1).

Conservatives remind us that our democratic republic and Western tradition have brought important values to this country, and they deserve an important part of the curriculum. The United States is a nation of immigrants and a nation of laws. Coming from different countries and family backgrounds, persons living here need to develop a common commitment—to become one people, one nation, indivisible, with liberty and justice for all. We deeply value our freedoms to think, speak, and worship as we choose. We also appreciate the opportunities to advance ourselves through knowledge and hard work. Likewise, conservatives remind us that respect for individual differences includes accepting students' religious beliefs that can be accommodated within the school. Students, in turn, must recognize that others may also have their own views. In the end, schools must maintain a respectful, appropriate, and safe learning environment for all. Finding the appropriate balance is not easy, but it is important.

Liberals remind us to have high expectations for all students' achievement. They recognize that not all students start from the same point, through no fault of their own. Schools can provide academic and social **scaffolding**—the extra time and academic and moral supports necessary to help economically and culturally diverse students overcome their educational limitations and learn to the highest levels. Liberal critics see equity and excellence as compatible and doable. Closing the achievement gap means schools must do things differently—teaching, staffing, curriculum, testing. The results will change both the lives of individual students and our society as a whole.

Critical theorists' core ideas have merit when we look at how U.S. schools have traditionally educated poor and minority students. Our success in fully educating disadvantaged and disenfranchised students has important implications for our own democratic society's well-being. We are living in a globalized world. Global systems of production, exchange, and technology bring people together economically. Divisive belief systems and social practices—such as nationalism, racism, sexism, and contempt for the disabled—keep people in poverty, leaving them without opportunities to advance and improve their lives. Democracy loses—unless the majority of people have access to the means to improve their own lives and the lives of their children.

When a society has too many people without the means or opportunities to improve their lives, social revolution becomes a reality. The many disadvantaged become increasingly resentful and angry about their situation. They blame those with the political power and economic means for keeping them down. With little to lose, the disenfranchised citizens may engage in violence against the society. The twentieth-century Communist Revolutions in Russia and China are cases in point. The bottom line: A democratic republic cannot long thrive—or even exist—without a well-educated, vibrant, widespread middle class, whose members have access to means of improving their lives. By taking this view, critical theorists sound much like the U.S. founding fathers.

Clearly, education can improve the quality of life for individuals, communities, and nations alike. Literacy—deep cognitive understanding of how to extract information from the printed page, spoken language, or computer screens—can empower people to take constructive action to improve their lives. Teaching for relevance and problem solving, when it focuses on students' daily lives, can produce meaningful engagement with the society. In this way, it helps students develop the tools they need for mature adulthood. Likewise, the curriculum needs to be to be critically understood and challenged for its application to real life. In addition, when teachers respect and understand their students' lives, they can help students learn what really matters. Necessary learning includes the attitudes, knowledge, and skills to transform disadvantaged students' lives so that they can move from poverty to economic self-sufficiency and responsible democratic participation.

Taking the best from these three perspectives, for U.S. schools to achieve their purposes and promises, they should do the following:

- Provide high-quality opportunities for all students to learn
- Develop student literacy and critical thinking to apply to curriculum, life experiences, and the larger society
- Create diverse classrooms with characterized by respect between teacher and students, and among students themselves
- Offer challenging and relevant learning activities (that have sense and meaning to students), and foster interpersonal skills
- "De-track" students from low-interest, low-challenge classes and provide them with opportunities (and support) to learn the important, high-status curriculum
- Increase educational scaffolding for those students who (because they did not have the early learning opportunities available to middle-class and upper-class children)

start from further back, learn differently, or more slowly so they can learn to high levels

- Teach for learning, using the insights about how students actually learn and providing the activities and quality feedback to help all students master and use what they are learning

- Move beyond completing worksheets, memorizing, and repeating to critical thinking, applying knowledge to real-world events, analyzing, synthesizing, evaluating, and creating

- Ask questions about current events and to what extent they represent—or deny—the democratic ideals upon which our country is founded

- Educate all our students to have the skills they need to lead more productive, creative, and satisfying lives, not just compliance inside the classroom or work setting

Our society cannot sustain a large gap between the poor and the rich. We cannot ignore the fact that our economically disadvantaged, minority students, and students with disabilities are not graduating from high school at high rates and are not performing well on national and international assessments. If we ignore these realities, we put our entire society and way of life at risk. Here is where education can be the agent for positive social change.

Educational critics ask, "What type of society do we want?" and "What is education's role in developing a democratic citizenry?" We can answer these questions more thoughtfully when we consider our critics' ideas.

Conflict—that is, courteous discussion of different viewpoints to reach consensus for the common good—is essential to living in a democratic society. We should neither fear nor blindly defend against our critics. We want to teach our students to think critically, listen carefully and respectfully, and act responsibly. Our society is not perfect, and we can help students develop the cognitive tools and interpersonal behaviors to make both their lives and our communities better. As educators and citizens, we can do no less. Public schools gain strong community support when they present their "official" curriculum within the larger context of "democratic education for a more democratic society" rather than as a means to advance the agenda of certain special-interest groups.

Activity 7.4

Education has long been a subject of debate among conservative, liberal, and critical theorist critics. Each group has a viewpoint about the type of society we should have and the way in which education should contribute to that society.

A. Divide the class into three groups, one for each of the three viewpoints. Collectively pretending to be running for a vacant seat on the local school board, each group will develop a 5- to 10-minute presentation for this class discussing the viewpoint that its political perspective promotes. Each group will address how its group sees the following issues:

The purpose of school in society

The value of traditional beliefs, values, and culture in school

The content of the curriculum

The type of instructional practices that should be used in the classroom

The family's role in educating its children

School as an agent of change for societal improvement

The role of the individual in getting a quality education

The school's role in preserving the "status quo"

Education, capitalism, and the free-market economy

Schools' role in reducing the "achievement gap" between minority and disadvantaged students and other students

Other issues presented by the group

B. After the group presentations, have the class vote on which candidate should win the school board seat—and explain why.

Activity 7.5

Do you consider yourself as having a conservative, liberal, or critical theorist perspective on education? Why? Does this surprise you? Sit down with two other people in your class who hold different perspectives. Discuss what you have in common in terms of education background and beliefs. How can taking the best of all perspectives help make education better for society at large?

Realizing Education's Purpose and Promise: Investment in Human Capital

Although U.S. education has many worthy purposes and goals, critics want to improve American society by changing our schools. No doubt any institution can improve. Nevertheless, the data show that viewing education as an investment in human capital is making our lives more satisfying and our communities demonstrably better places to live.

Emerging State of Investing in Human Capital

Education as an investment in human capital is the idea that educating everyone benefits the community. It is a relatively new concept. In earlier times, governments provided formal schooling to educate the social and financial elite, not the masses. Laborers, members of the working classes, and the poor remained largely undereducated, if they received any education at all.

Adam Smith's *The Wealth of Nations* (1776) formally introduced the notion of human capital.[33] In this seminal work, Smith discussed society members' learned abilities (education) as part of a society's resources. He viewed investment in human capital as providing workers with vocational training related to production. His original concept, which was quite revolutionary at the time, provided an early first step toward the larger view of educated workers' contributing to the economy and to society at large.

Two hundred years later (in the 1960s), Theodore W. Schultz's work on investment in human capital expressed the idea that laborers' primarily intellectual attributes have value.[34] Schultz, an agricultural economist, often visited farms and spoke with farmers.

---

[33] Smith, A. (1937). *The wealth of nations*, rev. ed. New York: Modern Library.
[34] Schultz, T. W. (1961, March). Investment in human capital. *American Economic Review, 51*, 1–17.

Figure 7.5	Theodore W. Schultz Saw Education as an Investment in Human Capital

AFP/AFP/Getty Images

After World War II, while interviewing an old, apparently poverty-stricken farm couple, he noticed their contentment. When he asked them why they were so satisfied with their lives—even though they were poor—they answered that they were not poor. They felt rich because they had used their farm to send four children to college and believed that education would make these children productive. This perspective led Schultz quickly to the concept of human capital as capital produced by investing in knowledge (Figure 7.5).[35]

To fulfill its purposes and promises, education requires a significant financial and cultural investment. Schultz suggested that investing in people's minds was economically valuable for the larger community. His theory of investing in human capital won the 1979 Nobel Prize for Economic Science. Schultz's work became the basis for considering education as an excellent investment—a significant contributor to a society's economic development.

Today, managers realize that better-educated workers make better employees. An educated citizenry makes many real, positive, and measurable impacts on society. Education, more than any other social investment, raises the standard of living by increasing employability and spendable income, while reducing a community's social services costs. In short, good education and community quality of life create a dynamic synergy. In addition, a good public education system is a major drawing card for local business development and expansion. Education enhances the quality of life not just for the educated individuals themselves, but for the entire community as well.

Convincing data clearly show that public education increases a community's economic well-being, safety, and overall quality of life. An investment in education is, therefore, essentially a community's investment in its own best interests. Increased education raises the individual's earning potential and employability, thereby giving the person the time, resources, and inclination to improve his

---

[35] Schultz bibliography retrieved October 18, 2006, from http://www.econlib.org/library/enc/bios/Schultz.html.

or her health, act as an informed and active voter, make monetary and time contributions to the community, and engage in a variety of cultural and leisure activities.

More immediately, education directly affects the personal living standard by influencing how much people earn. Figure 7.6 shows the increased median weekly earnings in 2006 along with the unemployment rate for each education level. As the figure shows, individuals with bachelor's degrees earned almost twice as much as those with only high school diplomas in 2006. Typically, the more the education a person has, the higher his or her income. The higher the level of education attained, the lower the likelihood of unemployment.

Every ethnic group gains economically from increased education. Figure 7.7 shows that while different ethnic and racial groups in the United States may earn

| Figure 7.6 | Education Level with Median Weekly Earnings and Unemployment Rate, 2006 |

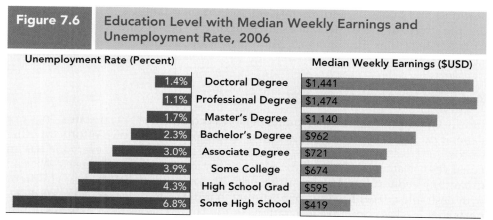

Source: U.S. Department of Labor, Bureau of Labor Statistics. (2007). *Occupational outlook handbook.* Washington, DC: Author. **www.bls.gov.**

| Figure 7.7 | The Payback of Education Rates, 2005 |

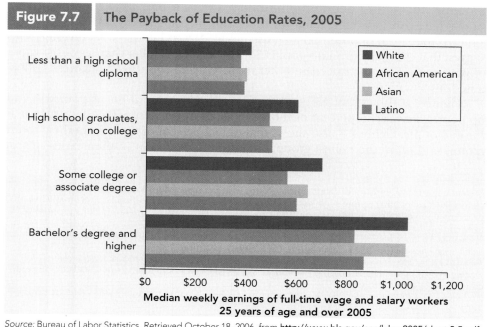

Source: Bureau of Labor Statistics. Retrieved October 18, 2006, from **http://www.bls.gov/cps/labor2005/chart 2-5.pdf.**

different amounts for the same level of education,[36] each group is making gains, and all ethnic group members earn more than their ethnic peers who have attained lower education levels.

Education is a major contributor to the U.S. economy's financial health. As a rule, citizens with higher levels of educational achievement earn more money, return more tax dollars to support government services, add more to the general consumer economy to enhance their lifestyles, and draw fewer resources from society than do those with less education.[37]

Is Education Still the Key to the American Dream?

One of our nation's most enduring myths sees the United States as the land of opportunity. For hundreds of years, immigrants have come here from around the world to find better lives for themselves and for their families. To these newcomers, the streets of the United States are figuratively "paved with gold." Within one or two generations, immigrants' children typically become part of the American mainstream.

America as a Meritocracy

In this version of American dream, a person's economic or social status does not depend on his or her parents, but rather on the individual's own efforts. In other words, America is a meritocracy. With direction and hard work, everyone has an equal chance at success, regardless of his or her family or circumstances. With an expanding economy and political freedom, those individuals (or their children) with desirable talents have the opportunity to join the middle class. One study reports that it takes about five generations in the United States for a person's family background influences to disappear.[38] To a large extent—as the human capital data suggest—this is still true. A growing body of research, however, questions whether this ideal of social mobility and economic opportunity is still a reality for many of our most economically disadvantaged students.

Slowing social and economic mobility. Over the past 10 to 15 years, several studies have concluded that it may be more difficult for children to use education as a means to rise out of poverty than it used to be. Newer international investigations suggest that children born into poor U.S. families have smaller chances of rising out of poverty than do their peers in other industrialized countries.[39] Figure 7.8 illustrates this situation.

Figure 7.8 shows that 45 percent of those who start out life as poor will end up poor. Likewise, 55 percent of those who start out richest will end up richest at the end of life. Figure 7.8 also shows that only 9 percent of those from the poorest groups end up in the richest group, and another 9 percent in the next-to-richest

---

[36] Unequal earning levels for different ethnic groups with the same education can have a variety of causes, such as inability to find high-paying employment in urban neighborhoods where many live or differential job descriptions (and salaries) for similar work. Here may be an example of a promise yet to keep.

[37] Owings, W. A., & Kaplan, L. S. (2006). School finance as investment in human capital. In *American public school finance* (pp. 95–117). Belmont, CA: Cengage Learning.

[38] Sawhill, I. (2006, September 19). *Opportunity in America: Does education promote social mobility? Proceedings.* Washington, DC: Brookings Institution. Retrieved October 31, 2006, from www.brookings.ed/comm/events/20060919.pdf.

[39] Viadero, D. (2006, October 25). Rags to riches in U.S. largely a myth, scholars write. *Education Week, 26*(9), 8.

| Figure 7.8 | Intergenerational Wealth, 1979–2000 | | | | | |

Moving On Up?

Percent

Origin Group Those who started in the...	...Ended Up in the					
	Poorest	Second	Third	Fourth	Richest	Total
Poorest	(45)	27	11	9	9	100
Second	24	35	20	14	7	100
Third	11	20	35	21	13	100
Fourth	7	11	23	33	25	100
Richest	5	6	9	25	(55)	100

Source: Viadero, D. (2006, October 25). Rags to riches in the U.S. largely a myth, scholars write. *Education Week, 26*(9), 8.

group; in contrast, only 5 percent of students from the richest group finish in the poorest group. People starting in the other groups have a better chance of moving up to a higher economic level. Over generations, people move up and down the social–economic ladder, but they do not travel far from where they began.

Even so, many individuals from other economic groups do move up to higher income and social levels—41 percent advance from the second poorest group, 34 percent advance from the third poorest group, and 25 percent advance from the second richest group. In this way, they increase their social mobility. In an information- and intelligence-based economy, in a globalized world, social and economic mobility without a strong education becomes increasingly less likely.

In his book *Class Counts*,[40] Allan Ornstein, a St. John's University professor and education writer, observes that public education is no longer the "great equalizer" of social and economic mobility. Although many people in America continue to believe in the possibility of social mobility—the idea that one generation or individual can and should rise above the previous generation's or family's attainment level—facts show that such movement is becoming increasingly difficult. Instead, mobility may depend more on one's social class than on one's education. Ornstein asks, if we reduce mobility based on merit, do we also reduce public schools' role as a means for talented but less affluent students to rise economically and socially? If the middle class cannot use public schools to advance their educational, social, economic, and political opportunities, what hope is there for less affluent students? And what does this trend mean for our larger society and our democracy?

Others offer modestly encouraging news about schools and economic mobility. In *Opportunity in America: The Role of Education*, the public policy Washington-based think-tank Brookings Institution notes that opportunities to move forward—or fall behind—remained high through the nineteenth and twentieth centuries but weakened in the 1980s.[41] Following up on this report, a 2008 Brookings Institution publication observed that lower college-going rates among poor Latino and African American children than among whites and Asians contribute to this situation.

---

[40] Ornstein, A. (2007). *Class counts: Education, inequality, and the shrinking middle class.* New York: Rowman and Littlefield.
[41] Sawhill, I. V. (2006). *Opportunity in America: The role of education.* Washington, DC: Brookings Institution. www.brookings.edu/es/research/projects/foc/20060913foc.htm.

A variety of reasons account for this discrepancy.[42] If a college degree is increasingly the ticket to improving or keeping one's relative economic position, this unequal access to higher education means fewer minorities will enter the middle class, which in turn limits their economic and social mobility.[43] The report concludes that "although education can and sometimes does boost the achievement and later the income of children from relatively poor families, the average effect of education at all levels is to reinforce the differences associated with the family background that children and adolescents bring with them to the classroom."[44]

Education's potential to increase social mobility is an important topic because statistics show that the income gap between America's poorest and richest has widened since the 1980s.[45] Greater inequality means it takes longer for income differences to disappear in later generations, a situation that jeopardizes the health of our entire society. "The United States could be in danger of creating a poverty trap at the bottom and an enclave of wealth at the top," says Isabel Sawhill, a senior fellow at the Brookings Institution.[46]

Slowing social and economic mobility has many causes. As we will discuss in Chapter 11, children from wealthier and middle-class families are more likely than poor or working-class children to have large vocabularies, attend preschool, and come to school with the cognitive skills, vocabularies, and attitudes needed to succeed in school. One study reports that parents who are high school dropouts spend $33 per year on their children, while high school graduates spend $600 per year, an 1,800 percent difference.[47] Similarly the schools attended by poor and rich children have different resources available. Thus the differences continue to compound throughout the grades, to poor and working-class children's increasing disadvantage.

Changing market conditions also factor into the discussion. The economy is no longer expanding at the post–World War II rate, and the marketplace is already populated with plenty of college graduates. College graduates' salaries remained high when they were in short supply and there were more professional and managerial jobs than there were people applying to fill them. In 1952, 7.9 percent of the work force had college degrees, with 2.33 college-level jobs available per college graduate.[48] In 2002, college graduates represented 25.9 percent of the work force.[49] Today, professional and service jobs are commonplace and often outsourced. Considering inflation, the typical college graduate household income was actually lower in 2005 than in 2000.[50] That is why so many middle-class families are able to maintain their quality of life only by having both husband and wife working full-time jobs.

A 2007 by the Educational Testing Service finds that the Americans' next generation, on average, will have lower literacy and math skills, and will experience greater income inequality than current working-age populations. In a labor market that increasingly rewards education and skills, this could mean tens of millions of

---

[42] These reasons include lack of high-quality preschools for eligible students, lack of academic preparation for college, lack of know-how about the college preparation and application process, and lack of financial resources or know-how to pay for college. See Haskins, R. (2008). Education and economic mobility. In J. B. Isaacs, I. V. Sawhill, & R. Haskins (Eds.), *Getting ahead or losing ground: Economic mobility in America* (pp. 91–114). Washington, DC: Brookings Institution. Economic Mobility Project. Retrieved September 22, 2008, from http://economicmobility.org/assets/pdfs/Economic_Mobility_in_America_ Full.pdf.

[43] Haskins, 2008.

[44] Haskins, 2008, p. 101.

[45] Viadero, 2006.

[46] Sawhill, 2006.

[47] Rouse, C. (2006, September 19). Cited in Sawhill, I., *Opportunity in America: Does education promote social mobility? Proceedings.* Washington, DC: Brookings Institution, p. 16.

[48] Freeman, R. B. (1976). *The over-educated American.* New York: Academic Press, p. 18.

[49] U.S. Census Bureau, American Community Survey (ACS). (n.d.). Ranking Tables 2002: Percent of People 25 Years and Older Who Have Completed a Bachelor's Degree. Retrieved November 20, 2009, from http://www.census.gov/acs/www/Products/Ranking/2002/R02T040.htm.

[50] Krugman, P. (2006, September 8). Winning over discontent. *The New York Times.* p. 49.

Americans who will be unable to qualify for higher-paying jobs.[51] Those jobs in our economy that require less than a college education need only short-term, on-the-job training, and they do not pay well.

From an economic viewpoint, the question is not whether people will find jobs, but whether they will be able to find jobs with long-term opportunities that will allow them to increase their economic and social mobility. Without significant increases in students' skill levels when they are ready to enter the job market, they will not be able to improve their lifestyles.

School quality and social mobility. Policies that address increasing school quality—including quality related to teachers, curriculum, and facilities—have the potential to improve social mobility. We will discuss many of these issues in the coming chapters. Improved teaching, curriculum, institutional practices, and facilities in disadvantaged neighborhoods would weaken the link between family socio-economic standing and children's educational and financial outcomes. In addition, ensuring family involvement with student learning is critical to improving students' mobility through the education system.

The processes required to create opportunities for social and economic mobility are highly complex. Indeed, it will take a whole series of interventions—involving schools, families, and society—to make a difference if all America's children are to receive the full promises that American education says are its purposes.

---

[51] Olson, L. (2007, February 7). ETS study warns of growing inequality in income, skills. *Education Week, 26*(22), 7.

Summary

Education has intellectual, social, political, economic, and personal purposes. In a democratic republic, education ideally provides a meritocracy in which individuals have equal chances to develop their abilities and advance in the society through their own talents and efforts. The degrees to which education fulfills these purposes are its promises to each student and the community.

People often disagree about what education's purposes are and how well education is fulfilling these promises. The natural tension between schooling's role in maintaining the status quo and its potential to bring about change lies at the heart of differing views of education and schooling. Those who support society as it is tend to stress school's role in preserving it. Those who believe that society needs improvement stress schools' role in either improving or transforming it.

In the decentralized school governance system employed in the United States, national education goals must be general enough to mean different things to different people, so that states can interpret and adapt them according to regional preferences and local circumstances. At the same time, these goals must be clear enough to give a common sense of national purpose and identity.

Struggles over curriculum, teaching, and policy are battles for power over children's thoughts and society's future direction. Knowledge is power. Whoever controls the knowledge—and the policies, textbooks, and lessons that convey that knowledge—holds the influence.

All critics—conservative, liberal, and critical theorists—offer us a perspective on how we can improve schools. While we need not agree with everything they say, each perspective has its merits.

Conservatives remind us that our democratic republic and Western tradition have brought important values of laws, freedom, and liberty to this country. They suggest that schools should acculturate all children to feel loyalty to our now-common heritage. Liberals remind us to focus on increasing achievement for all students, seeking equity and excellence for each. Critical theorists note that schools must help transform society to create more social justice.

Education is also an investment in human capital. An educated citizenry makes many positive impacts on society. Education, more than any other social investment, raises the standard of living. It increases employability and spendable income for all racial and ethnic groups. While today's schools are not perfect, education is fulfilling many of its purposes and promises.

Finally, scholars say that social mobility—opportunities to move forward (or fall behind)—has appeared to diminish in the United States since the 1980s. Reduced social mobility and few opportunities to attain a better quality of life through education combine to create a dangerous situation for democratic governments. Education has never been more critical to breaking or perpetuating the intergenerational poverty cycle. Until our students—and especially our poorest and most vulnerable children—receive the quality education we know how to provide, we are placing our own livelihoods and our country's future at risk.

Conclusions

- Education is a community's investment in its own best interests.
- U.S. public education is fulfilling many of its purposes and promises.
- Nevertheless, we have more to do before every student can benefit from education's value in increasing his or her quality of life and social mobility.

Teachers, Ethics, and the Law

Sooner than you think, you will sign a contract to become a teacher. A teaching contract creates a legal agreement between the new teacher and a school district. By signing this document, you accept certain legal rights, professional responsibilities, and ethical obligations that will underscore and guide your behavior.[1]

Schools accept a profound responsibility for educating students, and teachers play a unique role in their students' lives. Teachers are responsible for their students' physical and emotional safety as well as for helping them learn. Additionally, teachers serve as role models whose own behaviors children notice and copy. The state must balance individual teachers' and students' constitutional rights against the necessity of maintaining a controlled and safe learning environment. Courts have allowed schools to behave in reasonable ways to keep students safe, healthy, and learning. For teachers to carry out their professional actions within the law, they must first know how the law limits and protects teachers' and students' conduct.

This chapter reviews the ethics of teaching and legal considerations related to education. Relevant issues include codes of ethics, the teaching license or certificate, the teaching contract, teacher rights and responsibilities, student rights and responsibilities, and ways in which schools may limit freedom of speech and privacy. Disabled students' rights and sexual harassment in schools are discussed as well. Although this chapter does not cover every legal aspect future educators need to know, it presents a focused overview of key legal topics that may affect an individual's teaching career.

Focus Questions

- What is the value of having an Educators' Code of Ethics?
- What rights and responsibilities do teachers have?
- What does it mean to have a teaching license or certificate?
- What does it mean to have a teaching contract?
- How do teachers' constitutional freedoms, such as freedom of speech, freedom of religion, and protection from unreasonable search and seizure, operate in schools?
- What is "academic freedom," and what are its boundaries?
- Can teachers be required to submit to drug testing?
- Can teachers be sued for educational malpractice?
- Can teachers be sued for negligence?
- What are students' rights in the disciplinary process?
- Under what conditions can students, their lockers, or their cars be searched?

---

[1] We wish to thank our friends, David and Kern Alexander, for their help with this chapter. Much of the school law content is derived from their text, *American Public School Law,* sixth edition (2005) and seventh edition (2009), published by Cengage Learning. Text citations are from the sixth edition unless otherwise stated.

- What are students' privacy rights regarding their school records?
- What are students' rights concerning freedom of speech and expression in school (silent political speech, oral speech, school newspapers)?
- What are students' rights concerning student dress and appearance as related to their freedom of expression?
- What are students' rights concerning sexual harassment?
- What do you need to know about laws affecting students with disabilities?

The Importance of an Educators' Code of Ethics

Hippocrates, author of what is arguably the first code of ethics—the Hippocratic Oath—wrote, "First, do no harm." This is a concept that serves members of all professions well.

Professions unite their members through common training, shared values, mutual aspirations, and collective purposes. Professional expertise confers a degree of authority and power on its holders. But professional autonomy is never without societal limits. Because every profession affects the well-being of others who depend on those professionals' skills and services, professional behaviors have both technical and moral dimensions. Society holds practitioners accountable for both aspects through a professional code of ethics.

What Is a Code of Ethics?

Ethics can be described as the rules or widely accepted standards of practice that govern members' professional conduct. Ethics is not a series of laws imposed by the state, but rather a set of standards that is followed voluntarily. Ethics includes the norms, values, beliefs, habits, and attitudes that we choose to follow—that we as a society impose on ourselves. "Laws regulate behavior from the outside in. Ethics regulate behavior from the inside out."[2]

The word "ethics" is derived from the Greek word meaning "moral philosophy." To behave "ethically" means being able to *choose* the "right" behavior, whereas being "moral" means being willing to *practice* that right behavior. The tension between a profession's desire to control its own practice and the public's demand for accountability has led to many professions developing codes of ethics. **Professional codes of ethics** can be described as the rules that guide professional decisions and actions. These codes serve as both a foundation and a guide to professional behavior in morally ambiguous situations.[3]

Society grants a profession power and privilege only when its members are willing and able to contribute to the general well-being and to conduct their affairs in a manner consistent with broad social values. In this sense, the profession serves as a norm reference group for its practitioners. Its code of ethics visibly clarifies for practitioners and the general public alike the rules and norms that guide the actions of that profession's members. Medicine, law, accounting, pharmacy, teaching, and other

---

[2] Friedman, T. L. (2008). *Hot, flat, and crowded. Why we need a green revolution—and how it can renew America.* New York: Ferrar, Straus, and Giroux, p. 192.

[3] Frankel, M. S. (1989, February–March). Professional codes: Why, whom, and with what impact? *Journal of Business Ethics, 8*(2–3), 109–115.

professions have all developed their own codes of ethics to improve professional practice and maintain the public's confidence in their practitioners.

Teachers' Code of Ethics

When teachers enter the classroom, they represent the education profession to the local community and to the nation. From that standpoint, a teacher's professional and ethical behaviors are important on many levels.

Limitations of professional codes of ethics. While professional self-regulation is consistent with the tradition of self-government, it is not without shortcomings. Many professions have a poor record of reporting their own violators.[4] For the most part, professional codes of ethics are only as "ethical" and "moral" as the individuals following them.

National education association codes of ethics. A teacher's personal and professional ethical code and the faithfulness with which the individual puts these ideals into action will determine whether the person helps or hurts himself or herself and the profession. The National Education Association (NEA) has developed a Code of Ethics for the Education Profession. This ethical code is divided in two

Principle I: Commitment to the Student

The educator strives to help each student realize his or her potential as a worthy and effective member of society. The educator therefore works to stimulate the spirit of inquiry, the acquisition of knowledge and understanding, and the thoughtful formulation of worthy goals. In fulfillment of the obligation to the student, the educator

- Shall not unreasonably restrain the student from independent action in the pursuit of learning.
- Shall not unreasonably deny the student access to varying points of view.
- Shall not deliberately suppress or distort subject matter relevant to the student's progress.
- Shall make reasonable effort to protect the student from conditions harmful to learning or to health and safety.
- Shall not intentionally expose the student to embarrassment or disparagement.
- Shall not on the basis of race, color, creed, sex, national origin, marital status, political or religious beliefs, family, social or cultural background, or sexual orientation, unfairly

    Exclude any student from participation in any program.

    Deny benefits to any student.

    Grant any advantage to any student.

- Shall not use professional relationships with students for private advantage.
- Shall not disclose information about students obtained in the course of professional service unless disclosure serves a compelling professional purpose or is required by law.

[4] Frankel, 1989.

Principle II: Commitment to the Profession

The education profession is vested by the public with a trust and responsibility requiring the highest ideals of professional service. In the belief that the quality of the services of the education profession directly influences the nation and its citizens, the educator shall exert every effort to raise professional standards, to promote a climate that encourages the exercise of professional judgment, to achieve conditions that attract persons worthy of the trust to careers in education, and to assist in preventing the practice of the profession by unqualified persons. In fulfillment of the obligation to the profession, the educator

- Shall not in an application for a professional position deliberately make a false statement or fail to disclose a material fact related to competency and qualification.
- Shall not misrepresent his or her professional qualifications.
- Shall not assist any entry into the profession of a person known to be unqualified in respect to character, education, or other relevant attribute.
- Shall not knowingly make a false statement concerning the qualifications of a candidate for a professional position.
- Shall not assist a non-educator in the unauthorized practice of teaching.
- Shall not disclose information about colleagues obtained in the course of professional service unless disclosure serves a compelling professional purpose or is required by law.
- Shall not knowingly make false or malicious statements about a colleague.
- Shall not accept any gratuity, gift, or favor that might impair or appear to influence professional decisions or action.

A CLOSER LOOK

Review the NEA's Code of Ethics, Principles I and II, and answer the following questions.

1. Discuss why you think the teaching profession may or may not need a code of ethics. Why do most professions have a code of ethics?

2. Which statements do you consider vague? What are the different ways someone might interpret these vague statements? How would you clarify any statements you believe are not stated the way you would state them?

3. Are there areas of the teaching profession that the NEA's Code of Ethics does not address? What would you add? Answer now, and then answer this question again after finishing this chapter.

4. Do the principles and items appear to offer more protection to the profession or to the students? What examples can you cite to support this belief? Explain why you think this is so.

parts, or principles. Principle I contains a commitment to the student (the client), and Principle II contains a commitment to the profession at large.[5]

As with physicians, the first ethical principle is to do no harm. Teachers are advised to always act in the best interest of the client, the student.

Teachers, Ethics, and Social Networking Web Sites

Both current and prospective teachers may confront ethical issues when they put personal information online. In general, workers expect their supervisors to monitor them closely while they are on the job. After work hours, however, employees expect that as long as they break no laws, what they do is not the employer's concern. Unfortunately, the Internet, by its very nature, makes some off-the-job activities more visible to more people than was previously possible. This reality creates ethical concerns—and occasionally employment consequences—for educators.

Both preservice teachers and in-service teachers must understand that in today's world, the line between their personal lives and their professional lives is not black and white.[6] Teachers have lost their jobs and ended their opportunities to enter the profession because of material posted on their social networking pages. Even if teachers avoid losing their jobs and break no laws, the ethical concerns and potential abuses raised by communicating "inappropriately" with students through online social networking sites make the situation hazardous to teachers' reputation, effectiveness, and credibility.

Social networking and privacy. **Social networking sites** such as Facebook and MySpace are interactive Web sites designed to build online communities for individuals who have something in common—an interest in a hobby, a topic, or an organization—and who share a simple desire to communicate across physical boundaries with other interested people.[7] Most social networking sites include the ability to chat in real time, send email, blog, participate in discussion groups, and share files. Users can also post links to photos, music, and video files, all of which have the potential to create a virtual identity.[8]

The introduction of social networking has produced a cultural shift related to the idea of privacy. Some people today are willing to expose more about themselves to the general public. It is commonplace to see content related to alcohol, drugs, and sex posted on future teachers' social networking profiles.[9] A 2007 Pew study, titled "Digital Footprints," revealed that 60 percent of Internet users surveyed were not worried about how much information was available about them online. This finding represented a significant change from a 2000 Pew study, in which 84 percent of respondents expressed concern about "businesses and people you don't know getting personal information about you and your family."[10]

---

[5] http://ks.nea.org/profession/codeofethics.html NEA Code of Ethics. Retrieved October 2, 2009 from, http://www.nea.org/home/30442.htm

[6] Carter, H. H., Foulger, T. S, & Ewbank, A. D. (2008). Have you googled your teacher lately? Teachers use of social networking sites. *Phi Delta Kappan, 89*(9), 681–685. See this article for a more complete discussion of social networking and teachers.

[7] Carter, Foulger, & Ewbank, 2008.

[8] Although social networking remains very popular, a 2008 report by the Internet marketing research company comScore suggests that, on many social networks such as Facebook and MySpace, unique visitors and user engagement (measured by the number of minutes spent per visitor) are on the decline. See: Lo, K. (2008, February 6). Social networking sites: Declining in popularity? *Techsoup: The Technology Place for Non-Profits.* Retrieved October 2, 2009, from http://blog.techsoup.org/node/262.

[9] Carter, Foulger, & Ewbank, 2008.

[10] Stross, R. (2007, December 30). How to lose your job on your own time. *The New York Times.* Retrieved October 2, 2009, from http://www.nytimes.com/2007/12/30/business/30digi.html?pagewanted=1&_r=1.

Many teachers use social networking sites as an avenue to enhance their instruction.[11] Such sites allow teachers to establish deeper relationships with and understandings of students. Using this means of communication, teachers can remind students of upcoming homework, tests, and deadlines.[12] In contrast, other teacher social networking uses are coming under fire for what school districts consider "inappropriate activity," including candid photos, racy or suggestive song lyrics, and references to sex or to alcohol or drug use. Venting about personal frustrations at work has also caused problems.[13]

Risks of communicating outside the "controlled environment." Teachers who communicate with their students outside the controlled classroom environment must make decisions about what and how much personal information to reveal. While teachers may have control over the content they disclose on their university-housed Web pages, friends, strangers, or other students can post discrediting or defamatory messages on users' Facebook Web sites.[14]

Apart from banning teachers outright from using these sites to communicate with their students, some school districts have taken a range of disciplinary actions, including dismissal, against what they consider to be teachers' questionable uses of social networking sites.[15] Consider the following cases. In 2006, Tamara Hoover, an Austin, Texas, teacher, was fired from her high school art teacher position for "conduct unbecoming a teacher" when nude photographs of her were discovered on the Web site of her partner, a professional photographer.[16] In 2007, John Bush, a St. Augustine, Florida, middle school teacher, was fired over the content of his MySpace profile. The district superintendent claimed that the profile contained information that students and parents should not know about a teacher.[17]

Online social networking can even cause problems before someone enters the profession. In 2006, Stacy Snyder, age 25, a Pennsylvania college senior, was dismissed from the student teaching program at a nearby high school and denied her teaching credential after the school staff came across her MySpace photograph captioned "drunken pirate." The head shot, which was taken at a costume party, showed Snyder wearing a pirate's hat and sipping from a large plastic cup whose contents cannot be seen. A university official told her that the photo was "unprofessional" and could have offended her students if they accessed her MySpace page. Snyder filed a lawsuit in federal court in Philadelphia contending that her rights to free expression under the First Amendment had been violated and asking her college for her education degree and teaching certificate.[18] In December 2008, the court ruled against her.[19]

---

[11] Facebook now has 150 million members, and its fastest-growing demographic is the population age 30 and older. See Facebook. (2009). Facebook: Statistics. Retrieved February 18, 2009, from http://www.facebook.com/press/info.php?statistics.

[12] See Trzeszkowski-Giese, A. (2007, November 12). A Facebook education. *Teacher Magazine*. www.teachermagazine.org/tm/articles/2007/11/12/giese_first_web.h19.html; Warnings aside, teachers embrace Facebook. (2007, December 6). *Columbia (Missouri) Tribune*. www.columbiatribune.com/2007/Dec/2007 1206News003.asp. Retrieved October 2, 2009.

[13] Carter, Foulger, & Ewbank, 2008.

[14] Mazer, J., Murphy, R. E., & Simonds, C. J. (2007). I'll see you on "Facebook": The effects of computer-mediated teacher self disclosure on student motivation, affective learning, and classroom climate. *Communication Education, 56*(1), 1–17.

[15] Carter, Foulger, & Ewbank, 2008.

[16] Hoover: Caught in the flash. (2006, June 23). *Austin Chronicle*. Retrieved October 2, 2009, from http://www.austinchronicle.com/gyrobase/Issue/story?oid=oid%3A378611.

[17] Teacher fired over MySpace page. (2007, January 25). *Tallahassee.com*. Retrieved October 2, 2009, from http://www.tallahassee.com/legacy/special/blogs/2007/01/teacher-fired-over-myspace-page_25.html.

[18] Stross, 2007.

[19] The college granted Snyder an English—rather than an education—degree. See Krebs, B. (2008). Court rules against teacher in MySpace "drunken pirate" case: Security fix. Retrieved October 2, 2009, from *Washington Post*. http://voices.washingtonpost.com/securityfix/2008/12/court_rules_against_teacher_in.html.

Ethical behavior: A higher standard. Like it or not, teachers are held to a higher standard of moral behavior than is the population in general.[20] This expectation is reflected in the clauses of various state certification procedures, which mandate that teachers shall not "engage in conduct which would discredit the teaching profession." It is under these state clauses that teachers have been denied entry into or dismissed from their profession based on their behavior outside the classroom. Many states also have professional codes of ethics for teachers with guidelines for teachers' participation in social networking sites.[21]

Even when the law is clear, the higher standard to which teachers are held means they must rely on their professional ethics to govern their professional behaviors. Ethics regulates behavior from the inside out. Teachers need to always ask themselves how any behavior—whether inside the classroom or over the Internet—will protect students' well-being, motivate other teachers, and inspire public trust and confidence in education.

In a world where social connections and friendships are newly defined by user-generated content on the Web, it is yet unclear where privacy ends and professional life begins. Decisions about what and how to share private information cannot be made lightly, because their negative consequences for teachers—and for students—can last a lifetime. It is wise to be judicious before posting details about one's personal life online or participating in relationships with students outside clearly defined professional boundaries.

Activity 8.1

Placement of personal material on social networking sites may be part of the youth culture, but it also raises serious ethical and employment issues when viewed in a professional context.

A. Review your own social networking site from the perspectives of a future employer, a parent of a future student, and a future principal. Identify all "questionable" writings and images that may appear attractive to peers but that might appear "inappropriate" to an employer or client (parent).

B. Pair with a classmate to review each other's social networking sites through the eyes of a potential employer or a student's parent. What otherwise harmless words or images might these other parties consider "inappropriate"?

C. Report back to the class on your findings.

D. If you find items that might be "inappropriate," what will you do, and when?

Teacher Rights and Responsibilities

School law is a fast-growing field of study because states and courts keep making decisions that affect how states and localities can conduct education. Case law, the legal precedents that judges create in their written opinions when

---

[20] Carter, Foulger, & Ewbank, 2008.
[21] Check with your own state's professional teaching association for specific guidance.

they decide legal cases, influences virtually every aspect of education.[22] In case law, judges can either interpret statutory law or interpret prior judicial decisions.[23] As your teacher preparation and teaching experiences grow, the more familiar these issues will become to you, and the more informed decisions you can make.

A Legal Context

The United States Constitution, federal statutes, state constitutions, state statutes, case law, and regulations all influence educational practice. This chapter discusses how the Constitution's Tenth Amendment makes public schools' operation a state function. While states have substantial power to manage schools, their control is not absolute. Federal and state constitutions limit the state's authority to enact statutes controlling education's operations. In other words, if the state legislature enacted a law calling for a practice that conflicted with the federal or state constitution, a court of law would strike down the state statute.

Case law frequently references amendments to the Constitution. Many court cases that involve education's general or guiding practices come from the U.S. Supreme Court and focus on either the First or Fourteenth Amendment. The First Amendment, ratified in 1791, deals with freedom of religion, speech, press, and assembly. It reads:

> Congress shall make no law respecting an establishment of religion, or promoting the free exercise thereof; or abridging the freedom of speech, or of the press; or the right of the people peaceably to assemble, and to petition the Government for a redress of grievances.

This amendment is important to schools because it affects church–state relations, school prayer, religious exercises in schools, and individuals' right to practice their religion in schools. It also affects freedom of speech and freedom of the press, and becomes an issue when someone seeks a means to appeal some grievance that is government imposed.

The Fourteenth Amendment, ratified in 1868 and designed to promote the rights of newly freed slaves, addresses due process and equal protection. It reads in part:

> All persons born or naturalized in the United States and subject to the jurisdiction thereof, are citizens of the United States and of the State wherein they reside. No State shall make or enforce any law which shall abridge the privileges or immunities of citizens of the United States; nor shall any State deprive any person of life, liberty, or property, without the due process of law; nor deny to any person within its jurisdiction the equal protection of the laws.

This amendment guarantees that states cannot take away citizens' constitutional rights. It affects teachers' freedom of speech and freedom of religion, for example. The term "due process of law" has implications for teacher contract issues, student suspensions, and a host of other legal areas. Significantly, the last clause, known as *equal protection*, states that equal protection—that is, equal application—of the law shall not be denied to any *person* (not just a citizen) by a state.

---

[22] Case law is judge-made law. In contrast, statutes are laws passed by legislative bodies.
[23] Cases and digest research tutorials: Lesson one: Overview. (2001). Georgetown University Library. Retrieved October 2, 2009, from http://www.ll.georgetown.edu/tutorials/cases/one/2_overview.html.

Teaching License or Certificate

Each state has the authority to establish the criteria for teacher eligibility and certification.[24] For the most part, each state has developed its own specific certification requirements, though many states have reciprocal licensure agreements with other states. This **reciprocity** means if a person qualifies for licensure in a state that has a reciprocal agreement with another state, the individual qualifies for licensure in both states. For instance, if someone qualifies for a teaching license in Virginia, and Virginia has a reciprocal agreement with California, the individual also qualifies for a California teaching license. The general rule is that if a person satisfies all the requirements established for receiving a state teaching license, the licensing agency cannot arbitrarily refuse to issue a license to that individual.

Having a teaching license or certificate, however, does not guarantee its holder a teaching position. A teaching certificate is not a contract. Rather, **certification** is simply a state's way of saying that the certificate or license holder has met the minimum requirements to hold a teaching job. Once the individual has the license, it is that person's responsibility to persuade school district officials during an interview that he or she is the best-qualified candidate for the position.

Generally, states issue teaching licenses and keep them active for a specific period of time, usually five years. Over that period, teachers must prepare to renew the license by taking classes, participating in professional development activities, and updating and expanding his or her professional knowledge and skills. Because most states require a valid teaching license to obtain a teaching contract, a teacher's job may be in jeopardy if his or her teaching license expires.

What This Means for Teachers

Keeping one's teaching license up-to-date and not giving the school district cause (good reason) to request that the license be revoked are recommended professional practices.

Can my teaching license be revoked once it is issued to me? Yes. Most states have criteria that allow for revocation of a teaching license and have established a process to do so. Needless to say, an educator who loses his or her professional license will not be able to earn a living as a teacher. Revoking a license is a severe penalty, similar to a lawyer being disbarred or a physician losing his or her license to practice medicine.

States require a just cause to revoke a teaching license. These reasons may include conviction of a felony, moral turpitude,[25] and falsifying teaching credentials. Because community standards vary, the state may base these decisions on how the community reacts to certain situations. For example, in *Crumpler v. State Board of Education* (1991), an Ohio court decided that a conviction for stealing drugs and money was sufficient grounds for denying a teaching certificate.[26]

In 1982, a Florida court upheld the revocation of two teachers' licenses for growing 52 marijuana plants in a greenhouse because their actions violated the community's moral standards and impaired the teachers' classroom

---

[24] We use the terms "certification" and "licensure" interchangeably here, even while acknowledging that there are subtle, yet distinct differences between the two.

[25] *Moral turpitude* can be defined as conduct that is considered to be so base, vile, or depraved that it is contrary to community standards of justice, honesty, or good morals.

[26] 71 Ohio App. 3d 526, 594 N.E.2d 1071 (1991).

effectiveness.[27] Similarly, conviction of mail fraud was cited as grounds for revoking a teaching license in *Startzel v. Pennsylvania Department of Education* (1989).[28]

A clear example of how moral standards may vary from community to community is seen in *Erb v. Iowa State Board of Public Instruction* (1974).[29] In spring 1970, teachers Richard Erb and Margaret Johnson (both married, though not to each other) began an extramarital affair. Suspicious, Johnson's husband caught his wife and Erb during several rendezvous, had photos taken of the couple's illicit activities, asked his wife for a divorce, and requested that the school board fire Erb. Erb offered to resign, but the school board voted unanimously to reject his resignation. Owing to his excellent teaching evaluations and his wife's and student body's forgiveness, Erb's high standing in the community remained intact.

Although the State Board of Education and lower trial court voted to revoke Erb's teaching license, on appeal the Iowa Supreme Court disagreed, stating that the misconduct was an isolated incident in an otherwise unblemished past. Erb's conduct did not serve as an affront to public mores, he admitted the action, and he publicly stated his regret for his behavior. Ultimately, Erb kept his job and his teaching license.

A different community might have responded to Erb's behavior in a different way, of course. A fine line exists regarding which behaviors can result in losing a teaching license. Much depends on the exact details of the situation and the state in which the behavior occurs.

What This Means for Teachers

The best advice is always to make wise choices in personal conduct, because poor choices may cost teachers their jobs and their teaching licenses.

Can my teaching license be revoked if the state adds testing requirements later that I cannot pass? Yes. In *State v. Project Principle, Inc.* (1987), the court found that not passing a state-required test following a teacher license being issued may cause the individual to lose the license.[30] In 1984, the Texas legislature passed a bill requiring teacher competency testing. All practicing teachers and administrators were required to pass the Texas Examination for Current Administrators and Teachers (TECAT). A suit was brought claiming that not renewing licenses if individuals did not pass the TECAT violated teachers' existing contracts with their school systems and violated their equal protection and due process clauses. Agreeing with this logic, the lower court ruled that the state could not revoke teaching licenses if the teachers did not pass the TECAT.

The State of Texas appealed the decision. Ultimately, the Texas Supreme Court ruled that the state had the right to set competency testing requirements. Because such testing had a rational relationship to the state's objective of maintaining a competent teaching force in its public schools, it did not violate the equal protection clause. Furthermore, the Texas Supreme Court ruled that a certificate is not a contract to teach; it is merely a license.

---

[27] Adams V. State Professional Practices Council, 412 So.2d 463 (Fla. 1982).
[28] 1228 Pa. Commw. 110, 562 A.2d 1005 (1989).
[29] Supreme Court of Iowa. (1974). 216 N.W.2d 339.
[30] Supreme Court of Texas. (1987). 724 S. W.2d 387.

What This Means for Teachers

A teaching license is not forever. Its ongoing validity depends on the teacher continuing to successfully meet the state's requirements for keeping it.

A Teaching Contract

When teachers sign a contract, state statutes and State Department of Education regulations govern the employment conditions. Generally, the contract is between the teacher and the local school board. The contract will specify the nature of the job to be performed and the compensation to be paid. Some contracts are very specific and say, for example, "fifth grade teacher at Oak Hill Elementary School." Other contracts are less specific and may simply state, "teacher." Most often, the teacher cannot be assigned to teach a content area outside of his or her certification without the teacher agreeing to do so. Finally, once a contract is offered, it must be accepted within a reasonable time frame or the contract becomes null and void. The contract may or may not stipulate this time frame.

Most teaching contracts have a provision for teachers to serve a **probationary period**—usually three years. Some states have shorter probationary periods; others have longer ones. Generally, the range is from one to five years. Once the teacher satisfactorily serves the probationary period, states have a provision for tenure, sometimes called **continuing contract status.**

Tenure provides a degree of job security and a right of continued employment for teachers. Once tenured, a teacher cannot be dismissed without due process. **Due process** includes a formal hearing and presentation of proof of sufficient cause to meet the statutory requirements for removal from the position. The teacher has an opportunity to challenge the evidence.[31] Generally, the tenured teacher must be notified of the detailed charges in a timely manner and given sufficient opportunity to prepare a defense. The hearing must be held before an impartial body (which may be the school board unless bias can be proved). The teacher's attorney may cross-examine witnesses and challenge any evidence brought in the case. In addition, the teacher can appeal an unfavorable decision in court.

An untenured teacher, by contrast, may simply be notified that his or her contract will not be renewed. The employing school district may give no reason for the termination. However, if the employing school district gives an illegal reason, the teacher may decide to sue the school district.

Legal Issues Once Teachers Are Employed and Teaching

Teachers' rights sometimes come with complex responsibilities. Legal factors regarding academic freedom, free speech, teacher privacy, and freedom of religion may all affect how teachers do their jobs.

Freedom of Speech

On the one hand, as citizens of the United States, teachers have a right to disagree publicly with a school principal's decision. On the other hand, if a teacher in a school makes public comments about "what a stupid decision the principal made,"

---

[31] Alexander, K., & Alexander, M. D. (2001). *American public school law* (5th ed.). Belmont, CA: Wadsworth, p. 671.

the teacher may get into legal trouble if those comments disrupt the school's operation. Teachers' freedom of speech is subject to certain limits.

Do teachers have academic freedom in the classroom? It depends.
Academic freedom. The concept of academic freedom comes to American public education from German universities. It encompasses two separate aspects—the freedom to learn and the freedom to teach. In the United States, academic freedom is bound up in the First Amendment ideal of free speech. **Academic freedom** means that teachers have some choices in the teaching methods they use as long as the teaching methods meet professional standards. Teachers have the professional freedom to monitor and adjust their teaching strategies if their students are not mastering the content.

Academic freedom does *not* mean that teachers can say whatever they would like—or teach whatever they want—in the classroom. In *The Law of Schools, Students, and Teachers* (2003), Alexander and Alexander explain, "[A]cademic freedom . . . does not bestow upon the teacher and the student 'unlimited liberty' to do anything their hearts desire; rather the concept must be viewed in the total context of the legal purpose and conduct of the school. Although academic freedom and the First Amendment are not synonymous they are closely related."[32] For example, suppose a third-grade teacher wants to teach a unit about skin, muscles, and bones, but that content belongs in the fourth-grade curriculum. The teacher has no right to teach the subject out of the school system's established curriculum sequence.

Reviewing several court cases helps clarify teachers' academic freedom. In *Cockrel v. Shelby County School District, et al.*, 2001,[33] Donna Cockrel, a fifth-grade teacher, was teaching a unit on "saving the trees." Studying alternatives to wood pulp, the class discussed industrial hemp fibers (hemp is derived from the same plant as marijuana). At that time, popular actor Woody Harrelson was in the state to talk with the Kentucky Hemp Growers Association. With the principal's permission, the teacher asked Harrelson to speak to the class. During Harrelson's discussion, he

Figure 8.1	Teachers Have Choices in Teaching Methods as Long as They Meet Professional Standards

Stephanie Rausser/Iconica/Getty Images

---

[32] Alexander, K., & Alexander, M. D. (2003). *The law of schools, students, and teachers* (3rd ed.). St. Paul, MN: West, p, 51.
[33] 270 F.3d 1036 (6th Cir.2001), 53.

passed hemp seeds (which were illegal) around the class. Given the local and national media extensively covering this celebrity, the event received widespread publicity. Responding to several parents' complaints about the lesson's appropriateness, the school superintendent asked the Professional Standards Board to investigate the illegal hemp seeds incident and report back. The Board found insufficient cause to take any action against the teacher. At that point, the school district put a "controversial topics" policy into place in its schools.

Complying with the new policy, Cockrel received permission for Harrelson to return for another class discussion. The school board then fired her. Nevertheless, the court ruled that the teacher's speech was constitutionally protected as a matter of public concern, and that she could not be fired. The school board had violated its own policy; the teacher had not.

In another case, *Keefe v.* Geanakos (1969), a high school teacher gave his class copies of an article published in *Atlantic Monthly* that used a rather vulgar and literal term to describe an incestuous son.[34] The teacher explained the word's etymology to the class and clarified why the author had used that specific word in the story. Any students finding the article offensive were allowed to select an alternative reading. The school board dismissed the teacher, and he sued to recover his teaching position. The court agreed with the teacher in finding the article to be thoughtful; deleting the offending word would have made understanding the article impossible. The teacher was reinstated.

In *Board of Education of Jefferson County School District R-1 v. Wilder* (1988), the school district had a policy for approving material to be used in class that was outside the usual curriculum.[35] When a teacher failed to obtain approval for showing a class an R-rated film depicting nudity, sexual conduct, and drug use, the school board dismissed the teacher. The teacher then sued, stating that the school board's dismissal violated his Fourteenth Amendment due process rights and his First Amendment free speech rights. The court upheld the teacher's dismissal, stating that the school board's policy was a reasonable method for regulating possible inappropriate classroom materials.

Teachers may go beyond legal bounds when they select classroom material that is "offensive and unnecessary to the accomplishment of educational objectives . . . [where] . . . such questions are matters of degree involving judgment on such factors as the age and sophistication of the students, relevance of the educational purpose, and context and manner of presentations."[36] In other words, a teacher does not have total freedom to select materials that are not age or educationally appropriate.

What This Means for Teachers

Many school districts have approved curriculum and reading lists from which teachers must select books, articles, and reading materials. Teachers are advised to find out if their school board has a policy about selecting classroom materials, know what that policy is, and follow it. When in doubt about some particular content to use in class, teachers should first seek guidance from their department head, their grade-level leader, or a school administrator. Not following school board policy about classroom reading materials could be both unethical and insubordinate, and it could cost the teacher his or her job.

---

[34] 418 F.2d 359 (1st Cir.1969), 53,
[35] 960 P.2d 695 (Colo.1988), 54, 441.
[36] *Brubaker v. Board of Education, School District 149, Cook County, Illinois* (7th Cir.1974).

The *Cockrel* case mentioned "public concern." What is "speaking out on a matter of public concern," and how can it affect my job?

Speaking out in public. **Free speech** means that government must tolerate and cannot restrain the exercise of free speech in open public debate, regardless of whether that speech is offensive, tumultuous, or discordant.[37] Yet over the years, the U.S. Supreme Court has concluded that practical reality requires that government, at certain times and under certain conditions, be able to restrict employees' speech to fulfill its responsibilities to operate effectively and efficiently.

Defining what a *public concern* is can be tricky. Today, speaking out publicly as a teacher about tax increases or a proposed policy where public comment is encouraged is clearly a matter of public concern. The Supreme Court has decided, however, that a public school teacher or other school employee may be restrained in the exercise of speech depending on whether it involves a matter of public concern or private concern.

Early in American history, public employment was viewed as a privilege, not as a right. As such, many courts held that contracts between teachers and school boards curtailed certain teacher rights and freedoms. If a teacher spoke out on an issue that violated the contract's terms, the teacher could be dismissed and the courts would uphold the dismissal. Until 1968, school teachers were hesitant to become too involved in politics for fear that they would be penalized or even fired for such activities. In 1968, in its ruling in *Pickering v. Board of Education*, the U.S. Supreme Court decided that teachers have a right to speak out freely on matters of public concern.[38]

Marvin Pickering was a teacher at Township High School in Illinois. The locality was considering a tax increase to raise school revenue. Not liking how an earlier bond issue distributed funds between athletics and academics, Pickering wrote a letter to the editor of the local newspaper that was critical of how the previous tax increase had allocated funds. He alleged that the superintendent of schools tried to prevent teachers from opposing the proposed bond issue. Pickering's letter contained several factual errors.

The school board held a hearing to determine if Pickering's letter had "been detrimental to the efficient operation of the schools of the district," which, under state statute, required the teacher's dismissal. Finding this assertion to be true, the school board fired Pickering. In accordance with state law, it was required to hold a hearing on Pickering's dismissal. Although the hearing board found many of the school board's allegations that the letter's publication damaged the board's and superintendent's professional reputations to be false, the dismissal was upheld. The Illinois Supreme Court upheld his dismissal.

Eventually, the U.S. Supreme Court disagreed, noting that "without proof of false statements knowingly or recklessly made by him, a teacher's exercise of his right to speak on issues of public importance may not furnish the basis for his dismissal from public employment." Pickering's statements in no way harmed the school district's operations and did not affect the teacher's performance. The Illinois Supreme Court's decision was reversed, and Pickering won the case.

To guide lower federal courts in future cases of this nature, the Supreme Court stated what has come to be called the *Pickering* balance test. Writing in the Court's opinion, Justice Thurgood Marshall explained:

> The problem in any case is to arrive at a balance between the interests of the teacher, as a citizen, in commenting upon matters of public concern and the interest of the State, as an employer, in promoting the efficiency of the public services it performs through its employees.[39]

---

[37] Alexander & Alexander, 2005, p. 721.
[38] 391 U.S. 563, 88 S. Ct. 1731 (1968).
[39] 391 U.S. at 568.

In other words, a balance must be found between a person's rights to speak out on matters of public concern and an organization's interest in doing its job efficiently.

Fifteen years later in *Connick v. Myers* (1983), the U.S. Supreme Court clarified the limitations on public employees' free speech.[40] While a public employee's speech is protected when he or she is speaking out on a matter of public concern, balancing the employee's and state's interests, the First Amendment does not protect a public employee's speech or expression concerning a private or personal interest in matters of public concern. Even though this case did not involve educators, it is relevant because Myers was a public employee and the precedent established in this case has been cited in legal actions involving educators.

Assistant District Attorney Sheila Myers was told she would be reassigned to another area of criminal law. Opposing the transfer, Myers circulated a questionnaire to other assistant district attorneys about staff morale and related issues. She was told the questionnaire amounted to insubordination, and she was fired. The Supreme Court upheld her dismissal, stating that the matter was basically a personnel issue and not a public one. It became a personal issue because the questionnaire went out after the transfer was announced. The Court believed that Myers' First Amendment interest was outweighed by the disruptive nature of the questions she was circulating to colleagues, which "substantially interfered with the operation of the office."

Placing additional limits on teachers' speech, the ruling in *Stroman v. Colleton County School District* (1993) specified that teachers' First Amendment (free speech) rights do not extend to encouraging dishonest conduct and conduct that violates policy.[41] In this case, because he was upset about a change in the Colleton County School District's summer pay policy (from lump sum to bimonthly), teacher John Stroman wrote and circulated a letter to fellow teachers. He criticized the central office for fiscal mismanagement and being administratively "top heavy," and he encouraged teachers to participate in a "sick out" during the week of final exams.

Meeting with the superintendent and his principal the next day, Stroman admitted writing and circulating the letter, claiming that he was being treated unfairly in terms of his pay schedule. The superintendent promptly handed Stroman a dismissal letter dated that day, citing unfitness for teaching by proposing to and encouraging others to abandon their duties. Stroman sued to be reinstated as a teacher, claiming that his free speech rights were denied.

The Fourth Circuit Court of Appeals[42] affirmed the teachers' First Amendment free speech rights, but stated that a grievance (in this case, the change in summer pay policy) was not covered under the First Amendment. The court ruled that speaking out in self-interest about the summer pay changes made the matter one of self-concern and not public concern, eliminating the free speech rights claim. Stroman's dismissal was upheld.

This decision will have a major legal impact on teachers' rights to speak out on issues that are part of their official duties. At present, the courts appear to be moving more toward protecting employers than protecting employees in what might be considered free speech issues and employment.

What This Means for Teachers

When acting as a teacher or as a citizen, be careful what you say in a public forum about your teaching role and its employment context—because it might cost your job.

---

[40] 461 U.S. 138, 103 S.Ct.1684 (1983).
[41] 981 F.2d 152 (Fourth Circuit, 1993).
[42] There are 13 Circuit Courts of Appeal in the United States representing various geographic regions of the country. The Fourth Circuit Court of Appeals represents the mid-Atlantic states.

Can the school board require a dress code for teachers? Yes.
Professional dress code. Several court cases decided the issue of a teachers' dress code more than 30 years ago. The outstanding case specifically related to such a dress code was *East Harford Education Association v. Board of Education* (1977),[43] in which the Second Circuit Court of Appeals decided that a teacher dress policy is constitutional.

In this case, Richard Brimley, an English teacher, was reprimanded for not wearing a tie to his classes. Earlier, the school board had implemented a policy requiring male teachers to wear a jacket, shirt, and tie to classes. Female teachers were required to wear a dress, skirt, blouse, or pantsuit to classes. If teachers had other teaching assignments such as physical education, they could wear more appropriate clothing.

Feeling that the dress code deprived him of his free speech and privacy rights, Brimley stated that not wearing a tie to class assisted him with his teaching, helping his students relate more closely to him as a person not tied to conformity or the establishment. He claimed that not wearing a tie was his symbolic speech and, therefore, was constitutionally protected. The court disagreed with the teacher's assertions, stating that a "protected interest in Mr. Brimley's neckwear . . . does not weigh very heavily on the constitutional scales."[44] The court ruled that it is in the school board's interest to promote respect for authority and traditional values, as well as classroom discipline, by requiring teachers to dress in a professional manner. Promoting a dress code is a rational means of promoting these goals.

What This Means for Teachers

If your employing school district has a professional dress code, follow it if you want to continue your employment there. Express your individuality through effective instructional approaches.

Teacher Privacy

The word "privacy" is not found in either the Bill of Rights or the Constitution. Nonetheless, it is considered to be a basic and fundamental right, a logical offshoot of the constitutional protection against unreasonable search and seizure. Therefore, a compelling state interest must be demonstrated to warrant violating a person's privacy. The Fourth Amendment of the U.S. Constitution reads as follows:

> The right of the people to be secure in their persons, houses, papers, and effects, against unreasonable searches and seizures, shall not be violated, and no Warrants shall issue, but upon probable cause, supported by Oath or affirmation, and particularly describing the place to be searched, and the persons or things to be seized.

While teachers keep their right to privacy in schools, this right has certain limits.

Can my classroom, desk, closet, and file cabinets be searched? Yes.
Search of teachers' workspace. A teacher's right to privacy in the classroom comes under the concept of a workplace. In *O'Connor v. Ortega* (1987), the Supreme Court defined the **workplace** as "those areas and items that are related to work and are generally within the employer's control."[45] This would include offices, hallways,

---

[43] 562 F.2d 838 (2nd Circuit 1977).
[44] Quoted in Alexander & Alexander, 2005, p. 740.
[45] 480 U.S. 709, 107 S.Ct. 1492 (1987).

cafeterias, offices, desks, file cabinets, lockers, and other areas. In these locations, an employee does not have an expectation of privacy, and the school may search them.

The Supreme Court did not establish any ground rules on when or how an employer's "interest in supervision, control and the efficient operation of the workplace" would outweigh an employee's "legitimate expectations of privacy." It left to the lower courts the job of applying the simple "balance" formula on a case-by-case basis.

A teacher's personal effects, such as purses, briefcases, and closed luggage are not considered as belonging to the workplace. These items may not be searched without a warrant.

What This Means for Teachers

Because many workplace areas are not legally "private," wise teachers should only bring to school with them those items that they would not mind everyone knowing they have.

Teacher drug testing. The Fourth Amendment safeguards individuals against arbitrary and unwarranted intrusions into their privacy. It does not limit all searches and seizures, however—only those that are unreasonable. What is "reasonable" depends on the circumstances and the nature of the search and seizure itself. What is "reasonable" remains a critical question.

To search citizens, the police must have **probable cause**—a reasonable belief that a person has committed a crime. Due to schools' unique nature in which they serve *in loco parentis* (in the place of the parent), the standard for school searches is lower than that required for the police to search an ordinary citizen. In schools, the government has a special interest that allows warrantless searches based on **reasonable suspicion** (credible information from a reliable source)—a less demanding standard than probable cause. This standard of reasonable suspicion justifies searches of students and teachers on school property.

In addition, the increased prevalence of illegal drug use has prompted courts to define privacy rights in a new context that does not neatly fit with probable cause or reasonable suspicion. As a result, courts have formulated a new category of reasonable searches called **suspicionless searches,** which permit testing for drugs and alcohol without showing individualized suspicion.

As a teacher, can I be forced to take a drug test? Yes. In *Hearn v. Board of Education* (1999), the school district had a zero-tolerance policy for drugs and alcohol on school property.[46] During a routine "drug dog" search of the parking lot, the dog sniffed drugs in a teacher's car. The teacher claimed the search was illegal. The school district policy required that anyone suspected of having or having used drugs submit to a urine test within two hours; refusal to comply with the policy could result in the employee being fired. The teacher refused to take the urine test and was later fired. The teacher sued, and the court held that the search was legal based on the probable cause of the dog sniff identification of the vehicle.

Additionally, the U.S. Supreme Court has held that under certain conditions, suspicionless searches of persons employed in safety-sensitive positions may take place.[47] A federal court has ruled that teachers fall under the safety-sensitive positions and may be compelled to submit to drug searches in the form of urine testing.[48]

---

[46] 191 F.3d 1329 (11th Cir.1999).
[47] *Skinner v. Railway Executives Association* (S.Ct.1989) and National Treasury Employees Union v. Von Raab (S.Ct.1989).
[48] *Knox County Education Association v. Knox County Board of Education* (6th Cir.1998) 158 F.3d 361.

What This Means for Teachers

Teachers may be asked to submit to drug testing. They may refuse to do so, but they will probably be fired for not complying with the request.

Can school authorities test teachers for illegal drug use without having a reasonable suspicion of drug use? Yes. In *Knox County Education Association v. Knox County Board of Education* (1998), the U.S. Court of Appeals ruled that school authorities could conduct suspicionless drug testing of teachers.[49]

In this case, the court ruled that suspicionless testing was justified based on the unique role that teachers play in school children's lives. In the school setting, where teachers act *in loco parentis*, the public interest in drug testing outweighs teachers' privacy interests in not being tested. The court further pointed out that the teaching profession is by nature and of necessity heavily regulated, and teachers have a diminished expectation of privacy. The drug testing regimen employed in this school system was limited, narrowly tailored, and relatively unobtrusive in its monitoring and disclosure.

What This Means for Teachers

Prospective teachers must comply with school districts' drug and alcohol policies or be denied employment. Employed teachers risk job termination if they are found using an illegal substance or alcohol at a job-related function or on property owned by the school board.

Teachers' Freedom of Religion

As U.S. citizens, teachers have rights defined by the U.S. Constitution that accompany them into the classroom. Freedom of religion is one of these protected rights. As with freedom of speech, however, this right is not unlimited.

The First Amendment to the U.S. Constitution dealing with freedom of religion states:

> Congress shall make no law respecting an establishment of religion, or prohibiting the free exercise thereof . . .

The 1972 amendment to Title VII of the Civil Rights Act further expands this religious freedom:

> It shall be an unlawful employment practice for an employment agency to fail or refuse for employment, or otherwise to discriminate against, any individual because of his race, color, religion, sex, or national origin, or to classify or refer for employment any individual on the basis of his race, color, religion, sex, or national origin.

May I be required to teach something that goes against my religious beliefs? Yes. While these laws guarantee Americans freedom of religion, this religious freedom is not unlimited. In *Palmer v. Board of Education of the City of Chicago* (1980), a teacher refused to teach part of the city-designated curriculum, stating that to do so would violate her religious beliefs.[50] While the court acknowledged the teacher's

---

[49] Sixth Circuit, 1998, 158 F.3d 361.
[50] 603 F.2d 1271, 1274 (7th Cir.1979), cert denied. 444 U.S. 1026, 100 S.Ct. 689 (1980).

right to freedom of belief, it also pointed out the school district's interest in providing a proper education to all students. The ruling in this case further stated that teachers "cannot be left to teach the way they please." When a teacher has a religious belief that interferes with teaching the required class content, the content takes priority over the religious beliefs.

However, if a teacher's religious tenets prohibit the teacher from pledging to the flag, the teacher cannot be forced to recite the Pledge of Allegiance with the class as part of his or her professional duties. If school rules require the Pledge to be recited, the teacher may be required to be in the classroom with the students as they recite the Pledge of Allegiance.[51] The courts have continued to uphold teachers' freedom of religion as long as it does not encroach on students' rights and does not harm the school's good conduct.

What should teachers know about the courts' position on intelligent design? The U.S. Supreme Court and a federal court in Pennsylvania ruled that teaching creationism or intelligent design is unconstitutional teaching of religion in public schools.

Are teachers legally responsible for teaching intelligent design alongside evolution? No. In *Edwards v. Aguillard* (1987),[52] the U.S. Supreme Court ruled that requiring a "balanced" treatment of creation science and evolution science was unconstitutional because it violated the bar against teaching religion in public schools. Likewise, in *Kitzmiller v. Dover Area School District* (2005),[53] a federal court, in a strongly worded opinion, struck down as unconstitutional a local school board's attempt to insert teaching of intelligent design into the classroom as an attempt to "discredit evolution," which has the scientific community's support.

As a teacher, am I permitted to celebrate my religious holidays? Usually. As an employment practice, school boards must reasonably accommodate aspects of teachers' religious observances and practice unless it can be shown that such accommodations produce undue hardships on the employer's business. The teacher has the initial burden of proof to show that a school board's decision was religiously motivated or involved the denial of a religious freedom. If the teacher does so, the burden then moves to the school board, whose members must show they made a good-faith effort to accommodate the teacher's religious beliefs.

In *Wangsness v. Watertown School District No. 14-4* (1982), the court ruled in favor of a teacher who requested to be absent from school without pay for seven days to attend a religious festival.[54] The teacher's request was denied, but the teacher attended the festival anyway. Before leaving for the holiday, the teacher prepared lesson plans and met with the substitute teacher to review the lessons. The school district dismissed the teacher, and the teacher sued. The court found that the classes had run well in the teacher's absence, and the school district had not suffered a hardship due to the teacher attending the religious festival. The court determined that the dismissal was not warranted, and had violated the teacher's rights under Title VII.

In another case, *Pinsker v. Joint District No. 28J* (1983), a Jewish teacher requested more than the two days allowed to celebrate the religious holidays.[55] He showed that teachers of the Christian faith had more days to celebrate their holidays and that the school calendar was built around Christian holidays. The school board denied the teacher's request, and the teacher went to court. Eventually, the court found in favor of the teacher, stating that his Title VII rights were violated because the employer had punished an employee by placing

---

[51] *Russo v. Central School District No. 1*, 469 F.2d 623 (2d Cir. 1972), cert denied, 411 U.S. 932. 93 S/Ct. 1899 (1973).
[52] 482 U.S. 578, 107 S.Ct. 2573.
[53] 400 F. Supp. 2d 707.
[54] 541 F. Supp. 332 (D.S.D. 1982).
[55] 544 F. Supp. 1049 (D. Colo.1983).

the employee in a position in which a tenet of faith must be ignored to retain employment.

What This Means for Teachers

Teachers are allowed to be absent from school to practice their religious faith, but they need to ensure that their absence does not disrupt the school's learning environment. Before their absence during the normal school schedule, teachers must put plans in place to continue their students' learning. Teachers are advised to know and follow their school district's policies and procedures to facilitate their religiously motivated absences.

Can I wear religious clothing and accessories in class? It depends. State law and local policies determine the answer to this question. Some states see teachers wearing religious clothing and accessories as imposing their religious views on students in an area where the state should be neutral.[56]

A 1986 Oregon case related to teacher attire is especially noteworthy. In *Cooper v. Eugene School District No. 4J*, the court determined that the state can revoke a teaching license if a teacher violates the state regulations prohibiting teachers from wearing religious garb in school.[57] Janet Cooper, a teacher in Eugene, Oregon, converted to the Sikh religion. She began to wear the turban and the white clothing associated with her new religion, and she explained her life changes to her students. The administration warned her that her continuing violation of Oregon's state law prohibiting teachers from wearing religious dress in public schools could mean revocation of her teaching certificate.

Cooper continued to wear the religious clothing. Following state law, the superintendent suspended her from teaching and reported the incident to the state's Superintendent of Public Instruction; this official then held a hearing and revoked Cooper's teaching certificate. Cooper challenged the action. The Court of Appeals ruled in her favor, but the State Supreme Court of Oregon reversed the decision and upheld the revocation of her certificate.

So far, the courts have not agreed about teacher attire, largely because they are hesitant to invade the religious rights of either teachers or students. They are clearer about prohibiting situations where schools might appear to be endorsing a particular religion or even prayer. Courts weight interests in view of the particular facts in each case.

What This Means for Teachers

It is important for teachers to know and follow the state laws and local policies regarding their professional attire, wearing of religious garb or symbols, use of nondenominational prayer, or prominent display of religious books or other such items while teaching in public schools.

What could happen if I share my religious beliefs in class with my students? It depends. Teachers are employees of the school board. As government employees, teachers accept limits about sharing their personal religious beliefs with students. According to U.S. Supreme Court interpretations of the First Amendment, the state cannot endorse religion or promote one religion over another. When

---

[56] See *Hysong v. School District of Gallitzin Borough*, 164 Pa. 629, 30 A. 482 (1894); and *Commonwealth v. Herr*, 229 Pa. 132, 78 A. 68 (1910).
[57] 301 Or.358, 723 P.2d 298.

teachers speak as a teacher on school property, they are speaking to children who see them as authority figures. By sharing his or her religious faith with others, the teacher is implicitly endorsing a religion. This places impressionable students under pressure to accept the teacher's religion.

In two recent cases, in 2000 and 2007, two different U.S. Courts of Appeals ruled that teachers could not post "overly religious" materials on their classroom or school bulletin boards because that content violated the First Amendment's Establishment Clause and was not directly related to the curriculum.[58] If school administrators learn that a teacher is sharing his or her religion with students, the administrators can tell the teacher to stop this practice, for the reasons mentioned earlier. If the teacher continues to speak with students about his or her religious beliefs, the teacher can be fired for insubordination.

What This Means for Teachers

The teacher's job is to teach the content he or she was hired to teach and not to either subtly or overtly endorse the teacher's religion to students.

What are my rights and obligations as a teacher regarding Bible reading, prayers, and moments of silence in my classroom? It depends.
Religious activities in public schools. The U.S. Supreme Court has made decisions related to a variety of religious activities when they occur on school grounds. In *School District of Abington Township v. Schempp and Murray v. Curlett* (1963),[59] the Court found that state-enforced Bible reading and prayer in public schools were religious exercises and, therefore, unconstitutional. Likewise, in *Wallace v. Jaffree* (1985),[60] the Court ruled that a state-authorized period of silence for meditation or voluntary prayer is unconstitutional. In *Brown v. Gilmore* (2000),[61] however, the 4th Circuit Court of Appeals in Virginia found that a "minute of silence" was constitutional because its purpose was secular.

What This Means for Teachers

Teachers cannot lead prayers, Bible reading, or silent meditation in public schools. Teachers should check their school district's policy regarding any "minute of silence."

Other Legal Issues Affecting Teachers

Teachers also face legal issues arising from actions that occur while they are teaching.

Is there such a thing as "educational malpractice," and can I be sued if students do not learn in my class? No.
Educational malpractice. The good news here is that there has never been a successful suit for educational malpractice. Educational malpractice is a professional issue, not a legal one.

---

[58] *Lee v. York County School Division*, 484 F. 3d 687 (4th Cir. 2007), cert denied.128 S. Ct. 387 (2007); and *Downs v. Los Angeles Unified School District*, 228 F. 3d 1003 (9th Cir. 2000).
[59] 374 U.S. 203, 83 S. Ct. 1560.
[60] 472 U.S. 38, 105 S. Ct. 2479.
[61] 258 F. 3d 265 (4th Cir).

What This Means for Teachers

If students do not learn what the school district expects while those students are in a teacher's class, the issue of the teacher's ineffective practices will be addressed in the school and school district, rather than in court.

Can I be sued if my actions as a teacher cause harm to a student? Yes. **Teachers sued for harming students.** Not only may teachers be sued personally for causing student injury, but they may also lose their jobs. Harming another person is the subject of the legal arena called *torts*. A **tort** is a civil wrong or some type of harm that one person causes another person, outside of a contract, for which the courts may award damages.[62] Courts have not been hesitant to rule on torts. It is important to note that torts involve a civil—and not a criminal—wrong.

Most people are aware of the terms "assault" and "battery," but many do not understand the difference between the two. **Assault** is a mental violation or the threat that someone will receive a physical injury. **Battery** is what happens when the assault becomes physical. Almost every school district has regulations that protect students and teachers against assault and battery, and offending parties face severe consequences. Students who threaten to harm another person or who give an unlawful or unwanted touch with the intention of harming or offending another person could be suspended or even expelled from school. In addition, the victim may file criminal and civil charges against the student who threatened or hit that individual. Similarly, teachers who threaten to harm or who give an unwanted or unlawful touch with the intent to harm or offend a student could be fired from their jobs and may lose their teaching licenses. What is more, the teacher could be criminally or civilly charged as a result from the incident.

In *Spears v. Jefferson Parish School Board* (1994), the Louisiana Court of Appeals held the school district liable for a teacher's intentional act that resulted in emotional harm to a child.[63] In 1989, kindergartner Justin Spears and two friends became disruptive while their physical education class watched a movie. One of the coaches, Mr. Brooks, asked the boys to sit by him. They began to play with the teacher's hair and ears. He told the boys if they did not stop, he would "kill them." Brooks took two of the boys into an adjacent office while Justin remained behind with another teacher. The two boys asked Brooks how he would kill them; he responded by saying he would hang them. Brooks and the boys agreed to play a trick on Justin.

Returning to Justin, Brooks convinced him that the teacher had hanged his two friends. When Justin entered the office, one of the boys was on the floor with a rope tied around his neck pretending to be dead. Justin then began to cry, and Brooks tried to calm the boy down by telling him the boys were not really dead.

After this incident, Justin began to behave strangely at home, using infantile behaviors and becoming more attached to his mother. He refused to go to the bathroom alone, fearing Brooks would jump out of the mirror and harm him. A psychologist diagnosed Justin as having post-traumatic stress syndrome. The parents then sued both the school district as an entity and Brooks as an individual for this injury to their son. The trial court found in favor of the parents, awarding the family general damages of $100,000 for the additional therapy Justin would need, as well as money damages to the parents for losses they received from the incident.

---

[62] We will not examine contract law here.
[63] *Spears v. Jefferson Parish School Board*, 646 So. 2d 1104 (1994).

What if something happens in my classroom and someone gets hurt? Is that negligence on my part? Maybe. **What could happen to me?** It depends.

Negligence. As long as there are children, there will be accidents. Nonetheless, a student injury that results from an unintended accident does not mean that the supervising adult is legally blameless. **Negligence** is generally defined as conduct that is culpable because it falls short of what a reasonable person would do to protect another individual from a foreseeable risk of harm. In short, being a professional means minimizing the potential for injuries to occur by acting proactively in an informed manner to avoid potentially harmful situations.

A teacher is negligent when, without intending any wrong, he or she either acts or fails to take a precaution that under the circumstances an ordinary prudent and reasonably intelligent teacher ought to foresee would expose another person to unnecessary risk of harm. In certain school functions where children face greater risks, a teacher has an increased level of obligation or duty to the children.

For example, whenever pupils perform a dangerous lab experiment, the teacher has a greater responsibility to ensure the students' safety than when the teacher is supervising a study hall. Likewise, a woodshop teacher has a higher standard of care than a librarian because the risk of harm is greater when students are working with power tools than when they are reading books. Students face more dangers when they are running around the schoolyard than they do when they are sitting quietly studying in the classroom. Clearly, teachers' standards of care vary with the students' ages, situation, and circumstances.

No definite rules exist about what constitutes negligence. What is negligent in one situation may not be negligent under a different set of circumstances. The standards of conduct of the teacher are the key to making this determination. For teachers and other educators, the generally accepted standard of care would be that of a reasonably prudent *teacher*, not that of a reasonably prudent *layperson*.[64] As professionals, courts expect teachers to have more informed awareness and judgment about potential risks than would an ordinary person.

Of course, sometimes pure accidents occur in which someone is injured and no one is actually at fault. For instance, when a child closed a music room door, cutting

| Figure 8.2 | Being Professional Means Proactively Minimizing the Potential for Harm |

Andy Sacks/Stone/Getty Images

[64] Alexander & Alexander, 2005, p. 559.

off the tip of another student's finger, the court found no negligence had occurred; the event was merely an accident.[65]

What This Means for Teachers

Teachers are legally responsible the well-being of the students under their supervision. They must continually monitor the possibilities for student injury throughout the day and proactively remove threats to student safety. Teachers are held to a standard of care appropriate to reasonably prudent professionals, which is a higher standard of obligation than that applied to a person in general.

Student Rights and Responsibilities

Given that students enjoy many of the same constitutional rights as adults, courts have been very careful in ensuring that they protect students' constitutional rights.

School officials have broad authority to establish rules and regulations governing student conduct in the school setting. These powers are not absolute, however; they are subject to the standard of *reasonableness*. Generally, rules are considered reasonable if they are needed to maintain an orderly and peaceful school environment and advance the educational process.

In determining the enforceability of school policies, rules, and regulations, courts require school authorities to provide evidence to sufficiently justify their need to enforce these directives. Fair and reasonable exercise of administrative authority will stand up to a judge's scrutiny. Of course, determining exactly what is fair and reasonable depends on the situation.

Student Discipline and Due Process Rights

Courts have ruled that for schools to operate properly, teachers and principals must be given certain authority to maintain an orderly environment. Practically and legally, parents give schools some level of control when they enroll their children. Nevertheless, students do not lose all of their constitutional privileges when they enter the school building. Schools must balance the individual student's rights with those of the public good.

Just as parents must discipline their children from time to time, so teachers have the authority to guide, correct, and occasionally rebuke their students under the *in loco parentis* concept, unless state law or school board policy does not authorize such a role. Teachers are trained in how to maintain an orderly classroom environment. When students disrupt the learning process, teachers must discipline them. However, neither parents nor teachers have unlimited control over students: Child abuse is illegal whether it is committed by parents or by teachers.

For the most part, teachers' classroom management is preventive in nature; that is, it focuses on identifying and stopping small problems before they become bigger. When a student overtly and maliciously does not comply with classroom rules, the teacher usually refers the student to an administrator, who handles the misbehavior privately with the student. When punishment is required, detention, in-school suspension, or out-of-school suspension typically result. Under the *in loco parentis* principle, the rules must be reasonable ones. But what is reasonable? When the answer is unclear, the courts must decide.

---

[65] *Lewis v. St. Bernard Parish School,* 350 So. 2d 1256 (La. Ct. App. 1977).

Suspending a student from school disrupts his or her right to an education. According to the Fourteenth Amendment, due process is required if a citizen's right is being taken away.[66] In *Goss v. Lopez* (1975), the U.S. Supreme Court ruled that a temporary suspension of fewer than ten days from school requires **procedural due process**.[67] Students must be given oral or written notice of the charges, an explanation of the evidence against them, and an opportunity to present their side of the issue. Due process is required whenever a student is separated from school.

The due process procedures become even more formal when the school recommends a student for **expulsion**, which involves long-term or permanent separation from the school program. Similarly, the court's ruling *Honig v. Doe* (1988) gave special-needs students additional protections in situations involving disciplinary action, thereby limiting schools' ability to make unilateral decisions about removing a disruptive student with disabilities from school.[68]

Giving students their due process rights takes time. An administrator must speak with students and other teachers who may have witnessed the event, determine what actually happened, and decide a reasonable consequence. The administrator must then present the gathered evidence to the offending student and his or her parents or guardian to explain, justify, and document any disciplinary action taken. This process ensures that schools treat all students fairly and legally.

Corporal punishment. While the U.S. Supreme Court determined in *Ingraham v. Wright* (1977)[69] that corporal punishment in schools was acceptable, the public's acceptance of paddling (or spanking) in schools has declined substantially in recent decades. In fact, today a teacher or a principal may be charged with assault and battery for paddling a child in school. If convicted of criminal charges, the educator may be subject to a fine or imprisonment. If convicted on civil charges, the educator may have to pay monetary damages. Currently 29 states ban corporal punishment.[70]

What This Means for Teachers

For legal and ethical reasons, we advise teachers not to paddle or physically inflict discomfort on students. Additionally, such actions are not effective in teaching students more appropriate behaviors.

When are disciplinary actions considered to be child abuse? It depends. For many educators and parents, it is not clear precisely which actions make up "child abuse." Corporal punishment as a common-law school privilege often conflicts with most child abuse statutes. In *Arkansas Department of Human Services v. Caldwell* (1992), the court ruled that reasonable force in paddling a student does not constitute child abuse.[71]

In this case, an assistant principal in Mountain Home, Arkansas, paddled three fifth-grade students who had been caught smoking on the playground. The following afternoon, one child's mother noticed bruises on her daughter's

---

[66] There are two types of due process, procedural and substantive. We will deal only with procedural due process in this chapter.

[67] 419 U.S. 565, 95 S.Ct. 729 (1975).

[68] *Honig v. Doe* (1988), 484 U.S. 305, 108 S Ct. 592.

[69] 430 U.S. 651, 97 S. Ct. 1401.

[70] Stoddard, E. (2008, August 20). Corporal punishment seen rife in U.S. schools. *Reuters.* Retrieved August 20, 2008, from http://www.reuters.com/article/domesticNews/idUSN1931921320080820; The Center for Effective Discipline. (2008). U.S.: Corporal punishment and paddling statistics by state and race, states banning corporal punishment. Retrieved October 3, 2009, from http://www.stophitting.com/disatschool/statesBanning.php.

[71] 39 Ark.App.14, 832 S. W.2d 510 (1992).

buttocks, and reported these actions as suspected child abuse to the appropriate state agency. Because the bruises had resulted from the paddling, the case worker ruled the child abuse charges were substantiated and placed the administrator's name on the State Central Registry for Child Abuse. The administrator appealed to have her name removed. The court ruled that the paddling was not abusive and noted that reasonable paddling may be legal, although excessive punishment may be abusive.

Where allowed, the corporal punishment administered must be moderate, delivered with a proper instrument, and take into account the child's age, gender, size, and overall physical strength. Within these broad limits, a teacher must balance the seriousness of the offense with the extent of punishment assigned. Because teachers are usually present when student misbehavior occurs, and teachers normally know the manner, look, tone, gestures, language, setting, and general circumstances of the offense, courts will allow teachers considerable latitude in judgment. At the same time, courts will not tolerate punishment that is cruel and excessive. Any sign that teachers acted out of malice will override the teacher's *in loco parentis* privilege.

What This Means for Teachers

Teachers need to remain calm, even-tempered, emotionally objective, and professional at all times. Becoming upset with disruptive or disrespectful students to the point where teachers lose their cool and overreact to student behavior can place the teachers in professional and legal jeopardy.

Student Privacy: Search and Seizure of Student Property

Educators must occasionally decide whether to search a student's locker, desk, book bag, or pockets. At the heart of the issue is the right of privacy guaranteed by the Fourth Amendment, which states, "The right of people to be secure in their person, houses, papers, and effects, against unreasonable searches and seizures shall not be violated, and no warrants shall issue, but upon probable cause . . ."

Just as parents do not need to prove to a judge that they deserve a warrant so they can check their children's book bags or bedrooms, educators operating *in loco parentis are* held to the less rigorous legal standard of *reasonable suspicion*. Reasonable suspicion is based on receiving credible information from known (as opposed to anonymous) and reliable sources. Suspicion, by definition, implies a belief; it does not equal proof. The courts have ruled that students' right to privacy and freedom from unreasonable search and seizure must be balanced against schools' need to maintain order and provide a safe and secure environment for all students.

The reasonable suspicion standard is not unlimited, however. Public school officials have restraints on their rights to search students' persons[72], book bags, desks, or lockers. Some facts must provide reasonable grounds for performing the search, the search must be conducted to further a legitimate school purpose such as maintaining school discipline, and the search may not be overtly intrusive.

Can school officials search students' personal possessions? Yes, under certain conditions, school administrators can search students' personal possessions.

---

[72] In June, 2009. The U.S. Supreme Court ruled that school officials could not strip-search a student while looking for ibuprophen because it violated the 4th Amendment's prohibition against unreasonable search and seizure. See; Bravin, J. (2009, June 26), Court faults strip-search of student. *The Wall Street Journal/Law.* Retrieved August 14, 2009 from: http://online.wsj.com/article/SB124593034315253301.html

A landmark 1985 U.S. Supreme Court case, *New Jersey v. T.L.O.*, provides guidance for school administrators in the area of student searches and seizure of property.[73] In this case, a teacher found a 14-year-old freshman student, T.L.O. (her initials), smoking in the bathroom with another student. The assistant principal asked to see the girl's purse and found cigarettes, rolling papers, marijuana, a pipe, plastic bags, a substantial amount of money, a list of students who apparently owed the girl money, and two letters implicating her in selling marijuana at school. The parents sued, claiming the search unreasonable. On appeal, the U.S. Supreme Court ruled that a student search is permissible if it is "justified at its inception," reasonable, and "not excessively intrusive." What is reasonable, therefore, varies flexibly with the context.

What This Means for Teachers

Because school administrators have received professional training in the laws and practices regarding school discipline, teachers are advised to allow principals and assistant principals to conduct any reasonable searches of students' property or persons. The administrator may ask the teacher to remain as a witness to the search.

Can school administrators search student lockers? Yes.
Searching student lockers. In *State of Iowa v. Jones* (2003), the court ruled that annual, schoolwide locker cleanouts were permissible despite students' privacy interests and the lack of individualized suspicion.[74] During the locker cleanout in this case, marijuana was found in a student's locker. The court ruled that while students have a measure of privacy for their lockers' contents, the locker search was not overly intrusive and reasonable under the circumstances.

Can students expect privacy in their school lockers? No. In a similar case, *Isiah B. v. State of Wisconsin* (1993),[75] the Supreme Court of Wisconsin went still further, finding that a student does not have reasonable expectation of privacy when storing personal items in a school locker. In this case, a school security guard found a gun in a student's coat during a random locker search. The student, Isiah B., also admitted to having cocaine in the coat.

Since the ruling in the T.L.O. case, most courts have concluded that students have no expectation for privacy from search in school lockers. Schools make lockers available to students for the limited purpose of storing legitimate educational materials. Students' constitutional protections must be balanced against the necessity of maintaining a controlled and disciplined environment in which all children can achieve their education.

What This Means for Teachers

When assigning lockers to students, and periodically thereafter, teachers should remind their students that lockers are school property loaned to students to store books, coats, and educational materials. School officials can search lockers in the interest of maintaining a safe and orderly learning environment. Students' lockers are not "their" lockers, and should not be assumed to be "private."

---

[73] 469 U.S. 325, 105 S. Ct. 733 (1985).
[74] 666 N.W.2d 142 (2003).
[75] 176 Wis. 2d 639,500 N.W2d 637.

Student drug testing. Across the United States, illegal drugs affect students' health and safety. Controlling students' drug and alcohol use challenges school authorities, leading many school districts to seriously consider implementing drug testing programs.

In 1989, the U.S. Supreme Court made key rulings in two drug-related cases, concluding that a drug test—regardless of the method used to conduct the test—constitutes a search. Even so, such a search is legal because of the government's compelling interest in promoting public safety by minimizing accidents and protecting the public.[76] The Supreme Court did not hear a case involving drug testing in public schools until 1995.

Can schools randomly test student athletes for illegal drug use? Yes.

Does random drug testing of student athletes violate their privacy? No.

Random drug testing of student athletes. In *Vernonia School District 47J v. Acton* (1995), the U.S. Supreme Court ruled that schools could conduct random drug tests on student athletes.[77] According to the court's decision, student athletes voluntarily choose to participate in interscholastic athletics and, therefore, have no legitimate privacy expectations. In a later case, the Supreme Court extended the drug testing rule to include students beyond athletes.

Can all students who participate in competitive extracurricular activities be required to take random drug tests? Yes.

Random drug testing of students who participate in competitive extracurricular activities. In *Board of Education of Independent School District No. 92 of Pottawatomie County v. Earls* (2002), the U.S. Supreme Court ruled that a policy requiring all students who participated in competitive extracurricular activities to submit to a drug test was reasonable and did not violate the Fourth Amendment.[78] According to the Court, the policy reasonably served the school district's important interest in detecting and preventing students' drug use, and it was constitutional.

Student Records and Privacy Rights

Schools collect and keep student records for purposes including educational planning, counseling, program development, individualized instruction, grade placement, and college admissions, among other uses. Students' files typically include family background information, health records, progress reports, achievement test results, psychological data, disciplinary records, previous report cards, and other confidential material.

Do teachers and other educators have unlimited rights to use student records? No. Common law, specific state and federal statutes, and case law all limit the ways educators can access and use student records to protect students' privacy and rights.

The federal Family Educational Rights and Privacy Act (FERPA) of 1974 guarantees parents and students a degree of confidentiality and fundamental fairness in maintaining and using student records. FERPA was adopted to ensure that certain types of students' personally identifiable and sensitive information would not be released without parental consent. The act establishes standards for schools to follow in handling student records.

Parents have the right to inspect all records that schools maintain on their children, must have an opportunity to challenge these records' accuracy, and must consent before the school can release the student's records to agencies outside designated educational categories. Once a student reaches age 18 or enters postsecondary

---

[76] Essex, N. L. (2005). *School law and the public schools: A practical guide for educational leaders.* Boston, MA: Pearson, pp. 101–102.

[77] 515 U.S. 646, 115 S. Ct. 2386.

[78] 536 U.S. 822, 122 S. Ct. 2559 (2002).

school, the student may give consent in lieu of the parent to release his or her own records. Schools that do not follow the required procedures risk losing federal education funds.

What This Means for Teachers

Teachers must use care when they access and share information about students with other educators. Their purpose must be to help students learn. They must discuss only essential information and should speak only in private locations where others cannot overhear. Teachers must add only objective and accurate information to students' records. A teacher's grade book is considered an educational record that administrators and parents can review and challenge for accuracy and purpose; thus teachers are advised to keep this record accurate, appropriate, and up-to-date.

Students' Freedom of Speech and Expression

While free speech is a highly valued right, it is not absolute. Courts recognize that students keep their constitutional rights in school, although schools can regulate and balance them with the school's obligation to provide students with a safe and orderly learning environment. If the exercise of free speech creates a "clear and present danger" to the state, then schools can repress the speech without violating the individual's freedom. The ongoing tension between these two interests complicates the issue of free speech in schools, however.[79]

Can students express their political views silently and nondisruptively in school? Yes.

Silent political speech. In *Tinker v. Des Moines Independent School District* (1969), student speech became protected unless the public schools could justify a reasonable forecast of "material and substantial disruption."[80] In this case, which involved events that took place in December 1965, Mary Beth Tinker, John Tinker, (figure 8.3) and three other students were suspended because they wore black armbands to school to protest the Vietnam War, in violation of a hastily-made school policy banning wearing black armbands. The U.S. Supreme Court ruled in the students' favor, holding that armbands were a symbolic act of free speech protected by the First Amendment that did not disrupt the school environment.

In its ruling, the Court concluded, "It is hardly argued that either students or teachers shed their constitutional rights to freedom of speech or expression at the schoolhouse gate. . . . Students in school as well as out of school are 'persons' under our Constitution. They are possessed of fundamental rights which the State must respect just as they themselves must respect their obligations to the State. . . . To prohibit . . . expression of one particular opinion without evidence that it is necessary to avoid 'material and substantial interference' with schoolwork or discipline, is not constitutionally permissible."[81]

The *Tinker* ruling changed the relationship between administrators and students. It affirmed that school officials must respect students' civil rights in school. School officials cannot justify a ban on student activity unless the officials can reasonably and legitimately forecast substantial disruption to the school's orderly and safe learning environment.

---

[79] Schools should base their rules and regulations on the school's legitimate interests. If the rule's or regulation's purpose is unclear or nonexistent, courts say, then the rule should not exist.
[80] 393 U.S. 503, 89 S. Ct. 733 (1969).
[81] 393 U.S. 503, 89 S. Ct. 733 (1969).

| Figure 8.3 | Mary Beth and John Tinker's Black Armbands Were Protected Symbolic Speech |

Bettmann/CORBIS

Are all student speech and expressions protected while in school? No. **Profanity and lewdness: Not protected speech.** While the *Tinker* case affirmed students' rights to free political speech in school, not all student speech is permissible. In *Bethel School District No. 403 v. Fraser* (1986), the U.S. Supreme Court ruled that students' lewd and indecent speech is not protected by the First Amendment.[82] Likewise, in *Morse v. Frederick* (2007), the Court ruled that students' speech encouraging illegal drug use at a school function is not protected by the First Amendment.[83]

On April 26, 1983, Matthew Fraser, a student at Bethel High School in Bethel, Washington, delivered a nominating speech for a student elective office at a school assembly. Before giving the speech, the two teachers who reviewed it advised Fraser that the speech was "inappropriate" and that he should not deliver it or risk "severe consequences." Throughout the entire speech, Fraser referred to his candidate in terms of an elaborate, graphic, and explicit sexual metaphor.

A Bethel High School disciplinary rule prohibited the use of obscene or profane language or gestures in school. The next day, Fraser admitted and explained his conduct to the assistant principal. With the teacher witnesses' written statements and Fraser's admission, the administrator suspended Fraser from school. Fraser appealed the suspension and then brought suit, claiming protected speech as decided in *Tinker*.

The U.S. Supreme Court ruled that in this situation, *Tinker* did not apply. Students' silent political speech that did not disrupt the learning environment was not the same as a student's indecent speech and lewd behavior during a school assembly. Making a sexually provocative speech was offensive and had no political message. Such speech is not constitutionally protected.

In *Morse v. Frederick* (2007), Joseph Frederick, a high school junior, brought and displayed a sign reading "Bong Hits 4 Jesus" to a school-sponsored event. The school's Drug Free Schools and Communities policy required schools to promote drug-free messages. The principal confiscated the banner and suspended Frederick. The Supreme Court ruled that the First Amendment regarding free speech does not

[82] 478 U.S. 675, 106 S.Ct. 3159 (1986).
[83] 551 U.S. 127 S. Ct. 2618 (2007).

require schools to tolerate at school events any student expression that contributes to the dangers of illegal drug use.

What This Means for Teachers

Schools can place reasonable limits on students' language—and ban vulgar and offensive language—to ensure its appropriateness for school. Teachers' own conduct and language are considered as models for students' speech and actions. Teachers must use care in their vocabulary and comments while in school; that is, they must act professionally, especially when students can see or hear them.

Can schools regulate the content of student newspapers? Yes.
Free speech and student newspapers. Although a free press is essential to a democratic government's proper functioning, it has certain limitations. Published information is supposed to be true, without malice or harmful motives, and published for appropriate ends, no matter how difficult it may be for our society to ensure adherence to these goals. Similarly, courts tend to reject calls for prior restraint, in which a publication is censored before it can reach its readers.[84]

Freedom of the press in public schools, however, is governed by different constitutional precedents. In *Hazelwood School District v. Kuhlmeier* (1988), the U.S. Supreme Court ruled that schools may regulate the content of school-sponsored newspapers.[85]

Hazelwood East High School's journalism class published the school newspaper, *Spectrum*, which appeared every three weeks during the 1982–1983 school year. Typically, the journalism teacher submitted page proofs of each *Spectrum* issue to the school principal for review before publication. For the May 13 edition, the principal objected to two of the scheduled articles—one story about three students' pregnancies, the other about a divorce's impact on students at the school. The principal was concerned that the pregnant girls' identities would become known, the sexual references and birth control were inappropriate content for some younger students, and the divorcing family did not have the chance to respond and consent to the story before its publication. The principal did not allow the stories to be published, and the student authors filed suit.

The U.S. Supreme Court noted that while students have First Amendment rights to free speech, these must be applied in light of the school environment's special characteristics. The Court ruled that educators could exercise editorial control over school-sponsored student expression activities as long as there is a reasonably related pedagogical concern. Because the student newspaper was intended as a supervised learning experience for journalism students, school officials were entitled to reasonably regulate its content.

In the wake of the *Hazelwood* ruling, schools have been permitted to impose reasonable restrictions on students' (and teachers') speech in school newspapers, theater productions, and other expressive activities that are part of the school curriculum, whether or not they occur in a classroom setting. When supervised by faculty members, such activities are designed to impart particular knowledge and skills to student participants and audiences. Students' freedom of speech and expression in a school newspaper, therefore, is not solely determined by the requirements of *Tinker's* "material and substantial disruption" language. The Supreme Court ruled in *Hazelwood* that the principal was correct in deciding that the student authors and editors in question had not sufficiently mastered the ethical, moral,

[84] Alexander & Alexander, 2005, p. 385.
[85] 484 U.S. 260, 108 S.Ct. 562 (1988).

and legal restrictions that the journalism class taught about treating controversial and personal privacy issues. The principal had legitimate educational concerns.

Can students be disciplined for their speech on Internet/Web sites? Yes, if the school can show the off-campus Internet-distributed speech would substantially disrupt the school's operations.

The internet and student speech. Students' Internet-related behavior off campus can come under public schools' authority. In *Doninger v. Niehoff* (2008), a U.S. Court of Appeals for the 2nd Circuit in New York ruled that a school can apply disciplinary consequences to students when their off-campus Internet-distributed comments create a "foreseeable risk of substantial disruption" at the school.[86]

In spring 2007, Jamfest, a Connecticut high school's yearly music festival, experienced a series of planning setbacks that threatened to postpone or cancel the event. When Avery Doninger—a junior and incoming class secretary—was unable to meet with the school's principal, Karissa Niehoff, to discuss the problems, Doninger and three other students sent a mass email asking community members to speak to administrators about rescheduling the event. During a later conversation in the school hallway, the principal informed the Doninger that the event had been cancelled.

That night, Doninger wrote a LiveJournal blog post criticizing the school officials' handling of the issue, calling the school officials "douchebags," and asking that readers complain to the school superintendent, so as "to piss [her] off more" than the mass email had. In response to her blog post in which she made derogatory comments about school officials, the school barred Doninger from serving as senior class secretary and from speaking at her graduation. The Doningers sued.

In May 2008, the court ruled in favor of the school officials. It determined that regardless of the fact that Doninger wrote the blog while off campus, the blog could be considered on-campus speech. Because the blog related to school issues, it was reasonably foreseeable that other students and school administrators would become aware of it. The court then noted that school administrators have the right, in certain situations, to restrict on-campus speech to promote school-related goals.[87]

What This Means for Teachers

Student speech is constitutionally protected to the extent that it does not undermine the school's mission or substantially and materially disrupt the learning environment. Computer teachers, drama teachers, journalism teachers, and school newspaper, yearbook, and literary magazine sponsors must exercise appropriate editorial control over students' published or performed speech, because such speech raises legitimate pedagogical concerns. Even students' off-campus Internet-based speech can come under the school's authority. Teachers are advised to consult with their administrators when questioning the appropriateness of student speech.

Student dress and appearance. Courts tend to support school boards' authority to regulate student dress and personal appearance if the attire becomes so extreme as to interfere with a school's favorable learning environment. For instance,

---

[86] *Doninger v. Niehoff*, 514 F. Supp.2d 199 (D.Comm.2007).
[87] Walsh, M. (2008, June 11). Student loses discipline case for blog remarks. *Education Week, 27*(41), 7.

school districts have the right to require pupils to participate in physical education and to wear clothing appropriate for these occasions. Students may not, however, be required to wear "immodest" attire.[88] Nonetheless, courts disagree about how constitutional rights apply to cases involving students' appearance.

Can public school require students to wear school uniforms? Yes.
School uniforms. School officials face two irreconcilable issues when they investigate student attire: maintaining a safe and effective educational environment and respecting students' constitutional rights. In these situations, courts usually support the school.

Recently, in an attempt to mask differences between student groups, some schools have begun to require their students to wear school uniforms. Advocates for school uniforms cite statistics that show the incidence of gang activities, violence, and crime in schools drops dramatically after schools enact compulsory uniform policies.[89] Some students and parents, however, oppose these wardrobe requirements, claiming that the compulsory wearing of school uniforms denies freedom of expression and speech.

In the *Canady v. Bossier Parish School Board* decision (2001), the court ruled that a school's mandatory uniform policy does not violate students' First Amendment rights.[90] In its opinion, the court acknowledged that students have a constitutional right to free expression under the First and Fourteenth Amendments, and noted that a person's choice of clothing can be a constitutionally protected form of expression. However, the right to free speech is not absolute. In many cases, courts have concluded that school boards' regulation of student behavior outweighs individual students' right to free speech. Adjusting the school's dress code by adopting a uniform policy is a constitutional means for school officials to improve the educational process, so long as that policy is not directed toward censoring the expressive content of student clothing. Educators have an essential duty to regulate school affairs and establish appropriate standards of conduct, and this responsibility takes priority over students' choice of clothing to wear in school.

Sexual Discrimination and Harassment of Students

Sexual harassment of students by educators is a disturbing problem. Approximately 26 percent of all educator-misconduct cases involve sexual misconduct.[91] After a 7-month investigation, the Associated Press (AP) found 2,570 educators whose teaching credentials were revoked, denied, surrendered, or sanctioned from 2001 through 2005 following allegations of sexual misconduct. More than 80 percent of the victims were students. At least half of the educators punished by their states were also convicted of crimes related to their misconduct.[92]

The Education Amendments of 1972 contained Title IX, a law that specifically forbade discrimination based on gender.[93] Since the passage of the original legislation, the courts have expanded Title IX to address employee-to-employee, employee-to student, and student-to-student harassment. Over time, court cases have determined that a school district is obligated to take reasonable steps to prevent and stop sexual harassment by school employees or students.

---

[88] Alexander & Alexander, 2005, p. 375.
[89] Starr, J. (2000, January). School violence and its effects on the constitutionality of public school uniform policies. *Journal of Law and Education, 29,* 113.
[90] United States Court of Appeals, Fifth Circuit, 2001. 240 F.3d 437.
[91] Irvine, M., & Tanner, R. (2007, October 24). Sex abuse a shadow over U.S. schools. *Education Week, 27*(9),17.
[92] Irvine & Tanner, 2007, pp. 1, 16–19.
[93] Title IX prohibits discrimination not only within athletics and other extracurricular activities but also in regard to financial aid, testing, curricular offerings, pregnancy, and marital status.

If a teacher sexually harasses a student, can the student sue both the school district and the teacher as an individual for monetary damages? Yes.

Teacher-to-student sexual harassment. Two rulings established the case law regarding sexual harassment of students by adults in schools. In 1992, in *Franklin v. Gwinnett County Public Schools*, the U.S. Supreme Court ruled that students could recover compensatory and punitive monetary damages for sexual harassment under Title IX.[94] Further refining the scope of liability, in *Gebser v. Lago Vista Independent School District* (1998), the Supreme Court ruled that students could sue for monetary damages from the school district and the persons involved if the school knew about the alleged sexual harassment and failed to respond adequately.[95]

Starting in the fall of her tenth-grade year (1986), Christine Franklin was subjected to continual sexual harassment from Andrew Hill, a sports coach and teacher employed by the district. Among other allegations, Franklin claimed that Hill engaged her in sexually-oriented conversations, asking about her sexual experiences with her boyfriend and inquiring whether she would consider having sexual intercourse with an older man. Hill forcibly kissed her on the mouth in the school parking lot and telephoned her at home, asking her to meet him socially. Three times during her junior year, Hill took her out of class and to a private office where he subjected her to coercive intercourse.

School officials were aware of the sexual harassment, but they took no action. Indeed, they discouraged Franklin from pressing charges against Hill. Franklin filed an action against the school board for monetary damages. While the lower courts found for the school, the U.S. Supreme Court found for the student.

The Supreme Court unanimously held that damages were available under Title IX for intentional violations of the law. Where a student had been subject to sexual harassment, financial damages could be levied against the district and its supervisors as well as against the accused teacher. The case did not, however, specify the limits of that liability. The next case did.

In *Gebser v. Lago Vista Independent School District* (1998), the court ruled that school officials must take timely and positive actions in response to information that such inappropriate sexually harassing behaviors are occurring. A teacher's misconduct in sexually harassing a student does not make the school district liable under Title IX unless a school official had knowledge of the situation and responded with "deliberate indifference." If the school knows about the sexual harassment but does nothing to end it, the school and the individuals involved may be sued and collect damages.

In spring 1991, eighth-grader Alida Star Gebser joined a high school book discussion group led by Frank Waldrop, a high school teacher in the Lago Vista Independent School District. During the discussion sessions, Waldrop often made sexually suggestive comments to the students. These inappropriate comments continued in ninth grade when Gebser was assigned to Waldrop's class, where he addressed many of these remarks to her. In the spring, the teacher initiated sexual contact with Gebser. The teacher and Gebser had sexual intercourse several times during the rest of the school year and the next year, often during class time, although never on school property. Gebser never reported the relationship to school officials, although she testified that she realized Waldrop's conduct was improper.

In October 1992, when parents of two other students complained to the high school principal about Waldrop's inappropriate comments in class, the principal met with the parents, and the teacher apologized. The principal advised Waldrop to be careful about his classroom comments, but did not report the parents' complaint to the superintendent (who was also the district's Title IX coordinator). A few months later, a policeman discovered Waldrop and Gebser having sexual intercourse

---

[94] 503 U.S. 60, 112 S. Ct. 1028 (1992).
[95] 524 U.S. 274, 118 S. Ct. 1989 (1998).

and arrested Waldrop. The school district fired him, and the state education department revoked his teaching license. During this time, the district did not have a sexual harassment complaints policy or a formal antiharassment policy, as federal regulations required. Gebser and others filed suit against the district claiming damages under the Title IX statute.

The Supreme Court ruled that Title IX allowed damages only if a school official with authority to take corrective action had actual information about the harassment and showed "deliberate indifference" toward correcting the situation. The school district's liability was limited to situations in which the school had substantial control over both the harasser and the context in which the harassment occurred. Since school officials did not know about the sexual harassment, and did not act with deliberate indifference, the Court found for the school district and against the student. If sexual harassment occurred but the school officials did not know about it at the time, school districts and individuals cannot be held liable for financial penalties.[96]

Can school boards be held liable for student-to-student sexual harassment? Yes, but only when the school officials know about the harassment but do nothing to stop it.

Student-to-student sexual harassment. In *Davis v. Monroe County Board of Education* (1999), the U.S. Supreme Court ruled that a school board may be sued for damages in situations of peer-to-peer sexual harassment, but only when the educators acted with "deliberate indifference."[97]

LaShonda Davis, a fifth-grade student in Georgia, was subject to frequent sexual harassment from a fellow classmate. Starting in December, the male student tried to touch her breasts and genital area and made vulgar comments, such as "I want to get in bed with you." Similar conduct allegedly occurred on several later occasions, and LaShonda reported each of these incidents to her mother and to her classroom teacher. When contacted by the parent, the teacher assured Mrs. Davis that the school principal had been informed of the incidents. Nonetheless, no disciplinary action was taken against the offending student, and the offensive conduct continued.

After another harassing incident in February, the parent asked the principal how the school was going to stop this behavior. The principal stated, "I guess I'll have to threaten him a little bit harder." The offending student received no discipline, and the school did not separate LaShonda and the offender until after three months of reported harassment. The incidents finally ended when the student was charged with, and pleaded guilty to, sexual battery.

Mrs. Davis alleged that school officials failed to prevent LaShonda's suffering sexual harassment by another student. The school's complacency created an abusive environment that deprived her daughter of educational benefits promised her under Title IX of the Education Amendments of 1972. Furthermore, the school district had not instructed its personnel on how to respond to peer sexual harassment and had not established a policy on the issue.

The U.S. Supreme Court concluded that a person could collect punitive damages against the school board in cases of student-on-student harassment, but only where the school district acted with deliberate indifference to known acts of harassment in its programs or activities. Since school officials had knowledge of the sexual harassment and did not act assertively to prevent future harassment, the Court found for the student. Further, the damages are warranted "only for harassment that is so severe, pervasive, and objectively offensive that it effectively bars the victim's access to an educational opportunity or benefit."

---

[96] Alexander & Alexander, 2005, p. 463.
[97] 526 U.S.629, 119 S.Ct. 1662 (1999).

Student-to-student sexual orientation harassment. In *Nabozny v. Podlesny*, (1996), a U.S. Court of Appeals ruled that schools had a responsibility to protect students from antigay verbal and physical abuse.[98]

For four years, Jamie Nabozny was subjected to relentless antigay verbal and physical harassment and abuse by fellow students at his public high school in Ashland, Wisconsin.[99] Students urinated on him and pretended to rape him during class. When classmates found him alone, they kicked him so many times in the stomach that he required surgery. Although they knew of the abuse, school officials once said that Nabozny should expect it if he was gay. Nabozny attempted suicide several times, dropped out of school, and ultimately ran away. To make sure that other students did not go through the same kind of nightmare, he sued his former school.

The federal appeals court found that a public school could be held accountable for not stopping antigay abuse. In this case, the school had violated the student's Fourteenth Amendment rights to equal protection based on gender or sexual orientation. The case went back to trial and a jury found the school officials liable for the harm they caused to Nabozny. The case was ultimately settled for close to $1 million in damages.

What This Means for Teachers

When teachers observe or become aware of what may be sexually harassing behaviors toward students in school, whether from adults or other students, straight or gay, teachers must promptly inform an administrator about the situation. In turn, the administrator must promptly take affirmative action to resolve it.

Students with Disabilities

Today, disabled students have additional legal protections to ensure their right to a free and appropriate education. Although Congress passed legislation stating that special-needs students were entitled to a "free appropriate public education" (FAPE), it did not specifically define what an "appropriate education" meant. It deliberately left the definition broad and flexible, thereby allowing public schools to make this determination in accordance with the well-structured procedural process.

Do children with disabilities have unique educational protections? Yes. **Does "free and appropriate public education" require schools to maximize special-needs students' educational potential?** No.

A "basic floor of opportunity." In *Board of Education of Hendrick Hudson Central School District v. Rowley* (1982), the U.S. Supreme Court ruled that "free and appropriate public education" as specified in PL 94-142 and IDEA does not require a state to maximize each special-needs child's potential.[100] This was the first case in which the Supreme Court had an opportunity to interpret any of IDEA's provisions.

Amy Rowley, a deaf student in Peekskill, New York, had minimal residual hearing and was an excellent lip reader. Before she started kindergarten, Amy's parents and school administrators agreed to place Amy in a regular kindergarten class to

---

[98] *Nabozny v. Podlesny.* (1996). 92 F. 3d 446. Retrieved May 5, 2008, from http://caselaw.lp.findlaw.com/scripts/getcase.pl?navby=search&case=/data2/circs/7th/953634.html.

[99] Nearly nine out of ten lesbian, gay, bisexual, and transgender students experienced some form of harassment at school in the past year, according to a 2007 national survey of 6,200 middle and high school students. See Maxwell, L. A. (2008, October 15). Sexual orientation: The 2007 National School Climate Survey. *Education Week, 28*(8), 5.

[100] 458 U.S. 176, 102 S.Ct. 3034.

Figure 8.4   Amy Rowley Speaks with Her Mother, Who Is Also Deaf

Howie Swetz/The Journal News

see which supplemental services she would need. At the end of the trial period, all agreed that Amy should remain in the kindergarten class but with an FM hearing aid to help her participate in certain classroom activities. Amy successfully completed her kindergarten year.

Amy's first grade individualized educational program (IEP) kept her in a regular classroom with the FM hearing aid, and assigned her additional tutoring and speech services. Amy's parents agreed with this plan, but requested that Amy receive a qualified sign-language interpreter in all her academic classes instead of the other proposed services. After receiving an interpreter's services in kindergarten as part of a two-week experiment, the interpreter reported that Amy did not need his services at that time. After consulting with the school district's Committee on the Handicapped, which had heard evidence from both sides, the school administrators concluded that Amy did not need the interpreter in first grade.

The Rowleys demanded and received a hearing before an independent examiner, who heard the evidence and agreed with the school administrators. The interpreter was not necessary because "Amy was achieving educationally, academically, and socially" without such assistance. In an appeal, the New York Commissioner of Education also supported the school administrators' decision. The Rowleys then filed suit, claiming the denial of the sign-language interpreter constituted a denial of the "free and appropriate public education" guaranteed by law.

The U.S. Supreme Court found that the state does not have to maximize the child's potential, but rather provide a program that benefits the child. The Court observed that the special education act did not define "appropriate education" or offer a substantive prescription about the level of education to be given to children with disabilities. According to the Court, IDEA "generates no additional requirement that the services so provided be sufficient to maximize each child's potential 'commensurate with the opportunity provided other children.'" While this outcome might be desirable, ensuring that this goal is met was not the legislation's intent.

The original legislation intended to provide equal protection of the laws to children with disabilities. In passing IDEA, Congress intended to provide "a basic floor of opportunity" consistent with equal protection. As such, the Supreme Court ruled that the "basic floor of opportunity" that the act provided consisted of access to specialized instruction and related services that are individually designed to provide an educational benefit to the child with disabilities. IDEA left the primary responsibility for formulating students' education and choosing the educational methods to the state and local education agencies, which are expected to work in cooperation with the child's parent or guardian.

Do school districts have to pay tuition for disabled students to attend private educational facilities? Yes, sometimes. In 2007, for example, New York City paid for private schools for more than 7,000 severely handicapped children because it agreed that it could not properly instruct them. But this decision is quite expensive. According to New York officials, requests for tuition payments for special education students by parents who have placed their children in private schools on their own have more than doubled in five years, to almost 3,700 children in 2006, costing the city more than $57 million per school year.[101] The Supreme Court justices are likely to take up the issue soon, as reimbursement cases are now being argued in circuit courts.[102]

---

[101] Stout D. & Medina, J. (2007, October 11). With justices split, city must pay disabled student's tuition. *The New York Times. Education.* B1. Retrieved August 14, 2009 from: http://www.nytimes.com/2007/10/11/education/11school.html.

[102] See *Board of Education of New York City v. Tom F.,* and *Forest Grove School District v. T.A.* (No. 08-305), Also see Walsh, M. A. (2009, January 28). Sex-bias remedies upheld: High court to hear cases on student search, IDEA. *Education Week, 28*(19), 1, 18–19.

Summary

The state must balance individual teachers' and students' constitutional rights as citizens against the necessity of maintaining a controlled and safe learning environment. In keeping with this idea, courts have allowed schools to reasonably restrict teacher and student freedoms so as to keep students safe, healthy, and learning.

Society grants power and privilege to a profession only when their members are willing and able to contribute to the general well-being. A profession's code of ethics visibly clarifies for practitioners and the general public the rules and norms that guide the practitioners' actions. Because the professional entity is more stable, enduring, and visible than any one practitioner, the professional group has a collective moral responsibility to ensure that its members uphold the highest standards of practice.

Case law regarding teachers' freedom of speech, right to privacy, and freedom of religion significantly influences how teachers do their jobs. While teachers as citizens have a fundamental right to free speech, U.S. courts have allowed schools to set limits on this right if the state's interest in maintaining an efficient organization outweighs the employee's interest in exercising that right. These limitations affect teachers' academic freedom, their right to speak out publicly, their right to privacy in the workplace, and professional dress codes. Because teachers work in safety-sensitive positions, under certain conditions they may be required to undergo suspicionless searches and urine testing.

Criminal law also affects certain teachers' behaviors. Threatening to harm or physically harming students, or neglecting to anticipate and prevent harm to students in high-risk situations, can place teachers in legal jeopardy.

While students keep their constitutional rights in school, schools can regulate and balance those rights against the school's obligation to provide students with a safe and orderly learning environment. Schools must weigh the individual student's rights against the public good when making this determination. Students' rights issues include due process for suspensions and expulsions, privacy, drug testing, student records, free speech, sexual harassment, and disabilities.

Students retain their due process rights in schools. Before a student can be suspended, expelled, or involuntarily transferred to a specialized school, a serious breach of student conduct must have occurred, and the school district must have followed a procedure for allowing the student and family due process to hear the charges and present their view of events. If schools do not follow this process, the courts may not allow the student's suspension, expulsion, or transfer.

As in cases involving teachers, U.S. courts have ruled that students' constitutional right to privacy and freedom from unreasonable search and seizure must be balanced against schools' need to maintain order and ensure safety so as to permit learning. Public school officials can search students' persons, book bags, desks, or lockers if the search is based on reasonable grounds, advances a legitimate school purpose, and is not overly intrusive. Athletes or students who complete in interscholastic activities may be required to take random drug tests. Schools also have an obligation to take reasonable steps to prevent and stop sexual harassment by school employees or students. The federal Family Educational Rights and Privacy Act (FERPA) guarantees parents and students a degree of confidentiality and fundamental fairness in maintaining and using student records.

Students' free speech rights must be viewed in light of the school environment's special characteristics. Specifically, student speech is protected unless the public school can justify limiting this right based on a reasonable forecast of "material and substantial disruption" to the school's orderly and safe learning environment. Students' lewd and indecent speech and expressed advocacy for illegal behavior are not protected, however. Educators can exercise editorial control over school-sponsored student expression activities if there is a reasonably related pedagogical concern. Schools can discipline students for Internet-based speech that occurs outside school if it might reasonably be expected to disrupt effective school functioning. In addition, schools can regulate student dress and personal appearance that might reasonably interfere with a school's favorable learning environment.

Students with disabilities have additional legal protections. Cases being decided in U.S. courts continue to address issues specific to these students, such as the definition of a "free and appropriate education," separate school placement, related services, discipline, and tuition reimbursement.

Conclusions

- Ethics and law strongly influence how teachers and students conduct schooling.

- While teachers and students retain their constitutional rights to free speech, privacy, due process, equal protection, and religion while they within schools, courts continue to try to balance individuals' rights with schools' need to keep the learning environment safe, orderly, and efficient.

- Case law continues to affect the schoolhouse practices, and wise educators will stay current on the decisions that might affect their teaching and employment conditions.

Chapter 9

School Governance and Structure

As a people, Americans are hard working, **pragmatic,** and efficient—yet we prefer a little ambiguity when it comes to governing our public institutions. We have distributed accountability on purpose. "Anyone who has tried to change vehicle registration from Virginia to Maryland knows the true meaning of government by fragmentation," said Michael J. Fuerer, executive director and education policy maker with the National Research Council in Washington, D.C.[1] The same can be said for education.

The United States does not have one national education system like France, Italy, England, or Japan. Instead, American education is largely controlled at the state level. Currently, the United States has one federal Department of Education, 50 state education agencies and one for the District of Columbia, and 14,383 school districts.[2] Most states allow localities within the state to manage education. In short, education is a federal interest, a state responsibility, and a locally administered concern. Local school districts are the primary operating units of the American public school system.[3]

In this chapter, we review the U.S. schools' governance and structure from the federal government to the classroom. We discuss how state boards of education and local school boards function. We look at how state and local school superintendents, school board office personnel, school building administrators, and school support professionals influence teachers' classroom practice. Finally, this chapter considers how we structure schools.

Focus Questions

- What are the three areas of federal government's involvement in public education?
- What is the state's role in education?
- Which state leaders play key roles in shaping education policy and practice?
- What is the locality's role in education?
- Which local leaders play essential roles in shaping education policy and practice?
- Who are some key educational support persons who work with classroom teachers to promote student success?
- How are U.S. public schools structured?

---

[1] Fuerer, M.J. (2006, June 14). Moderation: A radical approach to education policy. Commentary. *Education Week, 25* (10), 36.
[2] The current number of school districts comes from the following source: Snyder, T. D., Tan, A. G., & Hoffman, C. M. (2006). *Digest of education statistics 2005* (NCES 2006-030). U.S. Department of Education, National Center for Education Statistics. Washington, DC: U.S. Government Printing Office, p. 129.
[3] In some localities, these entities are called school districts. In others, they are called school divisions or local agencies.

The Federal Role in Education

The U.S. Constitution defines the federal role in education. The Tenth Amendment to the U.S. Constitution reads as follows:

> The powers not delegated to the United States by the Constitution, nor prohibited by it to the states, are reserved to the states respectively, or to the people.

Because education is not specifically assigned as a federal government responsibility, it becomes a state and local responsibility. As a result, the United States has 50 different education systems, with each state directing its own.[4]

Brief History of the U.S. Department of Education

The U.S. Department of Education in Washington, D.C., is the primary federal agency responsible for overseeing state spending of federal education dollars. Following the Civil War, President Andrew Johnson established the U.S. Office of Education in 1867 to help strengthen growing federal support for education. A Commissioner of Education received an annual salary of $4,000 to head the Department, and three clerks were employed to help him at annual salaries ranging from $1,600 to $2,000.[5] Poor management, however, forced the first education commissioner to resign. Two years later, the Office of Education was transferred to the U.S. Department of the Interior and became the Bureau of Education. At the Bureau level, the focus narrowed to collecting information on schools and teaching to help states establish effective education systems.

In 1953, the U.S. Bureau of Education merged with other offices to become the Department of Health, Education, and Welfare (HEW). In 1979, President Jimmy Carter established the cabinet-level Department of Education, elevating its importance and influence.

In fiscal year 2008–2009, the U.S. Department of Education administered a budget of $1 trillion and employed 4,045 people. While this is a large operation, the federal share accounts for only 8 percent of the nation's total education budget. The state and local levels contribute the remaining 92 percent of education dollars.[6] The federal education budget represents only 2 percent of the total federal budget.[7]

The federal government has traditionally had little jurisdiction over state and local education policies or practices. The U.S. Constitution and federal legislation limit the federal role in education to three areas:

- Providing funding approved by Congress and monitoring states' compliance in using those funds
- Ensuring state and local compliance with federal laws
- Assessing student achievement at the national level

The Legislative Branch

Through its legislative branch, the federal government provides Congressionally approved funding and monitors the use of those funds. Over the years, the U.S. Congress has given public education a great deal of fiscal support. For instance, Americans

---

[4] The United States has 51 different education systems. The District of Columbia has its own education system, counting as the fifty-first.

[5] Grant, W. V. (1993, January). Statistics in the U.S. Department of Education: Highlights from the past 120 years. In T. D. Snyder (Ed.), *120 years of American education: A statistical portrait* (pp. 1–4). Washington, DC: National Center for Education Statistics. Retrieved October 3, 2009 from http://nces.ed.gov/pubs93/93442.pdf.

[6] The federal role in education. U.S. Department of Education. Retrieved October 3, 2009 from: http://www.ed.gov/about/overview/fed/role.html?src=In

[7] Center on Budget and Policy Priorities. (2009, April 13) Retrieved August 26, 2009 from: http://www.cbpp.org/cms/index.cfm?fa=view&id=1258nd

reacted with shock to the 1957 Soviet Union's launching of its Sputnik satellite. Our then-enemies, the Soviets, had beaten us in the "space race." Concerned citizens asked whether U.S. public schools had enough direction, drive, and resources to maintain our national security and global superiority in a threatening world.

In response, the U.S. Congress authorized a massive infusion of federal dollars into public education through the National Defense Education Act (NDEA) of 1958.[8] Congress believed that math and science education were essential to our national defense. NDEA also increased spending for foreign language learning, technology, and other "critical" subjects. These new monies came with strings attached, however: to receive the funds, states and localities had to agree to spend the dollars in compliance with the grants' terms. Federal spending audits in local school districts soon became commonplace as a result of this legislation.

Perhaps the most substantial federal education spending initiative occurred under President Lyndon Johnson's administration, when Congress passed the Elementary and Secondary Education Act (ESEA) in 1965. We now know this act by the name it was given in 2002: No Child Left Behind (NCLB). Seeking equity and excellence, NCLB intends to close the achievement gaps that exist based on students' race, economic status, and disability. NCLB was the federal government's first serious attempt to hold states, districts, and schools accountable for ending the unequal achievement among different student populations—especially poor, minority, and disabled students.

The 2002 NCLB currently contains six title categorical aid programs through which the U.S. Congress sends money specifically designed for certain student populations. The focus of these funding programs varies over time, changing with the reauthorization priorities. These categorical programs include funds to help states and local districts educate economically disadvantaged and other underserved children, improve teacher and principal quality, improve technology in schools, provide resources to children with limited English proficiency, develop drug and violence prevention activities, support community learning centers, implement promising educational reform, and develop additional educational assessments.[9]

Through Title grants, the U.S. national legislative branch sends states and schools federal dollars to help them accomplish their educational mission. Serving as incentives and resources, these federal monies tend to direct state and local educational efforts toward outcomes that the U.S. Congress, states, and localities deem as serving their best interests. They are clear examples of federal dollars reaching local classrooms.

The Judicial Branch

A second area of federal education involvement is the judicial branch of the U.S. government, which ensures that states comply with all federal laws and regulations. Sometimes this requires the U.S. Supreme Court to clarify the law.

Griffin v. County School Board of Prince Edward County. In *Griffin v. County School Board of Prince Edward County* (1964), the Supreme Court ruled that the practice of a state closing some of its public schools and contributing to the support of private segregated schools instead is unconstitutional.[10]

On April 23, 1951, Barbara Johns, a 16-year-old student in Prince Edward County, Virginia, led the 450 students at all–African American Robert R. Moton High School out of their classes in a two-week protest against the school's deplorable building conditions. Built in 1939 and designed to house 180 students, their

---

[8] Public Law 85-864.
[9] The information about the federal educational funding described in this chapter comes from the following source: *Consolidated state performance reports.* Washington, DC: U.S. Department of Education, Retrieved November 20, 2009, from http://www.ed.gov/admins/lead/account/consolidated/index. html#info.
[10] 377 U.S. 218, 84 S. Ct. 1226.

school was massively overcrowded. Rather than build a new African American high school, the Prince Edward County school board erected three large plywood buildings covered with tarpaper to accommodate the overcrowding. Called "tar-paper shacks" by the students and African American community, the shoddy buildings vividly symbolized the Moton students' unequal facilities, sparking their protest demanding a new high school. At one point, some classes were also held on an old school bus. The students contacted the National Association for the Advancement of Colored People (NAACP) for legal assistance. They filed suit alleging that they had been denied enrollment into public schools attended by white children and charged that Virginia's segregation laws denied equal protection of the Fourteenth Amendment.[11]

In 1954, the Prince Edward group was one of the plaintiffs in the landmark U.S. Supreme Court's *Brown v. Board of Education* decision, which ruled that the state's segregation laws were unconstitutional because they denied equal protection. That ruling did not end Prince Edward County's school segregation, however. In 1956, Virginia amended its constitution to permit public funds to assist students to go to either public schools or nonsectarian private schools. The General Assembly enacted legislation to close any public schools where "white and colored children" were enrolled together and to cut off state funds to such schools. When the Supreme Court of Appeals invalidated these laws in 1959, the Virginia General Assembly turned to a "freedom of choice" program, repealed compulsory attendance laws, and made school attendance a matter of local option.

Rather than submit to state and federal courts requiring Virginia public schools to accept children of all races, Prince Edward County decided it preferred to have no public schools at all. It refused to levy any school taxes for the 1959–1960 school year. The County's public schools did not reopen in fall 1959; in fact, they stayed closed for five years (although other public schools in Virginia were open and operating under the law). In the meantime, a private group, the Prince Edward School Foundation, was formed; it built and operated private schools for local white children who received county- and state-funded tuition grants and tax credits to attend these facilities. The vast majority of the county's 1,700 African American students and some white students went without formal education for five years, from 1959 to 1964.[12]

In 1964, the Supreme Court ruled in *Griffin v. Prince Edward* that local authorities had to fund public education and reopen the schools. The Court required that Prince Edward County enforce the nation's laws.

Plyler v. Doe.[13] Other education cases have gone to the U.S. Supreme Court to determine if states were correctly complying with federal laws. *Plyler v. Doe* involved the allocation of millions of dollars by the Texas state legislature to educate children of illegal immigrants. At the time of the court case, Texas was educating an estimated 50,000 school-aged children of illegal immigrants at an annual cost of approximately $100 million.[14]

In an attempt to save tax dollars, the Texas legislature argued that because these children were in the country illegally, taxpayers should not have to finance illegal activity—that is, the schooling of the children. Subsequently, in 1975, the Texas legislature revised its laws to withhold state education funds from school districts that enrolled children who were not legally admitted into the United States. The law also allowed local school districts to deny enrollment to these children. The local school districts could accept these students if they wished—but they would not receive state

[11] What happened in Prince Edward County? (2003). Longwood University. Retrieved November 20. 2009, from http://www.longwood.edu/news/bvb/princeedward.htm.

[12] What happened in Prince Edward County?, 2003.

[13] *Plyler v. Doe*, 457 U.S. 202 102 S.Ct. 2382 (1982).

[14] Owings, W., & Kaplan, L. (2006). *American public school finance.* Belmont, CA: Wadsworth, 2006, p. 261.

funding for them if they did. When opponents of this policy brought suit, the Texas Supreme Court agreed with the legislature's position.

Ultimately, this case went to the U.S. Supreme Court. As in *Brown v. Board of Education*, the Court decided the case based on the Fourteenth Amendment: "No State shall . . . deprive any person of life, liberty, or property without due process of law; *nor deny to any **person** within its jurisdiction* the equal protection of the laws". According to the justices on the Supreme Court, any *person* did not mean any *citizen*. Obviously, illegal immigrants are not citizens. They are, however, persons who cannot be deprived of equal protection under the law requiring compulsory school attendance.

Student Assessment at the National Level

The third area of federal involvement in education involves national assessment of students' academic progress.[15]

Until the 1960s, states generally educated their children as they saw fit. Even if educators were curious about how well their students were achieving compared to students in neighboring states, comparing K–12 student achievement on a state-by-state basis was impractical, untraditional, and largely irrelevant. Because students prior to the 1960s tended to leave school and find local employment, these individuals would have competed for jobs only with locally educated students. Thus attending more effective schools would have given them no special advantages.

National Assessment of Educational Progress (NAEP).
Matters on this front changed in the 1960s, when the Kennedy administration focused government accountability on student assessment. As expected, states and various educational agencies were actively suspicious of the federal government's plan to hold states responsible for its students' educational attainment. To reduce the states' misgivings about the potential for federal interference in local and state education, the Education Commission of the States (ECS) received the authority to design and conduct a national assessment.[16] Federal monies and the Carnegie Corporation would fund the project. In 1969, ECS received U.S. Office of Education assurances that it would give monies but not interfere with state policy or analysis. That compromise was sufficient for most states to allow federal involvement in collecting and monitoring student achievement data.

Today, the federal Department of Education oversees the National Assessment of Educational Progress (NAEP), also known as "the nation's report card." The NAEP data show regional, state, and national student achievement trends in the arts, civics, economics, foreign language, geography, math, reading, science, U.S. history, world history, and writing. Each state chooses a sample of students at identified grade levels in selected schools to take the NAEP tests.

No Child Left Behind and student assessment.
While the No Child Left Behind legislation is not officially considered to be student assessment at the national level as each state develops its own test, its influence over student testing across the country clearly shows how states are willing to comply with extensive federal rules for student achievement testing to secure more federal education dollars.

NCLB (2002) increases state and local school districts' accountability for all students' measured academic achievement in return for continued federal financial support. The act requires every state to develop a comprehensive system of standards and assessments in language arts, math, and science. All student subgroups[17]

---

[15] We will discuss student achievement and accountability in greater detail in Chapter 15. For the purposes of this section, we will briefly address the topic as one of the federal roles in education.
[16] Since 1983, Educational Testing Services (ETS) has held the NAEP contract.
[17] Subgroups include minority, low-income, special education, and English language learners.

must pass 100 percent of the state standards' assessments—and be performing at grade level—by the school year 2013–2014. Students are tested in grades 3–8 and once in high school in language arts, math, and science. The assessments measure student progress toward proficiency and determine school accountability, called adequate yearly progress (AYP), to close the achievement gaps. Each year, schools must show academic progress at all tested grades, in all tested subjects, by all tested student subgroups. If any one of the groups fails to make AYP (it can be a different subgroup from one year to another), the whole school receives a failing grade. To make the desired student achievement a reality, the law requires that only "highly qualified teachers"—that is, teachers with documented knowledge of the content they are teaching—be employed in all core subject classrooms.

The NCLB legislation purposely designed the rules so schools could no longer ignore the academic needs of disadvantaged student groups. Students in each subgroup must meet AYP expectations each year. By separating the achievement data in this way, increasing underserved student subgroups' achievement becomes a school priority. The school's own status depends on how well each student group meets the proficiency standards.

Most importantly, the No Child Left Behind Act expands the federal government's reach into state and local policies and practice. Many wonder if the federal government's regulation of local and state education with NCLB to such a great degree oversteps its constitutional boundaries. Discussion about this issue continues. Generally, if states agree to accept federal monies, they must comply with federal regulations.

The State Role in Education

Constitutionally, U.S. education is controlled at the state level. Figure 9.1 illustrates how most states are organized to administer the education function.

Every state has a legislative system similar to the federal government's three branches—executive, legislative, and judicial. Each state has a governor, a two-chambered legislature (except for Nebraska, which has a single chamber), a supreme court, and agencies that report to and are funded by the legislature. When we elect people to represent us in the legislative process, they pass many laws each year that directly affect education. For example, many years ago, Hawaiian legislators decided that they should have only one school district run by the state. As a result, Hawaii has no local school districts.[18]

California's Proposition 13 provides another example of how voters can give the state a significant role in schools. In 1978, California taxpayers voted to limit their local property tax rates. "Prop 13" resulted in a $6 billion cut in local property tax revenue. As a result, school districts lost, on average, half of their local funding. Overall, school revenues decreased by as much as 15 percent in wealthy districts and by 9 percent in lower-income districts.[19] The overall consequence was a shift in fiscal control of California's public schools from local communities to the state, with a decidedly negative impact on the state's education system.

Governors become the state's chief executive officer (CEO) or representatives to the state legislature. Some want to lower taxes. Others want to increase public services. In recent years, state legislators have acted on many educational issues, including the means by which the state will fund its schools, teacher licensure laws, school curricula, testing issues, consolidation of school districts, ways to accredit schools, and teacher retirement.

---

[18] Hawaii has a state-run school system with no local school districts. For a more complete discussion of Proposition 13 and the taxpayers' revolt, see Chapter 10.

[19] First to worst: Special challenge of Proposition 13. (n.d.). *The Merrow report*. New York: Public Broadcast System, Learning Matters Inc. Retrieved July 30, 2007, from http://www.pbs.org/merrow/tv/ftw/prop13.html.

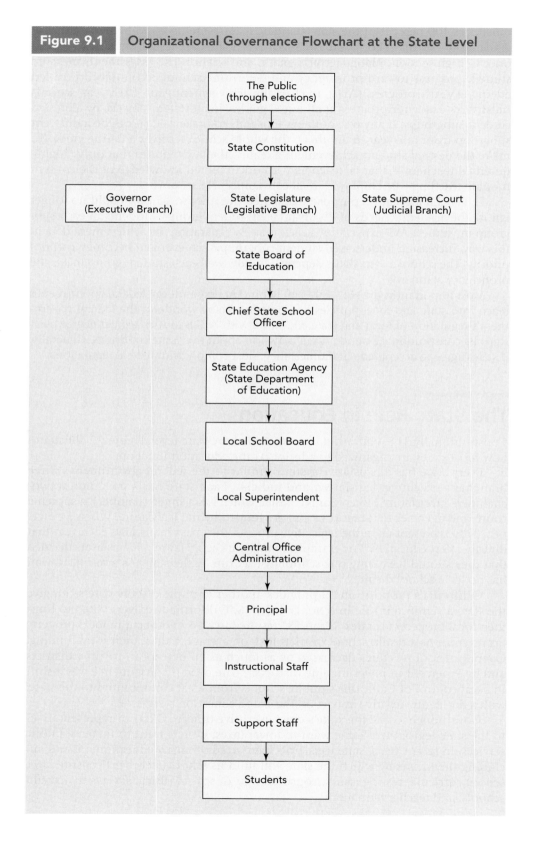

Figure 9.1 Organizational Governance Flowchart at the State Level

The Public

The public influences education at the state level through the election process. In the United States, our form of government is called a democratic republic. With this system, we elect people to represent us, and to make laws and enact policies that govern us. The Tenth Amendment to the U.S. Constitution makes education a state function. Therefore, each of the 50 states has its own constitution that details how the state will govern its education. By voting for representatives to the state legislature who hold certain beliefs about education, the public elects officials to enact their preferences about the type of education their state will have.

For example, in February 2007, Maine's Governor, John E. Baldacci, proposed consolidating the state's 283 school districts and 152 superintendents, with an average of 714 students per district, and replacing them with 26 regional centers, each of which would be governed by a 15-person, regionally-elected school board. Baldacci thought this change would "make educational and financial sense."[20] He claimed this consolidation would save $250 million in the first three years and allow local superintendents to focus on student achievement. In the opposite corner, local educators argued that the proposal would erode local control, cost hundreds of administrators their jobs, and force the smallest and most isolated schools to shut down. Currently, two-thirds of Maine's local property taxes go to support schools, so the consolidation might either reroute substantial tax dollars to education at the classroom level or reduce the tax rate.[21] Selecting either path reflects one's values and beliefs about what is in the public interest.

Regardless of who is elected, once the public has voted, much of the funding and legislation for education come from the state legislature.

The State Legislature

The legislature's education role varies from state to state, depending on the state constitution's wording. Basically, all state legislatures provide the laws and framework for how the state education system will function. Laws control how the state organizes and operates its department of education. Laws frame the procedures that localities must use to elect or appoint their school board members. Laws control how districts' structure their superintendents' contracts and define their role in overseeing the school district. And laws control the length of the school day and the school year, curriculum parameters, testing programs, licensure regulations, and other matters.

Most frequently, the state legislature decides how the state will fund its schools. The legislature is responsible for establishing, maintaining, regulating, and determining the school funding financing formula. Virtually every state requires a formula to equalize state funding between affluent and poor communities.[22] As a consequence, the state legislature establishes a basic floor level of education services that each locality must offer. Wealthier communities can afford to spend more on education than can poorer ones. Through its funding formula, the state finances more of the education costs for poorer areas and gives less state financial assistance to the wealthier ones. This equalizes school funding throughout the states.[23]

Table 9.1 shows how the sizes of school districts and the number of pupils per district vary across the states. The state legislature makes these decisions. For example, Maryland has, on average, more than 36,000 students per district; by comparison, North Dakota has, on average, fewer than 500 students per district. Obviously, population density has a role in deciding size as legislators make the final decisions.

---

[20] Tonn, J. (2007). Maine school consolidation plan under fire. *Education Week, 26*(23), 17, 21.

[21] Tonn, 2007.

[22] And the four commonwealths: Kentucky, Massachusetts, Pennsylvania, and Virginia.

[23] We will go into more detail about this issue in Chapter 10.

Table 9.1	Number of School Districts in Each State, 2005		
State	Number of Students	Number of Districts	Average Number of Pupils per District
Alabama	731,220	130	5,625
Alaska	133,933	55	2,435
Arizona	1,012,068	313	3,233
Arkansas	454,523	309	1,471
California	6,413,862	989	6,485
Colorado	757,693	178	4,257
Connecticut	577,203	166	3,477
Delaware	117,668	19	6,193
District of Columbia*	78,057	1	78,057
Florida	2,587,628	67	38,621
Georgia	1,522,611	180	8,459
Hawaii*	183,609	1	183,609
Idaho	252,120	114	2,212
Illinois	2,100,961	887	2,368
Indiana	1,011,130	294	3,439
Iowa	481,226	370	1,301
Kansas	470,490	302	1,558
Kentucky	663,885	176	3,772
Louisiana	727,709	68	10,702
Maine	202,084	283	714
Maryland	869,113	24	36,213
Massachusetts	980,459	350	2,801
Michigan	1,757,604	553	3,178
Minnesota	842,854	346	2,436
Mississippi	493,540	152	3,247
Missouri	905,941	524	1,729
Montana	148,356	438	339
Nebraska	285,542	518	551
Nevada	385,401	17	22,671
New Hampshire	207,417	178	1,165
New Jersey	1,380,753	598	2,309
New Mexico	323,066	89	3,630
New York	2,864,775	726	3,946
North Carolina	1,360,209	117	11,626
North Dakota	102,233	213	480
Ohio	1,845,428	613	3,010
Oklahoma	626,160	541	1,157
Oregon	551,273	199	2,770
Pennsylvania	1,821,146	501	3,635
Rhode Island	159,375	38	4,194
South Carolina	699,198	89	7,856

State	Number of Students	Number of Districts	Average Number of Pupils per District
South Dakota	125,537	172	730
Tennessee	936,681	136	6,887
Texas	4,331,751	1,040	4,165
Utah	495,981	40	12,400
Vermont	99,103	299	331
Virginia	1,192,092	134	8,896
Washington	1,021,349	296	3,451
West Virginia	281,215	55	5,113
Wisconsin	880,031	437	2,014
Wyoming	87,462	48	1,822
U.S. Total	48,540,725	14,383	3,375

*Washington, D.C. is not a state but does have its own school system.
Source: Snyder, T. D., Dillow, S. A., & Hoffman, C. M. (2008). *Digest of education statistics 2007* (NCES 2008–022). National Center for Education Statistics, Institute of Education Sciences, U.S. Department of Education. Washington, DC: U.S. Government Printing Office, Table 83, p. 117.

The Governor

Governors generally serve a four-year term.[24] At the state level, they serve much the same function as a company's chief executive officer (CEO) does. The governor's role is usually defined in the state's statutes or constitution. In general, governors' roles appear to be increasing in power as they assume greater responsibilities.

The governor's authority affects many areas of policy making. The governor can propose and veto legislation, veto appropriations, and set general policies and regulations that apply to all aspects of state government. The governor can make budget recommendations to the legislature. In addition, the governor influences educational policies through his or her appointment authority—that is, the ability to name individuals to head state agencies, boards, and commissions to oversee the state's operations. Education at all levels—elementary through college—is affected by these appointments. The governor's influence can also be felt through the governor's office staffing for the liaison with education and through the governor's implementing federal laws and aid.

Perhaps the governor's most important education appointments (unless the position is elected) are the Chief State School Officer and the State Board of Education members. By enacting their agendas in personnel and policy choices, governors exert powerful influence on directions given to the public schools.

The State Supreme Court

The state court system plays an important part in determining how public schools operate. Most state judicial systems consist of three levels, which are similar to the federal system. There is a court of original jurisdiction, an intermediate appellate court, and a court of last resort. Although these courts have different names in different states, the state's highest court is usually called the State Supreme Court.

The State Supreme Court is rarely involved in education issues, but when these judges are, their decisions are usually vital to the schools.[25] Generally, the

---

[24] Except in Vermont and New Hampshire, where the governors serve two-year terms. In all states except Virginia, governors may succeed themselves.
[25] Chapter 8 goes into greater detail about the courts' role in education.

State Supreme Court rules on whether the legislature's laws are consistent with the state's constitution. As the *Plyler v. Doe* case in Texas demonstrates, a State Supreme Court's decisions can have major educational and financial consequences for the state.

The State Board of Education

The State Board of Education is the policy-setting agency that oversees and directs the State Department of Education.[26] Depending on the state, the Board's name may vary. It is similar to the local school board's oversight of the local school division, but its impact is far broader.

All states have a State Board of Education.[27] In most states, governors appoint members to this Board. In some states, the state legislature appoints members; in other states, the general public elects State Board members. Still other states use a hybrid model combining election and appointment to the State Board of Education. Each state's constitution and laws define how the State Board operates. Some State Boards hire and fire the Chief State School Officer; in other states, the governor appoints the Chief State School Officer; and in a few states the public elects the Chief State Officer. In many states, State Board of Education regulations have the effect of law.

State Boards of Education create policies in a variety of ways and for an array of reasons. Most often, these policies are intended to respond to state educational issues, needs, or perceived educational crises. These issues come to the Board's attention through study sessions on topics that affect schools and students, from items brought forward by state and national trends and events, and from federal and state legislation.[28]

State Boards of Education and state legislatures frequently share responsibility for making educational policy. Students' interests are best served when these bodies work together in a collaborative fashion to improve teaching and learning in schools. In recent years, however, increased executive and legislative interest in education policy has blurred the lines of responsibility. Establishing a strong relationship between key members of the State Board, the governor's office, and the state legislature is very important to enhance communications and share responsibilities.[29]

While legislators introduce education policy initiatives with the best intentions, these initiatives are often delivered to the State Board without a comprehensive examination of existing policies addressing the issue or assessing those policies' effectiveness. State legislatures sometimes pass legislation in concept form, while leaving the specific details of how that concept should be implemented for the State Board to define. Because membership changes in legislatures, the governor's office, and State Boards of Education affect institutional memory and record of policies, multiple and occasionally conflicting practices designed to address the same concern may be produced. Consequently, maintaining records to assure continuity and accountability is a major Board concern.[30]

The Chief State School Officer

Each state has a Chief State School Officer. This position goes by different names, depending on the state: Superintendent of Public Instruction, Commissioner of

---

[26] Except in Wisconsin which does not have a State Board of Education.
[27] Except Wisconsin.
[28] Kysilko, D. (1999, January). Aggregating and tracking state board policies. In *Boardsmanship review*. Washington, DC: National Association of State Boards of Education.
[29] Kysilko, D. (2000, March). Building partnerships with the legislature. In *Boardsmanship review*. Washington, DC: National Association of State Boards of Education.
[30] Kysilko, 1999.

Education, or State Superintendent. It is also filled in a variety of ways. In some states, the governor appoints this person to carry out the governor's educational agenda. In others, the public elects this person directly. In still others, the State Board of Education appoints the individual. Alternatively, the governor may appoint the State Board of Education, which in turn appoints the state superintendent. The precise selection process employed often influences the way the chief officer enacts the role.

Although the Chief State School Officer's duties vary from state to state depending on the state's constitution, this person typically serves as the State Department of Education's chief administrator. As such, the Chief State School Officer recommends improvements to the State Department of Education, works with the governor in the state budgeting process, advises the state legislature on education issues, and ensures public schools' compliance with state regulations and statutes. He or she reports on the "state of education" within the state to the governor, the state legislature, and the public. Additionally, this official works with the Department of Education's licensure office to make recommendations regarding changes in licensure for educators.

The State Department of Education

Teachers generally do not have many dealings with the governor, the state legislature, the State Supreme Court, the State Board of Education, or the Chief State School Officer. Teachers do, however, deal with the State Department of Education, also known as the State Education Agency (SEA). The Chief State School Officer heads this agency, which is usually located in the state capital. The State Department of Education makes policy and program recommendations to the State Board of Education. It also constructs the guidelines (more general) and regulations (quite specific) that translate education-related laws passed by the legislature into workable practices for the public schools.

Additionally, the State Department of Education assures that the state is complying with the federal Department of Education's rules on federally funded programs. In the past, SEAs have provided curriculum and instruction assistance to schools. Since the early 1990s, however, budget cutbacks have reduced the number of SEA educators offering technical assistance to local schools. Nonetheless, SEAs continue to make certain that the local school districts are following exactly—are in compliance with—state and federal regulations regarding state testing, licensure regulations, and federal grants.

The Local Role in Education

Education is a state function that draws federal interest and that is administered at the local level. Most states allow the localities to administer neighborhood schools. This section discusses the role of the local school board, the local superintendent, the central office, the principal, teacher, and various educational support personnel—the positions and individuals with whom teachers are most closely involved.

The Local School Board

Local school boards play a critical part in preparing our children to be productive citizens and strengthening our communities. They aim to mirror the diverse communities they represent. All school boards derive their power and authority from the state. At the same time, all school boards generate their own "laws" by establishing the policies that govern their local schools. School boards everywhere are their communities' primary and—if state law permits—supreme educational authority.

Within every state except Hawaii, the local school board, as the local administrative unit, is responsible for implementing the state's policies and regulations. (Unique among the 50 states, Hawaii is a single state-run school district.) The state's power over the local school board depends on the state's constitution. In some states, it is possible for the state to "take over" local school operations. In such instances, the state would assume direct management responsibility for running the schools—from hiring personnel to designing the curriculum. In others states, this type of "takeover" of local schools is not constitutionally possible.

Boards of education are usually elected by the school district's residents but may also be appointed by mayors or other executives of jurisdictions such as cities or counties that encompass the school district. In the United States, most local school board members are elected. Through the election process, the community has the ability to change their representatives on the board and find people whose views more closely match their own values. Whether school districts have elected or appointed boards often has more to do with history than with any particular philosophical stand. When the current form of the school board was introduced in the early 1900s, municipalities that were incorporated as cities had appointed boards and all others had elected ones.

The local school district's power varies from state to state—again depending on the state constitution's wording. In some states, the local school board has the power to relieve the superintendent of his or her position and, if necessary, to change school policies.[31]

Likewise, the local school board's authority to request funding varies from state to state. Some local school boards have taxing authority to fund the school's operation. Others recommend funding levels, which the public must then formally approve. Still others make budget recommendations to the governing authority (a city council or board of supervisors, for example), which it may or may not follow.

Perhaps the local school boards' major responsibility is to hire the best superintendent of schools they can find. Other responsibilities include approving the local school budget and establishing school district policies. According to the National School Boards Association, a school board should be responsible for eight key areas:[32]

1. Setting a vision for the district
2. Establishing standards
3. Assessing student learning outcomes
4. Assigning responsibility for student outcomes
5. Dedicating resources to support the district's goals and objectives
6. Monitoring the organizational climate
7. Establishing trust among the stakeholders
8. Seeking ways to continue improvement in the seven previously mentioned areas

This eight-part framework relies on the perspective that no action is accomplished in isolation. As school board members make policy decisions, they try to pay attention to how these eight areas interact. When board members work together effectively, these eight components can optimize a local school board's ability to make positive and lasting school district improvements.

Most school board members are laypeople who volunteer their time or receive a modest stipend to meet once or twice a month to work for their local school system.

---

[31] Alsbury, T. L. (2003, December). Superintendent and school board member turnover: Political versus apolitical turnover as a critical variable in the application of dissatisfaction theory. *Education Administration Quarterly, 39*(5), 667–678.
[32] *Key work of school boards: School governance.* (2007). Alexandria, VA: National School Boards Association. Retrieved October 4, 2009, from http://www.nsba.org/site/page.asp?TRACKID=&CID=121&DID=8799.

Figure 9.2	School District Superintendents Inform and Advise Their School Boards

Jon Feingersh Photography Inc/Blend Images/Getty Images

For the most part, they rely on the district superintendent to give them information and recommendations upon which to act. Unfortunately, sometimes school board members overstep their responsibilities and try to micromanage the school system. This can lead to problems in role definition with the superintendent and may sidetrack the school board from its primary purposes.

While in previous years the local school board had considerable authority in curriculum policy, its authority has slowly diminished because of the federal government's increased involvement in school affairs, relevant court decisions, and special-interest groups' actions. Because board members often lack expertise in many education-related areas, many school boards tended to base their decisions on experts' (usually the superintendent's) recommendations and advice.[33]

Activity 9.1

After considering federal and state roles in public education, it is clear that states exert the most control over America's public education. What role should the federal government play?

A. Divide the class into two groups. One group will present arguments that the federal government should become more involved with public education. The other group will argue that the federal government should have a smaller role in education. Give clear reasons for each point and list them on the board.

B. After hearing viewpoints on both sides of the issue, have the class discuss their informed opinions about this topic.

---

[33] Robell, M., et. al. (1982). *Educational policymaking and the courts*. Chicago: University of Chicago Press.

Activity 9.2

Having state control of public education has both advantages and disadvantages.

A. As a class, list and explain the advantages and disadvantages of the United States adopting a national system of education instead of having 51 (50 states plus the District of Columbia) different education systems.

B. Discuss as a class what our schools and society would be like today if the U.S. Supreme Court had not made the decision that it did in *Brown v. Board of Education*.

C. Discuss the merits of the United States' current educational governance structure.

A CLOSER LOOK

Local school boards serve important educational and democratic functions. Read the following article, which was written by the National School Boards Association, and answer the questions that follow.

Do School Boards Matter?

What would happen if there were no school boards? That is not an idle question. Local school boards are part of the American landscape, yet they are increasingly under attack. Understanding what is at stake requires understanding why school boards exist. . . .

The school board is not an accidental creation. As Americans, most of us believe in the democratic concept of lay control of political functions, from the statehouse to Capitol Hill. The process begins with our local schools. We trust that reasoned people who are not "education experts" are qualified to set policy and govern the schools, to represent the "public" in public education. After all, education, in large part, reflects community values. Who better to set the policy and direction for this values-laden enterprise than local community members? That is why we elect (or, in some few cases, appoint) public-minded citizens to the local school board, where they are charged with articulating the needs of the community to the schools and the needs of the schools to the community. . . .

For generations, the public has trusted school boards to balance community goals and values with the needs of the children in their care. But that trust has frayed in recent years as the public schools have come under the nation's microscope. Today, 24 of 50 states have passed laws that allow for the takeover of districts with academic problems, and mayors in several urban centers are now in charge of their district's governance and operations.

The growing role of the state and federal government in education underscores the need for a representative local body specifically charged with providing a sound academic grounding for every student. This is the school board's mission, and it is a singular one. A system run by politicians is, by necessity, mired in and must compete with all of the other municipal services and priorities that demand a busy public official's attention. Not so with the school board, whose sole responsibility is education.

Transferring control of a school district's governance to a mayor, county manager, or state legislature also widens the gap between parents and the key decision makers who have direct oversight of public education. School boards are accountable to the public—96 percent of the 95,000 members in our nation's 14,890 school districts are elected. And, they are accessible. . . .

How difficult will it be for community members to have direct access to a mayor—especially in a large city such as New York or Philadelphia—to discuss a problem in their neighborhood school? . . .

When a board is divided on a critical issue in the community, it often means the community is divided. As with any form of government, the only way to build consensus is to discuss, debate, and, ultimately, make the best and most informed decision that is in the best interest of all children.

Those who support takeovers would prefer to squelch this town hall-style approach. They contend that putting career politicians in charge allows for radical, and necessary, changes in low-performing school districts. But those radical changes often require added resources—resources that have been stubbornly unavailable to districts, sometimes for decades.

A takeover also assumes—falsely—that states or mayors have the ability to effectively govern and manage a school district. Since 1988, 19 states have taken over 49 districts, and the results have been mixed. In New Jersey, for example, the state abolished the school board and took control of the Jersey City School District 13 years ago, but it has not been able to meet its own standards for making the district independent. West Virginia took over the Logan County School District in 1992, but the school board and administrators stayed on as advisors, and the district was returned to local control four years later.

The most effective districts are the ones that have a strong partnership among the schools, the community, and the home. The school board is your liaison, your partner. That's why school boards should continue to exist, evolve, and serve our children.

Source: *Do school boards matter?* (2007, January 3). Washington, DC: National School Boards Association. Retrieved April 22, 2009, from **http://www.nsba.org/MainMenu/Governance/WhySchoolBoards/ DoSchoolBoardsMatter.aspx**.

Questions

1. What reasons does the article give for allowing people who are not "educational experts" to set policy and govern our public schools? Do you agree or disagree this view? Why?

2. Describe several difficulties in giving governance of schools with academic problems to city majors, county managers, or state legislatures.

3. How would a school board run by politicians differ from one run by civic-minded individuals?

4. What are your thoughts about who should control public education?

The School District Superintendent

The local school board's most important responsibility is to hire an excellent superintendent of schools. The superintendent is the school system's CEO and reports to the school board. He or she is a crucial part of the governance team for the school system and an essential link in the chain connecting the school board to the school system's people, programs, and activities.[34]

---

[34] Campbell, D. W., & Greene, D. (1994). Defining the leadership role of school boards in the 21st century. *Phi Delta Kappan, 75*(5), 1–5.

Local school superintendents may be either appointed or elected. The Education Commission of the States reports that only Alabama and Mississippi have both elected and appointed local school superintendents. Cities tend to appoint their school superintendents, whereas county school systems tend to use a combination of elected and appointed school chiefs. Hawaii and Vermont have no local superintendents. The remaining 46 states tend to appoint their local superintendents.[35]

By and large, the superintendent oversees the school system's daily operations and advises the school board about policies and actions that need to be taken. The superintendent's specific responsibilities vary according to the school district's size; its location in a rural, suburban, or urban setting; and the superintendent's historical duties within the organization.

In small, rural areas, the superintendent may be a "jack of all trades": he or she may evaluate all principals and central office staff, and conduct professional development programs. In medium-sized suburban districts, two or more assistant superintendents may be available to assist and spread out the work. Large urban and suburban areas may have area superintendents and assistant superintendents who report to the district superintendent, shouldering some of the responsibilities associated with this position.

Superintendent responsibilities. The school superintendent's work is threefold:

- **Organize the school system for teaching and learning.** The superintendent must make certain that all students learn and achieve to high academic levels. He or she is responsible for developing and evaluating instructional programs and curriculum. The superintendent also influences curriculum policy by gathering and presenting data and responding to matters before the board of education, initiating programs for staff development, making district personnel aware of changes occurring in the schools, and moderating outside demands for change.[36]

- **Run the school system efficiently and effectively.** School systems are complex organizations that require not only good leaders, but also good managers. For example, the superintendent must develop and oversee the school district's budget and consider federal and state requirements when developing the courses offered by the school system. Similarly, the superintendent is responsible for ensuring the efficacy of the school district's organization.

- **Maintain good communication and relations with the school board.** The superintendent is the school board's primary advisor. Because the board members are laypeople, they rely on the superintendent and other specialists to give them the details and perspectives necessary to make informed decisions. Frequently, the superintendent serves as the school board's spokesperson in the community. Nonetheless, even when the board delegates many of its own powers to the superintendent and staff, especially in larger districts, the superintendent's policies remain subject to school board approval. When communication and relations break down between the superintendent and the board, the board may replace the superintendent. In reality, the superintendent works for the school board and is always subject to the board's approval for continued employment in that district.

---

[35] Local superintendents. (2008). In *Statenotes.* Denver, CO: Education Commission of the States. Retrieved October 4, 2009, from http://mb2.ecs.org/reports/Report.aspx?id=171.
[36] McNeil, J. (1996). *Curriculum: A comprehensive introduction* (5th ed.) Los Angeles, CA: Harper Collins College.

Some believe that the superintendent has lost much of his or her decision-making authority over curriculum policy in recent years because of the increased federal and state involvement in public education. Powers previously granted to superintendent have been taken away through the courts and the passage of various legislative acts.[37] Nevertheless, this role remains extremely important and highly challenging.

The District Central Office

The central office or school board office refers to the educators and support staffs who help the superintendent administer the school system. A typical central office organizational chart may look like Figure 9.3. It takes many people "behind the scenes"

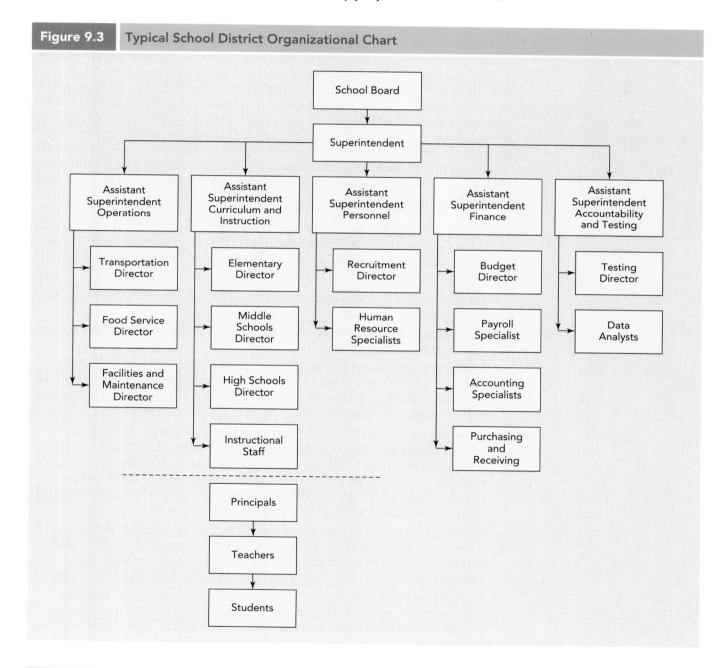

Figure 9.3   Typical School District Organizational Chart

---

[37] Andero, A (2000, Winter). The changing role of school superintendent with regard to curriculum policy and decision making. *Education, 121*(2), 276–286.

to support classroom teachers. While students appear at the base, the entire pyramid could be turned upside down with the students placed at the top, given that they are the focus of the entire educational enterprise.

Most teacher candidates rarely think about how the central office personnel work to make their classroom efforts more successful. Teachers need to be recruited, hired, and trained. Instructional items must be purchased, paid for, and inventoried. The achievement testing programs need to be coordinated, administered, interpreted, and analyzed to modify curriculum and instruction. Paychecks need to be processed correctly and delivered on time. Bus transportation routes need to be established and drivers hired, trained, and evaluated. Food needs to be ordered and delivered to the school cafeterias. Food service workers need to hired, trained, and supervised. Buildings need routine maintenance. The schoolyard grass needs to be cut. Leaking roofs and sputtering heating systems need to be fixed. The school district's budget needs to be developed and monitored so the school system does not overspend its limits. These functions and many others are coordinated at the central office level, long before most teachers even think about teaching their lessons to students.

Books, equipment, instructional supplies, and paychecks are only a small part of what it takes to operate a school system. Some critics of schools, however, claim that the central office's layered bureaucracy wastes taxpayers' money, diverting needed funds away from students. The truth is that administrative positions count for only 1.6 percent of all staff in schools. Gerry Bracey, an education writer and strong public education advocate, states that if every administrative position were eliminated, teachers could get a 5 percent raise and class size could be reduced by one student.[38]

Work responsibilities. Most importantly for teachers, school districts' central offices take charge of a variety of responsibilities that foster district-wide improvements in teaching and leadership. Many of these responsibilities focus on helping new teachers successfully adjust to their new role and work setting:

- Focusing on the district's instructional priorities and how the school district's employees will meet them.
- Communicating the school district's information to classroom teachers, parents, and the community.
- Fostering teacher leadership by giving teachers opportunities to serve the school district in curriculum development, working on school district committees, and making presentations illustrating their best programs and techniques at professional conferences
- Providing service and expertise to help teachers improve their professional practice. These measures include conducting the textbook adoption process, developing programs of studies, conducting formal teacher observations, assisting teachers who are having difficulties, conducting staff development, organizing district-wide activities such as science fairs, applying for grant-funded projects, and completing required state and federal reports.
- Ensuring consistency of practice among district schools through development of common goals, curricula, instructional texts, instructional practices, assessments, teacher training, programs for special populations, resource staff, and much more, so all students have equal and equitable opportunities to learn.
- Orienting new teachers to the districts' culture, expectations, and practices. Such orientations might include helping new teachers learn to hold high expectations for all students, understand the school district's curriculum, use instructional best practices, employ assessments to inform instruction, recognize

---

[38] Bracey, G. (1997). *Setting the record straight: Responses to misconceptions about public education in the United States.* Alexandria, VA: ASCD, p. 171.

and value diversity, and receive moral support from other new teachers who are also beginning their professional practice in the same school district.[39]

When one considers the many tasks that schools require to operate smoothly, it becomes clear that the central office function is an important one that enables the teachers to do their jobs well.

Activity 9.3

Figure 9.4 depicts the typical school district organizational chart. In this diagram, the school board sits at the top and the students sit at the bottom. Philosophically, all of the other parties' efforts are intended to benefit the students.

A. Discuss where principals, teachers, and students are on the organizational chart.

B. Who holds the most power and influence inside the school system? Which factors give these persons the most power?

C. Who holds the least power and influence inside the school system? Which factors contribute to this status?

D. How can teachers use and enhance their power and influence?

The Principal

Everyone knows the old spelling adage, "The principal is your pal." Principals' job descriptions vary from state to state depending on the laws and regulations. Virginia, for example, has defined the principal's position as the instructional leader of the school. Given the state testing conducted under the aegis of NCLB, most states now consider the principal's primary charges to be managing the school, ensuring that all students meet state achievement standards, and ensuring making certain that the school meets its AYP goals.

Teachers and their principals interact frequently. Larger schools have at least one assistant principal to help with these responsibilities, and teachers interact repeatedly with these personnel. Many of these principal–teacher interactions occur in faculty meetings and during the course of classroom observations. Most states require principals to observe teachers on a routine basis to make certain the curriculum is being taught effectively. As such, most principals or assistant principals observe classrooms formally at least twice a year, and perhaps more often before teachers are formally offered tenure, sometimes called continuing contract status. In addition, many principals informally stop by classrooms throughout the year to get a sense of the classroom climate and to monitor and support the teaching and learning process.

Principals affect student achievement. Principals can make a measurable difference in their schools' success. Three decades of school effectiveness research has concluded that successful schools have dynamic, knowledgeable, and focused principals. "Many of the most impressive examples of school-wide change and student achievement gains involve a talented principal who has brought together teachers, parents, and students . . . to improve teaching and learning,"[40] observes Jonathan Schnur, of

---

[39] Grove, K. F. (2002, May). The invisible role of the central office. *Educational Leadership, 59*(8), 45–47.
[40] Schnur, J. (2002, June 18). *An outstanding principal in every school: Using the new Title II to promote effective leadership*. National Council on Teacher Quality, p. 2.

New Leaders for New Schools. The Chicago Panel on School Policy's study of five years of school reform found that "the most distinguishing feature of improving [as compared to stable or declining] schools was [that] they were led continuously by strong principals who had a vision of improvement for their school."[41]

According to one national analysis of 15 years of school leadership research, an outstanding principal exercises a measurable, though indirect effect on school effectiveness and student achievement.[42] While indirect, the principal's role has a critical impact on teachers, and through teachers, on student achievement. The principal controls key factors affecting a school's instructional quality:

- Attracting, selecting, and retaining outstanding teachers
- Working with the school community to establish a common mission, instructional vision, and goals
- Creating a school culture grounded in collaboration and high expectations
- Facilitating continuous instructional improvement
- Finding fair, effective ways to improve or remove low-performing teachers
- Producing high measured student academic results aligned with state standards

Further, Robert Marzano and colleagues' meta-analysis of 30 years of research on principals' practices' effects on student achievement finds a significant, positive correlation between effective school leadership and student achievement. For the average school, having an effective principal can mean the difference between scoring at the 50th or 60th percentile on a given achievement test.[43] In addition, the study identified 21 leadership responsibilities, practices, knowledge, strategies, and tools that seemed to be linked to changes in students' test scores.[44]

Figure 9.4	An Outstanding Principal Has a Measurable But Indirect Effect on Student Achievement

Lacy Atkins/San Francisco Chronicle/Corbis News/CORBIS

[41] Hess, A. G. Jr. (1998, September). *Strong leadership is no. 1 catalyst.* Chicago: Voices of School Reform.

[42] Hallinger, P., & Heck, R. (1998). Exploring the principal's contribution to school effectiveness, 1980–1995. *R. School Effectiveness and School Improvement, 9*(2), 157–191.

[43] Marzano, R. J., Waters, T., & McNulty, Brian, A. (2005). *School leadership that works. From research to results.* Alexandria, VA: Association for Supervision and Curriculum Development.

[44] Viadero, D. (2003, October 1). Analysis teases out ways principals boost learning. *Education Week, 23*(5), 7.

In addition, principals have considerable operations management responsibilities for security, public relations, finances, personnel, transportation, and technology.

Principals' behaviors make a tremendous impact on teachers' work life. In fact, research indicates that a teacher's decision to stay at a school largely depends on the principal's leadership. Conversely, teachers cite a lack of administrators' support and weak or ineffective leadership as contributing factors in the negative working environment that add to teacher dissatisfaction and their decision to leave the profession.[45]

The Teacher

Chapter 1 discusses the role of the classroom teacher. It is important to know, however, that teachers have colleagues in the building who will assist in the teaching and learning process. Increasingly, school resources include other professionals to deliver services that support the teaching-for-learning process.

Support Staff

Teachers are not always alone with their students in the classroom. An array of skilled and specialized professionals may work with teachers to help make them and their students successful. Figure 9.5 shows the percentage of regular public schools that have support staff and the variety of resource professionals available. Not every school has every support role on-site, but most have specialized resource professionals available through the school district.

Figure 9.5 Percentage of Regular Public Schools with Student Support Staff

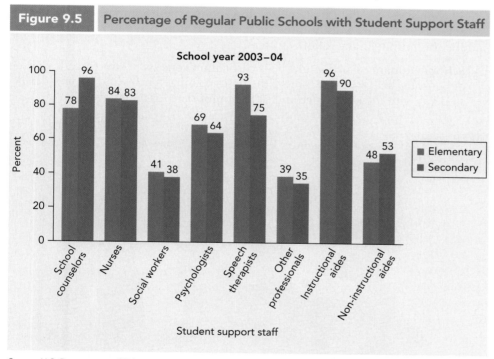

Source: U.S. Department of Education, National Center for Education Statistics. (2007). *The condition of education, 2007* (NCES 2007-064). Washington, DC: U.S. Government Printing Office, p. 72.

[45] Charlotte Advocates for Education. (2004, February). *Role of principal leadership in increasing teacher retention: Creating a supportive environment.* Charlotte, NC: Author, pp. 1–64. Retrieved October 4, 2009, from www.advocatesfored.org/principalstudy.htm; Ingersoll, R. M. (2002, June). The teacher shortage: A case of wrong diagnosis and wrong prescription. *NASSP Bulletin, 86*(631), 16–30; Public Education Network. (2004). *The voice of the new teacher.* pp. 1–37. Retrieved November 11, 2008, from www.publiceducation.org/pdf/PEN_Pubs/Voice_of_the_New_Teacher.pdf. National Commission on Teaching and America's Future. (2003, August 13). *Recruiting teachers for hard-to-staff schools: Solutions for the Southeast and the nation.* Chapel Hill, NC: Southeast Center for Teacher Quality. Retrieved on October 4, 2009, from http://www.teachingquality.org/legacy/HTSS_regional.pdf

The support professionals with whom teachers are most likely to work include school counselors, special education teachers, school nurses, school psychologists, reading specialists, and library media specialists. Each of these roles contributes a unique expertise that can help teachers do their jobs effectively.

School counselors. Today's school counselors provide academic counseling, career development, and personal–social counseling. Licensed professionals with a master's degree or higher in school counseling, school counselors are a major part of a school's education team. They are specifically trained to help maximize student achievement in schools. Professional school counselors develop strong rapport and largely confidential relationships with students to help them resolve or cope with problems and developmental concerns.

School counselors support teachers' success by helping their students learn the critical behaviors that help them do well in school. School counselors help students develop three types of skills:

- Cognitive and meta-cognitive skills such as goal setting, progress monitoring, and memory skills
- Social skills such as interpersonal skills, social problem-solving, listening, and teamwork skills
- Self-management skills such as managing attention, motivation, and anger

These three skill sets are the most powerful predictors of long-term school success and seem to separate high achievers from low achievers. As part of their role, school counselors can help students develop and use these approaches.[46]

School counselors work to provide services to students, parents, school staff, and the community in the following areas:

- **School Guidance Curriculum.** This curriculum consists of structured lessons designed to help students achieve the desired competencies and to provide all students with the knowledge and skills appropriate for their developmental

| Figure 9.6 | School Counselors Help Students Learn the Skills to Succeed in School |

David Young-Wolff/PhotoEdit

---

[46] Brigman, G., & Campbell, C. (2003, December). Helping students improve academic achievement and school success behaviors. *Professional School Counseling, 7*(2), 91–98.

level. Working collaboratively with K–12 teachers in their classrooms, professional school counselors systematically present the necessary information to students. Occasionally, counselors enact the curriculum with students individually and in small-group activities.

- **Individual Student Planning.** Professional school counselors coordinate activities designed to help students establish personal goals and develop future plans. This type of work includes planning for upcoming courses, further education and work experiences, and eventual careers. Typically, counselors work with the same group of students during their entire time in a particular school so they can build knowledgeable, strong, and caring relationships. With insight and trust gained from their positive rapport, counselors help young people construct a "big picture" for themselves and identify and begin taking the steps needed to get there, starting now.

- **Responsive Services.** *Responsive services* are preventive and/or intervention activities—usually consisting of individual or group counseling—that are intended to meet students' immediate and future needs. These needs can be prompted by events and conditions in students' lives. Counselors may consult with parents, teachers, and other educators and make referrals to other school support services or community resources. Additionally, school counselors can use peer helping and information sharing as tools to prevent or resolve problems that interfere with student learning.

- **System Support.** Schools counselors work with everyone in the school on behalf of students and teachers. Before the school year starts, they interact with the school administrators to identify the school's needs and detail how the school counseling program will be organized to address these needs. They frequently partner with teachers to conduct parent conferences. Professional school counselors engage in continual personal and professional development and are proactively involved in professional organizations promoting school counseling at the local, state, and national levels.

Developmental guidance and counseling program effectiveness is directly related to the counselor-to-student ratio within the program. The number of counselors needed to staff the program depends on the students' and community's needs and on the local program's goals and design. The American School Counselor Association recommends a maximum ratio of 1:250 counselor-to-students.[47] Each state decides the school counselor-to-student ratio for each grade level that it will fund. For instance, Virginia accreditation standards require secondary schools to employ one school counselor for every 350 students, one counselor for every 400 students at middle school, and one counselor for every 500 students at elementary school.[48] Depending on the state's requirements, counselors typically spend 60 to 80 percent of their time in direct service with students.

Research on school counselors and student success. As for teachers and principals, accountability, program evaluation, and obtaining data about student results are counselors' concerns.[49] Research substantiates the school counselor's ability to positively influence students through group counseling and classroom guidance, thereby changing their behaviors and increasing their achievement on classroom and standardized tests. When school counselor interventions target specific skills associated with school success and when school counselors use research-based

[47] *Student-to-counselor ratios.* (2006). Alexandria, VA: American School Counselors Association. Retrieved October 4, 2009, from http://www.schoolcounselor.org/content.asp?contentid=460.
[48] *Accreditation standards.* (2007). Richmond, VA: Virginia Department of Education, p. 39. Retrieved October 4, 2009, from www.pen.K12.va.us/VDOE/Accountability.
[49] Gysbers, N. G. (2004, October). Comprehensive guidance and counseling programs: The evolution of accountability. *Professional School Counseling, 8*(1), 1–14.

techniques to teach these critical skills, the outcomes for students show a marked difference, evidenced by positive changes in classroom performance.[50]

Based on empirical studies on students in grade levels K–12, students from 1954 to 2007 who participated in fully implemented guidance and counseling programs—as compared with students in less comprehensive or well-established programs—show markedly higher or more:

- Educational achievement[51]
- School success skills[52]
- Occupational level[53]
- Emotional stability[54]
- Preparation for the future[55]
- Enrollment in advanced math and science courses[56]
- Enrollment in vocational/technical courses[57]
- ACT scores on every scale of the test[58]
- Relations with teachers[59]
- Feeling safe in school[60]

In addition, schools with well-developed guidance and counseling programs have a more positive climate.[61]

School counselors are evaluated regularly. Their principals and central office supervisor usually collaborate in assessing their performance using basic standards of practice expected of professional school counselors who are implementing a school counseling program.

The Special Education Teacher

Today's public school students demonstrate a range of disabilities, including specific learning disabilities, speech or language impairments, intellectual disabilities (previously named mental retardation), emotional disturbance, multiple disabilities, hearing impairments, orthopedic impairments, visual impairments, autism spectrum disorders, combined deafness and blindness, traumatic brain injury, and other health impairments. After referrals, classroom interventions, rigorous screenings, and evaluations are complete, students may be classified under one of the various

---

[50] Brigman & Campbell, 2003.

[51] Cantoni, L. J. (1954). Guidance: 4 students 10 years later. *The Clearing House, 28,* 474–478; Wellman, F. E., & Moore, E. J. (1975). *Pupil personnel services: A handbook for program development and evaluation.* Washington, DC: U.S. Department of Health, Education, and Welfare; Lapan, R. T., Gysbers, N. C., & Sun, Y. (1997). The impact of more fully implemented guidance programs on the school experiences of high school students: A statewide-evaluation study. *Journal of Counseling and Development, 75,* 292–302; Lapan, R. T., Gysbers, N. C., & Petroski, G. (2001). Helping 7th graders be safe and academically successful: A statewide study of the impact of comprehensive guidance programs. *Journal of Counseling and Development, 79,* 320–330; Sink, C. A., & Stroh, H. R. (2003). Raising achievement test scores of early elementary students through comprehensive school counseling programs. *Professional School Counseling, 6,* 350–364; Campbell, C., & Brigman, G. (2005, February). Closing the achievement gap: A structured approach to group counseling. *Journal for Specialists in Group Work, 31*(1), 67–82; Webb, L., & Bregman, G. (2007, April). Student success skills: A structured group intervention for school counselors. *Journal for Specialists in Group Work, 32*(2), 190–201.

[52] Brigman & Campbell, 2003.

[53] Cantoni, 1954.

[54] Cantoni, 1954.

[55] Lapan, Gysbers, & Sun, 1997.

[56] Nelson, D. E., Gardner, J. L., & Fox, D. G. (1998). *An evaluation of the comprehensive guidance program in Utah public schools.* Salt Lake City, UT: State Office of Education.

[57] Nelson, Gardner, & Fox, 1998.

[58] Nelson, Gardner, & Fox, 1998.

[59] Lapan, Gysbers, & Petroski, 2001.

[60] Lapan, Gysbers, & Petroski, 2001.

[61] Lapan, Gysbers, & Sun, 1997.

special education categories. Special education teachers are prepared to work with students having certain disabilities that affect how they learn.

Because children with disabilities have more complex learning needs than their non-disabled peers, states have developed licensing standards for teachers who focus their work on these students. Special education teachers, therefore, are highly trained professionals who provide specially designed instruction to children with disabilities. Licensing requires the completion of a teacher training program and at least a bachelor's degree, although many states require a master's degree to qualify for this position.[62]

A small number of special education teachers work with students with intellectual disabilities or autism, primarily teaching them life skills and basic literacy. The majority of special education teachers work with children with mild to moderate disabilities, using the general education curriculum, or modifying it, to meet the child's individual needs.

As Figure 9.7 shows, since the enactment of PL 94-142, the percentage of students who qualify for special education services has increased from approximately 7 percent to 14 percent of all students. In terms of sheer numbers, total public school enrollment in 1975 and 2005 stood at 41.6 million and 48.5 million, respectively. Over the same period, the number of special education students increased from 2.9 million to almost 6.8 million.[63] This increase has created a large demand for special education teachers in U.S. public schools.

Special education teachers design and teach appropriate curricula, assign work geared toward each student's needs and abilities, and grade papers and homework assignments. They are involved in the students' behavioral, social, and academic development. They help special education students feel comfortable in social situations and learn socially acceptable behaviors. Preparing these students for daily life

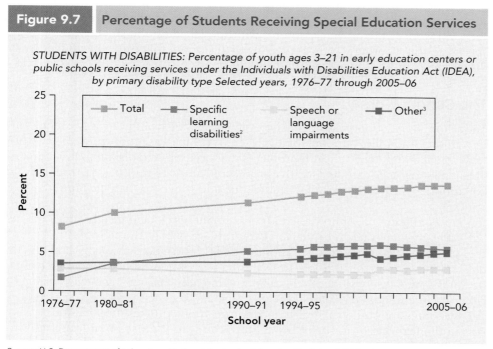

Figure 9.7 Percentage of Students Receiving Special Education Services

STUDENTS WITH DISABILITIES: Percentage of youth ages 3–21 in early education centers or public schools receiving services under the Individuals with Disabilities Education Act (IDEA), by primary disability type Selected years, 1976–77 through 2005–06

Source: U.S. Department of Education, National Center for Education Statistics. (2007). *The condition of education, 2007* (NCES 2007-064). Washington, DC: U.S. Government Printing Office, p. 28.

[62] Teachers: Special education. (2006, August 4). In *Occupational outlook handbook*. Washington, DC: U.S. Department of Labor, Bureau of Labor Statistics. Retrieved October 4, 2009, from http://www.bls.gov/oco/ocos070.htm.

[63] U.S. Department of Education, National Center for Education Statistics. (2007). *The condition of education, 2007* (NCES 2007-064). Washington, DC: U.S. Government Printing Office, p. 60.

after graduation is another important aspect of the job. In some instances, special education teachers assess students for possible careers or help them learn routine life management skills, such as balancing a checkbook.

Within the school, special educators deliver their services in a continuum of teaching settings. Increasingly, special education teachers work in general education classrooms using an **inclusion model**. In this model, students with disabilities receive most, if not all, of their instruction in a general education classroom. As a result, the percentage of U.S. students aged 6–21 with disabilities spending at least 80 percent of the school day in regular education classrooms increased from 45 percent in 1995 to 52 percent in 2005.[64] Special education teachers help general educators adapt curriculum materials and teaching techniques to meet disabled students' needs. Frequently, they plan lessons together. Sometimes they team-teach.

Other special educators teach special-needs students in **self-contained classrooms**. Approximately 48 percent of students with disabilities spend the majority of their school day in a classroom specifically set aside for children with disabilities.[65] The majority of special education teachers work in **resource rooms**, where they provide specialized instruction to students with disabilities who come in for part of the school day, either individually or in small groups.

A large part of a special education teacher's job involves interacting with others. These teachers communicate frequently with parents, social workers, school psychologists, occupational and physical therapists, school administrators, and regular education teachers. They coordinate the work of teachers, teacher assistants, and related personnel, such as therapists and social workers, to meet the students' individualized needs within inclusive special education programs.

Special education teachers represent a valuable resource for general education teachers. Because of their training, these teachers are creative problem solvers who bring expertise in curriculum, teaching strategies, and learning styles into the classroom. They will help you work with special-needs students in your classroom, or they will work in their own classrooms with special education students. Either way, special educators bring resources or skills to the school that can help students with disabilities achieve academically and socially.

The School Nurse

The school nurse supports student success by providing health care assessments, interventions, and follow-up care for all children within the school setting. They work with actual and potential health problems that occur in schools; provide case management services for students with chronic and short-term illnesses; and actively collaborate with teachers, parents, students, and others to manage family health issues.[66]

Here's an example of how a school nurse manages student health care. Students with diabetes have a school plan of care in place, which the school nurse helps them follow. These students often monitor their blood glucose levels several times a day and may require insulin injections during school hours. The school nurse must be familiar with every student's treatment regimen, including any devices or medical procedures required as part of the treatment.

By addressing students' health needs, professional nurses support student success in the learning process. In this context, the school nurse provides services to the entire school population, which may include infants, toddlers, preschoolers,

---

[64] U.S. Department of Education, National Center for Education Statistics. (2007). Indicator 31: What percentage of students with disabilities are educated in regular classrooms? In *The condition of education 2007* (NCES 2007-064). Washington, DC: U.S. Government Printing Office. Retrieved October 4, 2009, from http://nces.ed.gov/fastfacts/display.asp?id=59.

[65] U.S. Department of Education, National Center for Education Statistics, 2007. Indicator 31.

[66] *The role of the school nurse: Issue brief.* (2002). Silver Springs, MD: National Association of School Nurses. Retrieved October 4, 2009, from http://www.nasn.org/Default.aspx?tabid=279.

children with special medical conditions, traditional school populations, and, to a limited degree, adults within the school community.

The school nurse's responsibilities are profiled in the following subsections.[67]

Providing direct health care to students and staff. The school nurse provides care to injured or acutely ill students and staff, including administering emergency first aid, communicating with parents, and making referrals to other providers. The school nurse is responsible for administering student medications and performing health care procedures ordered by an appropriately licensed health care provider. The school nurse also assists faculty and staff in monitoring students' chronic health conditions.[68]

Providing screening and referral for health conditions. The school nurse often conducts screening activities to address students' health problems that might potentially become barriers to learning or treats symptoms of underlying medical conditions. Screenings may include vision, hearing, dental, postural, weight (body mass index), or other conditions.

Promoting a healthy school environment. The school nurse monitors student compliance with state immunization laws, assures appropriate exclusion from and reentry into school, and reports communicable diseases as required by law. The school nurse leads the school in implementing precautions for faculty and staff regarding blood-borne pathogens and other infectious diseases. This health care professional may also assess the school's physical environment and act to improve health and safety in areas including the playground, perform an indoor air quality evaluation, or review illness or injury patterns to determine a source of concern.

Promoting health with students, school, family, and community. The school nurse provides age-appropriate health information directly to individual students, groups of students, or classes as well as to school staff, families, and the community. Health promotion activities may include health fairs for students, families, or staff; consultation with food service personnel or physical education teachers regarding healthy lifestyles; and staff wellness programs.

As the school's health expert, the school nurse participates as part of students' individualized education program (IEP) and 504[69] teams and as part of student and family assistance teams. In his or her role as case manager, the nurse communicates with the family through telephone calls, letters, and home visits as needed. The school nurse also speaks with local health providers and health care agencies while ensuring appropriate confidentiality, develops community partnerships, and serves on area coalitions to promote public health.

State law usually regulates the nurse-to-student ratio required for a school; no national standard exists. The National Association of School Nurses recommends the following nurse-to-student ratios: 1:750 in general populations, 1:225 in student populations that may require daily professional school nursing services or interventions, and 1:125 in student populations with complex health care needs.[70]

The National Association of School Nurses recommends that all school nurses have a minimum of a baccalaureate degree and achieve School Nurse Certification. The school nurse needs expertise in pediatric, public health, and mental health nursing and must possess strong health promotion, assessment, and referral skills. School nurses also need to have knowledge of laws in education and health care

[67] *The role of the school nurse*, (2002). Silver Spring, MD: National Association of School Nurses.
[68] Knowing all that is needed to effectively conduct these functions' requires school nurses to participate in continuous professional development.
[69] Section 504 is a civil rights law that prohibits discrimination against individuals with disabilities. It ensures that the child with a disability has equal access to an education. The child may receive accommodations and modifications.
[70] *School nurse management of students with chronic health conditions: Issue brief*. (2006, June). Silver Spring, MD: National Association of School Nurses.

Activity 9.4

Schools have many personnel in support positions who are available to help teachers educate students to high levels of learning. These professionals include library media specialists, school counselors, school psychologists, reading specialists, school nurses, special education teachers, and many more.

A. Research the role of one of these positions that interests you. Determine what these personnel actually do in the school. Research their education and licensure requirements.

B. Interview one or two individuals in this line of work and see if a career in that field is something you wish to pursue further. Report your findings to the class.

---

that may affect children in the school setting. Each state sets its own eligibility and hiring requirements for this important school support person.

The Structure of Schools

Generally, local school boards decide how to structure their district's schools. Typically, schools are organized as elementary, middle, and high schools. Grade configurations vary substantially, however, as do schools' sizes. The local school board has much control over both these factors. Typically, elementary schools contain kindergarten through grade five. Middle schools typically house students in grades six, seven, and eight. Usually high schools have students in grades nine through twelve.

Most school boards take their role as stewards of their neighbors' tax dollars very seriously. Where local boards feel cautious about spending tax revenues, they choose efficiency as an operational value. They are likely to build larger schools, assuming that two or three big schools are more cost-effective to operate than four or five smaller schools. Conversely, school boards may decide that effectiveness as an operational value is more important that efficiency. Reflecting this perspective, they may decide to build smaller schools, citing research that smaller schools may be better for student achievement gains than larger schools. Members' beliefs and values as well as research findings contribute to board decisions about school structure.

Reducing School Size

What is the best size school to support student success? Research can help school board make decisions about this issue.

In 1987, after reviewing several studies, two researchers concluded that high schools should have no more than 250 students. Larger enrollments focused too much administrators' attention on control and order, harming the school climate. Additionally, the larger school population increased members' feelings of anonymity, making it more difficult to build a sense of community among students, teachers, and parents.[71] For instance, a 1994 study of 34 large New York City high schools showed that when students were organized into "houses" of approximately 250 students, attendance improved, student responsiveness in school increased, and grades went up.[72]

---

[71] Gregory, T. B., & Smith, G. R. (1987, January). *High schools as communities: The small school reconsidered.* Bloomington, IN: Phi Delta Kappa; Sousa, R., & Skandera, H. (2001, Summer). Why bigger isn't better. *Hoover Digest, 3.* Palo Alto, CA: Stanford University.

[72] Eichenstein, R., et al. (1994). *Project Achieve, part I: Qualitative findings, 1993–94.* Brooklyn, NY: New York City Board of Education.

Likewise, research has suggested that small and moderate-size high schools foster more positive social and academic environments compared to large high schools. This relationship is especially notable when it comes to economically disadvantaged students.[73] This research also suggests that students in very small high schools learn less than students in moderate-size (600–900 students) high schools. Learning also declines as school grows in size. Achievement decreases considerably in high schools with more than 2,100 students.[74]

Another study found that smaller is not automatically better when it comes to increasing student achievement. A 2008 federal study of high schools receiving grants to support forming "smaller learning communities" found that the proportion of students being promoted from ninth grade to tenth grade increased, participation in extracurricular activities rose, and the rate of violent incidents declined. The evaluation, however, found "no significant trends" in achievement on college entrance exams.[75] A similar study in Chicago concluded that while smaller schools have a more collegial, trusting, and innovative environment, this factor does not necessarily translate into instructional and curricular reform.[76]

Community affluence plays a role in school effectiveness, too. Studies have revealed that more affluent communities have effective student learning even with larger schools, whereas schools in low-socioeconomic neighborhoods or schools with high concentrations of minority students need be smaller in size to provide the most opportunities for their students to learn.[77]

Similarly, a seven-state study conducted by Ohio researchers for the Rural School and Community Trust in 2002 found that smaller schools reduce the harmful effects of poverty on student achievement. Smaller schools also help students from less affluent communities narrow the academic achievement gap between themselves and students from wealthier communities.[78]

Cost-effectiveness is also a consideration in determining school sizes. A 2000 study of more than 140 schools and 50,000 students in the New York City Public Schools found that small academic high schools had budgets per graduate similar to those of large high schools (more than 2,000 students). Smaller high schools had lower dropout rates. Researchers found that both small and large schools were cost-effective when looking at graduates as the outcome.[79]

It is true that smaller schools are more expensive to operate on a *per-pupil* basis. Researchers now argue, however, that small schools can be more efficient when measured on a *cost-per-graduate* basis. Cost-effectiveness is a relative term. With fewer dropouts, smaller schools graduate more of their students. Considering that high school dropouts are associated with substantial costs to society, including lower earnings, higher unemployment rates, greater reliance on welfare, and increased incarceration rates, small schools seem more cost-effective.[80]

---

[73] Gerwitz, C. (2006, August 9). Chicago's small schools see gains, but not on tests. *Education Week, 25*(44), 5, 18;

[74] Lee, V. E., & Smith, J. B. (1997, Autumn). High school size: Which works best and for whom? *Educational Evaluation and Policy Analysis, 19*(3), 205–227.

[75] Hoff, D. J. (2008, May 21). Study of small high schools yields little on achievement. *Education Week, 27*(38), 10.

[76] Gerwitz, 2006.

[77] Lee & Smith, 1997. Also see National Center for Education Statistics, (n.d.). Size of high schools. www.nces.gov/programs/coe/2003/section4/indicator30.asp.

[78] Johnson, J. D., Howley, C. B., & Howley, A. A. (2002). *Size, excellence, and equity: A report on Arkansas schools and districts.* Athens, OH: Ohio University College of Education, Educational Studies Department; Jimerson, L. (2006, September). *The hobbit effect: Why small schools work.* Arlington, VA: Rural School and Community Trust. The seven states were Alaska, California, Georgia, Montana, Ohio, Texas, and West Virginia.

[79] Stiefel, L., Berne, R., Iatarola, P., & Fruchter, N. (2000, Spring). High schools size: Effects on budgets and performance in New York City. *Educational Evaluation and Policy Analysis, 22*(1), 27–39.

[80] Lawrence, B. K., Bingler, S., Diamond, B. M., Hill, B., Hoffman, J. L., Howley, C. B., Mitchell, S., Rudolph, D., & Washor, E. (2002). *Dollars and sense. The cost effectiveness of small schools.* Cincinnati, OH: Knowledge Works Foundation. Retrieved October 4, 2009, from http://www.earlycolleges.org/Downloads/reslib79.pdf.

An Education Commission of the States (ECS) report details the benefits of reduced school size and draws five conclusions:[81]

- Under the right conditions, as schools get smaller, they produce stronger student performance as measured by attendance rates, test scores, extracurricular activity participation, and graduation rates.
- Smaller schools appear to promote greater levels of parent participation and satisfaction, and they increase parent–teacher communication.
- Teachers in small schools generally feel they are in a better position to make a genuine difference in student learning than do teachers in larger schools.
- There appears to be a particularly strong correlation between smaller school size and improved performance among low-income students in urban school districts. Smaller schools can help narrow the achievement gap between white, middle-class, affluent students and ethnic minority and low-income students.
- Smaller schools provide a safer learning environment for students.

Sometimes, larger schools create smaller schools by implementing the "school-within-a-school" concept. This approach may be a way to achieve the benefits associated with smaller school size without having to actually build expensive new school facilities. In this way, schools that personalize the learning environment for students can increase their engagement and academic achievement.

When considering the best school size to produce student achievement, school boards must consider the nature of their student body and decide whether they, as stand-ins for the larger community, prefer to pay now or pay later.

Consolidating School Districts

The debate about school size mirrors the debate about the best size for school districts. Larger school districts, their supporters contend, offer a broader tax base and reduce the educational cost per student. As a result, these districts can better afford high-quality personnel, a wide range of educational programs and special services, and good transportation. Over the past half-century, most studies of this issue have placed the most effective school district size at between 10,000 and 50,000 students.[82]

The twentieth century witnessed a trend toward consolidating smaller school districts in an effort to increase efficiency. In 1939–1940 (the earliest year for which data are available), slightly more than 117,000 public school districts existed in the United States. By 2004, that number had dropped to slightly more than 14,000, representing loss of more than 100,000 school districts—a decrease of almost 90 percent.[83]

School districts cite several reasons as driving forces for consolidation:

- **Size.** Larger schools, especially high schools, can accommodate broader curriculum offerings and specialized teachers.
- **Services.** Larger schools can justify hiring school counselors, deans of students, assistant principals, lead teachers, and specialists not typically available in smaller schools.

[81] *School size.* (n.d.). Denver, CO: Education Commission of the States. Retrieved October 4, 2009, from http://www.ecs.org/html/issue.asp?print=true&issueID=105&subIssueOD=0.
[82] Mertens, S. B., Flowers, N., & Mulhall, P. F. (2001, May). School size matters in interesting ways. *Middle School Journal, 32*(5), 51–55; Wahlberg, H. J. (1994, June–July). Losing local control. *Educational Researcher, 23*(5),19–26; Howley, C., & Bickel, R. (2002, March). The influence of scale. *American School Board Journal, 183*(3), 28–30; Andrews, M., Duncomb, W., & Yinger, J. (2002, June). Revisiting economics of size in American education: Are we any closer to consensus? *Economics of Education Review, 21,* 245–262; Pellicer, L, (1999, November). When is a school district too large? Too small? Just right? Lessons from Goldilocks and the three bears. *School Business Affairs, 65*(11), 4–6, 8–10, 26–29.
[83] National Center for Education Statistics. (1999). *Digest of education statistics, 1999.* Table 90. Retrieved July 21, 2008 from http://nces.gov/pubs2000/Digest99.

• **Economics.** Consolidating school districts lowers operating costs. Purchasing decisions can lead to significant savings when items are ordered in bulk; that is, the costs for books, paper, lab equipment, and art supplies may go down when schools can negotiate to buy them in larger quantities. Consolidation also allows schools to close older buildings, thereby saving money. Combining school districts can save money by reducing the number of higher-paid central office administrators. For example, instead of having three curriculum supervisors (one for each of the formerly separate school districts), a consolidated school district needs only one.

Figure 9.8 illustrates that larger schools are able to make more high-level, high-status courses available to students. These include dual-credit courses (simultaneous enrollment in a high school and college course), Advanced Placement (AP), and International Baccalaureate (IB) courses. Only 40 percent of high schools smaller than 500 students offer AP courses to their students, and none offers IB programs. By comparison, schools with 500 to 1,199 and schools with more 1,200 students provide more advanced-level offerings to their students.

When school districts merge, the resulting district serves more students. Table 9.2 compares the number of pupils per school district in 1940 and 2003. While the average school district in 1940 had approximately 217 students, school districts served more than 3,000 students on average in 2003.

In this 63-year period, the average number of students in school districts increased more than 1,500 percent—from 217 to 3,350. The number of public schools and school districts decreased, even as their size and efficiency increased (see Table 9.2 and Figure 9.9). Neighborhood schools and school districts gave way to larger ones covering multiple neighborhoods. Consolidation increased most districts' ethnic, geographic, and wealth diversity.

This changing structure posed crucial challenges for the localities affected. Feelings of community pride and ownership of local schools and school districts diminished as the schools and their leadership—and their children—moved farther away: Local

| Figure 9.8 | Percentage of Public High Schools Offering Advanced-Level Courses by Enrollment Size |

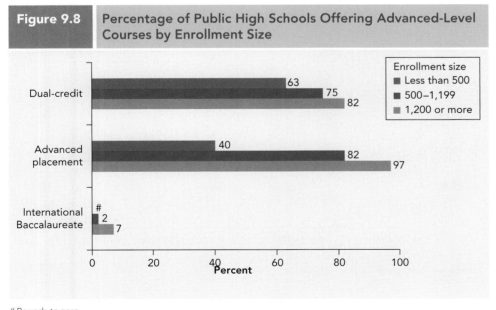

\# Rounds to zero.

Note: Dual-credit courses allow students to earn both high and postsecondary credits for a singlecourse. AP courses and their end-of-course examinations are developed and administered by The College Board and allow students to earn postsecondary credit. IB courses are defined ascourses that make up a 2-year liberal arts curriculum that leads to an IB diploma.

Source: U.S. Department of Education, National Center for Education Statistics. (2007). *The condition of education, 2007* (NCES 2007-064), Washington, DC: U.S. Government Printing Office, Figure 2, p. 6.

Table 9.2	Number of Pupils per School District, 1940 and 2007	
	1940	2007
Total number of students	25,434,000	49,644,000
Total number of school districts	117,108	13,862
Pupils per school district	217	3,581

Source: Snyder, T. D., Dillow, S. A., and Hoffman, C. M. (2009). *Digest of Education Statistics 2008* (NCES 2009-020). National Center for Education Statistics, Institute of Education Sciences, U.S. Department of Education. Washington, DC., p. 16. Calculations by author.

control was no longer local. At the same time, administrators and teachers worked with more diverse students. School climate and student achievement, once taken for granted in small local schools with relatively homogeneous student populations, suddenly became urgent issues. Many educators needed intensive professional development to gain the skills and attitudes needed to work effectively with students and their parents. In fact, distancing school districts from their communities has led some to call for replacing school boards with school councils, thereby returning public schools governance back to the "grassroots" level.[84]

Figure 9.9 shows how the number of public schools has changed over time as a consequence of both student population growth and school district consolidation. In 1939–1940, almost 250,000 public schools were in operation in the United States. Today, that number stands at approximately 96,000.[85] The number of one-teacher schools has declined dramatically.

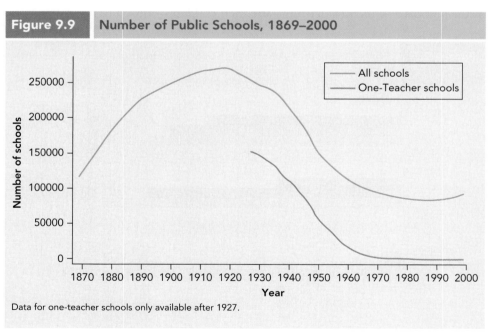

Figure 9.9	Number of Public Schools, 1869–2000

Data for one-teacher schools only available after 1927.

Source: Berry, C. (2003, October). *School district consolidation and student outcomes: Does size make a difference?* Cambridge, MA: John F. Kennedy School of Government, Harvard University, p. 31, Figure 2. Retrieved October 3, 2009, from http://www.ksg.harvard.edu/pepg/PDF/events/SBConfPDF/papers/PEPG_03-12Berry.pdf.

---

[84] Cunningham, W. G. (2003, June). Grassroots democracy: Putting the public back into public education. *Phi Delta Kappan, 84*(10), 776–779.
[85] Snyder, Tan, & Hoffman, 2006, p. 54.

The empirical literature on the effects of district size on student outcomes is small and mixed.[86] Some studies have found find that school districts with student enrollments between 2,000 and 4,000 students tend to be cost-effective, whereas districts enrolling more than 15,000 students achieve less cost savings.[87]

Organizing Schools by Grade Levels

When Americans think of how schools are organized by grade levels, we tend to think of elementary, middle, and high schools. The reality, however, is much more varied. Table 9.3 shows the breakdown of schools (the totals do not add up because of overlap in reporting).[88] In 2004, the United States still had 376 one-teacher schools.

Research on school grade configuration. Does a school's grade configuration affect student achievement? Do students achieve better in K–8 schools or in separate grades 6–8 middle schools? The research here is complicated and has yielded unclear results.[89] Little evidence exists to determine a cause-and-effect relationship between grade configuration and academic achievement. No empirical, large-scale studies have examined the relationship between grade configuration and student achievement as measured by standardized test scores.[90] The few studies that do exist

Table 9.3	Public Schools by Size and Type, 2007
Total (all public schools)	98,793
Elementary schools (beginning with grade 6 or below and no grade higher than 8)	68,990
Middle schools (grade spans beginning with 4, 5, or 6 and ending with 6, 7, or 8)	12,773
One-teacher schools	327
Secondary schools (no grade lower than 7)	23,436
Junior high schools (schools with grades 7 and 8 or grades 7 through 9)	3,112
High schools (three-year or four-year)	15,043
High schools (five-year or six-year)	4,048
Combined elementary/secondary schools (beginning with grade 6 or lower and ending with grade 9 or higher)	5,984
Other schools (special education, alternative, or schools not classified by grade spans)	383

Source: Snyder, T. D., Dillow, S. A., and Hoffman, C. M. (2009). *Digest of Education Statistics 2008* (NCES 2009-020). National Center for Education Statistics, Institute of Education Sciences, U.S. Department of Education. *Washington, DC.*, p. 154.

---

[86] Andrews, M., Duncombe, W., & Yinger, J. (2002, June). Revisiting economies of size in education: Are we any closer to a consensus? *Economics of Education Review, 21*(3), 245–262.
[87] Andrews, Duncombe, & Yinger, 2002.
[88] Some schools may be counted twice.
[89] Viadero, D. (2008, January 16). Evidence for moving to K–8 models not airtight. *Education Week, 27*(19), 1, 12.
[90] McEwin, C. K., Dickinson, T. S., & Jacobson, M. G. (2005). How effective are K–8 schools for young adolescents? *Middle School Journal, 37*(1), 24–28.

Activity 9.5

In groups, discuss and develop a written record of the elementary, middle (or junior high), and high school each group member attended. Answer the following questions:

1. How large was each of the schools you attended? How did it organize its grade levels? Within your group, were all schools organized in the same way? Were there differences?

2. What was your favorite level—elementary, middle, or high school? Why? Did the size of the school matter to you? How?

3. What was the principal's name for each of the schools? Do students from smaller schools remember their principals' names more frequently than students from larger schools?

4. Did you have a teacher who influenced you a great deal at each level or just at one or two of the levels?

5. What did you like about the sizes of your schools? Compare notes within the group and determine if there is a pattern.

6. What did you dislike about the sizes of your schools? Compare notes within the group and determine if there is a pattern.

7. Determine the average (mean) size for the schools students in your group attended. Is the average close to the national average? See Table 9.2 for reference.

8. By now you have some idea of what you would like to teach. Did favorable experiences in your school career lead you to what you would like to teach? If yes, at which grade levels did these experience affect you the most?

offered few clear policy guidelines.[91] In part, this is because their research methods do not allow readers to draw generalizable conclusions.[92]

Several recent research reviews have done a good job of summarizing the existing research. Because their findings are suggestive rather than conclusive, however, we should interpret these studies cautiously. They indicate that students in grades 6, 7, and 8 in K–8 schools had higher achievement than their counterparts in schools with middle school configurations, but both groups had the same achievement levels by grade 9.[93] Those students who demonstrated higher levels of achievement in K–8 schools may be reflecting their community's affluence rather than any school or instructional factors.[94] Additionally, a 2005 research review concluded that "no sequence of grades is perfect or, in itself, guarantees student academic achievement and healthy social and emotional development."[95] No particular grade configuration is the "magic bullet" to improving student achievement.

---

[91] Klump, J. (2006, Spring). What the research says (or doesn't say) about K–8 versus middle school grade configurations: Assessing the benefits of K–8 schools. *Northwestern Education, 11*(3). Northwest Regional Educational Laboratory. Retrieved October 4, 2009, from http://www.nwrel.org/nwedu/11-03/research/.

[92] The studies looking at whether students have better achievement in K–8 schools rather than in middle schools did not control for school size, socioeconomic factors, and other variables, so their results could be attributable to factors other than grade configurations.

[93] Abella, R. (2005). The effects of small K–8 centers compared to large 6–8 schools on student performance. *Middle School Journal, 37*(1), 29–35; Alspaugh, J. W. (1998). Achievement loss associated with the transition to middle school and high school. *Journal of Educational Research, 92*(1), 20–25.

[94] Viadero, 2008.

[95] Anfara, V. A. Jr., & Buehler, A. (2005). Grade configuration and the education of young adolescents. *Middle School Journal, 37*(1). p. 57.

Activity 9.6

Fiscal efficiency in government is an important concept, but one that is difficult to put into practice.

A. Imagine that your professor were elected governor of your state. The professor had run on a platform of fiscal efficiency in government. Now the candidate has to make these promises a reality. You and your classmates are a "group of advisors" who are trying to help the governor-elect examine the idea of consolidating school districts and schools to save money. Debate the merits and potential pitfalls of implementing such a school consolidation plan.

B. After the debate, discuss how this debate altered or reinforced your ideas and opinions of consolidating schools and school districts to save money.

Activity 9.7

Here are more topics for debate and discussion by your class:

1. States basically control education. Should the federal government be more involved in education? Debate this issue.

2. List and explain the advantages of the United States adopting a national system of education instead of having 51 different systems of education in our country (50 states plus the District of Columbia).

3. What would our schools and society at large be like today if the U.S. Supreme Court had not made the decision it did in *Brown v. Board of Education*? In *Plyler v. Doe*?

4. Imagine you were elected governor of your state. You ran on a platform of fiscal efficiency in government. Now you must assemble a group of advisors to examine the idea of consolidating school districts and schools to save money. Have a group of advisors debate the merits and potential pitfalls of implementing such a consolidation plan.

Summary

Unlike many other countries, the United States does not have a national education system. Instead, each state controls how education is operated—giving the United States 51 separate systems of education (50 states plus the District of Columbia). Put simply, education is a national interest and a state function operated at the local level.

The federal role in education has three key aspects. The first role is to provide Congress-approved funding. The second role is to ensure that states and localities are in compliance with federal laws. The third role involves assessing and maintaining data on student achievement.

Through their state constitutions, states control how education is established and operated. A State Department of Education, also known as the State Education

Agency (SEA), oversees the public school education function and monitors localities' compliance.

A local school board operates the schools in each locality. The local school superintendent functions as the chief executive officer of the school district. The local central office provides leadership and support for the schools. In addition, school districts employ many resource and support personnel in schools to help teachers educate students to high levels.

A variety of educational specialists work in schools to help teachers support student success. Each state sets the professional-to-student ratio for its schools. These specialists work in cooperation with general education teachers, using their professional skills to improve student learning and achievement.

School districts and schools vary in size and organization across the United States. The trend for the last 100 years has been to decrease the number of school districts by consolidating them. As a consequence of this trend, the number of schools has declined over the past century and average student enrollment has increased.

Structurally, schools tend to be organized as elementary, middle, and high schools. There is a great deal of variance in how schools organize grade levels, however.

Conclusions

- Political and educational influences well beyond teachers' classrooms affect what happens inside them.
- While the federal government has some input into school systems, the most influential forces are local.

Chapter 10

School Finance

Money plays a major role in educating America's students. Constructing and maintaining school buildings, purchasing equipment and supplies, and paying school staff and administrators are all costly. For the 2008–2009 school year, nation-wide public education at all levels cost $1 trillion.[1] In 2006, one in 75 adults was an elementary or secondary teacher.[2]

Although expensive, excellent education for all America's children is a good investment. When it comes to quality education, as a society we can pay now or pay later. Education is one of the largest determinants of an individual's life choices and chances. It affects students' future employment, income, health status, housing, and many other aspects of life. It is a critical investment in a community's—and our nation's—infrastructure.

It is the state and community's responsibility to ensure that all schools have the essential resources to provide positive learning environments. But this does not always happen. In his 1992 book *Savage Inequalities*, education writer Jonathan Kozol described conditions in several American city schools between 1988 and 1990:[3]

"East St. Louis High School was awash in sewage for the second time this year," wrote the St. Louis *Post-Dispatch* on Monday, in the early spring, 1989. The school had to be shut because of "fumes and backed up toilets." Fumes flowed into the basement, through the floor, and then up into the kitchen and the students' bathrooms. The backup . . . occurred in the food preparation areas.[4]

In the same week, the schools announced the layoff of 280 teachers, 166 cooks and cafeteria workers, 25 teacher aides, 16 custodians and 18 painters, electricians, engineers, and plumbers. . . . [T]he cuts will bring the size of the kindergarten and primary classes up to 30 students, and the size of fourth to twelfth grade classes up to 35 students . . . The school system . . . has been using more than 70 "permanent substitute teachers" who are paid only $10,000 yearly, as a way of saving money. . . .[5]

The science labs at East St. Louis High School are 30 to 50 years outdated. . . . The six lab stations in the room have empty holes where [water] pipes were once attached.[6] "I have no materials with the exception of a single textbook to give each child." . . . The high school has no VCRs. . . .[7]

What message do you think the students and teachers receive from a community that expects them to learn and thrive in this environment? How do you think learning in this school will impact the "achievement gap" between low-income and affluent students?

Large differences in educational attainment persist across income, race, and region. Even when similar schooling resources are available, educational inequalities continue

[1] (2009). The federal role in education. U.S. Department of Education. Retrieved August 26, 2009 from: http://www.ed.gov/about/overview/fed/role.html?src=In.
[2] Gallagher, J. J. (2007, April 4). Reform's missing ingredient: Building a high-quality support system for education: Commentary. *Education Week, 26*(31), 27, 29.
[3] Kozol, J. (1992). *Savage inequalities: Children in America's schools*. New York: Harper Perennial,
[4] Kozol, 1992, p. 23.
[5] Kozol, 1992 p. 24.
[6] Kozol, 1992, p. 27.
[7] Kozol, 1992, p. 29.

because many children from educationally and economically disadvantaged families come to school less prepared to start learning. They are unlikely to catch up without major educational interventions on their behalf.

Focus Questions

- In what ways is education an investment in U.S. infrastructure?
- What are the federal, state, and local contributions to school funding?
- How do school districts spend money (budgets)?
- What does "equity versus equality" mean in terms of school funding?
- How costly are teacher salaries?
- How can a "taxpayer revolt" negatively affect spending for education?
- How can wise spending positively influence student achievement?

Education as an Investment in National Infrastructure

Our country's wealth depends on an educated population. Education provides individuals with the ability to earn a living in career fields such as business, medicine, law, engineering, and services. Education is the profession that enables all other professions. It fuels the American economy's infrastructure like nothing else in our society. Any societal framework must be maintained to remain in working order, and education is no different.

Before considering the specifics of how we fund schools and identify ways to prevent *savage inequalities*, let's begin with the end in mind: Where can we see the effects of education dollars in our own lives and communities? How is education an important investment in our country's infrastructure? Education increases the value of the American economy by increasing the following characteristics of the country's residents:

- Earning potential
- Employability

Education decreases the following social costs that we underwrite with our tax dollars:

- Incarceration rates
- Childbirth and prenatal care
- Crime rates

We will briefly discuss how education has a positive impact on each of these factors.

Earning Potential

The 2007 Census Bureau figures show that people with higher educational levels earn more money than people with lower educational levels. Table 10.1 shows individual average income earnings in terms of both the **median**[8] (the middle value in

---

[8] The median is the halfway point—that is, half are above the figure and half are below it.

Table 10.1	Per Capita Income by Education Level for Persons 25 and Older, 2007	
Level of Educational Attainment	Median per Capita Income	Mean per Capita Income
Less than ninth grade	$18,868	$ 21,362
Grade 9–12 (no diploma)	$20,506	$ 24,721
High school graduate/GED	$27,384	$ 33,419
Some college (no diploma)	$31,789	$ 38,284
Associate's degree	$35,274	$ 41,475
Bachelor's degree	$46,435	$ 58,866
Master's degree	$55,445	$ 70,813
Professional degree	$85,857	$117,033
Doctorate degree	$78,212	$104,214

Source: U.S. Census Bureau. (2007). *Current population survey: 2007 annual social and economic survey: 2007.* Washington, DC: U.S. Government Printing Office, p. 59. http://pubdb3.census.gov/macro/032007/perinc/new03_001.htm.

a list of numbers) and the **mean**[9] (the numerical average). Income rises with educational level. Of course, as income rises, so do the taxes one pays to the government.

As you can see from Table 10.1, the median yearly income for a high school dropout (i.e., a person who drops out in grades 9–12 and does not receive a diploma) is $20,506. If we assume a 40-year work life for that individual based on constant 2007 dollars, that person would accumulate lifetime earnings of $820,240. Assuming that person paid a tax rate of 10 percent, he or she would have contributed $82,024 to the government's coffers.

The individual with a bachelor's degree would earn a yearly median income of $46,435—more than double what the high school dropout will earn. Assuming the same 40-year career in constant 2007 dollars, that person would have lifetime earnings of $1,857,400. Assuming this person has a good accountant and pays the same 10 percent tax rate, the college graduate will have paid $185,740 in government taxes, more than 2.25 times what the high school dropout would have paid.

The higher the education, the more taxes paid over a lifetime. A professional degree includes the M.D. that physicians obtain and the J.D. that lawyers have. If median attorney's salary is $85,857 and we assume the same 40-year career, the lawyer would earn $3,434,280 over his or her lifetime. Assuming the lawyer still pays 10 percent in taxes to the government, this tax bill totals $343,428, or 1.8 times more than what the college graduate pays. This is more than four times what the high school dropout would pay in taxes, assuming a constant 10 percent rate. From the standpoint of the government, an education is a very good investment, indeed.

Employability

Before one can earn a salary, one must first get and hold a job. Education increases employability and decreases unemployment rates. Individuals with lower educational attainment are more likely to be unemployed or underemployed than those with higher educational attainment.

---

[9] The mean is the true arithmetic average.

Table 10.2 shows the labor force participation rates by education level for people ages 20–24 and for those ages 25–64. The U.S. Department of Labor separates these figures by ages to account for students in college and graduate school.[10] At age 25, it is assumed that most formal schooling has been completed and that college graduates have found jobs.

Only two-thirds of high school dropouts are participating in the work force at either age grouping (66 percent and 78 percent for 20- to 24-year-olds, and 66 percent and 76 percent for 25- to 64-year-olds). The other one-third have not only dropped out of high school, but also dropped out of the work force. They are no longer seeking employment—and many may be receiving government services (e.g., welfare).

By comparison, approximately 85 percent of individuals with a college degree are participating in the work force and gainfully contributing to the economy and to the tax base supporting social service programs. The remaining 15 percent of college graduates who have left the work force include those who become parents and take time off from work to raise their children.

The unemployment rate represents the other side of labor force participation. Table 10.3 shows unemployment rates by education level. The unemployment rate for high school dropouts (7.6 percent) is more than three times higher than that for college graduates (2.3 percent) and more than twice that for high school graduates (4.7 percent). In times of recession, as in all economic downturns, unemployment increases.

Table 10.2	Labor Force Participation Rates, 2007	
Educational Attainment Level	**Labor Force Participation Rate**	
	Ages 20–24	Ages 25–64
Less than high school	66%	66%
Some high school or GED	78%	76%
Associate's degree	82%	84%
Bachelor's degree or higher	84%	86%

Source: Snyder, T. D., Dillow, S. A., & Hoffman, C. M. (2007). *Digest of education statistics 2006* (NCES 2007-017). National Center for Education Statistics, Institute of Education Sciences, U.S. Department of Education. Washington, DC: U.S. Government Printing Office, p. 566.

Table 10.3	Unemployment Rates by Level of Education, 2007
Level of Educational Attainment	**Unemployment Rate (percent)**
Less than high school	7.6
High school (no college)	4.7
Some college (no degree)	4.2
All educational attainment levels	4.0
Associate's degree	3.2
Bachelor's degree or higher	2.3

Source: Snyder, T. D., Dillow, S. A., & Hoffman, C. M. (2007). *Digest of education statistics 2006* (NCES 2007-017). National Center for Education Statistics, Institute of Education Sciences, U.S. Department of Education. Washington, DC: U.S. Government Printing Office, p. 557.

---

[10] Otherwise, the figures would be artificially low for college-age students in the tables.

As we can see from these data, education acts as an economic stimulus. By providing good income to support a positive quality of life—for the individuals themselves as well as for the community and nation through money given back in the form of taxes—education fulfills its promises for most individuals who engage it to fullest advantage. Education as an investment in human capital has benefits that extend even further than income and employability.

Public Social Costs

While education has the effect of increasing revenue both to individuals in the form of income and to the government in the form of tax dollars, it also tends to reduce public social expenses of unemployment costs, incarceration rates, and crime expenditures.

We have shown how education increases employability. Each increase in employability is associated with a reduced unemployment cost. Beyond this effect, however, further cost reductions are apparent.

For instance, the Alliance for Excellent Education estimates that if the 1.2 million students who drop out each year earned high school diplomas instead, states could save $17 billion in health care costs over the graduates' lifetimes. The nonpartisan Economic Policy Institute found that children who live in poverty but who receive high-quality early education have significantly fewer arrests than their peers without this opportunity. The nonpartisan Committee for Economic Development found that investing $4,800 per child in preschool can reduce teenage arrests by 40 percent. Meanwhile, the national nonprofit Coalition for Juvenile Justice reports that high school dropouts are three times more likely to be arrested than their peers who stay in school.[11]

In what is probably one of the best studies to date, Lochner and Moretti have determined that for each one-year increase in educational level, arrest rates and crime levels decrease by 11 percent. Specifically, murder and assault decrease by 30 percent, motor vehicle theft by 20 percent, arson by 13 percent, and burglary

Activity 10.1

Education is an investment in human capital—in having students increase their knowledge and skills so they can contribute to their own well-being as well as to their communities.

A. Divide the class into three groups. Each group will plan and deliver a persuasive oral and graphic presentation to an active senior citizen community explaining why these seniors should continue to pay taxes to support schools even though they no longer have children or grandchildren in the public schools. Using the chapter, each group will present visual and oral information about at least three of the following factors:

Education and employability

Education and earnings

Education and paying taxes

Education and crime

B. Each group should give its presentation to the class. For extra credit, they can deliver it to an actual community audience.

---

[11] Carroll, T. (2008, March 26). Education beats incarceration. *Education Week, 27*(29), 32.

by 6 percent. What is more, according to these authors, a 1 percent increase in the national graduation rate would save the nation nearly $2 billion each year in crime costs.[12] They conclude that increased education brings sizeable social benefits.

Sources of School Revenue

Public education is big business in the United States, accounting for more than $1 trillion in school-related expenditures in 2008–2009.[13] The total U.S. student enrollment in public elementary and secondary schools in 2008 was approximately 50 million.[14] Where does all the money come from to pay for these services? How is the money spent? How much do teachers earn?

Until recently, money for schools came from three government sources: federal, state, and local. Increasingly, more school districts are supplementing these sources from grants from various foundations. Although education is a state function, the state is not always the largest source of school revenues. Figure 10.1 shows the percentages of school funds that have come from federal, state, and local sources over the past 40 years.

In the 1970–71 school year, the local governments, on average, contributed slightly more than 50 percent of schools' total operating revenue. State governments accounted for approximately 40 percent of these revenues, and the federal government paid for slightly less than 10 percent. Over the next ten years, the state governments contributed more than the local government. Around the same time, the federal government's share began to drop. Since then, the federal share has remained relatively flat, and the local and state governments have switched places several times in terms of which entity contributed more.

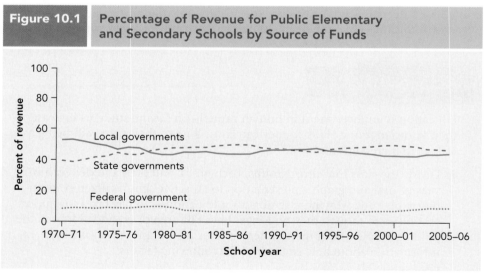

Figure 10.1   **Percentage of Revenue for Public Elementary and Secondary Schools by Source of Funds**

Source: Snyder, T. D., Dillow, S. A., & Hoffman, C. M. (2009). *Digest of Education Statistics 2008.* (NCES 2008-022). U.S. Department of Education. p. 59. Retrieved August 26, 2009 from: http://nces.ed.gov/pubs2009/2009020_2a.pdf

---

[12] Lochner, L., & Moretti, E. (2004). The effect of education on crime: Evidence from prison inmates, arrests, and self-reports. *American Economic Review, 94(1),* 155–189. Social savings costs are reported in this source in 2006 dollars.

[13] (2009).The federal role in education. U.S. Department of Education. Retrieved August 26, 2009 from: http://www.ed.gov/about/overview/fed/role.html?src=In

[14] Snyder, T.D., Dillow, S.A., and Hoffman, C.M. (2009). *Digest of Education Statistics 2008* (NCES 2009-020). National Center for Education Statistics, Institute of Education Sciences, U.S. Department of Education. Washington, DC., p. 62.

For the most part, American schools are a state function with a national interest that is operated at the local level. With the federal, state, and local governments all contributing to education, how does money come to school districts from each of the three government levels?

At the federal level, monies come back to the states once Congress has appropriated funds in an education budget. Those funds come from the federal taxes we pay.

At the state level, funding for the localities to help pay for schools is a bit more complex. A simple answer would be that states use their income taxes to provide these funds—but not all states have income taxes. Likewise, some states have no sales taxes. However a state raises revenues for its services, some mixture of those state funds goes to support education.

At the local level, the property tax is the predominant method for paying for schools. This tax dates back to the Massachusetts Law of 1647, which required landowners to pay a tax to support the local schools or face forfeiture of their acreage. At that time, the government taxed property because a person's estate was the basis for his or her income.

In the days when "land was money," property was a realistic proxy for income. Today, however, this is no longer the case for most of us. Very few of us now derive our income from our land. Instead, we earn our income from our place of employment, where that income is already taxed. Depending on the real estate market, most of us today will not realize any financial gain from our property until we sell it. That logic explains why some people object to using property taxes as the main revenue source for public schools. We will discuss taxpayers' resistance to property taxes and this movement's effects on school funding later in this chapter.

Increases in Education Spending

Education costs have been growing since we have been keeping figures on the subject. Figure 10.2 shows the increase in total dollars spent on education since 1960, the change in numbers of teachers, and the student–teacher ratio during the same period. In examining this figure, it is easy to see that school expenditures have risen as the number of teachers has increased. That relationship makes sense: It costs money to hire additional teachers. It is interesting to note that the student–teacher ratios have been declining since at least 1960.

Reasons for Increased Education Spending

Since 1960, public schools have hired more teachers for several reasons. In the 1960s, schools began serving more and increasingly diverse students as a result of court-mandated desegregation. This growth required hiring more teachers and providing more equitable teacher salaries.[15]

Additionally, during this time, more schools began to work with special-needs students, whose education requires a teacher to work closely with fewer students. While special-needs students as a percentage of the total student population increased from 9.7 percent in 1978 to 11.6 percent in 1990, and while the number of special education teachers rose by more than 50 percent during these same years, this increase was responsible for only 18 percent of the growth in school spending over this period, however.[16]

During these years, educators concluded that having more than 30 to 40 students in every class was not an effective environment for teaching and learning. As

---

[15] With desegregation, schools had to hire more teachers to reduce class sizes to more acceptable teacher–student ratios and increase African American teachers' salaries to levels comparable to what white teachers were earning.

[16] Hanushek, E. A., & Rivkin, S. G. (1997). Understanding the twentieth century's growth in U.S. school spending. *Journal of Human Resources, 32*(1), 35–68.

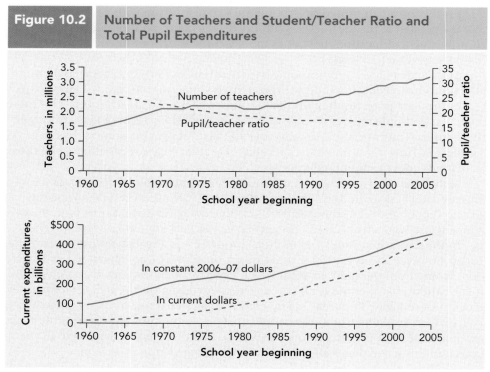

Figure 10.2 | Number of Teachers and Student/Teacher Ratio and Total Pupil Expenditures

Source: Snyder, T. D., Dillow, S. A., & Hoffman, C. M. (2009). *Digest of Education Statistics 2008.* (NCES 2008-022). U.S. Department of Education. p. 57. Retrieved August 26, 2009 from: http://nces.ed.gov/pubs2009/2009020_2a.pdf

a consequence, the pupil-to-teacher ratio declined: from 35:1 in 1890, to 28.1 in 1940, to 24.9:1 in 1960, to 20.5 in 1970, to 15.4 in 1990.[17] The two most important factors in the increased school expenditures since 1960 have been (1) the rising costs of instructional staff and (2) the declining pupil-to-teacher ratios as schools have attempted to raise school quality by reducing the pupil-to-staff ratios.[18]

In addition to the decrease in student–teacher ratios, increased student enrollments have affected U.S. school expenditures. Figure 10.4 shows the total student enrollment in U.S. public schools since 1960. From 1960 to 2004, total enrollments increased from 35 million to almost 50 million students. Along with greater expenditures devoted to the goals of decreasing class size and teaching more diverse and special-needs students, schools hired more teachers to meet the demand produced by increased student enrollments.

Knowing the full story behind the increasing cost figures helps to explain events with data. This consideration is especially important if you are considering a career in public education. Friends and family may think of you as an "inside expert," and ask you, "Why are education costs increasing so much?" and "Why are we spending more money and not getting better results?" The information in this chapter will help you successfully and convincingly answer these challenging questions.

National, Regional, and Local Education Expenses

How much does it cost to educate a child in the United States? The answer to this question varies widely according to the region, the state, and the locality. It also varies by the state and local wealth available to fund education: Affluent states and localities can fund education to higher levels.

---

[17] Hanushek & Rivkin, 1997, p. 41.
[18] Hanushek & Rivkin, 1997, p. 45.

| Figure 10.3 | Pupil/Teacher Ratios Have Been Reduced from 35:1 in 1900 (seen here) to 15:1 in 1990 |

Library of Congress

| Figure 10.4 | Total Enrollment in U.S. Public Schools, 1960–2007 (in millions) |

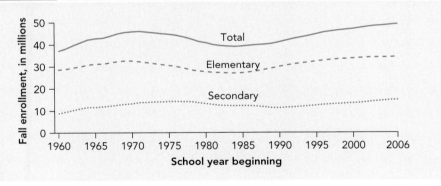

Source: Snyder, T. D., Dillow, S. A., & Hoffman, C. M. (2009). *Digest of Education Statistics 2008.* (NCES 2008-022). U.S. Department of Education. p. 57. Retrieved August 26, 2009 from: **http://nces.ed.gov/pubs2009/2009020_2a.pdf**

Activity 10.2

Education costs have increased for many reasons, including increased numbers of teachers and increased student enrollments.

A. Divide the class into two groups. Each group will develop a three-minute presentation to explain to your parents the increases in school expenditure since 1960, citing at least five specific reasons for this trend. Each group will also create a graphic illustration to support their presentation.

B. As a group, make your presentation. The class as a whole should then decide which group gave the more persuasive and convincing presentation and why.

Table 10.4 shows the average per-pupil expenditure for each state, the District of Columbia, and selected U.S. territories. Quite a variance appears in average state spending levels for each student. Among the states, New Jersey, on average, has the highest per-pupil expenditure ($14,917), and Utah has the lowest per-pupil expenditure ($6,110). When the territories are examined, the average per-pupil expenditure drops even lower. Note that these figures are averages within each of the states; inside each state, large differences also occur between districts.

Table 10.4	Per-Pupil Spending, Fall 2005		
State	Per-Pupil Spending	State	Per-Pupil Spending
U.S. average	$ 10,615	Nebraska	$10,359
Alabama	$ 8,755	Nevada	$ 9,514
Alaska	$ 13,538	New Hampshire	$11,615
Arizona	$ 7,749	New Jersey	$16,587
Arkansas	$ 9,278	New Mexico	$ 9,620
California	$ 10.068	New York	$15,837
Colorado	$ 9,897	North Carolina	$ 8,532
Connecticut	$ 15,219	North Dakota	$ 9,787
Delaware	$ 13,796	Ohio	$11,129
District of Columbia	$ 15,626	Oklahoma	$ 7,623
Florida	$ 9,854	Oregon	$ 9,632
Georgia	$ 9,909	Pennsylvania	$12,287
Hawaii	$ 10,758	Rhode Island	$13,015
Idaho	$ 7,343		
Illinois	$ 10.324	South Carolina	$ 9,864
Indiana	$10,2990	South Dakota	$ 8,649
Iowa	$ 9,730	Tennessee	$ 7,742
Kansas	$ 9,629	Texas	$ 9,248
Kentucky	$ 8,847	Utah	$ 6,629
Louisiana	$ 9,349	Vermont	$13,561
Maine	$ 11,638	Virginia	$10,809
Maryland	$ 12,202	Washington	$ 9,694
Massachusetts	$ 14,094	West Virginia	$ 9,658
Michigan	$ 11,208	Wisconsin	$11,309
Minnesota	$ 10,929	Wyoming	$13,471
Mississippi	$ 7,800	American Samoa	$ 3,837
Missouri	$ 9,388	Guam	$ 6,907
Montana	$ 9,415	Puerto Rico	$ 5,654

Source: Snyder, T. D., Dillow, S. A., & Hoffman, C. M. (2009). *Digest of Education Statistics 2008.* (NCES 2008-022). U.S. Department of Education. p. 262, Table 182. Retrieved August 26, 2009 from: http://nces.ed.gov/pubs2009/2009020_2a.pdf

Just as there are differences among states in per-pupil spending, so there is variance among districts in the same area. Figure 10.5 shows spending differences within six local school districts in the metropolitan Washington, D.C., area: Alexandria, Virginia; Arlington, Virginia; the D.C. Public Schools; Montgomery County, Maryland; Fairfax County, Virginia; and Prince George's County, Maryland. All are urban. Some are larger and some are smaller. Alexandria, Virginia, spends approximately 75 percent more per pupil, on average, to educate its children than does Prince George's County, Maryland.

| Figure 10.5 | Per-Pupil Spending in Six Selected Metropolitan District of Columbia School Districts, 2007 |

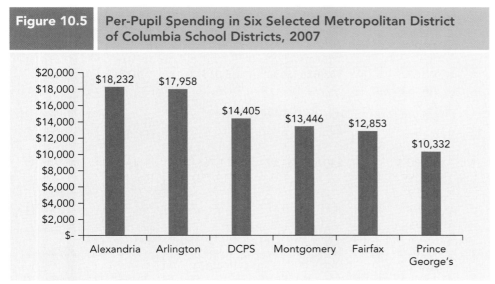

Source: Levy, M., (2007). Per student figures for District of Columbia public school system. Washington Lawyer's Committee for Civil Rights and Urban Affairs, p. 5. Retrieved August 26, 2009 from: **http://www.21csf.org/csf-home/** DocUploads/DataShop/DS_86.pdf

Activity 10.3

This activity will help you understand the differences in per-pupil spending. Divide the class into groups of six. Have each person or group (depending on class size), select one of the school districts listed in Figure 10.5. Using the data in the table in this activity, explain to the group why you think spending varies among these six school districts.[19] In your discussions, think about which school district might need to spend more per student for education. Use the following questions to guide you as you discuss your explanations.

Guiding Questions

1. What can you tell about the community by comparing the median household income?

2. What can you tell about the student populations by the percentage of students who qualify for free or reduced-price lunches? Do you think it costs more to educate students who qualify for special education services (those students with an individualized education program [IEP])? Explain your answer.

3. Do you think it costs more to educate students who do not speak English fluently yet (English language learners [ELL])? Explain your answer.

---

[19] Data obtained from www.quickfacts.census.gov/qfd/states and www.greatschools.com. All data are from the school year 2006–2007.

4. Based on what you can see, which school district needs to spend more to educate its students? Should districts with greater student needs receive more funding than districts with less needy students? Justify your answer.

School District Per-Pupil Spending	Total Population Number of Pupils in the School District	Racial Makeup of Student Population*	Median Income (% of Pupils Eligible for FRPL†)	Number of Students with IEPs (%)	Student–Teacher Ratio	Number of ELL (%)
Alexandria, VA $18,232	128,923 10,996	W: 54.8 AA: 22.5 A: 5.7 L: 14.7 O: 2.3	$56,054 (46%)	1,900 (17.3%)	9.6/1	2,223 20.2%
Arlington, VA $17,958	199,776 18,463	W: 63 AA: 8.8 A: 9 L: 16.1 O: 3.1	$66,626 (36%)	3,013 (16.3%)	10.8/1	5,165 28%
D.C. Public Schools $14,405	563,384 59,616	W: 30.8 AA: 55 A: 2.7 L: 7.9 O: 3.6	$40,127 (61%)	11,738 (19.7%)	NA	4,274 7.2%
Fairfax County, VA $12,853	1,010,4443 164,843	W: 62.3 AA: 9.3 A: 15 L: 12 O: 1.4	$83,890 (19%)	23,640 (14.3%)	12.5/1	30,032 18.2%
Montgomery County, MD $13,446	932,131 139,393	W: 57.9 AA: 16.4 A: 11.2 L: 11.6 O: 2.9	$76,957 (22%)	17,700 (12.7%)	14.9/1	13,228 9.5%
Prince George's County, MD $10,332	841,315 133,325	W: 23.7 AA: 61.1 A: 3.9 L: 13.6 O: 0.6	$55,129 (43%)	15,362 (11.5%)	15.9/1	8,311 6.2%

* W = white; AA=African American; A = Asian; L = Latino; O = other.
† FRPL = free or reduced-price lunch; it is an indication of the number students living in poverty.

Source: Compiled and calculated from: Alexandria City, VA public schools. Retrieved August 28, 2009 from: http://www.acps.k12.va.us/board/division-goals/goals-brochure.pdf; Washington area boards of education fiscal year 2008, Retrieved August 28, 2009 from: http://www.acps.k12.va.us/board/wabe.pdf; Arlingotn, VA public schools. Retrieved August 28, 2009 from: http://www.acps.k12.va.us/board/wabe.pdf; Washington, DC Public Schools, Retrieved August 28, 2009 from: http://dcps.dc.gov/portal/site/DCPS/menuitem.06de50edb2b17a932c69621014f62010/?vgnextoid=71a3f83a5f052210VgnVCM100000416f0201RCRD&vgnextchannel=39d1e2b1f0d32210VgnVCM100000416f0201RCRD&vgnextfmt=default; Fairfax County Public Schools, Retrieved August 28, 2009 from: http://www.schoolmatters.com/schools.aspx/q/page=dl/did=4013/midx=StudentDemographics; Montgomery County Public Schools, MD, Retrieved August 28, 2009 from: http://www.montgomeryschoolsmd.org/about/; Prince George's County Public Schools, Retrieved August 28, 2009 from: http://www.schoolmatters.com/schools.aspx/q/page=dl/did=5109/midx=StudentDemographics

Expenditures: How School Districts Spend Money

Operating a school system is a complex undertaking, whose costs go far beyond teacher salaries and supplies. The growth in school spending outside teacher salaries has increased from one-third of total expenditures in 1940 to more than one-half of school costs in 1990.[20] These funds go toward items such as administrative support and utilities to keep the lights, heat, and air conditioning running. They cover the expense of operating and maintaining school buses or buildings, ordering all the cafeteria food and supplies, and accounting for meal prices and student lunch payments. With virtually every school system having a different budgeting process, comparing how states and school districts spend money is informative.

Spending Categories

The *Digest of Education Statistics 2008* (which contains latest data available) separates education expenditures into ten defined categories to compare all states. The *Digest* also provides dollar amounts and budget percentages for each category, as seen in Table 10.5.

Instruction includes teachers, teaching assistants, curriculum support personnel in the schools, and anyone directly related to teaching children. This cost includes salaries, benefits, supplies, tuition reimbursement, and the like for all persons included in this category and for each employee of the other categories. As Table 10.5 shows, instruction is by far the largest budget category.

Table 10.5	National Average Pre-K – 12 Education Budgets and Associated Expenditures, 2005–2006
Budget Category	**Expenditure (%)**
Instruction	53
Student support	4
Instructional staff services	4
General administration	2
School administration	5
Operations and maintenance	8
Student transportation	3
Other support services	3
Food services	3
Enterprise operations	1
Capital outlay	11
Interest on debt	3
Total	100

Source: Snyder, T. D., Dillow, S. A., & Hoffman, C. M. (2009). *Digest of education statistics 2008* (NCES 2009-020). National Center for Education Statistics, Institute of Education Sciences, U.S. Department of Education. Washington, DC: U.S. Government Printing Office, adapted from Table 183, p. 263. Calculations by authors. The expenditure percentages total to 100 percent due to rounding.

---

[20] Hanushek & Rivkin, 1997, p. 39.

Student support includes school counselors, health care providers (school nurses), attendance personnel (the people who maintain attendance rolls and call students' home if they are absent to make certain they are really sick), school psychologists, and speech pathologists.

Instructional staff services include curriculum development, staff training, libraries, media, and technology centers. Again, this category takes into account all salaries, benefits, supplies, equipment, and costs associated with these functions.

General administration involves the personnel who administer leadership responsibilities at the central office level whose responsibilities are not delineated in other named categories. The school administration category includes building-level principals and assistant principals and their associated costs.

Operations and maintenance includes the cost of using and keeping up the buildings. Operations include electricity, heat, and insurance on the buildings and their contents. Maintenance includes custodial workers, building and grounds upkeep, and supplies and equipment needed to keep the building clean and in good order.

Student transportation involves all costs of operating the familiar yellow school buses. It includes the price of buses themselves as well as the drivers, mechanics, fuel, tires, and equipment required to transport students.

The other support services category includes business support for paying, transporting, or exchanging goods and services for the school district. It includes central office support for planning, research, evaluation, and information, staff, and data processing as well as other central support services. In some smaller school districts, a small number of employees may assume responsibility for several functions, so this category is relatively small. In larger systems, more administrators, supervisors, and coordinators work on these tasks. For instance, a large school district may have an assistant superintendent for planning, research, and evaluation with an entire professional and clerical staff to support this area.

Food services involve all the people, equipment, and supplies needed to feed students while they are at school. Someone must order the bulk food, plan menus, staff cafeterias, coordinate the federal free and reduced-price lunch information, and make certain that the operation does not lose money. Frequently, the school district's Food Service Department operates the largest chain of "restaurants" in the locality.

Enterprise operations involves expenditures for operations funded by the sales of products or services in the school. This would include the school bookstore, computer time, or leasing the building in the evening or weekends to civic groups.

Capital outlay includes expenditures for property, buildings, and alterations completed by the school district's staff or contractors. Interest on school debt includes all interest paid by school district.

Obviously, the operation of a school system and all of its finances are intricate and complex. They involve people, supplies, and processes that many teachers have never considered to be a part of education.

Recently, the advocacy group known as First Class Education has endorsed a proposal called the "65% Solution." It calls for 65 percent of all funds to go directly to classroom instruction. Members of First Class Education define "in the classroom" as classroom teachers and aides, general instruction supplies, activities such as field trips, athletics, music, and arts. Critics have claimed that the 65 percent concept is intuitive and not research based.[21] In fact, many educators do not favor this solution because it may force cuts to non-instructional personnel, such as school nurses, who provide valuable services in the schools.[22] Several states have endorsed this proposal, however.

Although it is not clear exactly what percentage of all revenue should go to classroom instruction, obviously most money should go where research informs us that money makes a difference to student learning. Later in this chapter, we will review research-based findings of how school spending can improve student achievement.

---

[21] Hoff, D. J. (2005, October). Group "65 Percent Solution" gains traction, GOP friends. *Education Week, 24*(7), 1, 18.
[22] Hoff, 2005.

Teacher Salaries

In education, salaries and benefits generally account for approximately 70 percent of the total budget. Because teachers are the largest group in education, most monies go to teacher salaries.

Table 10.6 shows the average teacher salary for each state from the 2007 National Education Association's *State Rankings*. These salaries are not distributed equally across schools. Experienced and more highly paid teachers tend to teach in more affluent schools. Table 10.6 averages the salaries to the state level to provide a comparison.

Table 10.6	Rank and Average Public School Teacher Salaries, 2008		
State	Average Salary	State	Average Salary
1. California	$63,640	27. Vermont	$45,337
2. Connecticut	$60,822	28. Florida	$45,308
3. New Jersey	$59,584	29. Nevada	$45,158
4. New York	$59,559	30. Texas	$44,897
5. District of Columbia	$59,000	31. Arizona	$44,700
6. Massachusetts	$58,257	32. Arkansas	$44,245
7. Illinois	$58,246	33. South Carolina	$43,891
8. Maryland	$56,927	34. Tennessee	$43,816
9. Rhode Island	$55,956	35. Kentucky	$43,646
10. Michigan	$55,526	36. Alabama	$43,389
11. Pennsylvania	$54,970	37. Kansas	$43,358
12. Delaware	$54,680	38. Iowa	$43,130
13. Alaska	$54,679	39. Louisiana	$42,816
14. Ohio	$51,937	40. Idaho	$42,798
15. Hawaii	$51,922	41. New Mexico	$42,780
16. Oregon	$50,911	42. Oklahoma	$42,379
U.S. Average	$50,758	43. Maine	$42,103
17. Wyoming	$50,692	44. Nebraska	$42,044
18. Georgia	$49,905	45. Missouri	$41,751
19. Minnesota	$49,718	46. Montana	$41,225
20. Wisconsin	$47,901	47. Utah	$41,156
21. Washington	$47,882	48. West Virginia	$40,531
22. Indiana	$47,831	49. Mississippi	$40,182
23. New Hampshire	$46,527	50. North Dakota	$38,822
24. North Carolina	$46,137	51. South Dakota	$35,378
25. Colorado	$45,833	Median Salary	$45,539
26. Virginia	$45,439	Range of Salaries	$28,262

Source: Data compiled from National Education Association (NEA). (2008 December). *Rankings and estimates: Ranking of the states 2008 and estimates of school statistics 2009.* Washington, DC: NEA Research, p. 18.

While Table 10.6 presents average salaries for all teachers in the state, the median salary (the salary at which half of teachers make more and half make less) is $45,539. The range between the highest and lowest salaries is more than $28,000. Over a 30-year career in education, the difference between being paid at the highest and lowest salary ends could translate into a $847,860 difference in lifetime earnings.[23]

How do teacher salaries compare with salaries in other jobs that require comparable skill and education? According to a report by the Economic Policy Institute, weekly pay for teachers ranges from 12.2 percent to 14.1 percent less than that for jobs with comparable skill and education requirements.[24] No doubt, this salary disparity discourages many well-educated and talented individuals from seeking careers as teachers.

Equity Issues in School Funding

Savage Inequalities' descriptions of blighted schools highlight equality and equity issues. Considering how schools' funds should be allocated and spent are critical concerns. Most of us believe in equal treatment for individuals, yet students come to school with different learning needs. Should all students receive equal funding? What is an adequate amount of funding to bring all students to high levels of learning and achievement?

Spending per Pupil

Earlier, we saw the 50 states' differences in per-pupil spending. Should every state spend the same amount per pupil? Similarly, Activity 10.3 had you think about whether needier school districts should receive more funding than less needy districts. Here lies the difference between equity and equality. Although the two concepts sound alike, they are very different. In its essence, **equity** is providing the services students actually need, whereas **equality** is providing the same services for all students regardless of the students' or locality's needs. Equity can be defined as a fairness issue for both students and taxpayers. The difference between equity and equality explains why equity, much more than equality, is a basic tenet of our school finance system.[25]

Adequacy is another money-related issue affecting fairness in school funding. **Adequacy** involves providing sufficient resources to accomplish the job of educating our children. A workable definition would be providing enough funds "to teach the average student to state standards, and then to identify how much each district/ school requires to teach students with special needs—the learning disabled, those from poverty and thus educationally deficient backgrounds, and those without English proficiency—to the same high and rigorous achievement standards."[26] How much funding is adequate? As a fiscal concept, adequacy is value driven, with people defining it subjectively according to their own priorities and opinions. Although attempts certainly have been made to quantify how much a state or school district needs to spend for its students, the actual figure remains unclear.

School funding adequacy has been a focus of active litigation. Since 1995, a number of school funding court cases have produced major changes in state

---

[23] $28,262 × 30 = $847,860.
[24] Allegretto, S., Corcoran, S., & Mishel, L. (2004). *How does teacher pay compare? Methodological challenges and answers.* Washington, DC: Economic Policy Institute, p. 2.
[25] Owings, W., & Kaplan, L. (2006). *American public school finance*, Belmont, CA: Cengage Learning, p. 146.
[26] Odden, A., & Picus, L. (2004). *School finance: A policy perspective* (3rd ed.). New York: McGraw-Hill, p. 25.

education policy around the country. School finance litigation has forced states to not only change the way they fund schools, but also to improve and update their states' assessment and accountability systems. As of February 2008, 45 states have been involved in some form of K–12 school finance litigation.[27] These suits addressed the state's role in assuring equitable spending among districts, providing suitable school facilities, and delivering adequate funding of programs designed for special education and at-risk students. Plaintiffs have won 20 of 28 adequacy cases since 1989. When used wisely, the money awarded in these cases has repeatedly translated into more resources for poorer districts and improved results for schools and students.[28]

Consider the following scenario from Table 10.7. Two relatively similar school systems have roughly the same amount of money coming to them from the federal, state, and local governments: $10,600 per student. The two systems have roughly the same capacity to fund education, as seen from the average family income, and both have the same number of students to educate.

Both school systems draw from upper-middle-class neighborhoods where parents expect their children to go to college. In school system A, 3 percent of the students have been identified as eligible for special education services—far below the national average. In school system B, 18 percent—six times as many—of the students have been identified as eligible to receive special education services, a rate higher than the national average.

If we look solely at the issue of equality, both school systems have the funds they need: $10,600 per pupil. If we look at the equity issue, however, the students' needs in school system B are greater than those in school system A. School system B must spend more money to meet the identified learning needs than does school system A. Equal funding for these systems may seem fair at first—until we consider the students' needs. Because of the varying student needs and the associated costs, treating these two systems equally on a financial basis would be neither fair nor equitable.

Consider this analogy. Imagine going to a physician who treats all patients equally. Each patient gets the same treatment at the same cost. It sounds ridiculous, because we expect to be treated on the basis of our differing health needs. We expect to care for a common cold differently than we care for cancer, and we realize that tending to cancer costs more than tending to a cold. We want and expect to receive the medical care we require. The same is true in education. While all students should have an equal opportunity for a good education, students require different levels services depending on their unique situations.

While education is expensive, providing poor and inadequate education for large numbers of students may be even more costly. Inadequately educated students bring steep public and social consequences. Money matters when it comes to

Table 10.7	Equality versus Equity Example				
School System	Average Family Income	Federal Revenue	State Revenue	Local Revenue	Percentage of Students Eligible for Special Education
A	$65,000	$1,050	$3,550	$6,000	3%
B	$65,100	$1,100	$3,450	$6,050	18%

[27] Rebell, M. A. (2008, February 13). Sleepless after Seattle? There's still hope for equal educational opportunity. *Education Week, 27*(23), 32–33.
[28] Rebell, 2008.

student achievement, a relationship confirmed by many studies.[29] The more money spent wisely on student learning, the more students learn.

The reality is that our society does not spend money equally or equitably to support all students' learning. Just as minority, low-income, and affluent students show "achievement gaps," the schools in which they receive their educations reflect serious "spending gaps."

Funding Inequalities

Most parents and students in affluent school districts would never consider crossing the threshold of schools such as those Kozol describes in *Savage Inequalities*. They expect their children's schools to be clean, rich in resources, with the best teachers that good (and regularly paid) salaries can provide. They make sure their schools have the funds to deliver on this expectation. As a result, schools serving different student populations often show large "spending gaps." School districts do not receive equal or equitable funding. Large differences exist between the funding available to educate low-income children as compared to affluent children. These disparities contribute strongly to the differences in their learning outcomes.

Approximately 50 percent of schools' local financial support comes from local taxes, mostly from property taxes. As a result, the wealthiest districts are able to spend as much as three times the per-pupil amount spent by the most economically disadvantaged districts.[30] In other words, students attending schools in districts with a lot of taxable wealth may have more money spent on their education than children attending schools with little taxable wealth. Making the situation more difficult, the recent trend has been for states to reduce education spending, leaving localities with the choice of either reducing services or increasing local taxes to fund education.[31]

The differences between districts with high property values and poorer districts in the region are profound and show up vividly in per-pupil spending. States in which school funding relies mainly on local property taxes place property-poor districts at a severe fiscal disadvantage. Although state and federal subsidies help high-poverty districts, they usually don't close the spending gap.

A 2009 report from the Editorial Projects in Education Research Center analyzed spending gaps in all 50 states. Alaska ranked highest with a $12,307 gap in per-pupil spending between high- and low-spending school districts in the state. West Virginia had the lowest gap, $1,895.[32]

Differences in per-pupil spending between and within states can only suggest the spending imbalances between school districts with large populations of minority students versus small populations of these students. Other studies have looked more closely at this disparity. In a 2006 national study, The Education Trust, an educational advocacy group, found that in 28 states, high-minority school districts received less state and local money for each child than did low-minority districts. Across the United States, schools spent $825 less per student in districts educating

[29] Baker, K. (1991). Yes. throw money at the schools. *Phi Delta Kappan, 72*(8), 628–631; Hedges, L. V., Laine, R. D., & Greenwald, R. (1994). Does money matter: A meta analysis of studies of the effects of differential school inputs on student outcomes. *Educational Researcher, 23*(3), 5–14; Verstegen, D., & King, R. (1998). The relationship between school spending and student achievement: A review and analysis of 35 years of production function research. *Journal of Education Finance, 24*(2), 243–262; Cooper, B., & Associates. (1994, Fall). Making money matter in education: A micro-financial model for determine school-level allocations, efficiency, and productivity. *Journal of Education Finance, 20,* 66–87; Fortune, J., & O'Neil, J. (1994). Production function analyses and the study of educational funding equity: A methodological critique. *Journal of Education Finance, 20,* 21–46; Verstegen, D. (1994). Efficiency and equity in the provision and reform of American schooling. *Journal of Education Finance, 20,* 107–131.
[30] Condron, D. J., & Roscigno, V. J. (2003, January). Disparities within: Unequal spending and achievement in an urban school district. *Sociology of Education, 76*(1), 18–36.
[31] For more on how schools are funded and the effects of school finances on student achievement, see Owings & Kaplan, 2006.
[32] Hightower, A. M. (2009, January 8). Securing progress, striving to improve. *Quality Counts 2009, Education Week, 28*(17), 44–47.

Figure 10.6 | School Funding "Gaps" Affect Student Achievement

Stephen Voss

Anonymous Donor/Alamy

the most students of color as compared with districts educating the fewest students of color.[33] Four states—New York, Illinois, Pennsylvania, and New Hampshire—under-supported their school districts with the highest minority rates by more than $1,000 per student per year.[34]

A 2006 study in Chicago's suburbs revealed some of the most glaring disparities in Illinois's school spending based on residents' wealth.[35] For example, one affluent school district spent $22,508 per student, compared with $8,675 in a different school district where property values were dramatically lower. Family income also correlates with school spending. Approximately 80 percent of suburban Chicago grade school districts with large low-income populations spent less than the state average of $8,765 per pupil for elementary districts in 2005.[36]

Consequently, wide, growing gaps in education quality appear in our school districts. Research shows that, depending on their location, some school districts receive *eight times* as much per-pupil funding as others.[37] This translates into differences in such areas as the teacher quality, class size, facilities' upkeep, the level of available technology, and other factors that can affect student outcomes and, ultimately, students' life chances.

Without a doubt, reliance on local property taxes is especially unfair to the African American, Latino, and Native American students who are disproportionately concentrated in the lowest-spending schools. Their families, on average, own less wealth and have lower per capita and family incomes than white Americans.[38]

---

[33] Wiener, R., & Pristoop, E. (2006). *How states shortchange the districts that need the most help: Funding gaps 2006.* The Education Trust.

[34] Weiner & Pristoop, 2006, p. 6.

[35] Rado, D. (2007, February 4). Disparities in school spending found in Chicago suburbs. Retrieved February 15, 2007, from http://www.chicagotribune.com/news/local/chicago/chi-0702040055feb04, 1,3512404.story?ctrack=1&cset=true.

[36] Rado, 2007.

[37] Verstegen, D. A. (2002 October). The new finance. School spending: The business of education. *American School Board Journal.* Retrieved February 21, 2007, from http://www.asbj.com/schoolspending/resources1002verstegen.html.

[38] Kayitsinga, J., Post, L., & Villarruel, F. (2007, July). *Socioeconomic profile of Michigan's Latino population: Demographic report no. 3.* Ann Arbor, MI: University of Michigan, Julian Samora Research Institute. Retrieved October 5, 2009, from http://www.jsri.msu.edu/RandS/research/drs/dr03.html; Fletcher, M. A. (2007, November 13). Middle class dream eludes African American families. WashingtonPost.com. Retrieved May 31, 2008, from http://www.washingtonpost.com/wp-dyn/content/article/2007/11/12/AR2007111201711_pf.html; *Civil Rights 101: Minorities by the numbers.* (2000). Washington, DC: Civil-Rights.org. Retrieved May 31, 2008, from http://www.civilrights.org/research_center/civilrights101/demographics.html.

In 2007, a team of economists recommended that adopting wide-scale, research-supported, effective pre-kindergarten through twelfth-grade educational interventions would gain $45 billion from increased tax revenues and reduced social costs over a high school graduate's lifetime.[39] The monies returned to the U.S. economy from these graduates' increased taxes as a result of their increased lifetime earning would be more than double the initial investment. Clearly, the benefits of society investing in an educational strategy of funding schools equitably outweigh the costs.

Increasingly, courts have recognized that public school funding practices are inequitable. School funding systems that rely too heavily on local property taxes have been determined to be unconstitutional, denying certain students equal protection under the law. As a result, the states try to offset these local wealth differences with their funding formulas. Nonetheless, Deborah Verstegen, an education finance scholar, writes, "There have been no new approaches developed or used to distribute state aid to school systems since the 1920s and 1930s."[40] What is more, in those days, less than one-third of the eligible population attended high school, much less graduated.[41] By comparison, in 2007 (the latest year for which data are available), 96.4 percent of all 14- to 17-year-olds were enrolled in school.[42]

The Cost of Educating Low-Income Students

Dollars do not tell the whole story. Talking about actual dollars per pupil or per school understates the inequity that high-poverty school districts suffer. To educate children growing up in poverty to common meaningful standards costs more than it does to bring more affluent students up to these standards. Children from low-income families have further to go than their more affluent peers to meet appropriate achievement expectations. They need more instructional time, and they especially need well-trained, effective teachers.

The Education Trust calculates that educating children from low-income families costs 40 percent more than educating their middle-class peers.[43] If states were to make this 40 percent adjustment to educate low-income students, school districts serving the largest concentration of minority students would still be receiving $1,213 less per pupil than their middle-class peers. Figure 10.7 shows the size of the funding gap in five states between the highest- and lowest-poverty districts between two typical classrooms, elementary schools, and high schools. The funding difference between two typical, 1,500-student New York high schools can be almost $3.5 million per year per school.

School districts make the fiscal inequities between high- and low-poverty schools worse by the ways they choose to spend the funds they do have. In a study of spending patterns in dozens of school districts in 20 states, two major patterns emerged. First, school districts spent less money on salaries in high-poverty schools than in low-poverty schools within the same district. Second, districts assigned a larger share of unrestricted funds to low-poverty schools. Apparently, resource-rich schools keep getting more; resource-poor schools get less.[44]

---

[39] Hoff, D. J. (2007, February 14). Economists tout value of reducing dropouts. *Education Week. 26*(2), 5, 15.
[40] Verstegen, D. (2002 Winter). Financing the new adequacy: Towards new models of state education finance systems that support standards based reform. *Journal of Education Finance, 27,* 749–782.
[41] Owings & Kaplan, 2006.
[42] U.S. Department of Education, National Center for Education Statistics, *Digest of Education Statistics, 2008* (NCES 2009-020), table 7, data from U.S. Department of Commerce, Census Bureau, Current Population Survey (CPS), October, 1970–2007. Retrieved August 26, 2009 from: http://nces.ed.gov/programs/coe/2009/section1/table-ope-1.asp
[43] Weiner & Pristoop, 2006, p. 6.
[44] Roza, M. (2006). *How districts shortchange low-income and minority students: Funding gap 2006.* Washington, DC: The Education Trust, pp. 9–10. Retrieved February 21, 2007, from http://www2.edtrust.org/NR/rdonlyres/CDEF9403-5A75-437E-93FF-EBF1174181FB/0/FundingGap2006.pdf.

Figure 10.7	Funding Gap Between High- and Low-Income School Districts

Per-Student Funding Gaps Add Up			
For example, when you consider the per-student funding gap for low-income students (without 40-percent adjustment for low-income students) in...	Between two typical classrooms of 25 students, that translates into a difference of...	Between two typical elementary schools of 400 students, that translates into a difference of...	Between two typical high schools of 1,500 students, that translates into a difference of...
New York	$57,975	$927,600	$3,478,500
Illinois	$48,100	$769,600	$2,886,000
Michigan	$14,325	$229,200	$859,500
North Carolina	$8,600	$137,600	$516,000
Delaware	$5,175	$82,800	$310,500

Source: Weiner, R., & Pristoop, E. (2006). *How states shortchange the districts that need the most help: Funding gap 2006.* Washington, DC: The Education Trust, p. 8.

Salary Inequalities

Typically, teachers in a school district receive salaries from a salary scale with increased monies paid for increased years of teaching experience and more academic credentials. Teachers with no or little experience and fewer advanced degrees receive lower salaries. As a result, schools with higher average teacher salaries tend to have the more experienced and well-educated teachers. Schools with lower average teacher salaries tend to have the newcomers with the fewest years of professional experiences. The result is a "salary gap" between teachers in affluent schools and teachers in low-income schools.

Figure 10.8 illustrates these salary gaps. In each city cited, the district spends less on teaching in its schools with high concentrations of low-income students. For instance, the gap between the average teacher salaries between the highest- and lowest-poverty schools in San Jose Unified is more than $4,000.

What is more, these examples are not the most extreme. A 2004 analysis of Baltimore City showed that teachers at one high-poverty school were paid an average of almost $20,000 less than teachers at a low-poverty school in the same district.[45]

These salary discrepancies affect classroom learning and school climate in varied ways. Some studies find that the most highly experienced and credentialed teachers are not randomly distributed within a school district. Instead, they are concentrated in high-SES (socioeconomic status) schools, which tend to have both higher per-pupil expenditures and higher teacher salaries.[46] Such schools may be more

[45] Roza, M., & Hill, P. (2004). How within-district spending inequities help some schools to fail. In *2004 Brookings Institute papers on education policy.* http://www.crpe.org/pubs/pdf/InequitiesRozaHillchapger.pdf.
[46] Condron & Roscigno, 2003; Haycock, K. (2000, Spring). No more settling for less. *Thinking K–16, 4.* 3–8, 10–12; Ingersoll, R. M. (June 2002). The teacher shortage: A case of wrong diagnosis and wrong prescription. *NASSP Bulletin, 86*(631), 16–30; Center for the Future of Teaching and Learning. (2003, December). *The status of the teaching profession 2003.* Santa Cruz, CA: Author. www.cftl.org.

Figure 10.8	Average Teachers' Salaries in High- and Low-Poverty Schools by School District, 2003–2004

District	Salary Gap
Austin*	$3,837
Dallas*	$2,494
Denver*	$3,633
Fort Worth*	$2,222
Houston*	$1,880
Los Angeles**	$1,413
Sacramento**	$4,846
San Diego**	$4,187
San Francisco**	$1,286
San Jose Unified**	$4,008

Sources: *Center for Reinventing Public Education Analyses, 2005
**Education Trust, Hidden Funding Gap, 2005, available at http://www.hiddengap.org/

Source: Roza, M. (2006). *How districts shortchange low-income and minority students: Funding gap 2006.* Washington, DC: The Education Trust, pp. 9–10.

attractive to teachers because of real or perceived differences in tangible resources, such as more books, more computers, wider availability of teachers' aides, and more achievement-oriented students.

Conversely, the least qualified, least experienced, lowest-paid teachers tend to work in schools with the highest number of low-income and minority students. Usually, new teachers start their careers at such high-poverty schools. In one 2003 study, students in the lowest-achieving schools were 4.5 times more likely to face under-prepared teachers than students in the highest-achieving schools.[47] High teacher and student turnover and a greater percentage of novice teachers working in the lowest-achieving, high-poverty schools contribute to both inconsistent instruction and the neediest learners working with the least experienced teachers.[48] With constant teacher turnover, principals can neither establish a culture for learning nor provide a skilled, experienced, and caring teacher corps to positively impact student achievement.[49]

As teachers gain experience and move up the pay scale, they often transfer to more affluent schools. District teacher transfer policies, sometimes written into teacher union contracts, aid this migration. Although teacher experience does not guarantee teacher quality, researchers agree that teacher effectiveness increases during the first three years in the classroom.[50] As a consequence, teachers' migration to affluent schools means that low-income and minority students have less chance of working with an experienced, effective teacher than do students in a more affluent school with few minority students.

---

[47] Center for the Future of Teaching and Learning, 2003, p. 6.
[48] Haycock, 2000; Ingersoll, 2002; Center for the Future of Teaching and Learning, 2003.
[49] Kaplan, L. S, Owings, W. A., & Nunnery, J. (2005, June). Principal quality: A Virginia study connecting Interstate School Leaders Licensure Consortium (ISLLC) standards with student achievement. *National Association of Secondary School Principals Bulletin.* Reston, VA: National Association of Secondary School Principals.
[50] Kane, T. J., Rockoff, J. E., & Staiger, D. O. (2007, Winter). Teachers certification doesn't guarantee a winner. *Education Next, 7*(1), 61–67; Ingersoll, R. (2003). *Is there really a teacher shortage?* Seattle, WA: Center for the Study of Teaching and Policy.

Facility Inequalities and Student Achievement

As Kozol vividly described in *Savage Inequalities*, low-income and minority schools frequently lack physically sound school buildings.[51] More money spent on school maintenance means a better upheld, repaired, and attractive building—and higher student achievement. One noteworthy study found a 5- to 17-point difference in standardized test scores for students who attended school in well-maintained buildings (with comfortable room and hall temperature, satisfactory lighting, appropriate noise levels, good roofs, sufficient space) as compared with students who attended school in poorly maintained facilities (too cold or hot rooms, inadequate lighting, high noise levels, leaky roofs, overcrowding), after controlling for the students' socioeconomic status.[52]

An earlier study found that if a school district were to improve its schools' conditions from poor to excellent, student achievement scores would increase an average of 10.9 percentile points. Working in "sick" buildings creates serious health issues for students and staff alike, which directly affects attendance rates and teachers' capacity to effectively instruct students. A reduced instructional investment in classrooms may be a source of student and teacher detachment, disengagement, and absences.[53]

Taxpayer Resistance to Funding Education

Historically, U.S. education has been almost exclusively a local concern. State legislatures set up local school districts to administer the schools and provide their young people with a "thorough and efficient" education. Community school boards implement state policy. The state gives the localities taxing powers to collect revenues to support schools, with the local property tax serving as the primary funding source. Coupled with state equalization assistance, basic state aid, and state and federal categorical aid, local property tax revenues pay for neighborhood public education.

Yet throughout history, virtually every political system has experienced its people's resistance to paying taxes. In 1773, the Massachusetts colonists led a tax revolt as they dumped British tea into Boston Harbor. Two hundred years later, beginning in the 1970s, taxpayer resistance to funding public schools became a popular issue.

While school financial referenda increasing local support for public schools were popular in the 1960s, the 1970s saw voters rejecting school funding increases. In fact, phrases like California's "Proposition 13" or Massachusetts's "Prop 2½" became shorthand for taxpayer anger over their high property taxes as voters took their frustration to the polls. During the 1970s, 23 states passed major fiscal limitations on school funding.[54]

Public Sentiment About Taxation

A well-developed body of research suggests that public sentiment about taxation reflects a number of factors. These include rational and economic self-interest, socioeconomic status, and the symbolic politics of ideology and partisanship.[55]

---

[51] Condron & Roscigno, 2003.

[52] Earthman, G. (2002). School facility conditions and student academic achievement. In *William Watch series: Investigating the claims of Williams v. State of California*. Los Angeles: UCLA Institute for Democracy, Education, and Access.

[53] Bernier, M. (1993, April). Building conditions, parental involvement, and student achievement in the District of Columbia public school system. *Urban Education, 28*(1), 6–29.

[54] Danziger, J. N. (1980, December). California's Proposition 13 and the fiscal limitations movement in the United States. *Political Studies, 28*(4), 599–612.

[55] Cataldo, E. H., & Holm, J. D. (1983). Voting on school finances: A test of completing theories. *Western Political Quarterly, 36*(4), 619–631; Reed, D. S. (2001, March). Not in my backyard: Localism and public opposition to funding schools equally. *Social Science Quarterly, 82*(1), 34–50.

People view public schools as providing young people with the intellectual knowledge and skills needed for their economic self-sufficiency and good citizenship. Taxpayers know that educated communities are safer and more prosperous. The higher the parents' education, the greater their support for their children's education and often for education in general. Conversely, rejecting taxation may be rooted not so much in its financial pinch on taxpayer, but rather in the voter's ideological or political views about paying higher (or any) taxes.[56] All of these variables play a role in taxpayers' views about funding schools through property taxes.

Several factors explain the taxpayer "revolts" that have occurred in recent decades:[57]

- Homeowners tend to vote.
- Property taxes may grow more rapidly than personal income. In California, for example, residential properties' assessed values were rising 10 to 20 percent annually and as much as 40 percent in some areas when the Proposition 13 revolt occurred. Property tax burdens can increase as much as 50 to 100 percent every three years.
- Residential real estate may see an increased tax burden relative to business and industrial real estate.
- Real per-pupil spending may rise dramatically, while student achievement scores do not.
- The school-age population and schools' political constituency may decline as compared with voters older than age 65.
- Attitudes come to favor the idea that older citizens living on fixed incomes should not be priced out of their homes through high property taxes.
- Voters lose confidence in the government's ability to spend tax dollars wisely for public goods and services.
- Large revenue surpluses make property tax increases appear unnecessary. For example, California had an estimated $3–6 billion revenue surplus in 1978.[58]
- Government at any level fails to provide meaningful tax reform to relieve taxpayers' discontent.[59]

Taxpayer Revolts and Low-Wealth Schools

When the localities pay less money to support their schools, the state must contribute more from the general tax funds. But taxpayer revolts tend to hurt low-wealth schools more than high-wealth schools. Affluent communities usually find innovative ways to provide additional resources to neighborhood schools. California's taxpayers' revolt provides a case study.

After a brief lag after Proposition 13 passed, California schools began to make up for the lost property tax revenues, largely through rapidly growing nontax fees and charges. These alternative resources were both less constrained and less visible to voters than taxes. Fees, rental income, grants from outside agencies directly to classroom teachers, and monetary donations by parents to teachers to buy supplies circumvented the state's budgetary limitations on school funding.[60] Although

---

[56] Reed, 2001.
[57] Danziger, 1980; Strauss, R. P. (2000). *School finance reform: Moving from the school property tax to the income tax.* Paper presented at the 88th Annual Conference on Taxation, National Tax Association, San Diego, CA. Retrieved November 22, 2009, from http://www.andrew.cmu.edu/user/rs9f/nta95a.pdf.
[58] Danziger, 1980, p. 604.
[59] Danziger. (1980). Ibid.
[60] Downes, G. (1992, December). Evaluating the impact of school finance reform on the provision of public education: The case of California. *National Tax Journal, 45*(4), 405–419.

| Figure 10.9 | Affluent Communities Usually Find Innovative Ways to Fund Extra School Resources |

Cindy Charles/PhotoEdit

little quantitative evidence is available, considerable anecdotal evidence indicates that schools' use of volunteer time increased, foundations were established to provide financial support for athletics and other extracurricular activities, and a variety of other methods (such as bake sales) were devised to get around the fiscal limitations.[61]

Taken together, this evidence supports the conclusion that individual actions to neutralize the schools' fiscal constraints play a major role in enabling high-wealth districts to keep their relative position of spending more resources per student and supporting higher student achievement. In contrast, less affluent communities are forced to rely on only the state's fiscal support. The end result is that taxpayer revolts make school funding more inequitable.

Spending for Student Achievement

Money matters when it comes to education.[62] Spending money wisely is associated with increased student achievement. Investments in the following critical areas pay off in student learning gains:

- Teacher quality
- Teacher salaries
- Reduced class size
- Professional development
- School facilities

Teacher Quality

We know what constitutes good teaching, and we know that good teaching can matter more than students' family backgrounds and economic status in terms of student

---

[61] Henke, J. T. (1986, Fall) Financing public schools in California: The aftermath of the *Serrano v. Priest* decision. *University of San Francisco Law Review, 21,* 1–39.
[62] For more on spending for student achievement, see Owings & Kaplan, 2006, pp. 315–338.

achievement.[63] Linda Darling-Hammond found that teacher quality variables such as full certification and completing a major in the teaching field are more important to student outcomes in reading and math than are student demographic variables such as poverty, minority status, and language background.[64]

Darling-Hammond identified the following teacher quality factors as being related to student achievement:[65]

- Verbal ability
- Content knowledge
- Education methods coursework related the teacher's discipline
- Licensing exam scores that measure basic skills and teaching knowledge
- Skillful teaching behaviors
- Ongoing professional development
- Enthusiasm for teaching
- Flexibility, creativity, and adaptability
- Teaching experience
- Asking higher-order questions (application, analysis, synthesis, and evaluation as opposed to recognition and recall questions) and probing student responses

As such, prospective teachers who want to be hired early in the process should highlight these skills in their résumés or portfolios and be able to discuss the research base that provides evidence of their efficacy.

Teacher Salaries

Teachers' long history of low salaries relates to supply and demand factors that date as far back as 1776.[66] At that time, the United States witnessed an oversupply

| Figure 10.10 | Teacher Quality Factors Are Important to Student Learning Outcomes |

JLP/Jose L. Pelaez/Ivy/CORBIS

---

[63] For more on teacher quality, see Kaplan, L., & Owings, W. (2003). *Teacher quality, teaching quality, and school improvement.* Bloomington, IN: Phi Delta Kappan; and Chapter 14 of this text.
[64] Darling-Hammond, L., (2000). Teacher quality and student achievement: A review of state policy evidence. *Education Policy Analysis Archives,* 8(1). Retrieved August 26, 2009 from: http://epaa.asu.edu/epaa/v8n1/
[65] Darling-Hammond, 2000.
[66] Johns, R., Morphet, E., & Alexander, K. (1983). *The economics and financing of education* (4th ed.). Secaucus, NJ: Prentice-Hall, p. 305.

of individuals trained to enter the clergy who were unable to find ministerial positions. These people subsequently entered teaching, created an oversupply of well-prepared instructors, which in turn depressed wages. This tradition of low wages for teachers continues today, effectively reducing the potential applicant pool.

The issues of teacher salaries and teacher quality are connected. It is difficult to link empirical evidence of increased teacher quality with higher teacher salaries because most school districts have salary schedules based on years of experience and earned academic degrees rather than on student achievement. As discussed previously in conjunction with the "salary gap" between high- and low-poverty schools, children in the highest-poverty schools are assigned to lower-salaried novice teachers almost twice as often as students in low-poverty schools.[67] Until 2002's No Child Left Behind law required teachers to hold bachelor's degrees in the subjects they were teaching, poor and minority students were more likely to have "out-of-field" teachers without majors or minors in the subjects they taught than were students in low-poverty schools.[68]

Likewise, research consistently affirms the relationship between teacher quality factors and student achievement. Briefly, these "quality" factors include teachers' academic skills and knowledge (especially their vocabulary), their mastery of the content they teach, their experience on the job (especially after the second year), their teaching effectiveness (pedagogy), and the interaction of these factors.[69]

According to Heather Peske and Kati Haycock of The Education Trust:

> No matter which measure we look at, the pattern is basically the same. In state after state, district after district, we take the children who are most dependent upon their teachers for academic learning and assign them to teachers with less of everything. Less experience. Less education. Less knowledge of content. And less actual teaching skill.[70]

Can increased teacher salaries make a difference in increased student achievement? Maybe. It is logical to assume that increased salaries will expand the potential teacher applicant pool. A basic capitalistic and free-market economy tenet is that higher wages attract more individuals seeking those jobs. If teachers' salaries increase, a larger applicant pool will seek teaching careers. An expanded applicant pool will include more individuals with higher levels of identified teacher quality factors. In fact, the Teaching Commission, a nonprofit group formed in 2003 to improve teaching, has recommended raising base salaries to make teachers' pay more competitive and attract higher-quality teachers.[71]

Reduced Class Size

The impact of class size on student achievement has been studied for many years. For example, Tennessee's carefully designed and managed experiments with class size reduction in primary grades showed positive results. This state's Student–Teacher Achievement Ratio (STAR) program involved more than 12,000 students

---

[67] "Novice" in this case refers to teaches with three years or less experience. National Center for Education Statistics. (2000, December). *Monitoring quality: An indicators report,* Cited in Peske & Haycock, 2006.
[68] Jerald, C. D. (2002). *All talk, no action: Putting an end to out-of-field teaching.* Washington, DC: The Education Trust.
[69] For more on teacher quality and student achievement, see Kaplan & Owings, 2001; Kaplan, L. S., & Owings, W. A. (2003, May). The politics of teacher quality. *Phi Delta Kappan, 84*(9), 687–692.
[70] Peske, H. G., & Haycock, K. (2006, June). *Teaching inequality: How poor and minority students are short-changed on teacher quality.* Washington, DC: The Education Trust, p. 11.
[71] Teaching Commission. (2004), *Teaching at risk: A call to action.* New York: Author, p. 26. Retrieved October 5, 2009, from http://www.csl.usf.edu/teaching%20at%20risk.pdf.

over four years. The findings from this highly controlled longitudinal study indicate that attending small classes for three consecutive years in grades K–3 is associated with sustained academic benefits in all school subjects through grade 8.[72] Similar results were found in studies of reduced class size in California.[73]

A review and synthesis of more than 100 class-size studies suggest that the most positive effects from small classes appear in kindergarten to third grade for mathematics and reading.[74] Most researchers believe that student achievement increases as class size is reduced from 30 to 16 students.[75] Nevertheless, although shrinking the number of students in a class can lead to higher test scores overall, it might not necessarily reduce the achievement gaps that exist between students in a given classroom.[76]

In reducing class size, however, it is important to consider teacher quality. Reducing class size without simultaneously improving the quality and effectiveness of what teachers do in the classroom to help all students learn to high levels would be expensive and unproductive. Even those who disagree over the research's implications agree that more scientific studies on class size are necessary.[77]

Professional Development

Once employed, professional development plays an important role in upgrading and retaining high-quality teachers. New teachers can get better, marginal teachers can improve, and successful teachers can strengthen their expertise when they participate in high-quality, ongoing professional development programs. Studies of NAEP data indicate that professional development programs related to cultural diversity, teaching techniques for addressing the needs of students with limited English proficiency, and teaching students identified with special education needs are all linked to higher math student achievement.[78]

Other studies show that when professional development is sustained over time and based on curriculum standards, teachers are more likely to adopt new and reform-based teaching practices. Subsequently, their students achieve at higher levels on standardized tests.[79]

Weiner and Pristoop of The Education Trust remark:

> It is unfair that children's educational horizons are limited by their neighborhoods' demographics. As state education systems grow into their responsibilities in a standards-based world, they need to ensure that budgets reflect fairness and that resources are targeted to districts with the most need. Aligning state education funding policies with goals would mark necessary, but not sufficient, progress towards equality of educational opportunity.[80]

[72] Nye, B., Hodges, L. V., & Konstantopoulos, S. (2000, Spring). The effects of small class size on academic achievement: The results of the Tennessee class size experiment. *American Educational Research Journal, 37*, 123–151.

[73] Stecher, B., Bornstedt, G., Dirst, M., McRobbie, J., & Williams, T. (2001, June). Class size reduction in California: A story of hope, promise, and unintended consequences. *Phi Delta Kappan, 82*, 670–674.

[74] Robinson, G. (1990, April). Synthesis of research on the effects of class size. *Educational Leadership, 47*(7), 80–90.

[75] Addonizio, M., & Phelps, J. (2000, Fall). Class size and student performance: A framework for policy analysis. *Journal of Education Finance, 26*, 135–156.

[76] Konstantopoulis, S. (2008, March). Do small classes reduce the achievement gap between low and high achievers? Evidence from Project STAR. *Elementary School Journal, 108*(4), 275–292.

[77] Jacobson, L. (2008, February 27). Class-size reductions seen of limited help on achievement gap. *Education Week, 27*(25), 9.

[78] Blair, J. (2000, October). ETS study inks effective teaching methods to test-score gains. *Education Week, 25*, 24–25.

[79] Hirsh, E., Koppcih, E., & Knapp, M.S. (1998, December). *What states are doing to improve the quality of teaching: A brief review of current patterns and trends.* Seattle, WA: Center for the Study of Teaching and Policy.

[80] Weiner & Pristoop, 2006, p. 9.

Summary

Education is a positive investment in our country's infrastructure. It provides a return on investment by increasing individuals' wages and growing government tax revenues. Education also reduces public social expenditures by decreasing social costs from unemployment, incarceration, and crime.

The revenue for education comes from three main sources—federal, state, and local. Federal revenues on average make up 9 to 10 percent of state budgets, while local and state revenues are almost evenly split in accounting for the rest. At the local level, property tax revenue constitutes the largest school revenue source.

How school districts spend money varies widely. One way to compare expenditures is by examining the state per-pupil expenditures. The variance in these expenditures is large—ranging from slightly more than $6,000 to slightly less than $15,000 per year. Budget categories vary from state to state for items such as instruction, transportation, and administration.

It is important to distinguish between equal and equitable spending. Our society has given education a mandate to provide for students' needs. For that reason, we do not spend equal amounts of money on each student. It costs more to educate some students than others; that is equitable spending. While we want to have equality of opportunity for all students, we want equitable treatment of all students. Unfortunately, our schools have equity problems in such areas as teacher salaries, resources, and school facilities. Lower-income and needier students tend to have less money spent on them than do richer and less needy students.

Adequacy involves providing sufficient resources to accomplish the job of educating our children. As a fiscal concept, adequacy is value driven and defined subjectively. Quantifying adequacy remains unclear.

Teacher salaries represent the largest expenditure in the education budgets. Average teacher salaries vary widely among states.. The district variance with states is also quite large.

Partly because property taxes provide the major revenue source at the local level and partly because the public does not understand school finance, taxpayer movements have tried to reduce education expenditures. Spending money wisely, however, can positively influence student achievement. Spending money for teacher quality, teacher salaries, smaller classes for primary grades, professional development, and better facilities is associated with student achievement gains.

Conclusions

- All educators should be knowledgeable about school finance so they can be intelligent advocates for education spending.
- Spending education funds wisely can increase student achievement and make a significant investment in a community's infrastructure.

Chapter 11

Equality of Educational Opportunity: Societal and School Practices

As we read in Chapters 4 and 5, American public schools were established in part to become the great social equalizers, placing any student on the path to social mobility and economic survival. If we look closely, however, we find that schools typically reinforce—rather than overcome—our communities' social, racial, and ethnic divides.

Although school doors open to all children, schools have never served all children or their families fairly or well. Both social class—as defined by parents' income, education, and occupation—and school practices influence student learning and contribute to the achievement gap. Differences in family resources, communication styles, and discipline practices distinguish the average families from different social classes.

In addition, we structure our schools to accomplish goals we set for them. Public school educators' naiveté about unfair school practices, societal barriers, and cultural values allow schools to limit certain students' access to the high-quality education they need and deserve. Frequently, educators do not see the schools' inequities because these practices are so familiar and well rationalized that they seem benign, neutral, normal, and appropriate rather than unfair.

This chapter looks at the various ways in which both society and schools may prevent minority and low-income students from getting the education they need. It also examines the practices educators can adopt to better support learning and higher achievement for all students.

Focus Questions

- How is the United States becoming more diverse, and what are the implications of this trend for everyone's quality of life?
- What are the historical perspectives on race, ethnicity, class, and U.S. education?
- How does socioeconomic status influence U.S. students' skills, outlooks, and opportunities?
- What are American public schools' contradictory roles?
- What is the relationship between social class and educational opportunity?
- How do parenting practices influence children's school success?
- How does attending a segregated school affect student achievement?
- How do teachers' expectations affect students' achievement?
- How do tracking, ability grouping, and restricted curricula affect students' achievement?
- How do discipline policies and practices affect students' achievement?
- How does school climate affect student achievement?
- How does multicultural education affect students' achievement?
- How can becoming aware of schools' inequitable and institutionalized practices affect students' achievement?

Increasing Diversity and Future Quality of Life

The United States is currently undergoing one of the most profound demographic transformations in our nation's history. The country's increasing racial diversity has serious consequences for our sense of national unity, democracy, and future economic prosperity. Our ability as a nation to make this transition successfully depends in large measure on the strength of our public education system.

Changing Demographics

The U.S. Census facts confirm our increasing diversity. The U.S. Census Bureau predicts that Latinos, African Americans, Asian Americans, Native Americans, Native Hawaiians, and Pacific Islanders will collectively become the majority population in the United States by 2042. The latest projections suggest that by 2050, minorities will account for 54 percent of the U.S. population, with non-Latino whites representing the remaining 46 percent, down from their current 64.7 percent share.[1] (See Figure 11.1.)

In addition, research finds that students from historically disadvantaged minority groups have only a 50 percent probability of finishing high school with a diploma. Nearly half the nation's African American and Latino student attend high schools with high poverty and low graduation rates.[2]

Implications of Changing Worker Demographics

Not successfully educating large numbers of minority students has major implications for the American work force. The National Center for Public Policy and Higher

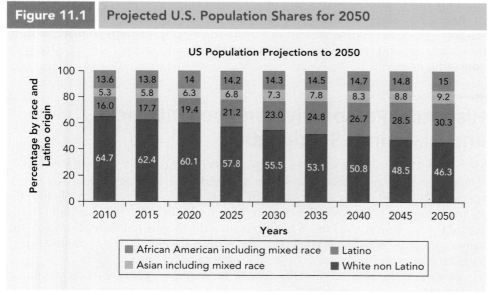

Figure 11.1 | **Projected U.S. Population Shares for 2050**

Source: *Minorities set to be US majority: U.S. population projections to 2050.* (2008, August 14). Washington, DC: U.S. Census Bureau. Retrieved November 22, 2009, from **http://news.bbc.co.uk/2/hi/americas/7559996.stm**.

---

[1] Bernstein, R., & Edwards, T. (2008, August 14). An older and more diverse nation by midcentury. *U.S. Census Bureau News.* Washington, DC: U.S. Census Bureau. Retrieved October 16, 2009, from http://www.census.gov/Press-Release/www/releases/archives/population/012496.html; Minorities set to be US majority. (2008, August 14). *BBC News.* Retrieved November 22, 2009, from http://news.bbc.co.uk/2/hi/americas/7559996.stm.

[2] Balfan, R., & Legters, N. (2006, July 12). Closing "dropout factories": The graduation-rate crisis we know, and what can be done about it. *Education Week. 25*(42), 42–43.

Education predicts that by 2020, the white working-age population will have declined to 63 percent of the total U.S. population (down from 82 percent in 1980). Because large numbers of younger workers will be members of ethnic minorities while larger numbers of white workers are retiring, the work force will shift from a majority of white workers to include more people of color.[3]

Unless this upcoming work force has the high-quality education and skills to earn strong and consistent wages, our whole society will suffer. This work force will support our economy through consumer purchases and taxes. It will also shape our society through income distribution as their wages contribute, through Social Security payments, to supporting retirees and disabled citizens. If tomorrow's workers have lower personal incomes than do present and retiring workers, our social networks may not be able to meet their obligations.

Unless we do something to close the education gap, the most highly educated generation in U.S. history could be replaced by a generation with far lower education levels (as measured by high school and college completion rates).[4] Many people's well-being and lifestyles will be reduced as a result.

A Complex Reality

According to Richard Rothstein, research associate with the Economic Policy Institute, "Policy makers almost universally conclude that these existing and persistent achievement gaps must be the result of wrongly designed school policies—expectations that are too low, teachers who are insufficiently qualified, curricula that are badly designed, classes that are too large, school climates that are too undisciplined, leadership that is too unfocused, or a combination of these factors."[5] In short, Americans have decided that the achievement gap is the result of "failing schools."

The reality, however, is much more complex. While certain school perspectives and practices do limit educational opportunities for poor and minority students in the United States, the larger social class–stratified society, a history of inequality, and even today's courts perpetuate inequities. Nonetheless, each student's personal future, as well as our nation's economy and security, will increasingly depend on those same minority children whom we are *not* effectively educating now.[6]

Historical Perspective on Race, Ethnicity, and Class in U.S. Education

More than 300 years ago, when Europeans arrived in the New World with their own language, culture, myths, and ideologies, the land was not empty. Native Americans speaking 300–350 different languages in North America greeted them.[7] Before the Pilgrims stepped off the *Mayflower* on to Plymouth Rock, the Spanish had already settled the Southwest; the French had populated the Mississippi Valley from St. Paul, Minnesota, to New Orleans, Louisiana; and African slaves had arrived in Jamestown, Virginia.

In spite of the cultural diversity already in place in America, our early political leaders envisioned a country with one unified history, shared mores, and a common

[3] Lewis, A. (2006, February). A new people. *Phi Delta Kappan, 87*(6), 419.
[4] Metropolitan Center for Urban Education, Steinhardt School of Education, New York University. (2005). With all deliberate speed: Achievement, citizenship, and diversity in American education. Retrieved April 23, 2009, from http://www.kwfdn.org/resource_library/getfile.asp?intResourceID=389.
[5] Rothstein, R. (2004, October). A wider lens on the black–white achievement gap, *Phi Delta Kappan, 86*(2), p. 106.
[6] Rothstein, 2004, A wider lens on the black–white achievement gap, p. 106.
[7] Larson, C. L., & Ovando, C. J. (2001). *The color of bureaucracy: The politics of equity in multicultural school communities.* Belmont, CA: Cengage Learning, p. 8

language. Indeed, the first colonists' Anglo-Saxon orientation set the stage for the symbolic politics of language and ethnic identity in the United States.[8] A European American tradition was born, and this background came to be the public schools' dominant culture.

From the 1600s to the 1800s, the U.S. frontier's physical and psychological openness allowed varied people to establish their own communities and preserve their Old World customs. Holding on to their ancestral mores and languages gave newcomers a strong and valued sense of who they were, even when living in an unfamiliar country.[9] If those emigrating to their community did not like these customs, they could move on to settle elsewhere.

Perspectives on Schools as Socializing Agencies

Throughout U.S. history, schools have served as a powerful agency to socialize ethnic and racial communities to white Anglo-Saxon Protestant norms. Developing a common heritage and loyalty to this country, unifying a diverse population, preparing students for citizenship in a democratic society, and teaching students to be economically self-sufficient were essential elements in ensuring this country's economic, social, and political survival. Portraying their own Western intellectual, political, historical, and cultural roots positively, public schools' curriculum deliberately minimized other cultures' realities, contributions, and worth.

While the members of many ethnic groups who immigrated to the United States by choice appreciated the schools helping their children to become Americans, not all ethnic communities welcomed this approach. Many groups did not want to be forced, taught, or encouraged to let go of their own cultural language, beliefs, and traditions. This was especially true for indigenous Native American communities, African Americans brought here against their will, conquered Mexican Americans in 1848, and Puerto Rican communities after the 1898 Spanish–American War.[10]

It is easy to see, therefore, how educators and students (along with their families and communities) could make different judgments about the same school practices. Educators acted in ways that they sincerely believed were best for the students and for society as a whole. Meanwhile, those students who were told to leave their family heritage at the schoolhouse door might have experienced their school-led Americanization differently.

Social Class and Opportunities for Children's Education

Since the nineteenth century, American schools have increased in number, affording knowledge and skills to all persons regardless of family background, race, class, gender, or national origin. This democratic ideology of providing equal opportunity to each citizen through a free public education has always been a highly motivating and worthy ideal. The question remains, however: To what extent is it actually happening?

Social Class

Social class and **socioeconomic status** (SES) are two terms used to distinguish a person's position in society relative to others within that society. Parental occupation,

---

[8] Ovando, C. J. (2003 Spring). Bilingual education in the United States: Historical development and current issues. *Bilingual Research Journal, 27*(1). Retrieved October 16, 2009, from http://brj.asu.edu/content/vol27_no1/documents/art1.pdf.
[9] Kloss, H. (1998/1977). *The American bilingual tradition.* Rowley, MA: Newbury House.
[10] Larson & Ovando, 2001, pp. 8–9.

educational level, income, housing value, and political influence are the basis for determining a student's social class or socioeconomic status. Socioeconomic level also includes parents' attitudes toward education, parents' aspirations for their children, and families' intellectual activities, such as taking cognitively stimulating trips to museums, historical sites, concerts, and other locations. A student's socioeconomic status is highly associated with academic achievement.[11]

Typically, the **upper class** is usually defined as wealthy persons with considerable money, property, and investments. At the level below the upper class, the **middle class** includes professionals, managers, and small-business owners (upper middle class) as well as technical workers, technicians, sales personnel, and clerical workers (lower middle class). Generally, the **working class**[12] includes skilled crafts workers (upper working class) and unskilled manual and service workers (lower working class). Skilled workers may either be middle or working class, depending on their education, income, and home neighborhood.

Recently, observers have identified an **underclass** group within the working or lower class. Many of its members are the third or fourth generation living in poverty. They depend on public assistance to maintain a relatively spare existence. The underclass tends to live clustered in inner-city slums or in rundown rural areas. After several generations without visible social or economic progress, members of the underclass usually lose hope of improving their economic and social situation.[13]

Social class differences in the United States appear in income, education, family and child-raising practices, occupations, place of residence, political involvement, health, consumer behavior, and religious beliefs. Additionally, class distinctions determine the quality of schooling students receive, their worldviews, and their relationships to others in society. Social class position creates a selective perception and set of experiences that shape a person's worldview and behaviors.

On a daily basis, social class differences may be difficult to recognize. Because observers see individuals only in limited situations, the patterns of class differences may not be clearly visible to outsiders. In addition, it is a mistake to generalize based on social class because many variations in attitudes, values, and beliefs exist within each category.

Because the United States has a powerful mythology about equal opportunity, many people try to hide their social class differences. Families buy larger houses or bigger cars than they can afford in an attempt to seem wealthier than they are. Students visibly parade their latest expensive footgear, wardrobe, and electronic toys to look like they are financially and socially well off. On the other side, affluent youths prize their tattered jeans and threadbare flannel shirts. The media present the illusion that the United States is an egalitarian society in which everyone has an equal chance to succeed by not portraying the desperately poor on TV except in documentaries.

People in the United States are stratified by more than social class, however: They are also stratified by race and ethnicity. Immigrants come from a variety of social class backgrounds. Generalizing that immigrant or minority populations are all poor or all come from the lower or working class would be incorrect.

---

[11] Coleman, J. S., Campbell, E., Hobson, C., McPartland, J., Mood, A., Weinfield, F., & York, R. (1966). *Equality of educational opportunity.* Washington, DC: U.S. Government Printing Office; Caldas, S. J. (1993). Reexamination of input and process factor effects on public school achievement. *Journal of Education Research, 84,* 325–326; Caldas, S. J., & Bankston, C. (1997, May/June). Effect of school population socioeconomic status on individual academic achievement. *Journal of Educational Research, 90,* 269–277; Rumberger, R. W., & Willms, J. D. (1992). The impact of racial and ethnic segregation on the achievement gap in California high schools. *Educational Evaluation and Policy Analysis, 14,* 377–396.

[12] While more respectful than the term "lower class", the term "working class" is a misnomer because most people of all social classes "work." The authors of this book sometimes use the term "low income" to refer to lower or "working" class social status, reflecting the group's economic situation.

[13] Jencks, C., & Peterson, P. E. (Eds.). (1991).*The urban underclass.* Washington, DC: Brookings Institution; Wooster, M. W. (1998, May–June). Inside the underclass. *American Enterprise,* 83–84.

| Figure 11.2 | Many Students Dress to Hide Their Social Class Differences |

Open Door Images/Creatas Images/Jupiter Images

Equal Opportunity in U.S. Schools

Equality of opportunity means that all members of a society are given the same chances to enter any occupation or social class and to compete for any place in society. It does not mean that everyone will have the same income and status. The close relationship between education and income indicates that education is truly an important factor in providing equality of opportunity[14]—but it is not the only factor, as we shall see.

Unequal starting lines. Providing actual equal opportunity requires all persons to start at the same place, as if all were running a race. In this perfect world, all runners would be physically fit and in excellent health. All would arrive wearing first-rate equipment. All runners would walk up to the starting line, take their positions, and take off at the starting gun at the same time. During this race, some people would lead, and others would follow. In this equality model, schools would guarantee that either everyone begins on equal terms at the starting line or schools can control the race to ensure that competition remains fair. In the first case, everyone must have an equal education before they reach the starting block. In the second, everyone must identify and develop their abilities during the race.

Of course, not all Americans actually begin at the same place. The American goal of equal opportunity has been an attempt to balance the equality ideal with the inherently unequal societal reality. Schools contribute to society's stability by promising to be the "great equalizer." Our society believes that getting a good education creates opportunities for students' economic and social advancement and political participation. For many students, this is true. For many others, it is not. Despite unequal realities, believing that schools give everyone the chance to achieve wealth and power allows people to rationalize that those who fail to reach those goals simply "did not work hard enough" or "did not take advantage" of these opportunities. This reasoning keeps our social system steady by shifting responsibility for the inequality from the institution and society to those without the money, power, or status.

---

[14] For data confirming the close relationship between education and income, see Chapter 10.

Contradictory Roles of American Schools

The roles of American schools often contradict each other. On the one hand, schools seek to transmit society's consensual values, beliefs, and skills to develop an educated, unified, and responsible democratic populace. On the other hand, schools are efficient sorting and selecting machines that track students and guide them into low-, middle- and high-paying occupations. What initially was intended as a unifying experience for diverse students has become one that increasingly separates students.

Sorting and selecting. In the early days of American schools, family economics did the sorting and selecting before students ever reached the common (elementary) school. A family's income and survival needs affected which students entered school at all and how long they remained there. Many students left school before finishing their studies to help support their families. Other students were not allowed to attend. As a result, those who remained in school were already among life's select.

Beginning in the late nineteenth century, all children in the United States were required to attend school. During their years there, schools "sorted and selected" students into their future occupational roles. Using what it considered "scientific," impartial, and professional opinions from teachers, guidance counselors, and standardized tests, schools classified students according to their individual talents or abilities. Educators then placed them into ability groups or "tracks" that would lead to appropriate education for their future societal roles and occupations.

Students determined to have the highest cognitive abilities (approximately 10 percent of those enrolled) received a rigorous academic education to prepare them for college and the few professional careers that required high-level reasoning and communication skills. The other 90 percent of the students received a less rigorous academic education appropriate to work on the farm and factories. Educators did not consider that not all students arrived at the schoolhouse door physically fit, healthy, properly shoed, fully trained, well coached, and ready for the same race.

A middle-and upper-class tilt. Because the educational system is inherently tilted to favor middle- and upper-class children, their parents believe that schools are doing right by their children. These parents assume that schools offer a level playing field, and that all children have equal opportunities within them. After all, their own children get to the starting line healthy, well outfitted, broadly experienced, and ready to race. In contrast, low-income children, children of color, and children with disabilities do not always come to the starting line equally as healthy or as well prepared. Because circumstances of poverty, minority status, or disability keep them from getting to the starting blocks fully equipped to run a competitive race with their better-prepared peers, these low-income, minority, and disabled children are denied opportunities for equal outcomes. Consequently, they are consistently underserved in public schools.

More recently, school programs have tried to overcome inequalities caused by differences in students' preparation for school learning. For example, schools may implement compensatory education, early childhood learning, and Head Start programs to overcome poverty's limitations on learning. These compensatory programs try to make up for students' unequal social conditions at home that make it impossible for these students to reach the starting line ready to complete before the race begins.

Research on Education, Social Class, and Opportunity

Do schools help students achieve equality of opportunity? Or do our schools reproduce and reinforce social-class differences? Does family income determine students' educational success and future income in spite of schools' historical attempts to provide equal opportunity? To some degree, the answer to all of these questions is "Yes."

Relationship Between Social Class and Educational Outcomes

An enduring relationship exists between social class and educational outcomes. It is usually true that average educational attainment (measured by years in school or dropout rates) and educational achievement (measured by grades and test scores) vary by social class.[15]

Higher social class, more education. In general, higher social class status correlates with high levels of education attainment and achievement.[16] A low-income child is roughly twice as likely to be a low academic achiever as a child who is not from a low-income family.[17] Nobel laureate economist James Heckman observes that the achievement gaps between the advantaged and the disadvantaged appear by age 5 and that schooling plays a minor role in creating or perpetuating the gaps.[18] The middle classes fall somewhere in between.[19]

Possessing educational credentials follows this same pattern. Upper-class individuals on average hold more academic credentials (college, master's, doctoral, and professional degrees) than members of the middle class, who in turn hold more credentials than working-class individuals.[20]

In addition, one study tracked students through their elementary years and found that poor children learned as much as their middle-class peers during the school year as measured by standardized tests. Unfortunately, African American, Latino, and low-income students tended to lose much academic ground over the summer when they were out of school. In contrast, middle-class children gained over the summer in reading and held their own in math. This suggests to researchers that the learning gap is probably not completely a school factor.[21]

Social Class Parenting Practices and School Success

It is not the social class label but the average group members' attitudes and behaviors that influence their children's school achievement. Young children's family environments (rather than income per se) are major predictors of cognitive, social, and emotional abilities.[22] Low income and skin color themselves do not influence academic achievement, but social class differences inevitably do.[23]

---

[15] Coleman et al., 1966; Jencks, C. (1972). Inequality: A measurement of the effect of family and schooling In America. New York: Basic Books; Natriello, G., McDilll, E. L., & Pallas, A. M. (1990). Schooling disadvantaged children: Racing against catastrophe. New York: Teachers College Press.
[16] White, K. R. (1982, May). The relationship between socioeconomic status and academic achievement. *Psychological Bulletin, 91*(3), 461–481.
[17] Wolf, A. (1978). The state of urban schools. Urban Education, 13 (2), 179–194.
[18] Heckman, J. (2008, June). *Schools, skills, and synapses* (NBER Working Paper No. 14064). Cambridge, MA: National Bureau of Economic Research, pp. 4, 12.
[19] Coleman et al., 1966; Goldstein, B. (1967). *Low income youth in urban areas: A critical review of the literature.* New York: Holt, Rinehart, & Winston; Persell, C. H. (1977). *Education and inequality: The roots and results of stratification in America's schools.* New York: Free Press; Persell, C. H. (1993). Social class and educational equality. In J. Banks & C. A. McGee Banks (Eds.), *Multicultural education: Issues and perspectives* (2nd ed., pp. 71–89). Boston: Allyn and Bacon.
[20] Coleman et al., 1966; Goldstein, 1967; Persell, 1977, 1993.
[21] Alexander, K. L., Entwisle, D. R., & Olson, S. (2001, Summer). Schools, achievement, and inequality: A seasonal perspective. *Educational Evaluation and Policy Analysis, 23*(2), 171–191; Viadero, D. (2006, November 15). Schools' role in achievement gaps scrutinized. *Education Week, 26*(12), 16. For more details, see McCall, M. S., et al. (2006, November). Achievement gaps: An examination of differences in achievement and growth. Northwest Evaluation Association. Retrieved February 19, 2007, from http://www.nwea.org/sites/www.nwea.org/files/AchGap_11.11.061.pdf.
[22] Heckman. 2008, p. 4.
[23] Rothstein, R. (2004). Class and schools: Using social, economic, and educational reform to close the black–white achievement gap. Washington, DC: Economic Policy Institute.

Rothstein observes that lower-class families show how occupational, psychological, personality, health, and economic characteristics interact and predict performance that differs, on average, from the performance of families from higher social classes. Although not every family in a particular social class uses all of the same practices, they are true for the group in general. Social-class lifestyle differences in average academic potential exist by the time children are 3 years old. This growth gap increases mostly during after-school hours and during the summer when children are not actually in classrooms.[24]

"Demography is not destiny, but students' social and economic family characteristics are a powerful influence on their relative *average* achievement."[25]

Differences in Child Rearing

Distinct differences in social-class-related child-rearing patterns affect students' academic performance as well. Research has shown that middle-and upper-class parents tend to include their children in adult conversations and ask their child's opinions. By contrast, low-income parents tend to speak less with their children. Accordingly, children raised by parents educated and working as professionals will, on average, ask their teachers more questions about the learning content than will children reared by working-class parents who speak less frequently with their children about their ideas and opinions and will build a larger vocabulary with which to understand the teacher's spoken words and the textbooks' written words.[26]

Reading to their children is another way that social-class-related parenting practices affect student learning. Middle- and upper-class homes usually have many books and periodicals. Parents not only read to children every day, but the adults also read themselves, whether the daily newspaper, magazines, professional journals, or novels. When these parents read to their children, they ask the children to respond to the content: "What do you think will happen next?" In these homes, children want to read because it is fun and interesting and because it is what grown-ups do. By comparison, full bookshelves, parents reading routinely for themselves and their children, and conversations about readings are less visible practices in working-class families.[27]

Differences in vocabulary. In an eye-opening study, two University of Kansas researchers visited homes of families from different social classes to monitor conversations between parents and toddlers. The researchers found that, on average, professional parents spoke more than 2,000 words per hour to their children, working-class parents spoke about 1,300 words, and welfare-recipient mothers (mothers who were unemployed but who received government assistance for housing and food) spoke about 600 words. By age 3, children of professionals had vocabularies that were nearly 50 percent larger than those of working-class children and twice the size of welfare-recipient children—a 30 million word gap.[28]

Even more important, children's vocabulary use at age 3 was predictive of their scores on language skills measures at ages 9–10. Cumulatively, the Kansas researchers estimated that by the time children were 4 years old and ready to enter

---

[24] Phillips, M. (2000). Understanding ethnic differences in academic achievement: Empirical lessons from national data. In D. W. Grissmer & J. M. Ross (Eds.), *Analytic issues in the assessment of student achievement* (NCES 2000-050, pp. 103–132). Washington, DC: U.S. Department of Education. Retrieved October 16, 2009, from http://nces.ed.gov/pubs2000/2000050a.pdf; Allington, R. L. & McGill-Franzen, A. (2003, September). The impact of summer setback on the reading achievement gap. *Phi Delta Kappan, 85*(1), 68–75.

[25] Rothstein, 2004, *Class and schools*, p. 16

[26] Rothstein, 2004, *Class and schools.*

[27] Rothstein, 2004, *Class and schools.*

[28] Hart, B., & Risley, T. (2003, Spring). The early catastrophe: The 130 million word gap by age 3. *American Educator.* Retrieved October 16, 2009, from http://www.aft.org/pubs-reports/american_educator/spring2003/catastrophe.html.

| Figure 11.3 | Reading to Children Prepares Them for Learning |

Dave & Les Jacobs/Jupiter Images

preschool, the typical child in a professional family would have an accumulated experience with 45 million words, compared to only 13 million for a typical child in a welfare-recipient family.[29]

Differences in disciplinary practices. Similarly, the Kansas researchers found that parental discipline practices differed by social class. Toddlers of professionals received an average of six verbal encouragements per scolding, whereas working-class children received two. Welfare-recipient children (children of parents who were not employed but who received government assistance for housing and food) received the reverse ratio: They received, on average, one encouragement for every two scoldings.[30]

It seems reasonable to expect that when these children go to school, their teachers cannot fully offset these early differences. Children with parents who encouraged them to build and use a vocabulary and to constructively use their initiative from an early age are probably more likely, on average, to understand teachers' language and directions, master vocabulary-based instruction and content more quickly, and take more responsibility for their own learning than are children who lack these previous experiences.

NAEP Results and Social Class. The National Assessment of Educational Progress (NAEP) also shows the close relationship between students' social class and their reading and math proficiency scores. Students with well-educated parents (one primary measure of social class) score much higher than students whose parents

[29] Hart & Risley, 2003.
[30] Hart & Risley, 2003.

have less education. Both math and reading scores show clear positive associations with parents' educational level and social class.[31]

Poverty and Education

Poverty is not just a lack of income. Indeed, poverty affects one's entire quality of life, bringing a constellation of variables that negatively affect children's schooling. These include health, housing, and multiple risk factors.[32]

Health issues. In addition to having low birth weight, children from poverty generally have poorer vision than middle-class children, partly because of prenatal conditions and partly because of how their eyes are trained as infants.[33] In addition, children of parents with less education (and from lower social classes) are prone to poorer oral hygiene, more lead poisoning, more asthma, poorer nutrition, and less adequate pediatric care.[34]

A 2009 study also found that poverty may affect children's brain functions. Compared to children from wealthier socioeconomic backgrounds, low-income children had a noticeably lower level of activity in the prefrontal cortex—the part of the brain that is important for creativity, reasoning, and problem solving. The stress from living in relative poverty may mean that these children are not realizing full brain development.[35]

These well-documented social class health differences may have a measurable effect on academic achievement. They affect language development, the ability to plan, remember details, and pay attention in school. The combined influences of parenting practices and more fragile health are probably very large.

Housing issues. The lack of affordable adequate housing for low-income families also affects school achievement. Urban rents have risen faster than working-class incomes. A Fall 2008 survey of 1,716 school districts nationwide found nearly all (95.4%) school districts reported increasing numbers of homeless students.[36] Children whose families have difficulty finding stable housing are more likely to move from place to place. In some schools in minority-dominated neighborhoods, student mobility rates have risen to more than 100 percent for every seat in

---

[31] Grigg, W., et al. (2003). *The nation's report card: Reading 2002.* Washington, DC: U.S. Department of Education, National Center for Education Statistics; Table 3.7, National Assessment of Educational Progress. p. 66. Retrieved February 13, 2007, from http://nces.ed.gov/nationsreportcard/pdf/main2002/2003521a.pdf; Braswell, J. S., et al. (2001). *The nation's report card: Math 2000.* Washington, DC: U.S. Department of Education, National Center for Education Statistics; Figure 3.ab, pp. 70–71. Retrieved October 16, 2009, from http://nces.ed.gov/nationsreportcard/pdf/main2000/2001517.pdf.

[32] For a fuller discussion of how poverty-related factors such as prenatal care health care, food insecurity, environmental pollutants, family stress, neighborhood characteristics, and extended learning opportunities strongly influence students' school success, see Berliner, D. C. (2009). *Poverty and potential: Out-of-school factors and school success.* Boulder, CO/Tempe, AZ: Education and the Public Interest Center & Education Policy Research Unit. Retrieved October 16, 2009, from http://epicpolicy.org/publication/poverty-and-potential.

[33] Barton, P. E. (2004). Why does the gap persist? *Educational Leadership, 62*(3), 9–13.

[34] Smith, J. P. (2005). Unraveling the SES–health connection. *Aging, Health, and Public Policy: Demographic and Economic Perspectives.* A supplement to *Population and Development Review, 30.* New York: Population Council; Ross, C. E., & Wu, C. L. (1996). Education, age, and the cumulative advantage in health. *Journal of Health and Social Behavior, 37*(1), 104–120; Rothstein, 2004, *Class and schools;* Mirowsky, J., & Ross, C. (2003). *Education, social status, and health.* Somerset, NJ: Aldine de Gruyter/Transaction.

[35] We have to view this conclusion with some skepticism because the study included only 26 children: Jacobson, L. (2009, January 7). Scientists track poverty's link to cognition. *Education Week, 28*(16), 4. For an article reporting on this study, see Kishiyama, M. M., Boyce, W. T., Jimenez, A. M., Perry, L. M., & Knight, R. T. (2009). Socioeconomic disparities affect prefrontal function in children. *Journal of Cognitive Neuroscience, 21*(1), 1–10.

[36] National Coalition for the Homeless. (2009). *Foreclosure to homelessness 2009: The forgotten victims of the subprime crisis.* Washington, D.C. Retrieved October 16, 2009 from: http://www.nationalhomeless.org/advocacy/ForeclosuretoHomelessness0609.pdf.

the school.[37] Student mobility is an important cause of low student achievement because students lose curricular continuity. Even the most experienced and well-trained teachers would have difficulty helping children who move in and out of their classrooms during the school year keep up with their classmates who are present and learning every day.

Multiple risk factors. A 2008 report found that children in families with multiple risk factors, such as poverty or having a teenage mother, are more likely to have high absenteeism during their early school years than children without those risk factors. At any grade, children experiencing any risk factor were more often chronic absentees—missing 10 percent of more of the school year—than children without these family risk factors. Frequently absent children fall further behind their peers in learning. The report also noted that children in poor health or who are members of ethnic or racial minorities were more likely than others to be exposed to "cumulative risk."[38]

Of course, these are generalities, not perfectly correlated with social class, and not true for all individuals. Every social group has its high and low achievers. In addition, overlaps certainly exist between lower- and middle-class children's average characteristics. Nonetheless, parenting and lifestyle differences between social classes do have a meaningful effect on students' achievement.[39]

These achievement gap differences by social class are not uniquely an American phenomenon. They can be found in any society where the occupational structure requires vastly different skills and work habits for employees in different strata. Such patterns are likely to influence how children learn, at what rate they learn, and which instructional approaches will be most effective in schools.[40]

Influence of Social Class and Ethnicity

The close relationship between social class, race, and ethnicity and school achievement leads researchers to ask: Which factor affects students' academic achievement more—the student's racial/ethnic background or the student's low socioeconomic status? The answer: Low SES has the most impact.

Social class accounts for much of the variation in educational achievement observed in terms of race and ethnicity. If one knows the student group's social class, one can accurately predict whether their achievement, ability scores, and college attendance rates will be high or low. Knowing students' racial or ethnic group, in contrast, does relatively little to improve this prediction. What is more, working-class white students as a group rate low in achievement and college attainment. Middle-class students, by comparison, rank relatively high on these variables.[41] Clearly, family income and parents' education level are the most influential social class predictors.

---

[37] Kerbow, D. (1996). Patterns of urban student mobility and local school reform. *Journal of Education for Students Placed at Risk, 1*(2), 147–169; Bruno, J., & Isken, J. A. (1996). Inter- and intraschool site student transiency: Practical and theoretical implications for instructional continuity at inner-city schools. *Journal of Research and Development in Education, 29*(4), 239–252.

[38] Family risk factors seen contributing to chronic absence. (2008, March 5). *Education Week, 27*(26), 10. The full report, *The Influence of Maternal and Family Risk on Chronic Absenteeism in Early Schooling,* is available online at www.nccp.org.

[39] On average, low-income students' achievement is below middle-class students' achievement. Nonetheless, some middle-class students achieve below typical low-income levels and some low-income students achieve above typical middle-class levels.

[40] Rothstein, 2004, *Class and schools.*

[41] McCallum, I., & Demie, F. (2001, Summer). Social class, ethnicity, and educational performance. *Educational Research, 43*(2), 147–159; Woessmann, L. (2004, March). *How equal are educational opportunities? Family background and student achievement in Europe and the U.S.* Paper prepared for the Harvard University conference on "50 Years After *Brown.*" Retrieved October 16, 2009, from http://www.ksg.harvard.edu/pepg/PDF/events/Munich/PEPG-04-15Woessman.pdf.

Segregation and Education

Although the landmark 1954 *Brown v. Board of Education* decision ruled against the "separate but equal" education of poor and minority students, courts in the 1990s began releasing school districts from 1970s desegregation orders. Today, segregation (and resegregation) is widespread and increasing, and court-ordered desegregation may soon be a memory.

Housing Patterns and Segregated Schools

Racially segregated housing has severely hampered school districts' ability to integrate their schools. Neighborhood schools, therefore, tend to teach very different student populations.[42]

Some argue that pursuing integration has led to residential segregation. As governmental agencies have sought to integrate schools, white families appear to have increasingly moved to districts with small African American populations.[43] One 30-year study traced the residential movements of African Americans and whites in urban and suburban communities from the 1960s onward and found that growth of the suburbs had increased the racial and economic isolation of central-city African Americans.[44] While the suburbs are more integrated than urban centers, segregated housing patterns often persist within the suburbs.[45] Accordingly, housing patterns make it more difficult to provide racially integrated schools.

Apart from housing, school districts sometimes find ingenious ways to promote policies and practices that create segregated schools. They manipulate school attendance zones, establish school sites in predominantly minority or white neighborhoods, and develop neighborhood school policies. All of these practices serve to create racially and ethnically segregated schools—and courts have found such discriminatory practices unlawful.[46]

U.S. Supreme Court and Recent Desegregation Orders

Over the past 20 years, courts have begun **vacating** (that is, annulling or voiding) their own desegregation orders, allowing schools to resegregate. Courts are declaring many school districts to be **unitary**, which means that they have, in theory, removed all vestiges of segregation from their school systems.[47] In accordance with this trend, the percentage of African American children attending schools that are mostly minority increased from 66 percent in 1991 to 73 percent in 2003.[48]

A series of 1990s U.S. Supreme Court decisions concerning Oklahoma City, Oklahoma; DeKalb County, Georgia; and Kansas City, Missouri, made clear that court-ordered racial desegregation was a temporary remedy for past discrimination

---

[42] Rivkin, S. G., & Welch, F. (2006). Neighborhood segregation and school integration. In E. A. Hanushek & F. Welch (Eds.), *Handbook of the economics of education.* (pp. 1019–1049). Amsterdam, The Netherlands: Elsevier.

[43] Rivkin, S. G. (1994). Residential segregation and school integration. *Sociology of Education, 67,* 279–292; Welch, F., Light, A., Dong, F., & Ross, M. (1987), *New evidence on school desegregation.* Los Angeles: Unicorn Research Association.

[44] Massey, D., & Denton, N. (1993). *American apartheid: Segregation and the making of the underclass.* Cambridge, MA: Harvard University Press.

[45] Rivkin, 1994.

[46] *Milliken v. Bradley* (1974) and *Keyes v. School District No. 1,* Denver (1973).

[47] When courts declare a school district "unitary," it means the district no longer has a dual school system. A school district does not achieve "unitary status," however, until it proves that its past discrimination has been removed and shows no discriminatory practices in student assignment, faculty, staff, transportation, extracurricular activities, and facilities. See *Green v. County School Board of New Kent County* (1968).

[48] Marcus, R. (2006, November 29). A slide toward segregation. *The Washington Post,* p. A23. Retrieved October 16, 2009, from http://www.washingtonpost.com/wp-dyn/content/article/2006/11/28/AR2006112801275_pf.html.

rather than a long-term strategy to promote equal opportunity.[49] In the Court's eyes, schools that lawfully complied with a court order to desegregate for a number of years had successfully made up for their long history of "separate but unequal" violations, even if they had not accomplished their long-term goals.[50] Under the Court's ruling, those localities were allowed to return to neighborhood schools, even if that meant many schools became resegregated.

In 2006, parents in Louisville, Kentucky, and Seattle, Washington, challenged their school districts' voluntary policies, which used students' race to help determine where children attend school.[51] In both cities, school planners were reassigning students from neighborhood schools to new ones based on racial composition to achieve racial balance. In a 2007 divided 5–4 decision, the U.S. Supreme Court ruled that school boards could not use a pupil's race in school assignment formulas.[52]

Chief Justice John Roberts argued, "The way to stop discrimination on the basis of race is to stop discrimination on the basis of race." He continued that any policy that requires sorting individuals into racial categories reinforces the notion that "race" is real, even though scientists tell us there is no such thing.[53] Clearly, school diversity remains a complex and challenging issue for courts as well as schools.

Segregated Schools and Students Academic Achievement

Overwhelmingly, the data show that attending predominantly minority schools harms students' academic achievement. In a 2006 study, economists Eric Hanushek of Stanford University's Hoover Institution and Steven Rivkin of Amherst College found that African American children are likely to attend schools that are more racially isolated, have more inexperienced teachers, and have higher student mobility rates than the schools that white children attend. African American students' achievement suffers as a result.[54] Hanushek and Rivkin concluded that the higher the schools' concentration of African American students, the more rapidly the "black—white achievement gaps" grow.

New research suggests that the brightest African American children may be the ones who lose the most ground academically in U.S. public schools. African American children tend to be taught in predominantly African American schools where test scores are lower on average and high-achieving peers are harder to find. In such settings, teachers aim instruction to the middle of the class, providing high-achieving students with fewer cognitively stimulating opportunities than they would receive in classrooms with a higher "middle."[55]

Other factors also contribute to poorer achievement for students in segregated school. Specifically, high-poverty schools are less likely to offer college-preparatory classes, have higher rates of teachers teaching out of their subject areas (before NCLB required "highly qualified" teachers in all core subjects), experience greater teacher

---

[49] *Dowell v. Oklahoma City* (1991); *Freeman v. Pitts* (1992), and *Missouri v. Jenkins* (1995).

[50] *Missouri v. Jenkins* (1995).

[51] Parents Involved in Community Schools v. Seattle School District and *Meredith v. Jefferson* County Board of Education.

[52] Greenhouse, L. (2007, July 1). In steps big and small, Supreme Court moved right. *The New York Times, 156*(53,992), 1, 18; Bravin, J. (2007, July 2). Court under Roberts limits judicial power. *The Wall Street Journal, 250*(1), A1, A12; *Parents Involved in Community Schools v. Seattle School District No. 1* and *Meredith v. Jefferson County Board of Education*, 555 U.S. (2007); Walsh, M. (2007, October 31). Use of race a concern for magnet schools. *Education Week, 27*(1), 8; Sacks, P. (2007, September 12). It's time to confront the class divide in American schools. *Education Week, 27*(3), 25.

[53] Burkholder, Z. (2007, October 24). Because race can't be ignored: Commentary. *Education Week, 27*(9), 29.

[54] Viadero, November 15, 2006, p. 16.

[55] Harris, D. (2006, November 24). Lost learning, forgotten promises: A national analysis of school racial segregation, student achievement, and "controlled choice" plans. Center for American Progress. Retrieved October 16, 2009, from http://www.americanprogress.org/issues/2006/11/lostlearning.html; Viadero, D. (2008, April 16). Black—white gap widens faster for high achievers. *Education Week, 27*(33), 1, 13.

turnover, have lower test scores, have less involved parents, and place less pressure on administrators to fire or transfer bad teachers.[56]

Clearly, economic segregation contributes to low achievement. Low-income children achieve less as the proportion of low-income children in their schools increases. The achievement drop is most severe when the subsidized-lunch population exceeds 40 percent.[57] Although there is no clear "tipping point" where student achievement falls once a school's poverty concentration passes a certain level, as the schools' proportion of students receiving free and reduced-price lunches exceeds 40 percent, the achievement decline grows steeper.[58]

Integrated Schools and Student Academic Achievement

On the flip side, minority students learn more in integrated schools. The 1966 Coleman study noted that African American students who attended predominately white northern schools during the late 1960s and early 1970s scored higher on standardized tests than did African American students who attended all–African American northern schools.[59] It seems clear that ambition and expectations for academic success among classmates positively influences peers to excel. Other studies have often reconfirmed these findings.[60]

Research has also identified evidence that racial integration helps minority students reach higher academic achievement and attain better long-term outcomes such as high school completion, college attendance and completion, employment, and lower rates of delinquency and teenage childbearing.[61]

Attending integrated schools increases students' opportunities to expand and build friendships with a variety of classmates who may view the world differently than they do. Having higher-achieving peers is positively associated with African Americans' and Latinos' learning gains. More peers with high achievement and higher aspirations tend to enroll in schools with lower percentages of minority students—that is, in integrated schools. In these ways, integrated schools benefit minority students.[62]

Segregation by Race, Class, and Income

Minority students often come from low-income, working-class families. The Harvard Civil Rights Project noted that segregation by race is very strongly related to segregation by class and income. Almost nine-tenths of segregated African American and Latino schools experience concentrated poverty. The average African American or Latino student attends a school with more than twice as many poor classmates than the average white student. Poverty levels are strongly related to school test score averages and many kinds of educational inequality. Because poverty and racial minority often occur together, it is poverty's influence on learning that largely affects minority students' achievement.

[56] Kahlenberg, R. D. (2001). *All together now: Creating middle class schools through public school choice*. Washington, DC: Brookings Institution Press.

[57] Lippman, L., Burns, S., & McArthur, E. (1996). *Urban schools: The challenge of location and poverty* (NCES 96–184). Washington, DC: U.S. Department of Education, Office of Educational Research and Improvement; Kahlenberg, 2001.

[58] Rothstein, 2004, *Class and schools,* p. 171.

[59] Ferguson, R. F., and Mehta, J. (2004, May). An unfinished journey: The legacy of Brown and the narrowing of the achievement gap. *Phi Delta Kappan 85* (9): 656 – 669.

[60] Crane, J. (1991). Effects of neighborhoods on dropping out of school and teenage childbearing. In C. Jencks & P. E. Peterson (Eds.), *The urban underclass.* (pp. 299-320). Washington, DC: Brookings Institution; Hanushek, E. A., Kain, J. F., & Rivkin, S. G. (2004). *New evidence about* Brown v. Board of Education: *The complex effects of school racial composition on achievement.* Revised draft, February 2004; paper presented at the Brookings Conference on Empirics of Social Interactions, January 2004.

[61] Hanushek & Rivkin, 2006; Mayer, S. E. (1991). How much does a high school's racial and socioeconomic mix affect graduation and teenage fertility rates? In C. Jencks & P. E. Peterson (Eds.), *The urban underclass* (pp. 187–222). Washington, DC: Brookings Institution Press.

[62] Harris, 2006, p. 18.

"The strong relationship between poverty, race and educational achievement and graduation rates shows that, but for a few exceptional cases under extraordinary circumstances, schools that are separate are still unquestionably unequal," write Professor Gary Orfield and Research Associate Chungmei Lee of the Civil Rights Project, Harvard University. "Segregation is an old issue but one that is deeply rooted and difficult to resolve and extremely dangerous to ignore."[63]

As the Civil Rights Project's Orfield and Lee observe, "Concentrated poverty is shorthand for a constellation of inequalities that shape schooling."[64] This syndrome of inequalities is so profound that a compelling relationship exists between a school's poverty level and its achievement test scores, independent of other factors.[65]

School Practices that Limit Opportunities for Equal Education

While societal factors such as social class, parenting practices, family income, housing patterns, and segregated schools affect students' preparation for learning and their eventual achievement in school, school practices pertaining to diverse students can also influence whether their opportunities are truly equal. Teacher expectations, tracking and ability grouping, curriculum selection, disciplinary practices, school climate, and quality of teachers all have tremendous impact on students and their future educational, employment, social, and lifestyle opportunities.

Teacher Expectations

Teachers' expectations about which students are likely or unlikely to succeed in school significantly influence how they teach diverse children. Research supports this theory.

Hawthorne study. The classic Hawthorne study illustrates how expectation affects performance. From 1927 to 1932, researchers at Western Electric's Hawthorne Plant in Cicero, Illinois, examined the workplace's physical and environmental influences (such as brightness of lights and humidity) and its psychological aspects (such as work breaks, group pressure, working hours, and managerial leadership). No matter which experimental manipulation was used, the workers' production improved. Researchers concluded that the workers enjoyed receiving the researchers' attention, also known as the "novelty effect."[66] Their conclusions have implications for educators:

- Individuals' aptitudes are imperfect predictors of job performance.
- The workplace is a social system made up of interdependent parts.
- Social factors strongly influence the amount produced, whereas workers' physical and mental factors address only their potential productivity.
- Informal organization affects productivity. Workers have a group life that can encourage or discourage productivity.
- Supervisors' relationships with workers tend to influence the way the workers carry out directives.
- Workgroup norms affect productivity. The group arrives at norms of what they consider "a fair day's work."

---

[63] Orfield, G & Lee, C (2006, January). Racial transformation and the changing nature of segregation. Cambridge, MA: Civil Rights Project, Harvard University. p. 4. Retrieved April 23, 2009 from: http://www.eric.ed.gov/ERICDocs/data/ericdocs2sql/content_storage_01/000019b/80/3d/42/4d.pdf.
[64] Orfield & Lee, 2006, p. 29.
[65] Rothstein, 2004, *Class and schools.*
[66] This phenomenon of improved performance without obvious intervention is now also known as the "Hawthorne effect" in honor of the initial Hawthorne studies.

Transferred into the school setting, the Hawthorne study suggests that teachers' expectations can greatly influence students' performance. Students' aptitudes are less important than their motivation to work in predicting their academic achievement. The classroom is a powerful social network, and students' feelings about both their teachers and their classmates have important implications for how much they are willing to work and succeed at learning.

Pygmalion in the classroom. Another classic study of teacher expectations was the subject of the book titled *Pygmalion in the Classroom.*[67] In 1965, Robert Rosenthal and Lenore Jacobson, a Harvard University professor and an elementary principal, respectively, told elementary school teachers that based on their students' standardized test scores, certain children were "late bloomers" and could be expected to be "growth spurters." In truth, the test did not exist, and children designated as "spurters" were chosen randomly. Rosenthal and Jacobson hoped this experiment would determine the degree (if any) to which changes in teacher expectations can produce changes in student achievement. In the end, the researchers found that when teachers expect students to do well, students tend to do well; when teachers expect students to fail, they tend to fail.[68]

Oakes' study on teacher expectations for students' futures. Jeannie Oakes, a University of California at Los Angeles education professor, found evidence suggesting that teachers (consciously or unconsciously) treat bright students as future peers and less bright students as future subordinates.[69] When asked to list the five most important lessons to be learned by high school students, the list for the bright students differed markedly from the list for the rest of the student population. Teachers hoped the brightest would learn to think logically and critically (important skills for future leaders). Meanwhile, they hoped that the less bright would learn good work habits, respect for authority, and practical or work-related skills (all important attributes for future subordinates).

Coleman study. Teacher expectations for students' achievement may have played a large role in the landmark Coleman Study. Coleman's teacher survey data suggested that achievement gaps in the same school between African American and white students were higher where most of the teachers had expressed preference for teaching college-oriented children of white-collar professionals.[70] They expected less achievement from their minority and poor students, and—in a self-fulfilling prophecy—they got it.

Preparation to Teach Diverse Students

In a 2007 survey conducted by the National Comprehensive Center for Teaching Quality and Public Agenda, most first-year teachers reported they were not well prepared to deal with the ethnic and racial diversity and special learning needs of children in their classrooms.[71] Although 76 percent of first-year teachers had received instruction in teaching ethnically diverse students, only 39 percent said that the training actually prepared them for what they would find in their classrooms. What

---

[67] Rosenthal, R., & Jacobson, L. (1968). Pygmalion in the classroom: Teachers' expectations and pupils' intellectual development. New York: Rineholt and Winston.
[68] Rosenthal & Jacobson, 1968.
[69] Oakes, J. (1985). *Keeping track: How schools structure inequality*. New Haven, CT: Yale University Press.
[70] Viadero, D. (2006, June 21). Fresh look at Coleman data yields different conclusions. *Education Week*, 25(41), 21.
[71] Rochkind, J., Ott, A., Immerwahr, J., Doble, J., & Johnson, J. (2008). *Lessons learned: New teachers talk about the jobs, challenges, and long range plans. Issue no. 3: Teaching in changing times*. Washington, DC: National Comprehensive Center for Teacher Quality and Public Agenda, pp. 7–14. Retrieved October 16, 2009, from http://www.publicagenda.org/files/pdf/lessons_learned_3.pdf.

is more, new teachers in high-need, low-income urban schools (47 percent) were actually less likely to complain about inadequate diversity preparation than those (32 percent) working in affluent communities.[72] Findings suggest that teachers headed for suburban schools are not well prepared for the diversity they will find.

This level of discomfort is not surprising. The teacher work force demographics do not match those of the students we teach. According to a 2005 National Center for Education Statistics (NCES) report, the teaching profession is approximately 75 percent female and 25 percent male.[73] Racially, the teaching force is even less diverse. Only ten percent of secondary teachers, 14 percent of K–6 teachers, 16 percent of principals, and 4 percent of superintendents are members of minority groups.[74]

Students bring to the schools an extensive range of languages, cultures, exceptionalities, talents, intelligence, and other factors that require an equally broad and varied teaching repertoire. When teachers do not receive professional education—either preservice or in-service—on how to most effectively educate diverse students, these educators are more likely to fall back on their own naive assumptions and their cultural norms to develop expectations for student achievement.

Tracking, Ability Grouping, and Restricted Curricula

Since the 1920s, most schools enrolling adolescents have offered a "tracked" curriculum—a sequence of academic classes that range from slow-paced remedial courses to rigorous academic ones with an array of electives, exploratory, vocational, and physical education classes. **Curriculum tracking** involves providing differential content and instruction for students based on various measures of intelligence and skill. This practice has been shown to have negative consequences for the future educational opportunities and schooling outcomes of children placed in the lower tracks, and especially for low-income, African American, and Latino children.[75]

Tracking. **Tracking** can be defined as sorting students into homogeneous groups according to their perceived abilities, past academic achievements, presumed educational needs, and expected vocational directions. Tracks can be identified by ability (high, average, or low) or by the kind of educational preparation they provide (academic, general, vocational). This process provides the basis for organizing schools.

Tracking differs from ability grouping in important ways. While almost all tracking is a form of ability grouping, not all ability grouping results in tracking. Generally speaking, tracking is rigidly determined. Once placed into a "track," the student tends to stay in it. In contrast, **ability grouping**, which also separates students into homogeneous groups according to perceived abilities, past academic achievements, and presumed educational needs, tends to be more flexible and related to the purpose of study. Students can change ability groups for different subjects or learning purposes by the day, week, or project.

How tracking affects students. Tracking limits students' access to quality curriculum, teachers, and learning experiences. Students' tracks propel them through the curriculum at different speeds. As a result, lower-track students fall further

---

[72] Rochkind et al., 2008.

[73] NCES Report, *Special Analysis 2005: Mobility in the Teacher Workforce*. Washington, D.C.: National Center for Education Statistics, U.S. Department of Education. Retrieved October 1, 2009 fromL http://nces.ed.gov/programs/coe/2005/analysis/index.asp

[74] Hodgkinson, H. (2006) *The whole child in a fractured world*. Alexandria, VA: Association for Supervision and Curriculum Development, p. 2

[75] Orfield, G., & Ashkinaze, C. (1991). *The closing door: Conservative policy and black opportunity*. Chicago, IL: University of Chicago Press; Fine, M. (1991). *Framing dropouts: Notes on the politics of an urban public high school*. Albany, NY: State University of New York Press.

behind and receive an increasingly different curriculum. They receive an education of less depth and less breadth, and they miss learning the prerequisites for more advanced classes. Students tend to stay in the track where they are placed. The weakest students in the lower tracks are essentially locked out of meaningful opportunities for high-level learning and become mostly likely to drop out of school.[76]

For example, high school students typically follow separate academic and vocational curriculum tracks intended to take them to different postsecondary destinations, either college or immediate work. The highest-achieving students go into the college preparatory, highly academic track. International Baccalaureate, Advanced Placement, or Honors students receive a rigorous math, science, English, social studies, and foreign language curriculum to prepare them for competitive college admissions. The lowest-achieving students are placed into the lowest track. Their curriculum tends to consist of remedial, repetitive, and less rigorous versions of academic subjects along with vocational training.

Tracking limits students' access to well-prepared, experienced teachers. In general, high-track teachers tend to be better qualified and more experienced.[77] Conversely, the least well-prepared, less experienced teachers usually find themselves teaching the low-track classes. The skills of teachers assigned to low-track classes appear to diminish over time, providing low-track students with lesser-quality instruction.[78]

Tracking limits students' access to quality learning experiences. Teachers tend to establish positive relationships with high-track students, whereas teachers in low-track classes focus more attention on classroom control.[79] Teachers in high-track classes are knowledgeable, more enthusiastic, and less critical. Their classrooms show greater variety in learning activities, better organization, higher interest, active student involvement, and more educational resources compared to low-track classrooms.[80]

Given the different achievement expectations that accompany tracking, low-track classes are typically "characterized by dull, passive instruction, consisting largely of drill and practice with trivial bits of information."[81] Students spend more time on routines and seatwork. Adam Gamoran, Professor of Sociology and Education Policy Studies at the University of Wisconsin–Madison, found that 25 percent of tracking-related learning differences were due to differences in curriculum and instruction.[82] In these ways, tracking produces a consistent pattern of academic disadvantage among low-track students.

Research Findings

Studies of how tracking and ability groupings affect achievement are one educational research's oldest traditions, in part because this area is characterized by considerable disagreement. The results are consistent but contradictory, depending on the study's methodology.

---

[76] Children's Defense Fund. (1988, January). *Making the middle grades work.* Washington, DC: Adolescent Pregnancy Prevention Clearinghouse.

[77] Oakes, J., Ormseth, T., Bell, R., & Camp, P. (1990). *Multiplying inequalities: The effects of race, social class, and tracking on opportunities to learn mathematics and science.* Washington, DC: National Science Foundation.

[78] Finley, M. K. (1984). Teachers and tracking in a comprehensive high school. *Sociology of Education, 57,* 233–243.

[79] Oakes, 1985.

[80] Brewer, D. J., Rees, D. I., & Argys, L. M. (1995 November). Detracking America's schools: The reform without cost? *Phi Delta Kappan, 77*(3), 210–215.

[81] Oakes, J. (1992, May). Can tracking research inform practice? Technical, normative, and political considerations. *Educational Researcher, 21*(4), 12–21.

[82] Gamoran, A. (1990). *The effects of track-related instructional differences for student achievement.* Paper presented at the Annual Meeting of the American Educational Research Association, Boston.

Tracking's impact on minority and low-income students. The research here is consistent. Tracking disproportionately excludes low-income African American and Latino students from opportunities to learn in high-track classes.[83] One study found that whites were six times more likely to be overrepresented in high-track classes while minorities were seven times more likely to be overrepresented in low-track classes.[84] In senior high schools, low-income, African American, and Latino students were underrepresented in college preparatory classes. More frequently, they were enrolled in vocational programs that train students to enter the lowest-level occupations. At all levels, minority and low-income groups were underrepresented in programs for gifted and talented students.[85]

On the other hand, studies have clearly demonstrated a positive relationship between de-tracking and the number of minority students, students who receive free or reduced-price lunches, and special education students who achieve a Regents (high status) diploma.[86] As a method of organizing students for instruction, tracking is neither equitable nor effective.

Tracking and achievement. Although students perpetually tracked into low-ability groups lose ground academically over the years, those kept in high-ability groups with an accelerated curriculum make learning and achievement gains.[87] Specifically, academically gifted students gain from being placed into fast-paced, high-ability groups.[88] Researchers suggest that these benefits result from the enhanced instructional and learning opportunities in these high-track classes rather than from their homogeneity.[89] In short, tracking hurts low-ability students but benefits highest-ability students.

Tracking and peer groups and attitudes. Over time, tracking fosters friendship networks linked to student group memberships.[90] Academically separating peer groups may lead to polarized attitudes among secondary students. High-track students tend to become more enthusiastic about school and more self-confident

---

[83] Heubert, J. P., & Hauser, R. M. (Eds.). (1999). *High stakes: Testing for tracking, promotion, and graduation.* Washington, DC: National Academy Press; Oakes, 1992.

[84] Oakes, J. (1990). *Multiplying inequalities: The effects of race, social class, and ability grouping on opportunities to learn math and science.* Santa Monica, CA: Rand.

[85] Oakes, 1992.

[86] Burris, C. C., & Welner, K. G. (2005). Closing the achievement gap by detracking. *Phi Delta Kappan, 86*(8), 594–598; Burris, C. C., Welner. K. G., & Murphy, J. (2008). Accountability, rigor and detracking: Achievement effects of embracing a challenging curriculum as a universal good for all students. *Teachers College Record, 110*(3), 571–608.

[87] Colangelo, N., Assouline, S., & Gross, M. (Eds.). (2004). *A nation deceived: How schools hold back America's brightest students.* Iowa City, IA: Belin Blank Center Gifted Education and Talent Development; Gagné, F., & Gagnier, N. (2004). The socio-affective and academic impact of early entrance to school. *Roeper Review, 26,* 128–139; Gamoran, A., & Mare, R. G. (1989, March). Secondary school tracking and educational inequality: Compensation, reinforcement, or neutrality? *American Journal of Sociology, 94,* 1146–1183; Goldring, E. B. (1990). Assessing the status of information on classroom organizational frameworks for gifted students. *Journal of Educational Research, 83,* 313–326; Hoffer, T. B. (1992, Fall). Middle school ability grouping and student achievement in science and mathematics *Educational Evaluation and Policy Analysis, 14* (3), 207–227; Kulik, J. A., & Kulik, C. L. C. (1992). Meta-analytic findings on grouping programs. *Gifted Child Quarterly, 36,* 73–77; Lubinski, D. (2004). Long-term effects of educational acceleration. In N. Colangelo, S. Assouline, & M. Gross (Eds.), *A nation deceived: How schools hold back America's brightest students* (pp. 23–37). Iowa City, IA: Belin Blank Center Gifted Education and Talent Development; Lubinski, D., Webb, R. M., Morelock, M. J., & Benbow, C. P. (2001). Top 1 in 10,000: A 10-year follow-up of the profoundly gifted. *Journal of Applied Psychology, 86,* 718–729; Rogers, K. (2004). The academic effects of acceleration. In N. Colangelo, S. Assouline, & M. Gross (Eds.), *A nation deceived: How schools hold back America's brightest students* (pp. 47–57). Iowa City, IA: Belin Blank Center Gifted Education and Talent Development; Slavin, R. E. (1990). *Achievement effects of ability grouping in secondary schools: A best evidence synthesis.* Madison, WI: Wisconsin Center for Educational Research.

[88] Gallagher, J. J. (1995, November). Comments on "The reform without cost?" *Phi Delta Kappan, 77*(3), 216–219.

[89] Oakes, 1992; Jaeger, R. M., & Hattie, J. A. (1995 November). Detracking America's schools. *Phi Delta Kappan, 77*(3), 218–219.

[90] Hallinan, M., & Williams, R. (1989). Interracial friendship choices in secondary school. *American Sociological Review, 54,* 67–78.

about their futures. Low-track students become more alienated.[91] These feelings foster significant differences in classroom climate.[92]

Tracking influences students' attainment and life chances in ways beyond their academic achievement. Track placements are quite stable, reflecting years of differentiated education. Students' early assignment affects their later course experiences. By high school, college-track students have better prospects for college attendance, school grades, and future high status occupations with financial and social rewards than their comparable non-college-track peers.[93]

Conclusions. The research shows that tracking harms low-tracked students by identifying students through questionable means and then rigidly keeping them in low-level courses with unmotivating curriculum and instructional techniques. This practice guarantees that these students will not learn what they need to learn to exit from the school system as educated individuals. It also reflects ingrained societal attitudes and beliefs about certain students that allow educators to have low expectations for their progress.

The Rationale Behind Tracking

If research confirms that tracking hurts low-track students' academic achievement and life options, one must wonder why schools continued the practice for so many years. Tracking continues because it reflects our society's cultural norms, accommodates integration requirements, reflects community "politics" and educators' mistaken ideas about intelligence, and makes fewer instructional demands on teachers.

Cultural norms. Tracking reflects widespread cultural assumptions and institutional norms about students' capacities, individual and group differences, and the school's role in addressing them.[94] One norm is that students' needs and capacities vary enormously, and ability grouping and tracking meet students' needs by placing individuals into learning situations appropriate to their intellectual capacities.[95]

Another norm is that each student generation has an ability distribution that roughly reproduces the skilled hierarchy found in a socially and economically diverse work force. According to this perspective, those students who are planning to immediately enter the labor force after high school graduation do not need the knowledge, reasoning, and communication skills essential for those individuals who are headed to college and the professions. Given this norm, tracking appears to the "logical" solution.[96]

Integration. In the early twentieth century, when schools began to educate immigrants' and working-class families' children, tracking was seen as the way to both accommodate the needs of these supposedly "lesser-ability" new students and still maintain the schools' role preparing middle and upper class college-bound students.[97]

---

[91] Oakes, J., Gamoran, A., & Page, R. N. (1992). Curriculum differentiation: Opportunities, outcomes, and meanings. In P. W. Jackson (Ed.), *Handbook of research on curriculum*. (pp. 570-608). New York: Macmillan; Oakes, 1985.

[92] Smith-Maddox, R., & Wheelock, A. (1995, November). Untracking and students' futures. *Phi Delta Kappan, 77*(3), 222–228.

[93] Gamoran et al., 1991; Vanfossen, B., Jones, J., & Spade, J. (1987). Curriculum tracking and status maintenance. *Sociology of Education, 60*, 104–122; Wolfe, L. (1985). Postsecondary educational attainment among whites and blacks. *American Educational Research Journal, 22*, 501–525.

[94] Oakes, J. (2005). *Keeping track: How schools structure inequality* (2nd ed.). New Haven, CT: Yale University Press; Oakes, J., Lipton, M. (1992, February). Detracking schools: Early lessons from the field. *Phi Delta Kappan, 73*(6), 448–454.

[95] Oakes, 2005; Oakes & Lipton, 1992.

[96] Oakes & Lipton, 1992.

[97] Oakes, J., & Lipton, M. (1999). Access to knowledge: Challenging the techniques, norms, and politics of schooling. In K. Sirotnik & (pp 131–150). R. Soder (Eds.), *To the beat of a different drummer: Essays on educational renewal in honor of John Goodlad*. (pp. 131–150). New York: Peter Lang.

In a similar vein, Ronald Ferguson, a Harvard University lecturer and researcher, suggests that schools have used tracking to accommodate integration requirements. He suggests that when poor and minority children enter a school with systematically different preparation and identity from those children the school usually serves, instructional quality, tracking, and ability grouping may be the school's way of providing an appropriate education for these newcomers.[98] Consequently, he concludes, "tracking and ability grouping are leading 'suspects' for why integration has not provided greater benefits for minority children."[99]

Tracking and politics. Tracking has a strong political component. Tracking brings labels and differences in status, expectations, and consequences for students' academic and occupational attainment into public view. For example, parents of students identified as gifted often exercise political clout, threatening "bright flight" or "white flight" to block attempts to remove tracking.[100] Professional parents who understand the benefits of high-track classes are highly successful at "working the system" to ensure that their children are placed in the top-track classes.[101] In this way, tracking becomes part of the students' and groups' struggle for comparative advantages as each party tries to corral socially valued school resources, opportunities, and credentials.

Tracking and teaching. Many people support tracking because they believe that it makes fewer demands on teachers. Tracking proponents assert that when teachers have a heterogeneous group of students, they must "teach to the middle," thereby hindering learning for students at the extremes—that is, struggling students and high achievers. These advocates do not consider that new research on constructivism and differentiated instruction which demonstrates that with planning and forethought, all learners' needs can be met in mixed-group classes.[102]

Rethinking Tracking

Relying on societal norms and other misconceptions, teachers see tracking as a logical practice. If teachers believe that if students' capacity to learn is unchangeable, and if the range in students' ability is very large, tracking appears sensible. Schools want to provide curriculum appropriate to students' abilities, so they separate students by ability and adapt curriculum and instruction accordingly. The fact that learning capacity seems to be unevenly distributed among groups—with low-income and minority group members showing less capacity to learn—appears beyond the schools' control.[103]

Undoing tracking in public schools involves a critical and unsettling rethinking of fundamental educational norms and cultural assumptions about who should and can achieve. In recent years, policy makers and educators have tried to end tracking. The National Governors' Association, the Carnegie Corporation, the College Board, and the National Association of Secondary School Principals, among others, all endorse de-tracking, identifying it as a barrier to many students' learning and path to college. Research findings from the American College Testing (ACT) program, which indicate that the reading and math skills needed for workplace success are comparable to those needed for success in the first

---

[98] Ferguson, R. F., & Mehta, J. (2004, May). An unfinished journey: The legacy of *Brown* and the narrowing of the achievement gap. *Phi Delta Kappan, 85*(9), 663.
[99] Ferguson & Mehta, 2004.
[100] Oakes, 2005.
[101] Unseem, E. L. (1992). Getting on the fast track in mathematics: School organizational influences on math track assignments. *American Journal of Education, 100*, 325–353.
[102] We will discuss constructivism more deeply in Chapter 15.
[103] Oakes & Lipton, 1999, p. 449.

year of college, supports these actions.[104] All students need the foundation of academic competencies necessary to learn additional skills as their jobs evolve or as they change positions throughout their careers—no matter which path they choose after graduation.

Implementing tracking reforms will require that competing interest groups create a collective advocacy for schools that serve all children well. It requires confronting likely opposition to a system that takes away comparative advantages enjoyed and effectively used by children whose parents are privileged by race and class. It means preparing teachers to work effectively with diverse students in a high-challenge curriculum. Confronting these issues is both an instructional and a political process that requires keen and sensitive leadership by educators.

Lower Teacher Quality and Equal Opportunity

Apart from tracking practices, research supports the idea that poor and minority students do not get their fair share of more experienced and capable teachers.[105]

Until 2002's No Child Left Behind law required teachers to have bachelor's degrees in the subjects they were teaching, poor and minority students were more likely to have "out-of-field" teachers—that is, teachers without majors or minors in the subjects they taught—than were students in low-poverty schools. In high-poverty secondary schools, for example, students were likely to have one in three teachers of a core subject without a major or minor degree in that subject as compared with students in a low-poverty school, who had a one in five chance of working with an unqualified teacher. Likewise, nearly half of the math classes in both high-poverty and high-minority high schools were taught by teachers who did not have a college major or minor in math or a math-related field, such as math education, physics, or engineering.[106]

Today, the situation remains difficult. Based on 2003–2004 data, researchers report that children in high-poverty schools are about twice as likely as those in more affluent schools to be taught by teachers who hold neither certification nor academic majors in their fields.[107]

Research consistently affirms the relationship between teacher quality factors and student achievement. Briefly, these "quality" factors include teachers' academic skills and knowledge (especially their vocabulary), their mastery of the content they teach, their experience on the job (especially after the second year), their teaching effectiveness (pedagogy), and the interaction of these factors.[108] Inequitably distributing quality teachers to schools is another way in which school practices poorly serve low-income and minority children.

---

[104] American College Testing. (2006). *Ready for college and ready for work: Same or different?* Iowa City, IA: Author. Retrieved October 16, 2009, from http://www.act.org/research/policymakers/pdf/ReadinessBrief. pdf; Olson, L. (2006, May 10). Skills for work, college readiness are found comparable. *Education Week, 25*(36), 1, 19. "Workplace success" in these studies refers to desirable occupations that pay enough to support a family of four and offer the potential for career advancement but do not require a four-year college degree.

[105] Peske, H. G., & Haycock, K. (2006, June). *Teaching inequality: How poor and minority students are short-changed on teacher quality.* Washington, DC: The Education Trust. Retrieved October 16, 2009, from http://www2.edtrust.org/NR/rdonlyres/010DBD9F-CED8-4D2B-9E0D-91B446746ED3/0/ TQReportJune2006.pdf.

[106] Jerald, C. D. (2002). *All talk, no action: Putting an end to out-of-field teaching.* Washington, D.C.: The Education Trust.

[107] Sawchuk, S. (2008, December 10). Out-of-field teaching more common in poor schools. *Education Week, 28*(15), 6. Out-of-field teaching appears to be most severe in grades 7 to 12.

[108] For more on teacher quality and student achievement, see Chapters 2 and 14, and the following sources: Kaplan, L. S., & Owings, W. A. (2001). *Teacher quality, teaching quality, and school improvement.* Bloomington, IN: Phi Delta Kappa Educational Foundation; Kaplan, L. S., & Owings, W. A. (2003, May). The politics of teacher quality. *Phi Delta Kappan, 84*(9), 687–692.

Retention and Equal Opportunity

Until around 1860, grouping students in grade levels was not common practice in the United States. Soon after the practice became routine, educators noticed that not all students progressed at the same pace. If students could not master the grade's content, they were **retained** or kept in that grade the following school year. Teachers believed that allowing more time to develop adequate academic skills would make students more successful.

By 1954, researchers had found no evidence of educational gain for retained students.[109] Other investigators agreed.[110]

According to the Education Commission of the States, research on retention notes that:

- Minority, male, urban and poor students are disproportionately (two to three times) more likely to be retained.
- Retention greatly increases students' likelihood of eventually dropping out.
- Retention lowers self-esteem and self-confidence.
- Retained students are likely to remain below grade-level proficiency levels.[111]

Studies show that retained students more often have lower SES backgrounds than do non-retained students. The Center for Child and Family Policy at Duke University estimates that as many as 2.4 million children in U.S. schools are retained each year. A disproportionate number of them are male, African American, and poor. The practice continues despite the research affirming its negative effects on children, especially minorities and the impoverished.[112]

Student Disciplinary Practices and Equal Opportunity

While educators view schools' prevailing disciplinary practices as unbiased, race neutral, fair, and objective, research is increasingly finding that disciplinary practices are culturally loaded.[113] Most school district discipline codes leave ample room for "professional judgment," allowing teachers' conscious or unconscious beliefs about their low-income and minority students to influence their discipline decisions.[114] Schools' zero-tolerance policies also demand strict compliance with established rules, without providing any discretion for extenuating or clarifying circumstances.

School discipline policies often inadvertently encourage discrimination. The schools' tendency to interpret all conflict as a threat to the institution's stability encourages educators to oversimplify conflict.[115] Thus teachers and administrators believe that any classroom disruption should be swiftly and efficiently ended. Behaviors that clash with the operating norms are viewed as aberrant and deserving of punishment. In this way, educators fail to notice problems and inequities that their organizations are creating, such as the disproportionately high suspension

---

[109] Goodlad, J. (1954). Some effects of promotion and non-promotion upon the social and personal adjustment of children. *Journal of Experimental Education, 22,* 301–328.

[110] Owings, W., & Magliaro, S. (1998, September). Grade retention: A history of failure. *Educational Leadership, 56,* 86–88.

[111] Retrieved October 16, 2009, from www.ecs.org/html/issue.asp?issueID=94.

[112] Meisels, S. J., & Liaw, F. (1993, November). Failure in grade: Do retained students catch up? *Journal of Educational Research, 87,* 69–77.

[113] Applied Research Center. (2000). *Facing the consequences: An examination of racial discrimination in U.S. public schools.* Oakland, CA: Applied Research Center; Noguera, P. (1997). Reconsidering the crisis confronting California black male youth: Providing support without further marginalization. *Journal of Negro Education, 65*(2), 219–236.

[114] Noguera, 1997.

[115] Larson, C. L., & Ovando, C. J. (2001). *The color of bureaucracy: The politics of equity in multicultural school communities.* Belmont, CA: Cengage Learning, p. 156.

rates of minority students, their overrepresentation in low-track classes, or the relationship between these facts.[116]

Current research finds that African American students are 2.3 times more likely to be suspended than white students.[117] A study of one state's 2006–2007 data found that school-year suspension rates averaged 18 percent in school districts with the poorest students compared to 1 percent in school districts with the wealthiest students. African American and Latino students statewide were suspended at three times the rate of white students that year, with 18 percent, 13 percent, and 4 percent being suspended, respectively.[118]

Data suggest that this cycle of misbehavior, disciplinary action, and removal from the classroom leads to lower achievement and more acting out in school.[119] Research shows that those students who are repeatedly suspended are at risk for less participation in positive extracurricular activities, increased placement in special education programs, and increased truancy.[120] Addressing the disparity in disciplinary practices, therefore, is an essential part of closing the achievement gap. While it is true that students must be held accountable for their behaviors, it is equally true that teachers should be held accountable for their classroom management skills and the learning climate they create for all students.

Disciplinary policies and practices offer a prescribed response to disturbing events, but they do not reveal the problems' causes or contexts, and they do not prevent the incidents from recurring. Looking at isolated incidents does not identify dysfunctional patterns within the system that need correcting.

School Climate and Equal Opportunities

Both academic and disciplinary practices affect school climate. **School climate** refers to the environment in which teachers' and students' behaviors occur within schools. School climate is the school's "feel" at the building and classroom level.[121] Some schools "feel" positive, encouraging, high achieving, and respectful of all its members; others do not.

School climate is a multidimensional construct. Teaching practices, student and faculty diversity, and the relationships among administrators, teachers, parents, and students all contribute to its formation. The number and quality of teacher–student interactions, students' and teachers' perceptions of the school's personality, environmental factors (such as the facility's attractiveness, cleanliness, and state of repair), the academic performance expected and received from all students, the school's size and feeling of safety, and the feelings of trust and respect among students and teachers all come into play. In total or viewed separately, these factors can have a positive influence on the learning environment—or they can create significant barriers to learning.

For example, tracking and retention affect school climate. They have a negative influence on the relationships among different groups within the schools, isolating students along cultural, racial, and economic lines. When the lower tracks

---

[116] Larson & Ovando, 2001.

[117] Hinojosa, M. S. (2008, March). Black–white differences in school suspension: Effect of student beliefs about teachers. *Sociological Spectrum, 28*(2), 175–193.

[118] Cho, J. (2008, August 8). New study: Out of school suspensions often harmful. *TheDay.com.* Retrieved October 16, 2009, from http://www.theday.com/re.aspx?re=5bd2af20-3728-4b50-bd39-161bd3bebd87.

[119] Barton, P. E., Coley, R. J., & Weglinsky, H. (1998, October). *Order in the classroom: Violence, discipline, and student achievement.* Princeton. NJ: Educational Testing Service, Policy Information Center, Policy Information Report; Myers, D. E. (1987, January). Student discipline and high school performance. *Sociology of Education, 60*(1), 18–33.

[120] Civil Rights Project. (2000). *Education denied: The devastating consequences of zero tolerance and school discipline policies.* Cambridge, MA: Harvard University Press.

[121] Although *culture* and *climate* are somewhat interchangeable terms, school climate refers mostly to the school's effects on students, whereas school culture refers more to the shared assumptions, values, and beliefs that influence the way teachers and other staff members work together.

are overwhelmingly populated by low-income and minority students while the upper tracks are predominantly populated with white and middle-class or affluent students, the two student groups do not have opportunities to move beyond stereotypes and get to know one another as persons. Separated daily by high- and low-status courses, teachers' behaviors toward them, and their relative expectations for success, students in the disparate groups tend to make uninformed judgments about one another. As a consequence, distrust and disrespect grow.

Ineffective school practices, antisocial behaviors, and academic failure reinforce one another. A pattern of academic failure provides few opportunities for the student to receive positive reinforcement. Students perceived as being at risk of antisocial conduct, particularly boys and impoverished minority students, "are more likely to be punished, excluded, and controlled than to have their problems addressed in a therapeutic manner."[122] From the failing student's perspective, school becomes a bad, unfair place. This perception increases the students' likelihood of wanting to escape, rebel, act uncooperatively, and display other disruptive actions. The cycle of bad grades and low expectations (perceived as disrespect toward the student) leads to disorderly student behaviors, suspensions, further failure, and eventual dropping out.[123]

When the school's psychosocial climate—in the halls, classroom, cafeteria, gym, and anywhere on campus—becomes negative, it can hinder students' achievement. All students want to feel safe, connected, well liked, competent, and valued. No students want to anxiously sense that they are in danger, whether physically or psychologically. In such conditions, students cannot learn. Further, when they perceive a threat, students react quickly, often disruptively. Fostering student academic achievement and development within a safe learning environment requires establishing and maintaining a school climate that positively meets a diverse student population's needs.

Research on school climate. Research on school climate shows that it can affect many areas and people within the school:

- A positive, supportive, and culturally conscious school climate in high-risk urban environments can significantly shape urban students' degree of academic success.[124]

- Positive school climate perceptions are protective factors for boys and may give high-risk students a supportive learning environment as well as prevent antisocial behaviors.[125]

- Positive interpersonal relationships and optimal learning opportunities for students in all demographic environments can increase achievement levels and reduce maladaptive behaviors.[126]

- Providing a positive and supportive environment for students is important for a smooth transition to a new school.[127]

---

[122] Brookover, W. B., Erickson, F. J., & McEvoy, A. W. (with Beamer, L., Efthim, H., Hathaway, D., Lezotte, L., Miller, S., Passalacqua, J., & Tomatzky, L. (1997). *Creating effective schools: An in-service program for enhancing school learning climate and achievement*. Holmer Beach, FL: Learning Publications.
[123] Barton, Coley, & Weglinsky, 1998, pp. 7–19.
[124] Haynes, N. M., & Comer, J. P. (1993). The Yale School Development Program process, outcomes, and policy considerations. *Urban Education, 28*(2), 166–199.
[125] Haynes, N. M. (1998). Creating safe and caring school communities: Comer School Development Program schools. *Journal of Negro Education, 65*, 308–314; Kuperminc, G. P., Leadbeater, B. J., Emmons, C., & Blatt, S. J. (1997). Perceived school climate and difficulties in the social adjustment of middle school students. *Applied Developmental Science, 1*(2), 76–88.
[126] McEvoy, A., & Welker, R. (2000). Antisocial behavior, academic failure, and school climate: A critical review. *Journal of Emotional and Behavioral Disorders, 8*(3), 130–140.
[127] Freiberg, H. J. (1998). Measuring school climate: Let me count the ways. *Educational Leadership, 56*(1), 22–26.

Figure 11.4	A Safe and Supportive School Climate Fosters Student Learning

Andreanna Seymore/Stone/Getty images

The worse the students believe they are performing in school, the higher the likelihood that they will engage in disruptive behaviors. Conversely, the better students believe they are doing, the lower the likelihood that they will act to disrupt or destroy their learning environment. Family and peer dynamics interact to shape the direction and severity of troublesome conduct.[128] Research supports the general conclusion that the greater the school's academic quality and more positive its emotional climate, the lower the level of school crime and violence.

Activity 11.1

Schools have expectations and engage in practices that sometimes limit low-income and minority students from receiving an equal or equitable education.

A. Separate the class into three groups: teacher expectations, tracking, school climate and student discipline. Have each group prepare and deliver a 5-minute presentation explaining the benefits and failings (inequities) of its topic and describing how it affects student achievement.

B. Discuss how students and teachers respond to one another's expectations with examples from your own observations or experiences.

C. Discuss ways in which teacher, administrator, or counselor expectations had either a positive or negative impact on your own school or life experiences.

---

[128] For more on the research underlying the relationship between academic failure and student misbehaviors, see McEvoy & Welker, 2000.

School Factors that Increase Opportunities for Equal Education

We have discussed a variety of factors that create a negative school climate, which in turn hurts students' achievement and behaviors. Now we will consider some factors that enhance students' opportunities for equal education.

Multicultural Education

Multicultural education encompasses more than just highlighting ethnic foods, holidays, heroes, and customs. Multicultural education is a response to the U.S. cultural pluralism and the absence of minority viewpoints in the public school curriculum and society.

Multicultural education. **Multicultural education** has many definitions. Some see it as the institutionalization of the cultural pluralism concept in the schools.[129] It explicitly promotes the Western values of democracy, freedom, human dignity, equality, and respect for diversity. It uses multiple, nonstereotyped perspectives and voices in primary sources to help all students understand and appreciate human differences and commonalities. It teaches students to recognize power and privilege inequities in society. Multicultural education means learning about, preparing for, and celebrating cultural diversity, or learning to be bicultural.[130]

From "melting pot" to pluralism. Multicultural education is a new approach to dealing with America's diversity. The massive wave of immigration that occurred from 1880 to 1920 in the United States put pressure on public schools to quickly assimilate these newcomers by imposing a strongly Anglo-centric curriculum. According to this perspective, students' mother tongues, cultural traditions, and values were to "melt away," replaced by a new American culture. Later, educators extended the 1960s Civil Rights Movement with various ethnic and racial groups wanting to include their voices, stories, and contributions in the school curriculum.

By the 1970s and 1980s, gender, class, language, ability, religion, and sexual orientation issues joined the multicultural education movement.[131] Each group wanted the same goal—a more democratic society in which each would have greater equality in all spheres of life.

Preventing miscommunications in school. Because the United States' ethnic and cultural diversity is not sufficiently reflected in educational decisions and practices, schools frequently fall out of sync with the populations whom they are supposed to serve. This disconnect is especially likely to occur when teachers and administrators come from the dominant culture, but students and their parents do not practice similar cultural standards.[132] Seeing the world in different ways often causes students, teachers, and parents to misinterpret one another's attitudes and actions.

---

[129] Baptiste, H. P. (1977). Multicultural education evolvement at the University of Houston: A case study. In F. H. Klassen & D. M. Gollnick (Eds.), *Pluralism and the American teacher: Issues and case studies.* (pp. 171–184). Washington, DC: American Association of Colleges for Teacher Education.

[130] Gay, G. (1994). *A synthesis of scholarship in multicultural education.* North Central Regional Educational Laboratory. Retrieved October 16, 2009, from http://www.ncrel.org/sdrs/areas/issues/educatrs/leadrshp/le0gay.htm.

[131] Rasool, J. A., & Curtis, A. C. (2000). *Multicultural education in middle and secondary classrooms: Meeting the challenge of diversity and change.* Belmont, CA: Cengage Learning.

[132] La Belle, T. J. (1976). An anthropological framework for studying education. In J. I. Roberts & S. K. Akinsanya (Eds.), *Educational patterns and cultural configurations: The anthropology of education* (pp. 67–82). New York: David McKay.

For instance, teachers may mistake students' background differences for intellectual inabilities and make pedagogical decisions accordingly. Because they do not understand some Latino ethnic styles, teachers may erroneously conclude that these students have limited critical thinking and reasoning abilities. Teachers may misunderstand Native American children's reluctance to operate on a tightly controlled time schedule or engage in highly individualistic and competitive activities as lack of initiative, motivation, and responsibility. Consequently, educators often engage in "miseducating practices" because they do not understand their ethnically, and linguistically diverse students' cultural characteristics.[133]

If students feel that the school environment is alien and hostile toward them or does not affirm and value who they are (as many students of color believe), they have difficulty concentrating as thoroughly as they might on academic tasks.[134] Psychological security and a positive feeling of self-worth are prerequisites for the more abstract need to know and learn.[135]

When teachers appreciate and understand their diverse students' assets, hold high expectations for their learning, and use a curriculum and instruction that invites and welcomes all students to participate in the American experience, occasions for miscommunications are lessened. In these ways, teachers practice **culturally responsive teaching**.[136]

Expanding the curriculum. Over time, educators came to realize that they might increase minority students' achievement by studying their relationship with the traditional school curriculum. They concluded that by teaching only selective aspects of U.S. history and culture and reinforcing students' prejudices and values, public schools indirectly contribute to perpetuating misunderstandings, tensions, and conflicts between groups. Teaching only one perspective, they reasoned, hurts both our students and our society as a whole. Expanding the curriculum to include minority voices and perspectives, in contrast, benefits all students' learning.[137]

James A. Banks, Professor at the University of Washington and pioneer multicultural educator, observed:

> Rather than excluding Western civilization from the curriculum, multiculturalists want a more truthful, complex, and diverse version of the West taught in the schools. They want the curriculum to describe the way in which African, Asian, and indigenous cultures have influenced and interacted with Western civilization.[138]

Typically, teachers implement multicultural education in small steps. Using an interdisciplinary approach, they select and explore relevant topics across disciplines. They supplement their existing curriculum with brief multicultural units. As they expand their offerings, teachers infuse the multicultural perspective throughout the curriculum.[139] Over time, it stops being an "add-on" and instead becomes a recognized part of what students learn. Teachers offer students instruction that matches their needs based on their age, race, gender, ethnicity, sociolinguistic backgrounds,

---

[133] Gay, 1994.

[134] Gougis, R. A. (1986). The effects of prejudice and stress on the academic performance of black Americans. In U. Niesser (Ed.), *The school achievement of minority children: New perspectives* (pp. 145–157). Hillsdale, NJ: Lawrence Erlbaum Associates, p. 147.

[135] Gay, 1994.

[136] For a fuller discussion of culturally responsive teaching, see the Knowledge Loom Web site, operated by the Education Alliance at Brown: http://knowledgeloom.org/practices3.jsp?location=1&bpinterid=1110&spotlightid=1110.

[137] Suzuki, B. H. (1984). Curriculum transformation for multicultural education. *Education and Urban Society, 16*(3), 294–322.

[138] Banks, J. A. (1991/1992, December–January). Multicultural education: For freedom's sake. *Educational Leadership, 49*(4), 34.

[139] Sleeter, C. E., & Grant, C. A. (1994). *Making choices for multicultural education: Five approaches to race, class, and gender* (2nd ed.). New York: Macmillan.

| Figure 11.5 | Professor James A. Banks, Multicultural Education Pioneer |

Courtesy of James A. Banks

and learning styles. Each school and its community determine where they stand on multicultural education and select the curriculum and teaching approach that best fit their needs.

Even while expanding the curriculum's content, teachers continue to provide students with instruction on basic academic skills, holding them to high expectations. They use teaching approaches and materials that are sensitive and relevant to the students' sociocultural backgrounds and experiences. Teachers encourage students to think critically, incorporate complexity, and respond to multiple ways of understanding information. In turn, students develop respect and appreciation for cultural diversity as their academic skills and achievement grow.

Multicultural education and student achievement. Research affirms the notion that multicultural education can increase students' basic and advanced academic skills. This type of education can improve mastery of reading, writing, and mathematical skills; subject matter content; and intellectual process skills such as problem solving, critical thinking, and conflict resolution by providing content and techniques that are more meaningful to ethnically-diverse students' lives and frames of reference. Using ethnic materials, experiences, and examples as students practice and demonstrate mastery of academic and subject matter makes the instruction more interesting, increases personal meaning, heightens the practical relevance of the skills to be learned, and improves students' time on task. This combination of conditions leads to greater student efforts, task persistence, skill mastery, and academic achievement.[140]

---

[140] Banks, J. A., & Banks, C. A. M. (1993). *Multicultural education: Issues and perspectives* (2nd ed.). Boston: Allyn and Bacon; Boggs, S. T., Watson-Gregeo, K., & McMillen, G. (1985). *Speaking, relating, and learning: A study of Hawaiian children at home and at school.* Norwood, NJ: Abex; Cazden, C. B., John, V. P., & Hymes, D. (Eds.). (1985). *Functions of language in the classroom.* Prospect Heights, IL: Wamland Press; Garcia, R. L. (1982). *Teaching in a pluralistic society: Concepts, models, strategies.* New York: Harper and Row; Greenbaum, P. E. (1985). Nonverbal differences in communication style between American Indian and Anglo elementary classrooms. *American Educational Research Journal, 22,* 101–115; Reys, R., Reys, B., Lapan, R., Holliday, G., & Wasman, D. (2003). Assessing the impact of standards-based middle grades mathematics curriculum materials on student achievement. *Journal for Research in Mathematics Education, 34*(1), 74–95; Rivette, K., Grant, Y., Ludema, H., & Rickard, A. (2003). *Connected Mathematics Project: Research and evaluation summary 2003 edition.* Upper Saddle River, NJ: Pearson Prentice-Hall.

| Figure 11.6 | Professor Sonia Nieto, Multicultural Educator |

Courtesy of Sonia Nieto

Becoming a multicultural person. Multicultural education is more than curriculum; it is a highly personal experience for students and their teachers.

Multicultural education emphasizes developing greater self-understanding, positive self-concepts, and pride in one's ethnic identity. Contributing to students' personal development adds to their overall intellectual, academic, and social achievement. Students who feel good about themselves are likely to be more open and receptive to interaction with others and to respect their cultures and identities. Research has repeatedly supported the relationship between self-concept, academic achievement, ethnicity, culture, and individual identity.[141]

Teachers must also become multicultural persons if they are to become effective multicultural educators. Sonia Nieto, Professor at University of Massachusetts and multicultural author, writes:

> That means looking critically at who you are, what you value, how you reflect those multicultural values, and then looking at your own biases. . . . [and thinking about] . . . the students who are sitting in front of us. Then we have to think about how to deal with those biases in a way that doesn't jeopardize the students we're teaching.[142]

To become a multicultural educator means learning more about oneself and one's views about cultural differences. It means understanding the school experience from diverse students' perspectives. It also requires creating learning opportunities that invite and motivate diverse students to participate as contributors to the common culture and learning rather than remaining passive outsiders to learning and to the "American experience." Although these are certainly emotionally and intellectually challenging tasks, completing them is necessary for a teacher's professional growth and effectiveness with all students.

Multicultural education and school climate. Multicultural education transforms school climate by improving relationships and increasing respect between mainstream and diverse students. Most students spend their formative years in

---

[141] Gay, 1994.
[142] Nieto, S. (n.d.). Commentary: Teaching multicultural literature. Workshop 1. Retrieved October 16, 2009, from http://www.learner.org/channel/workshops/tml/workshop1/commentary3.html.

ethnically and culturally isolated or encapsulated enclaves. Such separation often results in heightened group frustrations, anxiety, fears, failures, and hostilities when students eventually encounter others from different ethnic and cultural backgrounds in the classroom.[143]

Similarly, students born into the mainstream culture rarely have an opportunity to identify, question, or challenge their cultural assumptions because the school culture usually reinforces what they learn at home. As a result, mainstream Americans have few occasions to look at and consider their single-culture beliefs and perspectives, which all too often devalue and stereotype people of other cultures or social classes. This naive viewpoint limits their ability to function effectively within other American cultures—or in the many cultures found throughout the world.[144]

Multicultural education also improves relationships among diverse students. Many students have internalized the negative and distorted conceptions of their own and other ethnic groups. Students from groups of color may be convinced that their heritages have little of value to offer, while members of dominant groups may have inflated notions about their own culture's significance.

Multicultural education can ease these tensions by teaching students skills in cross-cultural communication, interpersonal relations, perspective taking, contextual analysis, understanding alternative points of view and frames of reference, and analysis of how cultural conditions affect values, attitudes, beliefs, preferences, expectations, and behaviors. These skills can help students learn how to understand cultural differences without making hasty and arbitrary value judgments about their intrinsic worth. Attaining these goals can be facilitated by providing students—and future teachers—with a variety of opportunities to practice their cultural competence and to interact with different ethnic peoples, experiences, and situations.[145]

"If we truly believe in democracy then we need to welcome those disparate voices—those voices of conflict and tension and difference—into the conversation," Nieto believes.[146] Multicultural education is not just about ethnic minorities, but about educating all students to live in a diverse nation and world. James Banks adds, "To fully participate in our democratic society, all students need the skills that a multicultural education can give them to understand others and thrive in a rapidly changing, diverse world."[147] Effectively creating a multicultural school climate,

A CLOSER LOOK

Leonard B. Stevens, an educator who has worked on school desegregation since the mid-1970s, takes issue with the U.S. Supreme Court's recent rulings to undo the *Brown* decision's attempts to end discrimination in education. Read his essay and answer the questions that follow.

> Now we have nine judges—the U.S. Supreme Court—assigned the task of deciding whether and how the nation's schools may (or may not) recognize the race of the children at the schoolhouse door. In essence, the argument is between those who would allow the schools to be color-conscious (in the interest of integrating the children), and those who would require the schools to be colorblind (in the interest of making race a forbidden consideration by government-financed schools under any and all circumstances, regardless of the intent of the schools).

[143] Gay, 1994.
[144] Banks, 1991/1992.
[145] Gay, 1994.
[146] Nieto, n.d.
[147] Banks, 1991/1992, p. 35.

The case for colorblindness is interesting in at least two respects.

First, its advocates place zero value on integrated education. To them, schooling is entirely an exercise of the intellect—it has nothing to do with developing citizenship traits or social attitudes or interpersonal skills or values. . . .

In effect, the advocates of colorblindness are saying society may be diverse, and children will become adults in this diverse society, but schools should not prepare them for it—and indeed we would prefer that schools did not: Leave that to parents (and to chance).

Moreover, by defining integrated education as valueless, the advocates of colorblindness reject out of hand all the research on the outcomes of integrated education, the quantity of which is not incidental, as well as the anecdotal stories of countless teachers and principals who work in diverse schools and will tell you at the drop of a question what diversity does for the climate of their schools and the social attitudes of their students. . . .

But the fact is a colorblind school policy would separate children into enclaves largely on the basis of race, culture, and income, which in turn would nurture attitudes on all sides more separatist than unified, and cross-race perceptions more distrustful than trustful. . . .

Second, the advocates of colorblindness are ahistorical—they erase history.

Clearly, a colorblind approach to social policy, including school policy, would be quite appropriate for a society with no history of invidious discrimination and no current vestiges of it.

But the history of the United States is exactly the opposite. No informed person would argue that racial discrimination never existed here or that all subtle remnants of discrimination have been redacted from our contemporary practices. Precisely for this reason—if we wish to work toward a colorblind society—we need to shape social policy so that it is directed at old discrimination patterns and the current end products of them, so as to eradicate from our collective attitudes and dispositions the worst of the past. It is akin to an alcoholic's entering a 12-step program: You first have to admit to the problem, then commit to curing it, then take the steps one day at a time to change course and thereby eventually change character. . . .

Horace Mann, the 19th-century educator from Massachusetts, saw schools as the great equalizer of society. Mann would have reminded them that there is more to school than "a mere capacity to read, write, and cipher" (point: be mindful of the benefits of integrated education); and that each generation has a duty to educate "a generation of wise and virtuous citizens."

Source: Leonard B. Stevens. (2007, February 14) To See or Not to See: Being Colorblind in a Color-Conscious Society. *Education Week, 26*(23):31.

Questions

1. How does Stevens define the different viewpoints on school desegregation between those who are color-conscious or colorblind?

2. How do the colorblind advocates argue their case, which favors ending the U.S. Supreme Court's desegregation orders? How do they view the role of public schools regarding this issue?

3. What does Stevens mean when he says that the colorblind advocates want to erase history and deny reality?

4. What are your views regarding the U.S. Supreme Court moving away from its *Brown* decision with its recent rulings? Explain your reasons.

curriculum, instruction, and positive teacher–student and student–student relationships can be a constructive means to change public schools' structure and learning environment to make equality of expectations and opportunities a reality for diverse students.

Becoming Aware of (and Ending) Inequitable School Practices

Parents know that not all schools are created equal. Homebuyers routinely ask realtors to show them houses in school attendance zones with high test scores. With few exceptions, most students end up replicating their parents' place in the social hierarchy.

Educators, in contrast, tend to believe that schools are fair systems of opportunity. Although well intentioned, teachers do not always see that the educational system is tilted in their favor.

Teachers accept their schools as fair. Teachers did not create the institutions in which they work; they simply fit themselves into their schools' existing patterns and norms. Most educators genuinely believe that schools provide a level playing field to all students. According to this perspective, it is the students' job to work hard, learn, and move ahead.

Likewise, educators are not often aware of the biased ideas that frame their perceptions and interactions with others. Educators generally believe that they are wholly objective professionals fully capable of interpreting situations and treating individuals in totally neutral and fair-minded ways. Future educators often come to the craft of teaching with little cross-cultural experience and knowledge, however, and tend to have limited visions of what teaching diverse students entails.[148] This lack of awareness creates one of the greatest obstacles to establishing more trusting and equitable relationships with the schools' multiple communities.

This type of thinking reflects a strong acceptance of "difference blindness."[149] Teachers try to see and treat every student the same way—seemingly "blind" to racial, ethnic, and gender differences. Because teachers were socialized as Americans and as transmitters of our cultural heritage, they simply do not see, understand, or value that other ways of knowing and understanding the world exist. Yet, when teachers are not aware that others see the world differently than they do, communication and trust become more difficult.

"Difference blindness" is a form of cognitive dissonance. **Cognitive dissonance** is a theoretical construct used to explain how people respond to information that does not coincide with their current understandings or beliefs.[150] According to cognitive dissonance theory, an individual can experience psychological tension or dissonance when new knowledge or information does not fit with what he or she already knows or believes. Because dissonance between opposing ideas is unpleasant, people are motivated to reduce it.

For example, a future teacher may try to make sense of two contradictory beliefs: the belief the individual always held, "Schools are fair and advance *all* students' best interests," and a newer belief, "Schools are unfair and are tilted to disfavor lower-income and diverse children." To reduce psychological discomfort, the future teacher may react in any of three ways:

- Change the new cognition to make it consistent with the preexisting cognition (i.e., deny or devalue the research that schools are unfair to lower income and diverse students)

---

[148] Sleeter, C. E. (2001). Epistemological diversity in research on preservice teacher preparation for historically underserved children. *Review of Research in Education, 25,* 209–250.
[149] Larson & Ovando, 2001.
[150] Festinger, L. A. (1957). *A theory of cognitive dissonance.* Evanston, IL: Row, Peterson.

- Add new cognitions to bridge the gap between the opposing cognitions (i.e., find additional information that supports the idea that many school practices disadvantage lower income and diverse children)
- Change his or her behavior (i.e., stop supporting institutional practices such as academic tracking altogether)[151]

Helping future teachers become fully aware of cognitive dissonance's internal discomfort *before* they experience it helps reduces their resistance to the unfamiliar ideas, prevents them from automatically rejecting the discrepant information, encourages their critical thinking, and promotes a classroom environment conducive to learning.[152]

It is important, therefore, for educators and prospective educators to consider ways the school, as an institution, may appear to those who do not share our norms or whom our practices harm. Unless we can see our schools' limitations and recognize when our unifying beliefs, systems, and practices are unfair to certain student groups, we will tend to interpret student failure or resistance as deviant or ill intentioned. Without full awareness of how our schools actually operate, educators' abilities to help all students become fully educated will remain limited.

Rethinking the difference-blind stance. Those who support the "politics of difference" claim that although people share a universal desire to be treated as full and equal citizens, people do not have equal needs or equal opportunities within an unequal society. For example, they argue that racial and ethnic minorities have a specific need to overcome and remove social inequities in society and school. Because most whites have not had to struggle against prejudice and discrimination in this society, they do not recognize these issues as either existing or valid. Instead, they use the difference-blind logic to silence or overlook these concerns. What is more, to recognize and admit such discrimination would create cognitive dissonance and the discomfort that goes with it.

Furthermore, those supporting the politics of difference assert that in an unequal society, a universal stance is not neutral, but rather aligns with and reflects the dominant culture's concerns and traditions. Indeed, this "professional neutrality" systematically ignores the institutional practices that keep schools and society unequal and inequitable. The dominant or majority culture becomes the mold into which all other cultures must fit.

For all these reasons, schools too often fail to take seriously their responsibility to educate all children. "Although we have expanded our geographical borders in many of our school systems, we have failed to expand our psychic circles of community."[153]

Instead of showing bias, becoming conscious of student differences can be a way of valuing, supporting, and genuinely relating to children rather than a way of diminishing them. Developing this awareness of difference is not easy. All people have an unconscious tendency to confirm what they believe and to explain away what they do not. They unconsciously magnify those features that fit with their expectations and overlook the rest. Difference, however, does not necessarily mean "less than."

Our cognitive maps and feelings about student differences affect the ways we interact with others. When we can critically examine how our own behaviors, systems, and practices may contribute to minority problems in school, we can truly become professional educators in a pluralist society. Recognizing and accepting student differences also helps educators become advocates for making schools better places for all students. Doing the right thing for all students requires more than having good intentions. When educators recognize that difference matters, they can willingly

---

[151] McFalls, E. L., & Cobb-Roberts, D. (2001). Reducing resistance to diversity through cognitive dissonance instruction: Implications for teacher education. *Journal of Teacher Education, 52*(2), 164–172.
[152] McFalls & Cobb-Roberts, 2001. The ultimate decision to accept or reject information is the learner's responsibility.
[153] Larson & Ovando, 2001, p. 82.

accept their responsibility for expanding their circle of care beyond the community insiders and work to address the system's inequities.

Reprise: Equality of Educational Opportunity

The gap between public schools' rhetoric and the reality encountered in today's school systems is large, but aware educators can help bridge it. Clearly, schools still retain their critical mission to equalize each student's opportunities for education and economic advancement. At a time when our national population is becoming increasingly diverse and the marketplace requires higher skill levels to survive and thrive, it becomes even more essential that educators and their communities turn the rhetoric of equal opportunity into reality. Increasing our awareness of how schools limit equal opportunity through its assumptions, norms, and practices is the first step. Looking at our own attitudes and behaviors as they contribute to or reduce the problems is the next.

It must be remembered, however, that schools are only one of the societal forces that influence students' learning. The larger society and its economic and political policies and actions also play significant roles. Nevertheless, schools must do what they can to remove obstacles to students' opportunities and provide necessary supports to help underserved students make the advances they need to become fully educated for twenty-first-century economic viability and democratic citizenship.

Activity 11.2

This chapter contains some difficult material to internalize.

A. Which parts of this chapter did you have difficulty accepting or believing?

B. Which parts of this chapter would you most like to share with one of your public school teachers? Why?

C. Which ideas do you think will most influence you when you are a teacher in your own classroom? As a teacher and leader in your school?

Summary

America has long tried to balance the ideal of equality with the reality of its unequal society. Large differences in income, family backgrounds, social and political power, and racial attitudes persist in this country, despite efforts to diminish them.

Schools hold contradictory goals. On the one hand, schools are charged with transmitting society's consensual values, beliefs, and skills to develop an educated and responsible democratic populace. On the other hand, schools act as talent-sorting machines that track students for low-, middle- and high-paying occupations. With few exceptions, most students end up replicating their parents' social status.

Students' social class is strongly related to their educational outcomes. In general, higher class status correlates with high levels of educational attainment and achievement, and lower class status with lower levels of educational attainment and achievement. The middle classes fall somewhere in between. Generally speaking, research shows that differences in social class culture, parents' education, and resources lead to different child-rearing practices. These factors, in turn, contribute to different educational outcomes.

In addition, school segregation hurts minority students' educational achievement. Today, housing patterns and the U.S. Supreme Court's rulings releasing school districts from their previous desegregation orders are making schools increasingly segregated.

Likewise, social beliefs, teacher expectations, tracking and ability grouping, disciplinary policies and practices, retention rates, teacher quality, and school climate all have significant effects on students' ability to thrive in school and their future educational, employment, social, and lifestyle opportunities. Research suggests that societal barriers and school practices place obstacles to minority group members' learning. Multicultural education and awareness of schools' inequitable norms and practices are two ways to begin overcoming schools' institutional biases and making cultural pluralism and higher achievement for all students a reality.

Conclusion

- Only when we can critically examine how our own attitudes, behaviors, systems, and practices may contribute to diverse students' problems in school, and we learn to act in ways to create more inclusive learning environments, can we truly become effective educators in a pluralist society.

Equality of Opportunity: Diverse Students' Perspectives

"Teaching and learning are cultural processes that take place in a social context,"[1] observes Geneva Gay, multicultural scholar. She elaborates: "To make teaching and learning more accessible and equitable for a wide variety of students, students' cultures need to be more clearly understood. Such an understanding can be achieved by analyzing education from multiple cultural perspectives and thereby removing the blindness imposed on education by the dominant cultural experience."[2]

Students' personal, familial, and cultural factors all influence how well they achieve in school. The achievement gap persists for students who are African American, low income, Latino, Native American, English language learners, and have special learning needs. While racial differences are not biological, they do have social and cultural implications. Apparently, members of any student group that largely differs from the typical white middle-class model around which public schools are organized face challenges to their school success. As outsiders to this norm, these students' unique family and societal histories, their cultural and peer influences, and sometimes their cultural and personal assets create a complex network of factors that determine how well students learn.

When teachers can recognize their own cultural beliefs, biases, and assumptions; acknowledge others' ethnic, cultural, and other differences in a nonjudgmental manner; and understand the ways in which schools reflect and perpetuate the larger society's discriminatory practices,[3] they can better provide the culturally supportive and high expectations classrooms in which all students can succeed.

Focus Questions

- How well are diverse student groups[4] achieving?
- How do people develop cultural and racial identities?
- What is the relationship between minority students' perceptions and their academic performance?
- How does stereotype threat relate to underachievement?
- How does oppositional culture theory relate to underachievement?
- What are low-income students' perspectives that influence their schooling?
- What are African American students' perspectives that influence their schooling?
- What are Latino students' perspectives that influence their schooling?

---

[1] Gay, G. (1994). A synthesis of scholarship in multicultural education. North Central Regional Laboratory. Retrieved October 17, 2009, from http://www.ncrel.org/sdrs/areas/issues/educatrs/leadrshp/le0gay.htm.

[2] Gay, 1994.

[3] Weinstein, C., Curran, M., & Tomlinson-Clarke, S. (2003). Culturally responsive classroom management: Awareness into action. *Theory into Practice, 42*(4), 269–276.

[4] In this chapter, we will respectfully use the self-referent terms that these groups prefer that others call them: children of poverty and low income, Latino, African American, Native American, students with disabilities.

- What are students with disabilities' perspectives that influence their schooling?
- How can teachers use diverse students' cultural and personal assets and foster resilience?
- How can teachers help diverse students succeed in school?

Diverse Students' Achievement

Not all American public school students are achieving at high levels. Looking at low-income and minority students' current academic performance provides a platform from which to move educators toward more effective ways of thinking about and working with these students.

Low-Income, African American, and Latino Students' Achievement

Looking at diverse students' academic achievement illustrates how well each student demographic group is learning in school. As discussed earlier in this book, the more years of education, the higher the employment rate and salaries.[5] Thus those individuals who leave school without a diploma will have a very difficult time moving themselves or their families out of poverty.

Achievement gaps between higher- and lower-income students persist throughout the elementary and high school years. Figure 12.1 depicts this disparity by using scores from the National Assessment of Educational Progress (NAEP) Reading Test.

Figure 12.1	Achievement of Lower- and Higher-Income Students, Grades 4–12

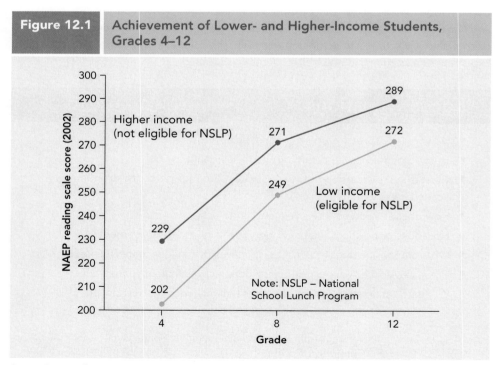

Note: NSLP – National School Lunch Program

Source: From cradle to career: Connecting American education from birth through adulthood. (2007, January 4). *Quality Counts 2007, Education Week, 26*(17), 5. Retrieved October 17, 2009, from http://www.edweek.org/media/ew/qc/2007/QC07_PressConference_Remarks.pdf.

---

[5] See Chapter 7, The Purposes and Promises of Public Education.

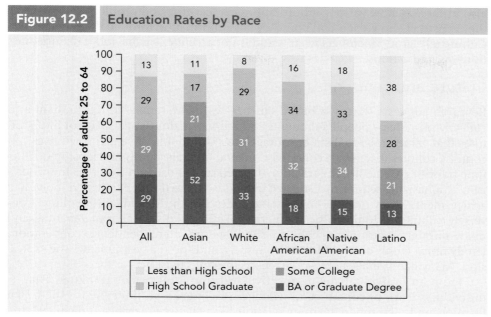

| Figure 12.2 | Education Rates by Race |

Source: From cradle to career: Connecting American education from birth through adulthood. (2007, January 4). *Quality Counts 2007, Education Week, 26*(17), 8. Retrieved October 17, 2009, from http://www.edweek.org/media/ew/qc/2007/QC07_PressConference_Remarks.pdf.

The figure shows that low-income twelfth graders read on a par with higher-income eighth graders (scores of 272 versus 271, respectively).

In addition, large disparities exist by race and ethnicity among different student groups in the degree to which they complete high school and go on to college. College completion is a strong indicator of future income and quality of life. This factor, in turn, affects how well the college graduates' children are likely to do in school, given that parents' educational level influences their children's school outcomes. As shown in Figure 12.2, more than 7 in 10 Asian Americans ages 25 to 64 and more than 6 in 10 non-Latino white adults have completed at least some college. In contrast, nearly 7 in 10 Latinos and half of African Americans have a high school diploma or less.

Too often, low-income, minority, and students with disabilities are considered "outsiders" to the mainstream culture. Looking more closely at the cultures, attitudes, and beliefs that affect these young people can help prospective educators better understand their students' frames of reference and find their cultural and personal resources to help them succeed in school.

Developing Cultural and Racial Identities

Our cultural heritage and backgrounds influence our lives in many ways. **Culture** is "the systems of values, beliefs, and ways of knowing that guide communities of people in their daily lives."[6] Culture always intersects with individuals' race, ethnicity, social class, gender, age, ability, status, and family traditions. These beliefs, shared traditions, language, values, and agreement about norms for living help people organize their world cognitively though language and other symbol systems. Culture

---

[6] Trumbull, E. (2005). Language, culture, and society. In E. Trumbull & B. Farr, *Language and learning: What teachers need to know* (pp. 33–72). Norwood, MA: Christopher-Gordon, p. 35.

also influences how various groups approach learning and problem solving, how they construct knowledge, and how they pass information through the generations.[7] Culture tells group members what is and is not acceptable behavior. It defines one's thinking and actions.

Culture and Learning

Research suggests that two broad cultural value systems—individualism and collectivism—shape people's thoughts and actions in almost all aspects of life.[8] Cultures that value individualism encourage their children to "live their own lives"; in contrast, cultures that favor a collectivist orientation make family and kinship ties lifetime priorities. Generally, the traditional American mainstream culture is individualistic, emphasizing self-reliance, rugged individualism, self-expression, and individual achievement. "Every man for himself" might describe the individualistic culture. Conversely, cultures including African American, Latino, Native American, Japanese, and many immigrant groups are collectivistic, stressing interdependence, cooperation, family unity, family and group success, respect, and social development.[9] The expression "Many hands make light work" reflects the collectivist perspective.

From an individualistic perspective, learning is an personal matter. That is, individuals learn or construct knowledge. Students are responsible for their own learning, and the primary learning relationship is between teacher and child. If the student needs help, he or she asks the teacher for help. Academic assessment measures progress through individual scores. The work itself is most important; relationships come second. Education's goal is for students to do well academically and to show that ability through good grades.[10]

In the alternative perspective, children from collectivist families are socialized to work toward group goals rather than personal goals. They may be used to working together as a group to help others with their tasks even before they consider their own assignments.[11] Their cultures emphasize learning embedded in a social context as students help one another, and group success—rather than individual achievement—is the goal.[12] Relationships are most important; academic tasks can be completed much more easily if students help and receive help from one another. Under this perspective, education's goal is to produce a good and knowledgeable person who respects others and does not place himself or herself above others in importance.[13] Social and ethical development and cognitive and academic develop are seen as integrated, rather than separate.[14]

---

[7] Rothstein-Fisch, C., & Trumbull, E. (2008). *Managing diverse classrooms: How to build on students' cultural strengths*. Alexandria, VA: Association for Supervision and Curriculum Development, pp. 2–3.

[8] Greenfield, P. M. (1994). Independence and interdependence as developmental scripts: Implications for theory, research, and practice. In P. M. Greenfield & R. R. Cocking (Eds.), *Cross-cultural roots of minority child development* (pp. 1–37). Mahwah, NJ: Lawrence Erlbaum Associates; Hofstede, G. (2001). *Culture's consequences: Comparing values, behaviors, institutions, and organizations across nations* (2nd ed.). Thousand Oaks, CA: Sage; Markus, H., & Kitayama, S. (1991). Culture and the self: Implications for cognition, emotion, and motivation. *Psychological Review, 98*, 224–253; Triandus, H. C. (1989). Cross-cultural studies of individualism and collectivism. *Nebraska Symposium of Motivation, 37*, 43–133.

[9] Greenfield, P. M. (1994). Independence and interdependence as developmental scripts: Implications for theory, research, and practice. In P. M. Greenfield & R. R. Cocking (Eds.), *Cross-cultural roots of minority child development* (pp. 1–37). Mahwah, NJ: Lawrence Erlbaum Associates; Lipka, J. (with Mohatt, G., & Ciulistet Group). (1998). *Transforming the culture of schools: Yup'ik Eskimo examples*. Mahwah, NJ: Lawrence Erlbaum Associates; Nelson-Barber, S., Trumbull, E., & Wenn, R. (2000). *The Coconut Wireless Project: Sharing culturally responsive pedagogy through the World Wide Web*. Honolulu, HI: Pacific Resources for Education and Learning; Rothstein-Fisch & Trumbull, 2008, pp. 10–12, 51.

[10] Rothstein-Fisch & Trumbull, 2008, pp. 12–13.

[11] Raeff, C., Greenfield, P. M., & Quiroz, B. (2000). Conceptualizing interpersonal relationships in the cultural contexts of individualism and collectivism. In S. Harkness, C. Raeff, & C. M. Super (Eds.), *New directions for child and adolescent development*. San Francisco: Jossey-Bass, p. 87.

[12] McLaughlin, H. J., & Bryan, L. A. (2003, Autumn). Learning from rural Mexican schools about commitment and work. *Theory into Practice, 42*(4), 289–295.

[13] Valdes, G. (1996). *Con respeto: Bridging the distances between culturally diverse families and schools: An ethnographic portrait*. New York: Teachers College Press.

[14] Goldenberg, C., & Gallimore, R. (1995). Immigrant Latino parents' values and beliefs about their children's education: Continuities and discontinuities across cultures and generations. *Advances in Motivation and Achievement, 9*, 183–228.

The basic difference between these two systems is the relative emphasis placed on individual versus group well-being. Every culture has both individualistic and collectivist values. Great variations appear within each culture, and both systems have advantages and disadvantages.[15] In addition, factors such as socioeconomic status (SES), rural or urban setting, and parents' formal educational level affect tendencies toward individualism versus collectivism. Specifically, higher SES, urban settings, and greater parental education are associated with greater individualism.[16]

Stages of Self- and Group Identities

Racial, ethnic, and cultural identities are defined as a sense of group collective identity based on a person's perception that he or she shares a common heritage with a particular racial, ethnic, or cultural group. These identities are critical parts of how persons see themselves both as individuals and as part of a larger group. Although the development of this group identity does not necessarily happen in an inflexible chronological sequence, scholars believe that most minority group members go through relatively similar stages.

For minority adolescents, race, ethnicity, and culture can play important roles in their identity development. Racial and ethnic attitudes among children appear to crystallize by about age 10.[17] Their home, community, and school experiences all contribute to how children come to view and value themselves as individuals and as minority group members.

| Figure 12.3 | Racial And Ethnic Attitudes Among Children Tend to Crystallize Around Age 10 |

Ariel Skelley/Jupiter Images

---

[15] Markus, H., & Kitayama, S. (1991). Culture and the self: Implications for cognition, emotion, and motivation. *Psychological Review, 98,* 224–253; Rothstein-Fisch & Trumbull, Elise, 2008.
[16] Hofstede, 2001.
[17] Rotheram, M. J., & Phinney, J. S. (1988). Introduction: Definitions and perspectives in the study of children's ethnic socialization. In J. S. Phinney & J. Rotheram (Eds.), *Children's ethnic socialization: Pluralism and development* (pp. 10–28). Newbury Park, CA: Sage.

Table 12.1	Racial and Cultural Identity Development	
Stages of Minority Development Model	**Attitude Toward Self**	**Attitude Toward Dominant Group**
Stage 1: Conformity	Self-depreciating or neutral	Group-appreciating.
Stage 2: Dissonance and Appreciating	Conflict between self-depreciating and group-appreciating	Conflict between self-depreciating and group-appreciating
Stage 3: Resistance and Immersion	Self-appreciating.	Group-depreciating.
Stage 4: Introspection	Concern with the basis of self-appreciation.	Concern with the basis of group-depreciation.
Stage 5: Integrative Awareness	Self-appreciating.	Selective appreciation

Source: Adapted from Sue, D. W., & Sue, D. (2008). *Counseling the culturally diverse: Theory and practice* (5th ed.). Hoboken, NJ: John Wiley & Sons, Table 10.1, p. 243.

Observers have noted that minority groups share similar patterns of adjustment to living in a culture that does not value them.[18] In past decades, African Americans, Asian Americans, Latinos, and Native Americans have experienced changes in the ways they view themselves within American society. Their sense of cultural oppression is the common unifying force. As a result, researchers have integrated various cultural identity models to identify common features that cut across minority populations.

Table 12.1 illustrates a conceptual framework to help educators understand their culturally diverse students' attitudes and behaviors. This model defines five stages of development that those outside the mainstream experience as they struggle to understand themselves in terms of their own culture, the dominant culture, and the oppressive relationship between the two cultures: conformity, dissonance, resistance and immersion, introspection, and integrative awareness. At each identity level, attitudes and beliefs reflect the individual's experiences at that stage.[19]

Conformity stage. Minority individuals strongly prefer the dominant cultural values over their own. They strongly identify with white Americans' lifestyles, value systems, and cultural and physical characteristics, while they disrespect, reject, or deny those most like their own minority group's.

Example: As a young man, Malcolm X, the 1960s African American leader, straightened and dyed his hair to look more like a white male.[20] Asian women sometimes undergo surgery to change the shape of their eyes.

Dissonance stage. Minority individuals receive information or have experiences that contradict the dominant culture's beliefs, attitudes, and values. The individual begins to question and challenge the conformity stage's attitudes and beliefs. The person becomes aware that racism exists. Not all aspects of the minority or majority

---

[18] Berry, G. (1965). *Ethnic and race relations.* Boston, MA: Houghton Mifflin; Sue, D. W., & Sue, D. (1999). *Counseling the culturally different: Theory and practice* (3rd ed.). New York: John Wiley & Sons; Sue, D. W., & Sue, D. (2008). *Counseling the culturally diverse: Theory and practice* (5th ed). Hoboken, NJ: John Wiley & Sons.

[19] Sue & Sue, 2008, pp. 242–243.

[20] Haley, A. (1966). *The autobiography of Malcolm X.* New York: Grove Press.

culture are good or bad. Feeling pride in one's minority culture changes the way the person sees himself or herself.

Example: An Asian American who believes that Asians are inhibited and passive meets an Asian leader who seems outgoing, dynamic, and articulate.

Resistance and immersion stage.
The culturally different individual tends to completely endorse minority-held views and rejects the dominant society's values and culture. The person actively seeks out information and artifacts of his or her own group's history that enhances the individual's sense of identity and worth. The person may feel embarrassed and angry that he or she once valued ("sold out") his or her own racial or cultural group and feels pride and honor about that group's cultural and racial characteristics.

Example: African American youth wear traditional African dashikis, plait their hair in customary African braids, or dress in urban styles.

Introspection stage.
The minority individual becomes uncomfortable with the rigid views of the resistance and immersion stage. The person no longer wants to hold back his or her own views and choices in an effort to please the group. The minority individual must choose between responsibility and loyalty to his or her own personal independence or group conformity.

Example: A Latino individual who develops a close friendship with a white person may feel considerable pressure from his or her culturally similar peers to end the relationship with "the Gringo"[21]

Integrative awareness stage.
Minority persons have developed an inner sense of security, a positive self-image, and confidence, and they can appreciate the unique aspects of their own culture as well as those of the dominant U.S. culture. Minority and white cultures are not always in conflict. The individual has greater control and flexibility, believing that there are both acceptable and unacceptable aspects in all cultures. The person is a member of his or her own racial or cultural group, of the larger society, and of the human race.

Example: A Latino can be good friends with other Latinos, whites, African Americans, and any other persons who have the qualities that make for strong, mutually respectful relationships.

Cultural identity development influences individuals' own identity development. Different persons experience these stages at different times and at varying rates, depending on their experiences and personalities. For this reason, teachers cannot expect all of their minority students to be at the same stage at the same time. Students may grow and change in their cultural or racial identity development throughout the year. When teachers understand that this process occurs, they can better understand and accept their diverse students as growing individuals.

Developing a White Racial Identity

White persons also have a racial/cultural identity. White persons in U.S. society have consciously or unconsciously learned racial biases, prejudices, misinformation, and negative stereotypes through cultural conditioning. Few think about what it means to be "white" in our society, rarely perceive race as belonging to them, or recognize the privilege that comes to them because of their white skin.[22] Because being white is the U.S. cultural norm, "it acts as an invisible veil that

---

[21]"Gringo" is a disparaging term for a foreigner in Latin America, usually a North American or English person.
[22]Katz, J. (1985). The sociopolitical nature of counseling. *Counseling Psychologist, 13,* 615–624.

limits many people from seeing it as a cultural system."[23] Being white is so interwoven into everyday living that whites, at times, cannot step outside and see their beliefs, values, and behaviors as creating a distinct cultural group.

White educators benefit when they can understand their own racial/cultural identity within a pluralistic society. Like minority persons, white people go through racial identity changes. The status of white racial identity development in any multicultural encounter affects the process and outcome of interracial relationships.[24] By going through the same stages as discussed previously in the minority racial/cultural identity development model (plus one earlier phase and one later phase), white persons experience their own racial/cultural self-awareness.[25]

Naiveté phase. During life's first three years, the child experiences immature, neutral, open, and spontaneous curiosity about race. Between ages three to five, the young white child begins to associate positive meaning with his or her own ethnic group and negative meaning with other groups, gradually developing a sense of superiority about the concept of whiteness from the media and significant others in the child's life.

Example: A white four-year-old meets an African American four-year-old on the playground, and they begin to play together. Their parents exchange quick glances and after a few minutes, the white parent exclaims, "It's time to go now!" and takes the child away.

Conformity phase. The white person consciously or unconsciously comes to believe that the white culture is the most highly developed, and that all other cultures are primitive or inferior. The person has minimal awareness of the self as a racial being and strong belief that his or her values and norms governing behavior are universal. The white person has limited accurate knowledge of other cultural or racial groups and tends to rely on stereotypes as the main source of information.

Example: A white person believes that "people are people," they are "color blind," and differences are unimportant, yet asserts that minority persons would not have problems if they "worked harder, assimilated better, or valued education."

Dissonance phase. The white person is forced to deal with the inconsistencies when confronted with information or experiences at odds with his or her denial of racial differences. The person must examine his or her own cultural values and see the conflict between upholding humanistic nonracist values and the person's own contradictory behavior.

Example: A person who consciously believes that "all men and women are created equal" and does not discriminate suddenly has qualms about having an African American family move next door or have his or her son or daughter date a person of color.

Resistance and immersion phase. The white person begins to question and challenge his or her own racism. The individual sees stereotypes portrayed and perpetuated in advertising, television, interpersonal interactions, and U.S. culture and institutions. The person recognizes how being white has provided him or her with certain advantages that are denied to various minority groups. The white person feels angry at the larger society and guilty about having been part of an oppressive system.

Example: A "white liberal" may want to paternalistically protect minority group members from abuse.

Introspective phase. The white person reflects on what it means to be white and accepts his or her whiteness. The individual recognizes that he or she has benefited

---

[23] Katz, 1985, pp. 616–617.
[24] Sue & Sue, 2008, p. 277.
[25] Sue & Sue, 2008, pp. 277–282.

from white privilege and may never fully understand the minority experience, but feels disconnected from the Euro-American group, too. The person speaks with and observes the white group but also actively creates experiences and interactions with various minority group members.

Example: The white person with minority friends feels unconnected and confused, making a transition from one perspective to another.

Integrative awareness phase. The white person understands self as a racial/cultural being, understands the social and political forces that influence racism, appreciates racial/cultural diversity, and shows increased commitment to ending racial/cultural oppression. The person develops a nonracist white Euro-American identity, values multiculturalism, and finds comfort with members of culturally diverse groups.

Example: A white person develops the inner security and strength needed to function in a multicultural society that only marginally accepts such an integratively aware white person.

Commitment to antiracist action phase. The white person enacts an increased commitment to end oppression, seeing "wrong" and actively working to make it "right."

Example: The white person objects to racist jokes; tries to educate family, friends, and coworkers about racial issues; and takes direct action to end racism in schools and at work.

Becoming aware of one's own white identity is an important characteristic of multicultural competence. If an educator does not notice a student's race or culture, then the teacher does not really see the child. Teachers working in a pluralistic society become able to develop better relationships with the diverse range of students they encounter in their classrooms when they can understand themselves and their students as persons with unique racial/cultural identities, values, and person/cultural assets who come together in schools for the common purpose of teaching and learning.

Limitations of the Racial/Cultural Identity Models

Cultural identity development is a dynamic process. Some persons show behaviors and attitudes characteristic of several stages at the same time. For example, they may exhibit conformity characteristics in certain situations, yet show resistance and immersion behaviors in other circumstances. Some persons move through the stages in a straight line at differing rates, whereas others may move back and forth between stages. These models are a conceptual framework intended to help understand student development[26]; they are not a set of fixed, rigid rules.

In addition, the cultural identity development model does not fit all minority situations. For example, recent Asian immigrants to the United States tend to hold very positive and favorable views of their own culture and already possess an intact racial/cultural identity.[27]

Racial/cultural identity models imply a value judgment that assumes that some cultural resolutions are healthier than others. For instance, the racial/cultural identity model suggests that the integrative awareness stage represents a higher form of healthy functioning. The models also lack an adequate consideration of gender, class, sexual orientation, and other group identities. Nor is racial/cultural identity a simple, global concept. Much evidence is mounting that while identity may move sequentially through identifiable stages, affective, attitudinal, cognitive, and behavioral components may not develop in a uniform manner.[28]

---

[26] Sue & Sue, 2008, p. 257.
[27] Sue & Sue, 2008, p. 257.
[28] Sue & Sue, 2008, p. 258.

Finally, sociocultural forces affect identity development. Many of the early African American identity development models arose as a result of perceived and real experiences of oppression in our society. The increasingly visible racial/cultural movements of Native Americans, Latinos, and African Americans happened at a time of heightened racial and cultural awareness and pride. The times themselves, in conjunction with the cultural forces in play, can greatly affect—that is, either facilitate or impede—cultural identity development.[29]

Research on Racial and Cultural Identities in School

Students' racial and cultural identities are strongly related to their behaviors. Specifically, students with positive racial and cultural identities are more likely to be successful in school. In a study of African American and mixed-race adolescents (ages 10–15), researchers found that racial and cultural identity was significantly related to the behavior adjustment among African American adolescents. Positive racial and cultural identity was associated with more active coping, fewer beliefs supporting aggression, and less hostile or combative behaviors.[30] Racial and cultural identity has also been significantly related to positive school adjustment.[31] Investigators have found that cultural minority adolescents who interacted more with peers of the same cultural background had more developed levels of cultural identity.[32]

Advanced levels of racial and cultural identity development are a significant predictor of positive social adaptation and emotional adjustment for African American and white adolescents.[33] This adjustment is a critical factor in school learning and appropriate behaviors. Moreover, racial and cultural identity and self-esteem/self-concept have positive relationships in middle school,[34] high school,[35] and college-age[36] students.

The research suggests that simply being a member of a racial or cultural minority group does not predict higher or lower levels of self-esteem. Instead, it is the *sense of belonging* that students feel toward their racial or cultural group that better predicts self-esteem.[37] Studies have shown that the stronger the sense of cultural or racial identity, the higher the individual's self-confidence and self-esteem. Conversely, those persons who have not examined or developed a clear sense of racial or cultural identity tend to have low self-regard and feelings of inadequacy. This relationship holds true for all racial and cultural groups.

---

[29] Sue & Sue, 1999, p. 142.

[30] McMahon, S. D., & Watts, R. J. (2002). Ethnic identity in urban African American youth: Exploring links with self-worth, aggression, and other psychosocial variables. *Journal of Community Psychology, 30,* 411–431.

[31] Phinney, J. S., Horenczyk, G., Liebkind, K., & Vedder, P. (2001). Ethnic identity, immigration, and well-being: An interactional perspective. *Journal of Social Issues, 57,* 493–510.

[32] Phinney, J. S., Romero, I., Nava, M., & Huang, D. (2001). The role of language, parents, and peers in ethnic identity among adolescents in immigrant families. *Journal of Youth and Adolescence, 30,* 135–153.

[33] Yasui, M., Dorham, C. L., & Dishion, T. J. (2004). Ethnic identity and psychological adjustment: A validity analysis for European American and African American adolescents. *Journal of Adolescence, 19,* 807–825.

[34] Carlson, C., Uppal, S., & Prosser, E. C. (2000). Ethnic differences in processes contributing to the self-esteem of early adolescent girls. *Journal of Early Adolescence, 20,* 44–67.

[35] Phinney, J. S. (1989). Stages of ethnic identity in minority group adolescents. *Journal of Early Adolescence, 9,* 34–49.

[36] Phinney, J. S., & Alipuria, L. (1990). Ethnic identity in college students from four ethnic groups. *Journal of Adolescence, 13,* 171–184.

[37] Helms, J. E. (1993). *Black and white racial identity: Theory, research, and practice.* Westport, CT: Praeger; McMahon, S. D., & Watts, R.J. (2002). Ethnic identity in urban African American youth: Exploring links with self-worth, aggression, and other psychosocial variables. *Journal of Community Psychology, 30,* 411–431; Phinney, J. S. (1992). The Multigroup Ethnic Identity Measure: A new scale for use with diverse groups. *Journal of Adolescent Research, 7,* 156–176; Martinez, R. O., & Dukes, R. L. (1997). The effects of ethnic identity, ethnicity, and gender on adolescent well-being. *Journal of Youth and Adolescence, 26,* 503–516; Phinney, J. S., & Kohatsu, E. L. (1997). Ethnic and racial identity development and mental health. In J. Schulenberg, J. L. Maggs, & K. Hurrelmann (Eds.), *Health risks and developmental transitions during adolescence* (pp. 420–443). New York: Cambridge University Press; Bracey, J. R., Bamaca, M. Y., & Umana-Taylor, A. J. (2004). Examining ethnic identity and self-esteem among biracial and monoracial adolescents. *Journal of Youth & Adolescence, 33,* 123–132.

Additional studies have found that social support from family and friends may be a means by which youths develop cultural identity, leading to a higher level of self-esteem.[38] When young people have positive family, community, and cultural support for their racial and cultural identity, the more ably they can resist and accommodate any negative social and media messages. Students who feel good about themselves and have a positive sense of their own value are more likely to work hard and have high achievement in school.

Activity 12.1

People develop a racial/cultural identity through various cognitive and emotional stages.

A. Using Table 12.1 and the discussion of minority and white racial/cultural identities, discuss with a partner how you personally experienced your own racial/cultural identity development.

B. Which commonalities do you find with your partner regarding these racial/cultural identity development experiences? Which differences?

C. As a class, discuss how your racial/cultural identity development experiences compare with those noted in the discussion of minority and white racial/cultural identity development and compared with one another.

D. Does your class have any personal findings that you would like to add to the stages or phases noted to make them more accurate or clear?

Activity 12.2

Developing a racial/cultural identity typically involves the stages described in the text, though not necessarily in the same sequence.

A. Divide the class into two groups. One group will work with the minority racial/cultural identity development model, and the other will work with the white racial/cultural identity development model. The groups should be racially mixed.

B. For approximately 20 minutes, each group should discuss the racial identity development described in its assigned table. Give examples from personal experience or observations that illustrate each stage.

C. Create a large graphic image or images to illustrate each stage and its meaning.

D. Present your graphics and explanations to the rest of the class.

E. As a class, discuss how the minority and white racial identity models are alike and how they differ.

F. Class members may volunteer to describe their own experiences in developing a racial identity, including the difficulties, the surprises, and their current phase in the process.

---

[38] Blash, R. R., & Unger, D. G. (1995). Self-concept of African American male youth: Self-esteem and ethnic identity. *Journal of Child & Family Studies, 4,* 359–373; Carlson, C., Uppal, S., & Prosser, E. C. (2000). Ethnic differences in processes contributing to the self-esteem of early adolescent girls. *Journal of Early Adolescence, 20,* 44–67.

Minority Students' Perceptions and Academic Performance

Students' perceptions and performances seem to have a chicken-and-egg complexity. Do minority students perceive and behave as they do because of how they are treated and taught in schools? Or are they treated and taught in schools because of the ways they perceive and behave? The answer seems to be both.[39]

In addition to the research-documented connection between SES and school success, group cultural patterns or the relationships between these groups and the larger society may also frustrate their identification with school. Claude Steele's stereotype threat theory and John Ogbu's ideas about "oppositional" culture describe how minority students' views and emotions influence their levels of academic achievement.

"Stereotype Threat" Theory and Underachievement

It may seem logical—but is actually inaccurate—to assume that the African American students' educational disadvantages affect only low-income students. In reality, even middle- and upper-class African American students have perceptions that limit their education.[40] Claude M. Steele, a Stanford University social psychology professor, has suggested that **stereotype threat** is a coping strategy that hurts high-striving, middle-income African American students' achievement. Put simply, stereotype threat is the idea that people tend to underperform when confronted with situations that might confirm negative stereotypes about their social group.

Stereotype threat occurs when an individual who really cares about doing well is placed in a circumstance in which a negative group stereotype could apply. For example, an African American student does not want to accidentally do something (such as perform poorly on an important exam) that might inadvertently confirm a stereotype (of ignorant African American students) to onlookers. The student does not want to embarrass himself or herself or cause onlookers to judge the individual harshly or treat the individual unfairly. This fear of confirming the stereotype may be distracting enough to the individual that the person actually makes careless mistakes.

In a series of ingenious experiments, Steele found that when students were told that the test they were about to take tended to produce achievement differences such that women and minority students scored at a lower level, that outcome was exactly what happened. In the control groups, where students took the same test but were not told about any expected performance differences among different student groups, no performance differences appeared.[41] These effects have been documented in more than 200 studies involving a variety of situations.[42]

In Steele's studies, highly capable students seemed to be trying too hard. They reread the questions and multiple choices and rechecked their answers more often than when they did not face stereotype threat. When this finding is applied to schools, it implies that when capable African American students take a difficult standardized test, their anxiety about not wanting to perform poorly may cause them to

---

[39] Evans, R. (2005, April). Reframing the achievement gap. *Phi Delta Kappan, 86*(8), 582–589.

[40] Steele, C. M. (1999, August). Thin ice: "Stereotype threat" and black college students. *Atlantic Monthly, 284*(2), 44–47, 50–54; Steele, C. M. (1997, June). Treat in the air: How stereotypes shape intellectual identity and performance. *American Psychologist, 52*(6), 613–629.

[41] Steele, 1997.

[42] Viadero, D. (2007, October 24). Experiments aim to east effects of 'stereotype threat'. *Education Week, 27*(9), 10.

make mistakes. In other words, their perceptions of the threat become self-fulfilling prophecies.

Sometimes students respond to stereotype threat by pretending that school is not important. Steele concluded that some students use **disidentification**—or withdrawal of psychic investment—to remove themselves from this perceived threat. Worried that society's negative perceptions and discrimination of their group will compromise their own futures if they appear to match the stereotype, these students try to avoid the humiliation of appearing less capable. Instead, they defensively pretend they are not interested or invested in schooling and its norms. They rationalize their poor performance as a lack of interest in the subject rather than as an inability to master it. They act cool and disinterested in an effort to save face. Such students may avoid situations that seem potentially threatening, setting up a negative spiral. Appearing not to care about school success may even become a group norm. In contrast, while these students respond to stereotype threat by underperforming, others work even harder to achieve.[43]

Interestingly, scholars have found evidence of stereotype threat occurring among elementary school girls taking mathematics tests, elderly people given a memory test, and white men being assessed on athletic ability.[44] White men who were outperforming African American and female students were themselves vulnerable to the stereotype threat. When researchers told them that

Figure 12.4	Stereotype Threat Undermines Capable Minority Students' Capacity to Succeed

Corbis/Jupiter Images

---

[43] Viadero, 2007.
[44] Viadero, 2007.

the same tests were being used to compare their abilities with those of Asian Americans, white male performance worsened.[45] Even something as subtle as asking students to indicate their race or gender on a test form can trigger the phenomenon.[46]

Critics challenge Steele's theory by asserting that students' vulnerability to stereotype threat and disidentification are universal characteristics; that is, they do not belong solely to African American or other underachieving minority students.[47] What is more, teachers can create learning environments that reduce stereotype threat's negative outcomes. Studies have found that students are more motivated to achieve when they believe that intelligence is malleable rather than a trait fixed at birth and that hard work and a positive outlook can improve their grades and close achievement gaps.[48]

Oppositional Cultures Theory and Underachievement

Low-income and minority students' underachievement is a very complex phenomenon with a variety of causes. John Ogbu, the late University of California–Berkeley professor, believed that although structural barriers and school factors affect minority school performance, minorities are also autonomous human beings who actively interpret and respond to their situation.[49]

To achieve is to "Be White." "Acting white" is a set of social interactions in which minority adolescents who get good grades in school enjoy less social popularity than white students who do well academically.[50] For example, when asked to identify acting-white behavior, African American students name actions ranging from speaking standard English and enrolling in an Advanced Placement or Honors class to wearing clothes from the Gap or Abercrombie & Fitch (instead of Tommy Hilfiger or FUBU) and wearing shorts in winter.[51]

Anthropologists Signithia Fordham and John Ogbu helped bring this phenomenon to public attention. They suggested an **oppositional culture theory** that seeks to explain why minority students often do poorly in school. According to their theory, African American students respond to institutionalized racism by believing that high achievement in school would cause them to lose their minority identity or betray their minority peers by "acting white."[52] Along the way, they come to value

---

[45] Singham. M. (1998). The canary in the mine: The achievement gap between black and white students *Phi Delta Kappan 80* (1), 9-15.

[46] Viadero, 2007.

[47] Evans, 2005.

[48] Good, C., & Aronson, J. (2003). The development of stereotype threat and its relation to theories of intelligence: Effects on elementary school girls' mathematics achievement and task choices (Unpublished manuscript). New York: Columbia University; Good, C., Aronson, J., & Inzlicht, M. (2003). Improving adolescents' standardized test performance: An intervention to reduce the effects of stereotype threat. *Journal of Applied Developmental Psychology, 24*(6), 645–662; Walton, G., & Cohen, G. L. (2007). A question of belonging: Racial, social fit, and achievement. *Journal of Personality and Social Psychology, 92*(1), 82–96.

[49] Ogbu, J. U., & Simons, H. D. (1998). Cultural–ecological theory of student performance with some implications for education. *Anthropology and Education Quarterly. 29*(2), 155–188.

[50] Fordham, S. (1996). *Blacked out: Dilemmas of race, identity, and success at Capital High*. Chicago: University of Chicago Press. Noguera, P. A. (2003). How racial identity affects school performance. *Harvard Education Letter, 19*, 1–3; Fryer, R. G. (2006, Winter). "Acting white": The social price paid by the best and brightest minority students. *Education Next, 6*(1). Stanford University: Hoover Institution. Retrieved October 17, 2009, from http://educationnext.org/actingwhite/.

[51] Neal-Barnett, A. (2001). Being black: A new conceptualization of acting white. In A, M. Neal-Barnett, J. Contreras, & K. Kerns (Eds.), *Forging links: African American children clinical development perspectives.* (75-88). Westport, CT: Greenwood.

[52] Fordham, S., & Ogbu, J. (1986). Black students' school successes: Coping with the burden of "acting white." *Urban Review, XVIII*, 176–206.

their minority identity, especially in terms of the ways in which they differ from the dominant white society.[53]

Other observers, however, place the blame for acting white squarely on the shoulders of African Americans. The Manhattan Institute's John McWhorter, for example, contrasts African American youth culture with that of immigrants (including blacks from the Caribbean and Africa) who "haven't sabotaged themselves through victimology."

These two theories—the former blaming acting white on a racist society, the latter blaming it on self-imposed cultural sabotage—have emerged as the predominant explanations for acting white among African Americans.[54]

One study gathered evidence of how "acting white" affects minority students' popularity. Figure 12.5 shows large differences in the relationship between academic achievement and popularity among whites, African Americans, and Latinos. At low grade-point averages (GPAs), ethnic groups show little difference, and high-achieving African Americans are actually more popular within their ethnic group than high-achieving whites are within theirs. But when a student achieves a 2.5 GPA (an even mix of B and C grades), clear differences start to appear. As the GPAs of African American students increase beyond this point, they tend to have fewer and fewer friends. An African American student with a 4.0 GPA has, on average, 1.5 fewer friends of the same ethnicity than a white student with the same GPA. A Latino student with a 4.0 GPA is the least popular of all Latino students, and Latino–white differences among high achievers are the most extreme. These findings were true for public school students but less true for private school students, however.[55]

Figure 12.5	Pressure to Be Average

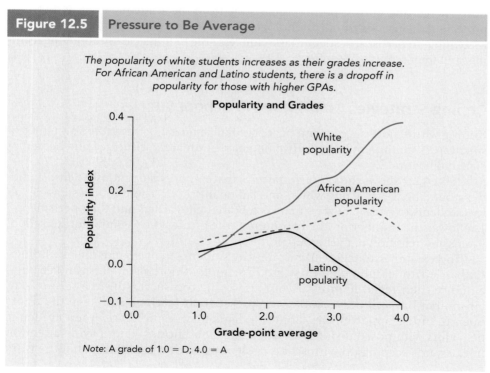

The popularity of white students increases as their grades increase. For African American and Latino students, there is a dropoff in popularity for those with higher GPAs.

Popularity and Grades

White popularity

African American popularity

Latino popularity

Note: A grade of 1.0 = D; 4.0 = A

Source: Fryer, R. G. (2006, Winter). "Acting white": The social price paid by the best and brightest minority students. *Education Next, 6*(1). Stanford University: Hoover Institution. Retrieved October 17, 2009, from http://educationnext.org/actingwhite/.

[53] Ogbu, J. U. (1995). Cultural problems in minority education: Their interpretations and consequences—part one: Theoretical background. *Urban Review, 27*(3),189–205.
[54] Fryer, 2006.
[55] Fryer, 2006.

These oppositional beliefs create dilemmas for minority students. They feel that they must choose between (1) conforming to the school's demands and rewards for certain attitudes and behaviors that are perceived as "white," especially mastering and using standard English and risking their community's rejection, or (2) accepting their community's interpretations and disapproval of or, at the least, ambivalence toward those mainstream (white) attitudes and behaviors and not getting the education they need.[56]

"Oppositional identities" appear in African American students from all socioeconomic backgrounds. Regardless of family income and social class background, any African American student may view school success as undermining his or her minority identity. In this way, middle- and upper-income African American youths may devalue academic pursuits and adopt self-defeating behaviors that jeopardize their academic success.[57]

At the same time, these general patterns do not hold true for all individuals. One study examined how African American adolescents' deductive reasoning and school performance were related their socioeconomic status, racial/cultural identity, and self-esteem.[58] The researchers found that better reasoning performance was associated with stronger—not weaker—racial/cultural identity.[59] The more comfortable the African American students were in their minority identity, the more effective their thinking.

Geneva Gay, a multicultural scholar, observes that if students feel that the school environment is alien and hostile toward them or does not affirm and value who they are (as many minority students believe), they will not be able to concentrate as intently as they might on academic tasks. The stress and anxiety that accompany this lack of support and affirmation are likely to drain these students' mental attention, energy, and efforts, pulling them away from the academic tasks and toward protecting themselves from (psychological) attack. As a consequence, they become less willing to persist at academic tasks and less able to think clearly about the learning, and their schoolwork suffers.[60]

Coping Strategies That Promote School Success

Coping with school success and peer acceptance does not have to be an either-or situation. A continuum links the two untenable extremes of "succeed and betray" or "fail and be loyal."[61]

Table 12.2 shows the various strategies that minority student use to find a middle ground between "acting white" and failing in school. These coping strategies allow students to behave in ways that keep both their teachers and their peers happy. The lower the number on the continuum, the greater the assimilation to school norms and rejection of peer group norms.

These coping strategies allow minority students to overcome the psychological barriers to learning that they find in school. Minority students can keep and enhance their racial identity by not appearing too successful in a "white" environment but still doing enough to please their teachers and keep the doors open to future opportunities. Some students may "camouflage" their academic behaviors with posed disinterest—reducing their efforts by not paying attention in class, not keeping up with school assignments, or complaining that the work

---

[56] Ogbu & Simon, 1998.
[57] Fordham & Ogbu, 1986.
[58] Chappell, M. S., & Overton, W. F. (2002). Development of logical reasoning and the school performance of African American adolescents in relation to socioeconomic status, ethnic identity, and self-esteem. *Journal of Black Psychology, 28,* 295–317.
[59] Ogbu, J. U. (1995). Origins of human competence: A cultural–ecological perspective. In N. R. Goldberger & J. B. Veroff (Eds.), *Culture and psychology reader* (pp. 245–275). New York: New York University Press.
[60] Gay, 1994.
[61] Ogbu, 1992.

Table 12.2	Ogbu's Continuum of Adaptive Strategies
Level on Continuum	**Adaptive Strategies**
1. Emulation of whites or cultural passing	Adopting "white" academic attitudes and behaviors or trying to behave like middle-income white students. This approach usually has a high psychological cost and isolation from African American peers.
2. Accommodation without assimilation	A student adopting this strategy behaves according to school norms at school but according to African American or other cultural norms at home and in the community.
3. Camouflage	Disguising true academic attitudes and behaviors by using a variety of techniques: becoming a class clown, pretending lack of interest in school, studying in secret, becoming involved in "acceptable" cultural activities such as sports. Good grades are attributed to "natural smartness" rather than hard work.
4. Involvement in church activities	Promoting school success while participating with one's own community and building an achievement-oriented peer group.
5. Attending private schools	For some, a successful way to get away from negative peer groups.
6. Mentors	Another success-enhancing strategy that encourages academic success while still feeling good about oneself as a minority group member.
7. Protection	A few students get the protection of bullies from peer pressure in return for helping the bullies with their homework.
8. Remedial and intervention programs	Some students succeed with extra time and assistance focused on achieving well in school.
9. Encapsulation	May become encapsulated in peer group logic and activities. These African American or other cultural minority students do not want to do the "white man's thing" and, as a result, often fail.

Source: Adapted from Ogbu, J. U. (1992). Understanding cultural diversity and learning. *Educational Researcher, 21,* 11.

is boring. Other students openly defy and challenge the teachers' authority. In these ways, they can be good students and still keep peer support. Along the continuum, students try to spit the difference between "selling out" and outright failing.

Ogbu's oppositional culture theory does not suggest that group membership alone determines school success or failure. While this perspective can help educators better understand why some minority students may behave the way they do, teachers should avoid basing their expectations about an individual's school performance and behavior on group membership. Students always should be treated as individuals. Educators must recognize and address minority students' mistrust of schools and fear of being seen as "acting white" without being disloyal to their peers or their own cultural identity.

Activity 12.3

Table 12.2 identifies nine ways minority students sometimes try to succeed in school without appearing to do so.

A. Distribute the nine continuum levels among class members (two to three students for each level) without telling one group which levels the other groups have.

B. Each group will discuss its continuum level and its adaptive strategies. The group members will identify several student behaviors that might represent this level and create a brief skit to illustrate it.

C. Groups will take turns acting out their level. Class members will guess which level and which strategies they are seeing.

D. Discuss these strategies and the continuum as a class. Which of these have any class members used? Have them explain their reasons and feelings for using them.

E. Discuss how teachers can use this awareness of these adaptive behaviors to help minority students succeed.

Low-Income Students' Perspective

The image of the United States as a classless or mostly middle-class society is an attractive media portrayal that hides our culture's pervasive social and economic stratification.[62] By downplaying economic insecurity and representing "the middle" as a "state of mind," the media encourage low-income individuals to identify with a politically neutralized universal middle class.[63] By giving very little broadcast time or print space to stories that openly discuss class-based privileges or power differences, the media portray the poor as either invisible or deficient outsiders (such as substance abusers, criminals, and sexually indiscriminant predators) who deviate from middle-class values or norms.[64]

Historical and Current Factors

While slavery and formal indenture are no longer legal, the United States has continued to maintain a society of "haves" and "have-nots." U.S. institutional practices, including schools, continue to support class stratification, providing differential treatment and opportunities for Americans of different social classes.[65] In the United States, socioeconomic status and social class distinctions influence every aspect of life, including the quality of a person's schooling, his or her employment opportunities, and the health and safety of the individual's family.

Social class differences in the home are clearly correlated with educational performance and student achievement. Poverty means fewer material resources in the home. Parents working a variety of jobs often have little time to spend

---

[62] Bullock, H. E., & Williams, W. R. (2001, Summer). Media images of the poor. *Journal of Social Issues, 57*(2), 229–246.

[63] Mantsios, G. (1998). Class in America: Myths and realities. In P. S. Rothenberg (Ed.), Race, *class, and gender in the United States: An integrated study* (4th ed., pp. 202–214). New York: St. Martin's.

[64] Bullock & Williams, 2001.

[65] Collins, C., & Veskel, F. (2004). Economic apartheid in America. In M. L. Andersen & P. H. Collins (Eds.), *Race, class, and gender: An anthology* (5th ed., pp. 127–139). Belmont, CA: Wadsworth/Thomson; Rose, S. J. (2000). *Social stratification in the United States*. New York: New Press.

with their children—to read to them, speak with them, and to build the large and flexible vocabulary students will need to achieve well in school.

Low-income families are also influenced by the cultural beliefs and values common to their ethnic groups and these ultimately influence how they see and act in the world.

Values, Behaviors, and Cultural Assets

Researchers agree that there is no such thing as a "culture of poverty." This term was coined in 1961 by Oscar Lewis in his book *The Children of Sanchez*, based on his study of a small sample of Mexican communities.[66] Since then, researchers around the world have tested this thesis empirically.[67] Others have analyzed the overall body of evidence focusing on the culture of poverty model.[68] These studies concluded that differences in values and behaviors among people in poverty are just as great as those between poor and wealthy people.[69] Nevertheless, the concept of a "culture of poverty," which began as an idea taken from small stereotypes, has become an unquestioned—albeit inaccurate—part of mainstream thinking.

Contrary to the stereotype, most people with low incomes have a strong work ethic and high motivation.[70] Approximately 83 percent of children from low-income families have at least one employed parent. Nearly 60 percent have at least one parent who works full-time throughout the year.[71] Many low-income adults must work two, three, or four jobs to earn the money necessary to maintain family life. According to the Economic Policy Institute, low-income working adults spend more hours working each week than their wealthier counterparts.[72] Every day, low-income parents and family members model high motivation and hard work for their children.

Low-income parents care about their children's education, just as more affluent parents do. Nonetheless, low-income parents may be less likely to attend school functions, participate in PTA meetings, or volunteer in their children's classrooms because they have less access to school involvement than more affluent parents. Although they care very much about their children's school success, these parents are more likely to work multiple jobs, work during the evening, have jobs without paid leave, and be unable to afford child care or public transportation. Teachers and schools need to take these realities into account if they value involving low-income families as much as they do wealthier ones in their children's education.[73]

Low-income and children from poverty speak a real language, even if it sometimes sounds different from standard English. All people, regardless of the language

---

[66] Lewis, O. (1961). *The children of Sanchez: Autobiography of a Mexican family*. New York: Random House.

[67] Billings, P. E. (1974). Culture and poverty in Appalachia: A theoretical discussion and empirical analysis. *Social Forces, 53*(2), 315–232; Carmon, N. (1985). Poverty and culture. *Sociological Perspectives, 28*(4), 403–418; Jones, R. K., & Luo, Y. (1999). The culture of poverty and African-American culture: An empirical assessment. *Sociological Perspectives, 42*(3), 439–458.

[68] Abell, T., & Lyon, L. (1979). Do the differences make a difference? An empirical evaluation of the culture of poverty in the United States. *American Anthropologist, 6*(3), 602–621; Ortiz, A. T., & Briggs, L. (2003). The culture of poverty, crack babies, and welfare cheats: The making of the "healthy white baby crisis." *Social Test, 21*(3), 39–57; Rodman, R. (1977). Culture of poverty: The rise and fall of a concept. *Sociological Review, 25*(4), 867–876.

[69] Gorkski, P. (2008, April). The myth of the "culture of poverty." *Educational Leadership, 65*(7), 32–36.

[70] Iverson, R. R., & Farber, N. (1996). Transmission of family values, work, and welfare among poor urban black women. *Work and Occupations, 23*(4), 437–460; Wilson, W. J. (1997). *When work disappears*. New York: Random House.

[71] National Center for Children in Poverty. (2004). *Parental employment in low-income families*. New York: Author.

[72] Economic Policy Institute. (2002). *The state of working class America, 2002–03*. Washington, DC: Author.

[73] Compton-Lilly, C. (2003). *Reading families: The literate lives of urban children*. New York: Teachers College Press; Lareau, A., & Horvat, E. (1999). Moments of social inclusion and exclusion: Race, class, and cultural capital in family–school relationships. *Sociology of Education, 72*, 37–53; Leichter, H. J. (Ed.). (1978). *Families and communities as educators*. New York: Teachers College Press.

and language varieties they speak, use a full range of language registers, or levels of formality.[74] Their languages are highly structured with complex grammatical rules.[75] What teachers often assume to be deficient English (such as Appalachian varieties or "black English") is no less sophisticated than standard English. Rather, these languages are appropriate for the students' home communities. Caring and respectful teachers can help these students learn to be "bilingual" by helping them with more formal language expression in "white talk" (standard English) so they can interact successfully in a variety of settings, including school and work.

Researchers have found that teachers too often look to these students' deficits rather than emphasizing their strengths. In addition, teachers often have lower classroom expectations for working-class and low-income students. Teachers tend to under-encourage these students and under-evaluate their work. School officials commonly steer low-income children into general education and vocational programs, thereby limiting their future options.[76]

While some low-income students beat the odds and succeed in school, cultural barriers still work against this achievement. Much remains to be done to reduce child poverty and allow more children to enter school ready to learn, achieve more highly, and continue their education through high school graduation and beyond.

Teachers cannot allow the "culture of poverty" myth to lead to low expectations for poor and low-income students. Relying on a deficit model and drawing on popular stereotypes would define these students by their weaknesses rather than by their strengths. Instead, when teachers consider the evidence and recognize low-income children and families' respect for education and hard work, and when students are properly motivated to achieve, teachers can provide the learning environment and enhance the personal, classroom, and familial assets that allow these students to learn and succeed in school.[77]

African American Students' Perspectives

Through our discussion of the theories advanced by Steele and Ogbu, we have already considered the broad influences on African American and varied minority students and some of their coping strategies. In this section, we examine several specific cultural factors unique to African Americans in the United States, considering how these factors can positively impact their success in school.

Historical and Current Factors

The United States built much of its society on forced labor. Legal in all parts of the United States by the early eighteenth century, slavery was the Southern colonies' dominant work force system. Colonists captured, imported, enslaved, beat, and killed hundreds of thousands of Africans so as to serve white economic needs. This practice continued for more than 244 years. White slaveholders preferred African

[74] Bomer, R., Dworin, J. E., May, L., & Semingson, O. (2008). Miseducating teachers about the poor: A critical analysis of Ruby Payne's claims about poverty. *Teachers College Record, 110*(1). www.tcrecord.org/PrintContent.asp?ContentID=14591.

[75] Gee, J. P. (2004). *Situated language and learning: A critique of traditional schooling.* New York: Routledge; Hess, K. M. (1974). The nonstandard speakers in our schools: What should be done? *Elementary School Journal, 74*(5), 280–290; Miller, P. J., Cho, G. E., & Bracey, J. R. (2005). Working-class children's experience through the prism of personal story-telling. *Human Development, 48,* 115–135.

[76] Becker, H. S. (1952). Social class variation in teacher–pupil relationship. *Journal of Educational Sociology, 25,* 451–465; Cicourel, A. V., & Kitsuse, J. L. (1963). *The education decision-makers.* New York: Bobbs Merrill; Eckert, P. (1989) *Jock and burnouts: Social categories and identity in high school.* New York: Teachers College; Rist, R. C. (1970). Student social class teacher expectations. *Harvard Educational Review, 40,* 411–451.

[77] For more on how teachers can support students from a collectivist family background, see Rothstein-Fisch & Trumbull, 2008.

slaves to indentured European servants because once purchased, slaves became their owners' permanent property.

Despite this enormously debilitating history, African Americans are showing significant gains in education, social status, income, life expectancy, and political viability:

- The percentage of African Americans completing high school rose from 20 percent in 1960 to 82.3 percent in 2007.[78]

- The percentage of African Americans completing college or more rose from 3 percent to 18.5 percent over the same period.

- Among African Americans, 17 percent age 25 or older hold at least a bachelor's degree,[79] and 5.1 percent hold an advanced degree (such as a master's degree, Ph.D., M.D., or J.D.).[80]

- The annual median income of single-race African American households in 2007 was $33,916, up from $32,876 (in 2007 constant dollars) in 2006.[81]

- Most African Americans are middle class.[82]

- African American life expectancy has soared from 34 years in 1900 to 73 years in 2008.[83]

- In 2008, Barack Obama, a African American U.S. senator from Illinois, won 53 percent of the broad electorate to become the 44th President of the United States.[84]

These data show that while African Americans are making meaningful advances, many are still struggling for educational and economic opportunities.

Values, Traditions, and Cultural Assets

The strength of the African American family is one of its most valuable assets. Although wide diversity exists within their community, African Americans typically place a high value on family, including extended family. More than one generation may live in the same home. Grandparents, aunts, uncles, and cousins may live together to share resources (money, information, and moral support) and overcome the economic disadvantages they all face. Child rearing is often undertaken by a large number of relatives, older children, and close friends. Within the African American family, family roles are adaptable, kinship bonds are durable, and a strong work ethic, achievement ethic, and religious orientation exist.[85] This family and kinship arrangement provides many positive benefits to its members, although

[78] U.S. Census Bureau. (2009). Educational attainment by race and Hispanic groups, 1960–2007. *Statistical abstracts of the United States 2009*, Table 221. Retrieved October 17, 2009 from: http://www.census.gov/compendia/statab/tables/09s0221.pdf

[79] U.S. Census Bureau (2009). Educational attainment by race and Hispanic origin. Table 221. The *2009 Statistical Abstract*. Retrieved October 17, 2009 from: http://www.census.gov/compendia/statab/tables/09s0221.pdf

[80] U.S. Census Bureau. (2007). Educational attainment by selected characteristics: 2005. *Statistical abstracts of the United States 2007*, Table 217, p. 144. Retrieved October 17, 2009, from http://www.census.gov/prod/2006pubs/07statab/educ.pdf.

[81] U.S. Census Bureau. (2009). African Americans by the numbers. Retrieved October 17, 2009 from: http://www.infoplease.com/spot/bhmcensus1.html.

[82] Nearer to overcoming. (2008, May 10). London, UK: *The Economist, 387*(8579)., 33–35.

[83] Nearer to overcoming, 2008.

[84] Noah, T. (2008, November 10). What we didn't overcome. Slate. Retrieved October 4, 2009 from: http://www.slate.com/id/2204251/

[85] Hildebrand, V., Phenice, L. A., Gray, M. M., & Hines, R. P. (1996). *Knowing and serving diverse families*. Englewood Cliffs, NJ: Prentice-Hall; McCollum, V. J. C. (1997). Evolution of the African American family personality: Considerations for family therapy. *Journal of Multicultural Counseling and Development, 25*, 219–229.

it does not look like the nuclear family of parents and children celebrated by the white culture.[86]

Spiritual beliefs play an important role for many African American families. Participation in religious activities brings opportunities for self-expression, leadership, and community involvement. The church, its pastor or minister, and its personnel help family members with social and economic issues as well as with religious concerns.[87]

African American men and women value behaviors such as assertiveness and flexible roles. Within families, males are typically more accepting of women's work roles and more willing to share in the responsibilities such as picking up the children from school. Despite widespread societal prejudice, many African American families have been able to instill positive self-images in their children.[88]

Some African American values reflect their African heritage, which stresses the group, community, cooperation, interdependence, and being one with nature.[89] In contrast, white middle-class values focus on individuality, uniqueness, competition, and control over nature.[90]

Education is a highly prized asset among African Americans, who see it as a way to achieve both personal and family goals. African American parents encourage their children to develop career and educational goals at an early age.[91] Education's importance becomes diluted when African American students experience schools' discrimination, when teachers display insensitivity to cultural differences, and when young people develop the defensive perspectives that make academic success appear disloyal to their group.

Latino Students' Perspectives

The Latino population in the United States shares a common language and cultural heritage, yet is characterized by different historical, economic, political, and racial variables. Latino groups include Mexican Americans, Cuban Americans, Puerto Ricans, and Central and South Americans. In schools, members of this group experienced legal discrimination and segregation until the 1954 *Brown* decision.

Historical and Current Factors

More than 60 percent of Latinos in the United States have Mexican ancestry. This population includes recent Mexican immigrants and U.S.-born Mexican Americans (also called Chicanos) whose ancestors lived in the American Southwest generations before Europeans set foot in North America. The United States won the southwest territories from Mexico in 1848, and the Mexicans living in these areas became U.S. citizens.

Puerto Ricans account for the second largest U.S. Latino community. In 1898, the United States won Puerto Rico from Spain during the Spanish–American War, and annexed the Spanish colony.

Cuban Americans represent the third largest Latino minority in the United States They tend to be more recent immigrants than either Mexican Americans or Puerto Ricans. Many Cubans came to this country as political exiles.

---

[86] Thomas, M. B., & Danby, P. G. (1985). Black clients: Family structures, therapeutic issues, and strengths. *Psychotherapy, 22,* 398–407.
[87] Sue & Sue, 2008, p. 336.
[88] Sue & Sue, 2008, p. 333.
[89] Todiscom, M., & Salomone, P. R. (1991). Facilitating effective cross-cultural relationships: The white counselor and the black client. *Journal of Multicultural Counseling and Development, 19,* 146–157.
[90] Sue & Sue, 1999, p. 245.
[91] Sue & Sue, 2008, p. 335.

Socioeconomically and educationally, these three Latino communities reflect differing levels of well-being. Generally speaking, Cuban Americans have attained a high socioeconomic level compared with other Latino groups.[92]

Values, Traditions, and Cultural Assets

Family and traditions are very essential parts of Latino life. Respect and loyalty to family, cooperation among family members, and nurturing and maintaining larger interpersonal relations within a wide network of family and friends all contribute to Latino students' sense of identity and well-being. Latino families are often large and very protective of their children. Family immersion is a cultural value for mutual support as well as a means to transmit their traditional culture to their young. Even the 25 percent of families headed by single females often depend on an extended family for help with young children.[93]

Latinos' strong families have a traditional clear division of responsibilities and roles. Generally, fathers are authoritarian. Men's roles include providing income for the household and making the major family decisions. Latinas are revered, holding a special respected position in their families, honored by their husbands and children for their strength and hard work while putting their families' needs about their own.[94] Adherence to these traditional roles is decreasing rapidly among urban families, however, as many women are required to act independently in the work setting, in some cases becoming the family's wage earner, and to deal with schools and other agencies.[95]

The Catholic religion is often a major influence and source of comfort. Latinos' beliefs in charity as a virtue, sacrificing in this world, and enduring wrongs done to you have many implications for their behavior.[96] As a result, many Latinos have difficulty behaving assertively and fatalistically feel their problems are "meant to be" and cannot be changed.[97] At the same time, their belief that "God helps those who help themselves" can prompt effective problem solving to support learning and achievement.[98]

Research shows that Latino parents believe it is their primary responsibility to raise well-behaved, moral, respectful children.[99] At teacher conferences, Latino parents tend to ask, "How is my child behaving?" before asking how well their child is achieving.[100] They know that if their child is well behaved, they as parents have done a good job in preparing their child for school. In addition, Latino parents have high aspirations for their children. Most want their children to complete college.[101] Nevertheless, Latinos generally have a lower socioeconomic status than whites and Asian Americans, and these students share some of the same challenges and obstacles to education as do low-income students.

---

[92] U.S. Census Bureau. (2004). Table 6.2, Educational attainment of population 25 years and over by sex and Hispanic origin type 2004. Retrieved October 17, 2009, from http://www.census.gov/population/socdemo/hispanic/ASEC2004/2004CPS_tab6.2a.html.

[93] Lewis, A. C. (1998, September). Growing Hispanic enrollments: Challenge and opportunity. *Phi Delta Kappan, 80*(1), 3–4.

[94] Seymour, M. N. (1977). Psychology of the Chicana. In J. C. Martinez (Ed.), *Chicano psychology* (pp. 329–342). New York: Academic.

[95] Sue & Sue, 2008, pp. 380–381.

[96] Yamamoto, J., & Acosta, F. X. (1982). Treatment of Asian-Americans and Hispanic-Americans: Similarities and differences. *Journal of the Academy of Psychoanalysis, 10*, 585–607.

[97] Sue & Sue, 2008, p. 382.

[98] Organista, K. C. (2000). Latinos. In J. R. White & A. S. Freeman (Eds.), *Cognitive-behavioral group therapy: For specific problems and populations* (pp. 281–303). Washington, DC: American Psychological Association.

[99] Reese, L., Balzano, S., Gallimore, R., & Goldenberg, C. (1995). The concept of educacion: Latino family values and American schooling. *International Journal of Educational Research, 23*(1), 57–81.

[100] Rothstein-Fisch & Trumbull, 2008, p. 53.

[101] Retish, P., & Kavanaugh, P. (1992). Myth: America's public schools are educating Mexican American students. *Journal of Multicultural Counseling and Development, 20*, 89–96.

Figure 12.6	Respect and Family Loyalty Contribute to Latinos' Identity and Well-Being

Michael Krasowitz/Photographer's Choice/

Teachers can help Latino students succeed in school if they look for and work with the students' cultural and personal strengths rather than their shortcomings. For example, when teachers recognize that Latino culture values the extended family and social network for self-definition, teachers can construct classroom practices that work *with* instead of *against* that orientation.[102] Peer helping and sharing are valued.[103] The family notion of working together for mutual benefit of all is easily applied to groupwork in schools. Saying, "Good work—your family will be proud of you," and encouraging the child to bring the work home to show the parents play to Latino students' cultural strengths.

Because authentic relationships matter to Latinos, teachers are more effective in encouraging Latino students to "care" about their schoolwork when these students experience genuine "caring" relationships and compassion from their teachers.[104] Teachers show real caring when they offer regular after-school consulting and tutoring, encourage students to ask questions and seek assistance.[105] Other effective practices include setting high expectations for achievement, attendance, and discipline; helping students envision a positive future; providing access to a rigorous curriculum; providing tutors and mentors for students; valuing students' linguistic and cultural heritage; and increasing parent involvement.[106]

Teachers need to understand that Latino parents' reluctance to attend teacher conferences may result from language difficulties, complicated by many low-income Latino parents' belief that they have no right to question the teacher or school decisions. This reluctance to meet should not be interpreted as a lack of caring or parent involvement in the child's education. Instead, scheduling conferences at flexible hours, making child care and interpreters available if the teacher is not

[102] Gay, G. (2006). Connections between classroom management and culturally responsive teaching. In C. M. Evertson & C. S. Weinstein (Eds.), *Handbook of classroom management: Research, practice, and contemporary issues* (pp. 343–370). Mahwah, NJ: Lawrence Erlbaum Associates.
[103] Delpit, L. (1995). *Other people's children: Cultural conflict in the classroom.* New York: New Press, p. 170; Rothstein-Fisch & Trumbull, 2008, p. 22.
[104] Valenzuela, A. (1999). *Subtractive schooling: U.S.–Mexican youth and the politics of caring.* Albany, NY: State University of New York Press.
[105] Calaff, K. P. (2008, June). Supportive schooling: Practices that support culturally and linguistically diverse students' preparation for college. *NASSP Bulletin, 92*(2), 95–100.
[106] Lockwood, A. T., & Secada, W. G. (1999). *Transforming education for Hispanic youth: Exemplary practices, programs, and schools* (NCBE Resource Collection Series No. 12). Washington, DC: NCBE; Gandara, P., & Biel, D. (2001). *Paving the way to postsecondary education; K–12 intervention programs for underrepresented youth* (NCES 2001205). Washington, DC: National Center for Education Statistics.

bilingual, and having face-to-face meetings rather than sending written materials (even in Spanish) helps develop trust between teacher and family.[107]

Special-Needs Students' Perspectives

Special-needs students come from all racial, ethnic, and socioeconomic spectra. Special-needs students are students who require supplemental services to effectively help them learn. The Education for All Handicapped Act of 1975 defines disabilities as involving mental, hearing, visual, speech, learning, emotional, orthopedic, or other health impairment. Amendments to this act in 2004 expanded the list of recognized disabilities.[108] These disabilities vary greatly in intensity and in the ways they affect students' life experiences and learning skills. Special-needs students bring the same racial, cultural, and socioeconomic factors and assets to the school equation as other students, along with their additional learning needs.

Historical and Current Factors

Historically, many cultures have ignored, exiled, exploited, or killed disabled persons. Many nomadic societies saw disabled persons' limitations as keeping them from contributing to the group's physical work. Some cultures viewed physical differences as deformities resulting from evil or sin living within the person or the family. Even advancing Western civilization viewed many disabled persons as unproductive. Placing disabled adults and children into asylums and institutions allowed them to stay out of the way and out of sight of the general populace. Although society saw these individuals as deserving pity and charity, their educational needs went largely unmet. Later, persons with disabilities were labeled "handicapped," implying dependence was an inevitable part of their lives.[109]

Beginning in the 1960s, rehabilitative counseling evolved into a profession whose members tried to help those with disabilities "fit" or adapt into society.[110] In addition, civil rights actions helped open doors for assimilating disabled persons into the larger society. At present, litigation about access and equity for the disabled continues.

The percentage of students with disabilities has increased from approximately 7 percent of all students in the 1975–1976 school year to approximately 14 percent by 2006. In 2006, 95 percent of students ages 6 to 21 served under IDEA were enrolled in regular public schools.[111] Approximately 1 million children are considered disabled in the three fastest-growing categories: speech and language impairments; autism and traumatic brain injuries; and health impairments (such as asthma, epilepsy, diabetes, and lead poisoning).[112] Nearly half of all children in special education programs are identified with "specific learning disabilities," the largest of the 13 special education categories.

---

[107] Sue & Sue, 1999, p. 289.

[108] The 2004 amendment includes students with physical or mental impairments that substantially limit one or more major life activities, students who have a record of disability, and students who are regarded as having a disabling condition. Special education laws and school practices are discussed more completely in Chapter 5.

[109] Hohenshil, T. H., & Humes, C. W. (1979). Roles in counseling in ensuring the rights of the handicapped. *Personnel and Guidance Journal, 58*, 221–227.

[110] Bowe, F. (1978). *Handicapping America: Barriers to disabled people.* New York Harper Row.

[111] (2009). U.S. Department of Education, National Center for Education Statistics. (2009). *The Digest of Education Statistics 2008* (NCES 2009-020), Table 51. Retrieved October 17, 2009 from: http://nces.ed.gov/fastfacts/display.asp?id=59

[112] Black, S. (2007, January). Research: A vigilant approach. *American School Board Journal, 194*(1), 33–35.

Cultural Assets of Special-Needs Students

Students with special needs are persons first. Thus they bring with them the individual personalities, talents, interests, and uniqueness that characterize their non-disabled peers from any family, neighborhood, and culture. They also bring their unique family and cultural assets. An effective teacher will not allow a special education label or assistive equipment to distract him or her from getting to know and nurture the student as a person who happens to have certain learning needs that the teacher and other specialists can help successfully address.

Language not only reflects attitudes, but can also shape them. The word *disabled* ignores the reality that persons with disabilities are people with abilities. Focusing on limitations through labels like *disabled* and *handicapped* reflects an outdated stereotype of persons who had no means of support other than by begging money from others, literally taking off their hats (caps) and asking others for charity (money) to survive. Over time, "cap in hand" evolved into "handicapped." As this derivation suggests, language can either focus negatively on what is missing or positively emphasize what is present.

Emphasizing a person's characteristic rather than the person as an individual is both disrespectful and inaccurate. For instance, describing someone as a "person with a disability" shows more respect and accuracy than referring to that individual as a "disabled person." Similarly, saying that someone *"uses* a wheelchair" leads to different assumptions about that individual's capacities compared to saying *"confined* to a wheelchair"—suggesting that the individual is helplessly imprisoned in the wheelchair rather than employing the wheelchair to help accomplish normal tasks.[113] Even when no insult is intended, language influences attitudes and behaviors. Lack of awareness of how word choices affect others can lead the speaker to inadvertently insult the person with a disability. It can also reflect the speaker's belief that the disabled person is not worthy of respect.

Many persons with disabilities find certain body language equally disrespectful. This includes touching someone's assistive device, such as a walker, wheelchair, or prosthetic without permission, speaking loudly to a person with a visual impairment, or communicating with a caretaker or interpreter who accompanies a disabled person rather than speaking directly with the person in question. Intentional or not, these insensitive behaviors send the message that persons with disabilities do not deserve esteem or have their own capabilities, thoughts, feelings, or rights.

When educators choose words to describe persons with disabilities, they are showing their attitudes about these students and their expectations for them. Teachers will be more effective with students when they focus on their assets. Becoming sensitive to verbal and nonverbal behaviors that express positive regard and high expectations for academic achievement can motivate students with disabilities to work hard and learn in your classroom.

Discarding the Deficit Model

Helen Keller, a woman who was deaf and blind (and whose life was later dramatized in a play and several movies called *The Miracle Worker*), campaigned relentlessly for social justice. In her work, she emphasized that it was others' attitudes about the disabled, rather than the disability itself, which caused problems. She wrote, "We have been accustomed to regard the employed deaf and blind as the victims of their

---

[113] Hayes, P. A. (2001). *Addressing cultural complexities in practice: A framework for clinicians and counselors.* Washington, DC: American Psychological Association.

Figure 12.7	High Expectations and Respect for Personal Assets Help Students with Disabilities Succeed

Stock Connection Distribution/Alamy

infirmities. Facts show that it is not physical blindness but social blindness which cheats our hands of the right to toil."[114]

The same "social blindness" often afflicts teachers when they are working with culturally and racially diverse students. This "blindness" is most evident when educators look at what these students *cannot do* rather than at what they *can and might do* with support from high expectations, respect for the personal and cultural assets they bring with them, and a variety of means to help them learn and achieve.

The deficit model is socially defined. It is based on the "normal" development of middle-class, usually white students whose homes and communities have prepared them for schooling long before they enter the classroom. Children who come to school without that preparation and without the continuing support of family members who can reinforce schooling's goals face teachers' expectations that students cannot easily meet. Instead of seeing human variation, teachers and schools have been institutionalized to see "pathology."[115] All too often, frustrated teachers quickly refer these students for special education evaluation for suspected "disability."

Viewing "disability" or cultural/racial difference as opposite from "normal" places false limits on our expectations for diverse students' achievement. The traditional or medical model of disability focuses on individuals' functional limitations or impairments as the cause of their disadvantages. For instance, a person has a "disabilty" because he or she has cerebral palsy, cannot walk, and must move around in a wheelchair. A student is "disadvantaged" or "at risk" because he or she represents a minority culture or has a low-income background. In this view, the person owns both the problem and the associated limits.

In contrast, the social model shifts the focus. Instead of looking at the individual's "lack of ability" or "otherness" as the problem, attention turns to identifying and remedying the disabling social, environmental, and attitudinal barriers. Today, for example, we modify public buildings to create wider doorways to rooms, wider private restroom stalls, and ramps to ease accessibility from the street. Likewise, we provide inclusive classrooms and multiple instructional interventions for struggling

---

[114] EDGE curriculum culture: Charity images. Education for Disability and Gender Equity. Retrieved April 9, 2007, from http://www.disabilityhistory.org/dwa/edge/curriculum/cult_contenta5.htm.
[115] Reid, K., & Valle, J.W. (2004). The discursive practice of learning disability: Implications for instruction and parent–school relations. *Journal of Learning Disabilities, 37*(6), 466–481.

A CLOSER LOOK

In "Discarding the Deficit Model," Beth Harry and Janette Klinger, college professors at the University of Miami, Florida, and the University of Colorado, Boulder, respectively, discuss how and why educators tend to look for "deficits" within the student who has learning difficulties rather than looking for (and fixing) "weaknesses" in the teaching and learning environments. Read this excerpt and answer the questions that follow.

. . . Many students have special learning needs, and many experience challenges learning school material. But does this mean they have *disabilities*? Can we help students without undermining their self-confidence and stigmatizing them with a label? Does it matter whether we use the word *disability* instead of *need* and *challenge*?

Language in itself is not the problem. What *is* problematic is the belief system that this language represents. The provision of special education services under U.S. law—the Education for All Handicapped Children Act in 1975 and the Individuals with Disabilities Education Improvement Act in 2004—ensured that schools could no longer turn away students on the basis of perceived developmental, sensory, physical, or cognitive limitations. However, the downside of the law is that it has historically relied on identifying a disability thought to exist within a child. The main criterion for eligibility for special education services, then, has been *proof of intrinsic deficit*. There are two problems with this focus: First, defining and identifying high-incidence disabilities are ambiguous and subjective processes. Second, the focus on disability has become so intertwined with the historical devaluing of minorities in the United States that these two deficit lenses now deeply influence the special education placement process. . . .

The disproportionate placement of some minority groups in special education continues to be a central problem in the field. . . . [T]he categories with the highest incidence of disproportionate minority-group placement are also those categories whose criteria are based on clinical judgment: Educable Mental Retardation, Emotional/Behavioral Disorders, and Learning Disability. The categories whose criteria are based on biologically verifiable conditions—such as deafness or visual impairment—do not show disproportionality by ethnicity.

Across the United States, African American students are represented in the category of Educable Mental Retardation at twice the rate of their white peers; in the category of Emotional/Behavioral Disorders, they are represented at one and one-half times the rate of their white peers. In some states, Native American and Hispanic students are overrepresented in the Learning Disability category.

The label of Learning Disability (LD) used to be assigned mainly to white and middle-class students. [Meanwhile] students with learning difficulties who were from low-income homes were more likely to end up in the Educable Mental Retardation category.

. . . The real problem is the arbitrariness and stigmatizing effects of the entire process. Students shouldn't need a false disability label to receive appropriate support. They also shouldn't acquire that label because they had inappropriate or inadequate opportunities to learn. And they shouldn't end up in programs that don't offer the truly specialized instruction they need. . . .

When a habit of looking for intrinsic deficit intertwines with a habit of interpreting cultural and racial difference as a deficit, the deck is powerfully loaded against poor students of color. Speaking about her African American 1st graders, one teacher in the study pointed out that "they don't know how to walk, talk, or sit in a chair. It's cultural!" Comments like this really don't refer to whether the students can or cannot do these things. Instead, they show that the manner in which the students do these things is unacceptable to the teacher. The teacher's focus on deficiencies predisposed her to see the students as limited by their culture and, ultimately, to refer almost one-half of her class of normally developing children for evaluation for special education.

Source: Harry, B., & Klinger, J. (2007). Discarding the deficit model. *Educational Leadership, 64*(5), 16–19.

Questions

1. Explain how the "deficit model" of student disabilities creates opportunities for exclusion.

2. Explain how the belief system's language of "disability" devalues the students it describes.

3. Describe how educators are using clinical judgment, I.Q. tests, and special education labeling to disproportionately place students of color into the Educational Mental Retardation, Educational/Behavioral Disordered, and Learning Disabled categories.

4. Explain how a poor classroom and school climate can contribute to students' learning difficulties.

5. Discuss your thoughts about the idea that teachers can make changes in their instructional practices that can help more students learn effectively—without needing to send students for a special education referral.

6. Discuss how the "deficit model" can also apply to other diverse students.

learners. We expand our curriculum to include authentic voices from culturally diverse groups who make up the American society. We look for and use our students' cultural and personal assets to employ in our efforts to educate them to twenty-first-century competence. When the environment (or people's attitudes) becomes the problem, we can fix it.

In short, the social model rejects the "deficit" language's belief system. It sees student difficulties and differences not as "pathology" or sickness, but rather as human variations.[116] Educators would do well to get rid of the deficit model in the way they approach the teaching and learning of all children.

Fostering Diverse Students' Resilience

Students growing up and living in challenging circumstances can overcome background limitations and happily succeed in the mainstream culture. **Resilience** can be defined as the process or capacity to have successful outcomes despite challenging or threatening circumstances.[117] Research finds that children who experience chronic adversity fare better or recover more successfully when they have a positive relationship with a competent adult, are good learners and problem solvers, are engaging to other people, and have areas of competence and perceived efficacy valued by self or society.[118]

---

[116] Harry, B., & Klinger, J. (2007, February). Discarding the deficit model. *Educational Leadership, 64*(5), 16–21.
[117] Masten, A. S., Best, K. M., & Garmezy, N. (1990). Resilience and development: Contributions from the study of children who overcome adversity. *Development and Psychopathology, 2*(4), 425–444.
[118] Masten, Best, & Garmezy, 1990.

Drawing Upon Students' Resources

Each student has an array of personal, family, and cultural resources from which teachers can draw to help the child succeed. Even if the child does not have money to buy goods and services, many more assets may be available. Emotional, mental, spiritual, physical, and relationship resources and knowledge of school's "unspoken rules" can help individuals become resilient.

Emotional resources such as stamina, persistence, and good decision making give children the ability to control their emotional responses, particularly to negative situations, without engaging in self-destructive behaviors. Mental resources include those abilities and skills such as reading, writing, and computing needed for daily life. Spiritual resources give children some belief in a divine purpose and guidance upon which they can rely for direction and support. Physical resources include good physical health and mobility or the capacity to use what abilities they have to influence and control their environment. Support systems include family, friends, and additional people who are available in times of need. Relationships and role models nurture the child and do not engage in self-harming behaviors. Finally, knowledge of unspoken rules is a critical awareness of the verbal and nonverbal knowledge, assumptions, and behaviors that in-group members continuously use to move easily through the system to meet their needs.[119]

School success requires large amounts of assets that schools do not necessarily provide. Teachers can informally assess each child in their classrooms through conversations, observations, student records, and other interactions to identify and employ these assets in the service of a high-quality education. The more resources each student has at hand, and the greater the extent to which the teacher can access and use these for teaching and learning, the more resilient the student is likely to become.

Making connections. Caring about young people and finding means to help them achieve will build connections between teachers and students. Educators have daily opportunities to develop relationships that can foster educational aspiration and performance. As a 2005 report for the Annie E. Casey Foundation observes:

> Some young people do well and stay in school despite tough circumstances. Researchers studying their resilience have found that children need personal anchors—stable, positive, emotional relationships with at least one parent or key person. . . . Teachers and other adults can play an important role in fostering resilience. They may mentor students . . . or they may play a role by offering emotional support during hard times, acting as the student's advocate when conflict arises in school or at home, or by providing an opportunity to pursue a special talent or interest.[120]

Educators' effectiveness with diverse students depends on their willingness to recognize students' skills, interests, aspirations, concerns, and cultural assets and to modify classroom rules, procedures, and activities in ways that build students' academic and interpersonal success. Maintaining a single cultural point of view can blind teachers to the potential sitting in front of them. Teachers need accurate information about each student and their students' communities and families if they are "to provide equitable opportunities for learning."[121] That is why learning about culture—our own, the school's, and our students' homes—is essential.

---

[119] Payne, R. (2008, April). Nine powerful practices. *Educational Leadership, 65*(7), 48–52.
[120] Annie E. Casey Foundation. (2005, July). *Kids Count indicator brief: Reducing the high school dropout rate.* Baltimore, MD: Author, p. 12.
[121] Weinstein, C., Curran, M., & Tomlinson-Clarke, S. (2003). Culturally responsive classroom management: Awareness into action. *Theory into Practice, 42*(4), 275; San Antonio, D. M. (2008, April). Understanding students' strengths and struggles. *Educational Leadership, 65*(7), 74–79.

Our role as educators is to understand the value systems and circumstances of all our students so that we can support them appropriately. Perhaps we can help students who accept disappointment too easily strive harder to achieve their desires—and help more economically fortunate students adjust to disappointment more resiliently.[122]

Strategies for Helping Diverse Students Succeed in School

Lisa Delpit, an educational leadership expert who focuses on education and race, writes that the clash between school culture and home culture comes into play in at least two ways:

> When a significant difference exists between the students' culture and the schools' culture, teachers can easily misread students' aptitudes, intent, or abilities as a result of the difference in styles of language use and interactional patterns. Secondly, when such cultural differences exist, teacher may utilize styles of instruction and/or discipline that are at odds with community norms.[123]

Such miscommunications limit students' access to learning. When teachers do not understand their students' potential, they will "underteach them no matter what the methodology."[124]

Likewise, Sonia Nieto, Geneva Gay, and Gloria Ladson-Billings write about **culturally responsive pedagogy**—the idea that students' backgrounds are assets that students can and should use in the service of their learning, and that teachers of all backgrounds should develop the skills to teach all students effectively.[125] Evidence is growing that all teachers—regardless of race, ethnicity, or gender—who care about, mentor, and guide their students can have a dramatic impact on those children's futures, even when these students face seemingly insurmountable obstacles related to poverty, racism, and other social ills.[126] Developing the personal and professional awareness, knowledge, and skills to use culturally responsive pedagogy is a paramount responsibility for all educators who want all our children to succeed.

A number of factors identified in the literature relate positively to helping minority students succeed in school.[127]

As a teacher, be willing to learn. Low-income, minority, and students with special needs may differ in attitudes, work habits, learning styles, and behaviors

---

[122] San Antonio. 2008, p. 77.
[123] Delpit, 1995, p. 167.
[124] Delpit, 1995, p. 175.
[125] Gay, G. (2000). *Culturally responsive teaching: Theory, research, and practice*. New York: Teachers College Press; Ladson-Billings, G. (1994). *The dream-keepers: Successful teachers of African American children*. San Francisco: Jossey-Bass; Nieto, S. M. (2002/2003, December/January). Profoundly multicultural questions. *Educational Leadership, 60*(4), 6–10.
[126] Flores-Gonzales, N. (2002). *School kids, street kids: Identity and high school completion among Latinos*. New York: Teachers College Press; Noddings, N. (1992). *The challenge to care in schools: An alternative approach to education*. New York: Teachers College Press; Stanton-Salazar, R. D. (1997). A social capital framework for understanding the socialization of racial minority children and youth. *Harvard Educational Review, 67(1)*, 1–40; Valenzuela1999.
[127] For more specifics about helping Native American students succeed in school, see the following source: Fore, C. L., & Chaney, J. N. (1998). Factors influencing the pursuit of educational opportunities in American Indian students. In S. M. Manson (Ed.), American Indian and Alaska Native mental health research. *Journal of the National Center, 8*(2), 54–59. Denver, CO: National Center for American Indian and Alaska Native Mental Health Research. Retrieved October 17, 2009, from http://aianp.uchsc.edu/ncaianmhr/journal/pdf_files/8(2).pdf, For more specifics about helping Latino students succeed in school, see the following source: Wainer, A. (2004). *The New Latino South and the challenge to public education: Strategies for educators and policymakers in emerging immigrant communities*. Los Angeles: Tomas Rivera Policy Institute. www.trpi.org. For more information about helping English language learners succeed, see the following source: Miller, P. C., & Endo, H. (2004, June). Understanding and meeting the needs of ESL students. *Phi Delta Kappan, 85*(10), 786–791.

from middle class white students. Be prepared to learn about them as individuals, as learners, and as members of specific families and cultures. The more you learn about them in these contexts, the more tools and insights teachers gain about how to help these students succeed in school.

Be welcoming. When teachers warmly and genuinely welcome working-class students, students of color, and students with disabilities into their classrooms and provide the supports needed to help them succeed, the positive learning climate will help all students focus and learn.

Be culturally sensitive and respectful. Understand the ways your students' cultural values, language, behaviors, social, and economic background may influence their attitudes and actions. See your students' cultural values and strengths as motivators and resources in the learning environment. Remember that communication styles vary with the culture, and don't misinterpret students' actions as disrespect, misbehavior, or inability to learn. Students may be choosing "not to learn" in an effort to maintain their sense of identity until the teacher can make the discussion more personally and culturally meaningful and respectful.

Build relationships based on respect. Holding high expectations, insisting on high-quality work, and offering supports to reach these goals demonstrate respect for students. Calling each student by name, answering students' questions, talking to each student respectfully, saying "Hello!" whenever the teacher notices the student, and helping the student when he or she needs it all show the teacher's respect. Words and gestures let students know whether the teacher really respects them—or not.

Assess each student's resources. Identify each student's assets, including financial, emotional, mental, spiritual, and physical resources; support systems; relationships; and role models. Use these resources to help support student learning. If certain students are not familiar with the school's "hidden rules," clearly teach them how to behave appropriately and successfully in the school environment.

Use culturally responsive pedagogy. Instructionally, one size does not fit all. Teachers with knowledge and understanding of their students' cultural backgrounds, values, and learning and interacting styles are more likely look for and use their strengths, not their deficits. For instance, noted educator Jaime Escalante, celebrated in the movie *Stand and Deliver,* prepared low-income Latino students to pass the Advanced Placement Tests by referring to their ancestors, entreating his students, "You *have* to learn math. The Mayans discovered zero. Math is in your blood!"[128]

Reduce the "cognitive load." Choose activities and assignments that allow students to draw on their prior knowledge and life experiences. Learning is always more effective when it is tied to the students' existing knowledge and experiences[129] and starts where the students are. Each student has his or her own educational and life history, and the more the teacher can have students use what they already know, the more they can extend their learning.

---

[128] As cited in Delpit, 1995, p. 164.
[129] Elmore, R., Peterson, P., & McCarthey, S. (1996). *Restructuring in the classroom.* San Francisco: Jossey-Bass; McLaughlin, M. W., & Talbert, J. W. (1993). Introduction: New visions of teaching. In D. Cohen & J. E. Talbert (Eds.), *Teaching for understanding: Challenges for policy and practice.* (pp. 1–10). San Francisco: Jossey-Bass; National Research Council. (2000). *How people learn: Brain, mind, experience, and school.* Washington, DC: National Academy Press; Wiggins, G., & McTighe, J. (1998). *Understanding by design.* Alexandria, VA: Association for Supervision and Curriculum Development; Wiske, M. S. (1997). *Teaching for understanding: Linking research with practice.* San Francisco: Jossey-Bass; Richardson, V. (2003, December). Constructive pedagogy. *Teachers College Record, 105*(9), 1623–1640.

Reduce the "cultural load." Build personal relationships with your students and their families, and make an effort to include aspects of each child's culture in the classroom on a regular basis. Start by pronouncing each student's name correctly, find out where each student is from, and gather a little background information about each one.

Reduce the language load. Keep the concepts and rigor high, but explain the language in simpler academic terms. Break up complex sentences into smaller ones, point out new and difficult words, define them, and explain how they are used. Give information both visually and verbally.

Don't underestimate students' ability to achieve well in your class. Just because diverse students' school behaviors may not be the same as those of white middle-class students, it does not mean that they lack the intelligence and motivation to learn at high levels when given a high-quality academic curriculum and any needed supports (encouragement, material, and extra time). Offer high expectations with high supports.

Identify past leadership experiences. Review with students any past formal or informal leadership experiences and connect these to the students' ability to make good decisions for themselves—including good decisions regarding schoolwork and the student's educational and work future.

Help students know themselves as students and learners. Give students useful but respectful feedback about what they are doing well and how they can improve. Students who can recognize and accept their own academic weaknesses and work to correct them are more likely to perform well in school.

Involve the parents or extended family. Research indicates that students are more likely to exhibit significant academic achievement when parents or family members are involved with their education.[130] This consideration is especially important for diverse students whose cultures place a high value on parents and extended family. Include flexibility in your schedule so that you can meet with parents who work during the day, greet them with a smile, find interpreters if needed to make understanding and communication easier, speak without education jargon, and provide bilingual information about school practices and ways that parents can help their children learn at home. Let parents know that you care about their children.

Work with parents as a team. Encourage parents to speak with their children in their native language at home and use family and community stories to complete school assignments, support students' adjustment to their new culture, know what is happening in their children's lives, and encourage student involvement in community events that help promote ethnic languages and cultures. Teachers can also invite parents to visit the classroom to talk about their cultures and display items from their countries.

Establish partnerships with community organizations and school liaisons. Finding and developing parent liaisons who are fluent in the languages spoken by students' families can facilitate relationships between schools, students,

---

[130] Henderson, A. T., & Berla, N. (Eds.). (1994). *A new generation of evidence: The family is critical in student achievement.* Washington, DC: National Committee for Citizens in Education; Epstein, J. L. (1991). Effects of students' achievement of teacher practices of parent involvement. In S. B. Silvern (Ed.). *Advances in teaching/language research. Vol. 5: Literacy through family, community, and school interaction* (pp. 261–276). Greenwich, CT: JAI Press; Henderson, A. T., & Mapp, K. L. (2002). *A new wave of evidence: The impact of school, family and community connections on student achievement, annual synthesis 2002* (Eric Document No. ED 474521). Austin, TX: Center of Family and Community Connections with Schools, Southwest Educational Development Laboratory.

and families. These intermediaries can teach parents about schools' "chain of command," assist counselors in interpreting immigrant students' home-country transcripts, help reduce miscommunications among staff and minority parents, and explain students' culture and values to staff.

Activity 12.4

U.S. minority groups have rich and varied cultures that can actively contribute to students' school success.

A. Divide the class into three groups and assign one group to each of the following minorities: African American, Latino American, and students with disabilities.

B. Identify and discuss the life-affirming cultural factors from each group that would support students' school success.

C. Discuss how can teachers use these family or community resources in culturally sensitive ways that would support this student group's school success.

D. Have each group present its findings to the entire class.

E. In a whole-class activity, discuss your findings.

Resetting Our Perspectives, Priorities, and Expectations

The process of learning involves more than intellectual ability and mastery of cognitive content. It also includes teachers' and students' psychological and emotional dispositions and the teaching and learning environmental settings or climates in which they occur.

Unequal educational opportunities still exist in American's schools. Increased understanding of students' social class, race, culture, and special learning needs can help educators better relate to all of their students and find resourceful ways to increase learning opportunities for each child.

"If we are to successfully educate all of our children, we must work to remove the blinders built of stereotypes, monoculture instructional methodologies, ignorance, social distance . . ."[131] In the words of a Native Alaskan educator, "In order to teach you, I must know you."[132]

---

[131] Delpit, 1995, p. 182.
[132] Cited in Delpit, 1995, p. 183.

Summary

Teaching and learning are cultural processes that take place in a social context. To make teaching and learning more accessible and equitable for a wide variety of students, students' cultures need to be more clearly understood. Minority, low-income, and special needs students possess valuable personal and cultural assets that educators can use to help them achieve.

Many low-achieving student groups come from cultures that differ from the U.S. white, middle-income norm on which public schools are based. Racial/cultural identity development is a cognitive, emotional, and behavioral process that continues throughout life. Racial and cultural identities are critical parts of how persons—both teachers and students—see themselves as individuals and as part of a larger group. Research shows that students with positive racial and cultural identities were more likely to be successful in school.

Culturally responsive teaching can help educators become more successful with a wider range of students. Knowing your students and showing respect and caring for them through setting high expectations, culturally sensitive instruction, use of students' personal and cultural assets, and a range of individualized supports can help them develop the resilience, attitudes, behaviors, and skills necessary to succeed in school and life.

Conclusions

- Developing a mature racial and cultural identity can increase students' school and social achievement.
- Diverse students come to school with a range of cultural and personal assets that culturally responsive teachers can use to help these young people learn and achieve well in school and in life.

Curriculum

What should students learn? Who decides if it worth learning? A 2008 national survey of almost 30,000 students at 100 randomly selected high schools found that cheating in schools is widespread—and getting worse. According to the survey, 64 percent of students cheated on a test in the past year and 38 percent did so at least twice. Thirty-six percent said they used the Internet to plagiarize an assignment. Despite such responses, 93 percent of the students said they were satisfied with their personal ethics and character.[1]

On another survey about cheating, some 50 percent of respondents said they don't think copying questions and answers from a test is even cheating.[2] They called it "borrowing."[3]

Many students cheat (or "borrow") because they feel the knowledge school is teaching them is useless. Kristi Mann, reflecting on her own experiences as a high school English teacher, says, "Perhaps our curriculum has become so irrelevant to real life that most students . . . would rather borrow the knowledge than commit to purchase it—learn it—for themselves."[4]

The curriculum is what we teach students in schools. Nothing is more important than deciding what to teach our young, because our continued existence as a society depends on these choices. Curriculum determines what our society considers to be "well educated." Yet unless students are highly motivated or clearly see the connections between what is personally interesting and relevant to them and the curriculum schools want them to learn, they will not learn it. In our complex world, high levels of learning are especially critical if students want more than limited life options. Understanding the concept and practice of curriculum, therefore, and being aware of how to make it meaningful to students are essential to making informed decisions as an educator and as a student.

Focus Questions

- What is curriculum and how does it contribute to meeting schools' purposes?
- What is the relationship between society and curriculum?
- What is the difference between *schooling* and *educating*, and how does it affect curriculum?
- How does the history of U.S. curriculum reflect intellectual, societal, and political influences?

---

[1] Associated Press. (2008, December 10). Student cheating found to increase. *Education Week, 28*(15), 4. For more information on this study, see *Ethics of American youth—2008 summary*. Los Angeles, CA: Josephson Institute. Retrieved October 18, 2009, from http://charactercounts.org/programs/reportcard/.
[2] Slobogin, K. (2002, April 5). Survey: Many students say cheating's OK. Education. *CNN.com*. Retrieved October 18, 2009, from http://archives.cnn.com/2002/fyi/teachers.ednews/04/05/highschool.cheating/.
[3] Mann, K. L. (2007, June 13). Thoughts on cheating. *Education Week, 26*(41), 33.
[4] Mann, 2007.

- What do curriculum thinkers Ralph Tyler, Hilda Taba, Benjamin Bloom, and Grant Wiggins and Jay McTighe have to say about both the learner and the curriculum?
- Which core curricula do our schools currently teach, and how well are our students learning them?
- How well do the arts contribute to education's goals?
- Which curriculum factors contribute to educating the whole child?

Curriculum and Educational Goals

What Is Curriculum?

For educators, no decision is more important that deciding what to teach and toward what end. Curriculum is at the core of any education system because it defines what schooling should accomplish. Once an education system has defined its curriculum, the teacher uses subject-matter and pedagogical knowledge to accomplish the curriculum's goals and facilitate student learning. In his book *What Works in Schools. Translating Research into Action* (2003), educational researcher Robert Marzano argues that having a "guaranteed and viable curriculum" is the number one factor for its impact on student achievement.[5]

Defining curriculum can be confusing because it can mean so many different things. The most common definition comes from the Latin root *currere*, which means "to run (around a racetrack)." For many students, curriculum is a race to be run, a series of obstacles (or courses) to be passed. Historically, curriculum referred to the subjects taught during the classical period of Greek civilization. In the mid-nineteenth century, it came to mean a course of study at a school or university. The twentieth century broadened the concept to include subjects other than the classics.[6]

Defining curriculum is also difficult because so many educational specialties call curriculum their professional home. Since the 1900s, the curriculum family has included people interested in subject content, teaching methods, teacher education, human development, social progressivism and conservatism, educational technologies, evaluation, and educational objectives.[7] With so many related but competing professional interests, agreeing on one common definition is challenging.

Two useful meanings for **curriculum** are as follows:

- Curriculum is all the learning that is planned and guided by the school, whether it is carried on in groups or individually, inside or outside the school.[8]
- Curriculum is a plan for learning.[9]

All agree that *curriculum* is the subjects that schools teach, whereas *pedagogy* is how the curriculum is taught. Curriculum is the program; instruction is the method. The two are separate but interdependent concepts.

---

[5] Marzano, R. J. (2003). *What works in schools: Translating research into action.* Alexandria, VA: Association for Supervision and Curriculum Development, p. 19.
[6] Marsh, C. J. (2004). *Key concepts for understanding curriculum,* 3rd ed. London, UK: Routledge, p. 3.
[7] Huebner, D. (1976). The moribund curriculum field: Its wake and our work. *Curriculum Inquiry,* 6(2), 153–167.
[8] John Kerr, as quoted Kelly, A. V. (1983/1999). *The curriculum. theory and practice.* 4th ed. London: Paul Chapman, p. 10.
[9] Taba, H. (1962). *Curriculum development: Theory and practice.* New York: Harcourt Brace and World.

Curricula don't just happen. Society uses curriculum to prepare its young people for adult responsibilities. Accordingly, states and localities decide what students should learn based on their beliefs about what students need to survive in a complex environment and what it means to be an educated person in that culture. The governing body selects people, serving as the larger society's agents, to write curriculum reflecting these values and beliefs. These persons may include professionals, politicians, or other community members.

Curriculum planning occurs in a social context and involves translating views about human nature and the nature of the universe into educational aims. Knowledge about how students learn and the educational process must be considered during this endeavor.

What Are Education's Purposes?

As discussed in Chapter 7, our society believes that education should accomplish many goals. Once we know schools' intent, we can select or develop the curriculum to help our students achieve these ends.

Our schools' purposes include (but are not limited to):

- **National goals**—to preserve traditional American values and encourage good citizenship, economic growth, and social stability by transmitting our cultural heritage and traditions.

- **Economic goals**—to socialize future workers for the workplace with appropriate attitudes, knowledge, skills, and behaviors.

- **Social goals**—to help create a better culture, in part, by helping students learn to thrive in a diverse, pluralistic society.

- **Personal goals**—to help students to live personally satisfying and socially productive lives by fully developing their minds.[10]

Schooling or educating? As schools select curriculum to accomplish these national, economic, social, and personal goals, they must also consider whether the schooling will merely teach subjects to students or whether the learning will educate their students. *Schooling* is not the same as *educating*.

Schooling is the program of formal instruction or training that occurs within a certain place (a classroom) and at a certain time (during the school day, during a certain number of days throughout the year). *Schooling* is legally defined in each state's laws. **Educating**, by contrast, encompasses more than what children should know or how much seat time passes between enrollment and assessment. Educating occurs all the time, even outside the confines of a designated building labeled the "school." "Educated" is how we want our children to be. This question, "What is an educated person?" has perplexed educators, philosophers, and parents for generations. Only after we answer this question can we create curricula and classrooms that strive to fulfill those intentions.

Education is not merely about the curriculum. It is about the human condition.[11] In the real world, knowledge does not appear in separate disciplines such as English, math, social studies, science, and art. For example, *language* involves more than just reading literature and learning correct grammar. Language develops proficiency in the written and spoken word, use of mathematical symbol systems, and understanding musical and graphic arts. All of these communication modes provide infinite ways to understand the world and to express ourselves. Accordingly, to

---

[10] Eisner, E. W. (1992, April). The misunderstood role of the arts in human development. *Phi Delta Kappan*, 73(8), 592

[11] Boyer, E. L. (1995). The educated person. in J. A. Beane (Ed.), *Toward a coherent curriculum* (pp. 16–25). Alexandria, VA: Association for Supervision and Curriculum Development.

become educated, students must see across disciplines to life's realities and innate coherence.

Likewise, Elliot W. Eisner, Stanford University Professor of Education and Art, writes, "What one wants . . . is to provide a curriculum and a school environment that enable students to develop the dispositions, the appetites, the skills, and the ideas that will allow them to live personally satisfying and socially productive lives. Education's most important results are not test scores or even skills performed in the classroom. They are the tasks students are able to complete successfully in the lives they lead outside of schools."[12] Education allows persons to become the architects of their own lives.

"In fact, students learn both more and less than what teachers intend to teach," says Eisner.[13] If they are to become *educated* as opposed to *schooled*, students will learn a lot more and in ways they take with them after the dismissal bell rings.

Activity 13.1

As discussed, *education* is different than *schooling*. They are different processes and get different results.

A. Working as a group, join your class members in defining the similarities and differences between *education* and *schooling*, using the information from this section, students' own experiences, and outside resources. In what ways are *education* and *schooling* different processes and different results?

B. Working as an individual, reflect on your own K–12 and college classroom experiences and decide which specific experiences contributed to your being *educated* and which contributed to your being *schooled*.

C. Again working as a whole class, discuss students' reflections on this topic. Which learning experiences were *schooling* and which were *education*? What qualities describe the differences between the two?

D. If you were a teacher, how would you try to ensure that your students were *educated* rather than *schooled*?

Until students find their studies personally meaningful, relevant, and interesting, they may be more likely to cheat—and less likely to learn. In this scenario, students may become schooled but will not become educated.

Depth or breadth? How does one decide what to include in a curriculum? Given the amount of time allotted in the school year and school day, should the curriculum be wide and thin, covering many topics superficially so students have a passing familiarity with many issues? Or should the curriculum include fewer topics but study each deeply so students truly understand and develop mastery over those subjects?

Those curriculum writers favoring breadth reflect the old saying, "Throw enough mud on the wall, and some of it is bound to stick." This view recognizes that not everything that is taught is learned. It suggests, nonetheless, that bombarding students with information is still a worthwhile effort because they will remember at least some of it.[14] For this theory's adherents, the traditional essentialist curriculum of different

---

[12] Eisner, E. W. (2003, May). Questionable assumptions about schooling. *Phi Delta Kappan, 84*(9), 651.
[13] Eisner, 2003, pp. 655–656.
[14] Brady, M. (2000, May). The standards juggernaut. *Phi Delta Kappan, 81*(9), 649–651.

subjects, each with many important topics studied apart from each other, is the right curriculum.

Those favoring depth follow the maxim, "Less is more." In the early twentieth century, mathematician, teacher, and philosopher Alfred North Whitehead asserted that dumping vast amounts of information on students was counterproductive. He argued that humans were not mentally equipped to handle a great deal of random, "inert knowledge." The young, he advised, need to study in great depth a relatively few really powerful ideas that encompass and explain major aspects of human experience.[15]

For instance, according to this view, students should learn broad concepts that cut across all fields of knowledge and find their inherent connections. Concepts such as patterns, structure, relationship, and system are central to all disciplines, including those not yet developed. By focusing on large-scale mental organizers, students become equipped to expand existing fields of study and to explore new intellectual territories. Unless persons can integrate what they learn with an often-used larger scheme or meaning, details are soon forgotten. In short, students tend to remember only the "big ideas."

Here or there? Educators who think that individuals learn by connecting new information to personally meaningful experiences believe in starting each student's learning "here." "Here" reflects where the student is, cognitively, socially, physically, and experientially. These curriculum writers would argue, for example, that second graders studying "society and family" would learn more by starting at home, looking at their own families' behaviors. They could study society in the field by asking focusing questions and then visiting their local shopping mall looking for answers.

The "there" adherents, in contrast, might formally teach American second graders about society and family in China, India, and ancient Greece—places far from the children's own experiences or present knowledge. Curriculum writers who stress "there" are thinking about the subject, not the learners. They believe that studying Chinese families and society are important concepts and do not consider whether the young students will find them meaningful or understandable.

Wise curriculum writers must ask and answer another question in making this decision: How do students actually learn? While it may be worthwhile for second graders to be able to locate China, India, and Greece on an atlas, real learning will come only by first developing authentic personal experiences with the concept of "society and family" and then extending it outward to the unfamiliar. Conceptually dealing with the complex, the abstract, and the remote is very difficult, especially for young learners. Immediate reality is a more practical place to begin to build the descriptive and analytical mental models that will eventually take students to wider experiences. This lack of personal meaning often frustrates and bores students, undermining their desire or effort to learn.

As with most false dichotomies, the "Depth or breadth?" and "Here or there?" questions do not require either–or decisions. If students are to achieve a full and accurate understanding, curriculum *depth* and *breadth*, and *here* and *there*, are all important. The real curricular issue is how to edit, organize, and place the information so that it will have the most meaning for the learner. Closely related is the challenge of finding the best means to connect students with the content so they will learn. The teacher is the critical factor in making these choices.

With these frames of reference in mind, it is time to consider the history of curriculum in the United States and key contributors to thinking about curriculum, and to survey the traditional curricula currently used in schools.

---

[15] Brady, 2000, p. 650.

Brief History of Curriculum in the United States

Curriculum is not neutral. Curriculum is "always part of a *selective tradition,* some-one's selection, and someone's vision of the knowledge that needs to be taught to everyone," says Michael Apple, Professor at the University of Wisconsin–Madison.[16] Fundamentally, curriculum is about values. The decision to define some group's knowledge as the most important says much about who holds the power in a particular society and the values they seek to transmit through schooling.

U.S. curriculum reflects an inherent tension between its focus on social control and transmission of our cultural history and its focus on developing the individual. On the one hand, we recognize that schools should acclimate students to the social order and allow them to learn its traditional values and culture. This is an important social and political responsibility that helps unite us as one nation with a common perspective. On the other hand, we talk about dignity of the individual, self-actualization, individual potential, and the reality that education frees individuals to become their fullest, most satisfied, and most productive selves. In all, we have sought to find the appropriate curricular balance among society, subject and child. This dynamic tension guides educational policy decisions at all levels and has influenced curriculum decisions for more than 100 years.

Pendulum Swings

Throughout American public school history, curriculum approaches swung along at least two dimensions—from subject centered to child centered, from studying subjects to prepare for college to studying subjects to prepare for work and life. Driving these swings was a key question: How could curriculum best prepare students to take their place in the larger society?

In colonial America, curriculum theory or practice was not an important topic.[17] The public school's core curriculum was subject centered. Pupils studied the classics—Greek and Latin, rhetoric, natural philosophy, ancient history, astronomy and trigonometry—to prepare select students for college and the ministry.

By the late nineteenth century, policy makers had begun to question the appropriateness of this curriculum. In 1893, responding to factors such as increased industrialization, immigration, and the United States' growing international profile, the Committee of Ten proposed a more up-to-date, subject-centered curriculum in language, math, science, and history. Two years later, the Committee of Fifteen proposed a more up-to-date elementary curriculum.

Moving away from the strictly subject-centered curriculum, the 1918 "Seven Cardinal Principles" emphasized social and personal adjustment necessary for functioning in life, including health; command of fundamental processes; worthy home membership; vocational preparation; citizenship; worthy use of leisure time; and ethical character.[18] School subjects became a means to promote learning relevant to diverse students' lives.

In the 1930s, during the Great Depression most states increased the compulsory school attendance age to 16; 14-year-olds could no longer (legally) find employment, so they went to school. Not surprisingly, the traditional classical curriculum did not suit this new school population. In response, the core curriculum shrank from being the entire school program for all students to being the high-status

---

[16] Apple, M. W. (1995). Facing reality. In J. A. Beane (Ed.), *Toward a coherent curriculum* (pp. 130–138). Alexandria, VA: Association for Supervision and Curriculum Development, p. 130.

[17] Franklin, B. M. (1977, Spring). Review: Curriculum history: Its nature and boundaries. *Curriculum Inquiry, 7*(1), 67–79.

[18] Mehl, B. (1960). The Conant Report and the Committee of Ten: A historical Appraisal. *Educational Research Bulletin, 39*(2): 29–38, 56.

studies in which only the college-bound students enrolled.[19] As a result, both a discipline-centered and more practical student-centered curriculum coexisted within public schools.

Throughout the 1950s, the discipline-centered, "back to basics" movement required schools to teach students the subjects as separate disciplines.[20] Schooling meant learning a set of facts that could easily be assessed by paper-and-pencil standardized tests. The Cold War and the Sputnik satellite's launch panicked U.S. policy makers, who suspected that the public schools' curriculum was jeopardizing the country's national security and economy. In an effort to catch up and surge ahead, gifted student programs grew in importance. School boards and administrators pushed for improved student test scores as proxies for higher achievement. Many influential thinkers reacted negatively to the progressive education approach that considered students' interests and real-world relevance as "soft" and "anti-intellectual."

A "humanizing" approach to curriculum made a temporary comeback in the late 1960s and 1970s. In the 1960s, the United States experienced internal unrest as the country grappled with issues such as racial discrimination, poverty, urban violence and the unpopular Vietnam War. Reflecting these societal influences, schools' emphasis turned from the academically talented to the educationally disadvantaged. Child-centered rather than subject-centered curriculum approaches again became popular.

A new wave of "back to basics," subject-centered curricula reappeared in the 1970s. Later, the highly critical 1983 report titled *A Nation at Risk*[21] brought additional attention to the presumed failures in the U.S. public education system. To reform and improve education, educators looked backward to an old solution—studying the academic disciplines as separate and rigorous subjects.

National Curriculum Standards

Discussions of national education goals and standards in the 1990s extended the 1980s' academic excellence movement. Policy makers saw the need for all schools to be held accountable for delivering a core set of high standards regardless of teaching styles and curricular emphasis.

Goals 2000, written by the U.S. state governors in 1989, introduced national curriculum standards as a way to ensure that schools met the nation's academic achievement goals. States could voluntarily comply and adopt these proposed standards. In response to this push, professional educational organizations developed academic subject area standards in almost all curricular areas.

Of course, national standards for content areas met with wide-ranging criticism. Many objected to federal intrusion into local schools. Others worried that the standards would be politicized, advocating only a certain interest group's viewpoints. Still others observed that the standards might narrow the school experience, with school districts giving formal approval only to easily described and tested content standards. In this case, critics worried, standards might result in *schooling* rather than in *educating*. Finally, critics complained that learning by standards would likely be subject centered rather than child centered, ignoring those dimensions that addressed students as individuals and that actually increased learning.

Ultimately, all curriculum changes reflect intellectual, social, and political dynamics. Decisions about what the curriculum is, does, and includes are highly selective decisions made by those with social and political influence. The dramatic swings from subject-centered curriculum to student-centered curriculum, and back again, are clearly evident in the history of the U.S. educational system. Unless the

---

[19] Goodlad, 1986/1987.
[20] This was an essentialist curriculum, as described in Chapter 5.
[21] National Commission on Excellence in Education. (1983). *A nation at risk*. Washington, DC: U.S. Government Printing Office.

curriculum both connects with students in meaningful ways and enforces account-ability for students mastering high-level and important knowledge and skills, the pendulum will continue to swing between the two approaches.

Notable Figures in American Curriculum

Many individuals have influenced U.S. curriculum thought and development.[22] In this section, we briefly highlight those individuals whose influence can be felt in how we view curriculum today—its content, planning, and attention to student learning.

Ralph W. Tyler

Since 1949, Ralph Tyler's (1902–1994) ideas have served as the pre-eminent design model for developing U.S. curriculum.[23] Tyler developed a curriculum rationale and recommended that curriculum writers at any educational level should answer the following four questions:[24]

- Which educational purposes should the school seek to attain?
- Which educational experiences can be provided that are likely to attain these purposes?
- How can these educational experiences be organized?
- How can we determine whether these educational purposes are being attained?

    Let's look at Tyler's four questions more closely.

Educational purposes. Curriculum developers identify their "educational pur-poses" when they select their general goals and more specific objectives. Educational purposes may address students' cognitive, affective, and psychomotor capaci-ties. Effective learning objectives (outcomes or results) might comprise students' behavioral, problem-solving, and expressive performances that correctly and ef-ficiently use the taught content and skills. Objectives may specify the desired level of intellectual rigor or complexity successful students should show for each do-main, as illustrated in Bloom's taxonomy (Figure 13.2 on page 418).

Educational experiences. Teachers decide what they will do with the content to create a meaningful learning opportunity for students. Ultimately, the question, "What is worth knowing?" will limit the options available to teachers and students.[25] Most importantly, children needed to be intellectually engaged, not merely active.

Organizing experiences. Organizing these educational experiences requires cur-riculum writers and teachers to consider how the current learning relates to the stu-dents' previous, present, and future learning. Organizing learning experiences must also take into account students' cognitive and affective age and maturity levels.

Assessing learning. Evaluation requires educators to consider how to gather, as-sess, interpret, and judge whether the desired learning has occurred. Educators can use the evaluation feedback to revise the curriculum. In this way, evaluation be-comes an integral part of the learning and curriculum process, for teacher and stu-dent alike, rather than just the last phase in a linear process.

---

[22] The viewpoints and individuals described in the Chapter 6, Philosophy of Education, all have impor-tant curricular implications.

[23] Chiarelott, L. (2006). *Curriculum in context: Designing curriculum and instruction for teaching and learning in context.* Belmont, CA: Thomson Wadsworth.

[24] Tyler, R. W. (1949). *Basic principles of curriculum and instruction.* Chicago, IL: University of Chicago Press.

[25] Chiarelott, 2006, p. 30.

Hilda Taba

A Professor of Education at San Francisco State University, Hilda Taba (1902–1967) believed in a concept-driven curriculum. She contributed a theoretical and pedagogical framework for curriculum development. Her work provided positive direction for increasing students' intellectual functioning and their critical and creative thinking.

Taba's 1962 book, *Curriculum Development. Theory and Practice*, attempted to bring order and meaning out of what she saw as curriculum chaos.[26] Influenced by cognitive psychology and the work of Ralph Tyler, Taba argued that learning was dynamic and interactive rather than static, thereby establishing a different paradigm from a simple transmission model of education and evaluation. She expanded Tyler's basic model to become more representative of curriculum development in schools.

Curriculum planning model. Taba recommended a seven-step curriculum planning model:[27]

1. Diagnose need.
2. Formulate objectives—into four distinct categories: basic knowledge, thinking skills, attitudes, and academic skills.
3. Select content.
4. Organize content—by using three levels: key ideas, organizational ideas, and facts.
5. Select learning experiences.
6. Organize learning experiences.
7. Determine what to evaluate and the ways and means of doing it.

Curriculum includes the content and learner. Taba's curriculum framework considered both the content and the learner. She organized curriculum around concepts and ideas. She believed that concepts and ideas—not unrelated facts—were the most durable form of knowledge. According to Taba, curriculum, therefore, should center on widely accepted ideas and concepts in the various disciplines, and students should learn by moving from the concrete and specific to the abstract and general.

To a large extent, Taba's emphasis on the learner reflects her experiences working with classroom teachers and students. She sought to ensure that teachers could make the curriculum adjustments necessary to help all students learn.[28] As teachers introduce new units, they should deliberately help students connect the content to their prior learning and experiences. This action will give students a bridge to the new content. If students still have a difficult time understanding the content, Taba suggested that teachers have the "moral obligation" to adapt the curriculum and instruction so each student can find that bridge to understanding.

Further, Taba stressed that actively using knowledge leads to learning. The best way to increase students' knowledge is to emphasize acquiring, understanding, and using ideas and concepts rather than memorizing facts alone.

Taba's ideas on curriculum development had a major impact on reform-minded curriculum developers in the 1960s and early 1970s. She introduced the notion of a "spiral" curriculum in which key concepts are referred to repeatedly throughout the grades. With each appearance, the curriculum introduced increasingly more abstraction and generalizations. Taba's ideas on curriculum development remain influential today.

---

[26] Taba, 1962.
[27] Taba, 1962, p. 12: Krull, E. (2003, October). Hilda Taba (1902–1967). *Prospects* (UNESCO, International Bureau of Education), *33*(4), 481–491.
[28] Denham, A., & Shutes, R. E. (1986, February). Too good to miss: Review of Hilda Taba: *Curriculum development: Theory and practice. English Journal, 75*(2), 97–98.

Figure 13.1	Actively Using Knowledge Leads to Learning

David Buffington/Photodisc/Getty Images

Benjamin Bloom

As noted by both Tyler and Taba, a good curriculum considers not only what to teach but how students learn it. Bloom's taxonomy helps educators design, deliver, and assess a curriculum that encourages **teaching for transfer**—that is, using what was learned to solve new problems, answer new questions, and facilitate learning new subject matter, often outside the classroom.

Benjamin Bloom (1913–1999), Distinguished Service Professor at the University of Chicago, attempted to identify and weigh the factors that control learning. In 1956, he headed a group of educational psychologists who developed a widely used classification of intellectual behaviors important in learning. These classifications are appropriate for any subject and their educational goals, objectives, and standards.

Bloom's taxonomy. Bloom based his taxonomy on the idea that not all learning objectives and outcomes are equal.[29] Bloom arranged complex cognitive skills in a cumulative hierarchy from simple recall on the lowest end to higher-order critical and creative thinking at the upper end. Figure 13.2 illustrates Bloom's classification system, both the original version and a revised version of his work.

The taxonomy was intended as a method of classifying educational objectives, educational experiences, learning processes, and evaluation questions and problems.[30] This schema helps curriculum developers and teachers distinguish more difficult from less difficult cognitive processes. Using this classification helps teachers select appropriate content and design students' learning activities to increase the cognitive skills that students develop and use in learning.

---

[29] Bloom, B. J. (Ed.). (1956). *Taxonomy of education objectives: The classification of educational goals. Handbook I: Cognitive domain.* New York: David McKay.
[30] Bloom, B. (1985). Benjamin Bloom replies: Bloom's taxonomy and critical thinking instruction. *Educational Leadership, 42*(8), 39.

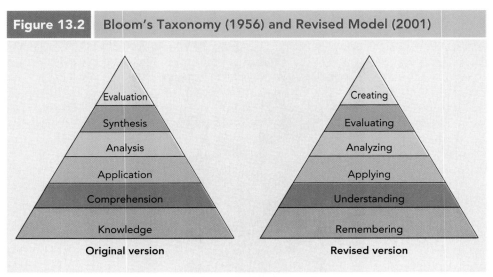

| Figure 13.2 | Bloom's Taxonomy (1956) and Revised Model (2001) |

Source: Forehand, M. (2005). Bloom's taxonomy: Original and revised. In M. Orey (Ed.), *Emerging perspectives on learning, teaching, and technology.* Retrieved October 18, 2009, from http://projects.coe.uga.edu/epltt/index. php?title=Bloom%27s_Taxonomy.

Let's first look at Bloom's original model more closely. Starting from the lowest level of thinking and moving up the pyramid toward the highest and most complex, students show:[31]

- **Knowledge**—rote memory, the recall of information in the form in which it was originally learned.

- **Comprehension**—the ability to explain a concept or define something in one's own words. Students understand when they build connections between the new knowledge to be gained and their prior knowledge. They can interpret, classify, summarize, infer, compare, and explain.

- **Application**—the ability to perform a skill or demonstrate an ability in a setting both similar to and different from the one in which it was learned.

- **Analysis**—the ability to determine the relevant elements in any problem or scenario. Analysis involves breaking material into its component parts and determining how the parts are related to each other and to an overall structure. This includes differentiating, organizing, and attributing.

- **Synthesis**—the ability to draw information from several sources and put elements together to form a coherent or functional whole, or reorganize elements into a new pattern or structure.

- **Evaluation**—the ability to develop a rationale for either position in a conflict that can be described as a moral dilemma. Evaluation involves making judgments based on criteria and standards, usually quality, effectiveness, efficiency, and consistency.

The cognitive hierarchy is cumulative, in the sense that each thinking level is more complex and comprehensive than the cognition required in the level before. Each level requires the student to master the less sophisticated thinking levels in the previous steps. For instance, *comprehension* is more intellectually demanding than *knowledge*. One must understand the relevant knowledge to comprehend, not just be able to recall and recite the information from memory. Next, one must understand the information before one can apply it in a new situation.

---

[31] Adapted from Bloom, 1956.

To produce meaningful learning, therefore, curriculum activities (and assessments) must include the higher thinking levels and use information and skills in meaningful ways, not simply recall facts. Once students understand and use the knowledge successfully, they can extend their thinking with it into analysis, synthesis, and evaluation, all of which are more intellectually rigorous and complex activities. Further, only with analysis, synthesis, and evaluation can individuals generate new ideas—that is, be creative.

Bloom's updated taxonomy. Bloom's cognitive model is still alive and growing. During the 1990s, Lorin Anderson (a former student of Bloom) and a new group of cognitive psychologists updated the taxonomy to reflect relevance to twenty-first-century work.[32] The changes, as can be seen in Figure 13.2, are small but meaningful. First, the revised version changes Bloom's nouns (*knowledge, comprehension*) into verbs (*remembering, understanding*) to make it simpler for teachers to design appropriate learning activities for students. Next, the 2001 version changes *synthesis* to *creating* and moves it to the top of the hierarchy.[33] With this new perspective, the highest level of understanding and learning—which employs all the cognitive steps before it—is to use learning to create something new.[34]

Using Bloom's taxonomy can also help educators prepare students for rigorous assessments. Applying the taxonomy to evaluation instruments, teachers can appraise their classroom and standardized assessments to see which type of thinking these exams require from the students. Developing students' application, analysis, synthesis, and evaluation skills with the learned content might lead students to achieve "proficient" rather than "basic" scores requiring lower-level recall or recognition. In addition, it may increase the students' likelihood of using the information in new settings, fostering transfer of learning outside the classroom.

| **Figure 13.3** | Application, Analysis, Synthesis, and Evaluation are Necessary if Curriculum is to Create Meaningful Learning |

Heinrich van den Berg/Gallo Images/Getty Image

---

[32] Anderson, L. W., & Krathwohl, D. R. (Eds.). (2001). *A taxonomy of learning, teaching, and assessment: A revision of Bloom's taxonomy of educational objectives.* New York: Addison, Wesley Longman, pp. 67–68.
[33] For a complete discussion of both models, see Krathwohl, D.. R. (2004, Autumn). A revision of Bloom's taxonomy: An overview. *Theory into Practice, 41*(4), 212–218.
[34] See Figure 13.2, the "revised" taxonomy.

Activity 13.2

Teachers use Bloom's taxonomy to design learning activities that require students to use a range of increasingly complex cognitive skills.

A. Divide the class into four separate groups. Using the 2001 revised taxonomy, each group will design a series of learning activities for a different children's story (such as Little Red Riding Hood, Goldilocks and the Three Bears, or The Three Little Pigs) using each step of the taxonomy (shown below), from remembering through creating for each story. Have the group first identify its story and the age of the students (pre-K, elementary, middle, high school) to whom they might teach their lesson.

Remembering: Teachers ask students to define, duplicate, list, memorize, recall, repeat, reproduce, and state.

Understanding: Teachers ask students to classify, describe, discuss, explain, identify, locate, recognize, report, select, translate, and paraphrase.

Applying: Teachers ask students to choose, demonstrate, dramatize, employ, illustrate, interpret, operate, schedule, sketch, solve, use, and write.

Analyzing: Teachers ask students to appraise, compare, contrast, criticize, differentiate, discriminate, distinguish, examine, experiment, question, and test.

Evaluating: Teachers ask students to appraise, argue, defend, judge, select, support, value, and evaluate.

Creating: Teachers ask students to assemble, construct, create, design, develop, formulate, and write.

B. After working for 15 minutes, groups should present their lessons to the class for their participation (as students) and feedback (as future educators).

Grant Wiggins and Jay McTighe

In 1998, Grant Wiggins and Jay McTighe, both former classroom educators, offered an innovative contemporary model for curriculum. Their model not only addresses which content to teach, but also considers the quality of student understanding and students' ability to use the content in new situations. Their framework helps teachers plan for student learning throughout the curriculum process.

Acknowledging influences of John Dewey and Ralph Tyler, Wiggins and McTighe integrate three major aspects of curriculum design—the material that teachers want students to learn, the assessment of whether students actually learned, and the learning experiences—written within a single planning schema.[35] This curriculum process keeps curriculum designers and teachers focused on the essential connection between learning and teaching.

Backward design. To this end, Wiggins and McTighe created a curriculum design model using a "backward design" approach.[36] They define curriculum as a specific blueprint for learning that is derived from content and performance standards. Curriculum shapes content into a plan for effective teaching and learning, from the viewpoints of both the learner and the desired achievements. Wiggins and McTighe specify what the learner will do, not just what the teacher will do.

Typically, teachers decide what they will teach, teach it to students, and then assess how well students learned what teachers taught. Wiggins and McTighe rethought this teaching, learning, and assessing process. In their model, shown in Figure 13.4, they

---

[35] Wiggins, G., & McTighe, J. (1998). *Understanding by design.* Alexandria, VA: Association for Supervision and Curriculum Development, p. vii.
[36] Wiggins & McTighe, 1998, pp. 7–19.

| **Figure 13.4** | Wiggins and McTighe's Backward Design Process |

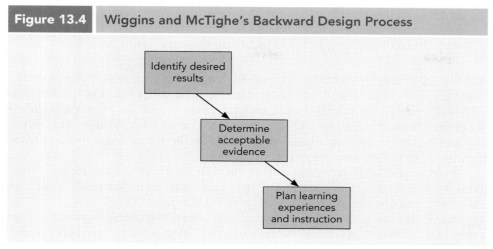

Source: Wiggins, G., & McTighe, J. (1998). *Understanding by design.* Alexandria, VA: Association for Supervision and Curriculum Development, p. 9.

begin "with the end in mind"—what teachers want students to be able to do—and proceed to the evidence teachers will accept that students have learned it. Only then do teachers consider the learning activities they must use so that students will learn the desired knowledge and skills. Because they know where they are going, teachers are better able to plan the journey to get there—hence the "backward" design.

Briefly, the backward design process includes three stages:[37]

- **Identify the desired results.** Teachers consider the instruction goals and content standards (national, state, district) and, as a result, make choices. They prioritize what should be "enduring" understandings important beyond the classroom, what is important for the student to know and do, and what is worth being familiar with. *Enduring understandings* are the "big ideas"—the larger concepts, principles, or processes—that lie at the discipline's heart and that have the potential for connecting with students. For example, the Magna Carta was a critically important document because it established that the law was more powerful than any person. Written law could limit governments' power and protect the individual's rights by guaranteeing due process under law.

- **Determine acceptable evidence.** What collection of evidence, gathered informally and formally, will show that the students understand and can use their knowledge in context through application, analysis, evaluation, or creation of new products? Evidence may include classroom checks for understanding, observations and dialogs, quizzes or tests, academic prompts, performance tasks or projects, and students' own self-assessments. Different types of assessments are appropriate to weigh different types of learning. For example, teachers might assess simple recall or recognition by giving a quiz or test (for content considered worth student familiarity). To evaluate more complex responses, teachers could use open-ended questions or prompts that require students to think critically (for content deemed important to know and use) or have students complete performance tasks or projects that require students to respond in authentic and complex ways with the learned content or skills (which demonstrate "enduring understandings").

- **Plan learning experiences and instruction.** With clearly identified results (specific "enduring understandings" and "big ideas") and appropriate evidence in mind (observations, tests, prompts, and projects), educators plan instructional activities. Teachers identify which activities will equip students with the needed knowledge and skills. They decide what should be taught and coached

---

[37] This is a simplified overview of Wiggins and McTighe's thinking. We refer the reader to the original source for more information.

and how to best do this in light of the students' maturity level and the desired performance goals. They also determine which materials and resources they need. Didactic teaching and feedback occur throughout this process.

Six facets of understanding. Of course, not all teaching aims for deep understanding. Sometimes familiarity is desirable, such as when learning the alphabet or developing a vocabulary. As Bloom's taxonomy reminds us, understanding progresses from recognition and recall to more complex knowledge uses including application, analysis, synthesis, and evaluation. Real knowledge involves using learning in new ways, sometimes called "transfer."

Wiggins and McTighe see *understanding* as a family of interrelated abilities. Table 13.1 describes Wiggins and McTighe's six facets of understanding, defines each facet, and gives examples of students using that facet.[38]

To this end, the backward design curriculum sees the textbook as a resource, not a map or a syllabus. Wiggins and McTighe observe that much student misunderstanding comes from a one-way, lock-step march through knowledge in textbooks. Teachers may assume that because the textbook's explanation is clear to them that it must be clear and understandable to their students. Wiggins and McTighe explain, "Most

Table 13.1	Wiggins and McTighe's Six Facets of Understanding	
Facet	Meaning (Definition)	Examples
Explanation	Provide thorough, supported, and justifiable accounts of phenomena, facts, and data. Knowledge is not just "what," but also "how" and "why."	An eighth-grade student explains with specific examples how photosynthesis is a life-sustaining process for plants, animals, and humans.
Interpretation	Tell meaningful stories, offer accurate paraphrases; provide a revealing historical or personal dimension to ideas and events; make it personal or accessible through images, anecdotes, analogies, and models.	An eleventh-grade student can show how *Huckleberry Finn* is a metaphor for white–African American relations during the era in which it was written; it is not just fiction.
Application	Using, adapting, or customizing knowledge to solve novel problems in realistic situations and making adjustments based on feedback.	A fifth-grade student can use knowledge of haiku poetry ideas and format to compose an original haiku.
Perspective	See and hear points of view through critical eyes and ears; see the "big picture," events, and ideas through a dispassionate and objective viewpoint.	A student explains the Israeli and Palestinian arguments for and against establishing an independent, Palestinian state on the West Bank.
Empathy	Make a disciplined effort to find value in what others might find unusual, strange, or implausible; perceive sensitively on the basis of prior direct experience. Empathy is not the same as sympathy, nor does it mean agreement.	A high school English student must explain why Romeo was so quick to kill himself when he thought Juliet was dead.
Self-knowledge	The wisdom to know one's ignorance and biases which inform as well as prejudice our understanding. The opposite of self-centeredness.	A student discovers that he or she is a visual learner, so he or she always has a paper and pencil ready to take notes, draw conceptual maps, and make other visual cues to help prompt understanding and retention.

Source: Adapted from Wiggins, G., & McTighe, J. (1998). *Understanding by design.* Alexandria, VA: Association for Supervision and Curriculum Development, p. 169.

---

[38] Wiggins & McTighe, 1998, pp. 44–62.

academic courses, organized around the content to be covered, are equivalent to giving cooks mere descriptions of finished meals. Such information, while complete in terms of the content, offers no explicit help in using the knowledge to accomplish cooking goals."[39] The misguided practice of relying solely on the textbook, instead of using it as a resource, may make the natural problem of misunderstanding worse.[40]

The backward design curriculum integrates content, assessment, and instruction with a focus on making the subject meaningful to students. Likewise, it recognizes that understanding is not a single concept, but rather a continuum; that is, understanding is a matter of degree, ranging from naive and simplistic to sophisticated and complex. Students show their understanding in varied performances and contexts. An education for understanding develops all aspects of understanding. With this approach, the learning comes with the *doing*, not the learning *about*.

Reviewing Contributions to Curriculum

Each of the persons discussed greatly added to educators' understanding of curriculum and learners. Table 13.2 summarizes their views on curriculum, emphasizing how each connected the curriculum to students.

Table 13.2	Summary of Contemporary Curriculum Contributors	
Curriculum Thinker	Views on Curriculum	Views on Learner

Tyler	• Developed curriculum rationale framework:
	  • Which educational purposes?
	  • Which educational experiences?
	  • How to organize these experiences?
	  • How to assess student learning?
		• Curriculum ideas considered how students learn.
		• Used psychological and philosophical insights to develop curriculum.

Taba	• Developed seven-step curriculum planning framework. • Curriculum is both subject centered and learner centered. • Curriculum should be organized around concepts and ideas, which are the most durable forms of knowledge. • Curriculum should be organized around four levels of generality in the continuum: specific facts and processes, concepts, basic ideas, thought structures. • Constructivist approach.	• Learning is dynamic and interactive. • Students learn by using knowledge. • Students learn from the specific and concrete to the general and abstract; curriculum should address this thought continuum. • Students can learn to think in ideas and concepts.
Bloom	• Developed cognitive taxonomy that described increasingly complex levels of understanding and learning. • Provided framework to clarify educational goals, content, learning activities, and assessments.	• Identified how students develop cognitive skills. • Addressed increasing levels of student cognitive understanding and increased transfer of learning to new situations.
Wiggins and McTighe	• "Backward design" curriculum framework to plan "big ideas," the assessments, and student learning activities. • Defined six levels of student understanding. • Appropriate to subject-centered or thematic curriculum. • Constructivist approach.	• Curriculum written from learners' viewpoint. • Identifying levels of student understanding is central to curriculum design and delivery.

[39] Wiggins & McTighe, 1998, p. 146.
[40] Backward design considers learning from the students' point of view.

Curriculum in the Schools

For the most part, today's public schools are subject centered, teaching to academic standards organized into subject disciplines. Each discipline has national standards that define what students at each grade level should know and be able to do. In this section, we take a closer look at each curricular area, identify the learning issues that each subject discipline confronts, and consider how well our students are achieving.

Math

Since colonial days, math has been part of the curriculum. Math is the most abstract discipline. It is based on numeric and conceptual relationships expressed through nonverbal symbols.[41] At the same time, math has practical applications, such as balancing a checkbook, making a family budget, or doubling a chili recipe. Fractions, decimals, and percentages are part of daily life.

Consensus on teaching math. While all states have math curriculum standards, they do not reflect a consensus of opinion about when students should learn particular mathematics topics. Mathematics learning expectations vary across states, including the grades in which different topics are taught. As a consequence, high-performing math student in one state may or may not have the same mathematics knowledge as a high-performing student in a neighboring state. This situation does not provide all students with an equitable opportunity to learn math.

Nor do math educators agree about how to teach math. As a profession, math educators occasionally engage in "math wars," pitting those who advocate teaching

Figure 13.5	Learning Math Concepts, Skills, and Problem Solving are All Necessary for Fully Understanding Math

David Lewis/istockphoto.com

---

[41] Jacobs, H. H. (2004). Development of a consensus map: Wrestling with curriculum consistency and flexibility. In H. H. Jacobs (Ed.)., *Getting results with curriculum mapping* (pp. 25–35). Alexandria, VA: Association for Supervision and Curriculum Development.

mathematics through real-world problems (what their critics call "fuzzy math") against those who prefer an emphasis on basic skills (what their critics call "drill and kill"). Overemphasizing either skills or problem solving leads to neglect of the other realm. Skills, concepts, and problem solving are all necessary, because each depends on the others for a complete understanding.[42] Owing to the state-by-state variations in math curriculum, interpreting student learning gains across the states—given that some students have had no opportunity to learn a math topic if it was not taught at a grade in which it was tested—is enormously difficult.[43]

Basing math curriculum on either concepts, skills, or problem solving has critical implications for national and international (i.e, outside the United States) math assessments. If students across the state or country are learning math in very different ways, at different grade levels, and to varying levels of comprehension and mastery, they may earn A's in class yet score poorly on standardized tests (which reflect different content, skills, and levels of complexity). These difficulties may be compounded in an international context. Countries whose students perform well in international comparisons do not choose between concepts, skills, or problem solving, but rather teach them all—concepts *and* skills *and* problem solving.

Measuring student achievement. The **National Assessment of Educational Achievement (NAEP)**, sometimes called "the nation's report card," compares student achievement in different states in math, reading, science, and social studies. These assessments describe student competency in a particular subject area on a continuum labeled from "basic" to "advanced:" They are not tied to any state's specific curriculum.

How well are U.S. students performing in math? Answer: In general, better, but overall, mediocre to poor.

Table 13.3 shows that the percentage of fourth-grade math scores at or above the "basic" level has increased since 1992, rising from 50 percent to 80 percent in 2005. The percentage of fourth graders performing at or above the "proficient" level rose from 13 percent in 1992 to 36 percent in 2005. During the same period, the percentage of eighth graders performing at or above the "basic" level rose from 52 percent to 69 percent, and those performing at or above the "proficient" level rose from 15 percent to 30 percent.[44] For twelfth-grade math, 61 percent of students nationwide scored at or above "basic" achievement in 2005, whereas only 23 percent scored at or above the "proficient" level.[45]

These data indicate that only 36 percent of fourth graders, 30 percent of eighth graders, and 23 percent of twelfth graders are doing solid academic work (the NAEP definition of "proficient") at their grade levels. The clear majority of students are only showing partial mastery of the required knowledge and skills needed for their grade.

Criticism of math curriculum. Critics look at this discouraging math achievement and complain that the U.S. math curriculum is "a mile wide and an inch deep." They suggest that the current curriculum tends to be too skill oriented, focusing mainly on the "one right way to get the one right answer" approach to solving problems.[46] It is broad but superficial and fragmented rather than coherent,

---

[42] Daro, P. (2006, February 15). Math warriors, lay down your weapons. Commentary. *Education Week, 25*(23), 34, 35.

[43] Reys, B. & Lappan, G. (2007).Consensus or confusion? The intended math curriculum in state-level standards. *Phi Delta Kappan, 88*(9), 678–680.

[44] Perie, M., Grigg, W. S., & Dion, G. S. (2005, October). *The nation's report card: Math 2005* (NCES 2006-453). U.S. Department of Education, Institute of Education Sciences, National Center for Education Statistics Washington, DC:. U.S. Government Printing Office. Retrieved October 19, 2009, from http://nces.ed.gov/nationsreportcard/pubs/main2005/2006453.asp.

[45] U.S. Department of Education, Institute of Education Sciences, National Center for Education Statistics. (2006). The *nation's report card: 12th grade reading and math.* Washington, DC: U.S. Government Printing Office. Retrieved October 19, 2009, from http://nces.ed.gov/pubsearch/pubsinfo.asp?pubid=2007468.

[46] Leinwand, S. (2009, January 7). Moving mathematics out of mediocrity: Commentary. *Education Week, 28*(16), 32.

Table 13.3	NAEP Math Achievement, 1992–2005				
	Percentage Scoring at or Above "Basic" Level		Percentage Scoring at or Above "Proficient" Level		
Grade	1992	2005	1992	2005
4	50	80	13	36
8	52	69	15	30
12	*	61	*	23

* Because of changes in the assessment content and administration, the results for 2005 grade 12 could not be compared directly with scores from previous years.

Source: Perie, M., Grigg, W. S., & Dion, G. S. (2005, October). *National Assessment of Educational Progress: The nation's report card: Mathematics 2005.* (NCES 2006-453). National Center for Education Statistics. Institute of Education Sciences, U.S. Department of Education. Washington, DC: U.S. Printing Office. Retrieved October 19, 2007, from http://nces.ed.gov/nationsreportcard/pdf/main2005/2006453.pdf. and for 12th grade, and http://nces.ed.gov/nationsreportcard/pdf/main2005/2007468_3.pdf.

jumping back and forth between topics at different grade levels.[47] For example, teachers are expected to introduce relatively advanced mathematics in the earliest grades, before students have had an opportunity to master basic concepts and computational skills. Conversely, the curriculum continues to focus on basic computational skills through grade 8 and perhaps beyond. Switching back and forth between basic and advanced topics confuses the logic presented in mathematics lessons—and the students who are trying to learn it.

Critics of this approach believe the mathematics curriculum should identify a progression of topics that build on the structure of mathematics, with topics in one year depending on topics covered in a previous year. Although there may not be one single "correct" sequence, math topics are not interchangeable. When the sequence does not reflect math's cumulative nature, students see the content as a meaningless list of facts that they learn for a test and then forget.

According to this view, students should be expected to master the basic concept of numbers and basic computational skills in the early grades before they tackle fractions or algebra. On an international level, children are expected to learn a relatively small number of topics at a given grade level. This approach permits deep coverage of each topic. For example, on average, second-grade students in high-achieving countries study nine math topics per year, whereas U.S. second graders are expected to learn twice as many topics in the same period.[48]

American students are not achieving well in math by international standards, either. Trends in International Math and Science Study (TIMSS)[49] results suggest that the top-achieving countries have coherent, focused, and rigorous mathematics curricula. A coherent curriculum helps students move from particular knowledge and skills toward an understanding of deeper structures, more complex ideas, and mathematical reasoning including problem solving. Adoption of a national set of world-class mathematics standards could help move U.S. schools in this direction.[50]

[47] Leinwand, 2009, pp. 32–33; Schmidt, W. H. (2005, Fall). The role of curriculum. *American Educator.* Washington, DC: American Federation of Teachers. Retrieved April 24, 2009, from http://www.aft.org/pubs-reports/american_educator/issues/fall2005/schmidt.htm; Schmidt, 2004.
[48] Schmidt, 2005.
[49] Gonzales, P., et al. (2004, December). *Highlights from the Trends in International Math and Science Study (TIMSS) 2003* (NCES 2005-005). National Center for Education Statistics, Office of Educational Sciences, U.S. Department of Education. Washington, DC: U.S. Government Printing Office; National Center for Education Statistics. Office of Educational Research and Improvement, U.S. Department of Education. (1998). *Pursuing excellence* (NCES 98-049). Washington, DC: U.S. Government Printing Office.
[50] Leinwand, 2009.

The following article is excerpted from Sean Cavanaugh's article, "'Math Anxiety' Confuses the Equation for Students," and describes how researchers have delved into causes and implications of fear of mathematics. Read the excerpt and then answer the questions that follow.

. . . In recent years, researchers and educators have delved further into the topic of "math anxiety," or the ways in which students' lack of confidence in that subject undermines their academic performance. Today, the issue is receiving renewed attention from academic scholars and others, who believe that developing a better understanding of the causes and implications of math anxiety is a key to improving achievement for many students.

Conceptual Barriers

Some evidence also suggests that anxiety is more of a factor in math than in other subjects....

Students feel more anxiety in math partly because they are dealing with so many concepts and procedures that are foreign to them . . . Once students realize they do not grasp a math concept, the internal pressure grows. Math entails certain conceptual barriers that lead people to read the same passage over and over again and not understand it. . . . by contrast, in reading a history lesson, students are likely to recognize vocabulary, themes, and ideas, even if they do not understand all the implications of a particular passage. . . .

Individuals with high levels of math anxiety tend to rush through problems, making them prone to errors. . . . Those math-anxious students also have far more difficulty on problems that require processes such as "carrying" numbers than on questions where such steps are not necessary.

In a 2001 study, . . . researchers concluded that math-anxious students struggle on problems involving carrying, borrowing, and long division. Those processes require a lot of working memory, they concluded, a function that is easily disrupted among students prone to math anxiety.

[A]nxious individuals devote attention to their intrusive thoughts and worries, rather than the task at hand. In the case of math anxiety, such thoughts probably involve preoccupation with one's dislike or fear of math, one's low self-confidence. . . . Paying attention to these intrusive thoughts acts like a secondary task, distracting attention from the math task.

Choking Under Pressure

Others have sought to better identify which students are most prone to the effects of anxiety in math . . . [S]tudents who had high amounts of working-memory capacity were, in fact, most susceptible to seeing their performance fall in math, on more complicated problems.

. . . Students with a good amount of working memory rely on "really intensive strategies" to solve math problems, such as keeping track of numbers in their heads as they move from step to step . . . That approach serves them well on relatively simple math problems, but not more complicated ones. . . .

In higher-pressure situations, such as timed tests, or where researchers put students under additional stress, those high-memory students fare more poorly. Performance pressure sucks the working-memory that has served them so well previously. By contrast, individuals with relatively little working-memory capacity do not seem to suffer as much . . .

. . . Although there has been little definitive research on what makes math anxiety worse, some scholars have suggested that math teachers or parents can ratchet up the anxiety of students by placing unrealistically high demands on them, or by showing annoyance when concepts aren't quickly mastered, while providing little academic support. . . . [M]ath anxiety is somewhat higher among women than men.

Source: Cavanaugh, S. (2007, February 21). "Math anxiety" confuses the equation for students. *Education Week, 26*(24), 12.

Questions

1. Have you ever experienced "math anxiety"? How does it affect your ability to learn math?
2. How does "math anxiety" interfere with trying to solve math problems in one's head?
3. How do you think math curriculum issues might contribute to students' "math anxiety"?
4. How can you as a future teacher use this information to help your students learn more successfully, regardless of the subject?

Language Arts

"No subject of study is more important than reading . . . all other intellectual powers depend on it,"[51] proclaims cultural historian Jacques Barzun. Focused, purposeful reading for meaning is an essential skill that all students need to learn if they are to succeed in school. Readers who can evaluate evidence in written material to find the answer to a provocative question or to garner support for an important argument do well at every grade level. College students and professionals also rely on these skills. Research has found that this type of engaged reading offers the best basis for effective student writing, which powerfully extends students' abilities to think and reason across disciplines.[52]

Veteran elementary teachers often comment, "In grades 1 through 3, students learn to read. In grades 4 and above, they read to learn." Researchers have called the obstacles children encounter during this transition the "fourth-grade slump" because it tends to occur when reading instruction shifts from basic decoding and world recognition to a focus on developing fluency and comprehension.[53]

The language arts include commonly used forms of communication—reading, writing, listening, and speaking. In the early grades (pre-K through early elementary), language arts instruction concentrates on teaching children how to read, write, and convey meaning with an emphasis on skill development. In later elementary grades, middle school, and high school, attention turns to developing meaningful and accurate communication, writing to learn, and reading to learn. The later grades emphasize developing reading strategies in various academic disciplines, including learning vocabulary, practicing methods of understanding content, and understanding each subject discipline's traits. Overall, language arts' principal goals are for

---

[51] Barzun, J. (1991). The centrality of reading. In M. Philipson (Ed.), *Begin here: The forgotten conditions of teaching and learning*. Chicago, IL: University of Chicago Press, p. 21.
[52] Hillocks, G. (1987, May). Synthesis of research on teaching writing. *Educational Leadership, 44*(8),71–82.
[53] Samuels, C. A. (2007, September 12). Experts eye solutions to "4th grade slump." *Education Week, 27*(3), 8.

Figure 13.6	The "Fourth Grade Slump" Occurs When Children Must Read to Learn

Jupiterimages

students to be able to read, comprehend, and communicate factual material—the skills upon which further education depends. Today's language arts are integrated with all subjects.

Reading achievement. How well are U.S. students achieving in reading? Answer: Mediocre and declining.

In reading comprehension, vocabulary knowledge, and critical thinking skills, NAEP reports that U.S. children's skills have remained at basically the same level for the past 30 years. The same is true internationally. While scores may rise a point or two, these gains are not statistically meaningful (see Table 13.4).[54] For twelfth-grade students, however, the reading results are especially disappointing. The percentage of students scoring at or above the "basic" level dropped from 80 percent in 1992 to 73 percent in 2005, and the percentage scoring at

Table 13.4	NAEP Reading Achievement, 1992–2005			
	Percentage Scoring at or Above "Basic" Level		Percentage Scoring at or Above "Proficient" Level	
Grade	1992	2005	1992	2005
4	62	64	29	31
8	69	73	29	31
12	80	73	40	35

Source: Adapted from data provided in Perie, M., Grigg, W. S., & Donahue, P. L. (2005, October). *National Assessment of Educational Progress: The nation's report card: Reading 2005* (NCES 2006–451). *NAEP 2005 assessment results: Reading grade 12: Executive summary. Reading performance declines for all but top performers.*

---

[54] Perie, M., Grigg, W. S., & Donahue, P. L. (2005, October). *National Assessment of Educational Progress: The nation's report card: Reading 2005.* Retrieved October 19, 2009, from http://nces.ed.gov/nationsreportcard/pubs/main2005/2006451.asp#section1.

or above the "proficient" level dropped from 40 percent to 35 percent over the same period.[55] This means than only 31 percent of fourth and eighth graders and only 35 percent of 12 graders are reading with solid comprehension skills at their grade levels.

Science

At a time when it seems as if everyone is discussing alternative fuels, cloning, global warming, and the use of biometric information to fight terrorism, science education is critical to economic, national, and worldwide survival. Yet after 15 years of standards-based reform, U.S. science education shows only modest improvement.

Differing views on science education. Since the 1950s, educators have debated whether students learn science more effectively through an emphasis on hands-on experimentation or through a more straightforward memorization and recitation of facts from teacher to student. They have also been unable to agree whether the science curriculum should include more or less material.

The 1993 Benchmarks for Science Literacy from the American Association for the Advancement of Science (AAAS), the 1996 National Science Education Standards, and the 2006 National Research Council all recommend that science curricula be pared down, so that students study a relatively small number of major concepts essential to understanding science and gradually build on them.[56] According to this view, science curriculum should present less content—not more—and should incorporate a realistic expectation of which science concepts and content students can learn deeply, meaningfully, and well.[57]

A 2006 National Research Council study also found that both approaches—hands-on experience and memorization—have merit, depending on the science topic. More importantly, the report recommends that standards, curriculum, and assessment developers should revise their framework to reflect better models of children's thinking and take better advantage of children's capabilities.[58] So far, these reform attempts have yielded only modest improvements in science performance on national tests and on international comparisons.

Learning science hinges on both curriculum and teaching methods. The 1999 **Trends in International Math and Science Study (TIMSS),** a math and science test of students in grades 4 and 8 in the United States and other countries, video study identified weaknesses in U.S. science teaching practices as compared with instruction in other, higher-achieving countries. In the TIMSS, researchers found that teachers in comparison countries clearly and consistently focused on science content and science ideas with activities selected to reinforce these concepts. In contrast, in the United States, content played a smaller role—and sometimes no role. U.S. teachers built lessons around engaging students in a variety of activities, often motivating ones, but these exercises were either weakly connected to science content ideas or not connected at all.[59] While U.S. science teachers were enthusiastic

[55] National Center for Education Statistics. Office of Educational Research and Improvement, U.S. Department of Education. (2006). *NAEP 2005 assessment results: Reading grade 12: Executive summary. Reading performance declines for all but top performers.* Retrieved October 19, 2009, from http://nationsre portcard.gov/reading_math_grade12_2005/s0201.asp.

[56] Cavanaugh, S. (2006, September 27). Panel points way to improving K–8 science learning. *Education Week, 26*(5), 14; Duschl, R. A., Schweingruber, H. A., & Shouse, A. W. (Eds.). (2007). *Taking science to school: Learning and teaching science in grades K–8.* Washington, DC: National Academies Press, Executive Summary.

[57] Bybee, R. W. (1995). Science curricular reform in the United States. In R. W. Bybee & J. D. McInerney (Eds.), *Redesigning the science curriculum.* Colorado Springs, CO: Biological Sciences Curriculum Study. Retrieved October 18, 2009, from http://www.nas.edu/rise/backg3a.htm.

[58] Cavanaugh, 2006, p. 14.

[59] Roth, K. (2007, October 10). Science teaching around the world: Lessons for U.S. classrooms. *Education Week, 27*(7), 9. Comparison countries in this study included the Czech Republic, Japan, Australia, and the Netherlands.

about having students be "hands-on," they were less focused on having students be "minds-on." In a 2008 study, researchers concluded that "depth" (focus on a few core topics within science courses) rather than "breadth" (study of a longer list of topics) was key to students' developing a strong understanding of science.[60]

Science achievement. With passage of the No Child Left Behind (NCLB) legislation, science education took a back seat in the curriculum (along with social studies and art) as elementary and middle schools increased class time devoted to reading and math, the first subjects to be tested under the federal law. Even when science testing became required, the results were not factored into the definition of **Adequate Yearly Progress (AYP)**, the federally determined level of achievement that schools must show.

How well are U.S. students achieving in science? Answer: There have been no meaningful gains in science achievement as measured by NAEP within the last decade. Twelfth graders' NAEP science achievement has actually dropped.

As Table 13.5 shows, approximately two-thirds of fourth- and eighth-grade students scored at or above the "basic" level and less than one-third scored at or above the "proficient" level in 1996 and 2005. The percentage of twelfth graders scoring at both at or above the "basic" level and at or above the "proficient" level has declined since 1996. In 2005, only 29 percent—less than one-third—of fourth and eighth graders, and less than one-fifth of twelfth graders, were achieving a solid understanding of science at their grade levels.

Looking at U.S. math and science achievement in national and international comparisons, Senator Lamar Alexander (Republican–Tennessee) concluded, "We are at risk of losing our brainpower advantage. If we lose our brainpower advantage, we lose . . . our standard of living."[61]

Table 13.5	NAEP Science Achievement, 1996–2005			
	Percentage Scoring at or Above "Basic" Level		Percentage Scoring at or Above "Proficient" Level	
Grade	1996	2005	1996	2005
4	63	68	28	29
8	60	59	29	29
12	57	54	21	18

Source: U.S. Department of Education, Institute of Education Sciences, National Center for Education Statistics. (2006, May). *The nation's report card: Science 2005*. (NCES 2006-466). Washington, DC: U.S. Government Printing Office, pp. 7, 19, 31. Retrieved October 19, 2009, from **http://nces.ed.gov/nationsreportcard/science/**.

Social Studies

One of public education's major goals is to teach students how to be effective and engaged citizens in a democratic republic. Even more importantly, education for twenty-first-century citizenship must prepare students to deal with rapid change; complex local, national, and global issues; intense cultural and religious conflicts; and the increasing global economic interdependence.

---

[60] Cavanaugh, S. (2009, March 11). "Depth" matters in high school science studies. *Education Week*, 28(24), 1, 16–17.
[61] Hoff, D. J., & Cavanaugh, S. (2007, May 2). Math–science bills advance in Congress. *Education Week*, 26(35), 23.

The National Council for Social Studies defines social studies as "the integrated study of the social sciences and humanities to promote civic competence."[62] Because civic issues—such as health care, crime, and foreign policy—are multidisciplinary in nature, social studies draws upon anthropology, archaeology, economics, geography, history, law, philosophy, political science, psychology, religion, and sociology. Occasionally, social studies uses appropriate content from the humanities, mathematics, and natural sciences.

Social studies achievement.   How well are U.S. students learning social studies? Answer: Not well.

Two reports, *The Nation's Report Card: U.S. History 2006* and *The Nation's Report Card: Civics 2006,*[63] reveal important and troubling data about U.S. students' achievement on NAEP's history and civics tests. The U.S. history assessment evaluates students' understanding of the development of America's democratic institutions and ideals—our democracy, culture, technological and economic changes, and role in the world.

As shown in Table 13.6, in U.S. history, students showed modest overall improvements in 2006 over prior years, with an increase in several percentage points in the number of students scoring at or above the "basic" level. This overall improvement was attributable to higher achievement by the lowest-scoring students.[64] No significant changes appeared in the percentage of students scoring at or above the "proficient" level. America's fourth, eighth, and twelfth graders know only very slightly more about history and civics (see Table 13.7) today than did such students in the 1990s.

In a related measurement, the 2006 NAEP civics assessment evaluated students' understanding of the democratic institutions and ideals necessary to becoming informed citizens. Because NAEP cannot directly address how well students practice their civic skills, this assessment sought to determine whether students can identify participation skills, recognize their purpose, explain how to use them, and specify how to best achieve the desired result.[65]

Table 13.6	NAEP U.S. History Achievement, 1994–2006			
	Percentage Scoring at or Above "Basic" Level		Percentage Scoring at or Above "Proficient" Level	
Grade	1996	2006	1996	2006
4	64	70	17	18
8	61	65	14	17
12	43	47	11	13

Source: Lee, J., & Weiss, A. R. (2006). *National Assessment of Educational Progress: The nation's report card: U.S. history 2006.* (NCES 2007-474). National Center for Education Statistics, Institute of Education Sciences, U.S. Department of Education. Washington, DC: U.S. Government Printing Office. Retrieved October 19, 2009, from http://nces.ed.gov/nationsreportcard/pdf/main2006/2007474.pdf.

[62] National Council for Social Studies. (n.d.), Silver Springs, MD.

[63] U.S. Department of Education, National Center for Education Statistics, Institute of Education Sciences. (2007, May). *The nation's report card: U.S. history 2006.* (NCES 2007-474). Washington, DC: U.S. Government Printing Office; U.S. Department of Education, National Center for Education Statistics, Institute of Education Sciences. (2007, May). *The nation's report card: Civics 2006.* Washington, DC: U.S. Government Printing Office.

[64] Lee, J., & Weiss, A. R. (2006). *The nation's report card: U.S. history 2006* (NCES 2007-474). Washington, DC: U.S. Government Printing Office. Retrieved October 19, 2009, from http://nces.ed.gov/nationsreportcard/pdf/main2006/2007474.pdf.

[65] Lutkis, A. D., & Weiss, A, R. (2007). *The nation's report card: Civics 2006* (NCES 2007-476). National Center for Education Statistics, Institute for Education Sciences, U.S. Department of Education. Washington, DC: U.S. Government Printing Office. Retrieved October 19, 2009, from http://nces.ed.gov/nationsreportcard/pdf/main2006/2007476.pdf.

Table 13.7	NAEP Civics Achievement, 1998–2006					
	Percentage Scoring at or Above "Basic" Level		Percentage Scoring at or Above "Proficient" Level		Percentage Scoring at or Above "Advanced" Level	
Grade	1998	2006	1998	2006	1998	2006
4	69	73	23	24	2	2
8	70	70	22	22	2	1
12	65	26	66	27	2	5

Source: Lutkis, A. D., & Weiss, A. R. (2007). *The nation's report card: Civics 2006* (NCES 2007-476). National Center for Education Statistics, Institute for Education Sciences, U.S. Department of Education. Washington, DC: U.S. Government Printing Office. Retrieved October 19, 2009, from **http://nces.ed.gov/nationsreportcard/pdf/main2006/2007476.pdf**.

As Table 13.7 shows, approximately two-thirds of fourth, eighth, and twelfth graders have at least a "basic" understanding of civics, according to the NAEP assessment. About one student in four at these grades has a "proficient" knowledge. Overall, eighth and twelfth graders' knowledge of civics has not changed since 1998.

Has civic education affected students' actual behaviors outside the classroom or testing situation—such as their voting behaviors? Answer: Only modestly. While schools are supposed to be preparing citizens, our 18- to 24-year-old voters are not likely to vote. In 2000, only 36 percent of that group voted for U.S. President. In 2004, only 47 percent voted. In the 2008 Presidential Election, however, an estimated 23 million voters ages 18 to 29 participated, resulting in an estimated youth voter turnout (percentage of eligible votes who actually cast a vote) of between 49 and 55 percent.[66]

Lack of civic and government knowledge is not just a problem found among recent high school graduates. In another survey, almost twice as many Americans could name the Three Stooges (73 percent) as could name the three branches of government.[67]

The only bright spot in these math, science, reading, and social studies assessments appears to be the modest increases in fourth graders' achievement in all these areas. The lowest-achieving students are making gains that put them at or above "basic" levels of knowledge. Experts attribute this development in large part to an intense national emphasis on reading in kindergarten through third grade, where improvements in reading comprehension would have the greatest impact on students' test-taking achievement.[68] As noted earlier, students who have successfully learned how to read in grades 1–3 are well prepared to "read to learn" in fourth grade and beyond.

---

[66] Kirby, Emily Hoban and Marcelo, Karlo Marcelo. (2006, December 12). Young Voters in the 2006 Elections. Washington, D.C.: Center for Information and Research on Civic Learning and Engagement. Retrieved October 18, 2009 from: http://www.civicyouth.org/PopUps/FactSheets/FS-Midterm06.pdf; and Center for Information and Research on Civic Learning and Engagement. (2008, December 19). Young voters in the 2008 Presidential election. *Circle Fact Sheet*. Boston, MA: Tufts University Retrieved October 18, 2009, from http://www.civicyouth.org/PopUps/FactSheets/FS_08_exit_polls.pdf); Lopez, M. H. (2006, September). *Quick facts about young voters: 2006*. Washington, DC: Center for Information and Research on Civil Learning and Engagement. We do not know yet whether this increased voting participation by 18 to 24 year olds will be a trend or an exception.

[67] New national poll finds: More Americans know Snow White's dwarfs than supreme court judges, Homer Simpson than Homer's Odyssey, and Harry Potter than Tony Blair. Zogby International. Retrieved October 18, 2009 from http://www.zogby.com/templates/printsb.cfm?id=13498.

[68] Matthews, J. (2007, May 17). Fourth graders improve history, civics scores; seniors make significant gains nationally. *The Washington Post*. p. A09.

The Arts

If we want to understand the values, morals, philosophies, aesthetics, and qualities of life in any particular historical period or geographic region (including our own), we must study their arts. Making art and actively appreciating the aesthetic dimensions of human creation transforms our world from a random, chaotic place into a purposeful and even beautiful environment.

Arts education includes teaching students how to use the tools and processes that produce works of art—such as using charcoal to draw a still life, reading sheet music, and singing choral harmony. Art also involves teaching students how the fine arts relate to history and culture, giving students occasions to explore the connections between arts disciplines and other subjects. Studying the arts can be highly entertaining, as when performing in and enjoying a school play or playing woodwinds in the marching band.

Several arguments support inclusion of arts education in curriculum. First, studying the arts has intrinsic value because the arts reflect what it is like to be human. Engaging in art-related activities gives us a better understanding of ourselves and of others. Second, studying the arts is intellectual and has cognitive benefits because it increases students' problem-solving abilities, critical thinking, expressive abilities, and creative skills.

The intrinsic value of the arts. The arts are worth learning for their own sake, as they provide benefits not available through any other means. Who cannot recall that special song that was playing on the radio or iPod when some momentous event occurred in his or her life? The arts open us up to a transcending dimension of reality that affects us deeply but that we find difficult to describe in words.

The arts also have personal value. They make the learning process exciting and exhilarating. Most students enjoy the arts, and their inclusion in curriculum makes learning fun. A comprehensive, articulated arts education program engages students in a process that helps them develop the self-esteem, self-discipline, cooperation, and self-motivation necessary for success in life.

The intellectual value of the arts. Arts help students think in different ways. Because so much of a child's early school years focus on acquiring language and

Figure 13.7   **Studying The Arts Has Intrinsic and Intellectual Benefits**

Tim Pannell/Tim Pannell/Corbis

math skills, children gradually learn, unconsciously, that the "normal" way to think is linear and sequential, the way words march across the textbook page: from left to right, from beginning to end, from cause to effect. As a result, students learn to value information gained through reasoning and second-hand experiences, such as reading a book or listening to a teacher's lecture.

Arts, in contrast, teach the value of learning directly through our immediate sensory input—seeing, touching, hearing, smelling, and moving. The person and the experience are directly connected, linking verbal and nonverbal, the strictly logical and the emotional. These connections give the person a better understanding of the whole. Likewise, arts education develops nonlinguistic skills in qualitative reasoning. Appreciating art requires a complex mental process of closely examining a work of art, attending to the emotional responses that these unique visual, auditory, or tactile qualities generate in the viewer, and inferring meaning from the art's specific combination of qualities.[69] This requires active meaning-making with many "right" answers and many ways of expressing them.

The arts offer ways of comprehending that do not take conscious information into account and that other academic studies do not include. In the arts, a flash of insight can be a valid source of knowledge. The arts provide students with tools for understanding a broad range of human experiences. They help students learn to adapt to and respect others' (often very different) ways of thinking, working, and expressing themselves. They teach students an array of communicative, analytical, and developmental tools for problem solving in human situations—this is why we speak, for example, of the "art" of teaching or the "art" of politics. Students learn the power of literature, visual arts, music, drama, and dance to reflect cultures and understand the interdependence of art with ideas and actions.

Arts develop such problem-solving abilities and thinking skills as analyzing, synthesizing, evaluating, and creating. In addition, they help develop students' cognitive competencies in elaborative and creative thinking, fluency, originality, focused perception and imagination. Arts education builds skills in analyzing nonverbal communication and making informed judgments about cultural products and issues. It gives students the tools they need to convey their thoughts and feelings in a variety of modes, giving them a vastly more powerful repertoire of self-expression.

Arts' immediacy and active involvement of the student's mind and body directs the learner's attention, without which no learning can occur. These "habits of mind" accustom students to taking multiple perspectives, to layering relationships, and to relating and constructing meaningful responses. Along the way, these habits help students extend their thinking and develop critical cognitive capacities and personal dispositions. Learning with the arts permits students to flexibly interweave the intuitive, practical, and logical modes of thinking.[70] It also helps students make decisions in situations where there are no official "right" answers.

Research on the arts and student achievement. A growing body of research has documented the habits of mind, social competencies, and personal dispositions inherent to arts learning. These studies' findings may not be as clear-cut as the standardized test results, but they offer empirical support for including an arts curriculum in any public schools that are truly interested in developing students' intellects and capacities as whole persons.

Studying the arts is highly related to high academic achievement. In a well-documented 2002 national study of more than 25,000 middle and high school students, researchers found that students with high arts involvement performed better

[69] Seigesmund, R. (2005, September). Teaching qualitative reasoning: Portraits of practice. *Phi Delta Kappan, 87*(1), 18–23.

[70] Burton, J., Horowitz, R., & Abeles, H. (2000). Learning in and through the arts: Curriculum implications. In E. B. Fiske (Ed.), *Champions of change: The impact of the arts on learning* (pp. 35–46). Washington, DC: Arts Education Partnership and the President's Commission on Arts and the Humanities.

on standardized achievement tests than did students with low arts involvement.[71] Multiple independent studies have found that students who studied the arts for more than four years scored as much as 59 points higher on SAT verbal tests and as much as 44 points higher on SAT math tests than peers with no coursework or experiences in the arts.[72]

In addition, an analysis of multiple studies confirms that students who take music classes in high school are more likely to score higher on standardized math tests, such as the SAT.[73] Similarly, students who are consistently involved in band or orchestra during their middle and high school years tend to perform better in math at grade 12. Students from low-income families who are involved with orchestra or band are more than twice as likely to perform at the highest math levels as their peers who are not involved in music.[74]

In 2002, *Critical Links: Learning in the Arts and Student Academic and Social Development* compiled 62 rigorous, experimental, peer-reviewed studies published in national professional journals on the academic and social effects of arts learning experiences in drama, dance, visual arts, music, and multi-arts with supporting data linking the arts with student achievement.[75] Overall, the researchers reported that arts learning has positive and measurable effects on math achievement, thinking skills, motivation, social behavior, and the school environment.

Do the arts make students smarter? While these studies draw attention to strong connections between arts and academic achievement, cautious interpretation of their findings is advised. A strong relationship is not the same as a cause-and-effect relationship. Headlines announcing "The Arts Make Kids Smarter" would oversimplify and overgeneralize these results. In fact, the results from these studies are correlational, not proof of a cause and effect.

Which factors might underlie this arts–achievement connection? Perhaps high-achieving students choose to participate in arts classes, rather than the arts classes themselves increasing students' measured SAT achievement.[76] Perhaps academically strong schools tend to have strong arts programs. Perhaps families who value academic achievement also value achievement in the arts. All of these explanations might explain the arts–achievement relationship. What is more, the arts call for multiple and conflicting interpretations that are fundamentally divergent. Standardized tests, in contrast, call for right-and-wrong answers and convergent thinking. Given

---

[71] Catterall, J. S. (2002). Involvement in the arts and success of secondary students. In R. Deasy (Ed.), *Critical links: Learning in the arts and student achievement and social development* (pp. 68–69). Washington, DC: Arts Education Partnership.

[72] Murfee, E. (1995). *Eloquent evidence: Arts at the core of learning.* Washington, DC: President's Committee on the Arts and Humanities, p. 3; College Board. (2005). *2005 college-bound seniors: Total group profile report,* Table 3.3; Vaughn, K., & Winner, E. (2000, Fall). *SAT scores of students who study the arts: What we can and cannot conclude about the association.* New York: College Board; (2005). *Critical Evidence. How the Arts Benefit Student Achievement.* Washington, D.C.: National Assembly of State Art Agencies and The Arts Education Partnership. p. 9. Retrieved October 18, 2009 from: http://www.aep-arts.org/files/publications/Critical%20Evidence.pdf.

[73] Vaughn, K. (2002). Music and mathematics: Modest support for the oft-claimed relationship. In R. Deasy (Ed.), *Critical links: Learning in the arts and student academic and social development* (pp. 130–131). ERIC (ED466413). Washington, DC: Arts Education Partnership.

[74] Catterall, J. S., Chapleau, R., & Iwanaga, J. (2002). Involvement in the arts and human development: Extending an analysis of general associations and introducing the special cases of intensive involvement in music and theatre arts. In R. Deasy (Ed.), *Critical links: Learning in the arts and student academic and social development* (pp. 70–71). ERIC (ED466413). Washington, DC: Arts Education Partnership.

[75] Deasy, R. J. (Ed.). *Critical links: Learning in the arts and student academic and social development.* ERIC (ED466413). Washington, DC: Arts Education Partnership. A complete version is available at http://www.aep-arts.org/files/publications/CriticalLinks.pdf; Deasy, R. J. (2003, January–February). Don't axe the arts! *Principal, 82*(3), 15–18. Arlington, VA: National Association of Elementary School Principals.

[76] Eisner, E. W. (1998, January). Does experience in the arts boost academic achievement? *Arts Education, 51*(1), 7–15; Viadero, D. (2008, March 12). Insights gained into arts and smarts. *Education Week, 27*(27), 1, 10–11.

these differences, one would not expect learning in the arts to translate directly into better achievement on standardized tests.[77]

Nevertheless, the research findings suggest that training in the arts might contribute to improving children's and adults' general thinking skills. The cognitive processes that give rise to the arts and those that give rise to the sciences may be interrelated. For example, both activities involve focusing attention and recognizing patterns.[78]

Providing a mind-centered curriculum. If schools want a curriculum designed to help children develop as productive thinkers and citizens, they must provide young people with the kinds of learning challenges that develop their minds to the fullest. To be most beneficial, arts need to become curricular partners with other subjects in ways that allow them to contribute their own distinctive richness and complexity to the learning process as a whole.

Education has social and personal as well as political and social goals. Its primary purpose is not to enable students to do well in school, but rather to prepare them to do well in the lives they lead outside of school.[79] Developing the mind is a form of cultural achievement in which schools play a critical role. An education that integrates the arts into curriculum can better prepare students to succeed in the world they are entering and enrich the lives they will lead. If schools are to be intellectual—rather than merely academic—places, the arts must be active parts of what and how our students learn.

Educating the Whole Child

The fact that this chapter does not review every public school curriculum is not meant to imply that those disciplines are not important to a fully educated person. Instead, we have looked at the traditional core curriculum taught in most schools, which provides the basis for national accountability and international comparisons—along with one unassessed discipline area—and their roles in advancing student learning.

The Search for Curricular Balance

Schools are cultures for growing minds, and the opportunities that schools provide influence the direction this growth takes.[80] The decisions that educators make about amount of time allotted to a field of study influences the kinds of mental skills children will have the chance to develop. As we have seen, the history of curriculum can be seen as a debate over which of three competing factors is most important—the individual child, the society, and the subject matter. The need to find the appropriate balance among these three essentials creates ongoing curriculum challenges.[81]

A disciplinary orientation to curriculum, which is the way that most public schools are organized, is especially attractive to professors and researchers who work within separate subjects' structure. It does not reflect the reality or convey the world's excitement, however, nor does it connect to students' own experiences or provide personal meaning or relevance that would motivate learning.

---

[77] Winner, E., & Cooper, M. (2000, Autumn–Winter). Mute those claims: No evidence (yet) for a causal link between arts study and academic achievement. *Journal of Aesthetic Education, 34*(3/4), 63.

[78] Viadero, 2008.

[79] Eisner, E. W. (2004, December/January). Preparing for today and tomorrow. *Educational Leadership, 61*(4), 6–11.

[80] Eisner, E. W. (1992, April). The misunderstood role of the arts in human development. *Phi Delta Kappan, 73*(8), 591–595.

[81] Schubert, W. H. (1995). Toward lives worth living and sharing: Historical perspective on curriculum coherence. In J. A. Beane (Ed.), *Toward a coherent curriculum: The 1995 ASCD yearbook* (pp. 146–157). Alexandria, VA: Association for Supervision and Curriculum Development.

Educators must teach students civilization's survival skills and balance the theoretical with the practical. Education needs to acknowledge the world's complexity, contradictions, and diversity. No subject stands alone in the real world—so why should it stand alone in the curriculum?

Educating the Whole Child

Every culture has debated education's aims. None, however, can produce final once-and-forever answers because education's aims are inevitably tied to a particular society's goals and ideals. In our pursuit of efficiency, we have remade ourselves into a collection of separate needs and attributes.[82] The same is true for our schools. Surely we should educate our students for more than reading and math proficiency.

Recently, Rothstein, Wilder, and Jacobsen synthesized nearly 300 years of American education policy making into eight broad categories. They surveyed a random sample of adults, school board members, and state legislators, asking respondents to weight each of the eight goals based on its relative importance in a comprehensive accountability system.[83] The eight categories include the following:

- **Basic academic skills**—reading, writing, math, science, history, civics, geography, and foreign language
- **Critical thinking and problem solving**—analyzing information, applying ideas to new situations, and developing knowledge using computers
- **Social skills and work ethic**—communication skills, personal responsibility, and getting along with others from varied backgrounds
- **Citizenship**—public ethics, knowing how government works, and participating by voting, volunteering, and becoming active in community life
- **Physical health**—good habits of exercise and nutrition
- **Emotional health**—self-confidence, respect for others, and the ability to resist peer pressure to engage in irresponsible personal behavior
- **The arts and literature**—participation in and appreciation of musical, visual, and performing arts as well as a love of literature
- **Preparation for skilled employment**—qualification for skill employment for students not pursuing college education

Those surveyed thought that "basic academic skills" and "critical thinking and problem solving"—the two "academic" categories—were more important (in combined percentage) than any other single goal.

Presently, our school curricula are not faithful to American education's goals, either those of today or those of yesterday. In our "test-mania," we now focus almost exclusively on basic academic skills (reading, math) and critical thinking. If we were faithful to what our communities say they want, we would be addressing the other six categories, too.

Contemporary research results support the view that educating the whole child requires teaching a well-rounded curriculum. A 2007 study found that exercise—such as occurs in physical education classes—boosts brain function and academic achievement in children and adolescents.[84] While the exercise itself

---

[82] Noddings, N. (2005, September). What does it mean to educate the whole child? *Educational Leadership, 63*(1), 8–13.

[83] Rothstein, R., Wilder, T., & Jacobsen, R. (2007, May). Balance in the balance. *Educational Leadership, 64*(8), 8–14.

[84] Viadero, D. (2008, February 13). Exercise seen as priming pump for students' academic strides. *Education Week, 27*(23), 14–15.

does not make children smarter, it puts the learners' brains in an optimal position to learn.[85] Similarly, a 2008 meta-analysis of 207 studies found that taking time to teach students to manage their emotions and to practice empathy, caring, and cooperation not only increased these behaviors, but also increased students' academic achievement as compared with a comparison group of students who were not exposed to these social–emotional programs.[86] Likewise, a 2009 investigation found that exposure to music, both in and out of school, is tied to higher student achievement in mathematics and reading even after controlling for prior school achievement and other factors.[87] Clearly, curricula such as these benefit the whole child—academic, social, and personal.

Success in basic academics does not necessarily result in more complex skills. For example, scores are now rising on state tests that tend to emphasize basic skills, but are not rising on the NAEP, which measures basic, proficient, and advanced skills.[88] Schools should be held accountable for teaching children first to basic levels, and then to proficient and advanced understanding. The existing accountability system unwittingly distorts curriculum by holding educators responsible solely for ensuring that students have basic skills. Perhaps our expectations are not set too high; perhaps they are set too low. Perhaps we are working feverishly to bring all students to the achievement "floor" when we should be trying to bring them all to the "ceiling." Holding schools accountable for each of the eight previously mentioned goal areas would create incentives for teaching a balanced curriculum that addresses the whole child.

Although educators today are almost entirely engaged in an *academic achievement discourse*, they would be more appropriately focused if they engaged in a *human development discourse*. Attention to human development would recognize that human beings travel through different stages of life, each with its own requirements for optimal growth.[89]

Children respond to educational situations not only intellectually, but also emotionally and socially. To neglect the social and emotional aspects of their development in the pursuit of measured academic performance is to ignore these young people's need to live satisfying lives.[90] It also limits their capacity to learn the prescribed content: If we fail to generate an affective link—personal meaning—for the information, it will be soon forgotten.

Schools need to approach curriculum in a way that is sensitive to these different developmental stages of life and each learner's unique needs. Curriculum also needs to reach beyond literacy, math, and science to include the arts, physical education, social skills training, and imaginative and ethical development. Such a curriculum would focus on the whole child. Future educators who fully understand the concept of curriculum and the need to educate the whole child can learn ways to meet local and state standards and to teach their subject in ways that students find meaningful.

In the human organism, all parts are interconnected. We need to recognize these connections when we teach. "Attention to such complex matters will not simplify our tasks as teachers but it will bring education closer to the heart of what

---

[85] Castelli, D. M., Hillman, C. H., Buck, S. M., & Erwin, H. (2007). Physical fitness and academic achievement in 3rd and 5th grade students. *Journal of Sport and Exercise Psychology, 29,* 239–252.

[86] Durlak, J. A., Weissberg, R. P., Dymnicki, A. B., Taylor, R. D., & Schellinger, K. L. (2008). *The effects of social and emotional learnings on the behavior and academic performance of school children.* Chicago, IL: Collaborative for Academic, Social, and Emotional Learning; Viadero, D. (2007, December 19). Social-skills programs found to yield gains in academic subjects. *Education Week, 27*(16), 1, 15.

[87] Southgate, D. E., & Roscigno, V. J. (2009). The impact of music on child and adolescent achievement. *Social Science Quarterly, 90*(1), 4–21.

[88] Lee, J. (2006). *Tracking achievement gaps and assessing the impact of NCLB on the gaps: An in-depth look into national and state reading and math outcome trends.* Cambridge, MA: Civil Rights Project at Harvard University.

[89] Armstrong, T. (2007, May). The curriculum superhighway. *Educational Leadership, 64*(8), 16–20.

[90] Eisner, E. W. (2005, September). Back to the whole. *Educational Leadership, 63*(1), 14–18.

really matter,"[91] proclaims Eisner. Likewise, *curriculum* is no longer about running a racetrack. As Jacqueline Grennon Brooks of Hofstra University so eloquently puts it, "Learning is not a race from point to point. It is a journey that changes pace, changes course, and, ultimately, changes us."[92]

Today, educators continue to look for the right balance in curriculum between the subject, the child, and the society. What young people need to know to become competent adults changes as the world changes. Public school curriculum must do the same. We all must deeply question our schools and our curricula. Each of us must ask what it means to be educated and what it means to be human. Then, future practitioners who deeply care about educating (rather than schooling) children as whole people can begin to find the answers.

---

[91] Eisner, 2005, p. 18.
[92] Brooks, J. G., Libresco, A. S., & Plonczak, I. (2007, June). Spaces of liberty: Battling the new soft bigotry of NCLB. *Phi Delta Kappan, 88*(10), 750.

Summary

Curriculum is the school's plan for learning, the subjects that schools teach. U.S. public school curriculum currently serves national, economic, social, and personal goals. States and localities decide what students should learn based on their beliefs about what students need to survive in a complex social and economic world and what it means to be an educated person.

Fundamentally, curriculum is about values. The curriculum and our ways of organizing it are always part of a *selective tradition*, someone's vision of the knowledge that needs to be taught to everyone. The decision to define some group's knowledge as the most important says much about who holds the power in a particular society and the values they want schooling to transmit.

Today's curriculum reflects certain intellectual traditions. The U.S. curriculum reflects an inherent and historical tension between its focus on social control and transmitting our cultural history and its focus on the individual. Until the early twentieth century, most curriculum thinkers believed that curriculum's purpose was to transmit the American cultural heritage and traditions to newcomers.

Since the late 1800s, changes in student populations, economic realities, and ideologies have affected schools' traditional core curriculum. In response to these trends, schools began offering more practical courses for students needing life-oriented skills, not just college-preparation. Over time, subject-centered and child-centered curriculum approaches alternated as policy makers and curriculum writers tried to define the curriculum that was best for the society, the subject discipline, or the individual. Among other curriculum thinkers, Ralph Tyler, Hilda Taba, Benjamin Bloom, and Grant Wiggins and Jay McTighe developed ways for curriculum writers and thinkers to integrate subjects, enduring concepts, thinking complexity, assessments, and learning activities into curriculum as a plan for learning.

Today's public schools are teaching a standards-based curriculum comprising separate disciplines that are usually taught and assessed independently. The typical "core curriculum" includes math, language arts, science, and social studies. Each of these disciplines is governed by national standards that indicate what students should know and be able to do by certain grades. Nonetheless, student achievement, as measured by "the nation's report card" (NAEP) or by international assessments on these subjects, is not as high as we would like.

The arts, although often marginalized in today's schools, are intrinsically meaningful and develop students' thinking skills and problem-solving abilities. A growing body of current research supports the links between education in the arts and a wide range of academic and social benefits. Our society has assigned many important goals to our educational system; to address these goals, schools' curriculum should educate the whole child.

Conclusions

- School curriculum reflects the larger society's views and values.

- If we want our children to be educated as whole persons (as opposed to schooled), we need to rethink how curriculum can best contribute to student learning and growth.

Chapter 14

Instruction

Becoming an effective teacher takes time. A young teacher writes,

> This is my fifth year teaching high school English. . . . Every single year has been a struggle . . .Yet, every single year, I have gotten better at this gig.
>
> This year, I realize that I enjoy teaching more than I dread it, more than it scares me—which in itself, is terrifying. The other day, my principal said, in front of the entire staff, that I am a "gifted teacher." My students inspire me. I think about them when I'm at the grocery store or in the gas station, and smile. Or I laugh out loud, and people give me funny looks. My students are improving as readers, writers, and thinkers, and it's because I know what I'm doing. This feels great.[1]

Who wouldn't want to have an enthusiastic, caring, and effective teacher like this? What prospective educator wouldn't want to become one? But becoming this successful and comfortable in the classroom does not happen overnight.

Having a license to teach does not make one an effective teacher. As in other fields, a professional license is only a minimum qualification and a promise to "do no harm." Teachers labeled as "highly qualified" who have met their credentialing standards may still provide their classrooms with a middling quality of instructional support, even if the learning atmosphere was emotionally positive.[2]

A growing cadre of researchers agrees that effective instruction probably has a greater impact on learning and achievement gaps than any other school factor. "Effective teaching," notes Harvard University Professor Richard Elmore "is voluntary, and therefore rare."[3]

While teachers need to thoroughly understand the subject material they will teach, they also need the skills that will help students learn it. Effective teaching can be learned, practiced, and mastered, by focusing on instruction.

Focus Questions

- In what ways is instruction purposeful decision making?
- What does the research say about teaching effectiveness and student achievement?
- What are the behavioral, cognitive, and constructivist learning approaches, and how do they influence today's classrooms?
- How do effective teachers provide high-quality instruction through planning and preparation?
- How do effective teachers provide high-quality instruction through the creation of an appropriate classroom environment?

---

[1] Guilmart, L. (2008, June 4). "An Impossible choice": A young teacher hits the five-year wall. *Education Week, 27*(39), 24.
[2] Jacobson, L. (2007, April 4). Study casts doubt on value of "highly qualified" status. *Education Week, 26*(31), 13.
[3] Richard Elmore, cited in Schmoker, M. & Allington, R. (2007, May, 16). The gift of bleak research: How the Pianta classroom study can help schools improve immediately. Commentary. *Education Week, 26* (37), 28.

- How do effective teachers provide high-quality instruction by teaching for student engagement?
- How do effective teachers provide high-quality instruction by reflecting on teaching?

Research on Teaching Effectiveness and Student Achievement

Pedagogy is the art and profession of teaching. Effective pedagogy involves three related areas: the teacher's instructional strategies, management techniques, and curriculum.[4] **Instruction** is the means by which teachers bring curriculum to life in the classroom. Even if the teacher has been given the standards-infused school district's curriculum, the teacher has tremendous influence over how to present it.

"The 'art' of teaching is rapidly becoming the 'science' of teaching."[5] Until recently, teaching had not been systematically studied in a scientific manner. At the beginning of the 1970s, however, researchers began to look at the effects of instruction on student learning. Before then, a widespread belief held that school really made little difference in students' achievement.[6]

Since then, research has shown that an individual teacher can have a powerful effect on his or her students *even if the school does not.* After reviewing hundreds of studies conducted in the 1970s, researchers Jere Brophy and Thomas Good confidently claimed, "The myth that teachers do not make a difference in student learning has been refuted."[7]

Teaching Effectiveness and Student Achievement

Conventional wisdom has long held that family backgrounds and economic status were the primary determiners of students' learning. In the last decade of the twentieth century, researchers found that, aside from a well-articulated curriculum and a safe and orderly environment, the individual teacher was the most influential school-related factor in determining which students learned and how well they learned. Consistently working with highly effective teachers can overcome the academic limitations placed on students by their backgrounds.

Many studies have quantified the effective teacher's influence on student achievement. This influence is relatively independent of anything else that occurs in the school. Researchers William Sanders and colleagues in Tennessee and William Webster and colleagues in Texas provide data from two different states that strongly affirm this conclusion. They found that having three consecutive years with effective versus ineffective teachers can make students' achievement appear to be either

---

[4] Marzano, R. J., Pickering, D. J., & Pollock, J. E. (2001). *Classroom Instruction that works: Research-based strategies for increasing student achievement.* Alexandria, VA: Association for Supervision and Curriculum Development, p. 10.

[5] Marzano, Pickering, & Pollock, 2001, p. 1.

[6] As we discussed in Chapter 5, the 1966 Coleman Report concluded that the quality of schooling a student receives accounted for only 10 percent of the differences in student achievement. The other 90 percent could be attributed to students' natural ability, socioeconomic status, and home environment. Christopher Jencks' *Inequality* came to similar conclusions.

[7] Brophy, J., & Good, T. (1986). Teacher behavior and student achievement. In M. Wittrock (Ed.), *Handbook of research on teaching* (p. 370). New York: Macmillan.

gifted or remedial, respectively.[8] The cumulative impact over three years of effective elementary teachers was estimated to produce (on a 100-point scale) a 35-point difference in reading achievement and more than a 50-point difference in math achievement as measured by standardized tests.[9] Consecutive years with highly effective teachers can produce dramatic achievement gains in all groups—low-, middle-, and high-achieving students. In a similar study , high school students working with the most effective teachers showed reading and math gains that exceeded the national median, while their peers with the least effective teachers showed virtually no growth.[10]

Sanders and his colleagues have observed that the individual classroom teacher is the essential factor in whether and how much students learn.[11] After analyzing the achievement scores of more than 100,000 students across hundreds of schools, these researchers concluded that more could be done to improve education by improving teachers' effectiveness than by modifying any other single factor. Conversely, if the teacher is ineffective, students working with that teacher will show inadequate academic progress, regardless of how similar or different they are in their academic achievement.[12]

One noteworthy 2004 study looked at teacher effectiveness in grades K–3. The four-year experimental study randomly assigned students to classes controlled for students' previous achievement, socioeconomic status, ethnicity, gender, class size, and presence (or not) of an aide in class. They found that students who have a teacher at the 75th percentile of pedagogical competence (an effective teacher) will outgain students who have a teacher at the 25th percentile (not so effective teacher) by 14 percentile points in reading and 18 percentile points in mathematics. Similarly, students who have a 90th percentile teacher (a very effective teacher) will outgain students who have a 50th percentile teacher (an average teacher) by 13 percentile points in reading and 18 percentile points in mathematics.[13] The more effective the teacher, the more his or her students' learning and measured achievement will increase.

Teachers who learn and practice sound instructional techniques can affect students' measured achievement. A 1996 National Assessment of Educational Progress (NAEP) study found that students of teachers who conducted hands-on learning activities outperformed their peers by more than 70 percent of a grade level in math and 40 percent of a grade level in science. In addition, students whose teachers had strong content knowledge and who had learned the

---

[8] Sanders, W. L., & Horn, S. P. (1995). Educational assessment reassessed: The usefulness of standardized and alternative measures of student achievement as indicates for the assessment of educational outcomes. *Education Policy Analysis Archives, 3*(6), 1–15. Retrieved October 30, 2009, from http://epaa.asu.edu/epaa/v3n6.html; Sanders, W. L., & Rivers, J. C. (1996, November). *Cumulative and residual effects of teachers on future student academic achievement.* Knoxville, TN: University of Tennessee Value-Added Research and Assessment Center; Webster, W. J., & . Mendro, R. L. (1997). The Dallas value-added accountability system. In J. Millman (Ed.), *Grading teachers, grading schools: Is student achievement a valid evaluation measure?* (pp. 81–99). Thousand Oaks, CA: Corwin Press; Webster, W. J., Mendro, R. L., Orsak, T. H., & Weerasinghe, D, (1998a). *An application of hierarchical linear modeling to the estimation of school and teacher effect.* Dallas, TX: Dallas Independent School District. Retrieved October 30, 2009, from: http://www.dallasisd.org/depts/inst_research/aer98ww2/aer98ww2.htm; Webster, W. J., Mendro, R. L., Orsak, T. H., & Weerasinghe, D. (1998b). *An application of hierarchical linear modeling to the estimation of school and teacher effects: Relevant results.* Dallas, TX: Dallas Independent School District. Retrieved October 30, 2009, from http://www.dallasisd.org/depts/inst_research/aer98ww2/aer98ww2.htm.
[9] Sanders & Rivers, 1996.
[10] Haycock, K. (1998, Summer). Good teaching matters—a lot. *Thinking K–16,* 3–14.
[11] Sanders, W., & Horn, S. P. (1994). The Tennessee value-added assessment system (TVAAS): Mixed-model methodology in educational assessment. *Journal of Personnel Evaluation in Education, 8,* 299–311; Wright, S. P., Horn, S. P., & Sanders, W. L. (1997). Teacher and classroom context effects on student achievement: Implications for teacher evaluation. *Journal of Personnel Evaluation in Education, 11,* 57–67.
[12] Wright et al., 1997, p. 63.
[13] Nye, B., Konstantopoulos, S., & Hedges, L. V. (2004). How large are teacher effects? *Educational Evaluation and Policy Analysis, 26*(3), 237–257; Marzano, R. (2007). *The art and science of teaching: A comprehensive framework for effective instruction.* Alexandria, VA: Association for Supervision and Curriculum Development, pp. 2–3.

professional skills needed to work with pupils from different cultures or with special needs tested more than one full grade level above their peers. Students whose math teachers stressed critical thinking skills, such as writing about math, scored 39 percent of a grade level higher. What is more, the teaching quality aspects measured have an impact 7 to 10 times greater than class size in affecting student achievement.[14]

Educators and policy makers agree that a clear, predictive relationship exists between teachers' basic skills—especially verbal ability—and student achievement.[15] They also agree that teachers' content knowledge affects student achievement. On the 1996 NAEP, students whose teachers had college majors or minors in the subjects they taught—especially in secondary math and science—outperformed students whose teachers lacked this content knowledge by about 40 percent of a grade level in each subject.[16] Similarly, evidence suggests that teacher content knowledge in English and social studies may be equally important.[17]

Content Knowledge

No evidence suggests that possessing content knowledge alone is enough to be an effective teacher.[18] While teachers need a strong knowledge base in the subject they teach, taking additional courses in that subject does not necessarily affect their own students' achievement.[19] Likewise, others have correctly noted that college majors vary in rigor, and a prospective teacher's college transcripts may not actually confirm that its holder possesses substantial content knowledge.[20] Therefore, although teachers' strong content knowledge and verbal skills have been linked to higher student achievement, teachers' content knowledge may be a necessary but not a sufficient condition for high-quality teaching and learning.[21]

Limitations in the research. As with all research, interpreting teacher effectiveness studies requires caution. Methodological weaknesses affect how we can interpret the data gathered by any particular study. After all, teachers are not randomly assigned to classes within schools. The most experienced, credentialed, and respected teachers usually receive assignments to upper-level and advanced courses. School culture, parents, and students expect mature educators with advanced degrees to teach these high-status, intellectually rigorous classes. Likewise, students cannot ethically be transferred from one teacher's classroom to another simply to provide the random conditions needed for an empirical study. Additionally, some of the teacher quality studies use highly sophisticated statistical models that estimate student gains and come with their own technical limitations. Even so, while

---

[14] Wenglinsky, H. (2000). *How teaching matters: Bringing the classroom back into discussions of teacher quality.* Princeton, NJ: The Milliken Family Foundation and Educational Testing Service, p. 31.

[15] Walsh, K. (2001). *Teacher certification reconsidered: Stumbling for quality.* Baltimore, MD: Abell Foundation; Darling-Hammond, L. (2000, January 1). Teacher quality and student achievement: A review of state policy evidence. *Educational Policy Analysis Archives, 8*(1). Retrieved October 30, 2009, from http://epaa.asu.edu/epaa/v8n1; Haycock, 1998; Whitehurst, G. J. (2002, March). *Scientifically based research on teacher quality: Research on teacher preparation and professional development.* Paper presented at White House Conference on Preparing Tomorrow's Teachers.

[16] Blair, J. (2000, October 5). ETS study links effective teaching methods to test-score gains. *Education Week, 20*(8), 24–25; Goldhaber, D. D., & Brewer, D. J. (2000, Summer). Does teacher certification matter? High school teacher certification status and student achievement. *Educational Evaluation and Policy Analysis, 22*(2), 129–145; & Wenglinsky, H. (2000, October). *How teaching matters: Bringing the classroom back into discussions of teacher quality.* Princeton, NJ: Milken Family Foundation and Educational Testing Service.

[17] Haycock, 1998.

[18] Berry, B. (2001, May). No shortcuts to preparing god teachers. *Educational Leadership, 58*(8), 32–36; Wilson, S., et al. (2002).Teacher preparation research: An insider's view from the outside. *Journal of Teacher Education, 53*(3), 190–204.

[19] Monk, D. H. (1994). Subject matter preparation of secondary mathematics and science teachers and student achievement. *Economics of Education Review, 13*(2), 125–145.

[20] Kanstoroom, M., & Finn, C. E. Jr. (Eds.). (1999, July). *Better teachers, better schools.* Washington, DC: Thomas B. Fordham Foundation.

[21] Kaplan, L. S., & Owings, W. A. (2003, May). The politics of teacher quality. *Phi Delta Kappan, 84*(9), 688.

recognizing and understanding research findings' limitations are important, the reality that excellent teaching practices can make a tremendous difference in student learning deserves serious attention.

Teacher Preparation and Student Achievement

Research shows that teachers' instructional preparation increases student achievement. Linda Darling-Hammond, Professor of Education at Stanford University, found that teacher preparation is a stronger correlate of student achievement than either class size, overall spending, or teacher salaries; indeed, this factor accounts for 40 to 60 percent of the total achievement differences after considering students' ethnicity and family wealth.[22] Additional studies show that both subject-matter knowledge and knowledge of teaching and learning strongly correlate with teachers' classroom performance.[23]

Teacher education coursework is sometimes more important than extra subject-matter classes in advancing students' math and science achievement.[24] David Monk, Professor of Educational Administration at Pennsylvania State University, found a positive correlation between students' achievement and their teachers' coursework in teaching methods.[25] Nonetheless, education classes do have a point of diminishing returns. Several studies have found that teachers with advanced subject-matter degrees, rather than advanced education degrees, have students who perform better in math and reading. This is especially true after elementary school, when students need a deeper understanding of increasingly more complex content.[26]

Additionally, teachers who clearly understand the learning process and adapt their instructional behaviors accordingly have students who learn more. When teachers systematically study how students learn and develop more effective teaching behaviors, their students' achievement increases. For example, investigators found that 73 percent of these teachers' students—especially the lowest achievers—showed the greatest (statistically significant) learning gains.[27]

Professional preparation includes classroom management skills. Teachers who cannot effectively manage their classrooms have students who learn less than their peers. Research suggests that teachers who lack classroom management skills, regardless of how much content they know, cannot create a classroom environment that supports student learning. For example, a study of the influence of teachers' different disciplinary practices on student achievement found that student classroom disorder results in lower achievement.[28]

In sum, the data supporting the impact of effective teaching practices on student achievement are credible and substantial. Both evidence and experience show that effective teaching requires a set of professional practices different from, yet connected to, the content taught. While the content knowledge is obviously essential, knowing *how* to teach the content makes a measurable difference in terms of student achievement.

---

[22] Darling-Hammond, 2000, p. 27.
[23] Guyton, E., & Farokhi, E. (1987, September/October). Relationships among academic performance, basic skills, and subject-matter knowledge and teaching skills of teacher education graduates. *Journal of Teacher Education, 38*(5), 37–42.
[24] Monk, D., & King, J. A. (1994). Multi-level teacher resource effects in pupil performance in secondary mathematics and science: The case of teacher subject-matter preparation. In R. G. Ehrenberg (Ed.), *Choices and consequences: Contemporary policy issues in education* (pp. 29–58). Ithaca, NY: ILR Press.
[25] Monk, D. H. (1994). Subject-matter preparation of secondary mathematics and science teachers and student achievement. *Economics of Education Review, 13*(2), 125–145. Monk conceded, however, that variations in the content of the college math courses made it difficult to draw definite conclusions.
[26] Johnson, K. A. (2000, September). The effects of advanced teacher training in education of student achievement. *Report of the Heritage Center for Data Analysis*, No. 00–09, pp. 1–17; Greenwald, R., Hedges, L. V., & Laine, R. D. (1996). The effect of school resources on student achievement. *Review of Educational Research, 66*(3), 361–396.
[27] Munro, J. (1999, June). Learning more about learning improves teacher effectiveness. *School Effectiveness and School Improvement, 10*(2), 151–171.
[28] Barton, P. E., Coley, R., & Wenglinsky, Harold. (1998). *Order in the classroom: Violence, discipline, and student achievement.* Princeton, NJ: Educational Testing Service.

Figure 14.1 Effective Instruction Has a Powerful Influence on Student Learning

Jose Luis Pelaez/Iconica/Getty Images

Differing Views on Teaching Practices

We have all had classes in which the teacher knew the subject very well but lacked the teaching skills to help you learn it. The relationship between curriculum (the content of education) and pedagogy (the process of teaching) is interdependent. Each factor is necessary but, by itself, is not enough to make an effective teacher. Each individual's view of how learning occurs influences how he or she ultimately understands and enacts teaching practices.

Three Learning Perspectives

In a broad sense, learning happens when experience produces a stable change in someone's knowledge or behavior.[29] It is a complex cognitive process. Different theories offer a range of explanations about what learning is and how a teacher produces it in the learner. Three general learning perspectives influence instruction—behavioral, cognitive, and constructivist.

- **Behavioral theories of learning** stress observable changes in behaviors, skills, and habits.

- **Cognitive theories of learning** emphasize internal mental activities such as thinking, remembering, creating, and problem solving.

- **Constructivist theories of learning** focus on how individuals make meaning of events and activities. Learning, therefore, is viewed as the construction of knowledge.

  Each perspective's application has different implications for teaching.

Behavioral Perspective on Learning

Influences on behaviorist thinking. B. F. Skinner's (1904–1990) work influenced the behavioral perspective. A psychologist, Skinner defined learning as a

---

[29] Hoy, W. K., & Miskel, C. G. (2008). *Educational administration: Theory, research, and practice.* Boston, MA: McGraw-Hill Higher Education, p. 43.

change in behavior brought by experience. **Behavior** is simply what a person does in a given situation. Skinner had little concern for the mental or internal processes involved in thinking or for the human psyche. He believed everything we do and are is shaped by our experience of punishment and reward. According to Skinner, the "mind" (as opposed to the brain) and other such subjective phenomena were simply matters of language; they didn't really exist. Skinner was strictly a behaviorist interested in how external forces influence behavior.

As a psychologist, Skinner experimented with pigeons. He used **operant conditioning** to reward a partial behavior or a random act that approached the desired behavior. For instance, if Skinner wanted a pigeon to turn in a circle to the left, he gave the pigeon a reward for any small movement to the left. When the pigeon caught on ("learned") and turned left to get the reward, Skinner gave the reward only for larger movements to the left, and so on. Soon, the pigeon had turned a complete circle before getting the reward.

Skinner compared this learning with the way children learn to talk. Children receive rewards—such as parents' smiles, laughs, and hugs—for making a sound that resembles a word until they can say the actual word clearly. Likewise, Skinner believed other complicated tasks could be broken down and taught in this way. He even developed teaching machines so students could learn bit by bit, uncovering answers for an immediate "reward." These machines were quite popular for a while, but eventually fell out of favor. Today's computer-based self-instruction uses many of the principles of Skinner's technique.

Behaviorist educators are concerned with the observable indications of learning. Looking for visible cause-and-effect relationships, they consider how external events—antecedents and consequences—change students' observable behaviors. The teacher's job is to modify the students' behavior by setting up situations to reinforce students when they exhibit desired responses. To behaviorists, learning involves a sequence of stimulus and response actions in the learner. By linking together responses involving lower-level skills, teachers can create a learning "chain" to teach students increasingly higher-level skills.

Behaviorist practices. Some of behaviorist educators' guiding principles are highlighted here:[30]

- Set clear and specific goals so you know what you want to reinforce.
- Give clear and systematic praise, but only if deserved.
- Recognize genuine accomplishments.
- Attribute students' success to effort and ability (rather than to luck) to build their confidence.
- Recognize positive behaviors in ways that students value.
- Give plenty of reinforcement when students attempt new materials or skills.
- Use a variety of reinforcers and let students select from among them.
- Try to structure the learning situation to remove something students don't like rather than to offer punishment For example, don't assign homework instead of assigning extra homework.
- Adapt the consequence to fit the misbehavior.

Direct instruction model. Behaviorist educators support a direct instruction model for teaching students basic skills. Basic skills include science facts, math computation, simple reading, and grammar rules.[31] These skills involve tasks that can

---

[30] Woolfolk, A. (2007). *Educational psychology* (10th ed.). Boston, MA: Allyn & Bacon.
[31] Rosenshine, B.., & Stevens, R. (1986). Teaching functions. In M. Whittrock (Ed.), *Teaching research on teaching* (3rd ed., pp. 376–391). New York: Macmillan.

be taught step-by-step and assessed by standardized tests. Steps in direct instruction proceed as follows:[32]

1. **Review and check the previous day's work.** Reteach if necessary.

2. **Present new material.** Teach in small steps with many examples and non-examples.

3. **Provide guided practice.** Question students. Give them practice problems and listen for misconceptions. Reteach if necessary. Continue guided practice until students answer approximately 80 percent of the questions correctly.

4. **Give feedback** and corrective information based on students' answers. Reteach if necessary.

5. **Provide independent practice.** Let students apply the new learning on their own, either in seatwork, cooperative groups, or homework. The success rate during independent practice should be approximately 95 percent. Thus the instructional presentation must effectively prepare the students for the work and guided practice, and assignments must not be too difficult. Students must practice the skills until they are automatic and the students are confident in their use.

6. **Review weekly and monthly.** Consolidate learning and include some review items as homework. Test often and reteach material missed on the tests.

Criticism of direct instruction. Direct instruction critics note that this approach does not work for more complex learning, such as is involved in writing creatively, solving intricate problems, or maturing emotionally. It is limited to lower-level objectives, ignores innovative teaching models, and discourages students' independent thought and action. According to these critics, the direct instruction perspective sees the student as an "empty vessel" waiting to be filled with knowledge rather than as an active constructor of knowledge.[33]

Answering critics, researchers have produced evidence showing that direct instruction can help students actively learn. Younger and less experienced learners need teacher direction and instruction to avoid developing incomplete and misleading ideas that might otherwise lead to knowledge gaps. In fact, evidence from empirical studies over the past half-century consistently indicates that direct instruction is more effective than less teacher-directed approaches.[34] Deep understanding and fluid performance, whether in solving math problems or analyzing literature, require models of expert performance and extensive practice with feedback—like that available in direct instruction. This instruction is less helpful only when learners have sufficiently high prior knowledge to provide "internal" guidance.[35] When students need to learn specific skills and behaviors, a teaching approach consistent with behavioral learning theory makes sense.

Cognitive Perspective on Learning

Cognitive research emerged with the mid-twentieth century's computer revolution and breakthroughs in understanding language development. Cognitive psychologists

---

[32] Rosenshine, B. (1988). Explicit teaching. In D. Berliner & B. Rosenshine (Eds.), *Talks to teachers* (pp. 75–92). New York: Random House; Rosenshine & Stevens, 1986.
[33] Anderson, L. M. (1989). Learners and learning. In M. Reynolds (Ed.), *Knowledge base for beginning teachers* (pp. 85–100). New York: Pergamon; Berg, C. A., & Clough, M. (1991). Hunter lesson design: The wrong one for science teaching. *Educational Leadership, 48*(4), 73–78.
[34] Kirschner, P. A., Sweller, J., & Clark, R. E. (2006). Why minimal guidance during instruction does not work: An analysis of the failure of constructivist, discovery, problem-based, experiential, and inquiry-based teaching. *Educational Psychologist, 41*(2), 75–86; Weinert, F. E., & Helmke, A. (1995). Learning from wise Mother Nature or Big Brother instructor: The wrong choice as seen from an educational perspective. *Educational Psychologist, 30*(3), 135–143.
[35] Kirschner, Sweller, & Clark, 2006.

study how people think, learn concepts, and solve problems. They also study how people process information, remember, and forget.

Current cognitive approaches suggest that one of the most important elements in the learning process is what the individual brings to the learning situation. What we already know determines in large part what we will attend to, perceive, learn, remember, and forget.[36] According to this view, knowledge is more than the end result of learning: A student's existing knowledge actually guides and scaffolds new learning.

Information Processing Model

The **information processing model** illustrates one cognitive perspective of how memory works. This model is based on the analogy between the mind and the computer. It includes three storage systems: sensory memory, working (short-term) memory, and permanent (long-term) memory. Effective teaching can help students to store experiences in permanent memory (learn it).

Figure 14.2 shows the three types of memory—sensory memory, permanent memory, and working memory—and how they interact. Sensory memory deals with temporary storage of data from the senses. Permanent memory contains huge amounts of information stored in such a way that it is available to us. Information may be stored verbally, visually, or both. Permanent memory is where students maintain their background knowledge, both academic and nonacademic. Working memory receives data from sensory memory (where it is held briefly—for approximately 20 seconds), from permanent memory (where it remains permanently), or from both.[37] As long as we focus conscious attention on what we have in working memory, we keep it active. All things being equal, the quality and type of processing that occur in working memory determine whether a particular piece of information will reach permanent memory—and be learned.

Working memory is, in some ways, like a computer screen. It is what you see and are thinking about at the moment. The more times a student practices or uses the information in working memory, the more likely that information is to eventually enter and become embedded in permanent memory, and, therefore, the more likely the student will be to remember it. In this way, information is learned.

The capacity of working memory is limited to nine new items, or chunks, of meaningful information at one time.[38] Working memory is also fragile. It must keep information activated or the material will be lost.

What happens in working memory makes a big difference in whether students ultimately remember (learn) the information. Each student must process the

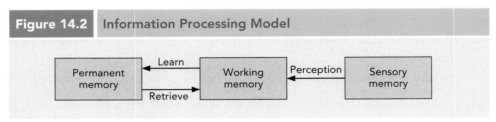

| **Figure 14.2** | Information Processing Model |

Source: Adapted from Marzano, R. J. (2004). *Building background knowledge for academic achievement: Research on what works in schools.* Alexandria, VA: Association for Supervision and Curriculum Development, p. 22.

[36] Ashcraft, M. H. (2006). *Cognition* (4th ed.). Upper Saddle River, NJ: Prentice Hall; Bransford, J. D., Brown, A. L., & Cocking, R. R. (2000). *How people learn: Brain, mind, experience, and school.* Washington, DC: National Academy Press.
[37] Ashcraft, 2006; Driscoll, M. P. (2005). *Psychology of learning for instruction* (3rd ed.). Boston, MA: Allyn & Bacon.
[38] Miller, G. A. (1956). The magical number seven, plus or minus two: Some limits on our capacity for processing information. *Psychological Review, 63,* 81–97.

information multiple times, add details, and make associations with other information. Students need approximately four exposures to information to adequately integrate it into their background knowledge. These exposures should come no more than two days apart.[39]

Nevertheless, practice alone is not enough to ensure that students remember information. Students must use the information in detail and with understanding, making new and varied connections to other meaningful information they already know. Elaborative rehearsal, or associating the information students are trying to remember with something they already know, improves working memory and helps move information into permanent memory. Thus, when teachers help students find personal meaning or relevance for something new, that information is more likely to be stored, remembered, and later recalled for use.

For example, if students are learning about U.S. nationhood, teachers might ask them to describe how their families celebrate the Fourth of July with parades, picnics, and fireworks. Students could also discuss the meaning of political separation from England as described in the Declaration of Independence. Then, teachers might show the class a DVD about the American Revolution. Students could draw pictures or perform skits to illustrate the idea of political separation. As illustrated by this teaching plan, to get the information and understanding into permanent memory, students must engage in the topic for more than one-class period and in a variety of ways.

Information processing approaches to learning consider the human mind to function as a symbol processing system. We convert sensory input into symbols and then process those symbols into knowledge, which can then be held in memory and retrieved. The psychology of learning is a major area of educational study and covers many more details than we discuss here. For our purposes, understanding the cognitive processes underlying student learning helps teachers design, deliver, and assess instruction that is more likely to increase student achievement.

Creating background knowledge. In his 2004 book, *Building Background Knowledge for Academic Achievement*, Robert Marzano looks at how academic background knowledge influences students' achievement and how educators can use this fact to help their students learn.[40]

What students learn depends on many factors—the teacher's skill, the students' interest, the content's complexity, and the students' existing knowledge about the subject. Research literature supports the idea that what students already know about the content is one of the strongest indicators of how well they will learn the new information.[41] What a person already knows about a topic is termed his or her **background knowledge**. Many studies have confirmed the relationship between background knowledge and achievement.[42] The reverse relationship also holds true: The less students already know, the less they will probably learn. In other words, the knowledge-rich get knowledge-richer, while the knowledge-poor do not.

---

[39] Nuthall, G. (1999). The way students learn: Acquiring knowledge from an integrated science and social studies unit. *Elementary School Journal, 99*(4), 303–341; Rovee-Collier, C. (1995). Time windows in cognitive development. *Developmental Psychology, 31*(2), 147–169.

[40] Marzano, R. J. (2004). *Building background knowledge for academic achievement.* Alexandria, VA: Association for Supervision and Curriculum Development.

[41] Marzano, 2004.

[42] Alexander, P. A., Kulikowich, J. M., & Schulze, S. K. (1994). How subject-matter affects recall and interest. *Review of Educational Research, 31*(2), 313–337; Bloom, B. S. (1976). *Human characteristics and school learning.* New York: McGraw-Hill; Dochy, F., Segers, M., & Buehl, M. M. (1999). The relationship between assessment practices and outcomes of studies: The case of research on prior knowledge. *Review of Educational Research, 69*(2), 145–186; Nagy, W. E., Anderson, R. C., & Herman, P. A. (1987). Learning word meaning from context during normal reading. *American Educational Research Journal, 24*(2), 237–270; Tamir, P. (1996). Science assessment. In M. Birenbaum & F. J. R. C. Dochy (Eds.), *Alternatives in assessment of achievements, learning processes, and prior knowledge* (pp. 93–129). Boston, MA: Kluwer; Tobias, S. (1994). Interest, prior knowledge, and learning. *Review of Educational Research, 64*(1), 37–54.

Figure 14.3   A Student's Existing Knowledge Guides and Scaffolds New Learning

H. Mark Weidman Photography/Alamy

Our ability to process and store information influences the extent to which our experiences create background knowledge. Consider this example: Two students visit the same natural history museum and see the same exhibits. The student with **high fluid intelligence** (an innate, enhanced ability to process and store information in permanent memory) will retain in permanent memory much information about early humans as tool makers, as hunters, and as group members. The student with **low fluid intelligence** (an innate, lesser ability to process and store information in permanent memory) will not. As a result, the student with the enhanced information-processing capacity has translated the museum experience into academic background knowledge. What is learned, however, does not depend solely on the amount of experience, but also reflects whether individuals can learn from it and do something with that experience.

Likewise, the more opportunities students have to add to their knowledge of content they will find in school, the more academic background knowledge they will have. The student who has visited the museum half a dozen times will have more academic background knowledge than the student who visits the same museum once or the student who never makes a visit.

Differences in students' access to these cognitive capacities and academically-oriented experiences will create differences in their academic background knowledge and in their academic achievement. Students' family and economic backgrounds play a large role in providing occasions for them to build academic-related background experiences. Limited access to academic background experiences, such as often occurs in low-income families, inhibits children's development of academic background knowledge.

Schools and teachers can make a difference in this regard. Teachers can provide students with academically enriching experiences and teach them cognitive techniques to increase their attention and learning.

Guiding principles. Guiding principles of the cognitive approach to teaching include the following points:

- Make sure to have the students' attention.
- Guide perception and attention by connecting it to students' prior knowledge.
- Help students focus on the most important information.
- Present information in an organized and clear manner.
- Help students connect new information to what they already know.
- Recognize and use strategies to overcome students' background resources and data limitations that restrain learning.
- Provide students with opportunities to learn meaningful and relevant vocabulary to build background knowledge.
- Provide opportunities for students to read and discuss relevant information in class with other students so as to further build their background knowledge.
- Give students opportunities to build their background knowledge through virtual experiences.
- Offer opportunities for students to use both verbal stories and visual images.
- Provide for review and repetition of information in different ways.
- Teach students how to use learning strategies and specific techniques to increase their learning.
- Focus on meaning, not memorization.

Criticism of the cognitive perspective. Although the cognitive revolution added "meaning" to the behaviorists' focus on human's external factors (and exclusion of internal mental factors from consideration),[43] the cognitive perspective has its critics. Evidence shows that the "mind as a computer" metaphor is not wholly correct. It discounts the mind's plasticity and downplays the varied experiences that influence children in infancy and early childhood, which greatly separate their learning capacities and background knowledge in later life.[44] Then, too, individual genetic and environmental differences exist in cognitive capacity and development.[45] Other cognitive critics argue among themselves about the finer points of biology and psychology as they apply to learning, such as whether cognitive development is more individual or social in nature.[46]

Constructivist Perspective on Learning

Constructivist learning theories address how individuals make meaning of events. The constructivist perspective suggests that learners create their own new understandings based on an interaction between what they already know and believe and the information and ideas with which they come into contact. Learning is a self-regulated process of resolving inner cognitive conflicts—by making meaningful connections between familiar knowledge and beliefs and the new data.[47] In this view, learning is seen as the student's cognitive construction of knowledge.

Drawing on a synthesis of current work in cognitive psychology, philosophy, and anthropology, constructivist theory defines knowledge as temporary, developmental,

---

[43] Bruner, J. (1990). *Acts of meaning*. Cambridge, MA: Harvard University Press.
[44] Bjorklund. D.F (1990). *Children's strategies: Contemporary view of cognitive development*. Hillsdale, NJ: Erlbaum Associates.
[45] Bjorklund, 1990.
[46] Anderson, J. R., Reder, L. M., & Simon, H. A. (1997, February). Rejoinder: Situated versus cognitive perspectives: Form versus substance. *Educational Researcher, 26*(1), 18–21.
[47] Fosnot, C. T. (1993). Preface. In J. G. Brooks & M. G. Brooks, *In search of understanding: The case for constructivist classrooms* (pp. v–vii). Alexandra, VA: Association for Supervision and Curriculum Development.

and socially and culturally mediated. Depending on their experiences, knowledge, and their intellectual structures at the time, individuals will develop a unique understanding of a given presentation. Research shows that people remember an experience based on what their preexisting knowledge and cognitive structures allow them to absorb—regardless of the teacher's intentions or the quality of the explanation.[48]

No single constructivist theory of learning exists, but rather multiple constructivist approaches. Understanding learning by any theory or teaching method requires understanding the constructivist ideas.

Influences on constructivist thinking. Swiss scholar Jean Piaget (1896–1980) studied children's cognitive development, including how they form knowledge. He viewed the mind as a dynamic set of mental structures that help us make sense of what we perceive. Through maturation and experience, children lay the new cognitive groundwork for new mental frameworks.[49]

Early progressive movements championed "child-centered" approaches and advocated much the same instructional philosophy as constructivists do today. In the late 1800s, Francis Parker led reforms in Quincy, Massachusetts, and at Chicago's Cook County Normal School that emphasized **learning in context**—that is, learning in settings where the knowledge naturally occurs.[50] Parker took his students on trips across the local countryside to learn geography rather than asking them to memorize and recite countries and capitals. Similarly, his students created their own stories for "reading leaflets," which replaced both the formal primers and the rote learning that went with them.[51]

Similarly, John Dewey routinely used the common childhood experiences as starting points for drawing his students into the more sophisticated forms of knowledge represented in the academic disciplines.[52]

All learning is constructivist. In reality, students are always constructing knowledge, and all learning is constructivist.[53] That is the way the human mind works, even when students are placed in rote learning situations (such as drill and practice) or in passive situations (such as lecture classes).[54] Because all pedagogy results in some kind of mental "construction" by learners if they are to remember any of it, it is technically inappropriate to identify particular approaches to teaching as "constructivist."

"Constructivist pedagogy," therefore, is less a teaching model than a descriptor for instructional strategies.[55] A host of labels for general teaching approaches are anchored in a constructivist philosophy. Among these are "teaching for understanding,"[56]

---

[48] Danielson, C. (1996). *Enhancing professional practice: A framework for teaching.* Alexandria, VA: Association for Supervision and Curriculum Development.

[49] Piaget, J. (1954). *The construction of reality in the child.* New York: Basic Books.

[50] Farnham-Diggory, S. (1990). *Schooling.* Cambridge, MA: Harvard University Press.

[51] Stone, M. K. (1999). The Francis Parker School: Chicago's progressive education legacy. In S. F. Semel & A. R. Sadovnik (Eds.), *Schools of tomorrow, schools of today: What happened to progressive education* (pp. 23–66). New York: Lang.

[52] Dewey, J. (1902/1956). *The child and the curriculum.* Chicago: University of Chicago Press.

[53] For a thorough discussion of constructivist pedagogy, see Windschitl, M. (2002). Framing constructivism in practice as the negotiation of dilemmas: An analysis of the conceptual, pedagogical, cultural, and political challenges facing teachers. *Review of Educational Research, 72*(2), 131–175.

[54] Von Glasersfeld, E. (1993). Questions and answers about radical constructivism. In K. Tobin (Ed.), *The practice of constructivism in science education* (pp. 23–38). Hillsdale, NJ: Lawrence Erlbaum Associates.

[55] Windschitl, 2002.

[56] Elmore, R., Peterson, P., & McCarthey, S. (1996). *Restructuring in the classroom.* San Francisco: Jossey-Bass; McLaughlin, M. W., & Talbert, J. W. (1993). Introduction: New visions of teaching. In D. Cohen & J. E. Talbert (Eds.), *Teaching for understanding: Challenges for policy and practice.* San Francisco: Jossey-Bass; National Research Council. (2000). *How people learn: Brain, mind, experience, and school.* Washington, DC: National Academy Press; Wiggins, G., & McTighe, J. (1998). *Understanding by design.* Alexandria, VA: Association for Supervision and Curriculum Development; Wiske, M. S. (1997). *Teaching for understanding: Linking research with practice.* San Francisco: Jossey-Bass.

"teaching for meaning,"[57] "authentic pedagogy,"[58] "progressive pedagogy,"[59] "child-centered teaching,"[60] and "transformative teaching."[61] Other models exist within specific subject areas. As can be seen, constructivist ideas are less a teaching approach than a range of instructional strategies that fit within many teaching models.

Constructing understanding. We construct, or build, our own understandings of the world in which we live as we interact with the world; reflect on our experiences with people, objects, and ideas; and draw conclusions. We synthesize our new experiences into what we have previously come to understand. Through this process, we create meaning for ourselves. This is human nature.

When an object, an idea, a relationship, or an event does not make sense to us, we respond in one of two ways. First, we may interpret what we see so that it fits within our present set of mental rules for explaining and ordering the world. Alternatively, we may generate a new set of rules that makes better sense for what we perceive to be occurring. Either way, our perceptions and rules constantly interact to shape our understandings, and both approaches contribute to learning.

For example, the first time a child visits the beach and tastes the salty ocean water, the child experiences water that tastes different from what he or she understands "water" from the home's tap or store's bottle to be. The new experience of "water" does not fit with prior understanding. The child must either build a new understanding of "water" (it can be salty) to accommodate the new ocean water experience or ignore the new information and keep the original understanding of water (the ocean is wet but it is not real water). Most likely, this experience and reflection lead to a new understanding in the way the child thinks about water.

Figure 14.4	Learning Occurs When Fresh Information Prompts Us to Rethink Prior Ideas

Terrie L. Zeller, 2009/Used under license from Shutterstock.com

---

[57] Knapp, M. S., & Associates. (1995). *Teaching for meaning in high-poverty classrooms.* New York: Teachers College Press.
[58] Newmann, F., & Associates. (1996). *Authentic achievement.* San Francisco: Jossey-Bass.
[59] Semel, S. F., & Sadovnik, A. R. (1999). Progressive education: Lessons from the past and present. In S. F. Semel & A. R. Sadovnik (Eds.), *Schools of tomorrow, schools of today: What happened to progressive education* (pp. 353–376). New York: Lang.
[60] Chung, S., & Walsh, D. (2000). Unpacking child-centeredness: A history of meanings. *Journal of Curriculum Studies, 32*(2), 215–234.
[61] Jackson, P. W. (1986). *The practice of teaching.* New York: Teachers College Press.

Learning, therefore, entails not discovering more, but rather interpreting events through a more complex cognitive schema. The more mature we become, the more sophisticated our understanding and meaning we give to people, events, and ideas. To wit, a teen might understand the chemical concept of salinity and apply it to ocean water. A physics student might study how salt solutions conduct electricity. Each level of understanding increases thinking's complexity.

In brief, authentic construction of knowledge involves applying, manipulating, interpreting, or analyzing prior knowledge to solve a problem that cannot be solved simply by routine retrieval or reproduction of what we know.[62] Such mental activity creates learning.

Constructivist instruction. Traditionally, American schools viewed learning as the process of students receiving and repeating (aloud or on written tests) newly presented information as evidence of learning. Constructivist instructional practices, in contrast, deliberately help learners to internalize and reshape new information into new understandings. Deep understanding occurs when fresh information prompts students to develop or enhance cognitive structures that enable them to rethink their prior ideas. Constructivist instruction does not look for what students can unthinkingly repeat, but rather for what students can do with the information to generate and demonstrate their understanding.

Compare a traditional with a constructivist approach to learning in a middle school classroom studying the Civil War. On the one hand, a teacher using the traditional approach might require students to write reports on the Battle of the Wilderness. Typically, these reports will paraphrase encyclopedia or Internet sites' battle accounts. On the other hand, a teacher using constructivist techniques might assign students to imagine that they are soldiers in the battle and write a detailed letter home telling their mothers or sweethearts about it. Students would then gather the information about the combat from various sources, coordinate versions from different perspectives, draw their own conclusions, personalize the information, and generate a written product. In this way, students in a constructivist classroom learn by using information in purposefully meaningful ways.

Teachers and students. In constructivist classrooms, teachers find deliberate ways of connecting students' own questions and interests with the curriculum through their instructional choices.[63] Teachers combine their understanding of how students learn with their own professional knowledge of a specific discipline so as to construct a framework for instruction. They encourage students to respond to texts and to one another, guiding students' attention and lending a "structuring consciousness" that helps students to think in increasingly complex ways about a range of possible perspectives. Research supports the belief that teachers in a constructivist classroom need to know their subjects well.[64]

Many students are not comfortable with constructivist instruction. They are accustomed to the lecture/discussion method, in which they sit back and "absorb" information, investing minimal effort or attention to the learning process. Participating in a constructivist classroom, by comparison, requires a greater intellectual and energy commitment from both teachers and students. It takes trust, time, experience, and the teacher's persistence in asking interesting questions, respecting and accepting the variety of student responses, and structuring students' thinking and work before students will find relevance and personal meaning in understanding and using what they are learning.[65]

---

[62] Newmann et al., 1996.
[63] Brooks, J. G., Libresco, A. S., & Plonczak, I. (2007, May). Spaces of liberty: Battling the new soft bigotry of NCLB. *Phi Delta Kappan, 88*(10), 749–756.
[64] Richardson, V. (2003, December). Constructive pedagogy. *Teachers College Record, 105*(9), 1623–1640.
[65] Students require more time to construct a concept that makes sense and has meaning to them and that is also consistent with the "official knowledge" than to simply be told about it. The former approach also requires more teacher planning time.

Assessment in constructivist instruction. Because every student constructs meaning differently, teachers who follow the constructivist path must ensure that every student understands the information correctly. Students' constructed meaning cannot be completely idiosyncratic, but rather must make sense or be verified by the larger public.[66] Ongoing, informal assessments are a means of checking for accurate understanding. Teachers can ask students questions to answer aloud or in writing and have students provide written products or artifacts that express their understanding.

Constructivist assessment methods may include clinical interviews, observations, student journals, peer reviews, research reports, construction of physical models, or performance in the form of inquiries, plays, debates, dances, or artistic renderings.[67] Such artifacts and performances require clear, well-designed, flexible evaluation rubrics, or specific criteria for increasingly successful completion. When teachers design these rubrics in conjunction with students, the process makes explicit what is valued in the learning process and how evidentiary criteria are linked to these values.

Principles of constructivist instruction. In constructivist classrooms, the following principles apply:[68]

- Students enjoy frequent opportunities to engage in complex, meaningful, problem-based activities.
- Teachers are familiar with students' prior knowledge and use it to help students assimilate new information by explaining or meaningfully extending their own experiences.[69]
- Teachers elicit students' ideas and experiences in relation to key topics, and then fashion learning situations that help students elaborate or restructure their current knowledge.
- Teachers provide students with a variety of information resources as well as the tools—technological and conceptual—necessary to advance their learning.
- Teachers make their own thinking processes explicit to learners and encourage students to do the same through dialog, writing, drawings, and other representations.
- Students are routinely asked to apply knowledge in diverse and authentic contexts—for example, to explain ideas, interpret texts, predict phenomena, and construct arguments based on evidence, rather than to focus on finding the predetermined "right" answer.
- Teachers offer opportunities for students to work collaboratively and use extended conversation, writing, and other expressive forms to think through and communicate information so it makes sense and has meaning.[70]
- Teachers use a variety of assessment strategies to understand how students' ideas are evolving and to give feedback on both the processes and the products of their thinking.[71]
- In addition to being an instructor, the teacher becomes a coach, guide, facilitator, and "mentor in a cognitive apprenticeship" who inspires and nudges students to do the active work of learning.[72]
- The classroom environment exemplifies the norms of trust, high expectations for intellectual accomplishment, and collaboration, for students and teachers alike.

---

[66] Newmann et al., 1996.

[67] Shepard, L. (2000). The role of assessment in a learning culture. *Educational Researcher, 29*(7), 4–14.

[68] Windschitl, M (2002). Framing constructivism in practice as the negotiation of dilemmas for analysis of the conceptual, pedagogical, cultural, and political challenges facing teachers. *Review of Educational Research, 72*(2), 131–175.

[69] Newmann et al., 1996, p. 285.

[70] Newmann et al., 1996, p. 285.

[71] Windschitl, 2002, p. 137.

[72] Newmann et al., 1996, p. 285.

Comparing traditional and constructivist classrooms. Not all valuable learning occurs through a constructivist process. Other types of learning, such as rote learning, have important roles as well. The instructional challenge is knowing when to use which approach. Nevertheless, all learning is somewhat constructivist in nature, because learners are continually integrating new information with old as they try to learn.

Table 14.1 illustrates how the constructivist and traditional classrooms compare in terms of teaching and learning.

Positive research support. Research studies have found positive results from students whose teachers use constructivist instructional practices. The National

Table 14.1	Comparison of Traditional and Constructivist Classrooms
Traditional Classrooms	**Constructivist Classrooms**
Teacher presents curriculum part to whole, with emphasis on facts and basic skills.	Teacher presents curriculum whole to part, with emphasis on big ideas and concepts.
Teacher values presenting the fixed curriculum.	Teacher encourages and values students questioning the curriculum.
Teacher asks students closed-ended questions with one right answer.	Teacher asks students open-ended questions with several "correct" answers.
Classroom focus is on the teacher and the information.	Classroom focus is on the students and information and helping them make the information personally meaningful.
The "right answer" is the fact or perspective presented by the teacher or the textbook.	Complex questions have multiple perspectives and truth is sometimes a matter of interpretation.
Instructional activities rely heavily on textbooks and worksheets.	Instructional activities rely heavily on primary data sources and hands-on experiences with materials.
Students are considered passive vessels into which the teacher "pours" information.	Students are viewed as thinkers with emerging ideas about the world.
Teachers generally lecture students to give them information.	Teachers generally interact with students about the information.
Teachers seek correct answers to validate student learning.	Teachers seek students' viewpoints so as to understand students' present ideas for use in later lessons.
Teachers view assessment of student learning as separate from teaching; assessment occurs almost entirely by testing.	Assessment of student learning is interwoven with teaching and occurs throughout via teacher observations of students at work, student performances, exhibitions, portfolios, and written tests.
Students work primarily alone.	Student work both alone and in groups.
Goal is for students to remember the information as presented.	Goal is for students to make the new information personally meaningful and make connections so they will remember, recall, and use the information later.

Source: Adapted from In Brooks, J. G., & Brooks, M. G. (1993). *In search of understanding: The case for constructivist classrooms.* Alexandra, VA: Association for Supervision and Curriculum Development, p. 17.

Research Council (NRC) states, "One of the hallmarks of the new science of learning is its emphasis on learning with understanding."[73] Likewise, a constructivist instructional approach can increase students' scores on standardized achievement tests. After conducting a rigorous study of 669 classrooms in 34 schools, the Washington School Research Center reported that a strong relationship exists between constructivist instructional practices and student achievement on the Washington Assessment of Student Learning (WASL).[74] The constructivist instruction predicts student achievement even beyond the effects of family income.

Assessment expert Mike Schmoker describes diverse schools in varied settings that use constructivist instructional practices which result in student success on exams.[75] Additionally, a comparative study of college environmental science courses using identical materials, learning resources, student questionnaires, and examinations reports that "students in constructivist classes performed significantly better on exams, rated the course higher, and participated more in campus and regional environmental support efforts than students in traditional classes."[76] Clearly, a relationship exists between students' high achievement and the use of constructivist teaching approaches in their classrooms.

Although constructivist instruction produces noteworthy student achievement gains, constructivist instruction is not widespread. It is especially rare in urban schools.[77] One study found that constructivist instructional practices were evident in only 17 percent of the observed classrooms, and found a negative correlation between constructivist teaching and school-level family income.[78] In short, students from wealthier family backgrounds were more likely to have teachers who used instructional practices that encouraged their making their learning meaningful than were students from less affluent families.

Constructivist criticisms and answers. Constructivist critics argue that constructivism is not a theory of teaching, that it suffers from a large disconnect between theory and practice, that it subordinates the curriculum to students' interests, and that it is inappropriate for teaching students from low-income and minority cultures. Let's consider these claims.

First, critics contend that constructivism is a theory of learning and not a theory of teaching. As a result, teachers can use any practices that they call "constructivist" but that may not involve either teaching or learning.[79] These critics are correct.

Next, critics point to a substantial disconnect between constructivist theory and its practice.[80] Critics claim that some advocates overgeneralize the constructivist concept and misapply it in learning situations. These critics are also correct. Mistaken beliefs such as "teachers should not be the experts," "teachers should not lecture

---

[73] Bransford, J. D., Brown, A. L., & Cockling, R. R. (Eds.) (2002). *How people learn: Brain, mind, and school.* Washington, DC: National Academy Press, p. 8.

[74] Abbott, M. L., & Fouts, J. T. (2003, February). *Constructivist teaching and student achievement: The results of a school-level classroom observation study in Washington.* Seattle, WA: Washington School Research Center, South Pacific University, Technical Report #5. Retrieved October 30, 2009, from http://www.spu.edu/orgs/research/ObservationStudy-2-13-03.pdf.

[75] Schmoker, M. (2002). The real causes of higher achievement. Southwest Educational Development Laboratory. Retrieved October 30, 2009, from www.sedl.org/pubs/sedletter/v14n02/1.html.

[76] Lord, T. R. (1999). A comparison between traditional and constructivist teaching in environmental science. *Journal of Environmental Education, 30,* 22–28.

[77] Darling-Hammond, L. (2006, October). Securing the right to learn: Policy and practice for powerful teaching and learning. *Educational Researcher, 35*(7), 18; Darling-Hammond, L., et al. (2005). Does teacher preparation matter? Evidence about teaching certification, Teach for America, and teacher effectiveness. *Education Policy Analysis Archives, 13*(42). Retrieved October 30, 2009, from http://epaa.asu.edu/epaav13n42; Elmore, R., & Burney, D. (1997). *Investing in teacher learning: Staff development and instructional improvement in Community District #2.* New York: National Commission on Teaching and America's Future; Wilson, S. M., Darling-Hammond, L., & Berry, B. (2001). *Teaching policy: Connecticut's long-term efforts to improve teaching and learning.* Seattle, WA: University of Washington.

[78] Abbott & Fouts, 2003.

[79] Richardson, V. (2003, December). Constructivist pedagogy. *Teachers College Record, 105* (9), 1623–1640.

[80] Windschitl, 2002.

to transmit information," "memorizing is always bad," and "students' idiosyncratic constructed meaning is more important than the 'official' knowledge" all misinterpret constructivist theory.

Widespread misconceptions about constructivist instruction *do* lead to poor teaching practices. Learning is an active process, but this does not mean that teachers should rarely if ever "teach" content to students.[81] In fact, lecture is a legitimate teaching methodology that can be stimulating and highly effective depending on the teacher's goals, the curriculum to be learned, the teacher's particular talents, and the students' characteristics.[82]

Likewise, rote learning is not always bad. It has the advantage of automatizing aspects of problem solving, thereby freeing the mind for more abstract thought. A student who has memorized the meaning of certain vocabulary words can more competently read and understand an essay that uses those words than a student who must constantly stop and look through a dictionary.[83]

Additionally, in their early stages of understanding, many educators naively place too much faith in students' abilities to structure their own learning.[84] They erroneously equate student interest and classroom involvement as sufficient—rather than necessary—conditions for worthwhile learning. Activities, as opposed to ideas, are their starting points for planning, and they mistakenly give little thought to an activity's intellectual implications.[85] Students' mastery of the content and ability to use it effectively in a variety of contexts is the ultimate goal, and the official curriculum remains the driver. Finally, critics question whether constructivist teaching practices impose an inappropriate culture and instructional approach on students who are not a part of the dominant society.[86] These critics are confused. While constructivism's psychological roots are certainly Western, liberal, and individualistic (Eurocentric), and while much of the current U.S. constructivist pedagogy developed within more affluent students, the lack of widespread constructivist instruction in low-income schools may have several causes.

To begin, many studies find that today's students of color and those from low-income families have the least qualified teachers, have only limited access to intellectually challenging curriculum, and are most likely to be taught in large classes in big, impersonal schools.[87] In classrooms where teachers are not familiar with students' interests and life experiences, they fail to build on local knowledge and may actually "disinvite" students to participate in classroom discussion.[88] In addition, because communication patterns differ from one cultural group to another,[89] and because constructivist teaching relies on students

---

[81] Anderson, J. R., Reder, L. M., & Simon, H.A. (1996). Situated learning and education. *Educational Researcher, 25*(4), 5–11.

[82] Baines, L. A., & Stanley, G. (2001, May). We still want to see the teacher. *Phi Delta Kappan, 82*(9), 695–696.

[83] Baines & Stanley, 2001.

[84] Prawat, R. (1992). Teachers' beliefs about teaching and learning: A constructivist perspective. *American Journal of Education, 100*(3), 354–395.

[85] Yinger, R. J. (1977). *A study of teacher planning: Description, theory, and practice.* Occasional Paper No. 84. East Lansing: Michigan State University, Institute for Research on Teaching.

[86] Eisenhart, M., Finkel, E., & Marion, S. (1996). Creating the conditions for scientific literacy: A re-examination. *American Educational Research Journal, 33,* 261–295; Delpit, L. (1986). Skills and other dilemmas of a progressive black educator. *Harvard Educational Review, 56*(4), 379–385; Delpit, L. (1988). The silenced dialogue: Power and pedagogy in educating other peoples' children. *Harvard Educational Review, 56*(4), 379–385; Lee, O. (1999). Science knowledge, worldviews, and information sources in social and cultural contexts: Making sense after a natural disaster. *American Educational Research Journal, 36*(2), 187–220.

[87] Darling-Hammond, L. (2004). The color line in American education: Race, resources, and student achievement. *W. E. B. Du Bois Review: Social Science Research on Race, 1*(2), 213–246.

[88] Windschitl, 2002.

[89] Au, K. H. (1980). Participant structures in a reading lesson with Hawaiian children: Analysis of a culturally appropriate instructional event. *Anthropology and Education, 11*(2), 91–115; Phillips, S. U. (1983). *The invisible culture: Communication in classroom and community on the Warm Springs Indian Reservation.* New York: Longman.

communicating in a variety of ways, middle-class white teachers may find it difficult to work with the discourse patterns favored by various ethnic and racial minorities,[90] and vice versa.

The constructive approach works best when learners have sufficiently high levels of prior knowledge to provide "internal guidance."[91] As discussed previously, studies show that low-income and minority students often have the least academic background knowledge as compared with more affluent students. For this reason, low-income and minority students need teachers who can actively structure their learning and provide essential background knowledge until the students gain the skills and knowledge store to do increasingly more themselves.

Urban teachers may incorrectly believe that because their students are so lacking in basic skills, they should be teaching for memorization and transmission of basic facts and skills rather than teaching for concepts, generalizations, connections, personal meaning, and deep understanding—all of which will actually motivate student learning and skill development. These factors argue for educators to find ways to make constructivist learning possible for minority and low-income students rather than to deprive these students of opportunities to learn in meaningful ways. Seeking equity and maintaining high expectations for all students' learning requires teachers to use constructivist, meaning-making learning approaches with minority and low-income students—indeed, with all students.

Effective teachers use a blend of constructivist, behavioral, and cognitive learning theories. One instructional approach does not fit all content with all students in all situations. Nevertheless, teachers with a strong knowledge base who understand how students learn will find many opportunities to use constructivist instruction approaches to ensure that their students learn to understand and apply concepts in meaningful ways—both inside and outside the classroom.

Activity 14.1

Understanding how learning occurs influences how one teaches. The three learning theories discussed here—behavioral, cognitive, and constructivist— have their own perspectives on how students learn and the instructional strategies to best accomplish this goal.

A. Break out into three groups. Each group should be assigned one of the three learning theories—behaviorist, cognitive, and constructivist.

B. Working with the other members of your group, identify, list, and describe the key beliefs, advantages, and disadvantages of the learning theory assigned.

C. Identify and discuss the learning situations (regarding content and learners) in which this approach is best used.

D. Working as a group, deliver a presentation to the class using the practices advanced by your learning theory.

E. Come together as a class to discuss these three learning theories and their contributions to instructional practice.

F. Decide under which learning theory you learn best, and give examples.

---

[90] Lee, O., & Anderson, C. (1993). Task engagement and conceptual change in middle school science classrooms. *American Educational Research Journal, 30*(3), 585–610.
[91] Kirschner, Sweller, & Clark, 2006.

Providing High-Quality Instruction

Although effective teachers make instruction look easy, it isn't. Effective teaching takes considerable preparation to identify the appropriate content for study, design the learning activities and assessments around it, and establish a classroom culture that supports learning. Teachers invest many hours preparing for quality instruction and learning. After delivering their lessons, teachers reflect professionally on what has occurred and make adjustments for the next day as well as for the next time they teach that or other lessons.

What Effective Teaching Looks Like

Charlotte Danielson, an education writer and consultant based in Princeton, New Jersey, has developed a framework for teaching that clearly represents all aspects of a teacher's daily responsibilities. Derived from the most recent theoretical and empirical research about teaching, her framework offers a "roadmap" to accomplished teaching and classroom organization practices.[92] We will use portions of this model to guide understanding of what effective instruction looks like.

Danielson's framework is public, generic, and holistic, and it fits any effective teaching methodology. She assumes that teaching is purposeful and professional. It is each teacher's responsibility, using the resources at hand, to have students learn important concepts and skills. Additionally, because the framework model is tied to actual teaching practices and is supported by a solid research background, many U.S. school districts currently use it for teachers' supervision, evaluation, and professional development.[93] Studies have consistently determined that teachers' ratings based on Davidson's rubric are positively and significantly related to student achievement.[94]

In this section, we discuss several essential behaviors that teachers use in planning and preparation, building a receptive classroom environment, delivering effective instruction, and conducting useful reflection. All of these aspects are key parts of delivering effective instruction.

Planning and Preparing for Teaching

During planning and preparing, teachers organize the content that students are to learn into a sequence of activities and exercises that make it accessible for students. At the same time, the teacher designs assessment techniques that reflect the

---

[92] Danielson, C. (2007). *Enhancing professional practice: A framework for teaching* (2nd ed.). Alexandria, VA: Association for Supervision and Curriculum Development; Danielson, C. (2002). *Enhancing student achievement: A framework for school improvement.* Alexandria, VA: Association for Supervision and Curriculum Development.

[93] School districts using Danielson's Framework for Teaching model include, among others, those in Newport News, Virginia; Chester, New Jersey: Cumberland, Maine; East Grand Rapids, Michigan; Kennett Square, Pennsylvania; Columbus, Indiana; Dubuque, Iowa; Riverton, Illinois; Greenwood, Arkansas; Grosse Ile, Maine; Douglas County, Colorado; Northfield, Vermont; Quakertown, Pennsylvania; and the Georgia Department of Education.

[94] Archibald, S. (2006). Narrowing in on educational resources that do affect student achievement. *Peabody Journal of Education, 81*(4), 23–42; Borman, G. D., & Kimball, S. M. (2005). Teacher quality and educational quality: Do teachers with higher standards-based evaluation ratings close student achievement gaps? *Elementary School Journal, 106*(1), 3–20; Gallagher, H. A. (2004). Vaughn Elementary's innovative teacher evaluation system: Are teacher evaluation scores related to growth in student achievement? *Peabody Journal of Education, 79*(4), 79–107; Kimball, S. M., White, B., Milanowski, A. T., & Borman, G. (2004). Examining the relationship between teacher evaluation and student assessment results in Washoe County. *Peabody Journal of Education, 79*(4), 54–78; Milanowski, A. T. (2004). The relationship between teacher performance evaluation scores and student achievement: Evidence from Cincinnati. *Peabody Journal of Education, 79*(4), 33–53; Milanowski, A., & Kimball, S. (2005, April). *The relationship between teacher expertise and student achievement: A synthesis of three years of data.* Paper presented at the annual meeting of the American Educational Research Association, Montreal, Quebec, Canada.

Figure 14.5	Planning for High Quality Instruction and a Supportive Classroom Culture Takes Time

instructional goals and document and evaluate student progress both during and after the teaching process.[95]

Knowing content and pedagogy. Teachers cannot teach what they do not know. When teachers know their subjects well, they tend to recognize which questions will interest their students and produce greater understanding. Teachers also identify where students are likely to become confused or make mistakes—such as the difference between area and perimeter in mathematics—so they can anticipate and prevent common student misperceptions.

Knowing the subject matter well is not enough, however. Teachers need to know which instructional techniques will work best for ensuring that students learn their content. Instructional practices must reflect current research on best pedagogical approaches within the discipline and require the teacher to continue professional learning.[96]

Knowledge of students. Effective teachers understand their students. Each age group has certain developmental characteristics—intellectual, social, physical, and emotional. Teachers must understand these general characteristics as well as individual exceptions that appear in their classrooms. Teachers need to be aware of their students' prior knowledge and the possible knowledge gaps, misunderstandings, and misconceptions that might interfere with learning.

Students vary individually in terms of their interests, talents, and preferred learning styles. Teachers need to recognize and understand these individual differences. Building on students' interests and strengths, teachers can connect them with the new content as well as develop a positive personal rapport. In this way, teachers address both the group as a whole and the individuals within it.

---

[95] Danielson, 2007, p. 27.
[96] For a more complete discussion, see the following sources: Ashton, P., & Crocker, L. (1987, May–June). Systematic study of planned variations: The essential focus of teacher education reform. *Journal of Teacher Education, 38,* 2–8; Byrne, C. J. (1983). *Teacher knowledge and teacher effectiveness: A literature review, theoretical analysis and discussion of research strategy.* Paper presented at the meeting of the Northwestern Educational Research Association, Ellenville, NY; Monk, D. H. (1994). Subject matter preparation of secondary mathematics and science teachers and student achievement. *Economics of Education Review, 13*(2), 125–145.

Selecting instructional outcomes. Teaching is purposeful. Instructional outcomes must be worthwhile, clear, relate to what the students are intended to learn, reflect a balance of different learning types, and be suitable for diverse learners. Instructional outcomes must represent learning central to a discipline as well as high-level learning for the students. They must also account for the district's curriculum, requirements of external mandates such as state testing or voluntary programs such as Advanced Placement or International Baccalaureate exams, and community expectations.

Teachers need to explicitly state these educational purposes in terms of student learning rather than student activity. The key question to ask is, "What will the students *learn* as a result of the instructional engagement?"—not just "What will the students *do?*"[97] These goals should be intellectually challenging and be capable of assessment to established performance standards.

Designing coherent instruction. Through their instructional design, teachers translate instructional outcomes into students' learning experiences. The sequence of these activities should be logical, progressing from easier to harder, simpler to more complex, from attention in one learning area to integration across several area.[98] "Easier" and "simpler," however, do not equate to "lower in intellectual level." The teacher's challenge is to find the meaningful and relevant connections to the student's prior learning before moving on to cover more complex material.

Since instructional outcomes vary, instructional strategies vary as well. Teaching students the steps in the scientific method is different from teaching students the procedure for cleaning lab beakers. Some lessons consist of presentations, whereas others have students work collaboratively on problem solving using the new information or skills. Accordingly, the teacher's role each day varies along with students' activities and grouping strategies.

Activities and assignments that promote student learning emphasize thinking and apply problem solving to real situations, permit a degree of student choice and initiative, and encourage depth (cognitive challenge) rather than breadth (superficiality).

Designing student assessments. Assessment plays a central role in learning. It has two related, but separate uses:

- Assessment determines whether students have achieved the instructional outcomes establishing during planning. This is assessment *of* learning.
- Assessment provides teachers and students with valuable information to guide future learning. This is assessment *for* learning.

Assessment requires clear criteria and standards about how it will evaluate students' work. Ideally, assessment methods should be part of the students' learning activities and should reflect real-world applications of knowledge and understanding. These approaches motivate student interest and efforts and give teachers deeper insight into how well students are learning.

Building a Receptive Classroom Environment

Establishing a classroom environment that supports students learning involves building relationships anchored in mutual respect and rapport. When a teacher has a good relationship with students, those students are more likely to accept the teacher's rules, procedures, and disciplinary actions. Establishing a classroom culture for learning includes managing classroom procedures and student behaviors.

---

[97] Danielson, 2007, p. 51.
[98] Danielson, 2007, p. 57.

Creating an environment of respect and rapport. An environment of warm mutual respect allows all students to feel safe and valued. Students know that the teacher and the other students will treat them with dignity. This emotional and physical safety allows students to take the intellectual and affective risks necessary to learn. Classrooms characterized by respect and rapport are friendly, open, and frequently humorous places, but teachers always remain the adults.

In learning environments, teachers' caring may be cloaked under a firm manner and business-like atmosphere. Students appreciate the difference between genuine adult caring and permissiveness. They know their teachers express their concern by insisting that all students achieve well, behave well, and not just "get by." Of course, caring takes many different forms. What is suitable for kindergarten students may be highly inappropriate for high school students. Teachers' personalities also vary, which greatly influences the environment in their classrooms.

To maintain a classroom of mutually respectful relationships, teachers need an appropriate mental set. In particular, they need "withitness" and emotional objectivity.[99]

Withitness means being "with it"—being aware of what is happening in all parts of the classroom at all times by continuously scanning the classroom. It also means intervening promptly and accurately when inappropriate behavior threatens to become disruptive, especially when the teacher is working with a small group or individual student.

Emotional objectivity means that teachers keep an even temper and calm demeanor. They are friendly, helpful, and congenial. They do not become visibly upset if students violate classroom rules, react negatively to disciplinary actions, or do not respond to the teacher's attempts to develop a relationship.[100] Teachers remain "matter of fact," not personalizing student mistakes or misbehaviors.

Establishing a classroom culture for learning. Classrooms characterized by a culture for learning are intellectually active places where teachers and students alike value the work. Teachers show a genuine enthusiasm for their subject and demonstrate respect and caring for their students. Students accept their teachers' insistence on high-quality work. Both parties take pride in their achievements. All teachers have the responsibility to establish such a climate in their classroom.

Classrooms with cultures for learning balance academic challenge with instructional support. Students want work that stretches but not overwhelms them. They expect to work hard and see success at the end of their journey. At the same time, good teachers provide a variety of supports by explaining the material until everyone understands and giving students varied learning experiences through which to master the information.[101]

A culture for learning encourages persistence—for students and teachers alike. Teachers are always searching for what works best with each student. They persist in trying to meet the individual needs of the problem student, the gifted student, the student with disabilities, the English language learner, and the frequently neglected pupil, all of whom too often fall between the cracks.[102]

---

[99] Marzano, 2003, pp. 93–94. The term "withitness" was coined by Jacob Kounin in 1983: Kounin, J. S. (1983). *Classrooms: Individual or behavior settings? Micrographs on teaching and learning* (General Series No. 1). Bloomington, IN: Indiana University, School of Education. (ERIC Document Reproduction Service No. 240 070).

[100] Nelson, J. R., Martella, R., & Garland, B. (1998). The effects of teaching school expectations and establishing a consistent consequence on formal office disciplinary actions. *Journal of Emotional and Behavioral Disorders, 6*(3), 153–161; Soar, R. S., & Soar, R. M. (1979). Emotional climate and management. In P. L. Peterson & H. J. Walberg, (Eds.), *Research on teaching: Concepts, findings, and implications* (pp. 97–119). Berkeley, CA: McCutchan.

[101] Students have different learning styles and accept teacher help in different ways.

[102] Haberman, M. (1995, June). Selecting "star" teachers for children and youth in urban poverty. *Phi Delta Kappan, 76*(10), 779.

Managing classroom procedures. An effective teacher plans and prepares for the classroom's organization with the same care and attention to detail he or she devotes to designing high-quality lessons. Classroom procedures and routines for distributing materials, moving students into workgroups, and taking attendance; thoughtful room arrangements; and effective discipline make a classroom run smoothly.

Teachers must appreciate the relationship between instruction and student conduct. When students are engaged in meaningful work and experience success in learning, they are not interested in disturbing the class. If students are bored or concerned that they will be embarrassed or humiliated, however, they may prefer to disrupt the class and distract others from learning. For such students, having the teacher send them out of the class is preferable to "looking foolish" in front of their peers. When teachers make learning more interesting, relevant, and successful for students, students can be constructively and successfully challenged.

A CLOSER LOOK

Margaret Metzger, an English teacher, wrote about classroom management and discipline as a letter to new teachers. Excerpts from her letter appear here. Read what she recommends and then answer the questions that follow.

A Confession

I still wince at my early attempts to "control" my classes. Here's what I painfully remember about myself as a young teacher, trying in vain to control classes.

- On the first day, I told a huge football player to change seats. I was stunned when he obeyed.
- I identified emotionally with the students rather than the teachers.
- I pretended competence, certainty, and adulthood—though I didn't feel any. I was still working out my own issues with authority figures, so it was hard to be one.
- I ricocheted between being a drill sergeant and Mary Poppins.
- Kids liked challenging me, and it was fun for them to see me squirm. Kids attacked my most vulnerable character flaws, and they could undo my self-esteem in a matter of minutes.
- One critical comment could haunt me for days.
- I thought everything was my fault.
- The kids who behaved worst got all my attention.
- Desperate, I used the curriculum, grades, and my own education to coerce (bully?) students.
- I was so afraid to admit failure that I didn't ask for help.
- The very idea of discipline exhausted me. I hated it.
- I felt terminally vulnerable.

Simple Principles of Survival

In the early years, I needed a few anchoring principles so that every problem didn't require a whole new philosophical debate with myself. Frankly, I didn't want to think about discipline, which I found—and still find—the most boring part of teaching. Here are my anchoring principles from those early years, with a few comments about each.

1. **Don't escalate, de-escalate.** Teachers, like parents, need to use a light touch. Let go of some infractions. Whisper instead of yell. Use humor. Change locations. Divide and conquer. Talk to students privately. Make a tiny hand movement. Call kids by name. Smile a lot. Listen. Listen. Listen.

2. **Let students save face.** A few generic phrases let everyone save face, they don't require me to articulate the problem or even to name it, and they allow me to keep the lesson going. Some of my favorites were and still are:

   • "It's a good thing I like you."
   • "Here's the deal: I'll pretend I didn't see that, and you never do it again."
   • "Consider yourself scolded."
   • "That's inappropriate."

3. **Insist on the right to sanity.** Roland Barth offers a great analogy for teachers. He talks about the airplane flight attendant who says, "In case of emergency, put the oxygen mask on yourself first, before you put the mask on the child." Barth says the same is true in schools: If we don't take care of ourselves, we can't save the children.

   So, instead of feeling overwhelmed, I tried—note the critical word *tried*—to figure out which behavior bothered me most. You need to know yourself as a teacher.

4. **Get help.** For the first several years, I felt too humiliated by my failures to ask for help. By the second year, I began to make alliances. I learned which guidance counselors really helped, which administrator trusted my judgment, and whether to trust the truant officer. I learned which teachers made good witnesses in difficult meetings. I began to feel not so alone.

5. **Get out of the limelight—or the line of fire.** Like dealing with unruly toddlers, keeping adolescents busy helps to control them. I am not proud of this.

Classroom Management Versus Classroom Discipline

Ideally, you want to anticipate and stave off discipline problems. Instead of merely reacting to bad behavior, we must create classrooms that eliminate the need for disciplinary action. This isn't totally possible. But certainly, some environments, some teacher attitudes, some assignments generate more cooperation than others.

Source: Adapted from Metzger, M. (2002, September). Learning to discipline. *Phi Delta Kappan, 84*(1), 77–84.

Questions

1. With which parts of Metzer's "Confession" do you most identify?

2. How can you prepare yourself to identify emotionally with the teacher rather than with the students? Which difficulties can you foresee if you don't?

3. Which of Metzer's "Survival Principles" have you observed your own teachers using? Which worked best with you? Which worked best with the rest of your class?

4. What is going to make these suggestions more difficult to put into practice than they seem?

5. Explain the difference between classroom management and student discipline.

Instruction for Student Engagement

While thoughtful planning and development of the appropriate classroom environment are essential components of teaching, **instruction**—the interaction between students and content—is the main event. With instruction, teachers put their plans for connecting students with content and their positive learning environment into action.

Instruction is a constellation of related behaviors. To engage students in the learning process, teachers must provide clear directions and explanations. They must skillfully use questioning and discussion and integrate assessment strategies into their instruction. Teachers must be flexible and responsive if they are to assure learning opportunities for all students. Finally, they must continuously reflect on their professional practice in an ongoing effort to improve their expertise and ability to help all students learn.

Communicating with students. Teachers' clear and accurate communications tell their students what they will be learning, why it is important, and what students will be doing to learn it. Students need unambiguous and accurate directions and procedures to guide their work and to prevent them from losing time by flailing about without knowing what to do or by starting the wrong activity.

Next, teachers must communicate clearly with students about the new content. As part of the lesson, teachers may need to present key background knowledge (information or vocabulary) to make the new lesson personally meaningful and relevant. They can present the new information in many different ways—orally, visually, or through discussion. No matter which strategy is used, the language and concepts must be appropriate to the students' ages and background and the specific discipline. Of course, teachers' language should always demonstrate correct usage and contain expressive vocabulary.

Using questioning and discussion techniques. Teachers' skills in questioning and leading discussions can help students explore new concepts, elicit evidence of student understanding, and promote deeper student intellectual engagement.

Poor questions tend to ask students primarily to engage in short-answer, low-level thinking as a way to see what they know after they have completed their homework or reading assignment. Poor questions are boring or narrow. Only a few students have the right answers. The teacher has a single correct answer in mind, even though several accurate answers are possible.

Effective questions, by comparison, rarely require a simple "yes," "no," or few-words response. Instead, they promote thinking by inviting students to formulate hypotheses, make connections between familiar concepts and new material, or challenge previously held views. Even when the question has a limited number of right answers—for instance, "Which different coins can you use to make 17 cents?"—an effective question is likely to encourage student thinking and extend learning.

Thinking of possible answers takes time. Experienced teachers allow students **wait time** to process the information before they must respond to a question and encourage all students to participate. Teachers often probe a student's answer, looking for clarification or elaboration with prompts such as "Could you give me an example of that?" or "Would you tell me more about what you mean?" These follow-up questions encourage students to think more deeply and convey respect for students and their ideas.

Engaging students in learning. Learning is a minds-on activity. **Student engagement** requires cognitive involvement with the content or active construction of understanding. The quality of student engagement results from carefully planning the learning experiences. "Engagement" is not the same as being "busy" or spending **"time-on-task."** Students may be completing a worksheet and be "on task" but not mentally engaged in significant learning.

Engagement must make sense to learners. Teachers continually help students make sense of and find meaning in what they are learning by connecting the content at hand to things students know and value—their prior knowledge, interests, concerns, and experiences. Teachers help students see connections among ideas by using examples known to students and by linking the content with their lives to emphasize its relevance.[103]

Physical materials may also encourage student engagement in learning. When students work with physical representations, such as using hands-on manipulatives in elementary school mathematics to understand place value, they are more likely to literally see and feel how the concept works. Of course, physical materials do not guarantee intellectual engagement: Hands-on must also be minds-on.

As discussed earlier, research has shown that learning requires multiple exposures to, and complex interactions with, knowledge.[104] Students also need varying experiences with the information if they are to truly learn it. When students can use their new information in visual or dramatic ways—representing the information in pictures or graphics, or by telling stories—instead of merely talking about it, they are more likely to learn and remember the content.[105]

Instructional materials and resources may contribute to student engagement. These items include everything from textbooks, maps, charts, the Internet, and lab equipment to classroom guests and field trips. Their primary value, however, lies in how teachers get students to cognitively interact with them to reach the instructional outcomes.

Research on student engagement. Research supports student engagement's importance in achievement.[106] One study concluded that students "cannot succeed in . . . school by remaining passive recipients of knowledge. . . . Without engagement, there is no learning."[107]

Researchers have established that students are significantly more likely to be engaged in activities that have inherent value—personal relevance and meaning—rather than those that rely on extrinsic values such as getting good grades. When teachers provide students with opportunities to make connections between real-world activities and their academic coursework, and when students have the freedom to explore issues that interest them, they remember more of what they learn, put more effort into their work, and are more involved in school.[108] Conversely, students withdraw personal effort from academic learning when they perceive that school curricula and systems do not reflect their own aspirations and culture or aim to help them fulfill their own purposes.[109]

Likewise, researchers have found that the type of student engagement affects how much of the lesson students will remember later. Table 14.2 highlights some examples of how well students remember material when it is taught via a variety of learning methods.

---

[103] Weiss, I. R., & Pasley, J. D. (2004, February). What is high-quality instruction? *Educational Leadership, 61*(5), 24–28.

[104] Marzano, 2003, pp. 112–113.

[105] Nuthall, 1999; Barrell, J. (2001). Designing the invitational environment. In A. Costa (Ed.), *Developing minds: A resource book for teaching thinking* (3rd ed., pp. 106–110). Alexandria, VA: Association for Supervision and Curriculum Development; Hicks, D. (1993). Narrative discourse and classroom learning: An essay response to Eagan's "Narrative of learning: A voyage of implications." *Linguistics and Education, 5*, 127–148.

[106] Lee, V. E., Smith, J. B., & Croninger, R. G. (1995). *Issues in restructuring schools: Another look at high school restructuring* (Issue Report No. 9). Madison, WI: University of Wisconsin–Madison, Wisconsin Center for Educational Research, Center of Organization and Restructuring of Schools; Newmann, F., Wehlage, G., & Lamborn, S. (1992). The significance and sources of student engagement. In F. M. Newmann (Ed.), *Student engagement and achievement in American secondary schools* (pp. 11–39). New York: Teachers College Press; Stigler, J., & Hiebert, J. (1999). *The teaching gap: Best ideas from the world's teachers for improving education in the classroom.* New York: Simon and Schuster.

[107] Clarke, J., & DiMartino, J. (2004, April). A personal prescription for engagement. *Principal Leadership, 4*(8), 19–23.

[108] Buck Institute for Education. (1999). *Project based learning handbook for middle and high school teachers.* Novato, CA: Author; Chard, S. C. (1998). *The project approach: Developing curriculum with children: Practical guide 2.* ERIC Documents ED.420363; Katz, L. G., & Chard, S. C. (2000). *Engaging children's minds: The project approach* (2nd ed.). Norwood, NJ: Ablex; Thomas, J. (2000). *A review of research on project-based learning.* New York: Simon and Schuster.

[109] Ogbu, J. U. (1987). Variability in minority school performance: A problem in search of explanation. *Anthropology and Educational Quarterly, 18*(4), 312–334; Fordham, S. (1988). Racelessness as a factor in black students' success: Pragmatic strategy or pyrrhic victory. *Harvard Educational Review, 58*(1), 54–84.

Table 14.2	Learning Methods Impact How Well Students Learn
Learning Method	**Retention in Students (percent)**
Lecture	5
Reading along with lecture	10
Audiovisual presentations	30
Discussion groups	50
Learning by doing	75
Learning by teaching others	90

Source: Adapted from NTL Institute for Applied Learning. Cited in Danielson, C. (2002). *Enhancing student achievement: A framework for school improvement.* Alexandria, VA: Association for Supervision and Curriculum Development, p. 24.

Focusing more closely on this issue, Robert Marzano (mentioned earlier in this chapter) and his colleagues determined which instructional practices produce the most students' learning.[110] Table 14.3 lists the nine categories of instructional strategies that affect student achievement and the estimated percentile gain students would receive if their teachers used these strategies as regular parts of their classroom learning activities.

Activity 14.2

Effective instruction intellectually engages students in learning. Research supports its value in increasing student achievement.

A. Working with a partner, identify and discuss 5 to 10 instructional factors from this chapter that teachers use which contribute to students' intellectual engagement in learning.

B. As a pair, present your list of factors to the class. Compile a "complete master list" of intellectually engaging learning factors.

C. In reviewing Table 14.2, which strategies work best for you as a student? Which ones do your professors use?

Using assessment in instruction. Academic achievement in classes where teachers provide effective feedback to students is considerably higher than the achievement in classes where no such feedback is delivered.[111] In fact, a review of almost 8,000 studies led one researcher to comment, "The most powerful single modification that enhances achievement is feedback."[112]

Rather than signaling instruction's end, assessment is integral to the instruction process. **Formative assessments** are especially valuable tools to promote learning. By continuously monitoring students as they work and checking for each one's understanding, teachers assess how well students comprehend what the teachers intend them to learn. While a student who gives the wrong answer has not fully

---

[110] Marzano, R. J., Pickering, D. J., & Pollock, J. E. (2001). *Classroom instruction that works: Research-based strategies for increasing student achievement.* Alexandria, VA: Association for Supervision and Curriculum Development, p. 7; Marzano, R. J. (2007). *The arts and science of teaching: A comprehensive framework for effective instruction.* Alexandria, VA: Association for Supervision and Curriculum Development.
[111] Marzano, 2003, p. 37.
[112] Hattie, J. A. (1992). Measuring the effects of schooling. *Australian Journal of Education, 36*(1), 9.

Table 14.3	Instructional Strategies That Increase Student Achievement	
Category	Specific Behaviors	Estimated Percentile Point Gain
Identifying similarities and differences	Assigning work that involves comparison and classification, metaphors and analogies.	45
Summarizing and note taking	Having students generate verbal summaries and written summaries, take notes (rather than copy teacher notes), revise notes by adding new information and correcting errors.	34
Reinforcing effort and providing recognition	Recognizing and celebrating progress toward learning goals throughout the unit; recognizing and reinforcing student effort.	29
Homework and practice	Providing specific feedback on all assigned homework; assigning homework for the purpose of having students practice the skills and procedures learned in class.	28
Nonlinguistic representations (graphic organizers)	Asking students to generate mental images, pictures, graphic organizers, physical models representing content, or to act out content.	27
Cooperative learning	Organizing students in cooperative groups and ability groups when appropriate.	27
Setting objectives and providing feedback	Setting specific learning goals at the unit's beginning and asking students to set their own learning goals; providing feedback on learning goals throughout the unit; asking students to assess themselves at the unit's end.	23
Generating and testing hypotheses	Engaging students in projects that involve generating and testing hypotheses through problem solving, decision making, investigation, and experimental inquiry tasks.	23
Questions, cues, and advance organizers	Before presenting new content, asking questions that help students recall what they might already know about the content or with direct links to content previously studied.	22

Source: Adapted from Marzano, R. J., Pickering, D. J., & Pollock, J. E. (2001). *Classroom instruction that works: Research-based strategies for increasing student achievement.* Alexandria, VA: Association for Supervision and Curriculum Development, p. 7; Marzano, R. J. (2003). *What works in schools: Translating research into action.* Alexandria, VA: Association for Supervision and Curriculum Development, pp. 82–83.

mastered the material, the wrong answer may give the teacher useful insight into which part of the information the student does not understand and offer direction about how to correct the situation.[113]

Feedback individualizes the instructional process. It ensures that each student knows the extent to which his or her performance meets the required standards. For example, students can review the teacher's comments on a writing sample or math solutions and use this information at once to increase what they know. As students assume increasing responsibility for their own learning, they are able to monitor their own progress and take corrective action without involving the teacher.

Helpful feedback is understandable, specific, accurate, meaningful, and timely.[114] It reflects clear criteria and standards of which students are fully aware. Global comments such as "nice work" are *not* helpful feedback. Feedback must be informational

---

[113] Danielson, 2007, pp. 86–89.
[114] Bangert-Downs, R. L., Kulik, C. C., Kulik, J. A., & Morgan, M. (1991). The instructional effects of feedback in test-like events. *Review of Educational Research, 61*(2), 213–238; Black, P., & Wiliam, D. (1998). Assessment and classroom learning. *Assessment in Education, 5*(1), 7–74; Madaus, G. F., Airasian, P. W., & Kellaghan, T. (1980). *School effectiveness: A reassessment of the evidence.* New York: McGraw-Hill; Madaus, G. F., Kellaghan, T., Rakow, E. A., & King, D. (1979). The sensitivity of measurement of school effectiveness. *Harvard Educational Review, 49*(2), 207–230.

and ongoing, giving students meaningful insight into what they are doing correctly and which errors they can fix. In general, the more delay that occurs in giving feedback, the less improvement in students' achievement.[115]

Teachers' feedback to students can take many forms: verbal, nonverbal, and written. Feedback may be subtle and informal such as written comments on corrected homework or more formal and systematic, such as report card grades or constructive comments during individual conferences.

Feedback has little value for students unless they use it. The degree to which students use feedback is highly related to their confidence as learners.[116] Confident students can accept and use constructive feedback to increase their knowledge. In contrast, students who are already discouraged about their academic abilities are likely to view feedback as more criticism and ignore it. If students don't accept the feedback, they cannot learn from it.

Demonstrating flexibility and responsiveness. Teachers continuously make decisions. If students are not familiar with a concept or event on which a teacher is basing an entire explanation, the teacher may need to stop and explain the necessary background information. If students become bored and sluggish, the teacher may have to pick up the pace. If students become confused and can't keep up, the teacher may have to slow down and return to the place where confusion began. If an activity is not appropriate for students, the teacher may choose to stop or modify the activity so that students can successfully complete it. As this discussion suggests, lesson adjustments may require either major or subtle changes.

Teachable moments—spontaneous events that give the class an opportunity for valuable learning—also require teachers' flexibility and responsiveness. A student may ask a relevant question but not one that the teacher had planned to discuss. The flexible and responsive teacher takes the time to answer it and connect it to the lesson. On other occasions, teachers may seize upon a major event and adapt their lesson to it.

For instance, on September 12, 2001, most teachers shelved their planned lessons and focused the class period on the prior day's events. They discussed the personal relevance: "What happened yesterday?" "Did you know anybody directly affected?" "How can you respond to overwhelming events that you cannot control?" They also considered larger issues: "How can people communicate with those who violently disagree to prevent and resolve conflicts?" "Why is it important that our Bill of Rights protects the freedom to practice one's religion?" Spontaneous events can provide a classroom springboard to valuable intellectual and emotional learning experiences. Flexible and responsive teachers can meet their instructional goals in an unplanned but ultimately unforgettable manner.

Even the most highly skilled and best-prepared teachers sometimes find that either the lesson is not going as planned or a teachable moment has appeared. The ability to develop and use an instructional repertoire and to have the confidence to make lesson changes in real time come with experience. Intellectual flexibility is a high-level skill. Experience and accurate reflection can help every teacher build this capability.

Reflecting on Teaching

While popular myth argues that great teachers are "born, not made," the truth is that effective teaching can be learned. Even when they are blessed with talent, great teachers work hard to be effective. **Reflection** is the continuous process of evaluating and learning from experience.[117] It is a mechanism for turning experience into

---

[115] Returning students' exams or essays several weeks after they turned them in—no matter how detailed and constructive the comments—is not timely. By then, most students have lost interest in the topic and will not find the feedback meaningful. See Marzano et al., 2001, pp. 96–99.

[116] Danielson, 2007, p. 87.

[117] Pinsky, L. E., Monson, D., & Irby, D. M. (1998, November). How excellent teachers are made: Reflecting on success for improve teaching. *Advances in Health Sciences Education, 3*(3), 207–215.

knowledge about teaching.[118] Through critical reflection, teachers assess their work's effectiveness and take steps to improve or enhance it.

Ongoing reflection is essential for building knowledge. After all, teaching encompasses a complex set of behaviors. Pulling them all together effectively to ensure a positive outcome is a very difficult and demanding endeavor. By thinking about what happened in the classroom, considering the consequences of their actions, and generating alternative approaches, reflective teachers systematically expand their skills' repertoire. As their knowledge develops, teachers have a larger array of information on which to draw for making decisions.

At the same time, their increasing knowledge base expands teachers' ability to use reflection effectively and to develop as teachers.[119] No matter how good a lesson, it can always become better. To suggest that a lesson can be improved is not to imply that the teacher's work was inferior, but rather engages a teacher in a key aspect of the work of every professional: self-analysis and improvement.

Teachers reflect during lesson planning, during the teaching episode, and after the teaching event. During planning, teachers consider the classroom, student, and content variables as they design their lessons. They think about how to create a positive learning environment, how to limit the content to a meaningful and manageable amount, how to involve the learners, how to assess what the students already know, and how to extend their learning from there.

During the teaching episode, teachers reflect as they monitor and modify their strategies as necessary to promote the maximum student learning. Finally, after the teaching event, teachers reflect on what went well and what they could do to make the lesson better. By focusing on both successful and unsuccessful teaching, educators can gradually improve their practice.

Reflection as a learned skill. Reflection requires purposeful and mature thinking. Novice teachers often have a difficult time reflecting productively. They tend to make global judgments, reporting that a lesson was "Okay" if students were busy and the day passed without any disciplinary incidents. Likewise, a beginning teacher may complain that the lesson was "terrible" without being able to say specifically why.

Skilled reflection is characterized by accuracy, specificity, and ability to incorporate the analysis into future teaching.[120] As teachers become more skilled at reflection, they recall more small events from their classes as evidence of the lesson's relative

| **Figure 14.6** | Reflection Requires Purposeful, Mature Thinking |

altrendo images/Altrendo/Getty Images

---

[118] McAlpine, L., & Weston, C. (2000, September). Reflection: Issues related to improving professional teaching and student learning. *Instructional Science, 28*(5), 363–385.
[119] McAlpine & Weston, 2000.
[120] Danielson, 2007.

effectiveness because they are better able to monitor and focus on what is happening at the time. What is more, teachers become better able to suggest specific remedies and predict when they will be able to put these measures into practice in their classrooms. Increased skills in reflection are most likely to emerge when the school environment feels safe and supports teaching changes that lead to increased student learning, and when the class seems appropriate to the revised teaching approach.[121]

Reflection requires that teachers not be defensive. Reflective teachers are comfortable with constructive feedback, either from themselves or from colleagues. They are not afraid to look critically at their own behaviors and seek ways to be more helpful to students' learning. These teachers often invite feedback on their teaching from other teachers or assistant principals. Learning to become a better teacher requires an open mind, accurate data, honesty, an increasing array of instructional approaches, and enough time to change teaching behaviors.

Mentors, coaches, and reflection. Mentors and coaches can help new teachers with reflection. Experienced educators' caring and skilled questioning can encourage beginning teachers to become more accurate, analytic, and insightful about their practice. This dialog can assist novices in learning both the essential habits of mind and a larger professional repertoire from which to make teaching decisions. The essential question is this: "If I had the chance to teach this content again with the same group of students, would I do it the same way or would I do it differently—and how?" After a while, novice teachers become more skilled in analyzing their own practice and have additional strategies to use with their lessons. Reflection becomes a habit of mind, a regular activity.[122]

At the same time, the mentors and coaches gain professionally by working with new teachers. Identifying specific teaching behaviors that affected student learning, observing how students respond, and seeking other approaches will deepen their own instructional knowledge. In this way, teachers evolve into a community of learners, each contributing to his or her colleagues' growth and effectiveness. Mature teachers' investment in their own school's improvement through mentoring novice educators is integral to their professional work, not an add-on.

Learning to teach is an ongoing process. Reflective teachers want to know more about the art and science of teaching and about themselves as effective teachers. They constantly improve lessons and think about how to reach particular children. Reflection produces a richer instructional knowledge base upon which to draw on during teaching. Reflection is an essential professional skill and habit that builds teacher competence and confidence even as it improves students' learning.

---

[121] Pinsky et al., 1998.
[122] Danielson, 2007, pp. 92–94.

Summary

Instruction is how teachers connect students with the curriculum. Teachers continually make instructional decisions that depend on their sophisticated understanding of the content to be learned, their students, the nature of learning itself, and the likely consequences of selecting different courses of action.

Research shows that teachers who learn and practice sound pedagogical techniques can enhance students' measured achievement. Thus effective teaching is the key to student learning.

Several learning theories have been developed. Behavioral learning theories stress observable changes in behaviors, skills, and habits. They support a direct instruction model for teaching students basic skills that involve tasks that can be taught in a step-by-step fashion and assessed by standardized tests. Cognitive learning theories, by comparison, emphasize internal mental activities such as thinking, processing information, problem solving, remembering, and forgetting. Constructivist learning theories focus on how individuals make meaning of events and activities. Research has found positive achievement results from students whose teachers effectively use certain behavioral, cognitive, and constructivist instructional practices.

Each of these learning perspectives has both supporters and critics. Expert teachers pick and choose from the constructivist, behavioral, and cognitive learning theories as appropriate to the content, the students, and their learning needs.

Effective teaching involves planning and preparation, creating an appropriate classroom learning environment, and delivering and reflecting on instruction. Preparing to teach requires identifying the appropriate content for study, knowing the students, selecting instructional objectives, and designing the learning activities and assessments. Teachers need to know which instructional techniques work best for their content and reflect current research on best pedagogical approaches within the discipline.

Effective teachers create a classroom environment characterized by mutual respect and rapport, establish a culture for learning, efficiently organize and manage classroom procedures, and manage student behavior effectively. Classrooms with cultures for learning are intelligence-friendly, safe, and caring places for all learners in which thinking and intellectual risk taking become the norm. They balance academic challenge with instructional support. When students are engaged in meaningful work and experience success in learning, they are not interested in disrupting the class.

Instruction comprises a constellation of related behaviors. Along with engaging students in the learning process, teachers must provide clear directions and explanations, skillfully use questioning and discussion, integrate assessment strategies into instruction, and remain flexible and responsive if they are to assure the most learning opportunities for all students.

Student engagement is an intellectual issue. Studies have established that students are significantly more likely to be engaged in activities that have inherent value—personal relevance and meaning—compared to activities that emphasize extrinsic values such as getting good grades. Research has also determined that active mental involvement in learning measurably increases student achievement. Academic achievement in classes where teachers provide effective feedback to students is considerably higher than the achievement in classes where it is not.

Finally, effective teachers learn by reflecting on their instruction, thereby turning experience into knowledge about teaching. By thinking about what worked well during instruction, what did not, and why, teachers assess their instructional effectiveness and take steps to improve it.

Conclusions

- More than 35 years of research overwhelmingly supports the idea that effective teachers affect students' achievement.
- We now know what effective teachers do to make learning happen.
- By understanding the nature of learning, the students, the content, and the instructional practices that increase learning, and by creating a culture that supports learning in each classroom, teachers can educate every child to high levels.
- Becoming an effective teacher requires continuous professional learning throughout one's career.

Chapter 15

Achievement and Accountability

Achievement and accountability are highly visible
topics. High-stakes testing, student proficiency, achievement gains, and schools'
responsibility for student learning are making headlines: "High Stakes Testing Is Putting
the Nation at Risk"[1]; "Study Questions NCLB Law's Links to Achievement Gains."[2] No
Child Left Behind (NCLB), the 2002 landmark federal education law, sets an ambitious
standard: All students tested in reading and math will reach grade-level proficiency by
2014. Yet even when Congress enacted the law, many educators, statisticians, legislative
aides, and others believed that this standard was unrealistic. NCLB deliberately left the
definition of "proficiency" vague so that each state could define "proficiency" for itself.
How realistic is it that every student meet the "proficiency" standard when no two states
agree on what it means?

"There is a zero percent chance that we will ever reach a 100 percent target,"
says Robert L. Linn, Co-director of the National Center for Research on Evaluation,
Standards and Student Testing at University of California at Los Angeles. "But
because the title of the law is so rhetorically brilliant, politicians are afraid to change
this completely unrealistic standard. They don't want to be accused of leaving some
children behind."[3]

Educators and politicians argue about whether this emphasis on testing and
accountability is actually increasing students' achievement. Recent reports have compared
NCLB state assessment data with results of the National Assessment of Educational
Progress (NAEP)—"the nation's report card"—in reading and math before and after
No Child Left Behind. The reports reveal that while student achievement on many state
assessments has improved over the past several years, the NAEP trend has remained
relatively unchanged; in fact, NCLB may have even slowed the achievement gains that
began to emerge in the mid-1990s.[4]

Future teachers do not have to feel intimidated by educational accountability.
Accountability is a shared responsibility. Assessment is an ongoing and integral part of the
teaching and learning process, not a once-a-year hurdle to be passed. Well-designed and
effectively used assessments can motivate students' interest and boost their achievement.
Larger than "tests and measurement," accountability involves helping students meet a
variety of clear, high standards in fair ways. Becoming knowledgeable about educational
accountability can help prospective teachers understand its benefits and limitations to
advance student equity and achievement.

---

[1] Berliner, D. C., & Nichols, S. L. (2007, March 14). High stakes testing is putting the nation at risk:
Commentary. *Education Week, 26*(27), 44, 32.
[2] Manzo, K. K. (2006, June 21). Study questions NCLB law's links to achievement gains. *Education Week,
25*(41), 11.
[3] Paley, A. R. (2007, March 14). "No Child" target is called out of reach. *Washington Post.* Retrieved
October 30, 2009, from http://www.washingtonpost.com/wp-dyn/content/article/2007/03/13/
AR2007031301781.html.
[4] Manzo, 2006, p. 11; Fuller, B., Wright, J., Gesicki, K., & Kang, E. (2007). Gauging growth: How to judge
No Child Left Behind. *Educational Researcher, 36*(5), 268–278.

- How do teachers use assessment to inform teaching and learning?
- What information belongs in an educational accountability system?
- What are the purposes of educational assessment?
- How do educational standards contribute to achievement and accountability?
- What are the principles of high-quality assessments and how do they affect classroom practice?
- What are the arguments for and against standardized testing?
- What are the ethical considerations in assessment?
- In what ways is accountability more than test scores?

How Teachers Use Assessment to Enhance Teaching and Learning

Parents, policy makers, and teachers want meaningful answers to all of the following questions:

- "How is my student doing?"
- "Are the schools succeeding or failing?"
- "What works best to help students learn?"
- "Do test scores prove the effectiveness of educational programs?"

Answering these reasonable questions requires teachers to have a variety of student achievement data available. An accountability system that contains test scores alone is incomplete without additional information about teaching practices and curriculum. A teacher or school system that answers these questions (or bases its accountability) on test scores alone is like a physician evaluating your health based on body temperature or blood pressure but ignoring weight, height, blood tests, or other medical indicators that are essential to a competent diagnosis.

Teachers can know if they or the schools are succeeding or failing only if they have access to multiple sources of data gathered over an extended period of time. They need information about the measurable elements of the educational process—the curriculum standards, the learning assignments, and samples of students' completed work. They also need information about the results—students' project grades, types of student support, and standardized test scores over many years. In addition, educators need to learn how to look beyond the final test results and provide insights based on observations, descriptions, and qualitative understandings that explain what has happened beyond the numbers. In the end, teachers must gather enough meaningful information and use professional judgments to make sense out of what is happening in the classroom for each student.

The Educational Assessment Learning Cycle

People tend to use the words "measurement," "assessment," and accountability" interchangeably. All of these terms relate to data and the process of evaluating progress in a concrete way, but they have rather important differences in meaning.

Measurement involves assigning numbers to observations according to rules that fit the circumstances. Measurement must be as objective as possible, but it can never be completely objective. For example, in a spelling bee, the judge counts the number of words that the student spelled correctly and assigns that number as the student's score. This part of the process is objective: The spelling is either correct or not. Deciding whether the student's spelling score of 16 is "poor" or "excellent," however, requires the teacher to use his or her judgment—that is, it is subjective.

Assessment is broader than measurement. The word "assessment" comes from the Latin root *assidēre*, meaning "to assist in the office of a judge." Assessment requires using professional judgment to determine what the measurement means. It is a comprehensive term that includes measurement, evaluation, and grading. **Educational assessment**, therefore, is a comprehensive process of describing, judging, and communicating the quality of students' learning and performances. As you see in Figure 15.1, assessment is the first step in a continual learning cycle that includes measurement, feedback, reflection, and change.

A well-designed assessment gives both teacher and student quality feedback about how well the student is mastering the assigned curriculum. Upon receiving the feedback, teacher and student reflect and try to understand what the results mean. Has the student learned successfully? On which aspects does the student need additional instruction, practice, and feedback? What do the student and teacher do next with this feedback to change their behaviors? Does the teacher need to work with the individual or with large numbers of students in the class who did not show mastery on this or other important aspects of the assigned learning?

Answering these questions requires teachers to gather more evidence, reflect, and analyze deeply before acting. It allows them to use achievement data to guide their daily instructional plans and classroom actions. Thoughtful teaching needs to be driven by evidence, not by test scores.

Accountability systems include much more than students' achievement test scores. **Holistic accountability** considers the factors that come before educational excellence, including teaching practices, curriculum practices, leadership practices, parent involvement, faculty communication and collaboration, and professional development. Thus accountability addresses all aspects of the teaching and learning process. We will discuss holistic accountability in more detail later in this chapter.

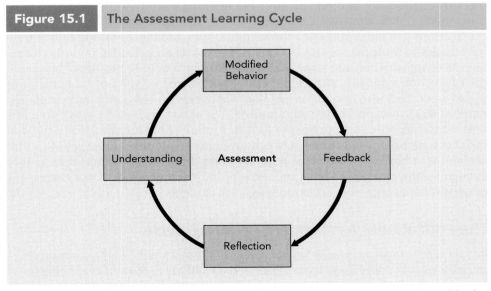

| Figure 15.1 | The Assessment Learning Cycle |

Source: Adapted from Frye, R. (n.d.). Assessment, accountability, and student learning outcomes. Retrieved October 30, 2009, from http://www.ac.wwu.edu/~dialogue/issue2.html.

Purposes of Assessment

The rationale for undertaking assessment is not merely to gather information. Rather, the intention is to combine data with professional judgment and relevant actions to create improvement. Assessment has several purposes, including making placement decisions, determining how well students attain curricular and instructional goals, and diagnosing student learning needs.[5]

Placement decisions. **Placement decisions** occur before instruction begins. The goal when making these decisions is to gather information on where to start and how to best teach students. Teacher awareness of what each student knows before trying to teach something new increases the likelihood that the teacher will be able to provide suitable instruction for each child. Data for placement assessment come from past records, observations of students' strengths and weaknesses, pretests, and student self-reports.

Likewise, assessments for placement are sometimes used as **gatekeepers** to determine who moves to the next grade or who receives admission to a college or profession. An increasing number of states are requiring high school students to pass one or more tests before they can receive a diploma. College admissions offices have long used the results of the American College Testing (ACT) program and the SAT as important data in making admissions decisions. Professions such as law, medicine, nursing, physical therapy, certified public accounting, and architecture require candidates to pass a specialized, standardized test before they are admitted to the profession. In the teaching profession, most state departments of education

| Figure 15.2 | Assessments are Sometimes Used to Make College Admissions Decisions |

Getty Images/Taxi/Getty Images

[5] Bravmann, S. L. (2004, March 17). Assessment's "Fab Four": They work together, not solo. *Education Week, 23*(27), 56.

require new teachers to pass a standardized test to become eligible to receive a teaching license.

Determining student attainment. Teachers use information from students' homework, classwork, projects, and a variety of tests to help determine how much students learned. Formative and summative assessments help establish whether students have mastered their required learning.

Formative assessments are assessment *for* learning. *Formative* does not refer to the content, but rather to the manner in which the assessments are used. As learners try to understand and apply their new knowledge and skills, teachers' formative assessments provide continuous and specific classroom feedback about students' areas of mastery and weakness as they relate to state standards. Formative assessments let everyone know where they stand in the learning process. Teachers can use this information to adjust instruction and to create appropriate work for groups of learners or individual students. Assessing *for* learning advances—not simply monitors—student learning in a variety of ways.[6]

The formative approach makes a measurable difference in student achievement. Research studies have defermined the following findings:

- Feedback improves learning when teachers give students ongoing responses and guidance about how to improve their class work and tests.[7]
- Students benefit more from feedback than from grades.[8]
- Consistent, formative practices are linked to significant achievement gains and a reduced achievement gap, especially for the lowest achievers.[9]
- Formative assessments motivate students in positive ways that reinforcement successful learning.[10]

Summative assessments involve the assessment *of* learning. Summative assessments are the final task at a unit's end used to make a concluding judgment about whether the student has met a certain required level of accomplishment. In addition to traditional examinations, teachers gather summative data through student demonstrations or performances, evaluating assigned projects and products, and systematically collecting portfolios that summarize students' achievements or progress. Capstone assessments, such as science fairs, recitals, or art shows, celebrate a milestone accomplishment or demonstrate how well a person has mastered a knowledge or skill.

Because summative assessments help teachers and students determine the extent to which students have achieved the instructional goals, they support assigning grades to report cards or to conferring certificates of mastery. To a limited degree, teachers can also use these data to help them judge their teaching effectiveness.

---

[6] Stiggins, R. J. (2002, June). Assessment crisis: The absence of assessment *for* learning. *Phi Delta Kappan, 83*(10): 757–765.

[7] Black, P., & Wiliam, D. (1998, October). Inside the black box: Raising standards through classroom assessment. *Phi Delta Kappan, 80*(2), 141–151.

[8] Black & Wiliam. 1998.

[9] Bloom, B. S. (1984, May). The search for methods of group instruction as effective as one-to-one tutoring. *Educational Leadership, 41*(4), 4–17; Black, P., & Wiliam, D. (1998, March). Assessment and classroom learning. *Educational Assessment: Principles, Policy, and Practice, 5*(1), 7–74; Black & Wiliam, October 1998, pp. 139–148; Meisels, S., et al. (2003). Creating a system of accountability: The impact of instructional assessment on elementary children's achievement scores. *Educational Policy Analysis Archives, 11*(9). Retrieved October 30, 2009, from http://epaa.asu.edu/epaa/v11n9; Rodriquez, M. C. (2004). The role of classroom assessment in student performance on TIMSS. *Applied Measurement in Education, 17*(1), 1–24.

[10] Danielson, C. (2007). *Enhancing professional practice: A framework for teaching* (2nd ed.). Alexandria, VA: Association for Supervision and Curriculum Development; Danielson, C. (2002). *Enhancing student achievement: A framework for school improvement.* Alexandria, VA: Association for Supervision and Curriculum Development.

Standardized tests will always be an important part of teachers' assessment repertoire as a means to find out if they are teaching the standard course of study in ways that support students' learning.[11]

Diagnostic assessment. **Diagnostic assessments** are a highly specialized intervention into student learning. They involve detailed and professionally prepared tests administered by a special education teacher, school psychologist, speech/language pathologist, occupational therapist, or regular teacher trained for this task. When a student experiences persistent learning difficulties despite the teacher's use of alternative instructional methods, diagnostic assessment is employed to determine the cause or causes of that student's ongoing learning problems. The findings enable teachers to develop plans for appropriate remedial attention to individual students and help them determine whether a student is eligible for special education or gifted services or accommodations.

Stephanie L. Bravmann, senior research consultant at the Center on Reinventing Education at the University of Washington, observes:

> Unlike formative assessment, which is intended to deal with the kinds of learning issues that respond to the classroom equivalent of bandages, hot-water soaks, or massage, diagnostic assessment helps find the underlying causes for learning problems that don't respond to purely palliative measures.[12]

Effective teachers learn how to balance assessment *for* and *of* learning. Teachers committed to educating each child appropriately collect and use ongoing student achievement data. This helps them understand each student as a learner on a daily basis and make the necessary adaptations to support learning every day. Additionally, teachers partner summative assessments with the other available student learning data to fairly and equitably support—not merely evaluate—student learning.

Educational Standards

Educational testing began in twentieth-century United States as an objective, relatively inexpensive tool to provide information for decision making about large numbers of people. Over time, its cost has grown exponentially. Recent press reports put the value of the testing market anywhere from $400 million to $700 million.[13] According to the Government Accountability Office (GAO), states were likely to have spent $1.9 billion to $5.3 billion between 2002 and 2008 to implement NCLB-mandated tests—and indirect costs of teacher time and test-prep activities raise these costs higher still.[14] This investment attests to the public's continued confidence in test scores as one measure of accountability and as a means to make important educational decisions.

Accountability is tied to educational standards. **Educational standards** clearly identify what students should know and be able to do. Accordingly, educational standards have become the foundation of curriculum and assessment in all 50 states, each of which has its own set of standards. Standards have come to be synonymous with rigor and setting high achievement expectations for all students.

---

[11] English, F., & Steffen, B. (2001). *Deep curriculum alignment: Creating a level playing field for all children on high-stakes tests of educational accountability.* Lanham, MD: Scarecrow Press.
[12] Bravmann, 2004.
[13] Testing our schools: The testing industry's Big Four. (2002). *Frontline.* Retrieved October 30, 2009, from http://www.pbs.org/wgbh/pages/frontline/shows/schools/testing/companies.html.
[14] Miner, B. (2004/2005, Winter). Keeping public schools public: Test companies mining for gold. *Rethinking Schools On-Line, 19*(2). Retrieved October 30, 2009, from http://www.rethinkingschools.org/archive/19_02/test192.shtml.

Educational Standards and Accountability

The emphasis on clear educational goals stems from the school effectiveness research conducted in the 1970s, which revealed that what students are taught in a specific subject and at a specific grade level varied greatly among schools and even among classrooms within a school.[15] For example, one report found that one elementary school teacher who was observed for more than 90 days did not teach fractions, despite the state mandate to teach the topic at that grade level. When asked about omitting the topic, the teacher replied, "I don't like fractions."[16] In a similar vein, another report showed a range of more than 4,000 minutes in the time spent on reading instruction in four fourth-grade classes.[17] Again, teacher preference accounted for such wide differences.[18] Across the country and within schools, students were learning according to teacher preferences and not based on high and clear educational benchmarks.

The focus of standards has now shifted attention from inputs to results. Before 1987, most standards focused on the curriculum, telling teachers what they should teach (inputs). In contrast, today's standards identify what students should know and be able to do when they finish a course, a grade, or a program (results). The standards-based education movement assumes that the only way to ensure that all students acquire specific knowledge and skills is to identify and teach to expected performance levels for specific knowledge and skills. "Standards," "benchmarks," "indicators," and "objectives"—all refer to what students should know and be able to do.

Setting standards, teaching to the standards, and assessing the extent to which students meet the standards provide the basis for public school accountability. This systematic approach connects curriculum, instruction, assessments, and professional development to a set of performance indicators that the teachers, administrators, parents, and students endorse. Student learning is at the center, and standardized tests are frequently the means to measure students' performance.

What is more, today's standards apply to all students. The current U.S. educational reform movement finds it unacceptable that only a small percentage of students achieve at high levels. Instead, schools must raise their expectations for all students' learning. This is not just the practical thing to do in a highly technological and global economy; it is the ethical thing to do if we want to make our society less stratified and provide more opportunities for talented and hard-working students from all racial, ethnic, and socioeconomic backgrounds to climb as high as their capabilities and energies will take them.

Why We Use Educational Standards

Many reasons exist for using educational standards. For example, such standards provide more accurate achievement measures than a comparison of students' scores to national norms. Meeting educational standards does not "sort and select" students into haves and have-nots. Instead, meeting educational standards provides the necessary intellectual challenge to above-average students, and this assessment

---

[15] Marzano, R. J., Pickering, D., & McTighe, J. (1993). *Assessing student outcomes: Performance assessment using the "dimensions of learning model.* Alexandria, VA: Association for Supervision and Curriculum Development.

[16] Fisher, C. W., Filby, N., Marliave, R. S., Cahen, L. S., Dishaw, M. M., Moore, J. E., & Berliner, D. C. (1978). *Teaching behaviors, academic learning time and student achievement.* San Francisco, CA: Far West Laboratory of Educational Research and Development.

[17] The actual range was from 5,749 to 9,965 minutes.

[18] Berliner, D. C. (1979). Tempus educare. In P. L. Peterson & H. J. Walberg (Eds.), *Research on teaching.* (pp. 120-135). Berkeley, CA: McCutchan.

process is fair to all students.[19] In this section, we discuss each reason for using these standards more fully.

Standards and national norms. First, standards are more accurate than norms as measures of student achievement. Garrison Keillor, the television and radio personality famous for "A Prairie Home Companion," greets his weekly audience with the words, "Welcome to Lake Wobegon, where all the women are strong, all the men are good-looking, and all the children are above average." This boast is a proud tribute to Lake Wobegon's All-American families, but it tweaks the popular notion of "norm." Bragging that all children are "above average" pokes fun at the idea of the **bell curve**, a statistical concept in which random scores spread out around a range from high to low, with half the scores above and half below the mean.

Figure 15.3 illustrates the bell curve and the statistical "norm" at the mean (average). The norm is the 34 percent below and 34 percent above (68 percent total) around the center line (50th percentile). The farther from the central line, the more outside the "norm." Because the Lake Wobegon population is not random (its fictional population has moved there by choice), the concept of "norm" does not apply. There's the joke! Likewise, all the children in this prairie town cannot be statistically "above average." The concept of *norm* is less funny, however, when it is applied to student achievement.

Only two ways exist to evaluate student performance. First, we can compare a student's performance to that of another student or to the average of a group of students. Second, we can compare the student's performance to an objective standard. When educators use the norm approach, they accept the logic of the **normal distribution** or bell curve.[20]

| **Figure 15.3** | **The Bell Curve: Finding the "Norm"** |

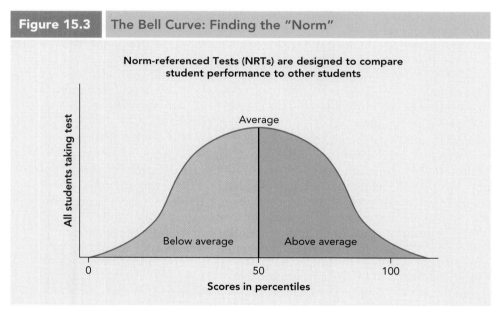

Source: Center for Public Education. (2007). Guide to standardized tests: Bell curve. National School Boards Association. Retrieved October 30, 2009, from **http://www.centerforpubliceducation.org/site/c.kjJXJ5MPlwE/b. 1698647/k.1A72/Guide_to_standardized_tests_Bell_curve.htm**.

---

[19] Reeves, D. B. (2004). *Accountability for learning: How teachers and school leaders can take charge.* Alexandria, VA: Association for Supervision and Curriculum Development, pp. 106–113; Reeves, D. B. (2000). *Accountability in action: A blueprint for learning organizations.* Denver, CO: Center for Performance Assessment, pp. 179–183.

[20] The J curve offers another way of looking at students' score distributions. In education, the classic bell curve represents the distribution of grades that occurs when small proportions of students get very low and very high marks and most students get average marks. A J-curve distribution implies that most students can occupy the rising part of the "J," which means most students can successfully learn and earn above-average marks . See Stewart, D. T. (2006). *The J curve: A new way of understanding why nations rise and fall.* New York: Simon and Schuster.

From a standards perspective, educators care only whether the student achieves the desired learning. They do not care whether the student is performing better or worse than his or her classmates and national peers. On normed tests, some students are expected to score at the top (showing high competence), but many others are expected to perform in the middle or at the bottom. Comparing results and determining one winner and many losers may make sense when only one baseball team can win the World Series or when only one country can win the Olympic gold medal in figure skating. It does not make sense, however, when the educational goal is for every student to be a winner—that is, to learn the necessary knowledge and skills that mark excellent learning. No teacher, parent, or employer wants his or her students to be in the "lower half" (below average).

Testing's central issue is accurately measuring students' performance and progress. This is accountability's most basic principle. Each student's challenge is to meet an objective standard. No one would want to be a passenger in an airplane flown by a pilot who merely scored "above average" on the Federal Aviation Administration (FAA) exam. No, we would all prefer to fly with an outstanding pilot such as "Sully" Sullenberger, who was able to save all on board his passenger flight in January 2009 by safely landing in the Hudson River after a "bird strike" disabled both plane engines. Viewed in this way, academic standards provide accuracy and an acceptable performance level that comparisons to the average or norm cannot offer. Meeting academic standards can determine a student's proficiency, and every student can meet this goal.

Standards and tracking. Standards do not "sort and select" students. If the standards define what every student should know and be able to do, then every proficient student has the opportunity to earn the top grade—and demonstrate capable knowledge and skills.

As discussed in Chapter 11, U.S. public schools have traditionally sorted and selected students to prepare them for future societal roles. Curriculum tracking is one example of how schools accomplish this task. This traditional sorting and selecting practice does not produce equitable results for minority and low-SES (socioeconomic status) students, who want schools help them create opportunities for social and economic mobility.

What is more, using norms or standards becomes an ethical issue when teachers focus on how the results will be used. With norms, teachers expect students to perform at higher or lower levels. The mindset that the lower scores are "normal" and "expected" means that teachers need spend no extra effort to bring lower-scoring students up to the proficiency level. As a result, lower-performing students remain perpetually behind. Using standards, by contrast, brings the mindset that all students must (and can) reach proficiency; that is, they must all achieve to the given standard. With the adoption of this perspective, teachers must invest extra time and use varied instructional and support practices with the lower-achievers so that they, too, reach the standard.

Norm-referenced high-stakes tests "are the equivalent of 'educational highways' with the smallest possible margin for error—an inch on either side—because *their* purpose is not to see that students 'arrive safely' but to nab them for violations," notes John Merrow, an education writer.[21] If the goal of U.S. public schools is to assure that each student arrives safely at the proficiency level, using assessments tied to educational standards rather than norm-referenced assessments is more likely to get them there.

Standards and "above-average" students. Although they may score highly on norm-referenced tests, many students classified as "above average" may not be able to write a coherent and persuasive essay, apply an algebraic concept to solve

---

[21] Merrow, J. (2001, May). Undermining standards. *Phi Delta Kappan, 82*(9), 659.

a real-world problem, or understand a complex literary passage's meaning. While "above-average" scores makes students and their parents feel good about their schools and their education, their expectations for proficiency are not high enough. They become inappropriately complacent when, in truth, their achievement as measured against academic standards may be inadequate.

Comparison to the average does not only hurt disadvantaged students; it also hurts higher-achieving students who score well on test but who still have much more to learn. They mistakenly believe because they can "beat" other students, they are successful and do not have to work harder to achieve a higher, more rigorous level of mastery. Standards keep the challenges high and learning continuing for nearly all students.

Standards and fairness. Standards communicate what students are expected to know and be able to do. **Benchmarks** identify specific expectations for certain grade levels or groups of grade levels. Scoring guides, sometimes called **rubrics**, provide the most specific expectations for students by identifying what they are supposed to accomplish on individual assignments and assessments. Students can reliably meet these expectations when the standards are clear and consistent and when the teaching is effective.

This system is fair because the rules do not change in the middle of the game. What students learn, study, and practice is what is assessed. What is also fair, ideally, is that every student—regardless of gender, race, ethnicity, social class, or parental education level—has the chance to meet the same standards and show proficiency.

In the real world, however, academic standards' integrity depends on the connection between standards and assessments. The state-approved tests must assess the same knowledge and skills that the teacher taught. Likewise, all students must have an opportunity to learn the state-approved curriculum and the standards set for that grade level. While different students and teachers may approach mastering the standards in varying ways and with diverse levels of support, all students should have access to what the community determines to be rigorous and excellent education. In contrast, if the state standards, the teacher-taught curriculum, and the assessments do not match, the system is fair to no one.

Types of Educational Standards

Standards make statements about the expected level of attainment or performance, but they may mean very different things to different people. World-class standards, real-world standards, content standards, performance standards, and opportunity-to-learn standards all define different expectations for achievement. Education standards also have their critics.

World-class standards. Educators and policy makers may think of standards as world-class goals based on the performances of exceptional individuals such as Fields Medal–winning mathematicians, Nobel Prize–winning scientists, Pulitzer Prize–winning authors, and Olympic gold medal–winning athletes. Elementary and secondary students are not expected to meet these extremely high standards, of course. Instead, school standards are statements of accomplishment and models of excellence meant to inspire ambition and greater effort.

Schools that adopt world-class standards take the long view. Educators see the curriculum as a developmental process. During each school year, students move toward the high standard. Teachers expect students to show improvement in many various ways over time as they advance toward increasingly greater mastery.

Real-world standards. Others believe that standards should be real-world goals that students can actually achieve in school. For instance, rigorous real-world standards for high school students reflect the knowledge and skills that will prepare them to enter and succeed in credit-bearing college courses or to gain entry-level positions in well-paying careers that offer opportunities to advance. By 2008, 22 states had aligned their high school standards with the real-world expectations of employers and postsecondary faculty. To get there, each state met with employers and college faculty, along with K–12 educators, to spell out what students need to know and be able to do to succeed after high school.[22] The knowledge and skills outlined in the standards will continue to evolve as the global economy changes, technology advances, and new challenges and opportunities emerge.

Content or discipline-based standards. Content or discipline-based standards describe what teachers and students should know and be able to do in subject areas such as reading, science, mathematics, social studies, history, geography, physical education, and the arts. Usually, these content standards emphasize the subjects' core components or big ideas that students of a certain age or grade level should know. They are often accompanied by standards stating what teachers should know about the content or subject so they can teach at the preschool, elementary, or secondary levels.

The first set of student standards was released in 1989 by the National Council of Teachers of Mathematics (NCTM). With federal support, a variety of professional associations and groups such as the National Research Council have since developed standards for preschool through grade 12 students. Many states have followed suit, developing their own content standards or adapting the national standards to their own state situations.

For example, four "big ideas" identified in the national social studies standards are culture; time, continuity, and change; people, places, and environments; and individual development. Statements spell out the specifics of what early-grades, middle-grades, and high school students are to learn, along with specific grade-level benchmarks. Similarly, the history content standards for "historical understanding" look like Table 15.1.

In addition to the knowledge acquisition statements, content standards often specify which thinking and process skills and strategies students and teachers should master. Table 15.1 gives examples of the history content standard for "historical understanding," the topics and benchmarks for Level I (grades K–2), and the knowledge/skill statements that let teacher and student know when they have mastered this standard. For instance, a first grader has partly mastered the standard for analyzing chronological relationships and patterns when the student can identify significant events in his or her own life.

Likewise, professional organizations representing arts, behavior studies, career education, civics, economics, educational technology, foreign language, geography, health, history, language arts, life skills, mathematics, science, physical education, and early childhood professional preparation have all developed standards based on national consensus.[23]

National standards. The U.S. Constitution assigns the responsibility of education to the states. Although each state sets its own content standards, collectively the state standards are converging to reflect a national consensus. Achieve, Inc., a bipartisan nonprofit organization begun in 1996 by U.S. governors and business leaders, finds that states have inadvertently created a "common core" of expectations in English/language arts and mathematics. When standards are anchored in the real-world

---

[22] Kraman, J., & Eresh, J. (2008, July). *Out of many, one: Towards rigorous common core standards from the ground up*. Washington, DC: Achieve, Inc.
[23] For an in-depth look at content standards, topics, and benchmarks, see Mid-continent Research for Education and Learning, (2007). *Content knowledge standards*. http://www.mcrel.org/compendium/browse.asp.

Table 15.1	Sample of History Content Standards and Benchmarks, Grades K–2
Historical Understanding	Understandings
Standard 1.	Understands and knows how to analyze chronological relationships and patterns
Topics	1. Chronological thinking; 2. Historical timelines
	Level I [Grade K–2] Benchmark 2. Knows how to develop picture timelines of their own lives or their family's history
	Vocabulary Terms A. picture timeline B. personal history C. family history
	Knowledge/Skill Statements 1. Knows that a timeline records significant events in chronological order 2. Knows significant events in own life 3. Knows when significant events in own life occurred relative to other events 4. Knows significant events in family's history 5. Knows when significant events in family's history occurred relative to other events

Sources: Mid-continental Research for Education and Learning. (2007). *Content knowledge* (4th ed.). Retrieved October 30, 2009, from http://www.mcrel.org/compendium/reference.asp?item=benchmark&BenchmarkID=116&subjectID=3.

demands of what students need to succeed in college and the workplace, commonalities appear. This apparent agreement among a critical mass of states on the kinds of complex knowledge and skills students need to master in those subjects suggest that a state-led effort toward setting common standards is feasible.[24] For moral, practical, and legal reasons, some also think it is desirable.[25]

Criticism of content standards. While content standards bring positive benefits to teaching, learning, and assessment, critics raise legitimate concerns about their use. The most important point is the large number of content standards to be taught and learned in the amount of time available in schools. For example, researchers at Mid-continent Research for Education and Learning (McREL) identified some 200 standards and 3,093 benchmarks in national and state-level documents for 14 different subject areas.[26] This material would take 15,465 hours to teach,[27] but U.S. public schools (K–12) have only 9,042 hours available to teach these standards and benchmarks.[28] Critics also express concern that the assessments tied to these

[24] Manzo, K. K. (2008, August 13). Achieve finds common core of standards in states. *Education Week, 27*(45), 6; Kraman & Eresh, 2008.
[25] Gordon, R. (2006, March 15). The federalism debate: Why the idea of national education standards is crossing party lines. *Education Week, 25*(27), 48, 35.
[26] Kendall, J. S., & Marzano, R. J. (2000). *Content knowledge: A compendium of standards and benchmarks for K–12 education* (3rd ed.). Alexandria, VA: Association for Supervision and Curriculum Development.
[27] Marzano, R. J., Kendall, J. A., & Gaddy, B. B. (1999). *Essential knowledge: The debate over what American students should know.* Aurora, CO: Mid-continent Regional Educational Laboratory.
[28] Marzano, R. J. (2003). *What works in schools: Translating research into action.* Alexandria, VA: Association for Supervision and Curriculum Development, pp. 24–25.

standards overrepresent easy-to-measure skills and underrepresent complex reasoning skills.[29]

To improve the situation, critics recommend that schools drastically reduce the amount of content teachers are required to address in class. Standards that are too large will inevitably lead to superficial coverage as teachers try to " force it all in" before the tests. With this approach, students will not fully learn what they need to know. What is more, assessments based on the standards will include questions on information and skills that students did not have an opportunity to learn—an unethical and harmful situation for students, teachers, and schools alike.

Professional educator standards. Professional education associations have also developed standards for teachers and other professional school personnel. These professional standards outline what educators should know and be able to do to teach or work as a school library media specialist, school counselor, principal, or other school professional. Prospective educators typically have to demonstrate the knowledge, skills, and dispositions of one or more sets of these standards before they can obtain a license to work in that field.

Standards may also include statements about the habits of mind or dispositions that teachers should nurture in students, such as curiosity, perseverance, tenacity, caring, and open-mindedness. For example, the Interstate New Teacher Assessment and Support Consortium (INTASC) standards for state licensure expect new teachers to demonstrate the following dispositions related to Principle 3 ("The teacher understands how students differ in their approaches to learning and creates instructional opportunities that are adapted to diverse learners"):

- The teacher believes that all children can learn at high levels and persists in helping all children achieve success.
- The teacher appreciates and values human diversity, shows respect for students' varied talents and perspectives, and is committed to the pursuit of "individually configured excellence."
- The teacher respects students as individuals with differing personal and family backgrounds and various skills, talents, and interests.
- The teacher makes students feel valued for their potential as people, and helps them learn to value each other.[30]

Similarly, INTASC specifies that four types of performance go along with these dispositions:

- The teacher identifies and designs instruction appropriate to students' stages of development, learning styles, strengths, and needs.
- The teacher uses teaching approaches that are sensitive to the multiple experiences of learners, and that address different learning and performance modes.
- The teacher makes appropriate provisions (in terms of time and circumstances for work, tasks assigned, and communication and response modes) for individual students who have particular learning differences or needs.
- The teacher can identify when and how to access appropriate services or resources to meet exceptional learning needs.

Performance standards. Performance standards are also statements about what a student or a teacher should be able to do in presentations that encompass combinations of knowledge and skills. Once teachers have identified the content

---

[29] Viadero, D. (2008, December 3). Researchers pitch policy ideas as power shifts in capital. *Education Week, 28*(14), 11.
[30] Retrieved October 30, 2009, from http://www.ccsso.org/content/pdfs/corestrd.pdf.

Figure 15.4	INTASC Standards Expect New Teachers to Appreciate and Value Human Diversity

Jose Luis Pelaez/Iconica/Getty Images

standard, they design performance standards so each student can show what he or she understands.

Because performance tasks require students to actively demonstrate what they know, performance assessments may sometimes be a more valid indicator of students' knowledge and abilities than a multiple-choice test. Answering a multiple-choice question correctly may require no more than recognizing or remembering a fact. Such tests require relatively low levels of thinking. Making an oral presentation, in contrast, requires the student to invest time; conduct research, analysis, writing, and practicing; make graphic illustrations to accompany the talk; and have sufficient subject knowledge to correctly answer listeners' questions.

Performance standards often differ from district to district and from classroom to classroom. Different educators prefer different levels of achievement specified in the rubrics. Some want rubrics with minimum national standards, whereas others prefer rubrics defining high levels of excellent performance. State and school district expectations as well as personal preference and professional judgments all factor into the choice of rubrics teachers use.

Determining Whether Students Have Met the Standards

Performance standards vary. Some specify a minimum level of performance or a range of performances ranging from unsatisfactory to outstanding. Other standards are expressed as a list of qualities, such as the organization and expression characteristics one would expect from a well-developed essay. Still other standards are stated as numbers, such as saying that a student must read a certain passage within 15 minutes and answer the related questions with 80 percent accuracy.

Educators sometimes use "cut scores" to identify the lowest acceptable score that still meets the standard. The **cut score** is a point somewhere on the continuum from the lowest possible score to the highest. Those students who fall below the cut

A CLOSER LOOK

Performance standards often use rubrics to give students clear information by which to develop and assess their performance tasks. This box highlights a rubric for conducting successful group work. Review the criteria and points assigned and discuss the questions that follow.

Rubric for Cooperative Group Work

4—Thorough Understanding

- Consistently and actively works toward group goals.
- Is sensitive to the feelings and learning needs of all group members.
- Willingly accepts and fulfills individual role within the group.
- Consistently and actively contributes knowledge, opinions, and skills.
- Values the knowledge, opinion and skills of all group members and encourages their contribution.
- Helps group identify necessary changes and encourages group action for change.

3—Good Understanding

- Works toward group goals without prompting.
- Accepts and fulfills individual role within the group.
- Contributes knowledge, opinions, and skills without prompting.
- Shows sensitivity to the feelings of others.
- Willingly participates in needed changes.

2—Satisfactory Understanding

- Works toward group goals with occasional prompting.
- Contributes to the group with occasional prompting.
- Shows sensitivity to the feelings of others.
- Participates in needed changes, with occasional prompting.

1—Needs Improvement

- Works toward group goals only when prompted.
- Contributes to the group only when prompted.
- Needs occasional reminders to be sensitive to the feelings of others.
- Participates in needed changes when prompted and encouraged.

Source: Adapted from Collaboration rubric: Teacher created rubrics for assessment. On-line professional development for K–12 teachers. (n.d.). University of Wisconsin–Stout. Retrieved October 30, 2009, from http://www.sdcoe.k12.ca.us/score/actbank/collaborub.html.

Questions

1. Which student behaviors or characteristics differentiate between those students who earn higher scores and those who earn lower scores?
2. Describe the role of leadership and initiative in conducting a successful cooperative group.
3. Describe the role you usually take in a cooperative group. Which point value would you typically receive?
4. Explain how having such a rubric explained to you as a student would affect your own behavior in the group.

5. Explain how a teacher could use this or a similar rubric to increase student learning in class.

6. Discuss what you think are the difficulties in teachers developing and using a strong rubric to increase quality teaching and learning.

score have not been able to demonstrate that they have met the standard. In short, the cut score separates those who met the standard from those who did not. Classifying students as having met the standard is relatively easy when the performance is either extremely high or extremely poor, but identifying passing somewhere in the continuum's middle is more difficult.

Deciding where to place the cut score is both an objective (psychometric) problem and a subjective (professional judgment and values) problem. The cut score's location needs to consistently allow educators to distinguish between those students who meet the standard and those who do not. Cut scores may carry a heavy weight for students, however—determining who graduates or who enters a profession, for example. Those who fall short of the mark do not receive the desired rewards. Furthermore, the procedures used to determine the cut score must withstand rigorous scrutiny because they will be challenged if they appear arbitrary or misplaced.

Other standards are not either–or propositions. Sometimes it is more astute to realize that there are greater and lesser degrees of competency rather than all-or-nothing performance. A student writer may have creative ideas, authentic "voice," and strong coherent organization, but may show inconsistent performance in terms of spelling and grammar. Even here, however, a point exists that separates those with some proficiency from those who lack it. Determining that precise spot between "just enough" and "not quite enough" is an objective and subjective decision.

As a result, a cut score or a passing score is often an arbitrary and unreliable benchmark. Professional and personal preferences or political philosophies can influence these points on the continuum. While no agreement exists on the best method for setting defensible standards on competency tests, the literature concludes that this activity is very difficult.

Opportunity-to-learn standards. Common sense tells us that for students to achieve, they must have appropriate opportunities to learn. Teachers' and students' awareness of content and performance standards will have little impact on achievement unless schools ensure that all students have the access and occasions to learn them.

Opportunity-to-learn standards define a set of conditions that schools, districts, and states must meet to ensure students have enough occasions to meet expectations for their performance.[31] Student achievement depends not only on students' abilities, but also on whether the student actually attended the class and whether the teacher has taught the subject in class with enough explanation, time, practice, and feedback in an appropriate learning environment necessary for students to learn it.

Opportunity-to-learn standards incorporate the following considerations:[32]

- **Content Coverage.** The more the assessment matches the information the students actually learned, the more mastery students will show.

- **Content Exposure.** The more time spent on instructional experiences and the more complete and meaningful the information, the more students will learn.

---

[31] Opportunity-to-learn standards are sometimes called *input* or *delivery standards*.

[32] Stevens, F. I. (1996). Closing the achievement gap: Opportunity to learn, standards, and assessment. In B. Williams (Ed.), *Closing the achievement gap: A vision for changing beliefs and practices* (pp. 77–95). Alexandria, VA: Association for Supervision and Curriculum Development.

- **Content Emphasis.** The more the teachers' emphasis closely matches the standards and the assessments, and the more teachers help students develop higher-order thinking skills, the more students will learn.
- **Quality of Instructional Delivery.** The more the teachers' classroom practices show cognitive understanding of the subject, structure presentations appropriately to students, relate new information to what students already know, monitor students' performance and provide corrective feedback during the lesson, and relate different parts of the lesson to each other, the more students will learn.

For instance, a student who is "tracked" into a lower-level course may not have a teacher who delivers the same standards-based curriculum that the students placed in a higher-level track receive. Likewise, a student who is frequently absent from school, whose teacher does not follow the school district's curriculum or pacing guide, or whose classroom is constantly disrupted by student outbursts does not have the same opportunity to learn as a student with perfect attendance, a teacher who closely follows the district's curriculum guide, and a calm, caring, focused, and orderly classroom environment. Even if the two students had identical academic abilities, the student in the latter class is more likely to master the expected standards. Clearly, differences in students' learning experiences can make tremendous differences in whether—and how much—they achieve.

Advocates of opportunity-to-learn standards often include this framework to include family support, the school environment, and student behavior. Educators monitor and measure the opportunity-to-learn standards by using teacher logs, observations, and surveys, as well as more structured interval testing and small-task assessment.

Regardless of how logical and important opportunity-to-learn standards appear, putting them into practice costs money. Currently, they are the subject of state legislation and court cases dealing with school finance, assessment, and unequal opportunity.[33]

Why Standards Differ

Educators and policy makers of good will may nevertheless disagree about standards' purposes. Business leaders want high school graduates with polished reading, writing, math, and interpersonal skills who are ready for work. Policy makers, for their part, think about the long-term societal needs: They want more rigorous academic standards that will guarantee students perform at high levels on international comparisons, keep the United States meeting world-class standards, and ensure a vibrant national economy in which U.S. workers earn high wages owing to their high-level skills.

Parents choose which standards they prefer based on their personal goals, family traditions, and expectations. Some parents expect their children to attend prestigious universities and aim for professional careers in medicine, law, engineering, or international banking. Others expect their children to get jobs immediately after high school.

School districts must reconcile these differing expectations when they adopt a set of learning standards. The process of setting standards is complex, both cognitively and socially. Nevertheless, developing clear standards allows the schools' communities to clarify their needs and aspirations. The standard-setting process becomes a community forum for discussing and negotiating what schools should do. Standards provide the criteria by which the locality holds schools, teachers, and students accountable. Given the mobility of today's workers, a persuasive case can be made for implementing national standards.

---

[33] Baratz-Snowden, J. C. (1993, Summer). Opportunity to learn: Implications for professional development. *Journal of Negro Education, 62*(3), 311–323; Elmore, R. F., & Fuhrman, S. H. (1995). Opportunity-to-learn standards and the state role in education. *Teachers College Record, 96*(3). 432–457.

Types of School Assessments

If standards are to have a real effect on schools and student achievement, other school elements must support them. These requirements for support include an articulated curriculum that spells out what students should learn and what teachers should teach. It includes professional development that connects teachers' instructional practices to this curriculum so they can better facilitate student learning. Finally, schools need a well-developed assessment process and materials that match the standards and the curriculum so as to monitor and measure how well students are learning the knowledge and skills the standards require.

Assessments come in a variety of styles and purposes. **Traditional assessments** commonly include paper-and-pencil formats with multiple-choice questions designed to compare students across the school district, state, or nation.[34] Their scores on these tests identify whether students have developed the core knowledge and skills the standards expect. Such standardized tests are the assessments traditionally used in the U.S. educational system. Although they are efficient, are relatively inexpensive to administer and score, and provide useful information about student progress and educational programs, they cannot measure many of learning's important aspects. They do not often assess higher-level thinking,[35] and they are not sensitive to students' ability to apply skills and knowledge to real-world problems. Likewise, the assessments provided through standardized tests do not support many useful teaching strategies.[36]

Performance or **authentic assessment** refers to a type of appraisal that requires students to enact, demonstrate, construct, or develop a product or solution under defined conditions or standards. Performance assessments capture aspects of students' learning that standardized tests cannot, allowing students to demonstrate what they know in a number of ways that meet standards in real-world settings. While performance tasks provide meaningful intellectual challenge as they promote using learning beyond the classroom and can be tailored to fit individual student interests, performance assessments, too, have their benefits and limitations.

Principles of High-Quality Assessments

Both traditional and performance assessments require certain essential technical and ethical components if they are to actually measure what they say they measure and if they are to be fair to students. Test developers, educators, parents, and policy makers expect the tests their students take to meet high-quality professional standards for fairness, reliability, validity, environmental limitations, and opportunity to learn.

Fairness. Children have an innate sense of fairness. No one wants to play in a game where the rules keep changing and are widely viewed as unreasonable. If the game score does not reflect their efforts, or if they receive penalties for events over which they have no control, children wonder if the game is worth the effort. The same holds true for testing.

Fairness means that everyone understands the rules of the game, the rules are applied consistently to each person, and everyone has the opportunity to play by

---

[34] Some traditional standardized assessments are being administered on-line as well as with paper and pencil fill-in the blanks.

[35] Kohn, A. 2000. *The case against standardized testing: Raising the scores, ruining the schools.* Portsmouth, NH: Heinemann; Schmoker, M. 2000. The results we want. *Educational Leadership, 57*(5), 62–65.

[36] Madeus, G. F. (1991, November). The effects of important tests on students: Implications for a national examination system. *Phi Delta Kappan, 73*(3), 226–231; Shepard, L. A. (1991, November). Will national tests improve student learning? *Phi Delta Kappan, 73*(3), 233–238. Shepard, L. A. (2000, October). The role of assessment in a learning culture. *Educational Researcher, 29*(7), 4–14.

| Figure 15.5 | Technically and Ethically Appropriate Assessments Must be Fair, Valid, and Reliable |

Charles Gupton/Flirt/CORBIS

the same rules. Standardized and performance tests, however, can sometimes be unfair.

A test is not fair when its items are biased. A test that shows provable and systematic differences in people's results based on group membership shows **test bias**. Test bias incorporates both psychometric and sociocultural factors, and both perspectives are necessary to draw a complete picture of test bias.

Psychometrically, a test demonstrates bias when it consistently under- or over-predicts how well someone or some groups will perform. Because it has better predictive validity for some groups than for others, such a test is not valid for certain populations. Typically, this type of test bias places students from low-income families, minority groups, students with disabilities, and English language learners at a serious disadvantage. Standardized tests often ignore the students' life experiences that may result in one group having an advantage over the others.

Testing is not fair when all students taking it have not had the school learning, family and cultural experiences, or biological equipment needed to help them perform well on this assessment. Any number of factors may work against students having a common experience that would place them on equal footing when taking a standardized test. Fairness in testing is, indeed, a complex and contentious problem.

Until the 1970s, most standardized tests writers were not so much culture biased as culture blind.[37] In other words, they did not recognize that ways of knowing the world—other than their way—existed. Since then, test publishers have made special efforts to remove these biased depictions and content to avoid offensive,

---

[37] Anastasi, A. (1976). *Psychological testing* (4th ed.). New York: MacMillan, pp. 58–59.

culturally restricted, or stereotyped materials. While important, documented cases of test bias exist, the legal and financial implications are so important in high-stakes testing that today's test developers carefully screen their tests in a concerted effort to reduce bias and increase validity.[38]

Educators must interpret traditional or performance test results within a context that includes the students' culture and the cultural assumptions under which the test was developed. How similar are our students to those in the norm group? Are minority students' scores low because of low test-taking motivation, poor reading ability, or inadequate subject knowledge? Depending on the testing's purpose, the appropriate norms to measure the scores against may be the general norms, subgroup norms based on persons with comparable experiential backgrounds, or the individual student's own previous scores.[39] The more differences between the individual student and the norm group—or the more the group depends on teacher instruction rather than home resources to provide the needed information and skills—the more caution with which one must interpret the results.

Validity. The most important question to be asked about any assessment is this: Does it really measure what it says it measures? **Validity** is the extent to which a test measures what it is supposed to measure. For instance, a measure of problem-solving ability should reflect how well learners can solve problems, not how well they can guess the correct answers. Three important types of validity are face validity, content validity, and concurrent validity.

Face validity is the appearance of validity. This is not a technical aspect, but rather a marketing one. For students to take tests seriously, tests need to look like "tests." For instance, a math test does not have face validity unless it includes obvious numbers and math problems.

Content validity focuses on whether the assessment provides an adequate sample or representation of the information that is supposed to be assessed. While a test can never duplicate every detail of the subject matter, tests usually sample all the important dimensions of the content reasonably well. For instance, if a teacher inadvertently omits a topic, or if the teacher gives a topic either too much or too little emphasis, the assessment may not have enough content validity.

Concurrent validity indicates the consistency or correlation between two independent measures of the same characteristic taken near the same time. Teachers can show an assessment has concurrent validity when the results of a teacher-made vocabulary test agree with the data from a standardized vocabulary test administered within a few days of the first test.

Reliability. To be valid, a test must be reliable; however, reliability does not guarantee validity. A test may produce consistent and repeatable results, yet the results may be meaningless and invalid. Reliability is an important technical aspect of high-quality assessments.

Reliability is the extent to which a test is repeatable and yields consistent scores. **Test reliability** is the consistency of scores obtained by the same persons when retested with the identical test or with an equivalent form. If a child is shown to have an IQ of 110 when tested on Monday and an IQ of 80 when retested on Thursday, little confidence can be placed on either score. Likewise, if a student identifies 40 of 50 words correctly in one set of words but identifies only 20 words correctly on an equivalent set, neither score can be taken as a dependable index of the student's verbal comprehension; after all, both scores cannot be

---

[38] Tanner, D.E. (2001). *Assessing academic achievement.* Needham Heights, MA: Allyn & Bacon, p. 269.
[39] Anastasi, 1976, pp. 59–60.

right. Conversely, high scoring reliability occurs when multiple scorings yield the same results.

A test score is subject to many unwanted, irrelevant influences, which explains why any single observation of a person gives only a rough estimate of the person's typical ability. Test scores may vary from one measurement to another for a variety of reasons—the student's attention or effort changes, the student is hungry or cold, the room is quiet or noisy. Likewise, test items may be more or less difficult for the student.

Environmental limitations. Every test imposes certain **environmental limitations**. These constraints include how much time students have to complete the test or product, whether they work independently, and whether they can use calculators, dictionaries, sheets with math formulas, or laptop computers. Can students stand up and stretch when they get tired? Can they walk around the room? Can they eat or drink while testing? Students need to know the limitations under which they will be assessed, and they must know this information ahead of time because it will affect their planning.

Test length is an important assessment limitation. Brief assessments cannot provide a complete picture of student performance, but the amount of time available for testing is always finite. This is especially true for testing younger students. A tension always exists between the number of test items needed for greater assessment precision, the students' maturity, and the information that educators want to know. Additionally, imposing shorter time limits can reduce the reliability of the test. Brief tests may be measuring how fast students produce the correct answers rather than how well the students understand the concepts supporting the questions that they might be able to answer correctly when they have enough testing time. In classroom testing, teachers want students to be able to show what they know without unduly worrying about time.

The testing conditions also affect students' results. A noisy, distracting classroom that is too hot or too cold can negatively influence students' thinking and final scores. Although some environmental conditions cannot be controlled, teachers can usually neutralize or reduce such factors as room temperature, noise, and visual stimuli (e.g., exciting posters or wall-mounted study guides) that might interfere with learners' performance.

Opportunity to learn. As discussed in conjunction with standards, high-quality assessments can be valid and reliable only when all students taking them have had the opportunities to learn the content being tested. Opportunity to learn is the single most powerful predictor of student achievement.[40] One cannot expect students to know what they have not been taught. This factor is not so much a technical aspect of the assessment instrument, but rather a reflection of the students' school, classroom, and home experiences.

Students have not had an adequate opportunity to learn if they have not received the allotted time of instruction needed for them to learn the subject matter at the level of depth necessary, if they have not received the appropriate content emphasis, or if they have not been given occasions to use higher-level thinking skills with the content. Further, unless the teachers' instructional practices helped students relate the new information to their prior knowledge, receive ongoing corrective feedback during the lessons, and have the lessons' parts related to other parts, the students will not have the opportunities to master the standards, correctly answer the assessment questions, or produce a meaningful, high-quality product or performance. Also, unless the school consistently provided an orderly

---

[40] Berliner, D. C., & Biddle, B. J. (1997). *The manufactured crisis: Myths, fraud, and the attack on America's public schools.* White Plains, NY: Longman, p. 55.

and academically focused learning environment, students will have been denied the opportunity to learn.

Teachers must seriously consider all of these factors when they interpret their students' test scores. Issues of fairness, validity, reliability, environmental factors, and opportunities to learn all play key roles in determining students' learning and their performance on assessments. No matter how well regarded the assessment instrument, other variables can confound and reduce the meaning of students' test results. Until these issues can be successfully resolved, teachers need to exercise caution in using these data to make important decisions about students.

Activity 15.1

High-quality assessments are fair, valid, and reliable; are administered under appropriate environmental conditions; and ensure that all students have had the necessary opportunity to learn. How would you as a college student determine if the assessments you take in your classes have these qualities?

A. Working in pairs, discuss occasions in your past when you had to take an important test that you did not think was fair, valid, or reliable; that was administered under proper conditions; or for which you did not have an adequate opportunity to learn. Which subject or skill was supposed to be tested? How did you feel while taking the test? How did the situation affect your scores? How were the test results used?

B. Working as a class, discuss how you might determine whether a test you had to take had fairness (lack of bias), validity, and reliability; was administered under appropriate conditions; and provided you with the opportunity to learn.

The Cases for and Against Standardized Testing

Standardized tests are an efficient and cost-effective way to assess large numbers of people from different backgrounds and learning experiences. As such, they have become a staple of school accountability. All teachers are likely to use standardized tests as part of their schools' efforts to monitor and assess students' progress. Yet critics openly challenge these tests for a variety of reasons. Both arguments for and against standardized testing deserve closer looks.

The Case for Standardized Testing

There are many reasons why standardized tests have become so popular with educators and the public. They include efficiency and cost-effectiveness; existence of a norm group for score comparisons; psychometric properties that make results meaningful; usefulness in measuring broad characteristics; and value as a factor in making important decisions.

Efficient and cost-effective for large numbers of people. Standardized tests allow educators to assess the performance of large numbers of people from a variety of backgrounds on some common trait or characteristic in a cost-effective way. They are "standardized" in that the administration and scoring procedures are the same ("standard") for all test takers. As a result, standardized tests are usually more convenient, require less time to administer and score, and are less expensive than most other types of assessments. Results are available quickly and can be used for informed decision making.

Comparisons with a norm group. Students' scores are compared to those of the typical group. This practice permits educators and parents to compare how well their students are performing relative to students in other localities and states across the country, or even internationally.

Validity and reliability that make scores meaningful. Standardized tests have technical qualities of validity and reliability that help make the data they generate useful. Educators can select those tests with sufficiently high levels of validity and reliability to justify their use for certain purposes.

Measurement of broad characteristics. Standardized tests usually help educators measure characteristics such as verbal or math achievement, analytical reasoning, and critical thinking that are not unduly sensitive to the inevitable, minor curriculum and experience differences that occur from one school to another. This permits educators to make comparisons and judgments about the performance and educational progress across several different groups.

Central component of making important decisions. Standardized tests have become high-stakes, high-profile assessments. Results from these tests are used to make decisions about whether students will graduate, become certified, or receive scholarships.

The Case Against Standardized Testing

Critics assert that no standardized test is accurate enough to be the basis for making important, life-altering decisions about students' futures or judgments about schools' effectiveness. Their concerns include standardized tests' limited measures of what matters, bias, misidentification of inferior and superior schools, curriculum narrowing, confusion of cause and effect, and "drill and kill" preparation. Other critics offer additional reasons to regard standardized tests with caution.

Limited measure of what matters. Simply because the tests are cost-effective and can quickly generate scores for large numbers of students does not mean that the resulting scores are meaningful. If standardized tests simply reflect the students' ability to take tests and vary depending on students' background characteristics, critics argue, they may not be worth their costs.

Bias. All assessments contain some bias and measurement error. Many minority students are educated in schools that do not reflect the norm group, so ethnic test bias may exist.[41] Certain test items are more likely to be correctly answered by children from affluent and middle-class families than by children from low-income families.[42] It is important for teachers to use caution when interpreting test scores for students who do not closely resemble the norm group.

Table 15.2 shows the percentage of test items linked to SES for different school subjects. Language arts, science, and social studies have the highest connection to students' outside school environments and experiences.

"Teaching to the test." **Curriculum narrowing** occurs when teachers are so focused on raising their students' test scores in certain content areas that they **"teach to the test."** Under pressure to raise students' English and math achievement, for example, teachers may have no time or rationale to teach anything except what will

---

[41] Tanner, 2001, p. 268.
[42] Popham, W. J. (2001). *The truth about testing: An educator's call to action.* Alexandria, VA: Association for Supervision and Curriculum Development, pp. 55–65.

Figure 15.6	Test Bias May Exist for Students Who Don't Match the Norm Group

Michael Newman/PhotoEdit

Table 15.2	Academic Subjects and Socioeconomic Status

Subject	Percentage of SES Items
Reading	15
Language arts	65
Mathematics	5
Science	45
Social studies	45

Source: Popham, W. J. (2001). *The truth about testing: An educator's call to action.* Alexandria, VA: Association for Supervision and Curriculum Development, p. 65.

be tested.[43] A 2008 Center on Education Policy research report found that many nationally surveyed elementary schools increased instructional time for English/language arts and mathematics (those subjects tested annually under the provisions of the No Child Left Behind legislation) by 43 percent on average and reduced time from social studies, science, art and music, physical education, and recess or lunch by 32 percent, on average.[44] These findings are similar to those obtained in previous studies demonstrating that the higher the stakes, the more "teaching to the test," often with harmful effects.[45]

---

[43] Music and art are among the first subjects for which no time remains in the school day after the intensive focus on math, reading, and science.

[44] McMurrer, J. (2008, February). *Instructional time in elementary schools: A closer look at changes for specific subjects.* Washington, DC: Center for Education Policy. Retrieved April 17, 2009, from http://www.cepdc.org/_data/n_0001/resources/live/InstructionalTimeFeb2008.pdf.

[45] Pedulla, J., et al. (2003, March). *Perceived effects of state-mandated testing programs on teaching and learning: Findings from a national survey of teachers.* National Board on Educational Testing and Public Policy, Boston College. Retrieved October 30, 2009, from www.bc.edu/research/nbetpp; Clarke M., et al. (2002, November). *Perceived effects of state-mandated testing programs on teaching and learning: Findings from interviews with educators in low-, medium-, and high-stakes states.* National Board on Educational Testing and Public Policy, Boston College. www.bc.edu/research/nbetpp. Cited in Neill, M. (2003, November). Leaving children behind: How No Child Left Behind will fail our children. *Phi Delta Kappan, 85*(3), 225–228.

"Teaching to the test" and curriculum narrowing not only affect what teachers present, but also influence the intellectual level of what they teach, limit the amount of time they invest in making learning make sense and have personal meaning for students, limit the opportunities for students to be creative with what they are learning,[46] and reduce the positive teacher–student interactions through which strong and caring relationships develop. The result is a seriously diminished education. This is especially true for high-performing students in low-performing schools who may lose ground academically even as they earn top grades and ace standardized tests. As teachers focus on helping the large number of low achievers or students in the middle meet the standard, the high achievers receive less attention. In turn, they continue to fall further behind their high-achieving peers in affluent public and private high schools where the primary focus remains on high achievement.[47]

Cause and effect. When policy makers and educators build accountability systems around test scores, they assume that higher test scores reflect better instruction—and identify better schools. This assumption is not necessarily correct.

Typically, state and school district officials test students in certain grade levels every year and compare the current year's test scores with previous years' test scores. If this year's eighth graders scored higher than last year's eighth graders, then officials and educators assume that this year's instruction has been more effective. In reality, it is not reasonable to compare the test performances of two sets of substantially different students.[48] The caliber of students fluctuates from year to year. Some groups of students are brighter and/or harder working than others. This year's apples are different from last year's oranges. As a consequence, year-to-year score differences do not necessarily reflect better or worse teaching. The existence of a cause-and-effect relationship between teaching effectiveness and test scores with year-to-year score comparisons cannot be confidently determined.

Superior and inferior schools. It is natural—but incorrect and unfair—for people to assume that schools whose students have high test scores are superior to schools whose students have low test scores. A "failing" school's staff may actually be doing an outstanding instructional job, but their efforts may not be reflected by their students' scores on a high-stakes achievement test. Students' scores may increase, but not enough to meet the cut-off mark or standard. If the school's students came from traditionally underserved families, they may have started out far behind the norm group and actually made notable achievement gains. Simply because their test results did not compare favorably with their more affluent peers does not mean the school, teachers, or students are "failing."

Likewise, identifying schools and teachers as successful simply because their students score well on standardized achievement tests is equally unfair and inaccurate. Much of what high-stakes tests measure is directly attributable not to what students learn in school, but to what they bring to school: their families' socioeconomic status or their inherited and nurtured academic aptitudes. Their high test scores do not prove that their school was effective. Until accountability systems include metrics that accurately reflect the contributions of those being judged, such as measuring how much progress a school's students make during the school year, and until

---

[46] Sternberg, R. J. (2006, February 22). Creativity is a habit: Commentary. *Education Week, 25*(24), 64, 47.
[47] Carnevale, A. P. (2007, September 26). No child gets ahead. *Education Week, 27*(5), 3; Viadero, D. (2007, August 1). Study: Low, high fliers gain less under NCLB. *Education Week, 26*(44), 7.
[48] Popham, 2001, pp. 50–53.

assessments use statistical methods that account for the disadvantages (or advantages) that students may bring to school because of the quality of their prior instruction or their family backgrounds, judgments about "superior" or "inferior" schools can be neither fair nor accurate.[49]

"Today's high-stakes tests often mask the actual quality of instruction in schools serving both low-income and high-income families,"[50] says educational assessment expert James W. Popham. This misidentification of schools leads to questionable recommendations for professional development. Skillful teachers in "failing" schools are told to change their instructional practices. Weak teachers in high-scoring schools may allow themselves to be carried along with the high esteem of working in a "good school" when, in fact, they should be significantly improving how they teach.

"Drill and kill." Teachers concerned with their students' performance on high-stakes tests often limit their instructional activities to lecture followed by relentless drilling of their students on the types of content and test items contained on the high-stakes test. The constant "skill and drill" often becomes "drill and kill"—that is, "killing" the students' interest in learning. While skill-and-drill instruction can help students develop low-level cognitive skills such as recognizing or remembering information, it is not fun, it lacks meaning, and it discourages many students from wanting to learn.

Even more, this "drill and kill" method of teaching has the worst impact on low-income and minority students, many of whom are in "low performing" schools. Many students who are performing two to five or more years below grade level are now expected to perform well on a grade-level test. Confronted with having to reach a seemingly unreachable goal, their schools are often the first to let go of the traditional curriculum and focus almost exclusively on "test prep." This approach does not provide the cumulative knowledge that students need to be educated or the meaningful approaches that support students' learning.[51]

How Tests are Used

More than 30 years ago, Donald T. Campbell, a noted Lehigh University professor, warned about the perils of measuring effectiveness with a single, highly important indicator. "The more any quantitative social indicator is used for social decision-making," he said, "the more subject it will be to corruption pressures and the more apt it will be to distort and corrupt the social processes it is intended to monitor."[52]

Important judgments about students, teachers, and school effectiveness are often based on a single test score. Overvaluing test scores for making important decisions promotes tests' misuse and often compromises the test scores' validity. Dozens of assessment experts have argued that high-stakes tests are psychometrically inadequate for the critical decisions that must be made about students, teachers, and schools. While standardized assessments offer many advantages, educators must employ informed caution in their use of these test scores.

---

[49] Toch, T., & Harris, D. N. (2008, October 1). Salvaging accountability: What the next President (and Congress) could do to save education reform. *Education Week, 28*(6), 36, 30–31.
[50] Popham, 2001, pp. 17–19.
[51] Kozol, J. (2007, September 13). NCLB and the poisonous essence of obsessive testing. *Huffington Post.* Retrieved October 30, 2009, from http://www.commondreams.org/archive/2007/09/13/3809/; Mitchell, B. (2002, September). World citizenship: A humane alternative to "drill and kill." *Phi Delta Kappan, 88*(9), 700–701.
[52] Donald T. Campbell, cited in Berliner, D. C., & Nichols, S. L. (2007, March 14). High-stakes testing is putting the nation at risk. *Education Week, 26*(27), 48, 36.

Activity 15.2

Reasons both favoring and discouraging the use of standardized tests exist.

A. Working individually, review the arguments against using standardized tests and identify three new things that you learned about their limitations that may affect how you view and use standardized assessments in your own classroom.

B. Separate the class into two groups. Given the pros and cons of standardized testing, one group should identify the purposes for which standardized testing should be used. The other group should identify purposes for which they should not be used.

C. After 10 minutes, the groups will report their findings to the entire class.

A CLOSER LOOK

Grant Wiggins, a curriculum and assessment authority, writes about how formative and authentic assessment can make teaching and learning more meaningful. He believes that tests teach what we value. Read the excerpt from his article and answer the questions that follow.

Here's a radical idea: We need more assessment, not less. . . .

Think of assessment, then, as information for improving.

This idea takes a while to get used to if you teach, test, and move on. The research could not be clearer, though: Increasing formative assessment is the key to improvement on tests of all kinds, including traditional ones. And more "authentic" and comprehensive forms of assessment provide not only significant gains on conventional tests but also more useful feedback (because the tasks are more realistic).

What do I mean by "authentic assessment"? It's simply performances and product requirements that are faithful to real-world demands, opportunities, and constraints. The students are tested on their ability to "do" the subject in context, to transfer their learning effectively.

The best assessment is thus "educative," not onerous. The tasks educate learners about the kinds of challenges adults actually face, and the use of feedback is built into the process. In the real world, that's how we learn and are assessed: on our ability to learn from results.

Good feedback and opportunities to use it are extremely important in this scenario. In their seminal report *Inside the Black Box: Raising Standards Through Classroom Assessment*, British researchers Paul Black and Dylan Wiliam showed that improving the quality of classroom feedback offers the greatest performance gains of any single instructional approach. "Formative assessment is an essential component," they wrote, and its development can raise standards of achievement. "We know of no other way of raising standards for which such a strong prima facie case can be made."

This just makes sense. The more you teach without finding out who understands the information and who doesn't, the greater the likelihood that only already proficient students will succeed. . . .

A good education makes knowledge, skill, and ideas useful. Assessment should determine whether you can use your learning, not merely whether you learned stuff.

Achieving transferability means you have learned how to adapt prior learning to novel and important situations. In an education for understanding, learners are constantly challenged to take various ideas and resources (such as content) they encounter and become adept at applying them to increasingly complicated contexts.

When I was a soccer coach, I learned the hard way about transfer and the need to better assess for it. The practice drills did not seem to transfer into fluid, flexible, and fluent game performance. It often appeared, in fact, as if all the work in practice were for naught, as players either wandered around purposelessly or reacted only to the most obvious immediate needs.

The epiphany came during a game, from the mouth of a player. In my increasing frustration, I started yelling, "Give and go!" "Three on two!" "Use it, use it—all the drills we worked on!" At that point, the player stopped dribbling in the middle of the field and yelled back, "I can't see it now! The other team won't line up like the drill for me!"

That's both a clear picture of the problem and the road to the solution: too many sideline drills of an isolated skill, and not enough testing of it; too great a gap between what the simplified drill was teaching and testing and what the performance demands. . . .

A good local assessment system does more than audit performance. It is deliberately designed to model authentic work and to improve performance. The aim of teaching is not to master state tests, but to meet worthy intellectual standards. We must recapture the primary aim of assessment: to help students better learn and teachers to better instruct.

Source: Wiggins, G. (2006, April). Healthier testing made easy. *Edutopia*. Retrieved October 30, 2009, from http://www.edutopia.org/healthier-testing-made-easy.

Questions

1. Explain how the best assessments are "educative."
2. Describe ways in which teachers can increase transfer of learning.
3. Explain how teachers can use assessment to *improve* performance rather than simply to *audit* performance.
4. In what ways is your professor making this course "authentic" for you and increasing the likelihood of transfer?
5. How is your professor using feedback and giving students opportunities to use it to increase their learning?

Achievement and Accountability

Traditional accountability systems use test scores as the primary indicator of educational quality. Educators and parents view these end-of-year test scores as the "results" of their students' learning, and often as the only important measure of their achievement. This perspective is shortsighted and misleading.

Accountability and Test Scores

Accountability includes assessment but is much broader in scope. **Accountable** means "to hold answerable for, to act in a creditable manner; and capable of being explained."[53] When a person is accountable, he or she is responsible for one's actions and obliged to answer for them. Educational accountability's primary aim is to improve student achievement. The bottom line for educational accountability is the answer to this question: Did students learn and achieve more than they might have without this specific educational system?

Considering test scores as education's "bottom line" is akin to the business model in which stock prices and reported earnings masquerade as quality indicators. In this view, critical factors such as accounting irregularities, deteriorating facilities, and restated earnings are "minor inconveniences." For instance, when Enron, a Houston energy company, collapsed in 2001 and wiped out more than $1 trillion of shareholder value, employees' retirement plans became worthless, college savings plans disappeared, and corporate leaders received convictions for fraud. Some employees of the company had used accounting tricks so clients and auditors would think Enron and its investors were in sound financial shape. The proverbial "bottom line" had been an illusion, and the focus on corporate "scores" had diverted attention from clear warning signs of larger, systemic problems.

In the same way, exclusive emphasis on test scores in educational accountability does not give a full and accurate picture of how well students are achieving. What is more, they offer no guidance about how to improve the performance of all players in the system.

Clearly, effective educational accountability systems encompass more than test scores. Teachers' jobs are more complex than what a single test can measure. **Effective accountability systems** are comprehensive, containing multiple measures of student achievement. Students' poor or excellent school achievement never has only one single cause.[54]

Student-Centered or "Holistic" Accountability

As mentioned earlier, student-centered or "holistic" accountability balances both quantitative and qualitative indicators: It presents the story behind the numbers. It focuses on the progress of individual students by placing traditional test scores into a context that gives the data meaning.[55] Low or high scores tell us little if we do not know, for example, the type of curriculum the student studied, the teacher's classroom experience and expertise in the subject taught, the teacher's instructional practices, the school's discipline climate, and the student's attendance in school during the year.

Holistic accountability includes a variety of background factors that contribute to educational excellence: [56]

- Teaching practices, including assessment, feedback, and collaboration
- Curriculum practices, including equity of opportunity for enrolling in advanced classes
- Leadership practices, including the use of resources to support the most important educational priorities (considering what teachers, administrators, school board members, and what other policy makers do)
- Parent involvement, including participation in school volunteer activities and meaningful home and community activities
- Faculty communication, including inter-grade and interdepartmental collaboration
- Professional development, including study of research, pedagogy, assessment, and content areas

---

[53] *The American Heritage dictionary of the English language.* (1970). New York: American Heritage, p. 9.
[54] Reeves, 2000, p. 8.
[55] Reeves, 2004.
[56] Reeves, 2004.

Holistic accountability is more motivating for teachers than other types of accountability. Teachers see holistic accountability as fair and meaningful because it includes indicators that they can directly manage or influence. They have a sense of control over the day-to-day learning they design for their students. When teachers know their success as educators will be judged based on a range of a student's learning activities and performances rather than on a single high-stakes test score, they feel less anxiety, stress, and resentment than if their entire year's work came down to how well each student scored on one 3-hour test.

Likewise, holistic accountability motivates students because it gives them more ways to succeed. They have more opportunities and formats in which to show what they have learned and can do. They can receive constructive feedback throughout the learning process and make continuous improvements. In addition, students often have occasions to choose their own topics, work partners, or performance methods as they show what they have learned. Throughout the school year, they know where they stand relative to the standard, and they know exactly what they must to do successfully reach it. Because they exert more control over their own learning and academic fate, students are more committed to learning.

Holistic accountability is comprehensive, showing the importance not only of teacher quality but also curriculum, principal leadership, parent involvement, student mobility, and other factors that traditional accountability practices ignore or obscure. All of these factors work together to build student success.

Finally, holistic accountability extends the value of traditional accountability. It focuses on improving teaching and learning rather than merely providing an educational evaluation and a published report. It recognizes that the purpose of student assessment is to improve student performance. We assess so we will know how to learn better and how to teach better. Poor performance on an appraisal inspires an improvement process, rather than leading to humiliation and blame. In this way, the assessment results spur the search to find the underlying causes of poor achievement and development of specific improvement strategies.

Every teacher should strive to help students be successful. Student success motivates students and teachers alike—after all, everyone wants to feel competent and empowered with new skills, information, and insights. When teachers and students can engage in continuous improvement, the accountability system is oriented toward achieving constructive ends rather than making judgments about failure.

Goals of Education and Accountability

Educational goals are broader than just "high reading and math scores."[57] While these subjects are critical disciplines that underpin most learning and work in our complex world, narrowing the curriculum down to these two areas actually increases the educational inequities that the accountability system is designed to remove. Teaching and assessing for learning should develop students' thinking skills, enhance their abilities to construct knowledge, encourage students to engage in disciplined inquiry, and inspire them to apply their classroom-derived knowledge to real-world situations.

Most school board members and state legislators say they want American students to learn critical thinking, social skills, citizenship and responsibility, physical and emotional health, preparation for skilled work, and appreciation for the

---

[57] Science has also been part of NCLB assessments since 2007.

arts and literature.[58] These are the essentials of a strong education necessary for continued learning, good citizenship, art appreciation, interpersonal skills, and economic self-sufficiency in a highly complex, information-rich world.

When schools receive sanctions based solely on their students' reading, math, or other single-subject scores, the accountability system inadvertently creates incentives to limit—or in some cases to entirely end—time spent on other important parts of the curriculum. Skewing of the curriculum toward reading, math, and test-prep activities disproportionately affects low-income and minority children, who need the most time and help becoming "proficient" in these test-targeted areas. This approach may actually widen the achievement gap in areas for which schools are not now being held accountable.[59]

In fact, American schools should be held accountable for their results. Our students, our economy, and our national security depend on all students learning to high and measurable levels the knowledge, skills, and habits of mind necessary for twenty-first-century viability. Nevertheless, when reviewing these broader goals, it is clear that basing school accountability only on student proficiency in reading and math is neither holistic nor in the best interests of the student and society.

Accountability is larger than evaluation or assessment. Educational accountability holds educators, parents, students, and the community answerable for providing the resources to support each student's achievement to high standards. Holistic accountability includes academic achievement scores as well as specific information on curriculum, teaching practices, and leadership practices. It weighs both quantitative and qualitative indicators, thereby delivering a fuller view of student learning. Our challenge is to find a workable balance between objectively and subjectively measured assessments for more comprehensive and valued educational ends.

An effective assessment program supports teaching and learning. Formative assessments that provide teachers and students with ongoing feedback about each student's learning can be highly effective tools to facilitate learning, motivate student engagement, and increase measured achievement. Teaching *for* learning and assessment *for* learning make teacher–student interactions more meaningful and productive for all involved. End-of-course standardized tests play an important role in this sense, but are not sufficient to ensure educational excellence for all students.

All students should be taught to high and well-defined standards. Both norm-referenced and criterion-referenced (standards based) assessments are useful tools to measure students' progress toward meeting these objectives. A combination of well-designed, cognitive-rich performance tasks can provide meaningful data about student achievement that complement the results gleaned from the more formal traditional assessments. Both types of data give meaning to student achievement. While teachers may adjust the assessments and teaching methods, they need to ensure that all students master the knowledge and skills reflected in these high standards.

Our assessments must reflect what we value. If we value learning to high standards, we must harness assessments *for* learning along with assessments *of* learning. We need assessment data to help us determine how well we are teaching and how well our students are learning. These data can help us improve teaching and learning only when we learn how to use them—and the sources from which they come—wisely.

---

[58] Rothstein, R., & Jacobsen, R. (2006, December). The goals of education. *Phi Delta Kappan, 88*(4), 264–272.
[59] Rothstein & Jacobsen, 2006.

Activity 15.3

Educational accountability is more than test scores, but the general public is often comfortable with the notion that end-of-year test scores are the key sign of a school's effectiveness.

A. Working as a class prepare a presentation to a local newspaper's education writer to help educate the community about educational accountability.

B. Working as a class, decide on five key arguments that you will present to the education writer to explain how educators value accountability but accountability includes, but is more than, end-of-year standardized test scores.

C. Divide the class into five groups, each of which will prepare the details and examples for its argument.

D. Present the entire public education talk to the class as a whole.

Activity 15.4

Effective schools have long disaggregated student demographic and achievement data to ensure that all student populations were achieving well. Activities 15.4, 15.5, and 15.6 will give you the experience of looking at such data closely to determine which school factors have the greatest impact on student learning and attainment.

Teachers learn how to use their students' achievement data to make instructional decisions. In these three activities, you have three sets of achievement data to analyze. The first is from Sym City Middle School, where you are following the students' progress as they move through grades 6 to 8. The students' test results have just come back from their last year at the middle school, grade 8. You also have available last year's data (grade 7) and data from two years ago (grade 6).

You are looking at one of the middle school's teams, which consists of an English, math, science, and history teacher. Each team has approximately 100 students, with each teacher having 25 students per class. Because the teachers teach four classes, they have a total of 100 students. All 100 students have the same four teachers for their four subjects. This arrangement provides teachers with time to discuss holistic assessment as a team. Students in this school are not grouped by ability; in other words, they are assigned to teachers randomly. There is not, for example, a high-ability group, two middle-ability groups, and a low-ability group. The test results are from the NCLB testing—a criterion-referenced test on which students must reach a certain passing score on the test.

Beside each teacher's name there is the percentage of the 100 students who passed the high-stakes test in the subject. Examine the trends over the three years and answer the questions at the end of the data. Remember that students are randomly assigned to classes and that the student population at this school is very stable—fewer than 1 percent leave the district each year.

Sym City Middle School			
	Grade 6 (2 Years Ago)	Grade 7 (1 Year Ago)	Grade 8 (Current Year)
English	Mr. Brown (90)	Mrs. Nguyen (67)	Mr. Green (88)
Math	Mrs. Rinaldi (77)	Mr. Papadopoulos (65)	Mrs. Dias (54)
Science	Mrs. Greenberg (73)	Mr. Davis (88)	Mr. Harvey (94)
History	Mr. White (62)	Mrs. Santos (80)	Mrs. Jung (89)

1. What is the trend in English achievement over the past three years? What are two possible explanations for the drop in student pass rates in the seventh grade? What reasons might explain the change from seventh to eighth grade in the pass rates?

2. What is the trend in math achievement over the past three years? What are two reasons that could explain what is happening?

3. What is the trend in science achievement over the past three years? What are two reasons that could explain this trend?

4. What is the trend in history achievement over the past three years? Which reasons might explain this trend?

Activity 15.5

NCLB requires collecting data beginning in third grade. As in the case earlier, students in June Cleaver Elementary School are randomly assigned to teachers; they are not grouped by ability. This elementary school has a unique variation on looping. *Looping* is the practice where a teacher stays with the same group of students over a multi-year time frame. In this school, the students stay in a group and move to the next grade level as the same group of students, but study under a different teacher.

Follow the 25 students in each class as they move from third grade to fifth grade. This time the test scores are norm-referenced tests and the score following the subject is the average percentile score that the students in the class obtained on the standardized test. Remember that the same group of students moves on with the same students in each class.

June Cleaver Elementary School			
	Grade 3: Mrs. Snow (2 Years Ago)	Grade 4: Mrs. White (1 Year Ago)	Grade 5: Mr. Troll (Current Year)
Reading	55th percentile	55th percentile	83rd percentile
Math	89th percentile	77th percentile	56th percentile
Science	77th percentile	79th percentile	78th percentile

1. What has happened with reading scores over the past three years? What might account for this trend?

2. What has happened with math scores over the past three years? What might account for this trend?

3. What has happened with the science scores over the past three years? What might account for this trend?

Activity 15.6

At Franklin County High School, all teachers are required to turn in summary data sheets at the end of the school year. At this school, all teachers are required to give a pretest at the beginning of the year to determine how much students know about the subject. They give a post-test at the end of the year to see how much the students have learned during the year.

The data sheet from a high school AP Chemistry teacher includes the students' pretest and post-test scores and the gain scores. The gain score is calculated by subtracting the pretest score from the post-test score. The data sheet also includes the four 9-week report card grades and the year grade in the course. Additionally, the data sheet lists the following items for each of the 20 students: ID number, race, free or reduced-price lunch status, and gender. Explanations are provided at the bottom of the data sheet for these categories.

Franklin County High School is an inner-city high school. Sixty-one percent of the population is female and 39% is male. Racially, the school is 66% African American, 15% white, 15% Latino, 3% Asian/Pacific Islander, and less than 1% classified as "other." The high school graduation rate is almost 80%. This is the only AP Chemistry class the school offers.

Franklin County High School

Teacher's Name: Mr. Williams   Subject: AP Chemistry   School Year: Current

ID Number	Gender	Race	FRPL	Term 1	Term 2	Term 3	Term 4	End-of-Year Grade	Pretest Score	Post-test Score	Gain Score
001	M	W	N	A	A	A	A	A	38	98	60
002	M	W	N	B	A	B	A	A–	16	86	70
003	M	W	N	A–	A–	A	A	A	21	96	75
004	F	W	R	B	B	B–	B–	B–	20	78	58
005	F	AA	F	C	C–	C–	C	C–	07	77	70
006	M	AA	R	B	B	B	B	B	11	83	72
007	M	L	F	C	C	C+	C+	C	03	68	65
008	M	AP	N	A	A	A	A	A	32	78	46
009	M	AP	N	A	A	A	A	A	38	87	49
010	M	W	N	A	B	A	B	A–	11	66	55
011	F	W	R	C	C	B	B–	C+	09	81	72
012	F	AA	R	D	C	D	C	D–	03	88	85
013	M	AP	N	A	A	A	A	A	49	80	31
014	F	O	N	B	B	B	B	B	30	98	68
015	M	W	N	A	A	A	A	A	15	70	55
016	F	W	N	B	B	B	B	B	05	90	85
017	F	AP	N	B–	B	B+	A	B+	09	94	85
018	M	L	R	C	C	C	C	C	02	92	90

ID Number	Gender	Race	FRPL	Term 1	Term 2	Term 3	Term 4	End-of-Year Grade	Pretest Score	Post-test Score	Gain Score
019	M	AA	F	D–	C–	B–	B	C+	01	93	92
020	M	W	N	A–	A–	A–	A–	A–	34	89	55
Average	65% M; 35% F	45% W; 20% AA; 20% AP; 10% L; 5% O	60% N; 25% R; 15% F						17.7	84.6	66.9

Gender: M = male; F = female.
Race: W = white; AA=African American; AP = Asian/Pacific Islander; L=Latino; O = other.
FRPL (free or reduced-price lunch status): F = free; R = reduced price; N = not eligible.
Terms: final term grades.
Pretest Score: score on pretest (first week of school).
Post-test Score: score on post-test (end of year).
Gain Score: point difference between pretest and post-test scores.

1. Do the demographics of the school match the demographics of the students in the class? What might explain the differences?

2. The average gain score from pretest to post-test was almost 67 points (66.9). Were there any differences in average gain scores for male and female students? How would you explain the differences?

3. Were there any difference in average gain scores for white, African American, Latino, Asian/Pacific Islander, and other students? How would you explain the differences?

4. Were there any differences in average gain scores for those eligible for free or reduced-price lunches and those who did not qualify for free or reduced-price lunches? How would you explain the differences?

5. Was there evidence that the gain scores were related to the end-of-year grade for the students? Were there differences among the different groups in gain score and end-of-year grades?

6. Were there differences in the pretest scores among the different groups? How could the differences be explained?

Summary

Over the past five decades, standards and test scores have come to define educational accountability in the United States.

Standards define accepted or valued definitions of academic success. Accountability is tied to educational standards that give a clear identification of what students should know and be able to do. Standards are more accurate than norms as measures of student achievement. Because standards vary from state to state, however, the United States has 50 different meanings of "proficiency."

Educators and policy makers rely on high-stakes assessments *of learning* to inform our decisions about accountability. These tests tell us how much students have learned, whether standards are being met, and whether educators have done the job they were hired to do. Such assessments of learning have been the practice throughout the U.S. for decades.

While standardized tests are assessments *of* learning, formative assessment is assessment *for* learning. Assessment for learning is ongoing and provides teachers and students with continuous feedback and evidence of student progress. Research has shown that assessment for learning can increase measured student achievement, especially for low-income and minority students. It can also help reduce the achievement gap. Both assessment *for* learning and assessment *of* learning are essential components of a complete accountability system.

Test developers, educators, parents, and policy makers expect the tests that students take to meet high-quality professional standards for fairness, reliability, validity, freedom from undue environmental limitations, and opportunity to learn. No matter how well regarded the assessment instrument, these and other variables can confound and reduce the meaning from students' test results. Because assessment data are used to make important decisions, ethical use of these instruments is extremely important.

Standardized tests offer certain advantages over other assessment methods. They are efficient and cost-effective for large numbers of people, permit student comparisons with a norm group, have validity and reliability that make their results meaningful, measure broad characteristics, and can gather data that are useful for educational decision making. Their limitations include psychometric test issues (such as bias and a limited measure of students' learning), curricular and instructional misuse (including narrowing the curriculum to the subjects tested and association with skill-and-drill instruction methods), and misunderstanding of results (confusing cause and effect, misidentifying superior and inferior schools).

Exclusive emphasis on test scores as a means of determining educational accountability does not give a full and accurate picture of how students are achieving. Effective accountability systems are holistic—that is, they are comprehensive, containing multiple measures of student achievement. They include academic achievement scores as well as specific information on curriculum, teaching practices, leadership practices, parental involvement, faculty communications, and professional development. They balance quantitative and qualitative indicators, providing the story behind the numbers. Holistic accountability is more motivating to students and teachers, recognizing that the purpose of student assessment is to improve student performance.

Americans want their public schools to develop students' capacities for literacy, numeracy, knowledge of government (so students can make informed choices as citizens), self-awareness and knowledge of the environment (so students can intelligently choose their life's work and act as responsible environmental stewards), advanced academic training for recreation, interests in all creative arts, social ethics, and interpersonal skills. Making schools accountable only for student proficiency in reading and math is neither holistic nor in the best interests of the student and society.

Conclusions

- Assessment is an integral part of the teaching and learning process.
- No single tool can fairly assess the entire complexity of individual students' performance.
- A variety of assessments as well as both school and community factors can be combined to produce a comprehensive, credible, dependable accountability system upon which to base important decisions and make meaningful educational improvements.

Chapter 16

Effective Schools

Reviewing our country's educational history with minority and low-income children can be discouraging. Sociological, economic, and cultural variables have often placed severe obstacles in the paths of minority and low-income students as they struggle toward learning. Too often, a variety of poverty-related issues put low-income students cognitively and academically behind their middle- and upper-class peers even before they arrive at school. Likewise, schools' traditional sorting and selecting practices and institutional norms have kept traditionally underserved students from entering the educational mainstream.

But this does not have to be the case. Research affirms that when teachers, administrators, and the community hold high expectations for students, effectively deliver a strong and appropriate curriculum, and provide high levels of support, learning typically improves. "We can, whenever and wherever we choose, successfully teach all children whose schooling is of interest to us. We already know more than we need to do that."[1]

In the early 1980s, educators began investigating whether schools might be able to increase low-income and minority students' achievement. They identified schools that successfully educated all students regardless of their socioeconomic status (SES) or family background. These schools were located in varying regions and in communities both large and small.

Investigators noted that these high-achieving schools had certain philosophies, policies, and practices in common: strong instructional leadership, a strong sense of mission, high expectations for all students, robust instructional behaviors, frequent monitoring of student achievement, a safe and orderly school environment, opportunities for students to learn, and positive home-school relations. Eventually, these attributes became known as the Correlates of Effective Schools. For almost 40 years, research has continued to support these basic beliefs.[2]

This chapter looks at the Effective Schools movement and the research-based practices that every school can employ to increase academic learning for *all* students. It provides an optimistic and realistic note on which to conclude a textbook for future educators.

Focus Questions

- How did the Effective Schools movement begin?
- Who are the key people who influenced the Effective Schools movement?
- What are the "Correlates of Effective Schools" and how have they evolved over the years?

[1] Edmonds, R. (1979, October). Effective schools for the urban poor. *Educational Leadership, 37* (1), 23.
[2] Lezotte, L. (2001). *Revolutionary and evolutionary: The Effective Schools movement.* Okemos, MI: Effective Schools Products Ltd., p. 2. For more information about effective schools, see *Journal for Effective Schools,* http://www.effectiveschoolsjournal.org/

- Which attitudes and behaviors make up "instructional leadership," and how do they contribute to students' achievement?
- Which beliefs and behaviors make up a "clear and focused mission," and how do they contribute to students' achievement?
- Which beliefs and behaviors make a "safe and orderly environment," and how do they add to students' achievement?
- Which beliefs and behaviors create a "climate of high expectations," and how do they contribute to students' achievement?
- Which beliefs and behaviors make up "frequent monitoring of student progress," and how do they contribute to students' achievement?
- Which beliefs and behaviors make up "positive home–school relations," and how do they contribute to students' achievement?
- Which beliefs and behaviors make up "opportunity to learn and students' time-on-task," and how do they contribute to students' achievement?
- What are the realistic expectations for effective schools?

The History of the Effective Schools Movement

Ronald Edmonds, the education professor and researcher who first defined the Effective Schools correlates, explains the rationale for the movement in this way:

> The very great proportion of the American people believes that family background and home environment are principal causes of the quality of pupil performance. In fact, no notion about schooling is more widely held than the belief that the family is somehow the principal determinant of whether or not a child will do well in school. . . . Such a belief has the effect of absolving educators of their professional responsibility to be instructionally effective.[3]

In other words, when teachers expect little achievement from certain students, they usually get it.

In the 1950s and early 1960s, the struggle against poverty, racial prejudice, and unequal educational opportunity grew more intense. After 1960, Congressional legislation attempted to address these problems. The ensuing efforts to document and remedy the unequal educational opportunity, especially for low-income and minority children, provided a major push for school effectiveness studies.

The Early Studies

The 1964 Civil Rights Act required the Commissioner of Education to conduct a nationwide survey of the availability of educational opportunity. The resulting 1966 report, *Equality of Educational Opportunity* (commonly referred to as "the Coleman Report" and discussed in Chapter 5), concluded that family background—not the school—was the major determinant of student achievement and life outcomes.[4] The Coleman Report suggested that schools were unable to overcome or equalize the disparity in students' academic achievement due to environmental factors. In 1972,

---

[3] Edmonds, 1979, p. 21.
[4] Coleman, J., et al. (1966). *Equality of educational opportunity.* Washington, D.C. U.S. Government Printing Office.

Christopher Jencks, a Harvard University professor, and his colleagues corroborated Coleman's findings."[5]

While these reports made for attention-grabbing headlines, their conclusions were wrong. Coleman et al.'s and Jencks et al.'s studies found that the higher a family's socioeconomic status,[6] the better its children's school achievement.

As a result, the belief that for academic achievement, "families matter and schools don't" has become part of our popular culture. In fact, Donald C. Orlich, an education assessment critic, believes that "many public school educators have uncritically accepted the hypothesis of familial effects, along with its corollary: that teachers cannot be held accountable for students' failure to learn when the students come from poor home environments."[7]

The Coleman and Jencks reports and the related literature prompted the federal government to create compensatory education programs and also stimulated work by researchers and educators who believed the opposite—that effective schools *could* make a difference in student learning *regardless* of students' family backgrounds or socioeconomic status. These later investigators developed a body of research that affirmed the school controls the factors needed to assure student mastery of the core curriculum, and the family plays a crucial role in promoting student learning.

Early Effective Schools Studies

For almost 40 years, researchers have gathered ample evidence that shows schools can and do make a powerful difference in students' academic achievement.

In the late 1970s, independent researchers in the United States launched investigations to demonstrate that schools could make a difference to low-income and minority students' achievement. They began to identify public schools whose graduates scored higher than the national average on standardized tests. Academic growth—not decline—characterized these schools. Soon, hundreds of studies and research-based analytic papers tried to identify these schools' characteristics or "correlates" that were unusually successful with students regardless of their parents' education or income levels.

So began the Effective Schools movement. The studies and reform efforts launched in the 1970s and early 1980s ultimately shared a common purpose: to identify those in-school factors that affect students' academic achievement. In addition, these studies were loosely coupled by the relatively small network of like-minded people conducting them and the relationship between studies. Each study built on the previous investigations' findings.

Types of effective schools research. Much of the effective schools research might informally be considered as **outlier studies**.[8] In statistical terminology, an *outlier* is something that lies at the far end of the distribution. In other words, an outlier school might be one where all students were eligible for free or reduced-price lunches, yet the student achievement test scores were extremely high.

Another vein of school effectiveness research focused on **case studies**. In these studies, investigators analyzed a small set of schools in depth. Typically, researchers organized the schools by outcome measures—that is, high-achieving schools versus low-achieving schools. The school characteristics in a group were then studied by demographic and survey techniques.

---

[5] Jencks surmised that students' achievement was primarily a function of the students' background. See Jencks, C., et al. (1972). *Inequality: A reassessment of the effect of family and schooling in America.* New York: Basic Books, pp. 255–256.
[6] Socioeconomic status is usually determined by considering parents' education and income.
[7] Orlich, D. C. (1989, March). Education reforms; Mistakes, misconceptions, miscues. *Phi Delta Kappan,* 70(7), 516.
[8] Scheerens, J., & Bosker, R. J. (1997). *The foundations of educational effectiveness.* New York: Elsevier.

Figure 16.1	Effective Schools Successfully Educated All Students Regardless of Socioeconomic Status or Family Background

Robert W. Kelley/Contributor/Time & Life Pictures/Getty Images

Outlier and case study investigations inevitably contained some methodological limitations. Small samples and statistical issues may yield results that vary widely. Nevertheless, these studies clearly show that effective schools are characterized by good discipline, high teacher expectations regarding student achievement, and effective administrator leadership.[9]

Ronald Edmonds and the "Effective Schools" Concept[10]

Until his death in 1983, Ronald Edmonds, an education professor at Michigan State University, was one of the key figures in the Effective Schools movement. Thomas L. Good and Jere E. Brophy—themselves noted educational psychology researchers—write that "Edmonds, more than anyone, had been responsible for the communication of the belief that schools can and do make a difference."[11]

Although Edmonds acknowledged that students' family background did make a difference, he refused to accept the Coleman Report's conclusions. In 1979, as Director of Harvard's Center for Urban Studies, Edmonds set out to find schools where students from low-income families were highly successful.

Effective schools correlates. In perhaps his most notable contribution to the education field, Edmonds articulated five school-level variables that are strongly

---

[9] Scheerens & Bosker, 1997.
[10] Crisci, P. E., & Tutela, A. D. (1990). Preparation of educational administrators for urban settings. *Urban Education, 24*(4), 414–431.
[11] Good, T. L., & Brophy, J. E. (1986). School effects. In M. C. Wittrock (Ed.), *Handbook of research on teaching* (3rd ed., pp. 570–602). New York: Macmillan, p. 582.

correlated with student achievement, more simply known as the five effective schools' "correlates":[12]

- Strong administrative leadership with attention to instructional quality
- High expectations for all students' achievement
- A safe and orderly climate conducive to teaching and learning
- An emphasis on basic skill acquisition
- Frequent monitoring and measuring of pupil progress so teachers and principals are constantly aware of pupil growth in relationship to the instructional objectives

Edmonds' five correlates of effective schools became the framework for thinking about school effectiveness for at least a decade and probably longer.[13]

Next, Edmonds defined an **effective school** as one in which low-income and minority students' basic skills are at least as well developed as the middle-class children's skills. An effective school has closed the achievement gap between low- and high-SES students. "To be effective, a school need not bring all students to equal mastery levels, but it must bring an equal percentage of its highest and lowest social classes to minimum mastery."[14] As Edmonds saw it, in an "effective" school, one could not guess a student's SES from reading test scores.

In addition, Edmonds found that schools that were instructionally effective for poor and minority children were "indistinguishable" from instructionally less effective schools on SES factors (i.e., father's and mother's education, category of occupation, percentage of white students, mean family size, percentage of intact families). The large student performance differences, therefore, could not be attributed to differences in pupils' social class and family backgrounds.[15] Instead, the differences came from the schools' practices. These findings directly contrasted with Coleman et al.'s and Jencks et al.'s conclusions that variations in student performance levels from school to school were only minimally related to the schools' characteristics.

Edmonds, along with Wilbur Brookover, Lawrence Lezotte, and others, looked for effective schools. They studied achievement data from schools in several major cities with student populations drawn mainly from poverty backgrounds. In one study, Edmonds and colleagues compared successful schools with similar schools in like neighborhoods where children were not learning or were learning at a low level, reaching the following conclusions:[16]

- Public schools can and do make a difference, even when the school population consists largely of students from poverty backgrounds.
- Children from poverty backgrounds can learn at high levels as a result of instruction and related practices delivered by public schools.
- Schools where all children are learning regardless of family background have common characteristics and processes.

Edmonds and colleagues determined that while effective schools were committed to serving all their pupils without regard for family background, they did not conduct "business as usual." They recognized the need to modify curricular design, text selection, teaching strategies, and a range of behaviors in response to differences in pupils' family background. Their clear sense of purpose, high expectations, focused and safe environments, and adapted instructional practices made measurable differences for their students.

---

[12] Edmonds, R. R. (1982, December). Programs of school improvement: An overview. *Educational Leaders, 40*(3), 4–11.
[13] Scheerens & Bosker, 1997.
[14] Edmonds, 1982, p. 4.
[15] Fredericksen, J. (1975). *School effectiveness and equality of educational opportunity.* Cambridge, MA: Harvard University, Center for Urban Studies.
[16] Lezotte, L., Edmonds, R., & Ratner, G. (1974). *Remedy for school failure to equitably deliver basic school skills.* Cambridge, MA: Harvard University, Center for Urban Studies; Association for Effective Schools.

While Edmonds' studies had methodological limitations,[17] their findings provided valuable lessons about how schools could make a difference in low-income and minority students' achievement level. Edmonds' review of the Effective Schools literature and his own investigations led him to conclude that no one model explained school effectiveness for the poor or any other social class of students. Also, the relationship between the Effective Schools correlates and increased student achievement was correlational in nature, not a cause-and-effect relationship. In these studies, both the correlates and higher student achievement appeared together; no evidence proved that one factor caused the other.

Edmonds' contributions were primarily thought provoking and conceptual.[18] He asserted that schools can and do make a difference in student achievement. The poor and minority students' failures were really educators' failures, he said. Edmonds' work and that of his colleagues in the United States and abroad motivated several decades of educators to improve their schools' capacities to help all children succeed.

Criticism of Edmonds' effective schools research. Edmonds' research into school effectiveness had its critics.[19] Skeptics questioned investigators' faith in Edmonds' five-step ("correlates") approach to improve student achievement. They also claimed that researchers and school leaders generally ignored Edmonds' own warning that "no one model explains school effectiveness and often treated his work as something to be replicated, confusing correlations with cause-and-effect factors that actually shape student achievement. Additionally, critics expressed concern about certain methodological issues in Edmonds' studies.[20]

More recently, researchers using sophisticated statistical models have determined that teachers can have more impact on student test scores than other school factors.[21] At the same time, methodological improvements in research studies have transformed Edmonds' initial narrow and managerial view of effective schooling into a more comprehensive notion of effective education, which encompasses classroom instruction as well as staff and community relations.[22]

Additional Effective Schools Findings

Over time, the list of effective schools "correlates" has expanded. In 1979, the Michigan Department of Education asked Wilbur Brookover and Lawrence W. Lezotte to investigate a set of eight Michigan schools characterized by consistent pupil performance improvement or decline. Trained interviewers visited schools and tried to identify the differences between improving and declining schools. The

---

[17] Edmonds' studies looked at relatively few and largely homogenous schools using norm-referenced tests, which made it difficult to see actual student learning gains or schools' effectiveness.

[18] Marzano, R. (2000). *A new era for school reform: Going where the research takes us.* Aurora, CO: Midcontental Research for Education and Learning, p. 13.

[19] Raptis, H., & Fleming, T. (2003, October 1). Reframing education: How to create effective schools. C. D. Howe Institute Commentary. Retrieved October 30, 2009, from http://www.accessmylibrary.com/coms2/summary_0286-11856261_ITM.

[20] For more on the critical reviews, see Purkey, S. C., & Smith, M. S. (1983, March). Effective Schools: A review. *Journal of Elementary Education, 83*(4), 426–257.

[21] Studies on teacher effectiveness have found that teacher effects explain more than the students' family backgrounds in producing student achievement. See Brophy, J. E., & Good, T. L. (1974). *Teacher–student relationships: Causes and consequences.* New York: Holt, Rinehart, and Winston; Mendro, R. A., Jordan, H. R., Gomez, E., Anderson, M. C., & Bembry, K. L. (1998). *An application of multiple linear regression in determining longitudinal teacher effectiveness.* Dallas, TX: Dallas Independent School District; Sanders, W. L., & Horn, S. P. (1995). Educational assessment reassessed: The usefulness of standardized and alternative measures of student achievement as indicates for the assessment of educational outcomes. *Education Policy Analysis Archives, 3*(6), 1–15: Sanders, W. L., & Rivers, J. C. (1996). *Cumulative and residual effects of teachers on future student academic achievement.* Knoxville, TN: University of Tennessee Value-Added Research and Assessment Center; Sanders, W .L., & Rivers, J. C. (2001). *EVAAS reports for educational assessment: Jefferson County Public Schools.* Cary, NC: SAS in Schools.

[22] Raptis & Fleming, 2003.

researchers found consistent differences between schools where students achieved well and where they didn't:[23]

- **Clear instructional focus.** Improving schools clearly accepted and emphasized the importance of the reading and math objectives, whereas declining schools gave less emphasis to such goals and did not specify them as fundamental.

- **High teacher expectations.** The staffs of improving schools tended to believe that *all* of their students could master the basic objectives. Teachers perceived that their principals shared this belief. Teachers at improving schools also expected that their students would complete high school or college, whereas teachers at declining schools had much lower expectations for their students' achievement and educational futures.

- **Commitment to and responsibility for student achievement.** In improving schools, teachers and principals were more likely to assume responsibility for and were committed to teaching the basic reading and math skills. Staffs at declining schools felt that teachers could not do much to influence their students' achievement and displaced the responsibility for skill learning to parents or students.

- **High time-on-task.** Teachers in improving schools spent more time on achieving reading and math objectives, while teachers in declining schools spent less time in direct reading instruction.

- **Principal as instructional leader.** In improving schools, principals were, more assertive in their institutional leadership role, more of a disciplinarian, and more regular in evaluating achievement of basic objectives. By comparison, principals in declining schools were more permissive, emphasized informal and collegial relationships with teachers, and emphasized general public relations rather than evaluating school effectiveness in providing a basic education for all students.

- **Accountability.** The improving schools showed greater acceptance of accountability and used measured student learning as one sign of their effectiveness.

- **Dissatisfaction with current achievement.** Generally, teachers in improving schools were less satisfied than staffs in declining schools. Staffs in declining schools were complacent and satisfied with current achievement levels.

- **Unclear role of parent involvement.** Differences in parent involvement levels were not clear. Improving schools had higher levels of *parent-initiated* involvement but less overall parent involvement.

- **Compensatory education.** Classroom teachers in improving schools focused on teaching reading. By comparison, classroom teachers in declining schools spent more time identifying students to be placed in compensatory reading activities and placed greater emphasis on programmed instruction.

The 1979 Brookover and Lezotte findings present a relatively clear profile of achieving schools that are congruent with other urban school studies. They showed that teacher and principal expectations and behaviors created the school conditions that allowed low-income and minority students to make achievement gains. They did not blame their students' low achievement on inherited, social, or family factors. At the same time, Brookover and Lezotte concluded that no single combination of variables will produce an effective school. Most importantly, these researchers found that pupil family background neither causes nor prevents elementary school instructional effectiveness.

---

[23] Brookover, W. B., & Lezotte, L. W. (1977). *Changes in school characteristics coincident with changes in student achievement.* East Lansing, MI: Michigan State University, College of Urban Development.

Limitations of the early effective schools research. Effective schools research finds common characteristics, but also shares serious limitations. The studies looked at too few schools with too-narrow student demographics to justify firm conclusions. The findings were correlational, rather than indicating a cause-and-effect relationship. Furthermore, researchers looking at middle-class students and secondary schools did not find the same results as those studying elementary schools.[24] Despite these limitations, the studies' consistent findings of the school effectiveness "correlates"—strong principal or staff leadership, high expectations for student achievement, a clear set of instructional goals, an effective schoolwide staff training program, an emphasis on order and discipline, and a system for monitoring students' progress—give substantial credibility to the diverse studies' findings.[25]

In spite of the cautions, many educators continued to mistakenly assume the cause-and-effect relationship exists between the Effective Schools correlates and student achievement. During the 1980s, this line of research had a major impact on educators' school improvement plans. Several implementation studies tried to change school-level behavior on one or more of the factors considered important to effective schooling, mistakenly assuming that the cause-and-effect relationship with student achievement held. Programs were initiated in Atlanta, Chicago, Minneapolis, Pittsburgh, San Diego, St. Louis, Washington, D.C., and many other smaller school districts.[26] Perhaps not surprisingly, these projects achieved mixed results.[27]

In light of both two decades of effective schools' research findings and the methodological criticism, in 1990 Levine concluded:

> The effective school correlates should be viewed more as prerequisites for attaining high and equitable student achievement levels. Their presence does not guarantee schools' success. All correlates must be present to make a difference.

> The correlates represented issues and challenges for their schools. They were not "prescriptions" or "recipes" for attaining a high achieving status. Enacting each correlate takes many steps, and no specific action or steps is right for every school.

> Much of the positive results at unusually effective schools involve teachers and administrators identifying and addressing obstacles to student learning. Changes one place usually create ripples elsewhere. Making sure that changes in one sphere do not create negative repercussions elsewhere takes constant monitoring and adjusting that cannot easily be written in a "to do" list.

> Schools cannot tackle all reforms at once or they would go into overload.[28]

Effective Schools Research in the 1990s

During the 1990s, educators made substantial conceptual and empirical progress in understanding explaining effective schools.[29] The new models were more specific about the school factors and their interactions. In addition, the definition of effective schools was expanded to include public and private elementary, middle, and high schools from communities with all social classes. These schools were located in rural, urban, and suburban settings and had various levels of support. This second generation of effective schools models and research not only focused on

[24] Wimpelberg, R. K., Teddie, C., & Stringfield, S. (1989). Sensitivity to context: The past and future of effective schools research. *Educational Administration Quarterly, 25*(1), 82–107.

[25] Purkey & Smith, 1983.

[26] Cuban, L. (1984). Transforming the frog into a prince: Effective schools research, policy, and practice at the district level. *Harvard Educational Review, 54*, 129–151.

[27] McCormack-Larkin, M., & Kritek, W. J. (1983). Milwaukee's project RISE. *Educational Leadership, 40*, 16–21; Marzano, 2000, p. 19.

[28] Levine, D. U. (1990). Update on effective schools: Findings and implications for research and practice. *Journal of Negro Education, 59*(4), 577–584.

[29] Teddlie, C., & Reynolds, D. (Eds.). (2000). *The international handbook on school effectiveness research.* New York: Falmer.

schools serving all types of students in all types of settings, but also emphasized growth in achievement and school improvement across all contexts. In fact, school effectiveness is now understood as sets of interacting variables.

In the 1990s, Jaap Scheerens and Roel Bosker, two professors of education at University of Twente, Netherlands, reviewed a number of school effectiveness models. They conducted one of the most quantitatively sophisticated reviews of the research literature on the myriad factors influencing student achievement.[30] Using a complex statistical model to organize their research, they produced a meta-analysis of an international literature base. Their findings identified a pattern of support across all literature bases for academic pressure to achieve, parental involvement, orderly climate, and opportunity to learn.

Likewise, University of Hawaii education professor Ronald Heck's 2000 and 2005 studies found that schools with higher-quality educational environments (principal leadership, high expectations, frequent monitoring of student progress and climate) produced higher-than-expected achievement gains after controlling for the students' characteristics.[31]

Nonetheless, the school's community and socioeconomic context do influence student achievement. Many observed differences in student performance can be attributed to characteristics of their schools and communities—even though these factors are beyond their schools' control. To help students learn, it is important for educators to understand and accommodate these outside factors.[32]

Implementing certain correlates without the others does not necessarily produce the desired results, however. A 2006 study found that school management structures that promote teacher cooperation, collegiality, and participation in decision making are not especially powerful determinants of student achievement at either the elementary or secondary levels.[33] Unless teachers have higher expectations for student learning or other Effective Schools correlates, teacher collaboration by itself will not significantly modify student achievement.

Another study shows that while principals' strong instructional leadership is important, its impact on school effectiveness is indirect.[34] Yet evidence continues to emerge that principal leadership is second only to teaching among the school-related factors in its impact on student learning.[35] Research on these issues is ongoing.

---

[30] Scheerens & Bosker, 1997; Scheerens, J. (1992). *Effective schooling: Research, theory, and practice.* London: Cassell; Bosker, R. J. (1992). *The stability and consistency of school effects in primary education.* Enschede: University of Twente; Bosker, R. J., & Witziers, B. (1995, January). *School effects, problems, solutions, and a meta-analysis.* Paper presented at the International Congress for School Effectiveness and School Improvement, Leeuwarden, the Netherlands; Bosker, R. J., & Witziers, B. (1996). *The magnitude of school effects: Or, does it really matter which school a student attends?* Paper presented at the annual meeting of the American Educational Research Association, New York.

[31] Heck, R. H. (2000). Examining the impact of school quality on school outcomes and improvement: A value-added approach. *Educational Administration Quarterly, 36*(4), 513–552; Heck, R. H. (2005). Examining school achievement over time: A multilevel, multi-group approach. In W. K. Hoy & C. G. Miskal (Eds.), *Contemporary issues in educational policy and school outcomes* (pp. 1–28). Greenwich, CT: Information Age.

[32] Heck, 2000.

[33] Miller, R. J., & Rowan, B. (2006). Effects of organic management on student achievement. *American Educational Research Journal, 43*(2), 219–253.

[34] Goddard, R. D., Sweetland, S. R., & Hoy, W. K. (2000) Academic emphasis and student achievement: A multi-level analysis. *Educational Administration Quarterly, 5,* 683–702; Goddard, R. D., Tschannen-Moran, M., & Hoy, W. K. (2001). Teacher trust in students and parents: A multilevel examination of the distribution and effects of teacher trust in urban elementary schools. *Elementary School Journal, 102,* 3–17; Goddard, R. D., LoGerfo, L., & Hoy, W. K. (2003, April). *Collective efficacy and student achievement in public high school: A path analysis.* Paper presented at the annual meeting of the American Educational Research Association, Chicago, IL.

[35] Leithwood, K., Louis, K. S., Anderson, K. S., & Wahlstrom, K. (2004). *How leadership influences student learning.* New York: Wallace Foundation. Retrieved October 30, 2009, from http://www.wallacefoundation.org/SiteCollectionDocuments/WF/Knowledge%20Center/Attachments/PDF/ReviewofResearch-Learning-FromLeadership.pdf.

Finally, the Effective Schools correlates are likely to have a cumulative impact on student achievement. One or two factors by themselves will not make much difference to important school and student outcomes.

Effective Schools Today

Effective schools research and practice continue today. Schools studied include the 90/90/90 schools, "No Excuses Schools" (such as KIPP Academies), "High Impact" schools, and Village Academies. While the school-related factors contributing to their success are largely identical to those in the Effective Schools literature, the present practitioners do not publicly place themselves within the Effective Schools movement. They represent elementary and secondary schools in various locations that are successfully raising low-income and minority students' academic achievement by using the Effective Schools correlates.

Effective Schools correlates consistently appear where public schools are effectively educating those students who have traditionally been underserved. This fact alone merits attention and, when possible, replication.

The Correlates of Effective Schools: Current Research Findings

The Effective Schools correlates evolved over time. The updated definitions incorporate the available research findings and represent a higher developmental stage than when they first appeared.[36] Let's look more closely at each of the correlates, see what the research literature has to say about their impact on student achievement, and describe what they look like in schools.

Strong Instructional Leadership

Strong instructional leadership is an essential component of effective schools. "Indeed, there are virtually no documented instances of troubled schools being turned around without interventions by a dynamic leader. Many other factors may contribute to such turnarounds, but leadership is the catalyst."[37]

In today's schools, the principal cannot be the only leader. As a "leader of leaders" rather than a "leader of followers," principals develop their skills as coach, partner, and cheerleader as well as organizational leader and manager. By consistently communicating and reinforcing the school's purpose in words and deeds, and by sharing leadership with teachers, the principal creates a professional environment in which teachers can thrive and contribute to the overall school goals and environment.[38]

Discussion and research. According to a national analysis of 15 years of school leadership research, an outstanding principal "exercises a measurable though indirect effect on school effectiveness and student achievement."[39] Similarly, a 2005 meta-analysis of 30 years of research on the effects of principals' practices on student achievement found a significant, positive correlation of .25 between effective school leadership and student achievement. For an average school, having an effective leader

---

[36] Lezotte, L. (1991). *Correlates of effective schools: The first and second generation.* Okemos, MI: Effective Schools.
[37] Leithwood, K., Louis, K. S., Anderson, S., & Wahlstrom, K. (2004). *Review of research: How leadership influences student learning.* New York: Wallace Foundation, p. 7.
[38] Lezotte, 1991.
[39] Hallinger, P., & Heck, R. (1998). Exploring the principal's contribution to school effectiveness, 1980–1995. *School Effectiveness and School Improvement 9*(2), 157–191.

can mean the difference between scoring at the 50th percentile on a given achievement test and achieving a score 10 percentile points higher.[40]

As the "official" school leader, the principal sets the climate, creates the expectations, clarifies the school's direction, and delivers the resources needed to make teaching and learning satisfying and successful endeavors. Effective school leaders build their organizational cultures through participatory decision making and collaborative planning, goal setting, and problem solving. As strong instructional leaders, they can help socialize teachers to take on broader responsibilities—such as assuring that each student learns to high levels and accepting leadership roles within their schools.

When the current school's practices and structures do not allow principals to reach these goals, strong instructional leaders don't downsize their vision or mission to fit. Instead, they change the school organization to permit the vision and mission to flourish. Giving teachers time each day to plan and work collaboratively with other teachers, designing a schedule that allows for extended student learning time and extended teacher planning time, and providing high-quality and relevant professional development tied directly to what teachers need to know and do to improve student learning in their specific curricula are ways that principals can modify the organization to support shared goals. Working with teachers, parents, and the community on school improvement planning is another way for principals to lead their schools in making positive changes.

When administrators create school cultures that welcome shared leadership, spirited and inventive teachers will willingly work as part of the team to bring improvements to their schools. When teachers participate in their schools' instructional leadership, they become less isolated. They gain satisfaction from knowing that they are improving their schools. All of these positive experiences spill over into their classroom teaching, helping teachers invest in their school rather than merely work there.

What it looks like in schools. How do teachers know when their principal is acting as an instructional leader?[41] Ways in which principals act as instructional leaders include these behaviors:

- Making student achievement the school's top goal and clearly (and repeatedly) expressing this goal
- Providing ongoing, two-way communication between school administrators with school personnel, students, and parents
- Regularly observing classroom instruction and providing feedback to teachers
- Offering helpful suggestions for instructional improvement as a part of the observation of classroom instruction
- Sharing leadership roles with teachers, using individual and team strengths
- Providing sufficient resources for effective instruction, including professional development
- Ensuring an effective, ongoing system for evaluating the school's progress toward its goals
- Systematically engaging staff in discussions about current research, theory, and practice
- Involving teachers in the design and implementation of important decisions and policies

---

[40] Marzano, R. J., Waters, T., & McNulty, B. A. (2005). *School leadership that works: From research to results.* Alexandria, VA: Association for Supervision and Curriculum Development.
[41] Several researchers have developed sets of principal leadership behaviors. See the following sources: Heck, R. (2000, October). Examining the impact of school quality on school outcomes and improvement: A value-added approach. *Educational Administration Quarterly, 36*(4), 541.; Waters, T., Marzano, R. J., & McNulty, B. (2003). *Balanced leadership: What 30 years of research tells us about the effect of leadership on student achievement. A working paper.* Aurora, CO: Mid-continent Research for Education and Learning.

- Actively seeking input from teachers, students, parents, and the community to develop the school's improvement plan
- Promptly and effectively handling student concerns and troubles

| Figure 16.2 | Principals Are Instructional Leaders in Effective Schools |

Michael Newman/PhotoEdit

Clear and Focused Mission

Today's school mission emphasizes teaching and learning an appropriate balance between higher-level learning and those more basic skills required for their mastery. The mission advocates *learning for all,* focusing on both the "learning" (what the student is doing and gaining) and the teachers' continuous professional growth. Results—not merely inputs—matter in this milieu.[42]

Discussion and research. School leaders begin to make their schools into positive learning environments for students and teachers by defining a compelling vision and a focused mission. A **vision** is an intelligent sense of what a better future can be; a **mission** is the purpose or direction pursued to reach that end.[43] "A vision is a target that beckons"[44] claim business leadership experts. For instance, in 1961, when President John Kennedy set the then-almost-unimaginable goal of placing a man on the moon by 1970, and when Bill Gates later aimed to put a computer on every desk and in every home, these leaders concentrated attention on worthwhile, highly challenging, and attainable achievements. A vision provides a bridge from the present to the future. Only when one knows where one wants to go can one plan how to get there.

Effective leaders bring vision into action by sharing it with others. An essential leadership skill is the capacity to influence and organize meaning for the organization's members. Leaders articulate and define what has previously remained unsaid. They invent images, metaphors, and mental models that help direct attention and energies. They depict a desirable future state of their organization for us.

Vision and *mission* are not always thought of as two separate things. Instead, they are both aspects of the same whole. Stephen R. Covey, author of *The Seven Habits of Highly Effective People,* sees a vision as telling where one wants to go, and a mission

---

[42] Lezotte, 1991, pp. 3–5.
[43] The Effective Schools movement did not use the term "vision." Its *mission* assumed *vision* as an integral part. To the members of this movement, a "clear and focused mission" meant challenging the conventional wisdom that students' achievement depended almost totally on their family backgrounds, which schools could not overcome.
[44] Bennis, W., & Nanus, B. (1997). *Leaders: Strategies for taking charge.* New York: HarperCollins, p. 82.

as telling how one will get there. Both deal with values and purpose and are different locations on the same continuum. One step is a prerequisite for the next.[45]

In an effective school, first the principal and then other school leaders champion a particular image or vision—expressed through a clear and focused mission—of what is possible, desirable, and intended. A persuasive, shared vision and a clear, focused mission compel the organization to attend to what is important and define where the organization intends to go.[46] Vision and mission create meaning for everyone in the organization and make the world understandable. They help explain why things are being done they way they are, and why certain things are considered good and rewarded while others are not.

Research shows that by fostering group goals, modeling the desired behaviors for others, and providing intellectual stimulation and individual support (through personal and professional development), principals directly affect a school's culture and climate and indirectly influence student achievement.[47] Nevertheless, while principals articulate the vision/mission, teachers are the essential agents who make a clear and focused mission work. Once the teachers and staff see the "big picture," the team members can understand how their own jobs relate to it. They can fit their skills and interests into the school's plan to help it get where it intends to go. All participants can use this goal to realize their own deepest desires for meaning, accomplishment, and self-fulfillment. With this clear and focused mission, teaching becomes more than a job: It becomes a means to enact teachers' values, and fully engage their energies and talents as they educate children for lifelong learning, mature awareness and behavior, and economic opportunities.

Involving teachers in the change process increases their investment in the school's success. It keeps effective and influential teachers in the school, despite the traditionally high turnover rate among teachers early in their careers.[48] Creating an atmosphere in which teachers are considered professionals and have opportunities to continue their professional development both inside and outside the school leads teachers—and their students—toward excellence.

What it looks like in schools. In an effective school with a clear and focused mission:[49]

- Everyone (teachers, students, parents, community) can tell you that student learning is the school's top goal.
- The school's beliefs and mission are clearly stated.
- The school's policies and practices are aligned with its beliefs.
- The school gives continual attention to every student's achievement.
- The school has a collaborative process for developing the school's vision, beliefs, mission, and goals that engages the school community in an in-depth study and assessment of important information sources and shared values.
- Student learning goals are high and measurable.
- The school regularly reports back to stakeholders about its progress toward meeting the mission's goals.
- Teachers have the materials, equipment, and professional development needed to do their jobs successfully.

---

[45] Covey, S. R. (1989). *The seven habits of highly effective people.* New York: Simon and Schuster, p. 106.
[46] Nanus, B. (2001). Why does vision matter? In Osland, J., S., Kolb, D. A., & Rubin, I. M. (Eds.), *The organization behavior reader* (7th ed., pp. 381–383). Upper Saddle River, NJ: Prentice Hall.
[47] Leithwood, K. (1994). Leadership for school restructuring. *Educational Administration Quarterly, 30*(4), 498–518.
[48] Darling-Hammond, L. (1997, September). Quality teaching: The critical key to learning. *Principal, 77*(1), 5–11.
[49] Heck, 2000, p. 542; Fitzpatrick, K. A. (1998, July). *Indicators of schools of quality. Volume 1: Schoolwide indicators of quality.* Schaumberg, IL.: National Study of School Evaluation, p. 149.

- Teachers present academic work in ways that students find interesting, varied, and actively involving.
- All students' learning includes both basic-level academic skills and higher-level cognitive abilities.
- Teachers use formative assessments to identify students needing additional help and the weaknesses they need to remedy; teachers then provide the specific assistance needed.
- Students receive enough time and help to master the basic skills.
- Students believe they are learning a lot in most of their classes.
- The achievement gap between middle-class and low-income and minority students is markedly decreasing or eliminated altogether.

Safe and Orderly Environment

Today's effective schools move beyond the absence of undesirable student behaviors, such as students fighting, to emphasize the presence of certain desirable behaviors. Now a safe and orderly environment is defined as including cooperative team learning, students helping one another, and all parties showing respect for and appreciation of human diversity and democratic values.[50]

Discussion and research. A safe and orderly environment is critical to effective schooling. It is essential that teachers and students feel physically and emotionally safe and comfortable if they are to have the psychological energy needed for teaching and learning. Without a minimum level of security and calm, a school has little chance of positively affecting student achievement.

Many studies have singled out a safe and orderly environment as essential to academic achievement.[51] In general, research finds the more safe and orderly the school climate, the higher the students' math and reading achievement levels. A secure and organized environment is significantly correlated with less student fear, lower dropout rates, and higher student commitment to their learning.[52]

Worry about safety shifts the brain's attention. When students and teachers worry about their personal safety, their focus insistently turns to protecting themselves. They become cautious and watchful, and they stay hyper-alert to potential dangers. At such times, the emotional parts of their brain are more fully aroused, and their cognitive areas become less active. In such environments, they cannot find extra energy to pay attention to teaching and learning. Achievement suffers.

Conversely, in a school with a safe and orderly environment, teachers and students feel no personal danger. Thus their cognitive capacities can become more fully engaged. The learning environment is well structured and business-like. Teachers are committed to teaching and learning. They set high but achievable goals for students. Likewise, students work hard on academic matters, are highly motivated, and respect peers who achieve academically.

---

[50] Lezotte, 1991, pp. 1–2.

[51] Chubb, J. E., & Moe, T. M. (1990). *Politics, markets, and America's schools.* Washington, DC: Brookings Institute; Mayer, D. P., Hoy, W. K., & Hannun, J. (1997). Middle school climate: An empirical assessment of organizational health and student achievement. *Educational Administration Quarterly, 33*(3), 290–311; Mullens, J. E., Moore, M. T., & Ralph, J. (2000). *Monitoring school quality: An indicators report.* Washington, DC: U.S. Department of Education, National Center for Education Statistics; Grogger, J. (1997). Local violence and educational attainment. *Journal of Human Resources, 32*(4), 659–692.

[52] Hoy & Hannun, 1997; Hoy, W. K., Hannum, J., & Tschannen-Moran, M. (1998, July). Organizational climate and student achievement: A parsimonious and longitudinal view. *Journal of School Leadership, 8*(4), 1–22; Hoy, W. K., & Sabo, D. (1998). *Quality middle schools: Open and healthy.* Thousand Oaks, CA: Corwin Press; Goddard, R. D., Sweetland, S. R., & Hoy, W. K. (2000). Academic emphasis of urban elementary schools and student achievement: A multi-level analysis. *Educational Administration Quarterly, 36*(5), 683–702.

What it looks like in schools. A school has a safe and orderly environment when it meets the following criteria:[53]

- The school is clean, inviting, and comfortable. Graffiti or disorder is promptly noticed and removed.
- Custodians clean the halls and common student areas after each time students use them throughout the school day.
- People at the school say that they feel safe.
- Students at the school tell visitors that they want to learn.
- Students sit in mixed race and gender groups in the cafeteria and classrooms.
- Teacher–student interactions are positive.
- Rules and expectations are clearly and visibly communicated (and frequently reviewed and enforced) to students (and parents), stressing mutual respect and responsibility.
- Teachers, administrators, and other adults are visible in the halls and common areas whenever students are using them, from morning entry to afternoon dismissal.
- The principal and administrators are aware of the details and undercurrents in running the school and use this information to solve and prevent problems.
- Students breaking rules receive fair and consistently administered consequences.
- Early recognition systems identify students with high potential for violence and extreme behaviors, and educators intervene to help solve and prevent problems.
- The school has low discipline referral rates and few (and declining) suspensions for disciplinary infractions.
- Student and faculty achievements are celebrated and recognized.
- All adults (principal, teachers, administrative personnel, custodians, cafeteria workers) help students learn self-discipline and responsibility.

| Figure 16.3 | Students Meet Regularly with In-School Adult Mentors to Discuss Concerns and Solve Problems |

Dennis MacDonald/PhotoEdit

---

[53] Adapted from Marzano, 2003, pp. 55–59; Heck, 2000, p. 545.

- Challenging students have in-school adult mentors with whom they regularly discuss concerns and solve problems.
- Students stay after school to work one-on-one with teachers to make up or gain more understanding about their schoolwork.
- Students and parents say that their teachers really care about them.
- Students and parents say students enjoy coming to school.
- Teachers and students are active in developing the school rules.
- The learning environment is cognitively challenging for all students.
- The school staff works cooperatively.
- The curriculum includes multicultural education.
- People in the building smile at one another freely and frequently.

Climate of High Expectations

To maintain a climate of high expectations for students, teachers must first hold high expectations for themselves. Ideally, teachers should accept responsibility for all aspects of their students' learning—the taught content, skills, and habits of mind. Likewise, schools must provide teachers with organizational "tools" to help them achieve successful learning for all. Lastly, schools as cultural organization must transform from institutions designed for "instruction" to institutions designed to assure "learning."[54]

Discussion and research. As students and teachers become involved in schooling's routines, both perceptions and expectations reflect and determine the goals they set for achievement; the strategies they use to meet those goals; the skills, energy, and other resources they use to apply these strategies; and the rewards they expect from making this effort.[55]

The research on effective schools reinforces the importance of teacher expectations in determining student performance. As discussed earlier, many other studies found comparable results.[56]

Researchers have found several relationships between teachers' expectations and student achievement:

- Teachers form expectations for student performance.[57]
- Teachers tend to treat students differently depending on these expectations.

---

[54] Lezotte, 1991.

[55] Ferguson, R. R. (2003). Teachers' perceptions and expectations in the black–white test score gap. *Urban Education, 38*(4), 460–507.

[56] Brookover, W. B., & Lezotte, L. W. (1979). *Changes in school characteristics coincident with changes in student achievement.* East Lansing, MI: Michigan State University, Institute for Research on Teaching; Edmonds, R. R., & Fredericksen, J. R. (1978). *Search for effective schools: The identification and analysis of city schools that are instructionally effective for poor children.* Cambridge, MA: Harvard University, Center for Urban Studies; Brophy, J. E., & Evertson, C. (1976). *Learning from teaching: A developmental perspective.* Boston, MA: Allyn & Bacon; McDonald, R., & Elias, P. (1976). The effects of teaching performance on pupil learning: Vol. I, final report. *Beginning teacher evaluation study, phase 2, 1974–1976.* Princeton, NJ: Educational Testing Service; Rotter, M., Maughan, B., Mortimore, P., Ouston, J., & Smith, A. (1979). *Fifteen thousand hours: Secondary schools and their effects of children.* Cambridge, MA: Harvard University Press.

[57] Brophy, J., & Good, T. (1970). Teachers' communication of differential expectations for children's classroom performance: Some behavioral data. *Journal of Educational Psychology, 61,* 365–374; Dusek, J. B., & O'Connell, E. J. (1973). Teacher expectancy effects on the achievement test performance of elementary school children. *Journal of Educational Psychology, 65,* 371–377; O'Connell, E., Dusek, J., & Wheeler, R. (1974). A follow-up study of teacher expectancy effects. *Journal of Educational Psychology, 66,* 325–328; Rist, R. (1970). Students' social class and teacher expectations: The self-fulfilling prophesy in ghetto education. *Harvard Educational Review, 40,* 411–451.

Figure 16.4	High Expectations for Students' Learning Leads to High Student Achievement

Tom & Dee Ann McCarthy/Encyclopedia/CORBIS

- Teachers' behaviors reflecting these expectations are related to measures of student academic achievement.[58]
- Teachers' perceptions of current students' performance as well as their judgments for students' future performance are generally accurate.[59]
- Once set, teachers' expectations change little.[60] In school, first impressions matter.
- Student characteristics such as physical attractiveness, socioeconomic status, race, use of standard English, and history of grade retention are related to teacher expectations for academic achievement.[61]

---

[58] Brophy & Good, 1970; Dusek, J. B. (1975). Do teachers bias children's learning? *Review of Educational Research, 45*, 661–684; Rosenthal, R. *On the social psychology of the self-fulfilling prophesy: Further evidence for Pygmalion effects and their mediating mechanisms.* New York: MSS Modular Publications; Rosenthal, R. (1976). *Experimenter effects in behavioral research* (2nd ed.). New York: Irvington.

[59] Egan, O., & Archer, P. (1985). The accuracy of teachers' rating of ability: A regression model. *American Educational Research Journal, 22*, 25–34; Hoge, R., & Butcher, R. (1984). Analysis of teacher judgments of pupil achievement level. *Journal of Educational Psychology, 76*, 777–781; Mittman, A. (1985). Teachers' differential behavior toward higher and lower achieving students and its relation to selected teacher characteristics. *Journal of Educational Psychology, 77*, 149–161; Monk, M. (1983). Teacher expectations? Pupil responses to teacher mediated classroom climate. *British Educational Research Journal, 9*, 153–166; Pedulla, J., Airasian, P., & Madaus, G. (1980). Do teacher ratings and standardized test results of students yield the same information? *American Educational Research Journal, 17*, 303–307; Good, T. L. (1987). Two decades of research on teacher expectations: Findings and future direction. *Journal of Teacher Education, 4*, 32–47.

[60] Ferguson, 2003.

[61] Cecil, N. L. (1988). Black dialect and academic success: A study of teacher expectations. *Reading Improvement, 25*(1), 34–38; Crowl, T. K. (1971). White teachers' evaluation of oral responses given by white and Negro ninth grade males [Doctoral dissertation, Columbia University, 1970]. *Dissertation Abstracts International, 31*, 4540-A; Dusek, J. B., & Joseph, G. (1983). The bases of teacher expectancies: A meta-analysis. *Journal of Educational Psychology, 75*(3), 327–346; Gaines, M. L., & Davis, M. (1990, April). *Accuracy of teacher prediction of elementary student achievement.* Paper presented at the annual meeting of the American Educational Research Association, Boston, MA. (ERIC Document Reproduction Service No. ED 320 942); Kenealy, P., Neil, F., & Shaw, W. (1988). Influences of children's physical attractiveness on teacher expectations. *Journal of Social Psychology, 128*(3), 373–383: Williams, J. H., & Muehl, S. (1978). Relations among student and teacher perceptions of behavior. *Journal of Negro Education, 47*, 328–336.

- Teachers who expect students to be low achievers attribute their improved achievement to luck, whereas teachers attribute the perceived high achievers' success to their ability.[62]

- Teachers overestimate the achievement of high achievers, underestimate the achievement of low achievers, and predict least accurately low achievers' responses.[63]

- The better the teachers know the students, the more accurate their expectations for student academic success, especially in the early elementary grades (grades 1 and 2).[64]

The more effectively teachers teach, the higher all their students achieve, and the less accurate teachers' initial predictions become about who will or will not learn. As teachers learn and apply more effective instructional practices that help more students learn, teachers become increasingly optimistic about their students' success; in turn, their students became more successful. Each player's positive expectation influences the other in a mutually reinforcing manner.[65] Studies find that the more inviting and responsive instruction is to children's efforts to improve, the less accurately teachers' initial perceptions and expectations will predict later success.[66] It is also possible that when teachers become more effective in their classrooms, they may treat all students as high achievers—providing them with similar praise and similar feedback, and making similar demands for work and effort.[67]

Community expectations also matter. Investigators have found that when a community pressures its schools to set higher expectations, all students' performance improves.[68] Sharing the high expectation for student achievement with the community in a clear and focused mission has a positive impact on student achievement.

In short, teachers' initial expectations about students' being high or low achievers weaken as teachers get better at their jobs and develop the expertise to have all their students successfully learn the curriculum.

What it looks like in schools. What do schools with high expectations for student achievement look like?[69]

- The school has developed a shared vision of a school with all students achieving at high levels, regardless of family background.

- The school has a very low dropout rate and a very high promotion or graduation rate.

- The school has standards and practices in place to avoid both grade retention and social promotion by keeping all students learning apace.[70]

---

[62] Peterson, P. L., & Barger, S. A. (1984). Attribution theory and teacher expectancy. In J. B. Dusek (Ed.), *Teacher expectancies* (pp.159–184). Hillsdale, NJ: Lawrence Erlbaum Associates.
[63] Coladarci, T. (1986). Accuracy of teacher judgments of student response to standardized test items. *Journal of Educational Psychology, 78*(2), 141–146; Hoge, R. D., & Butcher, R. (1984). Analysis of teacher judgments of pupil achievement level. *Journal of Educational Psychology, 76*(5), 777–781; Patriarca, L. A., & Kragt, D. M. (1986, May/June). Teacher expectations and student achievement: The ghost of Christmas future. *American Review,* 48–50.
[64] Raudenbush, S. W. (1984). Magnitude of teacher expectancy effects on pupil IQ as a function of the credibility of expectancy induction: A synthesis of findings from eighteen experiments. *Journal of Educational Psychology, 76*(1), 85–97.
[65] Guskey, T. (1982, July–August). The effects of change in instructional effectiveness on the relationship of teacher expectations and student achievement. *Journal of Educational Research, 75*(6), 345–349.
[66] Ferguson, 2003, p. 483; Guskey, 1982.
[67] Guskey, 1982.
[68] Brophy & Good, 1970; Good, T. L., & Brophy, J. E. (1987). *Looking in classrooms.* New York: Harper & Row.
[69] Waters, Marzano, & McNulty, 2003; Heck, 2000, p. 543.
[70] Owings, W. A., & Kaplan, L. S. (2001). *Retention and social promotion: A history and alternatives to two public failures.* Bloomington, IN: PDK Fastback Publication, Phi Delta Kappa.

- Teachers, administrators, and parents expect all students to learn a full range of skills—from basic mastery of needed skills to higher-level, complex problem solving. They also act on this belief.

- Teachers have confidence in their skills to help all their students master the basic and higher-level skills, regardless of their family background. Teachers also act on this belief.

- Teachers clearly inform students and parents of what students are expected to know and be able to do by the end of the unit or semester.

- Teachers help students use what they already know to learn new knowledge, develop new skills, and expand their understanding.

- Teachers use a variety of effective instructional approaches to ensure that all students learn.

- Students and teachers work together during class time and after school (if needed) to master the expected content and skills.

- The school has ongoing, collegial professional development tied to the classroom curriculum to help every teacher improve his or her instructional effectiveness.

- Students are encouraged to set high learning goals for themselves.

- Students and teachers believe that their effort is more important than their ability in producing their final achievement.

- Special-needs students receive regular instruction in the regular classrooms from the regular teacher with assistance from a collaborating teacher.

- English language learners receive support to learn academics in the regular classroom.

- Students and parents believe that their teachers have confidence in their ability to master the curriculum and expect them to do well.

- Students and parents say their schoolwork is challenging but feasible.

Activity 16.1

Effective schools have a climate of high expectations for students and teachers. Teachers' expectations influence student achievement.

A. Work in pairs to discuss your own experiences with teacher expectations and your responses as a student. Describe a time when a teacher held either an unfairly high or low expectation for your achievement.

B. How did this affect your opinion about the teacher? How did this affect your feelings about yourself as a student? How did this affect your achievement in that class?

C. Volunteers may share their experiences with teacher expectations with the whole class.

D. Working in groups of four, reflect on your own experiences with linguistically, ethnically, or culturally diverse individuals. How might these experiences—or lack of them—influence your own future expectations for these students?

E. Working as class, discuss how you as future educators will deal with the issue of teacher expectations and student achievement in your own classrooms and schools.

Frequent Monitoring of Student Progress

In today's effective schools, measurement of student progress has shifted away from predominant reliance on summative, standardized norm-referenced tests and toward including ongoing formative measurements of student mastery. In addition, teachers monitor students' learning by emphasizing more authentic assessments, including students' projects, performances, and portfolios.[71] Teachers pay increased attention to aligning the intended, taught, learned, and tested curriculum. Additionally, educators ask, "What is worth knowing?" and "How will we know when students know it?"

Discussion and research. Educational accountability has become the primary public space in which we focus on racial, ethnic, class, and educational inequities (as discussed in detail in Chapters 11 and 15). Annual standardized testing by itself, however, does not make schools "effective." Standardized tests are typically summative assessments, used at the end of the learning process. While they provide valuable information about student achievement, they cannot measure many of learning's important aspects. In fact, standardized tests sometimes narrow the range of cognitive skills used and remove knowledge from real-world uses.[72]

Likewise, standardized tests cannot identify individual students' specific learning weakness in ways and at times when teachers can quickly diagnose them and intervene to remediate and advance student learning. Effective schools use assessments in a wider variety of ways.[73]

Effective schools frequently monitor student progress to advance all students' learning, in addition to measuring it at instruction's end. Formative assessment can be a continuing and integral part of the teaching and learning process. Using a wide array of assessments throughout the school year—including observations, interviews, projects, portfolios, and presentations—teachers can support student achievement and increase the types and qualities of student learning.

Research supports the notion that these performance assessments offer a way to increase all students' achievement. One 2001 study found a significant relationship between students who received challenging intellectual performance assignments and those students' measured reading, math, and writing skills in grades 3, 6, and 8. These learning gains were observed regardless of the students' family income, race/ethnicity, and prior achievement.[74] Regular engagement with performance tasks also increases students' ability to use—that is, transfer—this knowledge for real-world problem solving.[75] However, although performance tasks and assessments appear to positively impact students' motivation to learn, teaching practices, and student learning, the evidence on this front remains largely anecdotal.[76]

While using performance assessments will not reduce the achievement gaps, the results of performance assessments will however, provide wider and more equitable data on which to base decisions about students and schools. These assessments can enhance equity by informing teachers more fully about how their students think and learn, as well as what they know. As teachers come to understand their students

---

[71] Lezotte, 1991.

[72] Stiggins, R. J. (2002, June). Assessment crisis: The absence of assessment *for* learning. *Phi Delta Kappan, 83*(10), 757–765; Stiggins, R., & Chappius, S. (2005, October). Putting testing into perspective. *Principal Leadership, 6*(2), 16–20.

[73] Stiggins, 2002; Stiggins & Chappius, 2005.

[74] Newmann, F., Bryk, A., & Nagaoka, J. (2001). *Authentic and intellectual work on standardized tests: Conflict or coexistence?* Chicago, IL: Consortium on Chicago Public Schools, pp. 21–28.

[75] Bransford, J. D., & Schwartz, D. L. (1999). Rethinking transfer: A simple proposal with multiple implications. Chapter 3. *Review of Research in Education, 24*(1), 61–100.

[76] *Assessment of student performance: Studies of education reform.* (1997, April). Executive summary. Retrieved October 31, 2009, from http://www.ed.gov/pubs/SER/ASP/studex.html.

as learners more fully, they will be more readily able to adjust their teaching to student needs and to create occasions for student success.[77]

What it looks like in schools. What do schools that use frequent monitoring of student progress look like?

- Indicators of students' and the school's achievement are visibly posted within the school.
- Teachers use a variety of assessments to guide and develop student learning, not merely to measure it.
- Teachers use feedback from student assessments to inform (and adapt) their instruction to meet individual student needs.
- Teachers give clear explanations about what students are to do and which criteria will be used for determining its quality before assigning work to students.
- Teachers promptly grade and return student work and give useful feedback.
- Teachers diagnose student learning difficulties early and act to reduce them.
- Students have an active role in assessing and evaluating their own progress.
- Students use prompt feedback to extend their learning.
- Students are constantly aware of how well they are learning and progressing.
- Students and parents understand how students' work is graded.
- The principal and leadership team monitor the effectiveness of curriculum, instruction, and assessment and their impact on student learning.
- The principal recognizes and celebrates teachers and students' accomplishments and acknowledges failures.

Positive Home–School Relations

In contemporary effective schools, the parent–school relationship becomes an authentic partnership. Both parents and teachers have much to learn from one another about how to best inspire their students to learn what the school teaches. To help them realize their mutual goal—an effective home and school for every child—educators and parents need to build genuine trust and engage in clear, two-way communication.

Discussion and research. "The way schools care about children is reflected in the way schools care about the children's families. If educators view children simply as *students,* they are likely to see the family as separate from the school. If educators view students as *children,* they are likely to see both the family and the community as partners with the school in children's education and development."[78]

More than 40 years of research has shown that family involvement is a powerful influence on student achievement.[79] Studies have documented that when schools work together with families to promote student learning, children tend

[77] Darling-Hammond, L. (1996). Cited in Winking, D. (1997). *Critical issue: Ensuring equity with alternative assessments.* North Central Regional Educational Laboratory. Retrieved October 31, 2009, from http://www2.tqsource.org/strategies/atrisk/leadership.pdf

[78] Epstein, J. L. (1995, May). School/family/community partnerships: Caring for the children we share. *Phi Delta Kappan, 76*(9), 701–712.

[79] For a review of recent research, see Epstein, J. L. (2005, September). *Developing and sustaining research-based programs of school, family, and community partnerships: Summary of 5 years of NNPS research.* Johns Hopkins University, National Network of Partnership Schools (NNPS). Retrieved October 31, 2009, from http://www.csos.jhu.edu/P2000/pdf/Research%20Summary.pdf.

to succeed not just in school but in life. These students attain the following results:[80]

- Earn higher grades and test scores and enroll in higher-level programs
- Attend school regularly and do more homework
- Are promoted, pass their classes, and earn more course credits
- Show higher math and improved reading proficiency
- Receive fewer placements in special education
- Have better social skills, show improved behavior, and adapt well to school
- Receive fewer disciplinary actions
- Have higher graduation rates
- Have greater enrollment in postsecondary education

Just as important, research shows that what a family *does* is more important to student success than what a family *is* or *earns*. Parental involvement is the most reliable predictor of academic achievement whether the child is in preschool or upper grades, whether the family is financially struggling or affluent, and whether

Figure 16.5	Over 40 Years of Research Show Family Involvement Is Powerful Influence on Student Achievement

Comstock Images/Jupiter Images

---

[80] Henderson, A, T. and Berla, N. (Eds.). (1994). *A new generation of evidence: The family is critical in student achievement.* Washington, D.C.: National Committee for Citizens in Education. p. 1. Retrieved October 31, 2009 from: http://eric.ed.gov/ERICDocs/data/ericdocs2sql/content_storage_01/0000019b/80/13/66/e0.pdf. Epstein, J. L. (1991). Effects of students' achievement of teacher practices of parent involvement. In S. B. Silvern (Ed.), *Advances in teaching/language research: Vol. 5. Literacy through family, community, and school interaction* (pp. 261–276). Greenwich, CT: JAI Press; Henderson, A. T., & Mapp, K. L. (2002). *A new wave of evidence: The impact of school, family and community connections on student achievement, annual synthesis 2002* (ERIC Document No. ED 474521). Austin, TX: Center of Family and Community Connections with Schools, Southwest Educational Development Laboratory. Retrieved October 31, 2009, from http://eric.ed.gov/ERICDocs/data/ericdocs2sql/content_storage_01/0000019b/80/1a/e3/85.pdf.

the parents finished high school or earned graduate degrees.[81] Regardless of family income, children succeed in school when their families are able to accomplish the following:

- Create a home environment that encourages learning
- Express high (but not unrealistic) expectations for their children's achievement and future careers
- Become involved in their children's education in school and in the community[82]

Family involvement can reduce the obstacles that low-income and ethnically diverse students typically encounter in school. Research shows that when schools support families to develop these three conditions, children from low-income families and diverse cultural backgrounds approach the school grades and test scores attained by students from middle-class families. They are more likely to take advantage of a full range of educational opportunities after graduating from high school. Even when only one or two of these conditions are in place, children do measurably better in school.[83]

Families clearly benefit from forging close ties to schools. The teachers they work with have higher confidence in the parents and higher expectations for the children. As a result, parents develop more confidence about helping their children learn at home, about the school, and about themselves as parents. In addition, when parents become involved in their children's education, they often enroll in continuing education courses to advance their own learning.[84]

Schools and communities benefit from stronger family–school ties as well. Schools that work well with families realize the following advantages:[85]

- Improved teacher morale
- Higher ratings of teachers by parents
- More support from families
- Higher student achievement
- Better reputations in the community

The bottom line: When parents are genuinely involved in their children's education, their children do better in school and in life.

What it looks like in schools. Joyce Epstein, Johns Hopkins Professor and Director of the university's Center on School, Family, and Community Partnerships, has developed a framework of parent involvement to help educators build more

---

[81] Henderson & Berla, 1994; Henderson & Mapp, 2002.
[82] Clark, R. (2002). Ten hypotheses about what predicts student achievement for African American students and all other students: What the research shows. In W. L. Allen et al. (Eds.), *African American education: Race, community, inequality and achievement—A tribute to Edgar G. Epps.* (pp. 155–178). Oxford, UK. Elsevier Science.
[83] Catsambis, S. (2001). Expanding knowledge of parental involvement in children's secondary education: Connections with high school seniors' academic success. *Social Psychology of Education, 5,* 149–177; Catsambis, S., & Beveridge, A. A. (2001). Does neighborhood matter? Family, neighborhood, and school influences on eighth grade mathematics achievement. *Sociological Focus, 34,* 434–457; Epstein, J. L., & Sheldon, S. B. (2002). Present and accounted for: Improving student attendance through family and community involvement. *Journal of Educational Research, 95,* 308–318; Sheldon, S. B., & Epstein, J. L. (2002). Improving student behavior and discipline with family and community involvement. *Education in Urban Society, 35*(1), 4–26; Sheldon, S. B., & Epstein, J. L. (2004). Getting students to school: Using family and community involvement to reduce chronic absenteeism. *School Community Journal, 4*(2), 39–56; Sheldon, S. B., & Epstein, J. L. (2005a). Involvement counts: Family and community partnerships and math achievement. *Journal of Educational Research, 98,* 196–206; Sheldon, S. B., & Epstein, J. L. (2005b). School programs of family and community involvement to support children's reading and literacy development across the grades. In J. Flood & P. Anders (Eds.), *Literacy development of students in urban schools: Research and policy* (pp. 107–138). Newark, DE: International Reading Association; Simon, B. S. (2004). High school outreach and family involvement. *Social Psychology of Education, 7,* 185–209.
[84] Henderson & Berla, 1994.
[85] Henderson & Berla, 1994, p. 1.

comprehensive school and family partnerships. Types of school–parent partnerships include parenting, communications, volunteering, learning at home, decision making, and collaborating with the community. Each type of involvement encompasses many different partnership practices and challenges and leads to different results.[86] Table 16.1 describes these variations and expected results.

Using this framework as a guide can help educators see their schools' strengths and build on them to create a comprehensive approach to parent and community involvement that can support student success. In reality, meanwhile, parent–school partnerships sometimes fail. If the school discourages parents, treats them as negative influences, or cuts them out of their child's education, those actions promote family attitudes that inhibit school achievement.

Relationships that must bridge cultures and languages require more effort to create and sustain. Educators need to learn their families' "funds of knowledge" and "cultural assets"—ways of knowing, learning, and acting—that exist within culturally and linguistically diverse families. In this way, teachers can see their students and families' strengths and opportunities rather than simply noticing deficits.[87] Programs and policies that want to improve student outcomes will be much more productive if they build on their families' strengths and enlist them as allies.[88]

Parent–school involvement tends to decrease as students move into higher grade levels. As students move from elementary to secondary school, all domains of family engagement suffer, with the school's support for home learning losing the most ground.[89] Teachers and administrators must make special and appropriate efforts to welcome parents, provide effective two-way communication between parents and educators, and support learning at home if they are to encourage family engagement with schools as children grow older.

When parents and educators work together successfully, the following behaviors are apparent:

- Teachers send home folders of student work weekly or monthly for parent review and comment.
- Parents and teachers hold formal conferences at least once a year.
- Teachers regularly call parents to discuss their child's progress and problems.
- Teachers schedule regular interactive homework that requires students to demonstrate and discuss what they are learning with a family member.
- Teachers understand and relate positively to students of diverse backgrounds.
- Teachers feel comfortable understanding and discussing parents' concerns about their child's academic, social, and behavioral progress.
- Teachers call on parents to use their talents and interests in school to help students learn.
- Teachers use their awareness of families' perspectives when developing policy and making decisions.
- Teachers and administrators continually look for ways to involve parents, students, and the community in school decision making
- Schools provide clear information in the parents' preferred language about ways parents can help student learn at home with homework, other curricular-related activities, program decisions, and planning at each grade level.

---

[86] Epstein, 1995.

[87] Colombo, M. W. (2006, December). Building school partnerships with culturally and linguistically diverse families. *Phi Delta Kappan, 88*(4), 314–318.

[88] Hoff, D. J. (2007, April 4). More parental power in revised NCLB urged. *Education Week, 26*(31), 23; Keller, B. (2006, September 20). Views differ over NCLB rules on involving parents. *Education Week 26*(4): 12–13.

[89] Constantino, S. M. (2007, March). Tips for moving parents to the secondary school. *Principal Leadership, 7*(7), 34–39.

Table 16.1	Six Types of Parental Involvement, Practices, and Expected Results		
Type	**Description**	**Sample Practices**	**Expected Results**
1. Parenting	Helps all families establish home environments to support children as students	Suggest home conditions that support learning at each grade level. Workshops, videotapes, recorded phone messages. Parent education. Home visits at transition points (grades 3, 5, 8). Neighborhood meetings to help families understand schools and schools understand families.	Students: Awareness of school's importance and family supervision; good or improved attendance. Parents: Understanding and confidence in their parenting, child and adolescent development, changes in home conditions for learning as the child moves through school. Teachers: Understanding family backgrounds, culture, concerns, and views; respect for families' efforts and strengths; understanding student diversity.
2. Communicating	Design effective forms of school-to-home and home-to-school communications about school programs and children's progress.	Annual parent conferences with follow-ups as needed. Parent/student pick-up of report card with conferences on improving grades. Language translators as needed. Weekly or monthly folders of student work sent home for review and comments. Regular schedule of useful notices, phone calls, newsletters. Clear information on choosing courses, schools, programs and activities within schools.	Students: Awareness of own progress and actions needed to maintain or improve grades; understanding of school policies on behavior, attendance; informed decisions about courses and programs. Parents: Understand school programs and policies; monitoring and awareness of child's progress; responding effectively to student's problems. Teachers: Appreciation for and use of parent network for communications; increased ability to elicit and understand family views on children's programs and progress.
3. Volunteering	Recruit and organize parent help and support for school activities.	School and classroom volunteer program to help teachers, administrators, students, and other parents. Parent room or family center for meetings, resources for families. Annual postcard survey to identify all available talents, times, and locations for volunteers. Class parent, telephone tree, or other means to provide all families with needed information.	Students: Skill in communicating with adults; increased learning of skills that receive tutoring or targeted volunteer attention. Parents: Understanding teachers' job; increased comfort in school and carry-over of school activities at home; self-confidence about ability to work in school and with children. Teachers: Awareness of parents' talents and interests in school and children; greater individual attention to students with help from volunteers.

(continued)

Table 16.1	Six Types of Parental Involvement, Practices, and Expected Results (*continued*)		
Type	**Description**	**Sample Practices**	**Expected Results**
4. Learning at Home	Provide information and ideas to families about how to help students at home with homework and other curriculum-related activities, decisions, and planning.	Information for families on skills required for students in all subjects at each grade. Information on homework policies and ways to monitor and discuss schoolwork at home. Regular schedule of homework that requires students to discuss and interact with families on what they are learning in class. Summer learning packets or activities.	**Students:** Gains in skills, abilities, and test scores linked to homework and classwork; homework completion; positive attitude toward school work; improved self-concept of ability as learner. **Parents:** Know how to support, encourage, and help student at home each year; understand each year's instructional program and what child is learning in each subject. **Teachers:** Respect for family time; recognize helpfulness of each family type; satisfaction with family involvement and support.
5. Decision Making	Include parents in school decisions, developing parent leaders and representatives.	Active PTA/PTO or other parent groups, advisory councils, or committees (curriculum, safety, school improvement) for parent leadership and participation. Independent advocacy groups to lobby and work for school improvements. District-level councils and committees for family and community involvement. Information on school or local elections for school representatives.	**Students:** Understanding that students' rights are protected; awareness of family representation in school decisions. **Parents:** Input into policies that affect child's education; feeling of ownership of school; awareness of parents' voices in school decisions. **Teachers:** Awareness of parent perspectives in policy development and decisions; view of parents as having equal status on committees and in leadership roles.
6. Collaborating with Community	Identify and integrate resources and services from the community to strengthen school programs, family practices, and student learning and development.	Information for students and families on community health, cultural, recreational, social support, and other programs or services. Information on community activities linked to learning skills and talents. Services to the community by students, families, and schools (e.g., recycling, art, music, drama). Participation of alumni in school programs for students.	**Students:** Increased skills and talents through enriched curricular and extracurricular experiences; awareness of careers and options for future education and work. **Parents:** Knowledge and use of local resources by family and child to increase skills and talents or to obtain needed services; interactions with other families in community activities. **Teachers:** Awareness of community resources to enrich curriculum and instruction; openness to and skill in using mentors, business partners, and community volunteers to assist students and enhance teaching practice.

Source: Adapted from Epstein, J. L. (1995, May). School/family/community partnerships: Caring for the children we share. *Phi Delta Kappan, 76*(9), 704–706.

- The school offers parents various options for involvement.
- The school provides clear information about the curriculum, assessments, and achievement levels and report cards as well as about community resources and services.
- Language translators are available at school for parent–teacher conferences.
- Bilingual or multilingual employees work in school locations and are ready to meet and greet parents.
- Parent volunteers from various student demographics work visibly in the school.
- Students better understand and follow school rules and policies because they have discussed these issues with their parents.
- The school schedules its events at different times during the day and evening so that all families can attend some throughout the year.

Opportunity to Learn and Student Time-on-Task

Time remains a difficult challenge for teachers. Insufficient time to learn the required material compromises students' opportunity to learn (OTL). While the curriculum expands, the time for teaching and learning does not. In most schools, teachers have too much content to teach without enough time to teach it in ways that students can learn it.[90] Effective schools may have to abandon less important content to make time for the most valuable areas as well as adjust the available time in the school day to make more of it available to those who need it to reach mastery.

Discussion and research. Of all school-level factors that affect student achievement, *opportunity to learn* has the strongest impact.[91] **Opportunity to learn** refers to equitable conditions or circumstances within the school or classroom that promote learning for all students. It includes providing the high-quality curricula, learning materials, facilities, teachers, and instructional experiences that enable students to achieve high standards and on the absence of barriers that prevent learning.

Much of the OTL research has focused on three types of indicators: curriculum, pedagogy, and instructional resources. The instructional content (curriculum) includes the degree and depth in which teachers cover academic material for different student groups. Pedagogical processes focus on how teachers organize classroom work and reflect teachers' varying skill levels. Instructional resources comprise the supplies used in delivering instruction, including curricular materials, technology, safe and secure school facilities, and time use. To some degree, these categories overlap.[92]

Curriculum and opportunity to learn. Having a guaranteed and viable curriculum are strongly correlated with academic achievement, yet are so interdependent that they may be considered as one feature.[93]

---

[90] Baratz-Snowden, J. C. (1993, Summer). Opportunity to learn: Implications for professional development. *Journal of Negro Education, 62*(3), 311–323; Elmore, R. F., & Fuhrman, S. H. (1995). Opportunity-to-learn standards and the state role in education. *Teachers College Record, 96*(3), 432–457; Berliner, D. C., & Biddle, B. J. (1997). *The manufactured crisis: Myths, fraud, and the attack on America's public schools*. White Plains, NY: Longman, p. 55; Stevens, F. I. (1996). Closing the achievement gap: Opportunity to learn, standards, and assessment. In B. Williams (Ed.), *Closing the achievement gap: A vision for changing beliefs and practices* (pp. 77–95). Alexandria, VA: Association for Supervision and Curriculum Development.

[91] Marzano, R. J. (2003). *What works in schools: Translating research into action*. Alexandria, VA: Association for Supervision and Curriculum Development, pp. 22–25.

[92] Venezia, A., & Maxwell-Jolly, J. (2007). *The unequal opportunity to learn in California schools: Crafting standards to track quality*. Berkeley, CA: University of California, Policy Analysis for California Education.

[93] Marzano, 2003, p. 22.

Schools actually have four curricula. The **intended curriculum** is the content specified by the state, district, or school to be addressed in a particular course at a particular grade level. The **taught curriculum** is the curriculum the teacher delivers in the classroom. The **attained curriculum** is the one the students actually learn, and the **tested curriculum** is the one about which students must answer questions on classroom and standardized tests. Any mismatches detract from students' learning and reduce their OTL.

It may seem surprising that the intended curriculum and the taught curriculum are not always the same. Public education provides teachers with much guidance on content standards for specific courses and grade levels. Yet teachers commonly make independent and individual decisions about what they will cover and to what extent. Different teachers omit or include different topics. This practice frequently creates sizeable holes in the curriculum—and in students' learning.

In a high-stakes testing environment such as that mandated by NCLB, it is very important that all students have opportunities to learn the same information and skills, to the same levels of depth and complexity—that they will see on assessments. Unless all students have the chance to learn the expected content to the same level of complexity that the assessment will measure it—or that real-world problem solving requires—they will not have the opportunity to learn.

Effective teaching and opportunity to learn. Improving students' opportunity to learn requires high levels of professional teaching competence. Teachers must know their subject and the standards to which they and their students will be held accountable. They must develop effective diagnostic skills to identify each student's learning obstacles in each required topic or skill. Teachers must deliver instruction in a variety of ways, adjusting their strategies to best suit the material and their students. They must design lessons that connect students to the content in ways that are meaningful and relevant to them. Students, in turn, must have occasions for demonstration, practice, and prompt feedback which they can immediately use to increase their learning. Further, these teachers and resources must be available to every student in every classroom. Achieving this feat requires teachers to become lifelong learners themselves, as they keep enhancing their professional expertise and expanding their repertoire of teaching skills.

OTL teaching also means that teachers form partnerships with parents and guardians, encouraging them to support students' good learning and study habits at home. Ideally, teachers and parents will frequently communicate about students' progress and academic programs.

Time and opportunity to learn. Time is another critical OTL variable. Robert Marzano, a noted education researcher and author, has found that most state, district, and school curricula are too large to fit neatly into the limits of the school day. In fact, researchers have identified some 200 standards and 3,039 benchmarks in national and state-level documents covering 14 different subject areas.[94] Classroom teachers estimated that it would take 15,465 hours to adequately address this content.[95] Assuming that most K–12 schools have a 180-day school year, with an average of 5.6 hours of class time each school day, teachers would have a maximum of 13,104 hours (13 years of instruction × 1,008 hours per school year) to address all of these standards.[96] Clearly, 15,465 hours of standards does not fit into 13,104 hours of instructional time.[97]

---

[94] Kendall, J. S., & Marzano, R.J. (2000). *Content knowledge: A compendium of standards and benchmarks for K–12 students* (3rd ed.). Alexandria, VA: Association for Supervision and Curriculum Development.
[95] Marzano, R. J., Kendall, J. S., & Gaddy, B. B. (1999). *Essential knowledge: The debate over what American students should know.* Aurora, CO: Mid-continent Regional Educational Laboratory.
[96] Marzano, 2003, p. 24.
[97] Marzano, 2003, p. 25.

What it looks like in schools. What does opportunity to learn look like in schools?

- Schools establish curricular priorities, ensure appropriate teacher assignments, and provide students with needed support.
- Teachers involve all students in synthesizing, generalizing, explaining, hypothesizing, and drawing conclusions to increase meaning and understanding.
- Teachers identify students' individual learning problems or misunderstandings early in the learning process and provide them with additional supports as necessary.
- Teachers use a variety of instructional strategies to meet students' diverse learning needs.
- Teachers receive the materials, equipment, and ongoing professional development necessary for their successful job performance.
- Teachers use effective classroom management and organizational strategies to maximize learning time.
- Teachers design challenging (but not unduly frustrating) learning tasks for students that are adjusted to accommodate students' unique learning needs while ensuring they achieve high levels of mastery.
- Classroom instructional resources for learning are equally accessible to all students.
- No public address announcements or other classroom interruptions occur during instructional time.
- Transitions between instructional activities and classroom routines occur smoothly with little time loss.
- Special education students are included in all academic classes and are supported with collaborative teaching.
- Students have opportunities to receive additional individualized assistance that addresses their specific learning challenges (e.g., teacher or classroom aide, peer tutor, interactive technology-based instructional resources aligned with the curriculum).
- Students who fail tests receive meaningful opportunities for remediation that focus on the test's knowledge and skills and give enough time to remedy any weakness in that area before retaking the test.

A Realistic Look at What Effective Schools Can and Cannot Do

Effective schools differ from other schools by integrating the elements that make school success achievable for all students—instructional leadership, a clear and focused mission, a safe and orderly environment, a climate of high expectations, frequent monitoring of student progress, positive home–school relations, and opportunity to learn. If policy makers and practitioners want to make a positive difference, they can focus on what excellent schools do and how they do it, and seek to replicate those practices in schools that are lagging behind.

Over the years, the Effective Schools movement has identified certain realities that affect the use of these correlates to improve schools:

- No one model of effective schools exists. No single set of variables can produce an effective school. Each school has its unique student and community factors that will influence how the correlates will work.

- The correlates are prerequisites—not guarantees—for attaining high and equitable achievement levels for low-income and minority students. They are proxies showing the school is moving toward being more effective in student achievement.

- The correlates interact in synergistic ways. They work together and influence one another in unique ways in different school environments.

- The correlates are challenges for schools to meet—not "recipes" to create high-achieving schools. Each correlate has many steps that must be implemented correctly for each school's unique situation and in recognition of its interplay with the other correlates.

- Schools must monitor and attend to all the correlates and the possible obstacles and repercussions their implementation may produce.

- Schools cannot undertake all of the correlates at one time, nor can they overlook implementing any one of them. Yet all of the correlates must eventually be present if student achievement is to increase.

- Each school's community socioeconomic context influences student achievement. Both family and school contribute to student learning.

- Minority and low-income students' skills in effective schools are at least as well developed as those of middle-class children. In effective schools, a child's socioeconomic status cannot be determined by looking at test scores.

The Effective Schools correlates appear repeatedly in effective schools at all grade levels, in separate regions, and among independent researchers. This consistency assures us that these correlates exist and have merit. That critics question the research methodology or claim that these schools' increased achievement scores may be random fluctuations simply means the effective schools correlates are not a panacea for all ills affecting the U.S. educational system, nor are they easily infused into schools across the board.[98] Likewise, the critics of the Effective Schools correlates have never sought to discount their merit or usefulness in promoting student learning.

Educators cannot completely close the achievement gap by intensively implementing the reforms advocated by proponents of the Effective Schools movement without also tackling the underlying social problems that affect the children who attend our schools.[99] "To pretend that schools can single-handedly overcome a lifetime of deprivation through a 'whole-school action plan' or through rigorous and intensive adherence to a particular reading program is more an exercise in ritualistic magic than an realistic solution to social, economic, and personal problems."[100] Many children come to school with issues affecting their health, mobility, housing, nutrition, parents' unemployment, family structure, medical and dental care—all of which have profound implications for how well they learn.

By themselves, these approaches cannot be completely successful. Six hours of daily instruction delivered over 180 days per year cannot overcome the effects of a deprived and impoverished home environment for 18 hours a day, 365 days a year. Nonetheless, the data show that when educators, parents, and communities integrate the Effective Schools correlates into their schools' daily life, they create important opportunities for more students learn the high-level knowledge, skills, and habits of mind necessary for twenty-first-century citizenship and self-sufficiency. If a democracy thrives only with an educated populace, such is the hope for public education's—and our nation's—future.

---

[98] Mathis, W. J. (2005, April). Bridging the achievement gap: A bridge too far? *Phi Delta Kappan*, *86*(8), 591.

[99] Borman, G., D., & Hewes, G. M. (2002, Winter). The long-term effects and cost-effectiveness of Success for All. *Educational Evaluation and Policy Analysis*, *24*(4), 243–266; Rothstein, R. (2004). *Class and schools: Using social, economic, and educational reform to close the black–white achievement gap*. New York: Teachers College Press.

[100] Mathis, 2005, p. 591.

Summary

Sociological, cultural, and school factors have often placed severe obstacles in the path to minority and low-income students' learning. Research affirms, however, that when teachers, administrators, and the community hold high expectations for students, effectively deliver a strong and appropriate curriculum, and provide high levels of support, learning and achievement typically improve. Effective schools can make a measurable difference with traditionally underserved students, increasing student achievement regardless of any particular student's family background.

The belief that schools cannot overcome the influence of family background is widespread and controversial. The 1966 Coleman Report and the 1972 Jencks et al.'s study concluded that students' academic achievement was primarily a function of their family background, which schools could not surmount.

Reacting to these reports, late 1970s and early 1980s research into effective schools began to identify public schools whose graduates scored higher than the national average on standardized tests regardless of their socioeconomic backgrounds. These findings directly contrasted with Coleman et al.'s and Jencks et al.'s conclusions.

Over the years, Edmonds, Brookover, Lezotte, and many researchers have compiled a list of school-based factors that contribute to high achievement for minority and low SES students:

- Strong instructional leadership
- A clear and focused mission, including a balance between basic skills and higher-level learning
- A safe and orderly school environment conducive to learning
- High teacher expectations for student achievement
- Frequent monitoring of student progress
- Positive home-school relations
- Opportunities to learn and student time-on-task

These early school effectiveness studies had methodological limitations, they were correlational studies that did not predict a cause-and-effect relationship. Since 1990, the effective schools models and research have expanded to include schools serving all types of students in various settings. In addition, school effectiveness is now understood as comprising sets of interacting variables. Once put into effect on a broader scale, the school effectiveness correlates are likely to have a cumulative impact on student achievement.

Conclusions

- The Effective Schools movement produced reliable findings about the characteristics of high-performing urban schools: clear goals related to student achievement, teachers and parents with high expectations, and a school structure and climate designed to maximize students' learning opportunities.
- Everything and everyone in the schools must emphasize successful teaching and learning if truly effective schools are to emerge.
- Research has shown that these in-school factors can overcome the inherent limitations of students' family backgrounds.

This page constitutes an extension of the copyright page. We have made every effort to trace the ownership of all copyrighted material and to secure permission from copyright holders. In the event of any question arising as to the use of any material, we will be pleased to make the necessary corrections in future printings. Thanks are due to the following authors, publishers, and agents for permission to use the material indicated.

Chapter 1. 24: Source: Davis, J, R. (1997). Better teaching, more learning. Phoenix: American Council on Education, Series on Higher Education. Retrieved July 30, 2009 from: http://www.ntlf. com/html/lib/btml_xrpt.htm.

Chapter 2. 41: Source: Ingersoll, R. (2003). Is there really a teacher shortage? Retrieved December 12, 2006, from http://www. ncctq. org/issueforums/atrisk/presentations/keynoteIngersoll. ppt#291,6, Beginning Teacher Attrition (Cumulative Percent Teachers Having Left Teaching Occupation, by Years of Experience). **42:** Source: Darling-Hammond, L., & Sykes, G. (2003). Wanted: A national teacher supply policy for education: The right way to meet the "highly qualified teacher" challenge. Educational Policy Analysis and Archives, 11(33). Retrieved October 9, 2009, from http://epaa.asu.edu/epaa/v11n33.

Chapter 3. 79: Source: Adapted from Sousa, D. A. (1995). How the brain learns. Reston, VA: National Association of Secondary School Principals, p. 11. **80:** Source: Sousa, D, A. (1995). How the brain learns. Reston, VA: National Association of Secondary School Principals, p. 15. **82:** Source: Caine, R. N., & Caine, G. (1991). Making connections: Teaching and the human brain. New York: Addison-Wesley, p. 102. **82:** Source: Sousa, D. A. (1995). How the brain learns. Reston, VA: National Association of Secondary School Principals, p. 18. **85:** Source: Caine, R. N., & Caine, G. (1991). Making connections: Teaching and the human brain. New York: Addison- Wesley, p. 104.

Chapter 6. 173: Source: Hirsch, E. D. Jr. (1996). The schools we need and why we don't have them. New York: Doubleday. Retrieved January 17, 2007, from http://mwhodges.home.att. net/tracy/tracy-hirsch.htm. **178:** Source: A. S. Neill's Summerhill School. Retrieved January 19, 2007, from http://www. summerhillschool.co.uk/ pages/school_policies.html.

Chapter 7. 225: Source: Bureau of Labor Statistics. Retrieved October 18, 2006, from http://www.bls.gov/cps/labor2005/chart 2-5.pdf. **225:** Source: U.S. Department of Labor, Bureau of Labor Statistics. (2007). Occupational outlook handbook. Washington, DC: Author. www.bls.gov. **227:** Source: Viadero, D. (2006, October 25). Rags to riches in the U.S. largely a myth, scholars write. Education Week, 26(9), 8.

Chapter 9. 278: Source: Snyder, T. D., Dillow, S. A., & Hoffman, C. M. (2008). Digest of education statistics 2007 (NCES 2008–022). National Center for Education Statistics, Institute of Education Sciences, U.S. Department of Education. Washington, DC: U.S. Government Printing Office, Table 83, p. 117 **284:** Source: Do school boards matter? (2007, January 3). Washington, DC: National School Boards Association. Retrieved April 22, 2009, from http://www.nsba.org/MainMenu/ Governance/WhySchoolBoards/ DoSchoolBoardsMatter.aspx. **291:** Source: U.S. Department of Education, National Center for Education Statistics. (2007). The condition of education, 2007 (NCES 2007-064). Washington, DC: U.S. Government Printing Office, p. 72. **295:** Source: U.S. Department of Education, National Center for Education Statistics. (2007). The condition of education, 2007 (NCES 2007-064). Washington, DC: U.S. Government Printing Office, p. 28. **301:** Source: U.S. Department of Education, National Center for Education Statistics. (2007). The condition of education, 2007 (NCES 2007-064), Washington, DC: U.S. Government Printing Office, Figure 2, p. 6. **302:** Source: U.S. Department of Education, National Center for Education Statistics. (2007). The condition of education, 2007 (NCES 2007-064), Washington, DC: U.S. Government Printing Office, Figure 2, p. 6. **303:** Source: Snyder, T. D., Dillow, S. A., and Hoffman, C. M. (2009). Digest of Education Statistics 2008 (NCES 2009-020). National Center for Education Statistics, Institute of Education Sciences, U.S. Department of Education. Washington, DC., p. 154.

Chapter 10. 309: Source: U.S. Census Bureau. (2007). Current population survey: 2007 annual social and economic survey: 2007. Washington, DC: U.S. Government Printing Office, p. 59. http://pubdb3.census.gov/macro/032007/perinc/ new03_001. htm. **310:** Source: Snyder, T. D., Dillow, S. A., & Hoffman, C. M. (2007). Digest of education statistics 2006 (NCES 2007-017). National Center for Education Statistics, Institute of Education Sciences, U.S. Department of Education. Washington, DC: U.S. Government Printing Office, p. 566. **310:** Source: Snyder, T. D., Dillow, S. A., & Hoffman, C. M. (2007). Digest of education statistics 2006 (NCES 2007-017). National Center for Education Statistics, Institute of Education Sciences, U.S. Department of Education. Washington, DC: U.S. Government Printing Office, p. 557. **312:** Source: Snyder, T. D., Dillow, S. A., & Hoffman, C. M. (2009). Digest of Education Statistics 2008. (NCES 2008-022). U.S. Department of Education. p. 59. Retrieved August 26, 2009 from: http://nces.ed.gov/pubs2009/2009020_2a.pdf **314:** Source: Snyder, T. D., Dillow, S. A., & Hoffman, C. M. (2009). Digest of Education Statistics 2008. (NCES 2008-022). U.S. Department of Education. p. 57. Retrieved August 26, 2009 from: http:// nces.ed.gov/pubs2009/2009020_2a.pdf **315:** Source: Snyder, T. D., Dillow, S. A., & Hoffman, C. M. (2009). Digest of Education Statistics 2008. (NCES 2008-022). U.S. Department of Education. p. 57. Retrieved August 26, 2009 from:http://nces.ed.gov/ pubs2009/2009020_2a.pdf **316:** Source: Snyder, T. D., Dillow, S. A., & Hoffman, C. M. (2009). Digest of Education Statistics 2008. (NCES 2008-022). U.S. Department of Education. p. 262, Table 182. Retrieved August 26, 2009 from: http://nces.ed.gov/

pubs2009/2009020_2a.pdf **317:** Source: Levy, M., (2007). Per student figures for District of Columbia public school system. Washington Lawyer's Committee for Civil Rights and Urban Affairs, p. 5. Retrieved August 26, 2009 from: http://www.21csf. org/csf-home/DocUploads/DataShop/DS_86.pdf **318:** Source: Compiled and calculated from: Alexandria City, VA public schools. Retrieved August 28, 2009 from: http://www.acps.k12. va.us/board/division-goals/ goals-brochure.pdf; Washington area boards of education fiscal year 2008, Retrieved August 28, 2009 from: http://www.acps.k12.va.us/board/wabe.pdf; Arlington, VA public schools. Retrieved August 28, 2009 from: http://www. acps.k12.va.us/board/wabe.pdf; Washington, DC Public Schools, Retrieved August 28, 2009 from: http://dcps.dc.gov/portal/site/ DCPS/menuitem.06de50edb2b17a932c69621014f62010/?vgnex toid=71a3f83a5f052210VgnVCM100000416f0201RCRD& vgnextchannel=39d1e2b1f0d32210VgnVCM100000416f02 01RCRD&vgnextfmt=default; Fairfax County Public Schools, Retrieved August 28, 2009 from: http://www.schoolmatters.com/ schools.aspx/q/page=dl/did=4013/midx=StudentDemographics; Montgomery County Public Schools, MD, Retrieved August 28, 2009 from: http://www.montgomeryschoolsmd.org/about/; Prince George's County Public Schools, Retrieved August 28, 2009 from: http://www.schoolmatters.com/schools.aspx/q/ page=dl/did=5109/midx=StudentDemographics **319:** Source: Snyder, T. D., Dillow, S. A., & Hoffman, C. M. (2009). Digest of education statistics 2008 (NCES 2009-020). National Center for Education Statistics, Institute of Education Sciences, U.S. Department of Education. Washington, DC: U.S. Government Printing Office, adapted from Table 183, p. 263. Calculations by authors. The expenditure percentages total to 100 percent due to rounding. **321:** Source: Data compiled from National Education Association (NEA). (2008 December). Rankings and estimates: Ranking of the states 2008 and estimates of school statistics 2009. Washington, DC: NEA Research, p. 18 **327:** Source: Weiner, R., & Pristoop, E. (2006). How states shortchange the districts that need the most help: Funding gap 2006. Washington, DC: The Education Trust, p. 8. **328:** Source: Roza, M. (2006). How districts shortchange low-income and minority students: Funding gap 2006. Washington, DC: The Education Trust, pp. 9–10.

Chapter 11. 337: Source: Minorities set to be US majority: U.S. population projections to 2050. (2008, August 14). Washington, DC: U.S. Census Bureau. Retrieved August 14, 2008, from http:// news.bbc.co.uk/2/hi/americas/7559996.stm. **368:** Source: Leonard B. Stevens. (2007, February 14) To See or Not to See: Being Colorblind in a Color-Conscious Society. Education Week, 26(23):31.

Chapter 12. 374: Source: From cradle to career: Connecting American education from birth through adulthood. (2007, January 4). Quality Counts 2007, Education Week, 26(17), 5. Retrieved October 17, 2009, from http://www.edweek.org/ media/ ew/qc/2007/QC07_PressConference_Remarks.pdf. **375:** Source: From cradle to career: Connecting American education from birth through adulthood. (2007, January 4). Quality Counts 2007, Education Week, 26(17), 8. Retrieved October 17, 2009, from http://www.edweek.org/media/ ew/qc/2007/ QC07_PressConference_Remarks.pdf. **378:** Source: Adapted from Sue, D. W., & Sue, D. (2008). Counseling the culturally diverse: Theory and practice (5th ed.). Hoboken, NJ: John Wiley & Sons, Table 10.1, p. 243. **387:** Source: Fryer, R. G. (2006, Winter). "Acting white": The social price paid by the best and brightest minority students. Education Next, 6(1). Stanford University: Hoover Institution. Retrieved October 17, 2009, from http://educationnext.org/actingwhite/. **389:** Source: Adapted from Ogbu, J. U. (1992). Understanding cultural diversity and

learning. Educational Researcher, 21, 11. **401:** Source: Harry, B., & Klinger, J. (2007). Discarding the deficit model. Educational Leadership, 64(5), 16–19.

Chapter 13. 418: Source: Forehand, M. (2005). Bloom's taxonomy: Original and revised. In M. Orey (Ed.), Emerging perspectives on learning, teaching, and technology. Retrieved October 18, 2009, from http://projects.coe.uga.edu/epltt/ index. php?title=Bloom%27s_Taxonomy. **421:** Source: Wiggins, G., & McTighe, J. (1998). Understanding by design. Alexandria, VA: Association for Supervision and Curriculum Development, p. 9. **422:** Source: Adapted from Wiggins, G., & McTighe, J. (1998). Understanding by design. Alexandria, VA: Association for Supervision and Curriculum Development, p. 169. **426:** Source: Perie, M., Grigg, W. S., & Dion, G. S. (2005, October). National Assessment of Educational Progress: The nation's report card: Mathematics 2005. (NCES 2006-453). National Center for Education Statistics. Institute of Education Sciences, U.S. Department of Education. Washington, DC: U.S. Printing Office. Retrieved October 19, 2007, from http://nces. ed.gov/nationsreportcard/pdf/main2005/2006453.pdf. and for 12th grade, and http://nces.ed.gov/nationsreportcard/pdf/ main2005/2007468_3.pdf. **427:** Source: Cavanaugh, S. (2007, February 21). "Math anxiety" confuses the equation for students. Education Week, 26(24), 12. **429:** Source: Adapted from data provided in Perie, M., Grigg, W. S., & Donahue, P. L. (2005, October). National Assessment of Educational Progress: The nation's report card: Reading 2005 (NCES 2006–451). NAEP 2005 assessment results: Reading grade **12:** Executive summary. Reading performance declines for all but top performers. **431:** Source: U.S. Department of Education, Institute of Education Sciences, National Center for Education Statistics. (2006, May). The nation's report card: Science 2005. (NCES 2006-466). Washington, DC: U.S. Government Printing Office, pp. 7, 19, 31. Retrieved October 19, 2009, from http://nces.ed.gov/ nationsreportcard/science/. **432:** Source: National Assessment of Educational Progress: The nation's report card: U.S. history 2006. (NCES 2007-474). National Center for Education Statistics, Institute of Education Sciences, U.S. Department of Education. Washington, DC: U.S. Government Printing Office. Retrieved October 19, 2009, from http://nces.ed.gov/nationsreportcard/ pdf/main2006/2007474.pdf **433:** Source: Lutkis, A. D., & Weiss, A. R. (2007). The nation's report card: Civics 2006 (NCES 2007-476). National Center for Education Statistics, Institute for Education Sciences, U.S. Department of Education. Washington, DC: U.S. Government Printing Office. Retrieved October 19, 2009, from http://nces.ed.gov/nationsreportcard/pdf/ main2006/2007476.pdf.

Chapter 14. 451: Source: Adapted from Marzano, R. J. (2004). Building background knowledge for academic achievement: Research on what works in schools. Alexandria, VA: Association for Supervision and Curriculum Development, p. 22. **458:** Source: Adapted from In Brooks, J. G., & Brooks, M. G. (1993). In search of understanding: The case for constructivist classrooms. Alexandra, VA: Association for Supervision and Curriculum Development, p. 17. **467:** Source: Adapted from Metzger, M. (2002, September). Learning to discipline. Phi Delta Kappan, 84(1), 77–84. **470:** Source: Adapted from NTL Institute for Applied Learning. Cited in Danielson, C. (2002). Enhancing student achievement: A framework for school improvement. Alexandria, VA: Association for Supervision and Curriculum Development, p. 24. **471:** Source: Adapted from Marzano, R. J., Pickering, D. J., & Pollock, J. E. (2001). Classroom instruction that works: Research-based strategies for increasing student achievement. Alexandria, VA: Association for Supervision and Curriculum Development, p. 7; Marzano, R. J. (2003). What works in schools: Translating research into action. Alexandria, VA: Association for Supervision and Curriculum Development, pp. 82–83.

Chapter 15. 478: Source: Adapted from Frye, R. (n.d.). Assessment, accountability, and student learning outcomes. Retrieved October 30, 2009, from http://www.ac.wwu.edu/~dialogue/issue2.html. **483:** Source: Center for Public Education. (2007). Guide to standardized tests: Bell curve. National School Boards Association. Retrieved October 30, 2009, from http://www.centerforpubliceducation.org/site/c.kjJXJ5MPIwE/b.1698647/k.1A72/Guide_to_standardized_tests_Bell_curve.htm. **490:** Source: Adapted from Collaboration rubric: Teacher created rubrics for assessment. On-line professional development for K–12 teachers. (n.d.). University of Wisconsin–Stout. Retrieved October 30, 2009, from http:// www.sdcoe.k12.ca.us/score/actbank/collaborub.html. **499:** Source: Popham, W. J. (2001). The truth about testing: An educator's call to action. Alexandria, VA: Association for Supervision and Curriculum Development, p. 65. **503:** Source: Wiggins, G. (2006, April). Healthier testing made easy. Edutopia. Retrieved October 30, 2009, from http://www.edutopia.org/healthier-testing-made-easy.

Chapter 16. 537: Source: Adapted from Epstein, J. L. (1995, May). School/family/community partnerships: Caring for the children we share. Phi Delta Kappan, 76(9), 704–706.